The Law of Consumer Protection and Fair Trading

'Suppose we turn goldsmiths?' said Schwartz to Hans, as they entered a large city. 'It is a good knave's trade; we can put a great deal of copper into the gold without anyone's finding out.'

The King of the Golden River JOHN RUSKIN

'If we had the Ten Commandments these days, there would have to be a Code of Practice attached to each of them.'

ANONYMOUS INDUSTRIALIST

'If the good Lord had wanted us to go metric, he'd only have had ten Apostles.'

SISTER INCARNATA, quoted by John Mortimer

Dedication

Emptori qui cavere debet, atque venditori cujus ignorantiam jus haud excusat.

The Law of
Consumer Protection and Fair Trading

Sixth Edition

Brian W Harvey MA, LLM (Cantab)
Solicitor, Emeritus Professor of Law at the University of Birmingham

Deborah L Parry BA (Law) (Sheffield)
Senior Lecturer in Law at the University of Hull

Butterworths
London, Edinburgh & Dublin
2000

United Kingdom	Butterworths, a Division of Reed Elsevier (UK) Ltd, Halsbury House, 35 Chancery Lane, LONDON WC2A 1EL and 4 Hill Street, EDINBURGH EH2 3JZ
Australia	Butterworths, a Division of Reed International Books Australia Pty Ltd, CHATSWOOD, New South Wales
Canada	Butterworths Canada Ltd, MARKHAM, Ontario
Hong Kong	Butterworths Hong Kong, a division of Reed Elsevier (Greater China) Ltd, HONG KONG
India	Butterworths India, NEW DELHI
Ireland	Butterworth (Ireland) Ltd, DUBLIN
Malaysia	Malayan Law Journal Sdn Bhd, KUALA LUMPUR
New Zealand	Butterworths of New Zealand Ltd, WELLINGTON
Singapore	Butterworths Asia, SINGAPORE
South Africa	Butterworths Publishers (Pty) Ltd, DURBAN
USA	Lexis Law Publishing, CHARLOTTESVILLE, Virginia

© Reed Elsevier (UK) Ltd 2000

A CIP Catalogue record for this book is available from the British Library.

ISBN 0 406 93062 7

Printed and bound in Great Britain by Hobbs the Printers Ltd, Totton, Hampshire

Visit Butterworths LEXIS *direct* at: http://www.butterworths.com

Preface

Recent years have seen a rapid increase in the volume of legislation to protect the consumer not only against fraud and dishonesty in commercial dealings but also against oppressive bargains and dangerous products. There is widespread public interest in 'consumerism' and an increasingly large number of professional and lay people are expected to be able to give advice on consumer problems and help to formulate consumer policy, both as regards UK domestic law and on the wider stage of the European Union, where a greatly increased enthusiasm for a more high profile concern for the consumer's welfare is clearly discernible. At the same time there has been debate among civil law jurists as to what sort of animal 'consumer protection law' is (see eg J Stuyck 'European Consumer Law after the Treaty of Amsterdam: Consumer Policy in or beyond the Internal Market?' (2000) 37 CMLR 367). Is it primarily a branch of public law in the form of consumer-orientated regulatory legislation imposing criminal penalties for breach, or is it just as much the study of such parts of the private law of contract, commercial law and tort as focus on the transaction between the supplier and the ultimate consumer and giving the latter the right to compensation? Anglo-American law would answer that it is both these things. Furthermore, the student will need some knowledge of the institutions that have been developed to promote consumer protection policy and enforce the regulatory side.

Accordingly, we have looked at the body of law which exists to protect the private consumer from (a) unsafe products, (b) qualitatively deficient goods and services, (c) fraudulent, misleading or undesirable trading practices, (d) insufficient information, and (e) economic exploitation through lack of competition or excessive prices. To understand the working of the law it is also important to examine the voluntary or statutory provisions for giving the consumer redress when he has a legitimate complaint, whether it be against a 'utility' provider formerly in the public sector or a producer of goods or services in the private sector. From this vast field we have necessarily had to be selective, particularly as to services. It could be argued, for instance, that the machinery regulating state welfare benefits is partly there to protect the consumer of these benefits, and certainly that public licensing systems relating to everything from taxi cabs to betting shops are an aspect of consumer protection. But the line has to be drawn somewhere, and the above topics are better dealt with in the specialist works that already exist, as are the intricate protective devices for those enjoying interests in land. In many of these more technical areas the 'consumer in the street' will often rely on professional advice, and if matters go wrong his first line of attack will be against his professional adviser – an aspect of consumer protection fully dealt with in this book.

In the preface to the first edition of this book by the first-named author (1979) it was mentioned that the justification of the then novel treatment of the social, political and (particularly) economic context of the laws and institutions concerning consumer protection in an introductory way was that 'many law students will not have studied economics before, and, with a few distinguished exceptions, authors of academic law books in England have given their readers little encouragement to think about the relationship between law and economics. Whilst extreme statements which would deny the study of law any normative role or intrinsic intellectual interest at all are to be deplored, a moment's thought will show that both parliamentary and judicial law-making rests on certain usually unexpressed economic or socio-political premises. Evaluation of a particular law's merits or demerits should not rest entirely on whether it appears to work well. It is also necessary to estimate the effect that any consumer protection law will have on, for instance, the economics of the production of the particular goods or services in question, and on consumer behaviour generally. It would be possible, given sufficient space, to deal with this wider dimension in far greater detail than we have done, but we have both kept in mind and tried to deal with it in a way comprehensible to the person without any previous training in economics.'

A number of people have read and commented upon parts of the text and it is not possible to mention everyone individually. But we would like to thank correspondents from the National Consumer Council, the British Standards Institution, the Citizens' Advice Bureaux, the National Federation of Consumer Groups, the Consumers' Association and the press office of the Office of Fair Trading who have given us specific assistance, as has the Department of Trade and Industry.

Detailed changes of case law and statute have affected almost every page of the former edition. Much rewriting and reordering of the material has been necessary. We have divided this task between us but are jointly and severally responsible for the whole.

September 2000   BRIAN W HARVEY

                                                         DEBORAH L PARRY

Contents

Contents

Contents

Contents

ABBREVIATIONS

In the footnotes we have made frequent reference to the following:

Miller, Harvey and Parry *Consumer and Trading Law:*
   Text, Cases and Materials . . . . M, H & P
Butterworths Student Statutes Commercial and
   Consumer Law . . . . BSSCCL

Table of statutes

Table of statutes

Table of statutes

Table of statutes

Table of statutes

xvii

Table of statutes

Table of statutes

Table of cases

Table of cases

H

Table of cases

M

PAGE

N

O

P

R

Table of cases

Table of cases

Table of cases

1 The historical, economic and philosophical background to consumer protection

The aim of this chapter is to introduce the economic and philosophical background to the widely accepted principle that the consumer of goods and services is entitled to protection under the law if the goods and services supplied to him for consideration are defective or falsely described. To be more precise, and as indicated in the Preface, the range of laws considered in this book are designed to protect the consumer in at least one of the following areas, namely against: a) unsafe products; b) qualitatively deficient goods and services; c) fraudulent trading practices; d) insufficient information to exercise a prudent buying decision; and e) economic exploitation through lack of competition or excessive prices.

The idea that the consumer is deserving of protection is not a new one in English law. A brief history of some aspects of trading law in England will perhaps assist in the appreciation of the impact of contemporary consumer protection law. It must be borne in mind, though, that the motivation for the early legislation was as much to protect the honest trader against dishonest competition as to protect the consumer.

1. HISTORICAL DEVELOPMENT

Roots

Early consumer protection machinery was closely linked to the then existing units of local government. The primary units of pre-nineteenth century local government were the county and the parish. The hierarchy of government would have been expressed as being the King in Parliament and, locally, the official dignitaries of the county – the Lord Lieutenant, the High Sheriff and the Justices of the Peace. The functions of the Justices of the Peace, as developed in the thirteenth and fourteenth centuries, were both judicial and administrative. In the sixteenth century their already increasing duties and jurisdiction were increased by giving them supervisory jurisdiction over the parish with regard to bridges and highways, and, a little later, the poor law, paving, lighting and cleansing of streets.

Outside this general scheme were the borough and the manor. A town which had secured its charter of incorporation and become a borough appointed its own justices and operated its own analogous system of local government through mayors, aldermen and burgesses. The manor was the residue of the feudal system of land tenure. Originally England had been parcelled out by William the Conqueror to his faithful followers, whose successors, after numerous subdivisions, were known as Lords of the Manor. Villeins within the Lord's demesne owed to him duties of service, and courts over which he presided regulated a large number of civil and criminal matters arising in the community. As the royal courts became established and offered a more efficient system of justice, manorial courts declined, but the manorial court known as the court leet had a persistent and important role in the main regulatory function of local government in the seventeenth century and beyond – the supervision of trading standards and the suppression of local nuisances. So, to summarise, the courts exercising functions which we would now associate with 'consumer protection' and 'public health' were primarily the petty sessional courts of the Justices of the Peace and the Manorial Courts Leet, whose jurisdiction was in practice concurrent.

The concept of consumer protection to the thinking person, throughout the eighteenth century at least, would mean a) protection from excessive prices levied on primary commodities, and b) protection from short measure. Protection from 'common nuisances' involving misuses of houses, streets and bridges is a separate area of activity which must be investigated by the historian of public health. (It is, of course, debatable how far the motivation for the regulation of trade came primarily from the honest traders seeking to preserve their own reputation and standards.)

Bread, beer, meat and fuel were singled out from earliest times as being commodities which the Crown, through the agency of the justices or other local courts, should regulate both as to quantity and quality. As to bread, a statute of 1709 recites that the existing law is so obscure that 'little or no observance hath in many places been made either in the due assize or reasonable price of bread, and covetous and evil disposed persons have for their own gain and lucre deceived and oppressed Her Majesty's subjects.' The justices of the peace or the mayors of boroughs were therefore empowered to fix the weight and price of bread and bakers had to mark their loaves with their size and quality. The price was to be fixed by reference to current market prices of grain, meal or flour. Setting the 'assize of bread' remained the function of the mayors or justices, together with the enforcement of criminal penalties for contravention, until the abolition of the assize in 1836 on the adoption of Adam Smith's principle that competition was the best regulator of these matters.

A somewhat similar system prevailed as regards the pricing, weighing and marking of coal from 1664. As regards ale, both the justices of the peace and the Courts Leet exercised jurisdiction over the price and measure of ale. This involved setting the price and ensuring that vessels made of 'wood, earth, glass, horn, leather, pewter, or some other good and wholesome metal', should be made and sized, and stamped or marked as a quart or pint (the half pint being nowhere mentioned, perhaps on the basis *de minimis non curat lex*). There is a reference in Shakespeare's *Taming of the Shrew* to Christopher Sly who is told that he would

> rail upon the Hostess of the house
> And say you would present her at the Leet
> Because she brought stone jugs, and no sealed quarts.

The Court Leet's contribution to the assessment of the ale and beer was made largely through the investigations of its officer styled an aleconner. The aleconner is one of the direct ancestors of the modern weights and measures inspector, though his job was perhaps more interesting in one respect in that he was under a duty to undertake spot checks of the quality of ale by tasting. His duties, all officially described in a contemporary record, were 'to examine bread, weights, measures, ale and beer for sale, and to return such as offend against the assize or standard, or vend unwholesome liquor.' The aleconner was in fact one of many officials that a larger Court Leet might appoint; the others might include Constables, Market-lookers, the Searchers and Sealers of Leather, the Pecksealers, the Town-crier, the Town Scavengers, Dog-muzzlers, Clerks of the Wheat, Fish and Butchery markets.

Courts Leet were the manorial criminal courts, established by an actual or presumed grant. The steward who presided over them was normally a lawyer and could punish by fine (called 'amercement') or even by imprisonment if the fine was unpaid. An important and lucrative feature was that all fines imposed belonged to the lord or the steward. Whilst their quasi-criminal functions have been abolished, they still retain the right preserved by section 24 of the Administration of Justice Act 1977 to sit and transact such business as was customary before the passing of that Act, some of which is quaintly spelled out in the Fourth Schedule to the Act.

Here are a few examples, taken from the contemporary record of the Court Leet of the Savoy, indicating the type of offences concerned with weights and measures and 'unfair trading' dealt with:

Terence McMahon amerced £10 for exposing for sale thirty-one penny worth of bread wanting thirty-one ounces assize (1709);

Upon the return of the Aleconners, Mrs Fossick, cheesemonger, for selling with scales no true ballance, to the great prejudice of the fair trader, amerced £2 (1766);

Richard amerced £20 for selling coal in sacks that want near 3 inches in length and near 2 inches in breadth of the standard or assize by law directed (1735);

Mary James, her weights being too light, amerced 5 shillings (1689);

Nicholas Baker, poulterer, amerced 3 shillings for vending and selling stinking and corrupt unwholesome pigeons (1694);

Upon the return of the fleshtasters, Mr Harrison, butcher, for exposing to sale fleshmeat not fit for Christians to eat, and refusing to remove the same, amerced 5 shillings (1761).

The development of uniform weights and measures

References in the above records to bread being too light or sacks of coal being too short of 'the standard or assize by law directed' remind us of the necessity of having constants by which weighing and measuring may accurately be assessed wherever the exercise is undertaken. For the need for accurate and widely understood weights and measures is as old as government. 'Without it there can be no civilisation and no society but the primordial. It is the first essential tool of material creation and the private and public economy are its dependants.'[1] The law and the administration designed to enforce it have for many years aimed at 1) standardisation of weights and measures, 2) control over the accuracy of the equipment used for weighing and measuring by traders, and 3) the protection of the consumer against short weight or short measure.

The search for a standard weight and measure has been a long one. The early inclination to measure weight by what a person could lift, quantities by grains of wheat and a measure by parts of the body, particularly the foot, led to many attempts at standardisation. Weight was essential for measuring gold and silver coins and bullion. By the reign of Henry VII the troy pound (of Mediterranean trade routes origin), ounce and pennyweight were established for silver, gold and some commodities. The main alternative system was avoirdupois, the pound consisting of 16 troy ounces or 7,680 grains. Wool had its own weight system. Sets of

1   O'Keefe *Law of Weights and Measures* (2nd edn, Butterworths), which contains an excellent and detailed history not only of the law (to which the authors are indebted) but of the emergence of weighing and measuring machinery.

weights were kept at the King's Treasury. Length measurements were equally slowly standardised. Edward I enacted in 1305 that '3 grains of barley, dry and round, make an inch, 12 inches make a foot, 3 feet make an Ulna' (Latin for 'elbow', later called a yard). Again the monarchs kept measuring rods in their Treasuries to set these standards, the yard-rod of Elizabeth I being the primary standard until 1824. Measurements of capacity were also crude and lacked uniformity. Measures such as gallons and pints were defined by the troy weight of the contents of the vessel containing threshed wheat, which varied with temperature and crop. In 1824 Imperial measurements were adopted, the Imperial Troy pound being 5,760 grains and the avoirdupois pound weighing 7,000 troy grains. The ounce was 1/16 of a pound, and the dram 1/16 of an ounce. A verified brass avoirdupois pound was constructed and deposited at the Treasury. Later in 1855 the Imperial standard Pound Avoirdupois of 7,000 grains was declared to be the only standard measure of weight. The Imperial gallon was standardised in 1824 by reference to ten pounds avoirdupois of distilled water weighed in air. The growth of science and technology has since required far more accurate measures. The metre is now defined as 'the length of the path travelled by light in a vacuum during a time interval of 1/299 792 458 of a second' (see Part I, Schedule 1 to the Weights and Measures Act 1985), and the yard is 0.9144 metres exactly. The four primary standards set out in section 2 of the Weights and Measures Act 1985 (yard, pound, metre and kilogramme) are in the custody of the National Physical Laboratory.

Of the two great measuring systems, the Imperial and the Metric, it is the latter with its more easily understood subdivision of weights and measures which has gained almost universal acceptance. Introduced into France by the Revolutionary Government of 1799 it spread throughout continental Europe, Russia, Japan, China and most other non-English speaking countries. Its key feature was to create a system of weights and measures based on a natural constant. The new linear unit, the metre, was to be one ten-millionth part of the distance between the North Pole and the Equator, (the earth's polar quadrant). At the same time a kilogramme standard was made to represent the weight of a cubic decimetre of pure water at a temperature of 4.44 degrees centigrade – thus linking weight with measurement. The system was decimal, using Greek prefixes for multiples of tens from the standard unit, deka- (10), hecto-(100), and kilo- (1,000), and Latin for sub-divisions in tens, deci- (one tenth), centi- (one hundreth), mili- (one thousandth). The litre, the derived unit of measure, was described as the volume of a cubic decimetre.

The United Kingdom legalised the use of metric terms in contracts in 1864 and by the Weights and Measures (Metric System) Act 1897 made metric weights and measures lawful in trade as an alternative to the Imperial system. Impetus towards metrication in the United Kingdom was added by the accession to the European Communities. The Weights and

Measures &c Act 1976 gave power to the Secretary of State by order to prohibit unauthorised Imperial units of weights and measures pursuant to the metrication policy of and under obligations imposed by EEC Units of Measurement Directives. Section 1 of the Weights and Measures Act 1985 (which consolidated the material provisions of the Weights and Measures Acts 1963, 1976 and 1979) and Schedule 1 to the 1985 Act set out the only units of measurement by reference to which any measurement involving length or mass may be made in the UK. Schedule 1 sets out definitions of measurements of length, area, volume, capacity, mass or weight and electricity. It also defines a number of traditional Imperial units which may not be used for trade. Further regulations made in 1995 (SI 1995/1804) provided for the almost complete phasing out of Imperial units of measurement for economic, public health, public safety or administrative purposes, mostly from 10 October 1995. Exceptionally the sale of loose vegetables was allowed by the pound until 31 December 1999 and the pint is allowed (indefinitely) for draft beer and cider and milk in returnable bottles, the mile, yard, foot and inch for road traffic purposes, the acre for land registration and the troy ounce for precious metals (reg 5). The law is more closely examined in chapter 13.

Enforcement

The statutory powers to enforce uniformity in weights and measures also have a long history. There is a reference to uniformity of measures of wine, ale, corn and cloth in Magna Carta in 1215. The Assize of Bread and Ale of 1266 laid down a scheme to control the amount of bread or ale obtainable for a farthing or penny respectively, depending on the current price of wheat, barley or oats. Short weight or quantity was punishable by a fine or in more serious cases flogging or the pillory. The attempt to control the weight of bread obtainable for a specified price continued until the Bread Act 1836 which required bread to be unadulterated and sold by weight. There were similar attempts to control the sale of almost all primary commodities of everyday life (particularly grain, cloth, wine, cheese, fish, honey, coal, salt and butter) in many cases dating from the fourteenth or fifteenth century. The vital step of penalising those using unjust balances was taken in the middle of the fourteenth century, towns having common balances and weights in the custody of the Mayor and Constable, but enforcement was sporadic. Excommunication after the Archbishop of Canterbury's promulgated anathema in 1428 if unequal-armed balances were used seemed to prove the most efficacious device.

The first part-time inspectors (or 'examiners') of weights and measures were appointed by justices at Quarter Sessions under Acts passed in 1795, 1797 and 1815. The present system, whereby inspectors have duties of verifying and stamping machinery as well as inspection, was established by Acts of 1834 and 1835. Inspectors were appointed by local magistrates. Local customs and a great deal of untidiness remained until the Weights and Measures Act 1878 provided for the appointment of a local authority inspectorate centrally supervised by the Board of Trade.

2. THE ECONOMIC CONTEXT OF CONSUMERISM[2]

Many assumptions are habitually made by those concerned with consumer protection as to the economic, philosophical and political nature of 'consumerism'. Statute law, comprising the State's view of the extent and nature of the protection which should be given to the consumer, proceeds on some of these assumptions but does not and cannot examine them. Nevertheless any informed view of the law, or an understanding of the writings on the philosophy of consumerism that follow, involve at least a nodding acquaintance with these assumptions, and an idea of how far they are open to challenge. A detailed analysis of any of these areas is outside the scope of this book; what follows is merely an attempt at looking at the 'context' of the law. It is appropriate to look first at some economic theories of consumer behaviour in the economy as a whole, explained in a way professional economists would regard as grossly over-simplified, but perhaps at some gain in comprehensibility to the layman.

Demand

There is alleged to be an economist who taught his parrot the distillation of a lifetime's study of the 'dismal science'. It merely repeated 'supply and demand'. As far as consumer behaviour is concerned we are dealing primarily with aspects of 'demand' in microeconomic theory.

Who is 'the consumer', the subject matter of this book? The Molony Committee on Consumer Protection regarded a consumer as one who purchases (or hire-purchases) goods for private use or consumption (para 2). The private consumer of services is equally 'a consumer', as the Molony Committee admitted, but this aspect of consumerism was rejected in the Report as a matter for investigation for reasons of practicability. (A transaction whereby goods are purchased from a retail shop does in any

---

2   On the persistent failure of law teachers to recognise the importance of the nexus between law and economics in the UK, see Ogus 'Economics, Liberty and the Common Law' [1980] JSPTL 42. There are now a number of texts incorporating the economic approach to law in this and other areas and the senior judiciary often consider micro-economic criteria when formulating policy issues.

case involve both goods and services, the mark-up over the wholesale price being the payment for the services involved in the purchase.) More recently it has been realised that the definition of 'a consumer' should be broadened to include anyone who consumes goods or services at the end of the chain of production, thus catching the otherwise excluded claimant in *Donoghue v Stevenson*,[3] for example. In some countries 'consumerism' embraces pressure groups concerned primarily with the environment and its preservation. However it is not practicable to discuss here such laws which protect the public generally and which do not give to the individual (except in rare cases) the right to take legal action against infringement. Nor is it appropriate here to discuss the government or public authorities as consumers, though they do of course 'consume' goods and services as do firms not publicly owned.

In economic theory the picture of consumer behaviour is drawn on a much larger canvas. The dramatis personae of economic theory consists of three groups – 'households', 'firms' and 'central authorities'. The stage on which they act is called 'the market'. When economists speak about 'the consumer' they refer to the group of individuals comprising the household. Unrealistically 'households' are deemed as consistent decision-taking units as individuals are. Again, perhaps unrealistically, households are assumed to know what they want and to act rationally. (Broadly these generalisations can be substantiated; on an isolated basis there will be found many aberrants.) So households are assumed to desire their well-being, 'satisfaction' or 'utility' as this concept is called. They operate in a market which is, for present purposes, an area over which buyers and sellers negotiate the exchange of a well-defined commodity.[4] In a competitive market the diversity of buyers and sellers is large enough to prevent any one of them being able to influence price, and this we assume to be the norm. In recent times neither completely free-market economies nor entirely centrally controlled, or 'command', economies have existed. But the degree of central control has significantly varied from one political bloc to another and from one country to another. The British economy is a mixed economy, so the consumer finds that in the case of some commodities he is facing a price and quality control dictated by the State or a public corporation (for example, the Post Office), in other areas price may be less controlled but subject at least to some regulation (eg rents of private housing), and in other areas price is dictated purely by market considerations (television sets, motor cars etc). Whether or not there is State regulation of price, quality and range of choice is, of course, a vital consideration in considering the shape and effectiveness of consumer protection in a given sphere.

3   [1932] AC 562. The case is discussed further in ch 6.
4   See Lipsey *An Introduction in Positive Economics* ch 6.

Three hypotheses can be deduced about the nature of a household's demand. Firstly, a household's demand for a commodity is influenced by the price of that commodity and the prices of other goods. Assuming other factors such as income and preference (or taste) remain constant, normally if price rises a lesser quantity will be consumed, often because a substitution can be made. Thus a typical household might react to high potato prices by buying fewer potatoes and more, cheaper, rice, or to high coffee prices by buying tea, in both cases as a substitute. Similarly, and bound up with this thesis, a fall in the price of (expensive) coffee should result in less (comparatively cheap) tea being consumed. The two commodities are said to be 'substitutes'. But if two sorts of commodity tend to be consumed together, so that a fall in the price of one increases demand for the other, the two commodities are termed 'complements'. Thus we would expect a fall in the price of motor vehicles to be accompanied by increased demand both for motor vehicles and petrol.

Secondly, a rise in the 'income' of the household is associated normally with a rise in demand. We say 'normally' because there are many exceptions to this. A household living well above subsistence level is unlikely to alter the quantity of salt consumed whether household income drops or rises (provided any drop is not too dramatic). And in some cases an inferior substitute might be abandoned in favour of a superior one, eg the demand of a household with increasing income for British sherry might cease altogether as Spanish sherry is substituted. Similarly, the total 'income' of the household marks the limit of its total spending in a given period. 'Income' here has to be defined very broadly to include savings, cash value of non-liquid assets and credit available. And as far as 'income' is concerned, the consumer's spending power is more likely in practice to be limited to the net 'take-home' sum received from all sources after tax and other deductions have been made – often called 'disposable income'.

Thirdly, the demand for a commodity depends upon the preferences, or taste, of the household. The question of varying taste is usually regarded as outside the realm of economic measurement, though taste and fashion are very real factors as far as production and marketing of goods are concerned and can be affected by advertising and publicity. Variations of taste are likely to lead to increase of demand for some commodities and decrease in demand for others.

Utility

The above three hypotheses help to explain, on a large scale, why consumers behave as they do. The concept of 'best value for money' is at the root of much of the legal and administrative machinery for consumer protection. It implies that the consumer will get the best return that he can for his expenditure just as a firm will seek to maximise the output from its inputs and, accordingly, its profit. How can this element of 'yield' that consumers are assumed to wish to maximise be measured? A fundamental concept, highly developed in the nineteenth century and still often referred to, is the concept of utility, particularly diminishing marginal utility.

Basic needs for housing, food, clothing and the like generate a large variety of specific wants. These wants can be satisfied by acquiring goods and services. The capacity of goods and services to satisfy wants is called 'utility'. Wants are subjective, and the concept of utility should not be confused with any objective assessment of 'usefulness'. Spectacles without which the wearer cannot see and eyeshadow without which the wearer will not be seen have equal utility for the person who wants each of them. But the intensity of demand, because of the level of satisfaction to be derived from the goods, is likely to affect the price of them unless supply of the goods can be increased to meet demand at the same price (ie supply is perfectly elastic). Therefore the relative price of commodities will be at least in part determined by the utility they have for consumers.

However, from the point of view of the individual consumer, a saturation point is likely to be reached if he consumes an ever increasing quantity of one good. To a thirsty person the first two pints of beer may be extremely satisfying, but after a certain number of pints in excess of this (depending on the capacity of the drinker) less and less satisfaction is derived. This principle applies to many commodities, even assuming there are no budgetary restraints because the beer is free or the consumer of the commodity has unlimited financial resources. So the principle of diminishing marginal utility is simply that although the utility derived from a good increases with the amount consumed, it does so less than proportionately. After a point utility starts to become reduced and continued consumption would confer a negative marginal utility (or a 'disutility').

Although this may seem somewhat abstract and unreal, the relevance of the theory to consumer behaviour may be seen by posing a series of choices. Which would you prefer – a visit to the opera or a hot bath? A person living in a comfortable house in Cornwall might prefer to go to the opera, since it is normally relatively inaccessible, whereas someone living in a cardboard box in a London street, equally musical, might prefer a hot bath. The consumer is not comparing the *total* utility of opera performances in general and of hot baths in general (although many opinion polls proceed on the assumption that such a comparison is a useful exercise); he is comparing the *marginal* utility of each commodity. To the affluent Cornishman, another hot bath has low marginal utility, perhaps zero marginal utility if he has already bathed that day. But to the bathless homeless person the marginal utility of a bath is high. Of course, choice of goods to satisfy various competing demands of the consumer is complicated by the fact that commodities vary in price per unit. So economists apply the principle of diminishing marginal utility to the behaviour of the household by saying that, to quote Lipsey, 'the household maximising its utility will so allocate its expenditure between commodities that the utility of the last penny spent on each is equal'.

It is fair to add that in the twentieth century economists invented more sophisticated ways of mapping consumer behaviour and choice. Because utility cannot accurately be measured, they have concentrated instead on preferences. Thus, for example, if food and clothing were rationed, it might be possible to show that consumers would prefer six points for food and four points for clothing, rather than five points each, out of a maximum of 10 points. The precise amount of utility is not measured when assessing the two combinations, but it is possible to plot by means of 'indifference curves' the areas in which consumers are indifferent to choice and those where they develop a distinct preference. The details of this need not unduly concern the layperson. The statement at the end of the last paragraph is the critical one in assessing consumer behaviour.

The courts have been asked to authorise the compensation of consumers disappointed by, for example, a spoilt holiday or lost photographs of a family wedding. In doing so the judges have recognised that consumers make purchases for the pleasure or utility they confer. This type of loss cannot be measured in the way normally employed in business law – by reference to the price paid or diminished profits. This concept of consumer surplus is fundamental to consumer law and can be seen explicitly recognised in, for example, *Jarvis v Swans Tours Ltd*.[5]

Consumer sovereignty and the generation of wants

To Adam Smith, 'the interest of the producer ought to be attended to only so far as it may be necessary for promoting that of the consumer' (*Wealth of Nations* 1776). Despite the scorn that has been poured onto the idea of 'consumer sovereignty' in the modern economy, for the reasons mentioned below, examples of how in a free market economy producers have to adjust to changing consumer preferences still abound. The mini-skirt manufacturer must adjust to the maxi (ie longer hemlines) or risk going out of business. In general terms the flow of consumer expenditure, directed by the preferences of numerous individuals, either increases or decreases pressures on producers. These pressures will be measured by the price mechanism which, at least in the short run, will increase as demand increases (and vice versa) until it settles at the point of balance of supply

---

5   [1973] QB 233, [1973] 1 All ER 71 – £125 damages for loss of entertainment and enjoyment of a holiday. See also Harris, Ogus and Phillips 'Contract Remedies and the Consumer Surplus' (1979) 95 LQR 581.

and demand. And as producers respond to increased demand, productive resources will be adapted (staff laid off and retrained, plant renewed or adjusted etc) in order to attract as much as they can of consumer spending.

The contrary thesis, developed by Galbraith in, for example, *The New Industrial State*, argues that the initiative now lies with the skilled 'technostructure' inside the corporation who can manipulate prices and demand. Others have pointed out that some products of large corporations still fail despite powerful promotion, and that, therefore, consumer sovereignty still fundamentally operates. The control which consumers exercise is, in truth, a matter of degree. The State, even in a mixed economy, can greatly affect consumer behaviour by its own spending, or, for example, increasing excise duties on alcohol and tobacco for reasons of revenue or public health or both, and demand is inevitably affected. In a centrally directed economy, such as that formerly in operation in the old Soviet Union, producers may be directed to concentrate on production which, in the State's view, is desirable (eg public education, recreation for working people, social security instead of luxury goods, drink, tobacco and so on). This system certainly avoids some 'abuses' occurring in free economies, but the incentive to satisfy consumers largely disappears in favour of the need to satisfy an insensitive bureaucracy. The Moscow queues for the bare essentials of life and the lack of choice for customers tenacious enough to get to the front were a sad and depressing feature of seventy years of a 'Communist' economy. And the proponents of the free market would add, in the words of Milton Friedman, that a free market economy 'gives people what they want instead of what a particular group thinks they ought to want'.

Another objection to the idea of consumer sovereignty is the thesis that their allegedly voluntary wants are 'created' by producers by advertising on TV or in newspapers, posters and the like, or by other methods such as door-to-door canvassing. This manipulates consumer preferences into areas which suit the producer. However, powerful though demand creation by advertising undoubtedly is, there are limitations to its effectiveness. Completely impractical clothing for the UK climate, or completely unpalatable food or drink would be rejected however subtle the advertising. And to the producer, the increased profit brought about by the increased demand must always exceed the often very considerable cost of advertising for the project to be worthwhile. Much will depend on whether the product itself is genuinely desirable and prolonged positive response will be primarily due to the making of the information available to the consumer, rather than 'puffing', which in an advanced free economy is likely to be controlled by a legal requirement that it should be lawful, decent and honest. To this extent, consumers retain their sovereignty.

In this connection, and associated with the colossal growth in technology over the last century, is a problem with which consumer protection is much concerned, namely the accuracy and extent of a consumer's knowledge about a product and the use of that knowledge when deciding to purchase goods. Watches, television sets, motor cars and many more consumer durables are difficult to judge objectively (disregarding the producers' advertising) by an ordinary individual without extensive initial testing which is normally impractical. Consumers may rely instead on a global brand name or trade mark of a large producer without considering less well publicised alternatives. This, too, exists as a powerful limitation to consumer sovereignty and underlines the importance of such organisations as the Consumers' Association which makes comparative information available on the quality and price of a range of competing products.

3. THE PHILOSOPHY AND POLITICS OF CONSUMERISM

In Britain it is conventional wisdom, adopted by the major political parties, that consumer protection is by and large 'a good thing'. Much of the law studied in this book emanates from Parliament and consists of measures over which there has been little political disagreement. Thus the Conservative Government introduced a Consumer Credit Bill to give effect to the main recommendation of the Crowther Committee on Consumer Credit and though this Bill fell with the Government in February 1974 the Bill was reintroduced with few substantive changes later in 1974 by the Labour Government.

However, if the student or practitioner of consumer protection is to have a broader appreciation of the subject than is likely to be afforded by a study of its detailed machinery, he or she should be able to answer such basic questions as – Why protect consumers? Against what are you protecting them? And by protecting them, towards what goal are you aiming? The US Special Committee on Retail Instalment Sales, Consumer Credit, Small Loans and Usury, in its Report had framed questions precisely along these lines:

> It is fair to ask precisely what it is that the consumer is to be protected from. Must he be protected from his own lack of knowledge or discipline which leads him to take advantage of easy credit to buy things he does not need or cannot afford? Is he to be protected from the 'fringe' operator who may take advantage of the ignorance and gullibility of the consumer to cause him to overbuy or pay too much?[6]

6   Page 9, cited Trebilcock 'Consumer Protection in the Affluent Society' 16 McGill LJ 263, an article fully exploring these problems to which the authors are much indebted.

Why protect the consumer?[7]

We have already seen that for many centuries it has been thought appropriate to protect the consumer against fraudulent or dangerous practices. This reflects a moral and religious ethic and is an appropriate function of the criminal law. As such the proposition is hardly controversial. More difficult to answer briefly is the question, – why 'protect' the consumer when there has been no fraud by the producer or seller? Examples of this sort of consumer protection are the implying of non-excludable terms as to quality in contracts for sale of goods or reopening of 'extortionate' credit bargains by the court under sections 137 to 140 of the Consumer Credit Act 1974.

The paternalism which this sort of legislation provision implies is normally justified in modern times by the idea of inequality of bargaining power. An important consumer protection measure in Australia was justified as follows:

> In consumer transactions unfair practices are widespread. The existing law is still founded on the principle known as caveat emptor – meaning 'let the buyer beware'. That principle may have been appropriate for transactions conducted in village markets. It has ceased to be appropriate as a general rule. Now the marketing of goods and services is conducted on an organised basis and by trained business executives. The untrained consumer is no match for the businessman who attempts to persuade the consumer to buy goods or services on terms and conditions suitable to the vendor. The consumer needs protection by the law and this Bill will provide such protection.[8]

Another aspect of consumer protection relevant to this question is the problem of claiming compensation against the large producer where the goods or services are defective. Litigation is disproportionately costly and

---

7   For a comprehensive study of the possible answers to this question (based on (i) the improvement of economic efficiency by remedying market failures and (ii) 'equity'), see Ian D C Ramsay *Rationales for Intervention in the Consumer Market Place* (OFT, Occasional Paper, December 1984). This study contains many further references to Commonwealth and USA monographs on aspects of the economics of consumer protection. Subsequent studies are referred to later in this chapter.

8   Senator Murphy, then Australian Attorney-General, introducing the Trade Practices Bill of the Commonwealth of Australia in the Senate – quoted John Goldring 'Consumer Protection and the Trade Practices Act 1974–5' 6 Federal L Rev at 288. For an analysis of the thinking of some European jurists on the province and function of consumer protection laws, see J Stuyck 'European consumer law after the Treaty of Amsterdam: Consumer policy in or beyond the internal market?' (2000) 37 Common Market Law Review 367–400.

troublesome to the small consumer. So policy has been to encourage producers to adopt codes of practice whereunder legitimate complaints are promptly dealt with on the one hand, and also encourage small claims and arbitration procedures to solve actual disputes expeditiously, cheaply and relatively informally.

The philosophy embodied in this type of consumer protection, which is to be found now in most of the developed jurisdictions in Europe and elsewhere in the non-Communist world, has been attacked at its roots by thinkers of both the left and the right.

A revealing slogan from the left describes this type of consumer protection as 'band-aid on the malignancy of capitalism'.[9] If non-centrally controlled production is regarded as against the interests of the 'substratum of society', a continuing function of capitalism disguised only in that it supplies material comforts to those who would otherwise be in the van of the revolution, the sooner it is destroyed the better. As Marcuse said of the American economy:

> Let me give a brief definition of what I mean by an affluent society. A model, of course, is American society today, although even in the US it is more a tendency, not yet entirely translated into reality. In the first place, it is a capitalist society. It seems to be necessary to remind ourselves of this because there are some people, even on the left, who believe that American society is no longer a class society. I can assure you that it is a class society. It is a capitalist society with a high concentration of economic and political power; with an enlarged and enlarging sector of automation and co-ordination of production, distribution and communication; with private ownership in the means of production, which however depends increasingly on ever more active and wide intervention by the government. It is a society in which, as I mentioned, the material as well as cultural needs of the underlying population are satisfied on a scale larger than ever before – but they are satisfied in line with the requirements and interests of the apparatus and of the powers which control the apparatus. And it is a society growing on the condition of accelerating waste, planned obsolescence and destruction, while the substratum of the population continues to live in poverty and misery.[10]

If this is believed, the present system of consumer protection is clearly merely propping up a corrupt system to supply palliative or cosmetic remedies to the abused substratum of society, remedies which fail to do

9   Quoted Goldring 6 Federal L Rev at 288.
10   H Marcuse 'Liberation from the Affluent Society' in Cooper (ed) *The Dialectics of Liberation* (1968).

Philosophy and politics of consumerism

anything to stop the system in its tracks. Consumer protection is also attacked, usually covertly, for being 'middle class', the middle classes for this purpose being defined as those with the opportunity and education to look after themselves. The implication is that the poor are out of reach of this movement since they are too ignorant or under too many pressures to resist exploitation.[11] Describing the attitude of consumer associations to this charge Eirlys Roberts wrote:

> Compassion for those poorer than themselves was not overt with the consumer associations. They were not social workers nor charity organisations. But it was there, and would show itself later in the perpetual attempt they would make to spread their membership beyond the middle classes, who showed some enthusiasm for joining them, to the working class, who showed very little.[12]

From the left to the right, the objection to at least some aspects of consumer protection is that it represents undue 'mollycoddling' of the consumer. In a laissez-faire economic system, the way in which production is affected by demand is not through regulation by law (except to stop fraud or dangerous goods and the like) but by the flow of consumer expenditure, activated by a series of voluntary choices, bringing pressure at various points. Part of the doctrine of consideration in law is that its adequacy cannot be questioned in legal proceedings. Neither law nor equity will, as a general rule, mend any person's bargain, even today. Linked with this is the belief in the therapeutic effect of the individual looking after his own interests rather than the 'nanny-state' trying, often at great expense and little result, to do this for him. The centrally planned economy, whose 'Nanny' is transmogrified into 'Big Brother' and under which the State decides what the consumer shall or shall not have, would represent the ultimate of objectionable control.

11   See David Caplovitz *The Poor Pay More* dealing with the expenditure of Negro and Puerto Rican families in New York State. See also 'Market Considerations and Consumer Protection Policy' xxiii Univ Toronto LJ 396 (Cayne and Trebilcock), and 'Why the Poor Pay More' National Consumer Council (1977). The argument can be taken further by saying that as natural resources are finite, unless production is centrally regulated the earth will be laid waste and man may not survive at all. See further Layton and Holmes 'Consumerism – A passing malaise or a continuing expression of social concern' 46 Austr Quarterly 6–25.

12   *Consumers* (New Thinkers Library) at 18. See also the OFT's published research on the classes of consumer (or perhaps more accurately, citizen) most likely to be prejudiced by the lack of capacity to obtain the best value for money: *Vulnerable Consumer Groups: Quantification and Analysis*, Research Paper 15 (R Burden, OFT 1998). On problems of access to financial services, see *Vulnerable Consumers and Financial Services: The Report of the Director General's Enquiry* (OFT, 1999).

The following extracts from an essay by Lord Coleraine are by no means necessarily antipathetical to a degree of consumer protection legislated for ad hoc as at present, but they do well explain the Conservative objections to the centrally directed economy desired by Socialists, Marxists or Neo-Marxists as the fundamental solution:

... a spontaneous order in the economic field does not depend upon the supposed infallibility of a few individuals at the centre, supported and nourished by a mass of information coming in from the periphery with varying degrees of unpunctuality and inaccuracy. It is created and sustained by the self-regarding activities of an almost infinite number of individuals, each of whom is in communication with only a very small number of others. Each one of these, in his turn, is linked to others again. Thus, the needs and ideas of a single person can be communicated through an endless chain to those utterly remote from him, of whose very existence he may be unaware; and everyone in the chain is free to respond to information reaching him, in any way he pleases – or not respond at all. It is this process, infinitely complex in its operation but infallible in its effects, which causes packets of tea, for instance, to appear in the grocer's shop in convenient sizes, with blends and flavours suited to the varying tastes of the housewife, and matched to the length of her purse, an operation which is carried out so smoothly that its complexity is not even suspected.

There are many who, admitting the greater efficiency of a spontaneous order, hold that the price exacted for it in terms of social cost is too high, and that even gross inefficiency is to be preferred to the suffering which follows the ruthless application of the principles of a free economy. Indeed, any exposition of the theory of a free economy can be counted on to arouse, even in those philosophically opposed to state intervention, dark mutterings about laissez-faire, or references to children aroused at three o'clock in the morning to work in textile mills, or to little chimney sweeps with cancer of the skin. But there are still such things as Factory Acts, and it is surely better to control the thoughtlessness, the cruelty or the cupidity of man by legislation than to attempt the impossible task of planning an economy in which there is not even the possibility of abuse.

A spontaneous economic order, then, is more efficient than an imposed order, and it need not be much less humane. It is necessary to stress again, however, that personal liberty is the necessary precondition for it. A spontaneous order is inconceivable without personal freedom and, in particular, without freedom of choice. The socialist dream, on the other hand, depends for realisation upon the limitation of freedom for the individual, and the dilution of his sense of responsibility for his own acts.[13]

The Crowther Committee addressed itself to the same problem in the field of consumer credit, and answered the question in a rather similar way:

> Given the principles of economic policy which we have advocated, our general view is that the state should interfere as little as possible with the consumer's freedom to use his knowledge of the consumer credit market to the best of his ability and according to his judgment of what constitutes his best interests. While it is understandable and proper for the state to be concerned about the things on which people spend their money and even to use persuasion to influence the scale of values implied by their expenditure patterns, it remains a basic tenet of a free society that people themselves must be the judge of what contributes to their material welfare.
>
> Our examination of the social effects of consumer credit has not uncovered any strong social reasons for departing significantly from this view. Since the vast majority of consumers use credit wisely and derive considerable benefit from it, the right policy is not to restrict their freedom of access by administrative and legal measures but to help the minority who innocently get into trouble to manage their financial affairs more successfully – without, however, also making conditions easier for the fraudulent borrower. The basic principle of social policy must, therefore, be to reduce the number of defaulting debtors. This is in everybody's interest.[14]

The decay of centrally planned economies

Since this debate between those favouring a 'command', centrally directed, economy and those favouring a free market was outlined in earlier editions of this book, colossal changes have occurred in the world economic order.

---

13 'For Conservatives Only' quoted in *How Conservatives Think* (1975). For a succinct political history of the Consumerist Ideology see Leonard Tivey 'The Politics of the Consumer', in R Kimber and J J Richardson (eds) *Pressure Groups in Britain – a reader* (1974). See also R Cranston 'Creeping Economism: Some Thoughts on Law and Economics' (1977) British Journal of Law and Society 103 (a critique of the Chicago School's free market approach to economic theory as applied to the legal system, with particular reference to consumer protection); T Sorrell 'The Customer is not Always Right' (1994) 13 Journal of Business Ethics 913 (a critique of morally questionable behaviour by consumers and its effect on businesses).

14 Cmnd 4596 (1971), paras 3.9.1 and 3.9.2.

The centrally directed economies of the Soviet Union and Eastern and Central Europe have either collapsed or were gradually transformed. Instead in the early 1990s, democratically elected governments were striving to 'privatise' their State run industry, one end product of which should eventually be a far more responsive meeting of consumer demand.

Plans for the conversion of 'command' to 'free' economies in Russia and Eastern Europe were nothing if not optimistic. Positive thinking is clearly needed, but the complexity of Western models, often taken completely for granted in the West itself, does not make for quick transplants. The free market needs carefully structured checks, balances and safety nets to make it work in a widely acceptable way. To take a few points, central to the understanding of the relationship between consumer and producer, free competition is essential to make markets work. But the supervisory mechanisms developed in the West to combat monopolies and restrictive practices have taken over a century to develop. And if competition works there will be business casualties. There must therefore be a safety net to supply income support to those thrown out of work. Much of the funding for this is a charge on central government taxation and taxation in a democracy has to be subject to limitations and principles of economic equity acceptable to the electorate. The Social Security system administered by the State similarly needs impartially administered and adjudicated rules. Businessmen themselves need a clearly understood legal system and an independent and knowledgeable judiciary – a product of years of tradition and training. The transition from a system where the all-powerful State (usually personified by supporters of the relevant party) was in effect unchallengeable was always likely to take more than 500 days to achieve, particularly in a country such as Russia with no tradition of democracy even before the 1917 revolution.

To revert to the problem of the First World, since the United Kingdom in common with the USA, Australia, Canada and other jurisdictions having similar systems of consumer protection is likely to have a mixed rather than centrally directed economy for the foreseeable future, our conclusion must be that the need for consumer protection in such an economy is part of its nature. A completely unregulated laissez-faire system is unacceptable as is a centrally directed one, and a pragmatic compromise is to compensate for the inequalities of bargaining power and technological expertise by giving the private consumer protection in specific areas by legislation.

Against what are you protecting the consumer?

Implicit in the suggested answers to this question is the concept of the prudent shopping decision. A decision is imprudent if the buyer buys goods which he does not need or cannot afford, or if he buys too much in quantity or pays too much as a result of slick salesmanship. The mischief of an apparently ever expanding economy involving ever increasing consumption the price of which is waste has now been the subject of a number of critical exposés – see for instance Vance Packard's *The Hidden Persuaders*, *The Status Seekers* and *The Waste Makers*. Galbraith uses what are philosophically similar arguments in advocating a decline in artificially contrived consumer demands (artificially contrived, that is, by producers' advertising and salesmanship as well as the psychological need to 'keep up with the Joneses') and a switch of productive resources into the public sector in response to an induced demand for better schools, better hospitals etc *instead* of more consumer durables. Galbraith supports the doctrine of diminishing marginal utility in relation to consumer wants in arguing that as more and more additional wants are satisfied the consumer *ought* to want less:

In the contemporary United States, the supply of bread is plentiful and the supply of bread grains even redundant ... And having extended their bread consumption to the point where its marginal utility is very low, people have gone on to spend their income on other things. Since these goods entered their consumption pattern after bread, there is a presumption that they are not very urgent either – that *their* consumption has been carried, as with wheat, to the point where marginal utility is small or even negligible. So it must be assumed that the importance of marginal increments of all production is low and declining. The effect of increasing affluence is to minimize the importance of economic goals. Production and productivity becomes less and less important.[15]

Logically this can be attacked by arguing that basing patterns of production on what a consumer *ought* to want is another way of saying that the economy ought to be centrally directed by the State, and even if the vast majority are incapable of taking independent prudent shopping (or non-shopping) decisions, to have freedom of choice, including the right to choose imprudently, entirely eliminated is also to eliminate personal freedom for the small minority who will always dissent from or challenge the norm.[16]

It can be seen that the question raises fundamental issues. If the law is to avoid venturing into the area of *regulation* of production so as to change society for better or worse according to taste, its role outside the criminal

15   Galbraith *The Affluent Society* quoted Trebilcock 16 McGill LJ at 268.
16   See eg Hayek *The Road to Serfdom*.

law must instead be primarily both to protect the consumer against misrepresentations of a contractual nature and to protect the prudent shopper on the basis of information. If all relevant information about a class of goods is available to the prudent shopper, together with information about the true cost of the goods if credit is available, then at least a prudent shopping decision can be made with the consumer's eyes fully open. In so far as the consumer's shopping decisions are made without information which could have been usefully obtained and assimilated, there is an element of 'consumer detriment'. The concept of 'consumer detriment' is, however, difficult to quantify and assess. Relying on the volume of consumer complaints per annum which happen to come to the notice of the authorities is hardly sufficient, though for many years the Office of Fair Trading has classified them into categories. This at least can indicate the market sectors where remedial action appears more urgent. The OFT's recent study, *Consumer Detriment* (OFT 296, February 2000) reveals much further thought on indicators of detriment and the problem of quantification. Its calculation that the estimated cost of all complaints in 1999 was between £5.6 billion and £11 billion, averaging at £1.5% of total household expenditure or £180 per adult per annum is a matter of great concern. The Director General of Fair Trading in his Annual Report for 1999 stated that increasingly sophisticated and widespread unfair trading is costing consumers billions annually, and defective goods and services specifically at least £8.3 billion a year (OFT, June 2000).

The body of consumer protection laws can also be usefully assessed by asking whether it is reconcilable with the economic concept of the 'perfect market'. If so, the proponents of the need for these laws have a ready made answer to the common assumption that they somehow interfere with a process that would be better left to automatic self-regulation. It is, therefore, worth examining the concept of the perfect market more closely.

The conditions for the operation of the perfect market may be summarised broadly as follows:

a)   there must be no monopoly;
b)   there must be no cartels;
c)   there must be freedom of entry into the market;
d)   it must be assumed that there are an infinite number of buyers – ie no buyer-monopoly;
e)   there must be product homogeneity – ie comparisons must be made between similar goods and public controls must affect similar goods equally;
f)   it must be assumed that all consumers have perfect knowledge – ie have all the requisite information to make informed choices between competing goods.

How far the UK's consumer protection and competition laws serve to promote the concept of the perfect market has been the subject of more detailed analysis elsewhere.[17] Suffice it to say here that the UK has for many years accumulated progressively more comprehensive anti-monopoly and cartel legislation and this is mentioned later in this chapter. The first four conditions mentioned above are consistent with the general objectives of the anti-monopoly provisions of the Fair Trading Act 1973 and the former Competition Act 1980, the Restrictive Trade Practices Act 1976 and the Resale Prices Act 1976, now almost entirely replaced by the Competition Act 1998. The condition as to ensuring that consumers have perfect knowledge of the market before the perfect market concept can operate is fundamental. In a highly technological society, the consumer cannot in reality be in possession of the requisite technological knowledge to assess the wide variety of goods in common domestic use, nor is there in reality any pre-buying opportunity to subject goods to scientific analysis. This is why, it may be argued, modern consumer law statutes tend to give the consumer inalienable guarantees of fitness and quality as well as guarantees as to the safe operation of the goods. The need for product homogeneity imposes a necessary uniformity on standard term contracts for goods sold to consumers and special terms, including exemption clauses, are heavily controlled or banned altogether.

The need for perfect knowledge also highlights the importance of the reports on comparative testing by the Consumers' Association and on comparative prices by some local authorities' consumer advice centres. Similarly it is reasonable to imply a measure of responsibility on the producer in respect of the quality of goods where this cannot readily be ascertained by inspection, as is commonly the case in English law. (Criminal misrepresentations and laws against unsafe goods are uncontroversially within the ambit of consumer protection, and have been for many years.) The Molony Committee, in substantial accordance with this philosophy, grouped their proposals for consumer protection as follows:

a)   arrangements to give the consumer a positive assurance that the goods on offer are safe (if safety is relevant) and of sound quality (shortly 'standards');

b)   the provision of information annexed to the goods which will assist the consumer to judge for himself whether or not they will satisfy his particular requirement ('informative labelling');

17   See B W Harvey 'Consumer Protection Laws and the Concept of the Perfect Market', John O'Keefe Memorial Lecture, Institute of Trading Standards, 1980. See also Siegan (ed) *Regulation, Economics and the Law* (1979), particularly ch 4; I D C Ramsey *Rationales for Intervention in the Consumer Market Place* (OFT Occasional Paper, December 1984); and various authors 'Legal Implications of Imperfect Information in Consumer Markets' (1995) 151 Journal of Institutional and Theoretical Economics, 31, 49, 52; *Consumer Detriment* OFT 296 (Feb 2000).

c)   the assessment of the merits of the goods on offer by independent agencies ('seals of approval' and 'comparative testing');

d)   the availability of adequate means whereby the justifiably aggrieved shopper may obtain fair redress;

e)   the restraint of misdescription of the significant characteristics of the goods on offer;

f)   the restraint of objectionable sales promotion methods, whether in the form of advertisements or otherwise, which are calculated to divert the shopper from a proper judgment of his best interests (Cmnd 1781 (1962) para 48).

The above discussion also indicates the alternative goals which a policy of consumer protection does or should aim towards. The Galbraith thesis is basically anti-materialist and would, it has been suggested, lead eventually to the sort of State-directed objectives which characterised the planning of an economy such as that of the now dissolved USSR. The philosophy of the UK's consumer protection policy (and that of Canada and Australia for example) is consistent with the more modest objectives indicated in the Molony Report above. But wider, anti-inequality of bargaining power, objectives are of increasing importance and may take the form of anti-monopoly legislation, encouragement of competition, control of excessive or misleading advertising, full disclosure requirements, powers to reopen extortionate bargains, better access to the legal system for the unrepresented consumer, and consumer education programmes.

Should (and can) a cost-benefit analysis be made?

Those to whom consumer protection is almost sacred would perhaps take the view that the consumer is now so much better off as a result partly of outstanding proselytisers such as Ralph Nader in the USA (and the privately mounted campaigns for safer cars and smoke-free zones in airliners) and partly of the official and voluntary framework of consumer protection that to question whether there should be financial limits to the umbrella of protection is unworthy. How can you measure, in financial terms, improvement of the human condition? However, the issue did not escape the Molony Committee, who stated with great cogency:

16. We received a great weight of criticism of the existing system of consumer protection, accompanied by suggestions for its replacement. Although we observed a measure of justification, as well as unanimity, in the criticism, we found that some of the suggestions were extravagant in the extreme – extravagant in terms of money cost as well as conception. The consumer, unlike some classes with claims on public bounty, is everybody all the time. The

consumer is the taxpayer, and we see small merit in creating an elaborate new system to assist him in one capacity when he would have to pay for it in the other. In so far as any increased cost fell on industry, recoupment from the consumer would be no less inevitable. Further, in considering bold suggestions for reshaping consumer protection arrangements it was necessary, in our opinion, not merely to balance the money cost, but also the degree of interference with production and distribution methods, against the benefits to the consumer claimed by the proponents of reform. These factors have weighed with us in favouring more stringent legal provisions in aid of the consumer rather than an extensive protective machinery, operating administratively at considerable cost.[18]

As regards the cost, in the UK part of this is met by those who subscribe to a particular group such as the Consumers' Association, but central government or local government revenue is now used extensively to service the Office of Fair Trading, the National Consumer Council, the Department of Trade and Industry itself, Citizens' Advice Bureaux, Local Authorities' Trading Standards and Consumer Advice Centres, and so on. The money to service these departments and agencies must be raised by taxes or borrowing. 'Compliance' cost to industry in respect of legislative regulation of their product or service can also be considerable and is, of course, passed on to the consumer in higher prices. Over-regulation can kill the goose that lays the golden egg.[19] In 1979, the Commercial Legislation Monitoring Group (an ad hoc group representing 18 leading businesses) estimated that consumer protection legislation might be costing £150 million per annum, or 14p per £100 of household expenditure. Subsidiary legislation, and in particular labelling requirements, were singled out for particular criticism. The National Consumer Council challenged these figures (commissioned from the Economist Intelligence Unit) and estimated the cost at nearer $^1/_2$p in every £10 of consumer expenditure, but the Monitoring Group's chairman was confident that the Group's higher figure was a reliable estimate.

In 1985 the Department of Trade published its own report based on the scrutiny of administrative and legislative requirements on businesses entitled 'Burdens on Businesses'. This identified a number of areas as being noticeably burdensome to small firms, particularly VAT and taxation procedures, employment protection and health and safety. Regulatory provisions falling under the head 'Consumer Law' were classified as

18 Cmnd 1781, para 16.
19 Consider, for instance, the effect of the introduction of most stringent fire regulations on the small hoteliers, many of whom were unable to find the capital needed for required improvements and went out of business. Greater safety is in fact being substituted for the choice of a less safe but cheaper hotel. And see Goldring 6 Fed L Rev at 290.

relatively light (11 mentions from respondents out of 200). There were mixed views produced by those surveyed on the fairness of regulatory consumer provisions and it was considered that little could be done to reduce the burden. It was suggested, though, that there should be 'greater use of common sense in balancing firms' and consumer interests'. Of a total of 200 firms surveyed, an estimate of £47,000 has been produced as the relevant overhead expense (see pp 31, 44 of the report).

Following the production of the 'Burdens on Businesses' report, an Enterprise and Deregulation Unit was established within the Department of Trade and Industry to implement the Deregulation Initiative, launched in 1985. A number of further initiatives followed based on the proposition that 'deregulation is vital to competitiveness. Rules can act as a deterrent to market entry, unnecessary requirements impose costs on business, and the burden of official forms and paperwork wastes management time. Bad regulation stands in the way of innovation, investment and jobs' (from 'Competitiveness: Forging Ahead' (Cm 2867, 1995)). The same paper pointed out that in 1994 some 1,467 regulations had been made, excluding commencement orders. To aid the 'weeding out' process the Deregulation and Contracting Out Act 1994 was passed which contained over 30 specific deregulation measures and, unusually, gave power to amend primary legislation by order subject to new Parliamentary scrutiny procedures.

The motivation behind this drive is to reduce the cost to business of complying with numerous statutory requirements. But this must not materially prejudice vital consumer and public protection against dangerous, fraudulent or misleading products – a balance must be struck between cost and benefit.

The election of a 'New Labour' government in 1997 brought a reassessment of the role of consumer protection legislation, mainly of an evolutionary rather than revolutionary character, spelled out in some detail in the White Paper (1999) 'Modern Markets – Confident Consumers' (Cm 4410). It states that the Government believes that the main body of consumer law will be adequate for the foreseeable future. However in some important areas such as financial services and food safety, new frameworks for regulation are being constructed. It also intends to 'look at' sale of goods and price marking laws. It goes on to state that the challenge is to meet new needs without distracting businesses from their focus on consumers by imposing unnecessary burdens. 'This is not in the interests of consumers who would suffer through either higher prices or reduced choice. Measures therefore need to be proportionate and targeted.' The system of regulatory impact assessments focuses attention on how far the harm identified will be reduced by a proposed measure, and comparing that to its expected costs both to business and the rest of society. Specifically on reducing burdens, it states that unrigorous or unnecessary regulations can act as obstacles to the competitiveness of businesses, particularly small ones. The areas of weights and measures law and consumer credit are picked out as being in need of simplification (see generally chapter 6 of the White Paper).

Despite the difficulty of the exercise, attempts have been made at least to construct models of how the cost component of such a cost-benefit analysis should proceed. The model constructed should serve to measure the social cost to the community of the corrective action being contemplated. So, for example, Layton and Holmes proceed as follows:[20]

Where legislation is concerned, more is not necessarily better. For the total cost of corrective action is made up of at least three elements. First there is the transactional cost that the customer incurs in terms of searching time,[1] inconvenience and risk; a cost which is presumably reduced as the intensity of regulation increases. But with the extension of legislation, a second cost becomes significant, that of enforcing and implementing the newly enacted orders. In turn, this spawns a third expense – that associated with the additional costs incurred by the business community in complying with all the relevant legal provisions. It would seem that in assessing any programme of consumer protection, we must consider the total of all three of these action components and seek to establish that particular balance between exploitation and over-protection that yields the minimum social cost to the community (see Fig 4).

Fig 4 Cost of protection

20 'Consumerism – A passing malaise or a continuing expression of social concern?' 46 Austr Quarterly 6 at 23–4. See also E P Belababa 'Unfair Trade Practices Legislation; symbolism and substance in consumer protection' 15 Osgoode Hall LJ 327.

Another Australian study[2] proceeds on the basis that 'the law of consumer protection is in substance the use of legal machinery to allocate consumer losses between the purchaser or user of goods and services and the vendor, manufacturer or others concerned with the production and distribution of goods and services'. This loss is both in Australia and the UK distributed in a somewhat random way. The loss falls on the purchaser if the seller or manufacturer effectively excludes contractual and tortious liability, or such liability does not necessarily arise in law – eg private sales of second hand motor cars, or where the State exacts criminal penalties without compensating the purchaser or user in respect of the deficient goods or services. Sometimes a user may obtain compensation in tort in respect of a manufacturer's negligence although a purchaser's right of action might be excluded by contract. In other cases the loss will fall on the seller, typically a retailer, where the purchaser pursues his non-excludable Sale of Goods Acts remedies against the seller but not the manufacturer, and the retailer finds his rights of indemnity barred by contract. As a further alternative, there may be an insurance fund on which consumers may claim in the absence of a remedy against the supplier, for example the compensation fund compulsorily covering the risk of defalcations by solicitors, or the 10-year protection against certain building faults by builders on the register of the National House Building Council. Here the cost of the loss is spread evenly amongst contributors to the scheme. The Australian study discusses the economic impact of the various loss distribution models and one conclusion is that the consumer is better served by a regulatory system that encourages rigorous quality control at the production stage rather than one which relies for its sanctions on the consumer having the energy and funds to activate a breach of warranty claim in respect of defects which a less rigorous production system allows to occur.[3] Voluntary codes of practice such as those initiated with various suppliers of goods and services by the Office of Fair Trading in London can be helpful in both improving standards and streamlining complaints procedures. This idea has led representatives of both industry and consumer organisations to propose diminishing the extent of regulation for technical matters through the criminal law and adopting instead a system mid-way between the criminal and civil law, perhaps through

1   By 'searching time' is meant the cost of ascertaining the quality of goods or services by the acquisition of information about them, including the resources spent in testing alternatives.

2   Merrilees and Cotman 'An Economic Analysis of Consumer Protection Law' (1976) Austr Quarterly (March) 79.

3   See also Jolowicz 'The Protection of the Consumer and Purchaser of Goods under English Law' (1969) 32 MLR 1, particularly at 7. The article is of fundamental importance, and proceeds in part on an analysis of the law as a system for the allocation of risks among the persons involved.

universally applicable codes of practice[4] (codes of practice are discussed in chapter 11). However, in more recent years this idea has not been pursued further than in the promotion of codes of practice within industry itself or through the OFT. As will be seen the 1999 White Paper (above) encourages businesses to promote customer service through effective codes of practice and outline 'core principles' are stipulated, with the Office of Fair Trading to have an enhanced role in their creation.

4.   MONOPOLIES

The detailed law of monopolies, mergers and restrictive practices is outside the scope of this book because of its complexity and its less direct importance to individual consumers, but a review of the economic and philosophical context of consumer protection would also be incomplete without at least some reference to monopolies.

In economic terms, consideration of monopolies involves the 'supply' side of the market place. In conditions of perfect competition the producer may assume that the price that he sells his goods at will be the market price. However, where either a single producer controls all the supply of a particular commodity or a combination of firms can control a very large proportion of total output, competition is imperfect and the monopolist may either fix the price (letting demand control output) or restrict output (letting demand determine the price). As regards output, even a monopolist must take account of consumer demand and diminishing marginal utility. Therefore as the volume of production, and hence supply, increases the price of each unit of output will fall. In order to maximise profits the monopolist will therefore cease to increase supply beyond the point where the marginal cost of producing each unit of production exceeds the marginal revenue obtained by selling it. Accordingly the disadvantages to the consumer of monopolistic supply are:

i)   Output is generally restricted to maximise profits and keep up price. Furthermore, trade unions in the industry can develop a stranglehold to the disadvantage of the consumer.

ii)   Consumers have less choice than they would have where perfect competition exists, and perhaps no choice at all as regards a particular commodity.

iii)   The existence of a monopoly discourages innovation. Dangerous competition which might result in more efficiency and lower prices is either bought up or stifled.

4   See in particular Gordon Borrie 'Laws and Codes for Consumers' [1980] Journal of Business Law 315 and David Tench *Towards a Middle System of Law* (Consumers' Association, 1981).

On the other hand, in some circumstances monopolies can be advantageous. Production can be better planned and trade stabilised. Distribution can be arranged economically, as would perhaps not be the case if, for instance, there were rival gas or electricity undertakings each with their own infrastructure and supply lines. It is also at least possible that since streamlined production and distribution save cost, the price of supply is lower than it otherwise would be.

In many countries anti-monopolies legislation exists. As long ago as 1890 the United States Government passed the Sherman Act and Theodore Roosevelt reinvigorated it in his 'trust-busting' operations at the beginning of this century. In the UK, besides the elderly provisions in the law of contract in respect of illegal arrangements in restraint of trade there are a number of statutes designed to secure the benefits of competitive trading conditions. The main ones are the Fair Trading Act 1973 and the Competition Act 1998.

In addition, the UK acceded to the Treaty of Rome on joining the European Economic Community on 1 January 1973, and this Treaty has as its major objective the elimination of customs barriers and free movement of 'persons, services and capital' (Art 3). Accordingly the UK is now subject to the competition policy of the EEC. In particular Article 81 (formerly 85) prohibits all agreements between undertakings, decisions by associations of undertakings and concerted practices which may affect trade between Member States and which have as their objective or effect the prevention, restriction or distortion of competition within the Common Market. The Article particularises five prohibited situations including those where the purchasing or selling prices are fixed or where markets or sources of supply are shared. The Article only catches agreements affecting trade 'between Member States', and the Commission has a circumscribed power to exempt certain agreements.

Monopolies

2 UK consumer protection law in the European context

1. THE EUROPEAN COMMUNITY DIMENSION

The impact of European Community Law on 'domestic' consumer protection law has now developed into a complex and discrete area of study. This chapter purports to do no more than introduce the reader not fully conversant with the EC framework to this topic and to illustrate developments with some examples. More advanced reading is mentioned in the footnotes.

A fundamental principle of the original European Economic Community and its founding Treaty, the Treaty of Rome, now referred to as the EC Treaty, may be expressed as being that all the players in the competition of selling goods and services in the single marketplace should be required to play on a *level playing field*. Otherwise a moment's thought will show that competition becomes distorted (by, eg hidden subsidies or legislative indulgences which put external competitors at a disadvantage) and it is the consumer, finally, who either pays more for goods and services than if there were true competition, or is denied choice in some way. Ideally the laws of member states in very wide areas including commercial law, safety law, environmental law and anything else affecting the costs of production and marketing ought to be the same. But as this is impracticable for political reasons, much of the energy of the EC institutions is put into formulating and, through the European Court of Justice, enforcing measures to harmonise these divergent laws. How far even this is truly practicable and enforceable is one of the key political questions of modern times.

2. EC INSTITUTIONS AND AIMS

The European Economic Community, now known as the European Community, was one of three Communities established between 1951 and

1957 by France, the German Federal Republic, Italy, Belgium, Holland and Luxembourg. With the approval of Parliament, the United Kingdom signed a Treaty of Accession in Brussels in 1972, to take effect from 1 January 1973. Denmark, the Republic of Ireland, Greece, Spain and Portugal, and more recently Sweden, Austria and Finland have also become members of the EC. The European Economic Community was by far the most important of the three Communities (the others being the European Coal and Steel Community and the European Atomic Energy Community).

The original economic objectives have since expanded towards a political union involving also social and financial factors. Two milestones may be noted. Firstly, a treaty known as the Single European Act was adopted in 1987 with the objective of making concrete progress towards European unity and amendments were made to the Treaty of Rome, some of which are discussed later. Secondly, the Maastricht Treaty, or Treaty of European Union (1992), was ratified by the UK in 1993 and given effect in UK law by the European Communities (Amendment) Act 1993. The UK has reserved its position on some of the later stages of the economic and monetary union proposed and the Treaty has been modified accordingly. Its adoption at all by the UK government without the preceding referendum held by some other member states remains politically controversial. Superimposed on this are some provisions strengthening consumer protection stemming from the Treaty of Amsterdam, which further amended the EC Treaty.

The Maastricht Treaty established a European Union immediately governed by a European Council, formerly the Council of Ministers. The Union (EU) consists of (1) the three existing communities (above), (2) the common foreign and security policy (FSP) and (3) the cooperation on justice and home affairs (CJHA). The European Community still continues to exist and areas such as competition law derived from the Treaty of Rome may still be referred to as 'EC' law. In addition, a European Economic Area has been established to include Norway, Iceland and Liechtenstein (but with Switzerland resolutely staying outside) and to which much EU law is designed to extend. This has its genesis in the European Free Trade Association (to which the UK formerly belonged) designed to promote free trade but rejecting the Treaty of Rome. The EEA evolved out of the idea that the EC and EFTA ought to move towards a closer relationship, and the present EEA agreement was signed in Oporto in 1992. The 'four freedoms', free movement of goods, services, capital and persons, apply throughout the EEA and there are provisions to remove non-tariff barriers to trade.

The main institutions of the EC are the European Council, the Commission, the European Parliament and the European Court. The European Court and the Court of First Instance (discussed in more detail below) have exclusive jurisdiction in the interpretation of Community law as between member states *inter se*, and also between member states and their nationals, or their nationals *inter se*, and the European Court is the supreme tribunal on matters of interpretation of the Treaty of Rome (the Treaty giving rise to the European Economic Community) and the other treaties constituting the European Communities. The Council is the final decision-making body for major Community questions, and most of its decisions are taken as a result of a proposal from the Commission. Proposals are normally transmitted by the Council to the European Parliament for debate and an opinion.

With regard to the European Court of Justice, as was said in *The Times* on 23 June 1990: 'Few people know much about the European Court of Justice. Most confuse it with the European Court of Human Rights in Strasbourg or the International Court of Justice at the Hague. Yet the Luxembourg-based court is at the centre of British ideas on European political union'. The European Court was brought to the forefront of public notice in 1990 when it reaffirmed that Community law prevailed over national law, including Acts of Parliament – see *R v Secretary of State for Transport, ex p Factortame (No 2)*[1] and *Factortame Ltd v Secretary of State for Transport*.[2] The European Court of Justice held that in stated circumstances an individual could claim compensation from his or her government if that government had failed to implement a Community directive by the time limit. As part of this principle, an interim injunction lay even against the Crown where, as in the *Factortame* case, the appellants were alleging that rights to fish under Community law were infringed by the quota provisions of the Merchant Shipping Act 1988. Here, the High Court had referred that question for preliminary adjudication under Article 177 (now Art 234) of the EC Treaty to the European Court, and the European Court held that the United Kingdom High Court had been right (despite having been reversed by the House of Lords) to suspend the operation of the 1988 Act as regards the appellants until the European Court had given a preliminary ruling to be implemented by the United Kingdom courts.

It will be seen from the above that the European Court's decisions are designed to guide the courts of member states on the interpretation of Community law (ie to decide whether those states have obeyed treaty obligations), review the legality of acts of the Commission and Council of Ministers (or their failure to act) and, as in the above decision, to give preliminary rulings on points of EC law for the national courts of member states. It has no power to enforce penalties, although perhaps because the United Kingdom has a good record of compliance compared to, say, Italy and Belgium, the United Kingdom Government proposed (successfully) that it should have the power to levy fines. Furthermore, EC

1   Case C-213/89 [1991] 1 AC 603, [1991] 1 All ER 70, [1990] ECR I – 2433.
2   [1990] 2 AC 85, [1989] 2 All ER 692.

EC institutions and aims

citizens have no power of *direct* access to the court on the matter of whether national law complies with EC law. The matter has to be referred on by a national court.

A new Court of First Instance has been established since 1989 to determine facts in complex cases and relieve the overburdened main court. It also determines all actions brought by legal or natural persons.

The main aims of the EC are referred to as the 'four freedoms', namely the freedom of movement of goods; the freedom of movement of persons; the freedom to provide services and the freedom of movement of capital. The law of the EC has developed so as to promote these objectives, together with that of the Common Agricultural Policy. In addition, and as outlined above, the Single European Act 1986, adopted by the heads of state or governments of the member states, is a treaty which envisages increasing the scope of Community authority into such areas as social policy, technological development and the environment. The treaty also envisages the adoption of measures aimed at establishing the internal market (ie an area without internal frontiers where there is free movement of goods, persons, services and capital). The object was to complete the internal market of the Community by the end of 1992. The Treaty on European Union at Maastricht in 1992 extended EC jurisdiction yet further, particularly in social matters.

3. EC LEGISLATION

How are laws in the EC transmitted to the United Kingdom? The answer to this question depends on the type of EC law which is being considered. The European Communities Act 1972 both applied existing Community law to the United Kingdom and made provision for the law of the Community to grow by:
a)   decisions of the European Court and
b)   legislation in the form of regulations, decisions and directives.
A regulation is binding in its entirety and directly applicable in all member states to which it is addressed, but the form and method are left to the national Government. A decision is binding in its entirety on those to whom it is addressed.

Directives are probably the most important source of EC law in the United Kingdom at present. Not being self-executing, a directive must be incorporated actively into the United Kingdom's domestic law (ie by statute or statutory instrument). An increasingly large volume of subsidiary legislation is now made under the European Communities Act 1972 pursuant to a directive. But a directive may also be implemented by primary legislation. An important example is Part I of the Consumer Protection Act 1987 which implements the Directive on Product Liability (85/374/EEC). As mentioned above, it is a matter of choice as to the method by which a directive is implemented in the United Kingdom's domestic law. If the matter is one of great importance, such as product liability, primary legislation may well be chosen. If the matter deals with detailed regulation of, for instance, labelling of food, the directive is more likely to be implemented by subsidiary legislation made either under the appropriate piece of primary legislation, eg the Food Acts, or under the European Communities Act 1972.

As has been mentioned, the European Court has developed the view that in some cases treaty provisions, decisions addressed to member states, directives and certain agreements between members and non-members can be 'directly effective'. This means, in effect, that an individual can enforce a right conferred by, for instance, a directive against the state if the state has failed to implement the directive properly, or at all. An unimplemented directive does not give individuals rights against each other. Only the state may be impleaded.[3]

The hierarchy of courts concerned with this type of legislation must be understood. If a question arises as to whether a directive has been correctly interpreted and implemented into the United Kingdom's domestic law by the appropriate deadline, this would be referred to the European Court of Justice, but in most other respects the fact that the directive has been implemented into the United Kingdom's domestic law, via its own primary or subsidiary legislation, gives the United Kingdom court jurisdiction over any matter of application or enforcement of those laws. As has been explained, in addition to the European Court's jurisdiction directly to enforce Community law, it is open to any court or tribunal in the United Kingdom to refer for a preliminary ruling points arising in domestic cases which might conflict with Community law (Art 234 of the EC Treaty).

The chronology of the legislative proposals affecting the consumer is that the Commission first prepares a preliminary draft of a directive or regulation, having consulted with governments, trade associations, consumer representatives and other appropriate bodies or persons. The draft directive or regulation is then sent to the Council, which consults the European Parliament and the Community's Economic and Social Committee (which has representatives of producers and consumers on its membership). There has also been a Consumers' Consultative Council and by virtue of a Commission Decision (2000/323) a Consumer Committee composed of representatives of national consumer organisations (one from each member state) and of European consumer organisations. The Commission may consult this Committee on all problems relating to the

3   See Miller, Harvey & Parry *Consumer and Trading Law, Text Cases and Materials* (hereafter, M, H & P) pp 14–17; ES Singleton 'Institutions and Procedures of the European Union After the Maastricht Treaty' (1995) 14 Trading Law 396.

EC legislation

protection of consumer interests at Community level. Neither they nor any other consumer body has any direct input into the legislative process. On occasion a draft directive or regulation is withdrawn, but if it proceeds it becomes law in the way described above.

4.   THE SINGLE MARKET

There was a great deal of speculation about the significance of '1992' in terms of the development of the idea of the Common Market, and this revealed widespread ignorance of what the significance of this date really was and on the wider question of how EC law directly affects the producer and thus the consumer.

Firstly, what was the significance of 1992? It was not about abolishing tariff barriers. Abolition of tariff barriers between member states, in terms of quantitative restrictions on trade within the Common Market, happened many years ago and has affected the United Kingdom since it joined the Common Market in 1973. But it was concerned with the abolition of non-tariff barriers in the form of physical, technical and fiscal barriers which prevent the completion of the 'internal market'. The (then) 12 separate member states, with a population well exceeding 300,000,000 people, still remained very much twelve separate markets. By 'internal market' we mean an area without internal frontiers in which the free movement of *goods, persons, services* and *capital* is ensured in accordance with the EC Treaty. This is made clear by Article 13 of the Single European Act, in force since 1987. By the end of 1992 the objective involved the removal of the remaining non-tariff barriers to one complete market. The deadline gave a focus to this essential objective which was in danger of becoming atrophied. The outcome was in reality, only partially successful – many frontiers remain, partly for security reasons. Political imperatives do not always point in the same direction as economic desiderata.

Many of the matters which were considered to be in need of addressing in order to achieve the internal market by the deadline of midnight on 31 December 1992 are of direct or indirect relevance to those involved as producers – and, in turn, consumers as their customers who want a market with the optimum range of choice of goods and services at the most competitive price possible. So, for instance, physical barriers, involving delays at the frontiers when goods are transported, have to be removed as far as possible. Where these delays are caused by administrative problems reforms are needed. A major step forward was the introduction of the single administrative document.

Technical barriers are important too. For instance, if most of the member states have different standards relating to goods which have to be complied with, the chances of achieving a single market are small. For a start, it can hardly be economic for manufacturers of mass-produced goods to make those goods to 15 or more differing standards. If there were one Community standard, manufacturing resources would inevitably be used much more efficiently.

This problem has been one of the most deep seated in the development of the EC. Individual states may have a particular reason for imposing specific standards, and if these reasons are founded on the basic requirements of health, safety, consumer and environmental protection, they may well withstand a challenge from within the EC. However, following the decision of the European Court in the *Cassis de Dijon* case[4] where the German Government attempted to ban the sale in Germany of Cassis because it did not contain the minimum quantity of alcohol required by German authorities for drinks of that class, the court held that a minimum alcohol requirement was not a *necessary* provision for the protection of public health. German domestic law in this respect was therefore held to be unenforceable, and a similar decision was later promulgated by the European Court as regards German legislative provisions restricting the use of the description 'bier' to beverages using particular ingredients.[5] The practical effect of the bier laws was to prevent the import into Germany of a large range of beers brewed in other member states, which were perfectly acceptable under the laws of those other states. The ensuing result was to partition the Common Market and dilute competitive pressure. The only possible justification for the German law was that public health was being protected in this way, but the European Court dismissed this argument as unsubstantiated. Indeed, it is difficult to see how a minimum alcohol content requirement could be said to be in the interest of public *health*, though it might be consistent with consumer protection. A better way of avoiding misleading consumers on such matters is by labelling requirements.

The end result of this is that protectionism introduced, perhaps under the guise of consumer protection or protection of public health, by an individual member state is likely to be struck down by the European Court unless it can be positively shown that health or other public policy principles are thereby prejudiced. The basis of the court's jurisdiction here is Article 28 (formerly 30) of the EC Treaty, with the exceptions mentioned above appearing in Article 30 (formerly 36). Article 28 prohibits quantitative restrictions on importations and all measures with equivalent effect and the relevant texts are as follows:

28. Quantitative restrictions on imports and all measures having equivalent effect shall, without prejudice to the following provisions, be prohibited between Member States.

4   See under *Rewe-Zentral A G v Bundersmonopolverwaltung*: 120/78 [1979] ECR 649.
5   *EC Commission v Germany*: 178/84 [1987] ECR 1227, [1988] 1 CMLR 780.

30. The provisions of Articles 28 and 29 shall not preclude prohibitions or restrictions on imports, exports or goods in transit justified on grounds of public morality, public policy or public security; the protection of health and life of humans, animals or plants; the protection of national treasures possessing artistic, historic or archaeological value or the protection of industrial and commercial property. Such prohibitions or restrictions shall not, however, constitute a means of arbitrary discrimination or a disguised restriction on trade between Member States.

It will be noted that the text of Article 30 does not refer directly to consumer protection, a concept which was not much in evidence when the Treaty was first designed and drafted. 'Public health' is the defence most usually argued. The court in effect weighs the conflicting policies of protecting the consumer and public health if there is a real threat to it by imported goods carrying a health or safety risk not affecting similar domestic goods on the one hand and the prejudice to the producer in the stifling of external competition on the other. Recent cases suggest that the court leans in favour of the pro-competition argument on the grounds of 'proportionality'. Using 'a sledgehammer to crack a nut' is not justifiable. A consumer can be informed that a drink, for example, has a higher alcohol content than its rivals (and thus perhaps a higher price) by mandatory labelling requirements. This is a neat application of the 'perfect knowledge' component of the concept of the 'perfect market' discussed in chapter 1, or, put another way, the 'protection' given to consumers by ensuring transparency in transactions.

A similar regime applies to prohibition of restrictions on the supply of services (Art 49) unless justified on the grounds of public policy, public security and public health (Arts 46 and 55). The concept of 'interest of the consumer' can be seen to be capable of dual interpretations. On the face of it laws apparently protecting the consumer may infringe Article 28 as involving quantitative restrictions on imports or 'having equivalent effect'. Consumers do not benefit from stifled competition. On the other hand there is a danger, unless Article 30 can be evoked, that the interest of the producer in a *free* market may swamp that of the consumer in a *safe* market.

5. THE CONSUMER INTEREST

As has been remarked above, the original EEC Treaty contains no direct and obvious provision designed to protect the consumer. Its purpose was to encourage and compel member states to operate a truly free market, though there were nods in the direction of public policy and public health. When the need to promote consumer protection legislation became pressing the powers given by Article 100 (now 94) were used, though this is very widely worded, providing for the issue of 'Directives for the approximation of such provisions laid down by law, regulation or administrative action in member states as directly affect the establishment or functioning of the Common Market'. It was under this somewhat inapt provision that directives on packaging or labelling of dangerous substances, solvents and cosmetics, control of the composition of articles coming into contact with food, product liability, contracts made away from business premises and consumer credit were in whole or part justified.

When the Single Market initiative presented a chance to amend the EC Treaty the opportunity was taken to insert a much more satisfactory Article 100A (now 95), an article which had the added administrative advantage of allowing the adoption of measures by a qualified majority vote rather than unanimity. The text empowers the Council, acting by a qualified majority on a proposal from the Commission in cooperation with the Economic and Social Committee, to adopt measures within the ambit of the (old) Article 100, and also states that the Commission, in its proposals concerning health, safety, environmental protection and *consumer protection*, will take as a base a high level of protection (old Art 100A(3)). Recent important directives on such matters as toy safety and price indications on goods, other than food, have been made under Article 95 (old 100A).[6]

6. PROMOTION OF THE CONSUMER INTEREST WITHIN THE EC

Consumer protection has increasingly in recent years been an important aspect of the Community's thinking and recommendations.[7] Within the Commission there is a Health and Consumer Policy Directorate responsible for representing the consumer interest in the Commission and formulating consumer policy. In addition, the Bureau Européen des Unions de Consommateurs is a federation of the consumer associations within member states and this also influences the Commission and undertakes studies for it. The Council and Commission also have to consult the Economic and Social Committee.[8] The creation by Commission Decision

---

6   See ch 9 on safety and price indications.

7   For an excellent review see J Stuyck 'European Consumer Law after the Treaty of Amsterdam' (2000) 37 Common Market Law Review 367–401.

8   In the UK the CECG (Consumers in the European Community Group) is an umbrella organisation which co-ordinates the research and representation of the UK consumer movement concerning EC policies. It has regular discussions with the Ministry of Agriculture, Fisheries and Food and the DTI and has direct links with Brussels through members serving on the EC committees mentioned above.

2000/323 of a Consumer Committee, representative of all member states has already been mentioned.

In 1975 the Council adopted a consumer protection and information programme listing five fundamental rights of the consumer. These are: 1) the right to protection of health and safety, 2) the right to protection of economic interests, 3) the right to advice, help and redress, 4) the right to information and education, and 5) the right to consultation and representation. A further draft resolution concerning the second programme of the EEC for a consumer protection and information policy was submitted to the Council on 26 June 1979. It was expressed as being intended to enable new tasks to be undertaken in the years 1980 to 1985. The programme was approved by the Foreign Affairs Council in May 1981. The second programme was particularly concerned with the following matters arising out of the basic rights adopted by the first programme. These are 1) the protection of consumers against health and safety hazards, 2) protection of the economic interest of consumers, 3) improvement of the legal situation of the consumer, 4) improvement of consumer information and education, and 5) appropriate consultation and representation of consumers during preparation of decisions which concern them. On the tenth anniversary of the adoption of the Community consumer programme a document entitled 'A New Impetus for Consumer Protection Policy' was issued proposing a further timetabled programme for reform of this area.[9] The Commission identified the deep economic recession of the 1980s as the main reason for slow progress but correctly added that the consumer needs protection in times of recession quite as much as when economies boom. In 1992 there was a Council Resolution on Future Priorities for the Development of Consumer Policy, these being integration of consumer protection with other common policies, consumer information and education, legal redress, safety and health, representation of consumers and economic interests. A second three-year action plan was subsequently devised for 1993–95.[10] But there were still no consumer protection titles in the treaties.

The Maastricht Treaty redressed the balance by adding a new Title (XVIII) on Consumer Protection, and this, as significantly amended by the Treaty of Amsterdam, now runs (in Art 153 of the EC Treaty) as follows:

See also H W Micklitz and Stephen Weatherill 'Consumer Policy in the European Community: Before and after Maastricht' (1993) 16 Journal of Consumer Policy 285 and S Weatherill *EC Consumer Law and Policy* (1997).

9 See Lawson (1986) 5 Trading Law 118 and (1987) 84 L S Gaz 39 for further detail. See also Peter Shears 'European Consumer Law: Limping Towards "1992"' (1992) 9 Trading Law 12.

10 A third action plan was published in October 1995 – see Com (95) 519.

Consumer protection

"(1) In order to promote the interests of consumers and to ensure a high level of consumer protection, the Community shall contribute to protecting the health, safety and economic interests of consumers, as well as promoting their right to information, education and to organise themselves in order to safeguard their interests.

(2) Consumer protection requirements shall be taken into account in defining and implementing other community policies and activities.

(3) The Community shall contribute to the attainment of the objectives referred to in paragraph (1) through:
(a) measures adopted pursuant to Article 95 in the context of the completion of the internal market;
(b) measures which support, supplement and monitor the policy pursued by the Member States.

(4) The Council, acting in accordance with the procedure referred to in Article 251 (co-decision procedure) and after consulting the Economic and Social Committee, shall adopt the measures referred to in paragraph (3)(b).

(5) Measures adopted pursuant to paragraph (4) shall not prevent any member state from maintaining or introducing more stringent protective measures. Such measures must be compatible with this Treaty. The Commission shall be notified of them."

The reference to 'the attainment of a high level of consumer protection' is significant as indicating the increasing emphasis on this topic. On the other hand Community regulative action is not the answer to every perceived problem. As has been shown in chapter 1, every protective measure has a cost which is likely to be borne by the consumer. This point seems to be recognised in the Council's Resolution on Consumer Policy 1999–2001 – 'the choice of measures to be taken at the Community level to safeguard the required high level of consumer protection should be based on the analysis of, in particular, the objectives to be achieved, the nature and scope of the issues to be covered, the potential costs and the benefits of action or lack of action and the developments in the market in order to make the best choice between the different legislative and non-legislative solutions.'[11]

---

11   OJ 1999, No C 206/1, recital 7, and see Stuyck, op cit, 393.

In connection with health and safety, Community directives on chocolate, some sugars, honey, fruit juices, and preserved milk and poultry health have (inter alia) been adopted by the UK and other similar proposals are under discussion. More generally, a directive aimed at harmonising consumer credit has also been promulgated, as have directives on 'doorstep selling', advertising and product liability (all discussed elsewhere in this book). A directive on package travel was adopted in June 1990 for implementation by the end of 1992.[12] It involves the licensing and bonding of all tour organisers, and confers various rights to accurate information on consumers. The Timeshare Directive[13] has also been incorporated into UK law – see the Timeshare Act 1992 as extensively amended by the Timeshare Regulations 1997.[14] There are also more recently adopted directives which extend, or will extend, yet further UK legislation on unfair contract terms, consumer guarantees, distance contracts and general product safety.

The OFT plays an important role in monitoring the application of the Community competition rules. It participates in meetings of the Community's Advisory Committee on Restrictive Practices and Monopolies.[15] The Competition Act 1998 is unusual in containing a 'mission statement', in section 60, undertaking that domestic competition law will be developed in a way consistent with that obtaining between members states of the Community.

What is the rationale for what is now a considerable body of EU law for the most part integrated into UK law by parliamentary legislation, usually regulations made under appropriate primary legislation such as the European Communities Act 1972? A glance at the recitals which precede these directives is instructive. Those applicable to the Directive on Aspects of the Sale of Consumer Goods and Associated Guarantees[16] include that:

- Article 153(1) and (3) of the Treaty provide that the Community should contribute to the achievement of a high level of consumer protection by the measures it adopts pursuant to Article 95 thereof;
- the internal market comprises an area without internal frontiers where there is free movement of goods, persons, services and capital and transactions by private persons are included;

12   See the Package Travel, Package Holidays and Package Tours Regulations 1992, SI 1992/3288, BSSCCL 766; M, H & P pp 171–6, 446–50; and below p 206.
13   94/47/EC, OJ No L280, 29.10.94, p 83.
14   SI 1997/1081, see BSSCCL 582.
15   See the Director General of Fair Trading's Annual Reports. The OFT also participates in the competition work of the OECD. Some of the earlier directives have been castigated by Sir Gordon Borrie, then the Director General of Fair Trading, as being irrelevant, retrograde and damaging to national interests. See Borrie *The Development of Consumer Law and Policy* (1984).
16   99/45/EC, OJ No L 171, 7.7.99, p 12. See further chs 6 and 7.

- by implication consumers resident in one member state should be free to purchase goods in the territory of another on the basis of a uniform minimum set of fair rules;
- in fact such laws are 'somewhat disparate' and such disparaties may distort competition;
- the creation of a set of minimum rules of consumer law, valid wherever the goods were purchased within the Community, will strengthen consumer confidence and enable consumers to make the most of the internal market;
- it is appropriate to approximate national legislation governing the sale of consumer goods and non-conformity with the contract without, however, impinging on national laws relating to contractual and non-contractual liability ...

and so on. This represents a policy of removing 'disparaties' which a reasonable non-national consumer might not suspect to be present but with a bow in the direction of the principle of proportionality. The core of each country's contractual code is generally not touched, though the legislation on unfair contract terms runs close to this borderline.

There is, despite the rhetoric and solid achievements of recent years, still a fundamental problem, namely that of enforceability. It is difficult to say who would feel more uncomfortable, a customer from the UK trying to exercise his rights as a disappointed consumer in Italy before the Italian courts or an Italian in a similar position in England. Linguistic fluency has, for a start, to be assumed, probably optimistically. Cases do not, in practice, depend entirely, or even predominantly, on legal argument. Facts have first to be established and proved in a way allowed by the relevant country's law of evidence or special small claims regime. If a local lawyer is involved, what is the system, if any, of dealing with recovery of costs? No one wants a time consuming Pyrrhic victory. Clients are sensibly advised against cross-border litigation unless substantial amounts of money are involved.

This problem has been extensively discussed; see, for example, the Commission's Green Paper on Access to Justice of 1993.[17] There is some progress towards a common system of availability of injunctions,[18] but a larger scale solution (such as perhaps a trans-European Ombudsman for consumer disputes with the resources to take up cudgels, on individuals' behalf, primarily outside the formal courts system) remains elusive.[19] However, a recent Council Resolution[20] states that, particularly in the light of the rapidly developing e-commerce market and the influence of a single currency (the euro) on cross-border transactions, there is a need to strengthen consumer confidence in the functioning of the internal market.

17 COM (93) 576.
18 See 98/27/EC, OJ No L 166, 11.6.98, p 51.
19 See Stuyck, op cit and Weatherill *EC Consumer Law and Policy*, ch 8.
20 2000/ C 155/01.

What is advocated is the development of voluntary, practical, efficient and inexpensive procedures for extra-judicial settlement of consumer disputes promoted at both the national and Community level. This should be without prejudice to the consumer's access to the courts and the 1968 Convention on Jurisdiction and the Enforcement of Judgments in Civil and Commercial Matters. In essence, member states are invited to encourage mechanisms for the out-of-court settlement of consumer disputes, create or designate a 'clearing house' to provide information and practical assistance to consumers to enable them to access out-of-court bodies or schemes nationally or in other member states, encourage the development of dispute settlement schemes, in particular with on-line application, and to encourage companies as well as economic organisations to act in affiliation or association with out-of-court bodies.

Following up the idea of utilising member states' systems for settlement of cross-border consumer complaints by utilising established out-of-court procedures, the Commission launched the European Extra-Judicial Network (EEJ-Net) in May 2000. The objective is that all on-going disputes of any value should be referable to a one-stop clearing house in the consumer's country. This would then put the consumer in touch with the parallel body in the supplier's country which would identify the appropriate out-of-court system. The DTI has reached agreement in principle that the UK's central clearing house should be jointly the National Association of Citizens' Advice Bureaux (NACAB) and the Local Authorities Coordinating Body on Food and Trading Standards (see ch 3). The UK has identified some 20 bodies, mostly arbitration-based or ombudsmen, which satisfy EU criteria as to being independent, transparent, adversarial (in the sense of allowing parties to present their case), effective (including being free or low-cost), non-exclusive of the courts of the supplier or of the consumer's residence and binding only if that is accepted in advance, and carrying the right to be represented. Other jurisdictions vary from having one single entity handling consumer complaints (Sweden) to 'hundreds' in Germany. (See 'Empowering the Euro-consumer' which includes charts, *Fair Trading* (OFT), August 2000, 15). Formidable practical problems, not least those involving language translation and communication remain unsolved. Nor is it obvious why reliance on out-of-court bodies of varying effectiveness and status is better than helping the non-resident consumer use an efficient small claims court-based system of universal rather than sectoral, applicability, where this exists. At least then enforcement is likely to be less problematic. But the EU seems determined that 'ADR' processes (see ch 8) are the way forward.

Outside the Community itself, the Council of Europe, now having 41 member states, was established in May 1949, having the membership of the UK and most of the other countries of Western Europe and some Central and East European states (eg Poland, Hungary, Czechoslovakia).

Its membership clauses insist upon a state's adherence to the principles of freedom and human rights. Rather overshadowed in importance by the European Union, it has, nevertheless, had an important influence in a number of spheres – see, for instance, the Convention on Product Liability adopted by the Council of Ministers of the Council of Europe at Strasbourg in 1976 and discussed in chapter 6. A draft chapter on consumer protection and assistance was adopted by the Consultative Assembly of the Council in 1973, and is similar to the EC consumer protection and information programme discussed above.

The important European Convention for the Protection of Human Rights and Fundamental Freedoms (1953) is interpreted and adjudicated upon by the European Court of Human Rights in Strasbourg as mentioned above, an entirely different court from the ECJ.[1]

Not to be outdone, in 2000 a draft EU Charter of Human Rights was unveiled with many provisions overlapping the existing Council of Europe Strasbourg model. The EU model would be enforceable by the European Court of Justice in Luxembourg and its detailed provisions could conflict with the Human Rights Act 1998, designed to 'bring rights home' – ie to lessen dependence on a non-UK court. Substantial opposition to this development can be expected except in so far as it can be regarded as purely declaratory rather than a step towards a Federal constitution for member states. It has also been pointed out that individuals at present have far less protection against abuse of human rights involving misuse of power by EU institutions than if such abuse is carried out by national authorities, since the latter are subject to the ECHR as members of the Council of Europe. The EU as an institution is not a party to the ECHR though if the EU did accede thereto there would be no real need for a separate (and in parts different) EU 'charter'.

7.   ADVERTISING – A CASE STUDY ON EC DERIVED LAW

After many years of long and complex negotiations the EC adopted a Council Directive on 10 September 1984 on misleading advertising. It was recognised that in the UK the combination of a substantial body of legislation including statutes dealing with trade descriptions, consumer credit, medicines and broadcasting and the self-regulatory system administered by the Advertising Standards Authority appeared to deal well with most problems which arise. The only positive proposal of the Report of the Working Party of the Department of Trade in 1980 on this topic was that there should be an injunctive procedure whereby the Director

1   The European Convention has now been incorporated into English Law – see the Human Rights Act 1998.

General of Fair Trading would be able to obtain court orders preventing publication of advertisements likely to deceive or mislead. This was seen as a reinforcement of the existing self-regulatory system. The EC Directive recognises the continuing role which self-regulatory bodies of this sort can play. In addition, the original 'unfair' advertising, a concept not recognised at present in UK law, was agreed to be left out for a further possible directive. However, a further Directive on Comparative Advertising (knocking copy)[2] amends the 1984 Directive and has led to the Control of Misleading Advertisements (Amendment) Regulations 2000.[3] These prohibit misleading comparisons, protect existing trade marks, and lay down other stipulations to prevent unfair comparisons.

The amended Directive's main requirement is that member states must establish procedures whereby those with a legitimate interest in prohibiting misleading advertising may either take legal action against it in the courts or bring the matter before an 'administrative authority' with competent jurisdiction and enforcement powers.

Government policy on implementation was that nothing should be done to hobble the ASA, which by its constitution and system of financing is regarded as more remote from industrial influence than, for example, a trade association enforcing a code of practice upon its members. As it operates on a non-statutory basis a great degree of flexibility is also maintained. The new powers which the Directive required to be introduced were therefore regarded as a 'long stop'.

Accordingly, subsidiary legislation made under the European Communities Act 1972[4] empowers the Director General of Fair Trading to consider complaints that an advertisement is misleading or, under the amendments to the Regulations, that a comparative advertisement infringes the tests of permissibility stipulated in regulation 4A, and in cases where he considers such measures to be necessary and taking into account all the interests involved, in particular the public interest, to institute proceedings in the High Court for an injunction prohibiting misleading advertising. The definition of 'misleading advertising' is taken from Article 2 of the Directive and is stated to mean any advertising which in any way, including its presentation, deceives or is likely to deceive the persons to whom it is addressed or whom it reaches and if by reason of its deceptive nature it is likely to affect their economic behaviour or which, for those reasons, injures or is likely to injure a competitor (reg 2(2)).

In making injunctions the court is also required to take into account all the interests involved and, in particular, the public interest. It then has

2 97/55/EC, OJ No L 290, 23.10.97, p 18.
3 SI 2000/914.
4 Control of Misleading Advertisements Regulations 1988, SI 1988/915 as amended by SI 2000/914.

power to include in injunctions provisions prohibiting future advertisements about the same goods or services as those which give rise to the injunctions and which are misleading in substantially the same respects. The court also has power to require persons concerned with the dissemination of advertising material to furnish evidence as to the accuracy of factual claims and to consider factual claims as inaccurate if evidence is not furnished or is insufficient. The court may grant an injunction without proof of loss or damage to anyone (reg 6(5)).

The DGFT as a precondition to court proceedings may require any complainant to satisfy him that established means of dealing with such complaints have been invoked (reg 4).

In the field of investment business advertising, the Securities and Investments Board were given similar powers to those given to the DGFT by rules made under the Financial Services Act 1986. Similar powers extend to advertising for which the Independent Television Commission and similar bodies have regulatory responsibility by virtue of the Broadcasting Act 1990 (commercial radio and television advertisements and cable advertisements). These bodies now have the additional duty of considering complaints about advertising alleged to be misleading in the sense of the Regulations and to take the necessary action, under their existing powers, to prevent the further dissemination of such advertising, taking into account all the interests involved and, in particular, the public interest, where they consider such action necessary. The bodies concerned are required to give complainants reasons for their decisions except where complaints are trivial or frivolous. In reaching their decisions the bodies will be entitled to regard factual claims as inaccurate if inadequate evidence is furnished by the advertiser as to the accuracy. This is in accordance with Article 6 of the Directive.

Modest activity has taken place pursuant to these Regulations, false nutritional or 'green' claims coming under particular scrutiny. Thus in *Director General of Fair Trading v Tobyward Ltd* [5] the DGFT had received complaints from Trading Standards Departments, the public and the ASA about a product of Tobyward Ltd called 'SpeedSlim' (which indicates the nature of the product). The court granted an interim injunction, later made permanent, restraining the publication of misleading advertisements for SpeedSlim and also any advertisement for any slimming product which is in similar terms or likely to convey a similar impression to the misleading claims.

5   [1989] 2 All ER 266, Ch D. The decisions of the ASA are, however, subject to judicial review – see *Butterworths Trading and Consumer Law*, Division 5, where a number of reported and unreported cases are abstracted.

Advertising – a case study on EC derived law

Hoffman J in this case expanded upon the meaning of 'misleading' thus:

'Misleading', as I have said, is defined in the regulations as involving two elements: first, that the advertisement deceives or is likely to deceive the persons to whom it is addressed and, second, that it is likely to affect their economic behaviour. In my judgment in this context there is little difficulty about applying the concept of deception. An advertisement must be likely to deceive the persons to whom it is addressed if it makes false claims on behalf of the product. It is true that many people read advertisements with a certain degree of scepticism. For the purposes of applying the regulations, however, it must be assumed that there may be people who will believe what the advertisers tell them and in those circumstances the making of a false claim is likely to deceive ... The other element, namely that the advertisement is likely to affect the economic behaviour of the persons to whom it is addressed, means in this context no more than that it must make it likely that they will buy the product.[6]

The Advertising Directive is one of those included in the Injunctions Directive,[7] and, in due course, other consumer bodies, in addition to the DGFT, will be able to seek injunctions.

The above material shows how an EC Directive was eventually implemented in the UK; it does not purport to give a full description of the law relating to advertising and its control. This is dealt with elsewhere in this book – eg see the discussion of the Trade Descriptions Act 1968 where relevant, in chapter 12 and, as to part of the civil law involved, the discussion of contract-based remedies for misstatement in chapter 5.

---

6   Ibid. at 270.
7   98/27/EC, OJ No L 166, 11.6.98, p 51. See also *Injunctions Directive: Implementation in the UK*, DTI, February 2000 and 'Widening the net' OFT, (2000) 26 Fair Trading 13.

3 The institutional framework of consumer protection

I. CENTRAL AND LOCAL GOVERNMENT

Central government

Introduction

As a generalisation it can be said that the role of central government in consumer protection is to promote legislative policy (often involving preliminary research), oversee the implementation of legislation and oversee the work of various government agencies. Very often actual enforcement is left to local authorities.

An oft-repeated criticism of the organisation of central government consumer protection machinery is that responsibility is spread over too many Departments, some of which have possibly conflicting responsibilities to industries supplying to the consumer. The Cooperative Party, in particular, as early as 1955 advocated a Consumers' Welfare Ministry but this idea was rejected by the Molony Committee (para 886 – 'we dismiss so grandiose a notion'). The Committee went on to recommend the establishment of a Consumer Council financed by government grant and this was established in 1963, concerned itself with consumer education and the promotion of consumer interests on a group (rather than individual) basis, but was abolished in 1971.

Central government was reorganised in 1970 and responsibility for consumer affairs passed to the new Department of Trade and Industry. A movement towards a separate Ministry for Consumer Affairs was made when Sir Geoffrey Howe QC was appointed as the first Minister for Trade and Consumer Affairs at the Department of Trade and Industry in 1972. Five junior ministers were appointed in other Departments concerned with consumer affairs (eg the Home Office and the Ministry of Agriculture,

Fisheries and Food) and given responsibility for the consumer aspects of the Departments' work.

In 1974, after the February election had returned a Labour Government, three new Departments were established to replace the Department of Trade and Industry, namely the Department of Industry, the Department of Trade and the Department of Prices and Consumer Protection (DPCP).

Further changes were made after the change of government in 1979. The new Conservative Government then abolished the DPCP and spread its functions amongst three divisions of the Department of Trade and Industry – the consumer affairs, competition policy, and metrology, quality assurance, safety and standards divisions. Transfer of functions from the Secretary of State for Prices and Consumer Protection to the Secretary of State for Trade was made by the Secretary of State for Trade Order 1979 by virtue of powers contained in the Ministers of the Crown Act 1975. After a further change of government in 1997, consumer affairs and competition continued to be under the aegis of an Under-Secretary of State within DTI, the Divisional Organisation including a Consumer Affairs Directorate. Very few Departments exercise no functions which affect the consumer, but the main Departments so concerned are these:

Department of Trade and Industry

The Secretary of State of this Department is responsible, amongst other things, for policy and legislation on consumer affairs including trading standards, fair trading, weights and measures, consumer credit and consumer safety. The Department also has responsibilities under the Prices Act 1974, and for monopolies, mergers and restrictive practices. Agencies and similar bodies for whose work the Secretary of State is responsible include the Office of Fair Trading (see below), the Competition Commission (which from 1999 succeeded the Monopolies and Mergers Commission), the British Hallmarking Council, the National Consumer Council and the Offices for regulation of the former public utilities such as water, gas and electricity. The Department also sponsors the British Standards Institution.

Office of Fair Trading

This is a government agency, established on 1 November 1973, the Director General of which is appointed by the Secretary of State. Its functions will be discussed in more detail in those parts of the book dealing with the Fair Trading Act 1973 (see ch 11) and elsewhere as appropriate. It is the administrative headquarters from which the Director General of Fair Trading exercises his various statutory responsibilities in connection with consumer protection, consumer credit, and monopolies, mergers and restrictive or anti-competitive practices. The OFT in addition exercises important functions relating to consumer education by publishing various informative leaflets or booklets which are available locally through Consumer Advice Centres or Citizens' Advice Bureaux. It produces numerous helpful publications, many giving guidance to consumers affected by defective goods or services (including credit problems), and holds seminars and conferences. The Office also acts as a clearing house for information received at ground level from local authorities and Citizens' Advice Bureaux on areas causing difficulty. It is funded by the Department of Trade and Industry.

In May 2000 the government announced plans for a new corporate structure which the Director General officially welcomed as being in line with the approach being taken to the statutory regulators and appropriate for an authority which increasingly needs access to a wide range of skills and expertise. Other comment in the press and from consumer interests was not so welcoming. Fears were expressed that the proposed new management board would be packed with the government's 'cronies' and would reduce the desirable independence of the Director General of Fair Trading.

The Home Office

The main function of the Home Office as regards consumer protection is the supervision of the control of explosives, firearms, dangerous drugs, poisons and liquor licensing. Legislation on shops is within its responsibility and it advises on fire hazards in consumer products.

The Department of Health

This Department is, of course, primarily concerned with the administration of the National Health Service and welfare services concerned with the aged, handicapped or children. As regards consumer protection it works with other Ministries and the Food Standards Agency in the area of food hygiene and safety, gives medical advice to government departments on chemical contamination of consumer products and is closely concerned with the control of drugs.

The Ministry of Agriculture, Fisheries and Food

A Board of Fisheries and Food was established in 1903 and in 1919 became a Ministry. In 1955 the Ministries of Food and Agriculture were amalgamated. As regards consumer protection the Ministry shares responsibility with the Department of Health, and with local authorities, in enforcing the Medicines Act 1968 and the regulations made thereunder. Regarding food safety, MAFF liases with the Food Standards Agency, with specific responsibility for such matters as animal welfare at slaughter; pesticide legislation and the operation of the pesticides approval system; and EC marketing standards, including schemes for organic foods.

Food Standards Agency

Created by the Food Standards Act 1999, the Agency came into existence on 1 April 2000. It has been created 'to protect public health from risks which may arise in connection with the consumption of food, and otherwise protect the interests of consumers in relation to food' (s 1(2)). It is led by a board, appointed to act in the public interest, and is accountable to Parliament through health ministers. It has several functions including providing advice and information on food safety and the protection of food quality standards and control of food labelling and advertising through enforcement and monitoring, in conjunction with local authorities. The Meat Hygiene Service is also accountable to the Food Standards Agency.

Local government

Enforcement

Responsibility for the enforcement of consumer protection legislation rests almost entirely with local authorities. As a general rule consumer protection functions are carried out by county councils in England and Wales, the London Boroughs and the regional or islands' councils in Scotland, and in Northern Ireland, Area Trading Standards Offices of the Department of Enterprise, Trade and Investment. Reorganisation by the Local Government Act 1972, operative from 1 April 1974, resulted in the number of authorities exercising these functions being reduced from 241 to some 88 in Great Britain.

By the Local Government Act 1985 the former metropolitan county councils were abolished. They had been responsible for a population of over one million, the largest weights and measures authorities ever to have been created in the UK, and the economies of scale achieved are generally regarded as having produced exceptionally efficient and well-equipped enforcement departments. These units have now been fragmented by being split up between the metropolitan district councils. Although the 1985 Act required the setting up of co-ordinating committees in the metropolitan districts, these are not thought to have been effective in maintaining standards. There is also power in the Act for the Secretary of State to establish by order a single authority in the metropolitan areas.

The Local Government Act 1992 provided for the effecting of further structural changes and established the Local Government Commission for England with power to recommend on-going structural, boundary or electoral changes. Section 17 then gives the Secretary of State power to effect such changes and some further reorganisation occurred (eg the reestablishment of the former sperarate counties of Hereford and Worcester). The policy favoured is illustrated by the Welsh situation where the Local Government (Wales) Act 1994 created 22 unitary authorities ('county councils' or 'county borough councils') to replace the former 8 county councils and 37 district councils. This has usually resulted in Trading Standards Departments combining with Environmental Health (and often other services). The process is similar to that following the abolition of the metropolitan counties in 1986 and to that currently in place in London. In England the former counties of Avon, Cleveland and Humberside with their 21 district councils ceased to exist on 1 April 1996 and are replaced by unitary authorities. 62 Scottish authorities also went.

The former Weights and Measures Departments are now generally called Trading Standards Departments or Consumer Protection Departments, and these departments are responsible for the enforcement of most of the legislation discussed in chapters 9, 10, 12 and 13, particularly the Weights and Measures Acts, the Trade Descriptions Act 1968, the criminal aspects of the Consumer Protection Act 1987 and the Consumer Credit Act 1974.

The Report of the Director General of Fair Trading covering the year 1999 reveals that there were 69 convictions under the Weights and Measures Acts (of which 32 concerned short weight or measure), 789 convictions under the Trade Descriptions Act 1968 (leading to penalties of £609,625, mainly for false trade descriptions of goods), 59 convictions concerning false price claims, and 483 convictions under the Food Safety Act 1990, mainly in respect of the labelling breaches and the supply of food not of the nature, substance or quality demanded. Much of the time of these departments is of course spent in 'preventive' activities such as the statutory weighing and verification of weights and measuring apparatus (including, for example, the retesting and stamping of petrol measuring instruments following price changes) or the submitting of articles of food for chemical analysis. Most trading standards departments take very seriously their duty to advise businesses on how to comply with consumer protection legislation, as well as enforcing the law against those blatantly breaking it. A decision to prosecute is usually first approved by the appropriate lay committee of Council members. District councils exercise certain functions concerning food hygiene and food safety and their joint responsibilities with county councils are described more fully in chapter 13.[1]

The United Kingdom is probably unique among EC member states in relying on local authorities for the enforcement of basic trading standards legislation such as weights and measures. The reasons are historical, as outlined earlier in this book. The advantage is greater local accountability and, perhaps, sensitivity to the needs of a particular area than could be obtained if the legislation were enforced by divisional departments of central government. But a serious disadvantage is the tendency to uneven levels of enforcement of and varying interpretations of the legislation in different local authority jurisdictions. In recognition of this growing problem, agreement was reached in 1976 between the Association of County Councils and the Association of Metropolitan Authorities to set up a new co-ordinating body (now incorporated as a private company) to be known as the Local Authorities Co-ordinating Body on Trading Standards (LACOTS). The main functions of this body are 1) to provide co-ordinated machinery for Trading Standards Departments in Great Britain to liaise with central government and industry on relevant technical issues, 2) to co-ordinate operational practice of local authorities at the technical level and ensure uniform enforcement of legislation, including particularly legislation emanating from the EC, and 3) to advise local authorities on interpretation and enforcement of specific legislation. The body now extends its remit to food law and has important European food law administrative functions. Invaluable co-ordinating and educational services are also provided to trading standards officers by their professional association, the Institute of Trading Standards Administration.

In order to mitigate the evident dangers of inconsistent decision-making as between, and duplication of investigative effort by, two or more authorities, LACOTS has issued guidelines on what is called the 'Home Authority Principle'. Thus, where a company requires advice from a Trading Standards Department as to legal matters within the Department's remit, its 'home authority' is identified and initial guidance or advice is given. If this is complied with the home authority would not then institute proceedings against that company concerning the particular product or service. Unfortunately, this informal 'estoppel' does not prevent another authority from doing so, but the 'home authority' should be consulted first.[2]

---

1   See the Food Safety Act 1990 and the Food Standards Act 1999 setting up the Food Standards Agency. See generally *Butterworths Law of Food and Drugs*, Div A(17).

2   The guidelines in their up-dated form are reproduced in *Butterworths Law of Food and Drugs* Div A(15). See also the important Enforcement Concordat (March 1998) drawn up by the Cabinet Office Access Business Group concerning the

In a report published in December 1999, the Audit Commission found evidence of varying standards in protecting consumers as between different Trading Standards Authorities (TSAs). The Commission suggested that national standards be set, with targets for achieving them. The Food Standards Agency is to set standards for the work of TSAs, in protecting buyers of food, while the Office of Fair Trading will be responsible for setting standards for consumer protection.[3] The Minister of Consumer Affairs also announced funding from the DTI for the training of Trading Standards Officers and for their examination qualification, the Diploma in Trading Standards, to ensure recruitment and high standards.

Consumer Advice Centres

The activities discussed above pertain to the *enforcement* of consumer protection law. In addition the Local Government Act 1972 (ss 137, 142) and the Local Government etc (Scotland) Act 1994 enable local authorities to provide *advisory* services for the general public. Much of the impetus for the establishment of the advice centres which now exist came from the Consumers' Association which was concerned to make the type of information to be found in *Which?* available to a wider, perhaps less middle-class, spectrum of the community. The CA advocated the setting up of advice centres to complement Citizens' Advice Bureaux and Weights and Measures Departments. Experiments were made in the London area from 1969 onwards, initially at the expense of the CA. The Advice Centre Servicing Unit of the CA was responsible for much of the information supplied to centres and the training of their staff.

About 120 consumer advice centres and about 300 local price survey schemes existed in 1976 aided by grants from central government. These included mobile units to operate in rural areas. These centres sought and, so far as they still operate, still seek both to assist consumers in getting satisfaction with complaints against retailers and other suppliers of faulty goods or services and to give pre-shopping advice primarily on the basis of price comparisons. The centres were also a source of information via printed leaflets on matters affecting consumers generally.[4]

---

activities of all central and local government enforcement agencies. The Concordat emphasises the duty of such agencies to give business help and advice. The text is set out in *Butterworths Law of Food and Drugs* Div A(17).

3   DTI Press Release p/2000/431, OFT Press Release PN 24/00, 22 June 2000.
4   A survey in *The Times* (24 November 1976) suggested that the Centres dealt primarily with complaints. In Wandsworth for example, about seven-tenths of complaints needed to be followed up and compensation of £1,777 was agreed with retailers in a year. Reactions of shoppers in London areas with Consumer Advice Centres ranged from ignorance of their existence to strong approval by those who made use of them. Because of their diminution since 1980, any impact tends to be local rather than national.

A change of policy occurred after the 1979 change of government. Shortly after taking office the Minister of State for Consumer Affairs announced that cash grants from central government for centres and local price surveys were to end from April 1980, at a saving of £3.5 million annually. The reason given was that the centres were thought not to be cost effective. Citizens' advice bureaux were the preferred vehicle for this type of advisory work, and financial support to them was doubled. Such centres as have been continued are financed from local authority revenue.[5] The NCC in its Report *Ordinary Justice* (1989, pp 52–53) found (in 1986) 29 remaining run by the trading standards departments of 20 local authorities. Otherwise, trading standards departments tend routinely to employ 'Consumer Advisers' who are not qualified trading standards officers but may hold the Institute of Trading Standards' Diploma in Consumer Affairs (DCA) and specialise in advisory, rather than enforcement work.

2. BODIES SPONSORED DIRECTLY BY THE GOVERNMENT

The National Consumer Council

A White Paper entitled *A National Consumers' Agency* was put forward by the DPCP in 1974.[6] It was argued that the disappearance of the Consumer Council, a body recommended by the Molony Committee, established by subvention in March 1963 with the function of (inter alia) informing itself about consumers' problems and to consider action to further and safeguard consumers' interests, and abolished in 1971, left a gap. This gap could not, it was argued, be adequately filled by the Director General of Fair Trading. Accordingly it was proposed to establish a National Consumers' Agency whose main function should be to represent the consumer interest in dealings with the Government, local authorities, the Director General of Fair Trading, industry and any other sphere in which the consumer voice ought to be taken into account before policies are formulated or implemented.

This bore fruit in the setting up early in 1975 of the National Consumer Council (with Associated Councils for Scotland, Wales and Northern Ireland), with the assistance of a government grant. This was £300,000 initially but rose to £1.51m in total in 1998–99, of which 70% went to the

---

5   It is the opinion of some trading standards officers that public requests for advice, primarily on civil matters, are still significant and tend to be made to any trading standards officer available. A survey by the NCC, however, suggested that 47 per cent of such complaints were dealt with by solicitors, as opposed to 17 per cent by Trading Standards Departments (see 'Simple Justice' p 17). See also *Ordinary Justice*, NCC, (1989) ch 2. Citizens' Advice Bureaux and Law Centres also supply much advice in civil matters which could involve litigation at a later stage.

6   Cmnd 5726.

NCC and the balance to the Scottish and Welsh Councils and the Consumers in Europe Group. The NCC received a supplementary grant of £26,000 for building maintenance and equipment and other income of £355,000 was raised from various sources including international consultancy work funded in part by the European Union. The Secretary of State for Trade and Industry has a general responsibility for its work, but it is non-statutory and independent of the Government. It has a part-time Chairman and Vice-Chairman.

The Council does not deal directly with consumer complaints but seeks, by making representations, and by representing the consumer on public and other bodies, to influence policies affecting the consumer. Its work to date includes major reports on consumer representation in the nationalised industries and on energy tariffs for domestic fuels and the difficulties caused to those on low incomes. Both reports were made at the request of the Secretary of State. In 1977 a report was published on behalf of the NCC in a book entitled *Why The Poor Pay More* based on research into the consumer behaviour of the poorest sector in Britain. Since then the Council has published a critical review of official forms and leaflets (*Gobbledegook*, 1980), and *Plain language, plain law* (1990), a guide to the Credit Unions Act 1979 which it promoted, a report on Country of Origin Marking, and two on small claims, *Ordinary Justice* (1989) and *Seeking Civil Justice, A Survey of People's Needs and Experiences* (1995) being of particular significance. In October 1981 its report entitled 'Service Please' recommended that all the consumer's existing rights should be re-enacted in one umbrella Act in an attempt to inform the consumer more clearly what these rights now are, which recommendation bore fruit in the Supply of Goods and Services Act 1982. Recent reports have scrutinised the quality of services supplied by local authorities, solicitors and the court system generally; self regulation in health care (1999); and the future for utility regulation (1998). The NCC interprets its remit sufficiently widely to cover many other matters of concern to the ordinary citizen, such as access to information, education, food quality, health and social services, housing and public utilities.

Key tests used by the Council are (a) access – can people actually get the goods or services wanted? (b) choice – is there any? (c) safety – are the goods or services a danger to health or welfare? (d) information – is it available so as to inform consumers' decisions (see ch 1)? (e) equity – are some or all consumers discriminated against? (f) redress – if something goes wrong, is there an effective system for putting it right? (g) representation – if consumers' decisions alone cannot affect the supply of goods or services, are there ways for their views to be represented?

The NCC publishes an annual report listing in more detail its activities and reports. The trend of policy advocated by the Council generally is from one of consumer protection to consumer intervention.

The establishment of the Council was not supported by the major opposition party at the time but the Council survived the 1979 change of government and continues to do much vigorous work in identifying and representing the consumer interest, particularly where this is not being fully taken into account in decisions or proposals of central government, public authorities and privatised industries.[7]

The Consumer Protection Advisory Committee

This Committee was established under the Fair Trading Act 1973 (s 3) and its work will be more fully discussed in chapter 11 dealing with that Act.

3.   VOLUNTARY ORGANISATIONS

Citizens' Advice Bureaux (CABx)

The first Bureaux were started in 1939, just before the outbreak of war, by the National Council of Social Services as a voluntary enterprise. The object of the service is much wider than 'consumer protection' as normally understood. Any personal problems on which individuals welcome independent, confidential, practical, often legal-based, advice (such as landlord and tenant problems, divorce and family problems, problems with the police, problems with social security claims) are within the ambit of the service. Enquiries concerning consumer problems of the sort discussed in this book account for about 18 per cent of the total of which 44 per cent was concerned with debt problems.

There are now 700 bureaux with over 1,000 outlets registered with NACAB (see below). The National Association receives central government finance (around £12 million in recent years). In addition local bureaux are heavily dependent on local authority funding (£46 million in 1997–98). Over 30,000 people work in the CAB Service, 90 per cent of whom are voluntary workers. Many bureaux have links with local solicitors, who may act as honorary legal advisers, and also have rota solicitor schemes whereunder solicitors alternate in giving free legal advice. On other occasions the CABx may assist people in filling in forms to enable them to get legal aid and advice from local solicitors in private practice. Bureaux workers themselves, after specialist training, play an increasingly important part in representing their clients in tribunals and county courts.

7   See *In the Absence of Competition* (1989), *Out of Court* (1991) – low-cost trade arbitration schemes, including British Telecom, *Paying the Price* (1994), a major review of water, gas, electricity and telephone regulation; and *The Future for Utility Regulation* (1998).

NACAB was incorporated as a company limited by guarantee in 1979. Its main charitable object is to encourage the provision of CABx providing a free, confidential and impartial service of advice, information and counsel for members of the public. It is its proud boast that it is now the world's largest independent advice-giving agency. (There are similar structures in Scotland and Northern Ireland.)

Local CABx are independent autonomous bodies and are represented through area committees on the Council of the National Association of Citizens' Advice Bureaux. The Council supplies the policy of the movement and NACAB provides them with a comprehensive and up-to-date information service on new legislation and administrative developments.

Initiated by allegations of political bias on the one hand, and requests for more public money on the other, in 1984 a Report on the Service was produced by the Lovelock Committee (Cmnd 9139 (1984)). This Report[8] contains much helpful information on the growth, work, aims and funding of the Service and prompted a constructive response from NACAB, 'Accepting the Challenge' (September 1984).

In 1997–98 some 6.2 million enquiries were handled. Their work is fundamental to the operation of a complex law-based social system.

Consumers' Association

The primary aim of the Consumers' Association, a company limited by guarantee and a registered charity, is to provide information to the consumer about products and services by testing them thoroughly and giving the reader, through its magazine *Which?* published by CA's trading subsidiary Which? Limited, a frank appraisal. This results in many cases in the recommendation of a 'best buy'. The Association was formally brought into being in 1957 and the inspiration for this type of exercise came primarily from the USA where since 1936 the Consumers' Union had been subjecting a wide range of goods to scientific testing and published the results to subscribers in the monthly Consumer Reports. This in turn was inspired by a book called *Your Money's Worth* by Chase and Schlink (1927) calling for the results of the tests made by the US Bureau of Standards to guide government purchasing policy to be made available to consumers generally.[9] Motivation was fivefold. Firstly, people should be encouraged

---

8   See M, H & P, pp 397–401. See also J Citron *Citizens' Advice Bureaux: For the Community by the Community* (1989); J Richards *Inform, Advise and Support: 50 Years of Citizens' Advice Bureaux.*

9   This plea was not finally granted until the (US) Freedom of Information Act 1966 made it a duty for government agencies and departments to give information to the public. Similar requests to the British government have been made and this has at last borne fruit in a Freedom of Information Bill.

to spend their money well amongst the variety of competing goods available. Secondly, it was regarded as desirable to do something towards reducing the inequality between the disadvantaged ordinary shopper and the technocratic manufacturer. Thirdly, there was the desire to improve Britain's economic performance by creating a more discriminating purchasing public for British goods which were not always of high quality. Fourthly, there was a resentment about the number of goods which were found to be unsatisfactory in some way and a desire to better the situation. Fifthly, there was a resentment of the power of advertising and the desire to find a means of choosing by rational rather than emotional means.[10] With the help of a charitable donation (£3,000) the first issue of *Which?* appeared in October 1957, issued to subscribers. At about the same time a rather similar magazine, *Shopper's Guide*, appeared under the sponsorship of the British Standards Institution, but ceased publication in 1963.

The number of subscribers to *Which?* runs currently at about 600,000. There are 'Sister' magazines to which members may subscribe. These are published by Which? Ltd, which is the trading subsidiary. In addition to its work 'on the ground' the Consumers' Association exerts a powerful influence in promoting public policy on consumer affairs, either by briefing members of Parliament, or representation on other bodies in the UK or in Europe. It was as a result of campaigning by CA that, for example, the Unfair Contract Terms Act was passed by Parliament in 1977 and the monopoly of solicitors to conduct conveyancing was ended in 1985. More recently, CA has campaigned to bring the Property Misdescriptions Act 1991 and the Cheques Act 1992 on to the statute book. CA also promoted the Private Member's Bill that became the Sale and Supply of Goods Act 1994. The Association is a member of the Bureau des Unions de Consommateurs, the European Office of Consumers' Unions and the Consumers International.

The Association is financed mostly by members' subscriptions. Ordinary members (those individual subscribers to specified CA publications who successfully apply to become true members of CA) elect the governing Council. Members of the Council may not be directly engaged in the manufacture, distribution and sale of goods or commodities or in the rendering of services to the public.

Under the Unfair Terms in Consumer Contracts Regulations 1999 the Consumers' Association is named as a qualifying body under Sch 1. It thus has power to apply to the court direct for an injunction to stop the use of an unfair term of a contract within the Regulations. This power is virtually unprecedented for what is essentially a 'private' body (see further ch 5).

---

10   The history of the movement is related by Eirlys Roberts in her book *Consumers* ch V.

Local consumer groups; the National Federation of Consumer Groups

Largely as a result of encouragement by the Consumers' Association there are some 12 local consumer groups in Great Britain, with about 220 other corporate or individual subscribers to the National Federation. The first one was established in Oxford in 1961. They are independent, voluntary and non-profit-making. Their aim is to encourage interest in consumer affairs locally and to campaign for better local shops, services and facilities as well as to encourage helpful existing ones. Many publish their own magazine. The co-ordinating body is the National Federation of Consumer Groups, formed in 1963, which also has close links with the DTI, the Office of Fair Trading and many other consumer organisations. The Federation obtains a grant from the Consumers' Association, a grant from the DTI and receives subscriptions from federated groups and associated bodies. A National Executive Committee is elected by local consumer groups to govern the Federation.

British Standards Institution

BSI originated in 1901 as the Engineering Standards Committee but was incorporated by royal charter under its present name in 1929. Its present charter dates from 1992. An independent, non-profit-making and non-political body, it is funded by sale of standards, subscriptions, testing and licence fees and associated training, information, consultancy, educational and promotional activities, and a grant-in-aid for Standards work from the DTI. Its objects may be summarised as 1) to co-ordinate the standardisation of materials, products and processes so as to simplify production and distribution and eliminate the wastage involved in an unnecessary variety of patterns and sizes of articles serving the same purpose; 2) to set up standards of quality for goods and services and promote British Standards; 3) to register marks of all descriptions in the name of the Institution. Its public relations department is responsible for educational work and for informing consumers about Standards and their impact.

A 'British Standard' is a published document laying down the specifications, testing or measurements with which an article must comply to ensure that it is efficient and suitable for the purpose. The Institution is responsible for over 16,000 published Standards, each one of which is drawn up after consultation with representatives of manufacturers, distributors and users. Over 90 per cent of BSI Standards' projects are directly concerned with the production of European and international standards. Compliance with Standards by manufacturers is usually voluntary, though in

Voluntary organisations

approximately 800 instances compliance is made compulsory by government regulation.

A manufacturer may claim that its goods are made in accordance with a certain British Standard by so stating and marking the goods with the BS number. But a more certain assurance of quality is where a manufacturer is licensed to apply a certification trade mark known as the 'kitemark' to his products. This involves testing for compliance by BSI and regular spot checks by BSI inspectors thereafter. Failure to meet the Standard results in withdrawal of the licence. The BSI 'registered firm' logo shows that a company's management and quality systems have been assessed as consistently meeting the requirements of ISO 9000. (Allied organisations also exist in Britain which provide certification schemes, particularly for electrical goods under the auspices of the British Electrotechnical Approvals Board.)[11]

An important feature of the consumer protection side of BSI is the work of its Consumer Policy Committee which comprises representatives of national consumer bodies and volunteer members of the public who work on standards where there is a consumer interest.

Other organisations to assist the consumer

There is a large number of organisations directly or peripherally concerned with assisting or protecting the consumer, and what follows is merely a brief selection of the more significant.

Advertising is in part controlled by legislation in the interests of consumer protection, but there are in addition comprehensive codes of practice promoted by the independent Advertising Standards Authority called the *British Code of Advertising and Sales Promotion.* Under the codes, advertisements must be legal, decent, honest and truthful, framed with a sense of responsibility to the consumer and conforming to the principles of fair competition. Detailed provisions apply to certain products, eg medicinal products, tobacco, consumer credit and mail order advertisements. Complaints about alleged breaches of the codes may be made to the Authority by the public which are then investigated and the results may be published, warning offenders. There are certain other sanctions which may be applied through the trade. Although the codes lack the force of law, they can be justified by the claim that they are designed to achieve high professional standards and good taste which it may not be practicable to make the subject matter of legislation.

---

11   Far more conformity has been required with safety requirements in domestic electrical equipment as a result of implementing the EC Directives on low voltage electrical equipment – see ch 9.

The Director General of Fair Trading presented a review of the UK's self-regulating system of advertising control to the Secretary of State for Prices and Consumer Protection in 1978. The review concluded that the system was working well overall and that there was no evidence to suggest that comprehensive legal controls were needed. However, some improvements were recommended and in particular it was considered that the Director General should be given reserve powers. A further report of a working party of the Department of Trade on the Self-Regulatory System of Advertising Control was issued in 1980 and the Consumers' Association published a paper on Self-regulation of Advertising Policy in June 1997.[12]

The adoption by the EC Council of Ministers on 10 September 1984 of a directive on misleading advertising has already been commented upon.[13] In the context of the control which the Director General of Fair Trading has been given under the Control of Misleading Advertisements Regulations 1988 the government has stated:

In those areas of advertising where the ASA currently provides the main control the Government see the new powers which the Directive requires to be introduced primarily as a 'long stop'. The Government hope that the effect will be to strengthen rather than diminish the authority of the self-regulation system.[14]

This attitude has been encouraged by the courts. Mr Justice Hoffmann, in *Director General of Fair Trading v Tobyward Ltd*,[15] where the first interlocutory injunction under the 1988 Regulations was granted, stated:

... the regulations contemplate that there will only be intervention by the director when the voluntary system has failed. It is in my judgment desirable and in accordance with the public interest to which I must have regard that the courts should support the principle of self-regulation. I think that advertisers would be more inclined to accept the rulings of their self-regulatory bodies if it were generally known that in cases in which their procedures had been exhausted and the advertiser was still publishing an advertisement which appeared to the court to be prima facie misleading an injunction would ordinarily be granted [at p 270].

There are numerous trade and professional associations whose functions include at least an element of consumer protection. To give some

12   Extracts from these publications are reproduced in M, H & P ch 10.
13   See ch 2. A further directive on misleading or unfair comparative advertising has led to amendments to the original Regulations in 2000 – see also ch 2.
14   Consultative Document, DTI, July 1985.
15   [1989] 2 All ER 266, Ch D. See further ch 2.

random examples, the National House Building Council, to which almost all house builders belong,[16] is an independent non-profit-making body whose aim is to improve the standard of house building and whose certificate is designed to ensure that the buyer does not suffer financially either from the financial failure of the builder or the seriously deficient building of the house. Its Council members are nominated by building societies, building employers' associations, consumer groups and the professions. It sets minimum standards of construction and has an inspection system of homes as they are built. A 10-year warranty is offered to protect buyers against losses, financed by means of a levy on builders.

The Association of British Travel Agents deals with complaints of disappointed travellers who have booked through members of the Association and provides replacement arrangements where a client is affected by the insolvency of his agent (see ch 11).

As regards professional bodies, the Law Society protects solicitors' clients against the dishonesty or insolvency of their solicitors through a compensation fund to which all practising solicitors contribute, and provides for compulsory insurance against negligence. It imposes strict disciplinary rules of conduct, breach of which may result in withdrawal of the right to practise, and there are independent systems for investigating complaints against solicitors regarding their standard of work (see ch 7).

Financial services have largely been omitted from this book because as regards investors they pertain to the raising of capital by offerors of financial services, and this is part of the apparatus of producers rather than consumers. But investors occupy a very similar position to consumers of services and investors have a considerable amount of protection against inadequate information about their investments or fraud. Once the capital is raised, providers of financial services sell them to consumers in the ordinary way – eg insurers through policies of various sorts, and where an industry is large and outside much consumer protection legislation[17] it may be justified to create special complaints mechanisms.

Since 1981 the financial sector has created a number of 'ombudsmen' in the private sector, typically financed by the subscriptions of those members of the particular sector joining the scheme.

The actual powers of these ombudsmen vary from scheme to scheme, but at the minimum they carry a voice which is listened to in an often seemingly insensitive corporation and at best they require the company to pay compensation (eg in insurance cases). As a rule, a customer is not

---

16 Expulsion from the Register, or non-membership, usually results in the unavailability of mortgage finance.

17 For example, ss 2 to 4 of the Unfair Contract Terms Act 1977 do not apply to contracts of insurance – see Sch 1. But the Unfair Terms in Consumer Contracts Regulations 1999 do so apply.

bound by the ombudsman's decisions and may resort to legal action if dissatisfied.

The effectiveness of these schemes (together with the Ombudsman for Corporate Estate Agents) was assessed in the Director General of Fair Trading's Report into Consumer Redress Mechanisms in November 1991. The report was critical of the bewildering variety of forms of redress in the financial sector, the varying standards of qualification required of ombudsmen, and the accessibility, simplicity and independence of some of the schemes. A new Financial Services Ombudsman Service is due to commence in 2001.

These services are further discussed in chapter 7.

4 Nationalised or privatised industries and the consumer

I. INTRODUCTION

The industries considered in this chapter were in their embodiment prior to privatisation examples of public corporations. By 'public corporations' is meant, briefly, bodies having a separate legal personality conferred usually by statute but occasionally by charter,[1] having a specific range of functions often involving a statutory monopoly of the supply of goods or services and, as regards management and finance, being independent of government except, in practice, on matters affecting national policy. This is not the place to endeavour to trace in detail the history of these corporations or assess their wider functions and significance.[2] Any survey now made must take into account the former Conservative government's privatisation policy which has deregulated (inter alia) the bus industry, telecommunications, British Gas, British Airways, water, electricity and rail services. In the case of telecommunications and gas supplies, both British Gas and British Telecom were dominant in their respective markets and the policy has been that, though privatised, they should be subject to a special regulatory regime some features of which are discussed below. Such machinery has not been necessary in, for example, the privatisation of the bus industry (outside London) by the Transport Act 1985. This Act swept away a regime which was regarded as bureaucratic and which had effectively prevented competition by granting de facto monopolies. Under the new policy any operator can run services on unsubsidised routes provided safety requirements are met and notices given of intention to run such services. Subsidies for unprofitable routes must be awarded on the basis of competitive tender. Bus undertakings run by local authorities or

---

1   For example, the British Broadcasting Corporation.
2   For a thorough survey, see Tivey *Nationalisation in British Industry*.

Passenger Transport Executives have been transferred into free-standing, unsubsidised organisations and the National Bus Company (NBC) was broken up and more than 60 subsidiaries sold off. In these circumstances the consumer's interests must be enforced in the same way as against any other private operator, leaving the consumer to pursue his rights through the courts and using, where appropriate, the Supply of Goods and Services Act 1982.

Of the many public corporations which until comparatively recently existed in Great Britain, those in which the consumer has a particularly direct interest were mainly created as part of the nationalisation programme of the Labour Government in the years immediately following the Second World War. The vehicle of the public corporation was chosen to manage such industries as coal, gas, electricity, transport and, after many years as a government department, postal and telephone services so as, in theory at least, to combine the virtues of commercial and independent business management with public accountability and ultimate public control. 'Public enterprise' is the cachet which most aptly conveys the hermaphrodite status and objectives of this type of public corporation. The movement to establish public corporations of this type went into reverse in the 1980s with the Conservative government's privatisation policy, as mentioned above.

2. THE IMPLICATIONS OF MONOPOLY POWER

There is an immediate apparent contradiction in the State's economic objectives when one compares the elaborate machinery in the monopolies, mergers and restrictive practices legislation and the rules of the EC to preserve an element of competition between producers in the consumer interest on the one hand, with the monopoly powers usually conferred by the nationalising statutes on the public corporations which supplied essential goods and services on the other. Thus for example the Coal Industry Nationalisation Act 1946 (s 1(1)(a)) stated that the duties of the National Coal Board were 'working and getting the coal in Great Britain, to the exclusion (save in this Act provided) of any other person'. Other everyday examples of these monopoly powers were 1) the carriage of rail passengers by British Rail and 2) currently in respect of the carrying of letters by the Post Office.[3]

---

3   'Subject to the following provisions of this Part, the Post Office shall have throughout the United Kingdom the exclusive privilege of conveying letters from one place to another, and of performing all the incidental services of receiving, collecting and delivering, letters' (British Telecommunications Act 1981, s 66(1)). The position of the Post Office is under review.

The reasons for conferring these monopoly powers on public corporations of this sort included considerations arising from the colossal capital investment because of the nature of the service provided, the social responsibility of suppliers of energy to the community[4] and to the workers within the industry. Although there are formidable difficulties in contriving a fair system of competition in these fields of economic activity, the view taken by the Conservative administration was that if the industry can be run profitably there is no intrinsic reason why ownership of it should not be vested in the public, through shareholdings, rather than in the State. The 'privatisation' policy adopted in recent years (and widely copied in a number of other countries) is discussed below. The legislation achieving the privatisation normally contains provisions at least narrowing down the areas in which the monopoly continues to exist.

Having pointed out the existence of legally enforceable monopoly powers it is necessary to qualify any impression that this necessarily put the consumer into a straitjacket in the market place. For example, the consumer considering the installation of domestic central heating has the choice as regards fuel between oil, gas, electricity and solid fuel. In theory at least, even assuming that the particular industry was monopolistic, there was strong competition between the various industries to provide fuel at favourable rates. But in practice government could interfere either, as in the period from 1972 to 1975, by holding down prices below break-even level as a contribution to macro-economic anti-inflation policies, or, for example, by reducing the public indebtedness of the then nationalised gas industry by raising gas prices so that as a result gas becomes less competitive with other sources of energy. Access to the capital market and the willingness to take risks with investment in response to actual or perceived potential consumer demand should, the then government believed, lead to a better service.

3. PROTECTING THE CONSUMER'S INTERESTS

There are a number of legal and parliamentary controls upon public corporations and an analysis of these controls is more appropriate to works

4   For example, the Gas Act 1948, s 1(1)(a) stated that it shall be the duty of every area board 'to develop and maintain an efficient, co-ordinated and economical system of gas supply for their area and to satisfy, so far as it is economical to do so, all reasonable demands for gas within their area'. The Electricity Act 1947, s 1(2) had a similar provision obliging boards 'to plan and carry out an efficient and economical distribution of those supplies to persons in their area who require them'. Professor Garner stated that 'there has yet been no litigant bold enough to ask for an order of mandamus against a public corporation, and it is perhaps doubtful whether he would achieve much by so doing': *Administrative Law* (4th edn) p 315.

on administrative law. But, to give brief examples, a member of the public may sue a public corporation in the ordinary way, and in particular the corporation will be vicariously liable in tort for the negligence or other civil wrongs of its servants. This may be negatived by a specific statutory immunity, such as the Post Office's in relation to liability in respect of actions or omissions 'in relation to anything in the post', under section 29 of the Post Office Act 1969 (as amended).[5] Similar exclusions in respect of telecommunications were made by section 23 of the British Telecommunications Act 1981 which excludes British Telecom's tort liability in respect of failure to provide a service or apparatus and errors in telephone directories. As has already been pointed out it is probably not possible for a member of the public successfully to sue the corporation itself in respect of any alleged breach of statutory duty to provide, for instance, an efficient and economical service. Professor Garner has called this type of provision 'a duty of imperfect obligation'. Alternatively the appropriate minister might be required in Parliament to answer members' questions, often made on behalf of constituents, provided in fact there is a responsible minister, and sometimes where there is no such direct responsibility. Opportunities for debate may also occasionally occur, for example where a constituent statute is made or revised, or where a motion of supply includes a vote for financial assistance to the public corporation. Between 1956 and 1979 a House of Commons Select Committee examined the Reports and Accounts of the Nationalised Industries, and from time to time investigated and reported on a particular public corporation, or on general matters such as relations with the public, discussed below. But neither the Parliamentary Commissioner for Administration ('the Ombudsman') nor the Commissions for Local Administration cover public corporations.

It was widely, if by no means universally, conceded that it was also appropriate to represent the consumer in an advisory capacity in the policy-making of public corporations. This can be justified either on the grounds that it may help to prevent the irresponsible use of monopoly power or on the more general ground of the inequality of technological knowledge between consumer and producer. The main way in which Parliament arranged for the consumer interest to be represented was by the creation of Consumer or Consultative Councils.[6] These were, for example, for solid

---

5   In *Harold Stephen & Co Ltd v Post Office* [1978] 1 All ER 939, the Court of Appeal refused to grant the claimant businessmen relief in respect of their mail detained by the 'blacking' action by Post Office workers.

6   Emanuel Shinwell, Minister of Fuel and Power at the time of the Coal Industry Nationalisation Act 1946, justified a Coal Consumers' Council by stating, 'It was necessary to take account of public opinion, and though such a Council might prove abortive, it would be a body which would *appear* to be useful, and that was an important factor'. See also Rutherford 'The Consumer Voice in Nationalised Industries' (1980) 130 NLJ 620.

fuel the Domestic Coal Consumers' Council (abolished by the Coal Industry Act 1994, section 24, this being the Act which enabled the British Coal Corporation to transfer coal-mining activities to the private sector) and postal services (Post Office Users' National Council ('POUNC')). The effectiveness of these bodies was the subject of debate though such independent surveys as have been made confirm that they could often deal effectively with consumer complaints.[7]

4. PRIVATISATION OF FORMERLY NATIONALISED INDUSTRIES

Major examples of the privatisation of formerly nationalised industries affecting the everyday activities of the consumer are the gas industry, the electricity industry, the water supply industry, the telecommunications industry and the rail industry. It is not practicable to consider the details of all these privatised concerns in a textbook of this non-specialised sort, but taking gas as typical of energy arrangements and rail as an interesting and controversial example of a non-utility, the general design will become clearer. A more general assessment will be found at the end of this chapter.

Gas

The gas industry is now considered in its nationalised and then privatised form. The arrival of a central supply of natural gas from the North Sea accompanied by a system of trunk pipelines prompted the reorganisation of the gas industry on a unitary basis, under the British Gas Corporation, by the Gas Act 1972. The BGC had the duty of meeting all reasonable and economic demands for gas, avoiding undue preference. The BGC had a virtual monopoly of supply to the approximately 13 million domestic gas consumers. It competed with private firms on appliance sales, servicing and contracting but enjoyed about 60 per cent of domestic gas appliance sales. Management of the industry was through 12 Regions each of which was divided into Areas.

The Gas Act 1948 had created 12 gas consultative councils on an Area basis. The 1972 Act preserved the regional structure by converting the Area Gas Consultative Councils into Regional Gas Consumers' Councils, and also set up a National Gas Consumers' Council (s 9). The National

---

7   See Consumer Consultative Machinery in the Nationalised Industries (Consumer Council, 1968); HC Paper (1970–71) no 514; Consumers and the Nationalised Industries (NCC, 1976); 'The Citizen and Public Agencies' (Justice, 1976); White Paper on the Nationalised Industries (Cmnd 7131 (1978)); Report on Non-Departmental Public Bodies (Cmnd 7797 (1980)); Consumers' Interests and the Nationalised Industries (DoT, 1981).

Council had a Chairman and not more than 30 members made up of the Chairmen of Regional Councils and other members appointed, after consultation, by the Secretary of State. The BGC had to inform the National Council of its plans, tariff proposals and other matters involving consumers generally and the Council could make representations to the Minister (ie the Secretary of State for Energy). The Council's statutory duty was to consider 'any matter affecting the interests of consumers of gas generally or any class or description of consumers of gas' (s 10(1)).

The Regional Gas Consumers' Council consisted of a paid chairman and between 20 and 30 members chosen from amongst local authority nominees and representatives of all classes of consumers in the area. Section 11 of the Gas Act 1972 required Regional Committees to appoint local, or district, committees to receive local representations and keep themselves aware of local requirements. Regional councils could make representations to the BGC or to the National Council, not to the Minister direct.

Under the then government's privatisation policy provision was made for dissolution of the BGC and the vesting of its property, rights and liabilities in a company nominated for this purpose by the Secretary of State and limited by shares (Gas Act 1986, s 49). This 'successor company' (ie British Gas plc) was designed to be widely owned by gas consumers and investments in its shares are authorised as being appropriate for trustees (s 59). The Gas Act 1986 also removed the privilege (ie monopoly) with respect to the supply of gas through pipes conferred on the BGC by the Gas Act 1972. It was open to any undertaking to supply gas to any premises provided the undertaking was authorised to do so under sections 7 and 8 of the Act as a 'public gas supplier'. Schedule 5 supplied a 'public gas supply code' with regard to the standard of service to be observed by public gas suppliers, 'the Gas Code' under Schedule 2B. There was, however, initially no competition in the domestic market for piped gas. Following the Gas Act 1995, full competition was introduced into the domestic market by 1998 and had already been introduced into the industrial and commercial markets. In early 1996 it was announced that British Gas would be split into two (as first proposed by a Monopolies Commission Report in 1993). One company focuses on the supply of gas and selected services in Britain, while the other continues to be Britain's single national transporter of gas. The change was welcomed by the Gas Consumers' Council as good for customers. By combining gas supply, appliance sales and central heating servicing in one company, a return to the concept of one-stop customer care could be expected.

In terms of competition, the domestic gas market has been transformed. By mid-2000 there were 23 different companies selling gas (and 16 selling electricity). The picture includes a number of 'dual fuel' companies, including British Gas, which sell both gas and electricity at an appropriate discount to buyers of both, and even 'affinity' company deals, such as Saga's, offering energy to members through a link-up with Northern Electricity and Gas.

A report by the National Audit Office in May 2000 found that the introduction of gas competition throughout Great Britain had been a major success. It had had the effect of real price reductions for consumers on average of £60 a year in 1999 (and between £35 and £45 per year for electricity customers). *Which?* undertakes useful surveys from time to time aimed at giving consumers the comparative data to make a prudent choice. Changing companies should be straightforward, generally involving four weeks' notice.

The 1986 Act also provided for the appointment of an officer known as a 'regulator', to be styled the Director General of Gas Supply (s 1) whose office was known as OFGAS. Amongst his duties were the fixing of maximum prices at which gas supplied by public gas suppliers may be resold, and provision was made for the publication of such prices to secure adequate publicity. If any person resells any gas supplied by a public supplier at a price exceeding the maximum price, the amount of the excess is recoverable by the person to whom the gas was resold.

The Act also contained the machinery for consumer representation. A new body corporate known as the Gas Consumers' Council was set up by section 2 to replace the old National Gas Consumers' Council. The Council consisted of a chairman and such other members as the Secretary of State might from time to time appoint. Such members were required to represent and consider the interests of consumers of gas supplied through pipes in the different areas of Great Britain and understand the needs of small businesses. Schedule 2 further described the status and duties of members of the Council which was funded by the Department of Trade and Industry. The Council had headquarters in London and regional offices in England, Scotland and Wales. An important feature was that it was independent of the regulator.

The Gas Consumers' Council (GCC) dealt also with complaints about appliances sold by British Gas, or servicing and repairs, which did not come within the jurisdiction of OFGAS. During 1999 the GCC dealt with 203,753 enquiries and 67,022 complaints. A monitoring of consumer opinion found 90% of complainants rating the GCC's services excellent or good. Details of complaints procedures should be found on the back of invoices.[8]

The Unified Scheme for Gas and Electricity

The pattern of the privatisation of electricity followed a somewhat similar sequence to gas. In particular, the Electricity Act 1989 1) provided a new

8   See *Consumer Redress Mechanisms* (OFT, 1991) para. 4.89.

system governing the generation, transmission and supply of electricity and 2) removed electricity from state ownership and control into a number of regionally based successor companies which were then floated off to the public.

The regulatory mechanism involved the appointment of a Director General of Electricity Supply (operating through an Office called OFFER). The duties of the Director included ensuring that all reasonable demands for electricity were met and protecting the interests of consumers in terms of prices, terms and quality of supply. Section 2 of the Act required the Director to appoint regional consumers' committees and an overarching national committee to review matters affecting consumers' interests. Nevertheless, if a consumer made a complaint to the supplier which could not be resolved it could then be taken up by the regional office of OFFER. The small print on the back of the invoice made it clear that OFFER was the first port of call and it was normally only if this produced no solution to the consumer's problem that the local Consumers' Committee was to become involved. Even then the Committee had no power to enforce the decision, though the Director had. It can be seen that a certain ambiguity pervaded the dual functions of OFFER in the consumer complaints field. The NCC in its Report *Consumer Representation in the Public Utilities* (1996) preferred the gas model, a regulator plus an external, independent consumer representative body, neither funded nor appointed by the regulator.

By May 1999 the electricity market had opened to full competition and 1.5 million customers had changed supplier. As has been mentioned, there were a number of dual suppliers. For this and other reasons it seemed logical to combine the regulatory and consumer function of gas and electricity into one body concerned with energy from these primary sources. The government's policy was described as, by virtue of the Utilities Act 2000, putting consumers at the heart of regulation and creating a new consumer body which will have a much sharper focus on championing the interests of all gas and electricity consumers, as well as giving new powers to the energy regulator.

Accordingly, section 1 creates the Gas and Electricity Markets Authority whose principal objective is to protect the interests of consumers of gas and electricity, wherever possible, by promoting effective competition in generation, transmission, distribution and supply. The office of the enhanced Director General is styled 'Ofgem'.

Section 2 of the Act creates the Gas and Electricity Consumer Council (inevitably, GECC), whose duties include providing advice and information to consumers, investigating consumer complaints, and developing proposals to improve industry service levels and help people in 'fuel poverty'. Section 22 of the Act provides that GECC is the main body for handling complaints not dealt with successfully by the supplier. In order to avoid clashes or overlapping of functions between the two independent bodies a memorandum of understanding was drawn up setting out the duties of each. Besides an HQ in London it is envisaged that GECC should have offices in Glasgow, Cardiff, Manchester, Newcastle, Birmingham and Bournemouth (Ofgem has a website giving more details – http://www.ofgem.gov.uk).

Rail services

Reorganisation of the railway industry was effected by the Railways Act 1993. Behind this Act lies a convoluted history and a series of controversial decisions by the then government. The continuing debate on how rail consumers can best be served can be better understood if the history of British railway organisation is outlined.

Prior to nationalisation in 1947, the rail industry had over 100 years' experience of privately-owned railway companies running their respective enterprises under, for much of the time, a great deal of government regulation. For a start, the companies themselves had to be created by private Acts of Parliament and they needed (and obtained) powers, amongst others, to acquire pieces of land compulsorily for construction. When operative, during the nineteenth century, a series of regulating authorities were created ('Railway Departments' and 'Railway Commissions'). Their duties included safety and the regulation of tariffs. During the First World War the importance of the railways as a military asset employed in transporting army personnel, equipment and the like, led to control being vested in the Minister of Transport. (The new 1993 Act also allows the Secretary of State to take control of the rail system in case of war or great national emergency (s 118).) After the war the Railways Act 1921 amalgamated the former railway companies into four groups: the London and North Eastern Railway Company; the London Midland and Scottish Railway Company; the Southern Railway Company and the Great Western Railway Company. A Railway Rates Tribunal arbitrated on matters relating to fares and the end result was a radical reduction in competition in the railways.

A further major reorganisation occurred on nationalisation in 1947 when, by the Transport Act 1947, the British Transport Commission (BTC) was created to provide an efficient, adequate, economical and properly integrated system of public inland transport for passengers and goods with due regard to safety of operation. Transportation by rail was but one part of the BTC, the rail governing body being known as the Railway Executive. Then by the Transport Act 1962 the monolithic functions of the BTC were broken up by the creation of the London Transport Board, the British Transport Docks Board, the British Waterways Board and, for rail, the British Railways Board.

But the 1962 Act was unable to deal with the fundamental problem of excess capacity and uneconomic services. This led to the historic investigation by Dr Beeching who was asked to set up a survey to show which services were profitable and which loss-making with a view to assessing whether it was possible for the rail industry to pay for itself. It then became apparent that the old railway system was uneconomic to a large extent and, inevitably, patently uneconomic services had to be cut and lines closed to make the railways more viable. On the basis of an assurance (not kept for long) that no services would be withdrawn until alternative services by road were in place (these being cheaper to subsidise), widespread rationalisation of services occurred in the early 1960s.

A change in Government in 1964 promoted the alternative idea that the main objective of the rail system was to provide services in accordance with socio-economic needs and within a system of integrated transportation. But the rail industry as a whole continued both to lose custom and lose money. The share of the passenger market dropped from about 20% in the 1950s to about 9% at the time of the 1993 Act. Freight market share fell from 40% to 7%.

Besides the aim of mitigating public expenditure, on the Second Reading of the Bill, later becoming the 1993 Act, the Secretary of State announced that the objective was to improve services for passengers and freight customers, while maintaining high safety standards and other necessary safeguards, including a commitment to the provision of subsidy to maintain loss-making but socially necessary passenger services, such as commuter lines and rural services. And as the preceding White Paper remarked (Cm 2012 (1992)): 'Too frequently and on too many lines, the quality of service fails to meet the travelling public's expectations … The industry is more insulated from the demands of the market than its private sector airline, coach and road haulage competitors. It therefore has fewer incentives to improve its performance and less freedom to respond to what the customer wants.' It was also accused of having the culture of a nationalised industry: a heavily bureaucratic structure; an insufficiently sharp awareness on the part of employees that their success depends on satisfying the customer; and an instinctive tendency to ask for more taxpayers' subsidy and to feel that public subsidy will always be there as a crutch whenever things got difficult. Inevitably (it was argued) public ownership also brings with it the constraints of public finance, not least given the many competing demands on the public purse.

These justifications for the privatisation policy are included because it is easy to forget, in the light of the bitter and persistent criticism which the privatisation of the rail industry attracted and to some extent continues to attract, how the industry was seen, and how it actually performed, before privatisation. But would privatisation be 'a poll tax on rails' or 'inordinately expensive, intensely bureaucratic – a nightmare' (as a former Chairman of British Rail predicted) or will it, as *The Economist* in 1996 suggested, be 'a consumer's dream – the start of a new era which will revolutionise Britain's under invested railway network'?

Whatever the answer, following the way railway policy unfolds will be enhanced by some understanding of the structure of the privatisation scheme in the 1993 Act. (Although, as will be seen, the Transport Act 2000 makes important modifications to the scheme, its main features remain intact. The primary feature of the new system is the creation of a new authority to develop the scheme and take over various powers and duties from the Franchising Director and the Regulator, particularly as regards consumer protection. But the Railway Act 1993 is not repealed; the changes are grafted on to it.)

Unlike conventional privatisations, there was no simple outright sale of British Rail in exchange for the issuing of shares. It was soon realised that outright privatisation was not possible. Some parts of British Rail were incapable of operating without subsidy in the foreseeable future. Instead, the business was divided into two primary services, the carriage of passengers and the carriage of goods. The nature of freight and parcels service operations permitted an outright privatisation by selling them off to the private sector. Passenger services are dealt with differently. The Act provides that passenger services are organised into franchised and non-franchised services. Franchised services are provided by private sector operators who make successful bids to operate them, or in certain circumstances by BR. Non-franchised services would continue to be operated by the British Railways Board as reorganised. The franchising operation, which is undertaken by the Franchising Director as an arm of the Secretary of State, involves an invitation to shortlisted respondents to a preceding invitation to submit a bid, either in the form of a fee payable to the Franchising Director or a fee payable by the Franchising Director, for the agreed level and standard of services. The overriding criterion is the bid which provides 'the best overall value for money'. Franchises may be from five to 15 years and the contract includes such matters as minimum frequencies, quality of service in terms of punctuality and the provision of compensation under the Passenger's Charter.

A further part of the scheme is that the role of 'Safety Watchdog' is to be fulfilled by the Health and Safety Executive, with compliance monitoring being the responsibility of a Railway Inspectorate. The onus for safety is firmly placed on the operators themselves and operators would have to satisfy Railtrack (see below) that the operator's safety systems are adequate. Section 117 of the Act applies the Health and Safety at Work etc Act 1974 to the railway system.

Another important and controversial feature of the scheme is to separate 'track and train' or 'wheel and rail'. BR's restructuring involves two units, the one responsible for providing passenger services until franchised, the other, 'Railtrack', responsible for the track and other railway infrastructure. The Act itself does not refer to Railtrack but the Secretary of State is given wide discretionary powers and 'Railtrack' is the product of the exercise of these. Railtrack was originally intended to continue as a nationalised element in the system but instead it became a government-owned company and its sale to investors occurred in 1996. Almost all Railtrack's revenues derive from usage charges paid by train operators, giving it a relatively assured income stream. This is designed to promote the long-term capital investment which has been so lacking under public sector management.

A more familiar feature of this privatisation scheme is the creation of a regulator. The Rail Regulator was put at the heart of the system and was given multifarious duties and functions, including establishing a relationship with the Franchising Director, the Health and Safety Executive and Railtrack on matters of competition, track accessibility, the level of charges and the process of safety validation. The Regulator functions as an independent body (contrasted with the Franchising Director who was an arm of the Secretary of State for Transport) and from the Office of the Rail Regulator. The Regulator (ORR) is financially accountable to Parliament and subject to the Parliamentary Ombudsman's jurisdiction. More specifically, the Regulator, by section 4, is charged with the protection of the interests of railway users, promoting efficiency, economy, competition and facilitating journeys made using more than one service operator (use of through tickets) and, in the case of private sector operators, otherwise than under franchise agreements, protecting interests of users in respect of prices charged and quality of service. The Regulator must also take into account safety and environmental concerns.

Besides the functions of the Regulator, what machinery existed to protect consumers sufficiently? The answer is that under section 2 of the Act the old Area Transport Users Consultative Committees created by the Transport Act 1962 were abolished and instead the Regulator was required to establish a number of committees, not exceeding nine at any one time, to be known as Rail Users Consultative Committees, of which there had to be one for Scotland and one for Wales. Each committee consisted of a chairman and not less than 10 nor more than 20 members, appointed by the Regulator after consultation with the Secretary of State and the chairman. Section 3 abolished the old Central Transport Consultative Committees of Great Britain and established instead a Central Rail Users' Consultative Committee consisting of a chairman and, as members, every person holding office as chairman of one of the consultative committees mentioned above, plus up to six other members.

The powers and duties of the consultative committees were to be found in sections 76–79 of the Act. As regards the Central Committee, section 76 empowered them to investigate any matter which related to the provision of railway passenger services (as defined) or to the provision of station services. Specific matters falling within the area of one of the consultative committees had to be referred to the relevant area consultative committee. The duty to investigate arose only if one of three possible conditions were satisfied: i) the representation was by a user or potential user of 'railway passenger services' and was not frivolous or vexatious; ii) the referral was from the Regulator and related either to passenger or station services; or iii) the matter was one which the Central Committee felt that it ought to investigate (as a central matter).

The committees were very much the creatures of the Regulator. For instance, if the Central Committee was unable to achieve satisfactory resolution of a complaint or had reason to believe that the holder of a passenger licence or a station licence was contravening, or was likely to contravene, any condition of the licence, the committee was under a duty to refer the matter to the Regulator. The same applied to Area Committees. This was, in effect, another way in which the Regulator could monitor compliance with the operating licence. Area Committees were obliged to submit a report relating to 'the quality of the railway passenger services, and the station services' provided within the relevant area *if* the Regulator so requested (s 77(6)).

The complexity of this privatisation scheme is indicated by the length of text needed to explain the bare bones. Consumer representation as such was not greatly different to that afforded under the old, nationalised, system. But the economic premise behind the whole scheme is that competition itself will be the consumer's main ally. Sceptics doubted whether the haste with which the reorganisation was pushed through and its very complexity would, even if it were theoretically possible, result in a rail system more trouble free and just as safe as before[9]. However, with franchise licences committing operators to replace old rolling stock with new trains and with a performance regime involving financial penalties for late running trains, it was thought that the public might in time see an improved service, particularly on well-used inter-city and commuter lines, if the system were allowed to develop.

Arrangements for consumer representation were, however, very much dependent on agreement between the Regulator and the committees as to

---

9   Public confidence was shaken by a bad accident involving the collision of two trains and killing 31 people near Paddington in October 1999. One of the trains passed a red signal. But similar accidents had periodically occurred in the immediately preceding era of British Rail. An enquiry was instituted under Lord Cullen. Having regard to the alarming fact that, apparently, about 600 trains a year pass red signals, Railtrack is to get £1.2 billion of public money to fit systems that would automatically stop trains passing them. This is part of a grant of £4 billion to improve and expand the carrying capacity of the rail network. The Rail Regulator is to monitor progress closely.

where the consumer interest lay, the Regulator keeping the whip hand. This was not the preferred model for the new millennium, and the new government chose this aspect to reform rather than reversing the whole privatisation, no doubt in part because of the political and economic consequences of funding the huge amounts needed to improve the system from taxation. The new system was certainly born with vociferous public opposition. It was also apparent, however, that there is little public awareness of the sophistication of the scheme as a whole. As John Swift, the first Regulator stated, 'What people have not yet realised is just how radical the Railways Act is'.

The government's proposals for reform are to be found in Part IV of the Transport Act 2000. This alone contains 53 sections and 15 schedules. To add to the complexities the modifications are grafted on to the Railways Act 1993 whose wording is frequently modified, repealed or added to and the two statutes have to be read together to make sense of the new provisions.

The first major feature is the creation of the Strategic Rail Authority ('the Authority'), a body which came to life in 'shadow' form before the Act was passed. It consists of a chair (Sir Alistair Morton) and between seven and fourteen other members (s 201). Its purposes are to promote the use of the railway network for the carriage of passengers and goods, to secure the development of the railway network and to contribute to the development of an integrated system of transport of passengers and goods (s 204). In formulating strategies it is under a duty to consult specified regional bodies and the Regulator, and it may be given directions and guidance by the Secretary of State. It is also under a duty to act in the way best calculated (a) to protect the interests of users, (b) to contribute to the achievement of sustainable development, (c) to promote efficiency and economy by providers, (d) to promote measures designed to facilitate passengers' journeys involving more than one passenger service operator (particularly through ticketing), (e) to impose on operators the minimum restrictions consistent with the Authority's functions, and (f) to enable railway services providers to plan the futures of their businesses with a reasonable degree of assurance. The Authority is also required to have regard to (a) the need to protect all persons from dangers arising from the operation of the railways, (b) the interests of the disabled, and (c) environmental issues (s 206). The Authority is also given power to make byelaws instead of such powers formerly exercised by train companies and Railtrack, confirmed by the Secretary of State. The Authority has the power to make uniform byelaws for the whole network (s 218 and Sch 20).

The Authority inherits all the functions (as outlined above), property, rights and liabilities of the Franchising Director, whose office is abolished (s 214 and Sch 16). There are elaborate provisions as to what happens where the Authority has invited tenders for services designated for franchising but considers that they could be provided more economically and efficiently other than by a franchise agreement – a statutory dialogue with the Secretary of State ensues (s 211 by amendment to s 26 of the 1993 Act). The British Rail Board's remaining properties, rights and liabilities are also vested in the Authority, with the right to manage or develop for sale property not required for railway purposes. There is power to dissolve the BRB (ss 217, 239). In addition to these accretions, the Authority acquires some powers formerly exercised by the Regulator – see below – particularly as regards consumer protection (see Sch 17).

The new scheme attempts to address the criticism that there was no clear division between the respective roles of the Rail Regulator and the Franchising Director in relation to the consumer. The Act transfers responsibilities for consumer protection to the Authority as successor to the Franchising Director. Although some detail needs to be added by subsidiary legislation the broad effect of the scheme is that, although licences to operate railway assets are still granted by the Regulator, the Authority will be responsible for the content of the licence as it relates to consumer protection. Control is through being able to refuse consent to the grant of a licence which does not make adequate provision for consumer protection, and it also has powers in relation to the enforcement, modification and revocation of licences.

What are the relevant consumer protection conditions? They are listed as follows: (a) conditions about fares (other than predatory fare pricing); (b) conditions about complaints against the operator by members of the public or liabilities of the operator to them; (c) conditions about insurance; (d) conditions about policing or security; (e) conditions about use of railway services such as timetable information, enquiries, sale of tickets, through ticketing and conditions of carriage; (f) conditions about liaison with the consumer bodies mentioned below, or (g) conditions for protecting the interests of the disabled. The Secretary of State can add further conditions by regulations (see generally Sch 17).

With regard to the consumer protection consultative committees mentioned above, these are renamed. The former Central Rail Users' Consultative Committee is renamed the Rail Passengers' Council and the Rail Users' Consultative Committees are renamed Rail Passengers' Committees. Responsibility for them is transfered to the Authority. This also inherits the code of practice concerning disabled rail users and the Rail Regulator's former power to make rules for penalty fares.

Meanwhile as the Transport Bill (on the basis of which the above comments are made) was proceeding through the legislature, the government announced that the Authority will receive from the companies operating rail facilities a percentage of their profits over an agreed level. There would be separate deals with each of the 25 franchises. Risk would be taken into account. The Secretary of State for Transport justified this by stating that the money obtained would be spent on the network to repay public investment. This policy was immediately attacked as reintroducing nationalisation by stealth, the government wanting both private investment of £34 billion and then some of the money back if the investment was successful. (This is surely the prerogative of taxing governments through the ages!) A network of future 'parkway' stations near major roads was also planned by the Authority.

The National Audit Office also did a survey showing decreased passenger satisfaction with almost every aspect of services since privatisation, including comfort, personal safety, information and ticketing; only catering and helpfulness of staff had improved. Punctuality of services was much criticised with the majority of operators on inter-city routes recording between 9 per cent and 16 per cent of trains more than 15 minutes late. The NAO criticised the original franchises as not being robust enough and not holding operators properly to account. It remains to be seen whether the new regime will achieve any better results.

Privatisation policy – some problems

Privatisation of British Gas provides one of the more recently available case histories on the effects of the Government's privatisation policy in the areas discussed in this book. The flotation of British Gas plc in 1986 resulted in the creation of about 5 million shareholders whose average holding was .00002 per cent of the total equity. It was pointed out at the time[10] that although this creates wider share ownership, the spread of the shareholders reduces rather than increases the ability of investors to influence the way British Gas behaves. The Japanese, by contrast, have arranged the privatisation of their Telecommunications System to favour the large investor rather than the small. And although John Moore, Financial Secretary to the Treasury, stated in 1983 that 'The primary objective of the government's privatisation programme is to reduce the power of the monopolist and to encourage competition', the machinery in the Gas Act 1986 for the promotion of competition appeared to be weak. Since 1982 industrial consumers have had the facility of buying gas directly from oil companies but it is still necessary to use the British Gas network to transport the gas to the factory. Domestic consumers had no alternative but to use British Gas. Although the industry could have been split up into regional companies with a separate transmission company, this would,

10 See Professor John Kay writing in the *Daily Telegraph*, 10 December 1986. See also Kay, Mayer and Thompson (ed) *Privatisation and Regulation, the UK Experience* (Clarendon Press 1986).

it is thought, have greatly reduced the value to the Government of the flotation of British Gas. Incentives to more efficiency include, of course, the prospect of insolvency or being taken over.

It was only recently that serious steps have been taken to allow other gas suppliers the chance to compete (as mentioned above). The water industry remains a series of monopolistic suppliers, there being no comprehensive national distribution grid. Consumer protection has hitherto been seen to be a sometimes uneasy alliance between the regulator, and, except for gas, non-independent advisory committees. Major statutory changes to create independent consumer bodies are presently being implemented as briefly described.[11]

The setting of prices by the industries' regulators is critical. The approved formula for pricing was known, shortly, as 'RPI-minus-X', which has the effect of making each industry limit its product price rises to x percentage points less than inflation. Thus, if inflation is at 6 per cent and x is set at 3, the industry may raise prices by the balance of 3 per cent. If the regulator considers that the monopoly profit is too high, x can be raised. BT's 'x' started at 3 per cent, rose to 4.5 per cent and then to 6.25 per cent. Similarly British Gas's rose from 2 per cent to 5 per cent. The regulator has to steer a difficult course between protecting the consumer and not discouraging investors.[12]

In July 1991 the Government published a White Paper entitled 'The Citizen's Charter – Raising the Standard'. Its aim was to raise the standards of quality and efficiency where the citizen as 'customer' consumed services (or encountered administrative machinery) for which government departments were responsible, or which were connected with monopolistic suppliers. Education, health, employment opportunities, the Inland Revenue, police and social services are beyond the scope of this book. But British Rail, London Underground and the Post Office received attention and 'mini-charters' proposing better performance monitoring and targeting, compensation schemes for disappointed customers and possible future privatisation or increased competition were discussed. This was 'rebadged' by the new government as 'Service First'.[13] Additionally the

11 See DTI *A Fair Deal for Consumers: Modernising the Framework for Utilities Regulation* (Cm 3898 (1998)); also A McHarg 'Separation of Functions and Regulatory Agencies: Dispute Resolution in the Privatised Utilities' in M Harris and M Partington *Administrative Justice in the 21st Century* (1999); C Graham *Regulating Public Utilities* (Hart, 2000); and T Prosser (1999) 62 MLR 196.
12 See *The Regulation of BT's Prices*, Consultation Document of OFTEL, 1992.
13 See A Barron and C Scott 'The Citizen's Charter Programme' (1992) 55 MLR 526; C Scott 'Regulation Inside Government: Rebadging the Citizen's Charter' [1999] Public Law 595.

European Commission is concerned to develop norms with minimum service quality in 'services of general interest'.[14]

As regards the utilities which are the subject matter of this chapter, the Competition and Services (Utilities) Act 1992 was hurried through Parliament prior to its dissolution and raised the powers of the regulators of the various offices up to the level of the strongest.

It was probably true to say, in summary, that initially it was the *management* of these industries which had been privatised. They became no longer directly accountable to the government and they have the ability to raise private capital. But except in the case of fragmentation of the bus industry[15] the formerly nationalised industries remained monolithic until the mid 1990s, substantially free from the prospect of competition and, unlike the old regime, government regulation. The public perception appeared to be of industries involving vital services to consumers run primarily for the benefit of shareholders and with 'fat cat' directors paying themselves unjustifiable salaries and bonuses. Against this background it is easy to forget the strike-prone, apparently grossly overmanned, unresponsive to the consumer and inefficiently State-run utilities and rail services, which many saw as the pre-privatisation picture. Whether the existing services will deteriorate as a result of cutting costs further to meet such competition as has now been introduced, or whether the consumer can expect lower prices, keen service, uninterrupted supplies and cleaner and more efficient trains, remains to be conclusively shown. The issue is certainly not a simple one and taxes most advanced democracies. It is how to deliver a service requiring huge capital investment, and being of vital social importance, in a way which delivers the best possible service to the consumer with nil cost or the least possible cost to the taxpayer; and whether ownership of the enterprise should be vested in the government or in private shareholders with management independently overseen by a regulator. The addition of a real element of competition into formerly nationalised industries such as gas, electricity and telecommunications lends a comparatively new dimension to the hitherto monolithic profile, and there is concrete evidence of consumer benefit.

14 See COM (96) 443 Final; S Whittaker 'Unfair Contract Terms, Public Services and the Construction of a European Conception of Contract' (2000) 116 LQR 95.
15 Achieved by the Transport Act 1985 and mentioned above.

5 Supply of goods and contract-based remedies

When a consumer is supplied with goods which are subsequently discovered to be unsuitable for their intended purpose or of defective quality or not to comply with the supplier's description, may the consumer recover some or all of the money paid? Or more seriously still, where the goods cause damage to the consumer or whoever uses the goods, may the injured person recover damages for the injuries?

For the answer to the first question it is necessary to examine the relevant parts of the law of contract as developed by the judges and as adjusted and amended by the legislature in the form of the sale and supply of goods legislation and the Misrepresentation Act 1967. The answer to the second question depends primarily on the development of the law of negligence in tort together with what might loosely be called the statute law of products liability. There is some danger in isolating parts of the complex body of contract and tort law and the sale and supply of goods legislation because one happens to be analysing the legal consequences of a transaction from the consumer's point of view. For instance, it must be borne in mind that, whilst it can generally be assumed that where a consumer buys goods from a seller there has been a valid contract of sale of goods, occasionally this may not be the case. An apparently valid contract may be nullified or vitiated by some factor such as an operative mistake, or incapacity to contract, or illegality. Similarly, in cases where traders refuse to redeem 'money-off' vouchers and such like, it is often important to analyse the actual or attempted purchase and sale transactions, bearing in mind that it is well established that goods on display in shops and marked at a price are not 'offered' to the customer. It is the customer who makes the offer for the article to the shopkeeper, who may or may not accept,[1] though display of goods at a false price may give rise to *criminal*

---

1   *Pharmaceutical Society of Great Britain v Boots Cash Chemists (Southern) Ltd* [1953] 1 QB 401, [1953] 1 All ER 482, CA.

liability under the Consumer Protection Act 1987, considered in Chapter 12. Knowledge of the principles of contract and tort must therefore be assumed since it is not appropriate in this book to attempt a global examination of them. Nor shall we attempt to deal with those provisions of the Sale of Goods Act 1979 which deal in detail with the transfer of property, risk of loss and proprietary remedies which are more appropriately left to works on commercial law.

I. INTRODUCTION

Two associated principles permeated the nineteenth century development of contract – freedom of contract and, at ground level, *caveat emptor*, let the buyer beware. The idea of freedom of contract was part of the laissez-faire doctrine of liberal classical economics. Just as to the liberal interference with religious freedom was anathema, so was interference with business. The duty of a government was to preserve law and order, promote foreign trade and defend the country from its enemies. Industry was left to look after its own interests, the inefficient going under in favour of the more cost-effective producer, except that the State could legitimately act against privileged monopolies which interfered with free competition. A perfect market responded automatically to the total pressure of self-interested but enlightened buyers and sellers. The system was manifestly sufficiently flexible to cater, at a price, for the needs of even the most individualistic consumer. Prices were the measure of the balance between supply and demand, cost and utility. 'Planning' and other collectivist intervention by government was unnecessary and harmful.[2] This philosophy was reflected by the judiciary. In an oft-quoted passage, Sir George Jessel, in 1875, said:

> … if there is one thing more than another which public policy requires, it is that men of full age and competent understanding shall have the utmost liberty in contracting, and that their contracts, when entered into freely and voluntarily, shall be held sacred and shall be enforced by Courts of Justice.[3]

The doctrine was harsh but, in terms of national wealth, highly successful. It still permeates many aspects of the law of contract; the parties will be held bound in the absence of some material vitiating factor, however bad a bargain the buyer or seller has struck. But, without overtly replacing it,

2   For a short but excellent account of the rise and decline of laissez-faire see Cairncross *Introduction to Economics* ch 34.

3   *Printing and Numerical Registering Co v Sampson* (1875) LR 19 Eq 462, cited in Cheshire, Fifoot and Furmston's *Law of Contract* (13th edn) at p 11, chs 1 and 2 of which are an excellent introduction to the development of the law.

the twentieth century has seen increased intervention by both the judiciary and the legislature on behalf of the consumer.[4] This is in recognition of the fact that, in many transactions, there is a significant inequality of bargaining power between the buyer and the seller. It is accordingly unrealistic to ascribe to the buyer a freedom to contract and agree detailed terms when in practice there is little choice but to accept those terms. In other spheres, of which the contractual relationship between landlord and tenant or employer and employee are graphic examples, the State has intervened in favour of the tenant or employee respectively to give him a protected status irrespective of the terms of any contract.

2. EXPRESS TERMS

Undertakings and promises contained in a contract are known as terms of the contract, and may be express or implied by law or as a consequence of the presumed intention of the parties. As regards express terms, if the parties intended, or are deemed by the court to have intended, that a particular statement was to have a contractual and binding effect, the statement will be a term of the contract. Breach of a term will result in the claimant being entitled to damages and, in some cases, rescission of the contract. Otherwise, the statement will be construed as a mere representation made before the contract was entered into and not forming part of the contractual promise. The claimant's remedies are then dependent on a) being able to prove that the statement was a misrepresentation and b) the character of the misrepresentation, discussed below. There is often difficulty in deciding whether a statement is a term or a representation.[5] The attitude that the court tends to take is to regard statements as terms if the maker of the statement has greater expertise than the other party, or where the statement is of vital importance and is made with distinct promissory intention, or at a crucial stage of the pre-contract negotiations. But if the seller asks the buyer to verify the truth of a statement, such as where the seller of a boat said it was sound but advised the buyer to employ a surveyor to check it,[6] or in the ordinary case where the vendor or his agent states that his house is sound but leaves the purchaser free to have it surveyed, the statement will not normally be regarded as a term of the contract. Statements of unverifiable opinion are neither terms of the contract nor even material representations.

---

4   The history of this development is well outlined in Borrie and Diamond *The Consumer, Society and the Law* (4th Edn) ch 1. See also Jolowicz (1969) 32 MLR 1.
5   See M, H & P pp 18–28.
6   *Ecay v Godfrey* (1947) 80 Ll L Rep 286, KBD (Lord Goddard).

Three examples of how the Court of Appeal construed statements made in the course of selling a car in different ways may be noticed. Firstly, in *Oscar Chess Ltd v Williams*:[7]

> The seller, a private person, sold his car to the buyers, who were car dealers, stating that it was a 1948 Morris and the registration book confirmed this. In fact it was a similarly styled 1939 model and the registration book had, presumably, been altered by a previous owner. The 1939 model was worth £115 less than a 1948 model. It was held that the seller's statement was not a term of the contract, and being a mere innocent misrepresentation, no damages were recoverable.

By contrast, in *Dick Bentley Productions Ltd v Harold Smith (Motors) Ltd*:[8]

> The buyer, Dick Bentley, had been looking for a 'well vetted' Bentley car. The defendants, through their respective companies, sold him a Bentley which their manager told him had been owned by a German baron, had been fitted with a replacement engine and gearbox and, since that time, had done only 20,000 miles. The car turned out to be a considerable disappointment and the buyer brought an action for damages. The county court judge awarded him £400 on the basis that the statement as to the mileage that the car had done was a term of the contract classified as a warranty, and the warranty had been broken, the car having actually done nearly 100,000 miles. This judgment was upheld by the Court of Appeal.

Thirdly, in *Beale v Taylor*:[9]

> A private motorist advertised his car for sale, describing it as a 'Herald convertible, white, 1961, twin carbs'. Unknown to either party the car was in fact the rear half of a 1961 Herald and the front half of an earlier model, and the seller was not regarded as careless in not knowing this. The private buyer was held entitled to recover damages for breach of the contractual term (possibly implied, as discussed below) that the car was a 1961 Herald.

Various attempts have been made to distinguish these cases. For instance Lord Denning suggested that in the *Oscar Chess* case the private seller

---

7   [1957] 1 All ER 325, [1957] 1 WLR 370, CA (by a majority).
8   [1965] 2 All ER 65, [1965] 1 WLR 623, CA; M, H & P p 20.
9   [1967] 3 All ER 253, [1967] 1 WLR 1193, CA; M, H & P p 91, and see *Cehave NV v Bremer Handelsgesellschaft mbH, The Hansa Nord* [1976] QB 44, [1975] 3 All ER 739, CA.

was not penalised because he was not at fault, but in the *Dick Bentley* case the expert seller could have and should have verified the information. But this distinction is not possible to make in *Beale v Taylor*, where the fact that the seller appeared for himself in court may not have helped him, the *Oscar Chess* case not being cited. We are therefore left with the guidelines suggested above as supplying the best prediction of how a court will construe what was said in a particular transaction.

Once it has been determined that a particular statement is a term of the contract, it is classified as a *condition*, a *warranty* or a '*hybrid*' term[10] according to its importance. A condition is a vital term of the contract, breach of which entitles the claimant to terminate the contract if he so wishes and sue for damages in respect of past breaches. A warranty is described, by the Sale of Goods Act 1979 section 61, as an agreement collateral to the main purpose of the contract. It is, in other words, a part of the contract not so vital that failure to perform it goes to the substance of the contract. The remedy for breach of warranty is damages only. A 'hybrid' term is one which, in a complex contract, can legitimately be treated either as a condition or warranty, the evaluation to be made primarily in the light of the parties' intention, express or implied, at the time of the contract, irrespective of the event resulting from the breach.[11]

In cases of hire-purchase, it may be that the customer is persuaded by the dealer to enter into a hire-purchase agreement with a finance company, to whom the dealer then sells the car outright. The courts have classified this arrangement as a) a hire-purchase agreement between the customer and the finance company and b) a collateral contract embodying a warranty between the customer and the dealer. (The consideration is the entering, by the customer, into the hire-purchase agreement, thus enabling the dealer to sell the car to the finance company.) If the dealer wrongly warrants the goods sound, the customer may recover damages from the dealer under contract (b). Thus in *Andrews v Hopkinson*:[12]

The customer wished to take a second-hand car on hire-purchase terms. The dealer recommended it by saying, 'It's a good little ' bus.

---

10   See generally M, H & P pp 28–33; *Sale and Supply of Goods* Law Commission Working Paper No 85 pp 26–34; Law Com No 160 (Cm 137) paras 2.22–2.31 for useful discussions.

11   See *Bunge Corpn v Tradax SA* [1981] 2 All ER 513, [1981] 1 WLR 711, HL, where the court was unsympathetic to construing the effect of a commercial term (a stipulation as to time limits) in the light of the gravity of the events which occured. This is a problem unlikely to be met in ordinary consumer contracts; it seems unlikely that a condition implied under the Sale of Goods Act could be 'hybrid' or 'innominate'. Compare *Hong Kong Fir Shipping Co Ltd v Kawasaki Kisen Kaisha Ltd* [1962] 2 QB 26, [1962] 1 All ER 474, CA, favouring the view that evaluation should be in the light of the events occurring.

12   [1957] 1 QB 229, [1956] 3 All ER 422, Leeds Assizes.

I would stake my life on it. You will have no trouble with it.' The dealer then sold the car to a finance company, which entered into a hire-purchase agreement for the car with the customer. The car was in fact in a dangerous condition, owing to defective steering, and the customer shortly afterwards collided with a lorry, wrecking the car and injuring himself. It was held that he was entitled to recover damages for breach of the undertaking given to him by the dealer.

3. IMPLIED TERMS

There are a number of situations where, apart from statute, a court will be prepared to read into a contract an implied term or terms – ie a condition or warranty not expressly stated. This would be in accordance with the presumed intention of the parties, or in accordance with trade usage, or in compliance with the pattern of previous dealings between the parties, or where the court otherwise deems it just to do so.[13] Many of the cases on implied terms relate to contracts between vendor and purchaser of land or landlord and tenant and the like, rather than 'consumer' transactions.

Of fundamental importance, when assessing the remedies of the disappointed buyer of goods, is the part of the Sale of Goods Act 1979 ('the 1979 Act') implying various terms into contracts of sale of goods unless the parties agree to the contrary. The original Sale of Goods Act 1893 ('the 1893 Act') was significantly amended by the Supply of Goods (Implied Terms) Act 1973 ('the 1973 Act'), the main object of which was severely to limit the seller's right to exclude these implied terms. This aspect is dealt with later.[14] The Act also applied these terms, suitably adjusted, to contracts of hire-purchase, and these provisions were re-enacted, with minor amendments, by the Consumer Credit Act 1974 (Schedule 4, para 35). The Sale and Supply of Goods Act 1994 further amended the 1973 Act, to keep it in line with the Sale of Goods Act 1979, see below. The 1973 Act will not specifically be discussed further except to point out that the debtor is better protected than the buyer in that the debtor's rights are not diminished by the possibility that the goods have been 'accepted' shortly after delivery. The 1973 Act also imposed obligations on the supplier of goods on redemption of trading stamps that are to the same general effect

---

13 See *The Moorcock* (1889) 14 PD 64, CA; *Hollier v Rambler Motors (AMC) Ltd* [1972] 2 QB 71, [1972] 1 All ER 399, CA; *Reed v Dean* [1949] 1 KB 188 (a hired motor launch is impliedly warranted fit for the purpose of the hiring).
14 See below, p 126.

as the implied terms under a contract of sale or hire-purchase (s 16, amending the Trading Stamps Act 1964).[15]

The sale of goods legislation was subsequently consolidated by the Sale of Goods Act 1979.[16] Following the Law Commissions' Report, *Sale and Supply of Goods*,[17] which recommended changes to aspects of the 1979 Act and related statutes, an amending Act, the Sale and Supply of Goods Act 1994 ('the 1994 Act'), came into force from 3 January 1995. The major effect of the 1994 Act is to replace the implied term of 'merchantable quality' with a new term of 'satisfactory quality' in the 1979 Act and related Acts. It also makes changes to 'acceptance' and remedies for business buyers under the 1979 Act. Since the 1994 Act is an amending Act, its effects will be discussed, where relevant, as part of the discussion of the 1979 Act. The likely impact of the EC Directive on Certain Aspects of the Sale of Consumer Goods and Associated Guarantees[18] will also be considered.

It is not always the case that ownership or possession of goods is obtained under a sale of goods contract governed by the 1979 Act. A sale of goods contract is defined in section 2(1) of the 1979 Act as:

> A contract by which the seller transfers or agrees to transfer the property in goods to the buyer for a money consideration called the price.

If, therefore, ownership of goods is transferred for non-money consideration, for example other goods or a service (as in barter or exchange); if the possession but not ownership is transferred as, for example, in simple hire; or if goods plus services are supplied, as in work and materials contracts, then the Sale of Goods Act 1979 does not apply. Instead, implied terms similar to those in the 1979 Act, regarding the nature of any goods supplied, are incorporated by the Supply of Goods and Services Act 1982 ('the 1982 Act').[19] These terms will be discussed in this

---

15 It is proposed to repeal the Trading Stamps Act 1964 and to amend the Supply of Goods and Services Act 1982 to include trading stamps transactions under 'transfers of goods' under s 1 of the 1982 Act, see *Draft Regulatory Impact Assessment: For consultation on repeal of the Trading Stamps Act 1964 and associated provisions*, DTI, Spring 2000; http://www.dti.gov.uk/consumer/law/3b.htm.

16 See BSSCCL p 428.

17 Law Com No 160, Scot Law Com No 104, Cm 137, May 1987.

18 99/44/EC, OJ No L 171, 7.7.99, p 12.

19 As amended by the Sale and Supply of Goods Act 1994. See BSSCCL p 462. The 1982 Act was based, in part, on the Draft Supply of Goods (Implied Terms) Bill contained in the Law Commission Report No 95 *Implied Terms in Contracts for the Supply of Goods*.

chapter whilst the implied terms in the 1982 Act relating to any service element of a contract are discussed in chapter 7.

The contracts covered by the 1982 Act are those 'for the transfer of goods' and for 'hire of goods'. A 'contract for the transfer of goods means a contract under which one person transfers or agrees to transfer to another the property in goods, other than an excepted contract' (s 1(1)). Excepted contracts are those for the sale of goods, hire-purchase agreements, goods received on redemption of trading stamps,[20] goods transferred by deed with no additional consideration and contracts by way of mortgage, pledge, charge or other security (s 1(2)). By section 6 a 'contract for the hire of goods' is defined as a 'contract under which one person bails or agrees to bail goods to another by way of hire, other than an excepted contract'. The excepted contracts are hire-purchase agreements and trading stamp agreements.

Title

To outline each implied term in turn, referring in each case to the sections of the 1979 Act and the 1982 Act, we commence with section 12 of the 1979 Act, which deals with implied undertakings as to title. It is, of course, vital in any commercial transaction that the buyer is assured that the goods which are to be bought are the unencumbered property of the seller.

In practice it is quite common to find cases where, for example, a buyer has innocently bought a car which is subject to an undischarged hire-purchase agreement or an antique which has been stolen. The normal rule here is nemo dat quod non habet, ie good title cannot pass to a buyer unless the seller has good title. To this rule there are some significant exceptions. For example, in the case of a seller who is not the true owner of goods, good title may, nevertheless, in specified circumstances be passed to the buyer if the seller is in possession of them with the owner's consent.[1] In cases of the sale of cars, a private purchaser in good faith of a car which is in fact 'owned' by the seller under a hire-purchase or conditional sale agreement obtains a good title as against the true owner if the private purchaser took without notice of the agreement.[2] In other cases, where

---

20   It is proposed to repeal this exception, see *Draft Regulatory Impact Assessment: For consultation on repeal of the Trading Stamps Act 1964 and associated provisions*, DTI, Spring 2000; http://www.dti.gov.uk/consumer/law/3b.htm.

1   Sale of Goods Act 1979, s 24, BSSCCL p 443, and Factors Act 1889, ss 8 and 9, BSSCCL pp 67–68. For discussion of sales by buyers in possession with consent: see ch 10.

2   Hire Purchase Act 1964, s 27(2), BSSCCL p 123; if the hirer sells to a trade purchaser who sells to a bona fide private purchaser, the latter is still protected (s 27(3)); the topic is further discussed in ch 10.

goods are stolen and the thief convicted, the court may order the restoration of the goods to the true owner under the Theft Act 1968, section 28(1).[3] It is in these circumstances, in particular, that the buyer will look for redress to the seller, assuming that he is in a position to make compensation.[4]

In cases where there is no indication other than that the seller intended to pass a full title to the purchaser, section 12(1) of the 1979 Act states that there is:

> an implied term[5] on the part of the seller that in the case of sale he has a right to sell the goods, and in the case of an agreement to sell, he will have such a right at the time when the property is to pass.

Section 12(2) also implies terms[6] of freedom from encumbrances and of the right to quiet possession, which are likely, only occasionally, to be useful in view of the more fundamental implied terms above.[7] Section 12(3) deals with the uncommon case where the seller contracts to transfer only such title as he or a third party may have, in which case limited versions only of the two terms mentioned above apply.

As to remedies where a condition as to the right to sell applies, there is an apparent difficulty where the goods have been accepted by the buyer, who then wishes to reject the goods and have a refund of the money paid. This is because section 11(4) of the 1979 Act states that: 'where a contract of sale is not severable and the buyer has accepted the goods (as to which see s 35 and the discussion of 'acceptance' below) the breach of any condition to be fulfilled by the seller can only be treated as a breach of warranty, and not as a ground for rejecting the goods and treating the contract as repudiated ...'. The normal consequence of this is that the buyer, who has accepted, is limited to obtaining damages, which may amount to less than the purchase price. However, as regards the condition of title, it was held in *Rowland v Divall*,[8] where a buyer of a stolen car had to return it to the true owner, that there was a total failure of consideration, since what the buyer bargained for, ownership of the car, had never been

---

3   The wrongful possessor of the goods is in any event liable to the true owner for the tort of wrongful interference with goods under the Torts (Interference with Goods) Act 1977, BSSCCL p 396.
4   Under the Theft Act 1968, s 28(3) the court may order payment to the buyer of stolen goods out of the money in the thief's possession when apprehended.
5   In England, Wales and Northern Ireland this term is a condition: s 12(5A).
6   In England, Wales and Northern Ireland, these are warranties: s 12(5A).
7   In *Microbeads AC v Vinhurst Road Markings Ltd* [1975] 1 All ER 529, [1975] 1 WLR 218, CA, the buyer having validly bought goods was prejudiced in his use of them by a patent acquired by a third party. This was held to be a breach of a warranty for quiet possession.
8   [1923] 2 KB 500, CA.

transferred at all. He was therefore entitled to a full repayment, although the car had been used for four months.[9]

The equivalent section in the 1982 Act dealing with title in contracts for the transfer of goods is section 2. In cases where there is an intention to pass full title there is an implied condition that the transferor has a right to transfer the property (s 2(1)) and implied warranties of freedom from encumbrances and quiet possession (s 2(2)). If it is intended that only limited title passes, then there are modified warranties of freedom from encumbrances and quiet possession (s 2(3)-(5)).

In contracts for the hire of goods there is clearly never any intention to pass title. Instead there is an implied condition that the bailor has a right to transfer possession and an implied warranty of quiet possession save for disturbance by the owner or other persons with a known or disclosed charge or encumbrance (s 7).[10]

Description

It is clear that where the seller sells goods by reference to a description of them, the buyer should have a remedy if the goods fail to comply with the description.[11] It could be argued that the description should be regarded as an express term[12] but section 13(1) and (2) of the 1979 Act categorises it as an implied term:

13 (1) Where there is a contract for the sale of goods by description, there is an implied term that the goods will correspond with the description.

(1A) As regards England and Wales and Northern Ireland, the term implied by subsection (1) above is a condition.

(2) If the sale is by sample as well as by description it is not sufficient that the bulk of the goods corresponds with the sample if the goods do not also correspond with the description.

Formerly section 14(2) of the 1893 Act stated that the implied condition of merchantable quality only applied where the goods were 'bought by

9   In *Mason v Burningham* [1949] 2 KB 545, [1949] 2 All ER 134, CA, it was held that a buyer of a stolen typewriter was entitled not only to have her money back but to claim the cost of a repair she had paid for on the basis that there was a breach of warranty of quiet possession.

10   For an early common law authority on this see *Lee v Atkinson and Brooks* (1609) Cro Jac 236.

11   See M, H & P pp 87–95.

12   It is designated as an 'express warranty' in the USA's Uniform Commercial Code, art 2–313(1)(b).

description', and this was an encouragement to the courts to interpret sales by description liberally. The terminology is obviously appropriate to mail order sales and other cases where the seller has not seen the goods before buying. But the courts have made it clear that a sale by description can occur even where the buyer has seen and examined the goods:

> ... a thing is sold by description, though it is specific, so long as it is sold not merely as the specific thing but as a thing corresponding to a description, eg woollen under-garments, a hot water bottle, a second-hand reaping machine, to select a few obvious illustrations [per Lord Wright in *Grant v Australian Knitting Mills Ltd*].[13]

Dixon J in the High Court of Australia was equally explicit in the same case:

> In the ordinary course of a sale over the counter by a shopkeeper to a customer, who calls for an article of a given description, inspects the specimens produced, and buys one, the transaction is a sale by description.[14]

However, it will not always be the case that sales of specific goods, with verbal or even written descriptions applied, will be held to be by description. In *Harlingdon & Leinster Enterprises Ltd v Christopher Hull Fine Art Ltd*[15] the Court of Appeal decided that, for section 13 to operate, the description had to be influential in the sale, thereby becoming an essential term of the contract. There must be a common intention on the part of both parties for the description to become a term. In the words of Slade LJ:

> If the court is to hold that a contract is one 'for the sale of goods by description', it must be able to impute to the parties (quite apart from section 13(1) of the 1979 Act) a common intention that it shall be a term of the contract that the goods will correspond with the description [at pp 584, 751].

To help determine this issue the presence or absence of reliance on the description by the buyer was relevant. In this case a painting, stated to be by Gabriele Munter, was sold by an art dealer, who had no knowledge of the artist, to another dealer who had inspected the painting. The painting was found to be a forgery. In dismissing the buyer's claim of a breach of section 13, the court, by a majority, decided that, viewing the transaction

13 [1936] AC 85 at 100, PC (sale over the counter of some men's underwear held sale by description).
14 (1933) 50 CLR 387 at 418.
15 [1991] 1 QB 564, [1990] 1 All ER 737, CA, M, H & P p 88. See also Lawrenson (1991) 54 MLR 122.

Implied terms

objectively, there was no reliance by the buyer on the description applied by the seller.

The Molony Committee questioned whether sales in a self-service supermarket would qualify as being 'by description'[16] and the 1973 Act[17] accordingly added a new provision, now (slightly reworded) section 13(3) of the 1979 Act, which states:

> A sale of goods is not prevented from being a sale by description by reason only that, being exposed for sale or hire, they are selected by the buyer.

It may, therefore, be concluded that in shop sales in the normal way, goods with labelling of any sort to identify them would be sold by description, but goods such as greengroceries not labelled would probably not be sold by description where selected, without assistance, by the shopper. Where *quality* is concerned the point will now usually be academic since the implied term of satisfactory quality, more usually involved, is no longer confined to sales by description. However, one case where the description term may be of crucial importance is where the sale is a private one. Both the terms relating to quality of goods considered below apply only to sales in 'the course of a business', but section 13 is not so confined. It may, therefore, supply a buyer with the necessary ground for action in a case such as *Beale v Taylor*[18] where, it will be recalled, that the seller, who advertised what transpired as his hermaphrodite car in a motoring journal, was a private motorist, not a dealer. The buyer recovered damages for breach of condition, presumably assessed as the difference between the actual value of the car and the price paid. Where *quantity* is concerned the court may insist on exactitude if this is commercially reasonable:

> If the written contract specifies conditions of weight, measurement and the like, those conditions must be complied with. A ton does not mean about a ton, or a yard about a yard. Still less when you descend to minute measurements does ½ inch mean about ½ inch. If the seller wants a margin he must, and in my experience does, stipulate for it.[19]

16   Cmnd 1781, para 441.
17   Supply of Goods (Implied Terms) Act 1973, s 2.
18   [1967] 3 All ER 253, [1967] 1 WLR 1193, CA; M, H & P p 91; see above, p 88. The cause of action was actually the alleged breach of the s 13 implied term, but it is not entirely clear from the report whether the court regarded the advertised description also as an express term.
19   *Arcos Ltd v E A Ronaasen & Son* [1933] AC 470 at 479, HL per Lord Atkin. See also the Sale of Goods Act 1979, s 30, as amended, BSSCCL p 445, which confirms the buyer's right to reject for wrong quantities (where a business buyer is involved only if shortfall/excess is not slight).

It is important to note, however, that where there is a business buyer and the effect of the breach is slight, the buyer may not have a right to reject the goods, but only a right to damages.[20]

The equivalent sections relating to description in the 1982 Act are section 3 for contracts for the transfer of goods and section 8[1] for contracts for the hire of goods.

Satisfactory quality[2]

The *caveat emptor* principle was firmly embedded into the 1893 Act, and it is now restated in section 14(1) of the 1979 Act (as amended):

Except as provided by this section, and section 15[3] and subject to any other enactment, there is no implied term about the quality or fitness for any particular purpose of goods supplied under a contract of sale.

There are similar provisions for contracts for the transfer of goods and the hire of goods in sections 4(1) and 9(1) of the 1982 Act respectively. However, the twin implied terms of satisfactory quality (formerly merchantable quality) and fitness for purpose, particularly as broadened since the 1973 and 1994 Acts, have substantially eroded the caveat emptor principle.

From January 1894 to January 1995 the implied term in section 14(2) was one requiring goods to be of 'merchantable quality'. The Law Commissions examined this provision in detail in their Report *Sale and Supply of Goods*[4] and recommended that the term be remodelled and renamed as 'acceptable quality'. When the Sale and Supply of Goods Bill was introduced to enact these proposals, the words 'satisfactory quality' were chosen for the substitute term. It was felt there could be confusion between 'acceptance' under section 35 and 'acceptable quality' and reasonable purchasers might be more tolerant over defective goods making them 'acceptable' whereas 'satisfactory' imposed a higher standard. The replacement implied term applies to all contracts made on or after 3 January 1995. It is, however, likely that reference will often be made to many cases decided on merchantable quality in assessing the meaning of satisfactory quality. It is

20   See s 15A, discussed below, p 113.
1   Restating the pre-Act position, see *Astley Industrial Trust Ltd v Grimley* [1963] 2 All ER 33, [1963] 1 WLR 584, CA.
2   See M, H & P pp 95–108.
3   1979 Act, s 15 and 1982 Act, ss 5 and 10 deal with sales by sample, and imply terms i) that the bulk shall correspond in quality with the sample and ii) as to satisfactory quality except as regards defects apparent on examination.
4   Law Com No 160, Scot Law Com No 104, Cm 137, 1987, Part 3.

Implied terms

suggested that all successful claims under the previous wording would also be successful under the current wording and that some, previously unsuccessful, claims would now be successful.

The implied term[5] of satisfactory quality, in its amended form, is comprised in section 14(2) of the 1979 Act, which states:

> Where the seller sells goods in the course of a business, there is an implied term that the goods supplied under the contract are of satisfactory quality.

The equivalent provisions in the 1982 Act are sections 4(2) (transfer of goods) and 9(2) (hire contracts).

'In the course of a business'

It has already been noted that this excludes private sales. Business is defined to include 'a profession and the activities of any government department (including a Northern Ireland Department), or local or public authority'.[6] The purpose of the wide wording of the phrase was 'to ensure that the conditions implied by section 14 are imposed on every trade seller, no matter whether he is or is not habitually dealing in goods of the type sold'.[7]

There has been considerable academic debate over whether transactions ancillary to the normal course of a seller's business, such as the selling off of items of equipment used in a business, are included within the wording of the section. The Court of Appeal, in *Stevenson v Rogers*,[8] considered the sale of a fishing vessel by a fisherman. It was decided that the words of section 14(2) were to be construed broadly – 'at their wide face value'.[9] There was no reason to restrict the application of the section to situations where there was some degree of regularity of dealing in the item sold. It could, therefore, apply to sporadic sales which are no more than incidental to the seller's business. The court declined to follow the approach of the Court of Appeal in *R & B Customs Brokers Co Ltd v United Dominions Trust Ltd*.[10] Here the same phrase was examined in the context

---

5   In England, Wales and Northern Ireland, this is a condition: s 14(6).

6   1979 Act, s 61(1); similarly 1982 Act, s 18(1).

7   *First Report on Exemption Clauses* 1969 (Law Com No 24) para 31. See M, H & P p 96.

8   [1999] QB 1028, [1999] 1 All ER 613, CA. See also Brown (1999) 115 LQR 384; De Lacy (1999) 62 MLR 776; MacDonald [1999] 3 Web JCLI; Sealy (1999) 58 CLJ 276.

9   Per Potter LJ at pp 1039, 623.

10   [1988] 1 All ER 847, [1988] 1 WLR 321, CA; M, H & P p 357. See below p 129.

of the Unfair Contract Terms Act 1977, section 12, to determine whether a company buying a car was doing so 'as consumer' or not. It was held that if a transaction was only incidental to the main business activity of the company, a degree of regularity was required before it was considered an integral part of the business and thus 'in the course of a business'.[11] Having examined the different origins of section 14 of the 1979 Act and section 12 of the 1977 Act, their different purposes and the intentions of the Law Commission, in proposing, and Parliament, in enacting, the measures, Potter LJ, in *Stevenson v Rogers*, concluded:

> To apply the reasoning in the *R & B Customs* case in the interests only of consistency, thereby undermining the wide protection for buyers which section 14(2) was intended to introduce, would in my view be an unacceptable example of the tail wagging the dog.[12]

The implied terms of section 14[13] apply, therefore, in any sale by a business seller, regardless of whether that type of goods is regularly supplied by the seller or is, for example, the salesman's car or a piece of redundant office equipment from the doctor's surgery. It is only sales by private individuals which receive no protection under section 14.

'Satisfactory quality'

The starting point for discussion of the meaning of this term is section 14(2A)[14] which states:

> For the purposes of this Act, goods are of satisfactory quality if they meet the standard that a reasonable person would regard as satisfactory, taking account of any description of the goods, the price (if relevant) and all other relevant circumstances.

This test has some similarities with the previous definition of merchantable quality.[15] It is an objective test, which means that the views of the

11   This construction derives from the criminal sphere: *Davies v Sumner* [1984] 3 All ER 831, [1984] 1 WLR 1301, HL; M, H & P p 609. See p 386.
12   At pp 1041, 626.
13   Presumably also ss 4 and 9 of the 1982 Act and s 10 of the 1973 Act.
14   The equivalent provisions in the 1982 Act are s 4(2A) for transfers of goods and s 9(2A) for hire.
15   Which was found in s 14(6): 'Goods of any kind are of merchantable quality within the meaning of subsection (2) above if they are as fit for the purpose or purposes for which goods of that kind are commonly bought as it is reasonable to expect having regard to any description applied to them, the price (if relevant) and all the other relevant circumstances.'

reasonable purchaser are considered, not necessarily those of the actual purchaser. One significant change with 'satisfactory quality' is that much less emphasis is placed on fitness for purpose. As will be seen below, this is only one factor to be taken into consideration, whereas previously, under merchantable quality, it was a very prominent factor.[16]

Some decisions on merchantable quality may continue to be of assistance. For example, in *Godley v Perry*[17] a six-year-old boy bought a cheap polystyrene catapult from a stationer. It fractured without abuse on his part shortly after purchase, blinding him in one eye. It was held that this was a breach both of the fitness for purpose condition (see below) and the condition of merchantable quality, and the boy recovered £2,500 damages. In *Wilson v Rickett, Cockerell & Co Ltd*[18] a consignment of 'Coalite' was bought by a consumer and this exploded when put in the grate owing to the extraneous presence of a charge of high explosive. It was held that the merchantable 'Coalite' could not be separated from the unmerchantable explosive. The entire goods were not of merchantable quality and the buyer could recover damages accordingly. But in *Heil v Hedges*[19] the presence of a harmful parasite worm in pork chops, which caused illness when the buyer ate the chops half-cooked, was held not to render the chops unmerchantable since the worm would have been killed had the chops been properly cooked. It is suggested that this type of case would be decided similarly even after the change to 'satisfactory quality', since it is 'reasonable to expect' that pork will be properly cooked.

To assist in determining whether or not goods are of satisfactory quality under the test in section 14(2A), section 14(2B) provides a list of factors which may be considered, where relevant:

> For the purposes of this Act, the quality of goods includes their state and condition and the following (among others) are in appropriate cases aspects of the quality of goods–
> (a) fitness for all the purposes for which goods of the kind in question are commonly supplied,
> (b) appearance and finish,
> (c) freedom from minor defects,
> (d) safety, and
> (e) durability.

The equivalent provision in the 1982 Act is to be found in section 18(3). The list is not a finite list, other factors may also be relevant, and no one

---

16   See, for example, *B S Brown & Sons Ltd v Craiks Ltd* [1970] 1 All ER 823, [1970] 1 WLR 752, HL; discussed further at p 101.
17   [1960] 1 All ER 36, [1960] 1 WLR 9, QBD.
18   [1954] 1 QB 598, [1954] 1 All ER 868, CA.
19   [1951] 1 TLR 512, KBD.

factor takes precedence. Not every factor will be relevant in each case; for example the Law Commission suggests that, when selling manure, appearance and finish may be of less significance.[20]

The reference in section 14(2B)(a)[1] to fitness for purpose links closely with the previous meaning of merchantable quality, but differs in some very significant ways. It is only one factor to be considered and is not the dominant factor. Also the new wording refers to fitness for *all* the purposes for which the goods would usually be used, which means that if an item has three or four common uses but will only perform one of them, it is unlikely to be of satisfactory quality.[2] This is to be contrasted with the position under merchantable quality where, in the House of Lords' decision in *B S Brown & Sons Ltd v Craiks Ltd*,[3] it was suggested that goods were merchantable if they were commercially usable, even if not usable to the full extent of the buyer's expectations. If the buyer seeks goods for a particular purpose this may involve the implied term under section 14(3) also, see below.

Appearance and finish, under section 14(2B)(b) are newly incorporated into the Act,[4] although some judicial reference was made to them in cases on merchantable quality. In *Bernstein v Pamson Motors (Golders Green) Ltd*[5] Rougier J stated: 'No buyer of a brand-new Rolls-Royce Corniche would tolerate the slightest blemish on its exterior paintwork, the purchaser of a motor car very much at the humbler end of the range might be less fastidious' (at p 228). Also *in Rogers v Parish (Scarborough) Ltd*[6] Mustill LJ referred to 'pride in the vehicle's outward and interior appearance' as relevant factors in assessing the merchantability of a new car.

Much will depend upon the intended use of the goods in question. Highly visible goods, such as fitted kitchen units and furniture, will have appearance and finish as a more significant factor, whereas with pipe-work and cables, which will be concealed, it will be of little significance. It is important to recognise that not all imperfections of appearance will amount

---

20 Law Com No 160, Cm 137, 1987, para 3.41, M, H & P p 101.
1   See further Law Com No 160, Cm. 137, 1987, paras 3.31 –3.35, (M, H & P pp 99–100) and 6.24–6.27.
2   A seller may avoid problems by making clear any limitations with the goods, see s 14(2C)(a) below p 104, or by modifying the price.
3   [1970] 1 All ER 823, [1970] 1 WLR 752, HL. See also *Millars of Falkirk Ltd v Turpie* 1976 SLT (Notes) 66, Ct of Sess.
4   See further Law Com No 160, Cm 137, 1987, paras 3.38–3.43, M, H & P pp 100–101.
5   [1987] 2 All ER 220, QBD, M, H & P p 104.
6   [1987] QB 933 at 944, [1987] 2 All ER 232 at 237, CA; M, H & P p 102. See also *Jackson v Rotax Motor and Cycle Co* [1910] 2 KB 937, CA; (dented and scratched motor horns held unmerchantable).

Implied terms

to a breach of contract, for example those involving second-hand items, pottery, natural products etc.[7]

Section 14(2B)(c) concerns a newly-identified aspect of quality: freedom from minor defects.[8] It links with the previous sub-paragraph and it will be a question of fact whether or not a number of minor defects are sufficient to amount to a breach of the implied term. A *de minimis* principle will apply. The Law Commission stated: '... it should be emphasised that the reference to minor defects will not guarantee that goods which contain minor defects will always fail the test of acceptable [enacted as satisfactory] quality.'[9] The problem which a buyer faces is that, if the defects are insufficient to establish a breach of section 14(2) (assuming the item is fit for its purpose), in the absence of any express term, there will be no remedy available, as section 14(1) prevents any other implied term concerning quality or fitness arising. This problem was highlighted by the Consumers' Association in its report 'Merchantable Quality: What does it mean?'[10] and has only been partially improved by the new wording of section 14(2B)(c).[11]

Safety aspects of goods were never specifically mentioned in the statute until the 1994 Act changes were introduced. Subsection (2B)(d) of section 14 now makes it clear that safety is a relevant factor regarding quality.[12] There are close links here with Part I of the Consumer Protection Act 1987, regarding tortious liability,[13] and Part II of that Act regarding criminal liability.[14]

The final new statutory factor to be considered is durability (s 14(2B)(e)).[15] Clearly much will depend upon the type of product involved and what buyers would reasonably expect of the product.[16] Breaches involving this factor will often only come to light some considerable time after the purchase of a product. It will be up to the buyer to establish that,

---

7   See further Law Com No 160, Cm 137, 1987, para 3.40, M, H & P p 101.
8   See further Law Com No 160, Cm 137, 1987, paras 3.38–3.43, M, H & P pp 100–101.
9   Law Com No 160, Cm 137, 1987, para 3.42.
10   November 1979.
11   It is suggested that cases like *Millars of Falkirk Ltd v Turpie* 1976 SLT (Notes) 66, Ct of Sess; (buyer had no remedy for slight leak on the power steering on his new car) could now be decided differently.
12   See further Law Com No 160, Cm 137, 1987, paras 3.44–3.46, M, H & P p 101.
13   See further ch 6.
14   See further ch 9.
15   See further Law Com No 160, Cm 137, 1987, paras 3.47–3.61; M, H & P pp 114–116.
16   In *Thain v Anniesland Trade Centre* 1997 SLT (Sh Ct) 102, Sheriff Court; it was decided that when buying a 5–6 year old car with 80,000 miles on the clock, durability would be considered as a matter of luck; it was not a quality a reasonable person would demand of it. The car, which appeared fine when purchased, had shown signs of wear in the gear box within two weeks of purchase. The buyer's claim was rejected and the car found to be of satisfactory quality.

at the time when the product was purchased, it did not measure up to the durability requirements reasonably to be expected of it. The Law Commission stated: 'when goods are supplied they must have those qualities which will enable them to last in reasonable condition for a reasonable time.'[17]

The combined effect of section 14(2A) and (2B) is that a number of factors must be taken into account when deciding whether or not a product is of satisfactory quality. There is no one overriding factor and the effects of the test will vary depending upon the type of product and the particulars of the contract involved. Prior to the 1994 Act changes, the courts had been recognising that goods are purchased to fulfil a variety of expectations of buyers and the test of merchantable quality was being applied in a broader, more consumer-orientated way. For example, in the purchase of a new car in *Rogers v Parish (Scarborough) Ltd*[18] Mustill LJ declared:

> Starting with the purpose for which 'goods of that kind' are commonly bought, one would include in respect of any passenger vehicle not merely the buyer's purpose of driving the car from one place to another but of doing so with the appropriate degree of comfort, ease of handling and reliability and, one may add, of pride in the vehicle's outward and interior appearance. What is the appropriate degree and what relative weight is to be attached to one characteristic of the car rather than another will depend on the market at which the car is aimed.

The fact that a defect was repairable or that a vehicle could be started and driven from A to B did not necessarily mean it was merchantable. A number of factors were considered relevant in *Bernstein v Pamson Motors (Golders Green) Ltd*:[19] the intractability of the defect, the time which a repair took, the potential danger involved, the risk of knock-on effects and the price.

Second-hand goods involve more flexibility of treatment, since used goods may be expected to be less efficient or less long lasting than new goods and this is reflected in the price. But the courts latterly applied the same test of merchantable quality as applied in *Rogers v Parish (Scarborough) Ltd*[20] to second-hand cars. In *Shine v General Guarantee*

17 Law Com No 160, Cm 137, 1987, para 3.55.
18 [1987] QB 933 at 944, [1987] 2 All ER 232 at 237, CA; M, H & P p 102. The case concerned a new Range Rover car costing £16,000 which had engine, gearbox and bodywork defects. After some 5,500 miles and six months of driving the claimants rejected the vehicle. The court found that even though the vehicle was driveable it was not of merchantable quality and had been validly rejected by the claimants.
19 [1987] 2 All ER 220, QBD; M, H & P p 104. Here a new Nissan Laurel, costing about £8,000, seized up after 142 miles due to a blockage in the lubrication system.
20 [1987] QB 933, [1987] 2 All ER 232, CA; M, H & P p 102.

Corpn Ltd (Reeds Motor Co (a firm), third party)[1] the expectations of the purchaser of a second-hand enthusiast's car were examined in addition to the condition of the car to determine if it was merchantable. In applying *Rogers*, the court found that the car, which had been submerged for over 24 hours, treated as an insurance write-off, and was without a rust-proof warranty, was unmerchantable. Since the new wording of section 14(2) takes more factors into consideration and places less emphasis on whether or not the item is 'usable', the approach taken in these cases is likely to continue in future cases.

Exceptions

Section 14(2C) indicates three situations in which there will be no implied term of satisfactory quality:

> The term implied by subsection (2) above does not extend to any matter making the quality of the goods unsatisfactory–
> (a) which is specifically drawn to the buyer's attention before the contract is made,
> (b) where the buyer examines the goods before the contract is made, which that examination ought to reveal, or
> (c) in the case of a contract of sale by sample, which would have been apparent on a reasonable examination of the sample.

The first case is where the defects are specifically drawn to the attention of the buyer before the contract is made. The only room for argument about what is, otherwise, a clear-cut and justifiable defence by the seller, is whether the extent of a particular defect had been made clear, even though it had been mentioned 'specifically'. The wise seller will specify defects in writing and not minimise them, as can be seen, for example from the catalogue of any good antiquarian bookseller:

> VALERIUS FLACCUS, Argonautica. 72 leaves, 40 lines, Roman letter, folio, 18th century Italian vellum boards (joints cracked), a few very small worm holes, and small ink stain on title page covered with a slip of paper, large stain on verso of A4, Bologna, 1498 – £750.

---

1 [1988] 1 All ER 911, CA. See also *Business Application Specialists Ltd v Nationwide Credit Corpn Ltd (Marn Garage (Camberley) Ltd, third party)* [1988] BTLC 461, CA. For discussion of the various new and second-hand car cases see Stephenson (1988) 6 Tr Law 172; Barlow (1990) 7 Tr Law 140; Whincup (1988) 138 NLJ 7; and Thomas (1989) 139 NLJ 1188.

Second, lazy buying seems to be encouraged by excepting the case where the buyer has examined the goods before the contract is made, as regards defects which that examination ought to reveal. If the buyer apparently imprudently does not examine the goods at all, he preserves his full right to reject for unsatisfactory quality. There is considerable academic debate on whether the quality of the examination is assessed objectively (as in *Thornett and Fehr v Beers & Son*)[2] or, more likely, subjectively, taking the word 'that' to mean the actual examination undertaken by the buyer.[3] It is consequently no less than prudent, for instance, that the Code of Practice for the motor industry states that 'dealers should provide all reasonable facilities to enable prospective customers or their nominees to carry out an examination of the car prior to sale, in order that any defects which ought to be revealed at the time of the sale are made known to both parties'.[4] There are of course many cases where examination is not possible at all, such as where there are harmful chemicals in the fabric of underpants[5] or arsenic in beer,[6] and the exception will accordingly have no relevance.

The third exception was newly introduced by the 1994 Act to clarify the relationship between section 14(2) and section 15 (see below) in the case of sales by sample. There is no implied term of satisfactory quality where there is a sale by sample, if the defect would have been apparent on a reasonable examination of the sample, whether or not any such examination has actually occurred.

Fitness for the purpose

The reforms made by the 1973 Act to the 1893 Act, and the subsequent consolidation in 1979, have resulted in the renumbering in the 1979 Act of the original subsections of section 14 of the 1893 Act. The former implied term of merchantable quality was contained in section 14(2), and that subsection now contains the implied term of satisfactory quality. The former implied term of fitness for purpose was comprised in section 14(1)

2   [1919] 1 KB 486, KBD (barrels of vegetable glue examined externally only; no liability in respect of defect discoverable had the barrels been opened).

3   See eg *Chitty on Contract* (1999, 28th edn) para 43-085; Atiyah *Sale of Goods* (9th edn) pp 136–7; Howells and Weatherill *Consumer Protection Law* p 139.

4   Reproduced in *Butterworths Trading and Consumer Law* Div 5, para 5[3908]. Note potential difficulties where a defect is discovered and notified prior to sale but sale proceeds as indicated by Dillon LJ in *R & B Customs Brokers Co Ltd v United Dominions Trust Ltd (Saunders Abbott (1980) Ltd, third party)* [1988] 1 All ER 847, CA, at p 851.

5   *Grant v Australian Knitting Mills Ltd* [1936] AC 85, PC.

6   *Wren v Holt* [1903] 1 KB 610, CA. See also *Preist v Last* [1903] 2 KB 148, CA (burst hot water bottle).

Implied terms

and is now to be found in section 14(3). This point must be borne in mind when studying older cases if confusion is to be avoided. The current section 14(3) runs:

> Where the seller sells goods in the course of a business and the buyer, expressly or by implication, makes known to the seller ... any particular purpose for which the goods are being bought, there is an implied term that the goods supplied under the contract are reasonably fit for that purpose, whether or not that is a purpose for which such goods are commonly supplied, except where the circumstances show that the buyer does not rely, or that it is unreasonable for him to rely, on the skill or judgement of the seller ....[7]

In England, Wales and Northern Ireland the implied term is a condition (s 14(6)).

In the course of a business

The meaning of this phrase has been discussed above under 'satisfactory quality'.

The purpose

In ordinary consumer transactions the courts will readily hold the buyer impliedly to have made known his purpose. Obviously one buys food to eat it,[8] a catapult in order to shoot with it,[9] underclothing to wear[10] or a car to drive it. As to cars, the following case is illustrative of both the implicit nature of making known the purpose, and the fact that this condition too applies in appropriate circumstances to sales of second-hand goods. In *Crowther v Shannon Motor Co (a firm)*,[11] a young man bought an eight-

---

7   See M, H & P pp 108–113. The equivalent sections in the 1982 Act are s 4(4)–(6) for transfer of goods and s 9(4)–(6) for hire contracts.
8   *Frost v Aylesbury Dairy Co* [1905] 1 KB 608, CA (milk infected with typhoid germs probably without fault on seller's part, but held not fit for purpose); *Chaproniere v Mason* (1905) 21 TLR 633, CA (solicitor broke teeth on a stone in a bath bun; bun unfit for purpose of eating); *Wallis v Russell* [1902] 2 IR 585, CA – poisonous crabs unfit, though possibly a case of expressly making known the purpose, since the buyer asked for 'two nice fresh crabs for tea' – see Maurice Healy *The Old Munster Circuit* (1st edn) p 209, for the bizarre background detail.
9   *Godley v Perry* [1960] 1 All ER 36, [1960] 1 WLR 9, QBD, see above.
10   *Grant v Australian Knitting Mills Ltd* [1936] AC 85, PC, see above.
11   [1975] 1 All ER 139, [1975] 1 WLR 30, CA; M, H & P p 113.

year-old Jaguar car from a dealer which had 82,000 miles on the odometer. The dealer commended it, saying that the engine was 'hardly run in'. 2,300 miles and three weeks later the engine seized up. The previous owner, when contacted, described the engine as 'clapped out'. The claimant-buyer claimed that the car was not fit for his purpose under what was then section 14(1) of the unamended 1893 Act. It was held that the buyer impliedly made known the purpose for which he wanted the car and had relied on the seller's skill or judgement. As a question of fact and degree the implied term had been broken. It is significant to note that the price paid was £390 and the damages awarded were £460, more than then could have been obtained had there been criminal proceedings and a compensation order by the magistrates' court, as discussed later in the book.

If the buyer requires goods for a particular purpose then this must be expressed. For instance, in *Baldry v Marshall*[12] the buyer claimed to reject an eight cylinder Bugatti car for breach of the implied condition of fitness. He had specified his purpose as being to acquire a fast, flexible and easily managed car which would be comfortable and suitable for ordinary touring purposes, which the Bugatti was not. Similarly if the buyer has some peculiarity, such as an abnormally sensitive skin, he will not be entitled to rely on this condition if he fails to reveal this and the goods are fit for the purpose of a normal buyer.[13] This will be the case whether or not the buyer is aware of the abnormal feature or idiosyncrasy.[14] The Act specifically states that the goods supplied must be 'reasonably' fit for the purpose.

In general, consumer cases will involve a much higher degree of expertise in the seller than the buyer may be expected to have. The courts are correspondingly more inclined to imply the condition on the basis, no doubt, that it is not 'unreasonable' for the buyer to rely on the seller in these circumstances. In some commercial cases, where the goods are bought for resale, this may not be so. As Lord Wilberforce stated, the authorities show that the conditions respectively in sections 14(2) and 14(3) are 'readily and untechnically applied to all sorts of informal situations – such as retail sales over the counter of articles whose purpose is well known – and are applied rather more strictly to large-scale transactions carried through by written contracts'.[15] The private consumer can take comfort from the first part of this statement.

12 [1925] 1 KB 260, CA.
13 See *Griffiths v Peter Conway Ltd* [1939] 1 All ER 685, CA; M, H & P p 109 (coat caused buyer dermatitis, but only because her skin was particularly sensitive). The principle is that the buyer's statement must be sufficient to allow the seller to exercise his skill and judgement.
14 *Slater v Finning Ltd* [1997] AC 473, [1996] 3 All ER 398, HL.
15 *Henry Kendall & Sons (a firm) v William Lillico & Sons Ltd* [1969] 2 AC 31, HL at 123 (manufacturers had bought groundnut extract, without previous experience of it, from suppliers for making up poultry food which because of a too high

Quality and fitness

In many cases a buyer will be able to bring a successful action for breach of the implied terms of both quality and fitness, as in *Godley v Perry* above where the defective catapult was neither merchantable nor fit for the purpose. But if the buyer examines the goods, the right to sue in respect of satisfactory quality may be lost and it would be necessary to rely on the fitness provision provided it could show that the buyer did not rely solely on his or her own skill or judgement.[16] Similarly, if there is no preliminary advice given by the seller it may be difficult to show that the buyer relied in any way on the seller's, as opposed to the manufacturer's, skill or judgement.

It should also be noted that both implied terms apply to goods 'supplied' under the contract. Whilst containers are normally sold with the goods contained therein, and there is liability where, for instance, a defective bottle breaks and injures the buyer,[17] this would still be the case where the bottle was returnable and remained the property of the seller, since he would still have 'supplied' the bottle under the contract.[18] In addition to the packaging and its contents, the Queen's Bench Division in *Wormell v RHM Agriculture (East) Ltd*[19] held that the instructions supplied with a chemical weed killer were part of the 'goods'. If the instructions were missing, inaccurate or misleading so that the chemicals were not reasonably fit for their purpose, a breach of section 14(3) would be established, as it was in this case. On appeal the Court of Appeal took the view that the purchaser was prepared to take the risk that his crops might be damaged by the spray (as indicated in the instructions) and so, rather surprisingly, also took a risk that the spray might not work effectively (a fact not mentioned in the instructions). There was, thus, no breach of the implied terms.

---

concentration of a substance, poisonous to poultry but not cattle, killed a number of the ultimate buyers' birds. Despite a comparable level of expertise between manufacturer-buyer and supplier the groundnuts were held unfit for the purpose of use for cattle and poultry). See also the somewhat similar decision concerning foodstuffs unsuitable for mink in *Ashington Piggeries Ltd v Christopher Hill Ltd* [1972] AC 441, [1971] 1 All ER 847, HL.

16 See eg Dillon LJ in *R & B Customs Brokers Co Ltd v United Dominions Trust Ltd (Saunders Abbott (1980) Ltd, third party)* [1988] 1 All ER 847, CA, at p 851.

17 *Morelli v Fitch and Gibbons* [1928] 2 KB 636; *Aswan Engineering Establishment Co v Lupdine Ltd (Thurgar Bolle, third party)* [1987] 1 All ER 135, [1987] 1 WLR 1, CA (on facts no breach of s 14(3) when pails containing glue melted in the heat, either because of no reliance or, if reliance, pails suited normal purpose and no special purpose declared).

18 *Geddling v Marsh* [1920] 1 KB 668, KBD.

19 [1986] 1 All ER 769, [1986] 1 WLR 336, QBD; M, H & P p 110; revsd [1987] 3 All ER 75, [1987] 1 WLR 1091, CA.

Sample

Section 15 is concerned with sales by sample, applying to both business and private sellers. Here there are two terms implied in contracts where there is a sale by sample, for example curtain material, wallpaper, carpets etc. First, it is implied that the bulk of the goods supplied will correspond in quality with the sample that has been provided. Second, the goods must be free from any defect which makes their quality unsatisfactory which would not be apparent from a reasonable examination of the sample, whether or not the sample has, in fact, been examined.[20] Thus defects in the printing of fabric or wallpaper, which do not appear in the shop sample but which are present in the full roll, would be claimable if of sufficient seriousness. The terms are conditions in England, Wales and Northern Ireland. The case of *Godley v Perry*[1] is one where, inter alia, section 15 applied to the purchase of the catapult by the shopkeeper from the wholesaler.

Liability without fault

Where there has been a breach of any of these implied terms, there is no effective defence by the seller of 'reasonable care'. Liability is strict. 'If there was a defect in fact, even though that defect was one which no reasonable skill or care could discover, the person supplying the article should nevertheless be responsible, the policy of the law being that in a case in which neither were to blame, he, and not the person to whom they were supplied, should be liable for the defect.'[2] Of course, in most consumer sales the defendant will be the retailer who may well be blameless, a position which hardly accords with common sense in cases where the wrong clearly originates with the manufacturer. A survey undertaken on behalf of the Office of Fair Trading in 1988 showed that 40 per cent of those asked who would be responsible if an electric kettle had been bought which did not work either did not know or were incorrect.[3] As it stands at present the buyer's remedy is against the seller, and if that seller is a retailer he must

20 See also s 14(2C)(c) discussed above.
1 [1960] 1 All ER 36, [1960] 1 WLR 9, QBD, see above.
2 *Randall v Newsom* (1876) 45 LJQB 364 at 365, per Blackburn J and *Frost v Aylesbury Dairy Co Ltd* [1905] 1 KB 608, CA. See also statements to the same effect in *Henry Kendall & Sons (a firm) v William Lillico & Sons Ltd* [1969] 2 AC 31, [1968] 2 All ER 444, HL and *Ashington Piggeries Ltd v Christopher Hill Ltd* [1972] AC 441, [1971] 1 All ER 847, HL. It is clear that the state of technical knowledge at the time (the 'state of the art' defence in negligence) is not a defence to an action under s 14. This fact is often overlooked in the debate on strict product liability in tort referred to in ch 6.
3 See Bee Line February 1989, p 28. Also Jolowicz (1969) 32 MLR 1 at 5.

rely on his similar rights under the 1979 Act against the wholesaler and so on until in this indirect (and economically very inefficient) way the manufacturer may[4] be made ultimately to bear the cost of the defect. This, in fact, remains the position for defective goods as opposed to dangerous goods since the implementation of the Consumer Protection Act 1987.[5] The Department of Trade and Industry consultation paper *Consumer Guarantees*[6] did canvass the possibility of making manufacturers or importers liable, with the seller, under the Sale of Goods Act for the quality of goods but no further developments have occurred.

Effects of the European Directive

By 1 January 2002, it is necessary for the Government to implement the Directive on Certain Aspects of the Sale of Consumer Goods and Associated Guarantees.[7] This applies to consumer goods[8] supplied to consumers (natural persons acting for purposes which are not related to trade) by sellers (who are selling in the course of trade, business or profession). Article 2 concerns the requirements as to contractual obligations. It stipulates that the seller must deliver goods which are 'in conformity with the contract of sale'. By Article 2.2:

> Consumer goods are presumed to be conformity with the contract if they:
> (a) comply with the description given by the seller and possess the qualities of the goods which the seller has held out to the consumer as a sample or model;

---

4 Note the problem of a retailer who cannot identify his source of supply as in *Lexmead (Basingstoke) Ltd v Lewis* [1982] AC 225, [1980] 1 All ER 978, CA; revsd *sub nom Lambert v Lewis* [1981] 1 All ER 1185, HL; M, H & P p 62.

5 See further ch 6.

6 February 1992.

7 99/44/EC, OJ No L 171, 7.7.99, p 12. See also R Bradgate 'Consumer Guarantees: the EC's draft Directive' [1997] 1 Web JCLI, http://webjcli.ncl.ac.uk/1997/issue1/bradgate1.html; P Shears, F E Zellers and S N Hurd 'It will be the biggest change to consumer rights for 20 years!' [2000] JBL 262; C Twigg-Flesner 'The EC Directive on Certain Aspects of the Sale of Consumer Goods and Associated Guarantees' [1999] 7 Consum LJ 177; C Twigg-Flesner and R Bradgate 'The EC Directive On Certain Aspects of the Sale of Consumer Goods and Associated Guarantees – All Talk and No Do?' [2000] 4 Web JCLI http://webjcli.ncl.ac.uk/2000/issue2/flesner2.html.

8 Any tangible movable item, with the exceptions of goods sold by way of execution or by authority of law, or water or gas where not sold in a limited volume or set quantity or electricity (art 1(2)).

(b)   are fit for any particular purpose for which the consumer requires them and which he made known to the seller at the time of conclusion of the contract and which the seller has accepted;

(c)   are fit for the purpose for which goods of the same type are normally used;

(d)   show the quality and performance which are normal in goods of the same type and which the consumer can reasonably expect, given the nature of the goods and taking into account any public statements on the specific characteristics of the goods made about them by the seller, the producer or his representative, particularly in advertising or on labelling.

The existing implied terms of correspondence with description, fitness for purpose, satisfactory quality and sample would seem to need little amendment in order to satisfy the requirements of Article 2.2 (a), (b) and (c). Specific reference, will, however, need to be made to the effects of public statements about the goods made by the producer under Article 2.2(d). Article 2.4 prevents the seller being bound by public statements where no actual or reasonable knowledge of the statement, on the seller's part, can be established, where the statement is corrected prior to purchase or where the consumer has not been influenced by the statement. This will also need enactment.

Claims are prevented if, when the contract was concluded, the consumer was aware of the lack of conformity or could not reasonably have been unaware of it (similar to s 14(2)(C)) or if the lack of conformity arises from materials supplied by the consumer (art 2.3). Finally, lack of conformity caused by incorrect installation by a seller, or under his responsibility, and inadequate installation instructions[9] for do-it-yourself consumers, are to be treated as the equivalent of lack of conformity of the goods (art 2.5). It is not clear whether this, apparently strict, liability will be applied to what, under current law, are classified as work and materials contracts or will be confined to sale of goods contracts as defined in the 1979 Act. Currently, in a work and materials contract, the supplier is only under an obligation to use reasonable care and skill regarding the installation (service) element of the contract.[10]

Under Article 5(3), unless proved otherwise, a lack of conformity which becomes apparent within six months of delivery will be presumed to have been present at the time of delivery, unless the presumption is incompatible with the nature of the goods or the lack of conformity. For consumer durables the presumption is useful as it will restrict arguments about faults

9   Similar to *Wormell v RHM Agriculture (East) Ltd* [1986] 1 All ER 769, [1986] 1 WLR 336, QBD; M, H & P p 110; revsd [1987] 3 All ER 75, [1987] 1 WLR 1091, CA; above p 108.

10   See further Supply of Goods and Services Act 1982 s 13, discussed in ch 7.

being due to wear and tear rather than being present at the time of delivery. In the case of perishable goods, in particular, it will, however, often be the case that the presumption is incompatible; such goods often not being expected to last more than six months anyway.

The requirements of the Directive are in addition to any other rights consumers may have under contract or tort and it is possible for stricter measures to be adopted to ensure a higher level of protection (art 8). Sellers will retain their rights of action against others in the distribution chain, according to their national laws (art 4). The Directive is included amongst those for which injunctions may be sought under the Injunctions Directive.[11] It is proposed that the Director General of Fair Trading should be the lead authority.

Remedies – rejection and damages[12]

The remedies available for the breach of an implied term in a contract for the supply of goods currently depend, in part, on whether the term is classified as a condition or warranty. In addition, differences may occur depending upon which statute governs the contract. The Sale of Goods Act 1979 defines the word 'condition' indirectly in section 11(3) (see below) and the word 'warranty' specifically in section 61(1).[13] Neither of these terms is defined in the Supply of Goods (Implied Terms) Act 1973 (for hire-purchase contracts) or the Supply of Goods and Services Act 1982 (for transfer of goods and hire). The omission of any definition in the 1982 Act was based on the recommendations of the Law Commission in its 95th Report *Implied Terms in Contracts for the Supply of Goods* (para 25), on the grounds of convenience and consistency with the 1973 Act. The whole area of remedies for breach of implied terms was discussed extensively in the Law Commission Working Paper No 85 *Sale and Supply of Goods* and the final Report of the same name (Law Com. No 160, Scot Law Com No 104).[14] The Sale and Supply of Goods Act 1994, based on the Law Commissions' recommendations, has introduced restrictions on the right to reject in non-consumer sales and changes to the meaning of 'acceptance', which will be discussed below. Changes to United Kingdom

11 Directive 98/27/EC, OJ No L 166, 11.6.98, p 51. See also *Injunctions Directive: Implementation in the UK*, DTI, February 2000 and 'Widening the net' OFT (2000) 26 Fair Trading 13.

12 M, H & P pp 123–142.

13 A warranty is 'an agreement with reference to goods which are the subject of a contract of sale but collateral to the main purpose of such contract, the breach of which gives rise to a claim for damages, but not to a right to reject the goods and treat the contract as repudiated'.

14 See also M, H & P pp 126–127, 135–136; Atiyah pts VI and VII.

law which are necessary to implement the European Directive[15] are also indicated.

Rejection

The primary remedy for breach of either an express or implied condition is for the buyer to reject the goods and reclaim the price in full. In addition damages for breach of contract in respect of losses not too remote, in the light of the principles of contract law may be claimed. Looking first at sale of goods contracts, the right to repudiate the contract for breach of condition, rather than simply to reject performance as tendered and leave the seller the option of replacing the goods as some authorities suggest,[16] though nowhere explicitly stated, seems to be clearly inferred from the wording of section 11(3) of the 1979 Act (which refers to 'a condition, the breach of which may give rise to a right to treat the contract as repudiated'), and by section 54 (which preserves the buyer's right to recover money paid where the consideration for the payment of it has failed).

Alternatively, the buyer may treat the breach of condition as a breach of warranty and retain the goods but claim damages for the breach by way of reduction of the purchase price, or by action if the price has been paid, or both (s 53). Section 15A[17] has introduced a restriction on the right to reject where a non-consumer buyer is involved. If the breach of a condition relating to quality, fitness, description or sample is 'so slight that it would be unreasonable for him to reject' a buyer who does not deal as consumer (as defined in s 12 of the Unfair Contract Terms Act 1977[18]) may only treat the breach as a breach of warranty and claim damages. It is up to the seller to establish that the breach is slight and that the buyer is not dealing as consumer.[19] This provision only applies in the absence of an express or implied contrary intention of the parties.[20] In sale of goods contracts there are further, similar restrictions on rejection of goods where wrong quantities have been delivered under section 30.

15 Directive on Certain Aspects of the Sale of Consumer Goods and Associated Guarantees, 99/44/EC, OJ No L 171, 7.7.99, p 12.
16 The right to repair or replace defective goods was considered 'uncertain' as to its existence or extent by the Law Com Working Paper No 85 para 2.38.
17 Applicable to contracts made on or after 3 January 1995. The equivalent sections in the 1982 Act are s 5A for contracts for the transfer of goods and s 10A for hire contracts.
18 S 61(5A) of the 1979 Act and s 18(4) of the 1982 Act respectively. For 'dealing as consumer' see below p 128.
19 Ss 15A(3) and 61(5A) of the 1979 Act and ss 5A(3), 10A(3) and 18(4) of the 1982 Act respectively.
20 S 15A(2), 1979 Act, ss 5(A)(2) and 10(A)(2) of the 1982 Act respectively.

Where the buyer has 'accepted' the goods, as mentioned above under the discussion of title, he will have no option but to treat the breach of any condition (express or implied) as a breach of warranty (s 11(4)).[1] The concept of acceptance[2] is explained primarily by section 35 of the 1979 Act (as substituted by the 1994 Act). A number of different factors need to be examined. The first two situations when acceptance occurs are:

35(1) The buyer is deemed to have accepted the goods subject to subsection (2) below–
(a) when he intimates to the seller that he has accepted them, or
(b) when the goods have been delivered to him and he does any act in relation to them which is inconsistent with the ownership of the seller.
  (2) Where goods are delivered to the buyer, and he has not previously examined them, he is not deemed to have accepted them under subsection (1) above until he has had a reasonable opportunity of examining them for the purpose–
(a) of ascertaining whether they are in conformity with the contract, and
(b) in the case of a contract of sale by sample, of comparing the bulk with the sample.

The concept is thus based on the buyer's conduct. An express acceptance is unequivocal and may occur if a buyer signs a delivery note or 'acceptance' note. To ensure that a consumer buyer still has time to examine the goods, as permitted by subsection (2), even after signature in a delivery note, additional protection is given under subsection (3):

(3) Where the buyer deals as consumer[3] or (in Scotland) the contract of sale is a consumer contract, the buyer cannot lose his right to rely on subsection (2) above by agreement, waiver or otherwise.

In the case of a business buyer, it would be possible for the right of examination under subsection (2) to be lost by signature on a delivery note, but the buyer also has rights under section 34 (as amended) to examine the goods.[4]

1 This is subject to the right of partial rejection under s 35A, see below p 116.
2 See Law Com Working Paper No 85 paras 2.48–2.60; Law Com No 160 paras 2.40–2.49.
3 As defined in the Unfair Contract Terms Act 1977, s 12: see below p 128.
4 'Unless otherwise agreed, when the seller tenders delivery of goods to the buyer, he is bound on request to afford the buyer a reasonable opportunity of examining the goods for the purpose of ascertaining whether they are in conformity with the contract and, in the case of a contract for sale by sample, of comparing the bulk with the sample.'

Two examples of acts which, prior to the 1994 Act changes, were suggested[5] as being inconsistent with the seller's ownership were the reselling of the goods and where the buyer tried to get the seller to repair defective goods. Under the new wording of section 35 neither of these actions, in themselves, amount to acceptance:

> (6) The buyer is not by virtue of this section deemed to have accepted the goods merely because–
> (a) he asks for, or agrees to, their repair by or under an arrangement with the seller, or,
> (b) the goods are delivered to another under a sub-sale or other disposition.

It is to be noted, however, that repair by a third party, including the manufacturer, may well be considered as an 'act inconsistent with the seller's ownership'.

The majority of consumer cases will fall under the third head of acceptance:

> (4) The buyer is also deemed to have accepted the goods when after the lapse of a reasonable time he retains the goods without intimating to the seller that he has rejected them.
> (5) The questions that are material in determining for the purposes of subsection (4) above whether a reasonable time has elapsed include whether the buyer has had a reasonable opportunity of examining the goods for the purpose mentioned in subsection (2) above.

Subsection (4) is worded in the same way as the earlier version of section 35 in deeming acceptance where the buyer retains the goods without intimating[6] that he has rejected them 'after the lapse of a reasonable time'. The word 'reasonable' provides a desirable flexibility which a court would apply by reference to such factors as whether the goods have been used and have deteriorated and whether the buyer has been unduly tardy in going back to the seller. Thus, for example, in *Leaf v International Galleries*[7] a buyer discovered that a picture that he had bought of Salisbury Cathedral, which was honestly represented by the seller to have been by Constable, was not a genuine Constable. Denning LJ stated:

5   Law Com No 160 para 2.47.
6   Rejection must be unequivocally expressed, see *Lee v York Coach and Marine* [1977] RTR 35, CA; M, H & P p 128 (two solicitor's letters requesting repairs and suggesting a right to reject not sufficient for rejection).
7   [1950] 2 KB 86, [1950] 1 All ER 693, CA.

Implied terms

I think it right to assume in the buyer's favour that this term was a condition and that, if he had come in proper time he could have rejected the picture . . . In this case the buyer took the picture into his house and, apparently, hung it there, and five years passed before he intimated any rejection at all. That, I need hardly say, is much more than a reasonable time. It is far too late for him at the end of five years to reject this picture for breach of any condition. His remedy after that length of time is for damages only. [At pp 89, 694].

The introduction of subsection (5) has, however, potentially changed the provision by highlighting the time a buyer has had to examine the goods to assess conformity with the contract and to compare the bulk with a sample. Until case law develops it is not certain how the courts will interpret this. Some commentators suggest that the consumer may be permitted a much longer period for examination where, for example, items for a new baby are bought some weeks or months in advance of its arrival or winter clothing is bought in summer sales and early use could not reasonably be expected. It might, however, be that the courts' approach remains similar to that in *Bernstein v Pamson Motors (Golders Green) Ltd*,[8] which suggested that section 35 (as originally worded) did not refer to a reasonable time to discover the defects, it meant a reasonable time to inspect the goods and try them out generally. Rougier J stated: 'The complexity of the intended function of the goods is clearly of prime consideration here. What is a reasonable time in relation to a bicycle would hardly suffice for a nuclear submarine'.[9] He held that three weeks and 142 miles driven in a new car was a reasonable time and that acceptance had occurred.

A final new aspect of section 35 is subsection (7), which deals with 'commercial units':

Where the contract is for the sale of goods making one or more commercial units, a buyer accepting any goods included in a unit is deemed to have accepted all the goods making the unit; and in this subsection 'commercial unit' means a unit division of which would materially impair the value of the goods or the character of the unit.

Examples of commercial units would be a set of volumes of an encyclopaedia or a pair of shoes.[10]

Section 35A[11] of the 1979 Act links with section 35(7) and deals with the right of partial rejection of goods. Unless the parties agree otherwise,

8   [1987] 2 All ER 220, [1987] BTLC 37, QBD; M, H & P p 130.
9   At pp 231, 50.
10   See Law Com No 160, paras 6.12–6.13.
11   Newly inserted as of 3 January 1995 by the Sale and Supply of Goods Act 1994, s 3.

where a buyer could reject goods for a breach which affects some or all of the goods, acceptance of some of the goods, including all unaffected goods, does not now prevent the buyer from rejecting the remainder of the goods. This prevents the previous problem that buyers encountered where they had to accept or reject all the goods in a batch, unless the contract was severable.

It is a common fallacy that the buyer can, currently, require the seller to repair defective goods. The statutory rights of the buyer are presently limited to rejection and/or damages. A right to require the seller to repair will, however, need to be created to implement the Sale of Consumer Goods Directive.[12] Where the buyer does have the right to reject the goods, section 36 makes clear that he is not bound to return them to the seller, but it is sufficient if he intimates to the seller that he refuses to accept them.

In contracts other than sale of goods, for example hire-purchase, work and materials, hire and barter, the right to reject the goods is not governed by any statutory measure. Instead it is subject to the common law doctrine of affirmation[13] whereby once a person has been held to have affirmed the contract he may only sue for damages. In *Farnworth Finance Facilities Ltd v Attryde*,[14] a case concerning affirmation in a hire-purchase contract, Lord Denning MR indicated that: 'affirmation is a matter of election. A man only affirms a contract when he knows of the defects and by his conduct elects to go on with the contract despite them.'

Effects of the EC Directive

As indicated above, changes to United Kingdom law on remedies are necessary to implement the Directive on the Sale of Consumer Goods and Associated Guarantees.[15] Under Article 3, where goods are not in conformity with the contract of sale,[16] consumers have four possible avenues of redress: repair, replacement, reduction in the price or rescission. The primary rights are free[17] repair or replacement by the seller, unless this is impossible or disproportionate (art 3(3)). Neither repair nor replacement would be possible if a product, which is no longer available for sale, self-destructs. A remedy is disproportionate if:

---

12 99/44/EC, OJ No L 171, 7.7.99, p 12, see below.
13 See Law Com Working Paper No 85 paras 2.61–2.63 (reproduced in M, H & P pp 135–136) and Law Com No 160 paras 2.50–2.52 for summaries of the doctrine.
14 [1970] 2 All ER 774 at 778, [1970] 1 WLR 1053 at 1059, CA; M, H & P p 136.
15 99/44/EC, OJ No L 171, 7.7.99, p 12.
16 Discussed above at p 110.
17 Included here are the costs of postage, labour and materials.

it imposes costs on the seller which, in comparison with the alternative remedy, are unreasonable, taking into account:

- the value the goods would have if there were no lack of conformity,
- the significance of the lack of conformity, and
- whether the alternative remedy could be completed without significant inconvenience to the consumer.

It may often be the case that to replace an item is a disproportionate remedy compared to a repair, in particular if there is an easily corrected breach and if replacement causes considerable expense to the seller, who might be left with an item which cannot be resold. Repairs or replacements must be completed within a reasonable period of time and without any significant inconvenience to the consumer, taking into consideration the nature of the goods and the purpose for which they are required. The provision of substitute items, eg courtesy cars, whilst repairs are undertaken would be of assistance here.

Price reductions and rescission are secondary remedies, available if the consumer is not entitled to repair or replacement, if the seller has not completed a repair or replacement within a reasonable time or if the remedy has not been provided without significant inconvenience to the consumer (art 3(5)). Rescission is not available where the lack of conformity is minor (art 3(6)), avoiding the possibility of minor breaches being used as an excuse for a refund because the consumer discovers that the item could be purchased more cheaply elsewhere. It may be the case that a repair or replacement is originally sought but, because of delays or inconvenience, subsequently a price reduction is also requested.

Instead of the current rules regarding acceptance, discussed above, the Directive will permit *any* available remedy to be sought where a lack of conformity is apparent within two years of delivery (art 5(1)). This, for the purposes of rescission, is much more generous than 'lapse of reasonable time' under section 35(4) of the 1979 Act. It is, however, possible for member states to require a consumer to inform the seller of a lack of conformity within two months from the date of detection of the lack of conformity to be able to claim a remedy. This is similar to the concept of affirmation and may be incorporated into the United Kingdom implementing legislation. It is open to member states to provide more generous time limits than the Directive stipulates (art 8).

Damages

Where damages are claimed for breach of condition or warranty in the circumstances discussed above, section 53(3) of the 1979 Act lays down a rule applicable in the many consumer cases. If the claim is for loss due to defects in the goods under sections 13 and 14 of the 1979 Act, or in respect of broken express warranties:

> In the case of breach of warranty of quality such loss is prima facie the difference between the value of the goods at the time of delivery to the buyer and the value they would have had if they had fulfilled the warranty.

In consumer cases the courts would normally take the difference between the contract price and the diminished value of the defective goods, either on a rough estimate or with the help of expert evidence.[18] The phrase 'at the time of delivery' should be noted, since it precludes increasing the claim in respect of inflationary rises in the cost of repairing or replacing the goods since the time of delivery. It is to be noted that the Sale of Consumer Goods Directive,[19] in providing the remedy of a reduction of price for goods not in conformity with the contract, provides no further details regarding how this is to be assessed.

Where there are consequential losses which may involve physical damage to the buyer or his property as a result of defective goods, or where the breach is of a condition other than a 'warranty of quality', the heads of loss for which the buyer may claim are those within section 53(2), modelled on the first part of the leading case in contract on remoteness of damage, *Hadley v Baxendale*.[20] The subsection states:

> The measure of damages for breach of warranty is the estimated loss directly and naturally resulting, in the ordinary course of events, from the breach of warranty.

To take a few examples of where consequential damage has been recovered, in *Bernstein v Pamson Motors (Golders Green) Ltd*[1] the claimant was awarded the cost of returning home after the car broke down plus loss of a tank of petrol (£32.90), five days' loss of use of his car (£50) and £150 for a totally spoilt day out in the car. In addition the car had been fully repaired. No diminution in value of the car was established so no damages were awarded under section 53(3). In *Godley v Perry*,[2] a case already referred to, a boy who lost his left eye because of a defective cheap catapult which

---

18 'It seems to me that one can very rarely arrive at an accurate figure of unsound value' per Devlin J in *Biggin & Co Ltd v Permanite Ltd* [1951] 2 KB 314 at 438, CA.
19 99/44/EC, OJ No L 171, 7.7.99, p 12, see above.
20 (1854) 9 Exch 341, Exchequer.
1   [1987] 2 All ER 220; QBD, M, H & P p 130, see above.
2   [1960] 1 All ER 36, [1960] 1 WLR 9, QBD.

Implied terms

broke with a dog-tooth fracture, recovered £2,500 in respect of pain and suffering, the loss of his eye and the discomfort of daily removal of his artificial eye. In *Wilson v Rickett, Cockerell & Co Ltd*,[3] also discussed above, the claimant's room and furniture were damaged by the explosive 'Coalite' and she recovered £117 for the damage done. All these losses arise 'directly and naturally' from the breach. If the parties are aware, at the time of making the contract, of 'special' losses which would arise on breach, as under the second part of *Hadley v Baxendale*,[4] these may also be recovered (s 54). In *Hardy v Losner Formals*[5] a spoilt wedding dress led to general damages of £650 for the distress caused to the bride and £25 special damages.

If the seller fails or refuses to deliver goods to the buyer then damages can be claimed under section 51. According to subsection (2):

> The measure of damages is the estimated loss directly and naturally resulting, in the ordinary course of events, from the seller's breach of contract.

If there is an available market in the goods concerned then subsection (3) awards damages on the basis of the difference between the contract price and the market price at the time of delivery or when delivery was refused.

As was the case with rejection, there are no statutory provisions relating to damages in the 1973 Act and the 1982 Act. Damages for breach of implied terms in work and materials, hire, barter and hire-purchase contracts will be assessed in a similar way to those under the 1979 Act. For example in *Phillips v Kannike-Martins Associates*[6] a model suffered hair loss and damage due to a chemical treatment at her hairdressers going wrong. She was awarded general damages of £3,500 and special damages of £6,000. In *Harrison v Howard Morgan (t/a Flamingoes)*[7] a wedding reception booked by the bride's mother, where insufficient food was provided resulting in visits to a local fish and chip shop, led to an award of £85 compensation for the lack of food and £400 for distress and inconvenience. Finally, in *Ruxley Electronics and Construction Ltd v Forsyth*[8] damages of £2,500 for loss of amenity were awarded to the owner of a newly-constructed swimming pool, which had been built nine inches shallower than the contract specified. The court decided that to insist on reinstatement

3   [1954] 1 QB 598, [1954] 1 All ER 868, CA.
4   (1854) 9 Exch 341, Exchequer.
5   [1997] CLY 1749, Shoreditch County Court.
6   [1993] CLY 1470, Central London County Court.
7   [1993] CLY 1365, Blackwood County Court.
8   [1996] AC 344, [1995] 3 All ER 268, HL. See B Coote 'Contract Damages, *Ruxley* and the Performance Interest' (1997) 56 CLJ 537.

(at a cost of £36,000) was unreasonable in proportion to the benefit to be gained, the pool still being usable at the reduced depth and the owner did not intend to rebuild it. Instead the owner could claim the diminution in value of the pool as built in comparison with the pool as contracted for, but on the facts there was no difference in value. The court recognised that a breach might lead to disappointment, where the consumer does not gain all the pleasure or benefit that was hoped for from the contract. An award for loss of amenity would compensate for such intangible losses.

4. MISREPRESENTATION

Whether a seller's or supplier's statement about goods to be sold constitutes a promissory term of the contract or is merely a misrepresentation can be problematic, and the way the courts tend to find a solution has already been discussed. If the statement complained about is found to have no promissory effect but was a mere representation, the buyer still has useful remedies provided he can show that the statement was at least one of the factors that induced him to contract. If the buyer pays no regard to the statement or was aware that it was untrue, no complaint can be made.[9] The statement, to give rise to legal effects, must be more than an unverifiable opinion and must not be a mere advertiser's 'puff' – *simplex commendatio non obligat.*

Where a misrepresentation has been made, remedies depend on its nature. A fraudulent misrepresentation is one made either knowingly, or without belief in its truth, or reckless as to whether it be true or false.[10] The buyer will often find this element of fraud by the seller difficult to prove and certainly dangerous to allege since heavy costs may be involved in the event of failure. However, if successful the buyer is entitled to seek the discretionary remedy of rescission of the contract and an indemnity for any expenses, and is entitled, as of right, to damages for the tort of deceit. At common law, if the misrepresentation was made innocently, without intention to deceive and not recklessly, the buyer had no right to sue for damages. Further, it was often found that because of delay, the impossibility of restoring the goods in the same condition as when the contract was made, or the acquisition of rights to the goods by an innocent third party, that the equitable right to rescind the contract had also been lost.[11] The

---

9   See *Horsfall v Thomas* (1862) 1 H & C 90 (buyer bought dangerously defective gun, the seller having tried to conceal the defect, but no misrepresentation (by conduct) because buyer had not examined the gun).
10   *Derry v Peek* (1889) 14 App Cas 337, HL.
11   See, for example, *Long v Lloyd* [1958] 2 All ER 402, [1958] 1 WLR 753, CA; M, H & P p 132.

House of Lords, in 1963[12] mitigated the rigour of this principle by holding that there are circumstances where careless advice can give rise to an action in tort based on the negligent misstatement. The doctrine can be used where there is also a contractual relationship between the parties.[13] In the ordinary case of misrepresentation made by the seller or supplier to the buyer it will rarely now be necessary to go beyond the Misrepresentation Act 1967 which significantly increased the buyer's remedies in respect of innocent misrepresentations.

Section 2(1) of the Misrepresentation Act 1967 states that where there is an operative misrepresentation which, had it been made fraudulently, would have made the person making it liable to damages,

> that person shall be so liable notwithstanding that the misrepresentation was not made fraudulently, unless he proves that he had reasonable ground to believe and did believe up to the time the contract was made that the facts represented were true.

Thus if a misrepresentation has been made honestly but negligently – in the sense that the maker of the statement must disprove negligence by showing reasonable belief in its truth – damages may be awarded.[14] The existing remedy of rescission is available as well as damages, or as the only remedy where there is no element of negligence.

Subsection (2) gives the court a discretion to award damages in lieu of rescission, in addition to any damages awarded under subsection (1), though damages awarded under subsection (2) must be taken into account in awarding damages for negligent misrepresentation under subsection (1) (s 2(3)). The Act does not affect the pre-existing equitable limits to

12 *Hedley Byrne & Co Ltd v Heller & Partners Ltd* [1964] AC 465, [1963] 2 All ER 575, HL.

13 See *Esso Petroleum Co Ltd v Mardon* [1976] QB 801, [1976] 2 All ER 5, CA; M, H & P p 22; *Batty v Metropolitan Property Realisations Ltd* [1978] QB 554, [1978] 2 All ER 445, CA. The usual rule in professional cases was that a client must sue his negligent solicitor in contract not in tort, see *Clark v Kirby-Smith* [1964] Ch 506, [1964] 2 All ER 835, Ch D. However, in *Midland Bank Trust Co Ltd v Hett, Stubbs and Kemp (a firm)* [1979] Ch 384, [1978] 3 All ER 571, Ch D, Oliver J held that an action against a firm of solicitors for not registering an option to buy land lay both in contract and tort. Concurrent liability has been confirmed by the House of Lords in *Henderson v Merrett Syndicates* [1995] 2 AC 145, [1994] 3 All ER 506. See further ch 7 at p 191.

14 Damages are to be assessed on a tortious basis, using the test applicable in the tort of deceit – that is any loss flowing from the misrepresentation, even if not reasonably foreseeable. Authority for this is *Royscot Trust Ltd v Rogerson* [1991] 2 QB 297, [1991] 3 All ER 294, CA. This is more generous than the position under the law of negligence, see *Smith New Court Securities Ltd v Citibank NA* [1997] AC 254, sub nom *Smith New Court Securities Ltd v Scrimgeour Vickers (Asset) Management Ltd* [1996] 4 All ER 769, HL.

rescission mentioned above – excessive delay, impossibility of restoring the goods in the same condition as when supplied, or where an innocent third party has acquired rights to the property. Following *Zanzibar v British Aerospace (Lancaster House) Ltd*[15] it is possible to claim damages under section 2(2) even where the right of rescission has been lost.

5. EXEMPTION CLAUSES AND UNFAIR TERMS

Introduction

There has long been something of a war of attrition between large-scale sellers of goods, or suppliers of services, and their customers with regard to exemption clauses and onerous terms. We are here concerned with two types of terms: first, exemption clauses affecting the buyer's rights if the goods bought are defective and, second, terms that are onerous or unfair to consumers. (Exemption clauses in contracts for services are dealt with in chapter 7.) Such clauses are normally only found in 'standard form' contracts which the consumer must take or leave without alteration and where there is marked inequality of bargaining power between manufacturer-supplier on the one hand and consumers on the other.

Statutory control of exemption clauses, in the form of the Unfair Contract Terms Act 1977 and the Unfair Terms in Consumer Contracts Regulations 1999,[16] has had, and will continue to have, a considerable impact on the use and effectiveness of exemption clauses. Before analysing these statutory measures, the protection offered by the common law is worth examining. When looking at a particular exemption clause it is important to consider whether it is binding at all. The wording may, for instance, not be apt to cover the event complained of,[17] or the exemption clause may not be incorporated into the contract at all,[18] or it could be inconsistent with express undertakings that have been given at the time of making the

---

15   (2000) Times, 28 March, QBD.
16   SI 1999/2083, replacing SI 1994/3159 as of 1 October 1999.
17   Exemption clauses are construed by the courts contra proferentem, ie ambiguities are construed against the person relying on the exemption clause. See eg *Wallis, Son and Wells v Pratt and Haynes* [1911] AC 394, HL ('no warranty express or implied' does not protect against breach of implied condition); and *Andrews Bros (Bournemouth) Ltd v Singer & Co Ltd* [1934] 1 KB 17, CA (exclusion of conditions and warranties implied do not include express conditions).
18   Usually because it is introduced after the offer has been accepted – see *Chapelton v Barry UDC* [1940] 1 KB 532, [1940] 1 All ER 356, CA (deck chair hire document receipt), and *Olley v Marlborough Court Ltd* [1949] 1 KB 532, [1949] 1 All ER 127, CA (notice in hotel bedroom too late).

contract.[19] Even where a clause appears part of the contract, by inclusion in a written document provided by one party to the other; if this contains onerous provisions these may not be enforceable in the absence of evidence to show that they have been fairly and reasonably brought to the attention of the other party. This can be seen in the case of *Interfoto Picture Library Ltd v Stiletto Visual Programmes Ltd.*[20] Here a provision in a delivery note sought to impose a penalty of £5 per day per item for each day any colour transparencies were retained beyond 14 days. This led to a bill for £3,783.50 being sent to the defendants. The court held the term was not part of the contract for the hire of the transparencies. The court took the view that nothing was done to draw the defendants' attention to this clause which was described by Bingham LJ as 'unreasonable and extortionate' (at pp 445, 357). An award based on a quantum meruit was substituted.

If an exemption clause is incorporated into the contract it is generally not a defence to plead that the clause was not understood[1] or read, particularly if signed.[2] In this event, in order to do justice in cases where buyers or hire-purchasers of goods have been denied any remedy because of a comprehensive and binding exemption clause, the courts steadily enlarged the idea of 'fundamental breach' of contract, a topic fully discussed in the standard textbooks on contract. The idea originates from the self-evident proposition that 'if a man offers to buy peas of another, and he sends him beans, he does not perform his contract';[3] no exclusion clause can avail the seller since beans are not merely defective peas and there is complete failure of consideration. The problem is often one of identity. Is an object suffering from a long line of defects still recognisable as that object? In the well-known case of *Karsales (Harrow) Ltd v Wallis,*[4] the defendant having inspected a car which was then in good order, was eventually delivered, under a hire-purchase contract, with a 'shell' which had a broken cylinder head, burnt out valves and two broken pistons. This had been towed in late at night. The defendant had signed a contract

---

19   *Couchman v Hill* [1947] KB 554, [1947] 1 All ER 103, CA (statement that heifer was 'unserved' in auction catalogue overrode general disclaimer in conditions of sale); *J Evans & Son (Portsmouth) Ltd v Andrea Merzario Ltd* [1976] 2 All ER 930, [1976] 1 WLR 1078, CA (oral assurance that goods would be carried on deck overrode exemption clause giving carriers complete freedom of transportation and exemption from liability for loss).

20   [1989] QB 433, [1988] 1 All ER 348, CA; M, H & P p 317. See also *Thornton v Shoe Lane Parking Ltd* [1971] 2 QB 163, [1971] 1 All ER 686, CA.

1   *Thompson v London, Midland and Scottish Rly Co* [1930] 1 KB 41, CA (claimant illiterate).

2   *L'Estrange v F Graucob Ltd* [1934] 2 KB 394 (signed contract not read but contained effective comprehensive exemption clause). See the critical analysis of this principle in [1973] CLJ 104 (Spencer).

3   Per Lord Abinger CB in *Chanter v Hopkins* (1838) 4 M & W 399 at 404.

4   [1956] 2 All ER 866, [1956] 1 WLR 936, CA.

containing an exemption clause excluding all express or implied conditions and warranties as to roadworthiness or fitness for purpose. It was held that the claimants were disentitled to rely on the exemption clause since there had been a fundamental breach of contract. 'In the true meaning of words a car that will not go is not a car at all'.[5] But the House of Lords has re-affirmed, in *Photo Production Ltd v Securicor Transport Ltd*,[6] that the 'doctrine' of fundamental breach is one of interpretation only. In the particular case the court refused to apply it where the parties were of equal bargaining power and well able to insure against the risk, the subject matter of the purported exemption clause. As a working rule for consumers, it is safer to assume that a breach of the implied term of satisfactory quality or fitness is not likely to be classified as fundamental, provided the object contracted for is recognisably delivered. Nor, as will be seen next, is the private consumer of goods likely to need to rely on the doctrine to escape from the meshes of exemption clauses, owing to the relieving provisions of the Unfair Contract Terms Act 1977. Indeed, Lord Denning, in *George Mitchell (Chesterhall) Ltd v Finney Lock Seeds Ltd*,[7] having provided a useful catalogue of the various techniques used to defeat exclusion clauses including fundamental breach concludes that: 'We should no longer have to go through all kinds of gymnastic contortions to get round them'.[8]

Freedom of contract

In accordance with the theory that there should be freedom to contract in any form between parties of full capacity, the 1979 Act gives the parties the right to negative or vary such provisions as those implying terms as to the quality of goods. Section 55(1) states as follows:

> Where any right, duty or liability would arise under a contract of sale of goods by implication of law, it may (subject to the Unfair Contract Terms Act 1977) be negatived or varied by express

5   Per Birkett LJ at 869, 942. Parker LJ elaborated on this dictum by suggesting that not every defect temporarily rendering a car unusable would amount to a fundamental breach, 'but where, as here, a vehicle is delivered incapable of self-propulsion except after a complete overhaul ... it is abundantly clear that there was a breach of a fundamental term' (at 871, 943). For an example, where cleaners who lost a customer's carpet were disentitled to rely on an exemption clause because of a fundamental breach, see *Levison v Patent Steam Carpet Cleaning Co Ltd* [1978] QB 69, [1977] 3 All ER 498, CA. As mentioned in the text, since the passing of the Unfair Contract Terms Act 1977 there can be few cases where the consumer would need to rely on arguing fundamental breach.

6   [1980] AC 827, [1980] 1 All ER 556, HL.

7   [1983] QB 284, [1983] 1 All ER 108, CA; M, H & P p 319.

8   At pp 299, 115 respectively; M, H & P p 322.

agreement, or by the course of dealing between the parties, or by such usage as binds both parties to the contract.

The same is true in contracts for the transfer or hire of goods. Section 11(1) of the 1982 Act has very similar wording. The freedom to exclude the implied conditions and warranties on standard form sales agreements was for many years objected to by consumer organisations, and these objections were supported by the Molony Committee, paragraph 435 of whose Report states:

> The overriding argument in favour of prohibiting 'contracting-out' is that it enables well-organised commerce consistently to impose unfair terms on the consumer and to deny him what the law means him to have.
>
> This benefit is obtained without the consumer knowing how he is being treated. If a particular consumer is alive to the position he will find it difficult, and sometimes impossible, to avoid submitting to the terms of business universally adopted. Because the percipient customer is in a small minority the trades concerned can afford to refuse to modify their usual terms at his behest. He possesses no bargaining power of sufficient weight to compel. This is the essence of the case for intervention in support of the consuming public. We endorse the soundness of the case and accept the need to ban 'contracting-out'. To be effective the prohibition must extend to the efforts of any person to relieve the retailer of liability whether made before, at or after the moment of sale. The prohibition we have in mind is not a dictate supported by criminal law but a denial of legal effect to provisions relieving the retailer of statutory liabilities. The safeguard thus provided would be additional to any other rule of law … annexing obligation to a contract of sale.

The Law Commission also studied and reported on the position, and the Supply of Goods (Implied Terms) Act 1973 was based on the Commission's First Report on Exemption Clauses[9] to which passing reference has already been made. The 1973 Act amended section 55 of the 1893 Act by adding to it a number of subsections the primary purpose of which was to prohibit contracting out of the then implied conditions relating to description, quality and fitness in sales to consumers. The Act did not prevent exclusion or restriction of other obligations under the 1893 Act, such as to deliver the goods in reasonable time under section 29, and this remains the position.

---

9   (1969) Law Com No 24. See also M, H & P pp 323–324.

The current position is stated by the Unfair Contract Terms Act 1977 ('the 1977 Act'), a private member's bill based on the draft bill contained in the Law Commission's Second Report on Exemption Clauses (1975) and the Unfair Terms in Consumer Contracts Regulations 1999[10] ('the 1999 Regulations'), which implement the European Directive on unfair terms in consumer contracts.[11]

Unfair Contract Terms Act 1977[12]

The 1977 Act generally only applies to 'business liability' as defined in section 1(3) as amended.[13] This is liability for breach of obligations or duties arising a) from things done or to be done by a person in the course of a business or b) from the occupation of premises used for business purposes, subject to certain exceptions for recreational and educational uses. Purely 'private' transactions are, therefore, usually outside the scope of the Act. An exception under section 6 is discussed below.

Exclusions of statutory implied terms

Sections 6 and 7 of the 1977 Act contain similar provisions to deal with attempts to exclude or restrict statutory implied terms relating to title, description, quality and fitness of the goods and sample. Section 6 governs contracts for the sale of goods, under the 1979 Act, and hire-purchase, under the 1973 Act. Section 7 governs other contracts where ownership or possession of goods is transferred, primarily work and materials, barter, and hire under the 1982 Act.

Title

The implied undertakings as to title provided by section 12 of the 1979 Act (sale of goods) and section 8 of the 1973 Act (hire-purchase) are protected by section 6(1) of the 1977 Act and those under section 2 of the 1982 Act (work and materials and barter) by section 7(3A).[14] In each case any attempt to exclude or restrict the liability by a contract term is rendered void. In other contracts (eg hire under s 7 of the 1982 Act) liability in respect of the right to transfer ownership or possession of the goods, or to have quiet

10   SI 1999/2083.
11   93/13/EEC, OJ No L 95, 21.4.93, p 29.
12   BSSCCL p 409. See MacDonald *Exemption Clauses and Unfair Terms*.
13   By the Occupiers' Liability Act 1984, s 2.
14   As inserted by s 17(2) of the 1982 Act.

possession, is protected by subjecting any exemption clause to a reasonableness test (s 7(4) of the 1977 Act).[15]

Description, quality, fitness and sample

As against a person dealing as consumer (see below), the implied undertakings as to conformity with description, sample, quality and fitness, contained in sections 13, 14 and 15 of the 1979 Act (sale of goods) and sections 9, 10 and 11 of the 1973 Act (hire-purchase), are non-excludable by virtue of section 6(2) of the 1977 Act. Similarly, the equivalent terms for work and materials and barter (ss 3, 4 and 5 of the 1982 Act) and hire (ss 8, 9 and 10 of the 1982 Act) are non-excludable (s 7(2) of the 1977 Act).

In all cases where a person is not dealing as consumer the implied undertakings are excludable if the term satisfies a reasonableness test (s 6(3) of the 1977 Act for sale of goods and hire purchase, s 7(3) for supply of goods contracts).

Before examining what is meant by 'deals as consumer', it is worth noting that, whilst section 7 of the 1977 Act only applies to business liability (see s 1(3) and above), section 6 applies to *all* contracts of sale and hire-purchase, not purely those containing 'business liability' (s 6(4)). Thus exemption clauses inserted in contracts for sale of goods between two private individuals will be affected by section 6.

'Dealing as consumer'

Section 12(1) indicates that a person 'deals as consumer' in relation to another party if a) he neither makes the contract in the course of a business nor holds himself out as doing so; and b) the other party does make the contract in the course of a business; and c) in the case of contracts of sale of goods, hire-purchase, or the miscellaneous contracts such as hire, barter and exchange obliquely referred to by section 7 of the 1977 Act, the goods in question are of a type 'ordinarily supplied for private use or consumption'. Sales by auction or competitive tender are excluded.[16] It is for those claiming that a party does not deal as a consumer to show that he does not (s 12(3)).

---

15 As amended by s 17(3) of the 1982 Act.
16 Section 12(2). It is important to note that it is standard practice in salerooms to stipulate that lots must be taken with all faults and misdescriptions, any statements as to description being statements of opinion only. There is sometimes a right to return deliberate forgeries within a stipulated short period. The position is extensively discussed in Harvey & Meisel *Auctions Law and Practice* (2nd edn).

A problem to which the disparate treatment of consumer and non-consumer sales might give rise is that, whilst a consumer can ignore a purported exemption clause caught by section 6 of the 1977 Act, a retailer who buys from a wholesaler or manufacturer may find that the clause is binding on the 'reasonableness' test. It is unlikely that a retailer (if without insurance) in similar circumstances to the one in *Godley v Perry*[17] would be in a position to bear heavy damages. This would, in turn, gravely prejudice the consumer in the absence of an alternative right of action against an intermediate wholesaler, or the manufacturer – who could be abroad and difficult to sue.

With regard to consumer sales with which we are primarily concerned, it should be noted that sales by private sellers of second-hand goods are not 'in the course of a business'. Such a seller would only be free, when selling to a consumer, to exclude or restrict the implied term of compliance with description under section 13 of the 1979 Act if the term was reasonable. The other implied terms of satisfactory quality and fitness are not applicable in this situation. The buyer must also not be one buying, or holding out to be buying in course of a business, for example for resale. Problems may arise in deciding whether, for example, a professional person buying an asset partly for business and partly for private use (such as a doctor's car) would be buying the asset 'in the course of a business'. However, two decisions suggest that the courts apply the provision liberally in the consumer's interest. In *R & B Customs Brokers Co Ltd v United Dominions Trust Ltd (Saunders Abbott (1980) Ltd, third party)*[18] a new car was bought from the defendants on credit. The claimants, as purchasers, were a private company of shipping brokers, and the car was for the directors of the company. The car proved defective in that it leaked. The court held that the claimants were 'dealing as a consumer' and thus the exclusion clause (which specifically did not apply to a buyer who dealt as consumer) was inoperative. Applying the criminal case of *Davies v Sumner*,[19] a case concerning the Trade Descriptions Act 1968, section 1; the court took the view that to fall outside the category of a consumer sale by virtue of the company's buying in the course of business, the buying of cars must form at the very least an integral part of the buyer's business. If only incidental to the business, a sufficient degree of regularity is required. Only in those circumstances could the buyer be said to be on an equal footing with the seller.[20] In the words of Dillon LJ:

17   [1960] 1 All ER 36, [1960] 1 WLR 9, QBD; M, H & P p 357, considered above, p 100.
18   [1988] 1 All ER 847, [1988] 1 WLR 321, CA.
19   [1984] 3 All ER 831, [1984] 1 WLR 1301, HL; M, H & P p 611, see p 386.
20   A similar result was achieved in the earlier case of *Peter Symmons & Co Ltd v Cook* (1981) 131 NLJ 758, QBD. See further 'Business or Consumer? A Trap for the Unwary' D Parry (1988) 6 Trad Law 270; I Brown 'Business or Consumer?'

Exemption clauses and unfair terms

... there are some transactions which are clearly integral parts of the business concerned, and these should be held to have been carried out in the course of those businesses; this would cover, apart from much else, the instance of a one-off adventure in the nature of trade where the transaction itself would constitute a trade or business. There are other transactions, however, such as the purchase of the car in the present case, which are at the highest only incidental to the carrying on of the relevant business; here a degree of regularity is required before it can be said that they are an integral part of the business carried on and so entered into in the course of that business.[1]

A further illustration of the fact that the apparent status of the buyer can be misleading, arises in *Rasbora Ltd v JCL Marine Ltd*.[2] Here a private individual contracted to buy a boat which was later sold to a company incorporated in Jersey by the buyer, for the purpose of the transaction, thus avoiding VAT. The original contract was clearly a consumer sale and the court held that, despite the substitution of the corporation as the final buyer, this did not alter the character of the original transaction to a non-consumer sale. The position under the 1977 Act is to be contrasted with that under section 14(2) and (3) of the Sale of Goods Act 1979 as decided in *Stevenson v Rogers*.[3]

Section 12 of the 1977 Act also stipulates that the goods must be of a type ordinarily supplied for private use or consumption. It will normally be clear into which category goods fall; a motor car or television set will qualify but a lorry or a large computer would be unlikely to. The word 'ordinarily' could conceivably give rise to problems over the years as buying patterns change.

Reasonableness

The concept of reasonableness is incorporated into exemption clauses in non-consumer transactions under sections 6(3) and 7(3) of the 1977 Act. Section 11 of that Act provides the explanations of the test. Section 11(5) makes it clear that:

> it is for those claiming that a contract term or notice satisfies the requirement of reasonableness to show that it does.

---

1   [1988] JBL 386; and discussion of the Consumer Transactions (Restrictions on Statements) Order 1976, SI 1976/1813, below at p 135.
1   At pp 854, 330.
2   [1977] 1 Lloyd's Rep 645, QBD.
3   [1999] QB 1028, [1999] 1 All ER 613, CA; see p 98.

Thus the clause is deemed unreasonable unless proved otherwise.[4]

The basic test of reasonableness for a contract term is:

> that the term shall have been a fair and reasonable one to be included having regard to the circumstances which were, or ought reasonably to have been, known to or in the contemplation of the parties when the contract was made (section 11(1)).

Section 11(2) specifies that for sections 6 and 7, in assessing whether the clause is then reasonable, regard should be had to the matters specified in Schedule 2 to the 1977 Act. These 'guidelines' are (summarised):

a) the relative strength of the bargaining positions of the parties, taking into account alternative means by which the customer's requirements could have been met;

b) whether the customer 'received an inducement to agree to the term', or whether he could have entered into a similar contract with other persons not containing such a term;

c) whether the customer knew or ought reasonably to have known of the existence and extent of the term (having regard, among other things, to any trade custom or previous course of dealing);

d) if liability is excluded if some condition is not complied with (eg giving notice of a claim within a time limit), whether it was reasonable to expect that compliance with that condition would be practicable;

e) whether the goods were manufactured, processed or adapted to the special order of the customer.

In addition where the restriction relates to a person's liability to pay a maximum sum of money, regard must be had to the resources available to him to meet the anticipated liability, and to how far it was open to him to insure against the risk (s 11(4)).[5]

Two cases examined the reasonableness of clauses under section 55(4) and (5) of the Sale of Goods Act 1893/1979 (the predecessors of section 6 of the 1977 Act). In *R W Green Ltd v Cade Bros Farms* the terms of a contract of sale limiting liability to repay the price between seed potato merchants and a farming business were upheld as being reasonable. The ground was that the form of contract had been in use for many years with the approval of the negotiating bodies acting on behalf of both seed potato merchants and farmers.[6] The *Cade* case was distinguished in *George Mitchell*

---

4   See *AEG (UK) Ltd v Logic Resource Ltd* [1996] CLC 265; see also (1997) 60 MLR 582, (Bradgate) and *Sheffield v Pickfords Ltd* (1997) 16 Tr LR 337, CA.

5   Product liability insurance of £50 million made a limitation clause of £100,000 appear unreasonable in *St Albans and District Council v International Computers Ltd* [1996] 4 All ER 481, CA.

6   [1978] 1 Lloyd's Rep 602, QBD. A term imposing a short time limit for claims was, however, held unreasonable as to latent defects.

(Chesterhall) Ltd v Finney Lock Seeds Ltd [7] where the defendants sought to limit liability for supplying cabbage seeds which proved to be commercially useless. Here the clause had been inserted, by the seed merchants, without negotiation with the farmers and there had been negligence on the part of the seed merchants or their suppliers. Factors considered by the House of Lords included the relative bargaining strength of the parties, the opportunity to buy seeds without a limitation of liability, the ease and cheapness of insurance available to the defendants and the defendants' negligence. In particular the court, in deciding the clause was unreasonable, noted that in other cases of seed failure a negotiated settlement in excess of the limitations imposed would be agreed with an aggrieved farmer, though this had not been achieved in this case. Lord Bridge examined the role of the appellate court in assessing the reasonableness of a clause and said:

> … the court must entertain a whole range of considerations, put them in the scales on one side or the other and decide at the end of the day on which side the balance comes down. There will sometimes be room for a legitimate difference of judicial opinion as to what the answer should be, where it will be impossible to say that one view is demonstrably wrong and the other demonstrably right. It must follow, in my view, that, when asked to review such a decision on appeal, the appellate court should treat the original decision with the utmost respect and refrain from interference with it unless satisfied that it proceeded on some erroneous principle or was plainly and obviously wrong.[8]

Liability arising in contract

The 1977 Act also attempts to deal with exemption clauses purporting to relieve the party in breach from the consequences of that breach. Section 3 applies where one party to a contract deals as a consumer or on the other's written standard terms of business. As against that party, the other cannot by reference to any contract term a) when himself in breach of contract, exclude or restrict any liability of his in respect of the breach; or b) claim to be entitled either to render a contractual performance substantially different from that which was reasonably expected of him; or c) in respect of the whole or any part of his contractual obligation, render no performance at all, except, in any of the cases mentioned above, in so far as the contract

---

7   [1983] QB 284, [1983] 1 All ER 108, CA; M, H & P p 319; affd [1983] 2 AC 803, [1983] 2 All ER 737, HL; M, H & P p 365.
8   [1983] 2 AC 803 at 816, [1983] 2 All ER 737 at 743; M, H & P p 365.

term satisfies the requirement of reasonableness. The requirement of reasonableness is partly the same as that discussed above. This is that the term shall have been a fair and reasonable one to be included having regard to the circumstances which were, or ought reasonably to have been, known to or in the contemplation of the parties when the contract was made (s 11(1)). There is, however, no specific requirement to refer to the guidelines in Schedule 2, although reference has been made in a number of cases.[9]

Section 3 gives rise to a number of difficulties of interpretation. It will be seen that the section applies in two circumstances; firstly where one of the contracting parties deals as a consumer (as defined by s 12 of the Act above); and secondly the section applies where one party contracts on the other's written standard terms of business. There is no statutory definition of 'written standard terms of business'. The Law Commission's original comment (see Law Com No 69, para 157) explains why: 'We think that the courts are well able to recognise standard terms used by persons in the course of their business, and that any attempt to lay down a precise definition of "standard form contract" would leave open the possibility that terms that were clearly contained in a standard form might fall outside the definition.' This issue would only be of importance where both parties were businessmen, since a person dealing as a consumer is already protected. It is thought that the phrase would cover standard form contracts prepared by professional and trade associations to be used by all those engaged in the relevant profession or trade and those prepared by individual contractors for use in all cases. Stannard J in *Chester Grosvenor Hotel Co Ltd v Alfred McAlpine Management Ltd*[10] stated: 'What is required for terms to be standard is that they should be regarded by the party which advances them as its standard terms and that it should habitually contract in those terms.' It is common to find such standard form contracts in daily use in commerce, both as to conditions of sale and conditions of purchase. Occasionally it can be difficult to establish which of two conflicting sets of standard conditions have actually been incorporated in the contract – see *Butler Machine Tool Co Ltd v Ex-Cell-O Corpn (England) Ltd*.[11]

A second problem of interpretation concerns the nature of the exemption clauses covered by this section and which are subject to the requirement of reasonableness. Taking each in turn, with regard to clauses which, when one party is in breach of contract, exclude or restrict any liability of his in

9   See eg *Rees Hough Ltd v Redland Reinforced Plastics Ltd* (1984) 27 BLR 136, QBD; *Keeton Sons & Co Ltd v Carl Prior Ltd* [1986] BTLC 30, CA, cited in Law Com No 156 (1986) para 3.8; *Stewart Gill Ltd v Horatio Myer & Co Ltd* [1992] QB 600, [1992] 2 All ER 257, CA.
10   (1991) 56 BLR 115, QBD (Official Referee's business).
11   [1979] 1 All ER 965, [1979] 1 WLR 401, CA.

respect of the breach, this is essentially aimed at the restriction of the exercise of rights or remedies to which the other party might otherwise then be entitled. Examples are provisions in carriage contracts that the carrier shall not be liable for loss from a consignment unless advised of the loss in writing within seven days from the date of delivery, or a term in a building contract that the builder's liability for failure to complete within the contract period shall not exceed £X. In *St Albans City and District Council v International Computers Ltd*[12] an unsuccessful attempt was made to limit liability for unsatisfactory computer software to £100,000, when losses of £1.3 million were caused. The clause was judged unreasonable on the grounds of unequal bargaining power. The defendants were insured and were better loss bearers and the figure of £100,000 could not be justified, both because a higher limit of £125,000 was then currently used and, in any event, the amount was small considering potential risk and absolute loss.

With regard to the other types of exemption clause mentioned in this section, an example of rendering a contractual performance substantially different from that which was reasonably expected of him would be the circumstances in issue in the case of *Anglo-Continental Holidays Ltd v Typaldos (London) Ltd*.[13] The facts of the case occurred before the Unfair Contract Terms Act 1977 came into force. The defendant travel agents agreed to book, for the claimants, cruises on a named ship following a fixed itinerary. There was a clause, printed on the back of their handbook, which read: 'Steamers, Sailing Dates, Rates, and Itineraries are subject to change without prior notice'. On the basis of this clause, the defendants offered the claimants cruises on a different ship following a different itinerary. In the event the Court of Appeal held, probably as a matter of construction, that the defendants could not rely on the clause to alter the substance of the arrangement. Minor variations in itineraries, or in other contracts for goods or services, would probably be excluded from the scope of this section by the use of the words 'substantially' and 'reasonably'.

With regard to the purported exclusion of liability for rendering no performance at all in respect of the whole or any part of a person's contractual obligation; it is probably already the position at common law that a clause purporting to exclude all one's obligations is void, since this would amount to a mere declaration of intent – see *Firestone Tyre and*

12 [1995] FSR 686, QBD; affd [1996] 4 All ER 481, CA. See also E Macdonald 'The Council, the Computer and the Unfair Contract Terms Act 1977' (1995) 58 MLR 585.

13 [1967] 2 Lloyd's Rep 61, CA; M, H & P p 351. See also *Askew v Intasun North Ltd* [1980] CLY 637. The county court held in this case that a clause in the defendants' brochure, entitling the defendants to change the place of holiday, did not exclude liability since it was inadequately worded.

Rubber Co v Vokins & Co Ltd.[14] This principle would not necessarily apply to the question of non-performance of part only of the contractual obligation. The Law Commission, in the explanatory notes to their draft Bill in similar language to the form that the 1977 Act eventually took, comment that 'this would apply to various terms excusing non-performance or entitling a party to cancel a contract'. (See also paras 141–146, on which the above examples are founded.) It must finally be emphasised that such exemption clauses are not void but are deemed to be unreasonable until the person relying on the contract term or notice in question satisfies the court to the contrary on the basis of the statutory definition of the reasonableness test.

In the construction of section 3, there is every reason to think that courts would be more likely to regard such clauses as being reasonable where the contract is a commercial one between two traders of roughly equal bargaining power than where the party complaining was dealing as a consumer. In *Stag Line Ltd v Tyne Shiprepair Group Ltd, The Zinnia*[15] the clause in question sought to exclude liability for economic loss which arose after wrong materials were used in the repair of a ship. The court, in view of the bargaining positions of the two business parties, decided the clause was reasonable. The views of Lord Wilberforce in *Photo Production Ltd v Securicor Transport Ltd*,[16] where he favoured commercial undertakings of equal bargaining strength being allowed to apportion the risk as they wished, were supported.

Since the passing of the 1977 Act some abuses relating to void exclusion clauses have continued and attracted the attention of the Director General of Fair Trading. In particular, a seller might be tempted to purport to exclude a buyer's right to reject defective goods by a 'no refunds' notice, or any other notice purporting to take away the rights conferred by the sale of goods legislation ('goods returned for credit notes only', 'once sold goods may not be returned' were once common examples). Many consumers, being ignorant of their rights, would be disposed to accept this. As a result of a proposal by the Director and a supporting Report of the Consumer Protection Advisory Committee in 1974, an order was made under the Fair Trading Act 1973, section 22.[17] This makes it a criminal offence in the case of sale of goods or hire-purchase to display this type of notice, or display similar advertisements – or label goods and containers with similar notices.[18] It is also an offence to supply statements either about the

14 [1951] 1 Lloyd's Rep 32.
15 [1984] 2 Lloyd's Rep 211, Commercial Court, QBD.
16 [1980] AC 827, [1980] 1 All ER 556, HL.
17 Consumer Transactions (Restrictions on Statements) Order 1976, SI 1976/1813, as amended by SI 1978/27; BSSCCL p 701.
18 In *Hughes v Hall* [1981] RTR 430, QBD, M, H & P p 385, sales of second-hand cars 'sold as seen and inspected' were held to infringe the terms of this order

retailer's obligations to the buyer or to supply statements made by third parties (eg in manufacturers' guarantees) unless that statement is accompanied by a further statement that the consumer's statutory rights are not affected. The offence carries a maximum penalty of £5,000 on summary conviction and a fine or imprisonment not exceeding two years, or both, on conviction on indictment (Fair Trading Act 1973, s 23, as amended). There is no such protection for contracts governed by the Supply of Goods and Services Act 1982.

The comparative absence of legislative protection given to buyers from private sellers can also be abused by a business seller purporting to be a private seller and contacting buyers through classified advertisements in newspapers. This practice was referred to the CPAC by the Director. The supporting CPAC Report[19] resulted in the Business Advertisements (Disclosure) Order 1977[20] similarly making non-disclosure of business status a criminal offence.

Misrepresentations

The 1977 Act (s 8) also amended the statutory provisions dealing with clauses exempting a party to a contract from liability for misrepresentations by substituting a new section 3 into the Misrepresentation Act 1967 (and a new s 8 into the Misrepresentation Act (Northern Ireland) 1967). The former provision stated that any such exemption clause must be 'fair and reasonable', the criteria for which were not stated. This section was criticised, but has given rise to little litigation.

Section 3 now reads as follows:

If a contract contains a term which would exclude or restrict
a)   any liability to which a party to a contract may be subject by reason of any misrepresentation made by him before the contract was made; or

---

since prima facie such a phrase negates the implied condition of compliance with description under the Sale of Goods Act 1979, s 13. In contrast *in Cavendish Woodhouse Ltd v Manley* (1984) 82 LGR 376, QBD, the words 'bought as seen' were held not to amount to an offence as they reflected the fact that the customer had seen the goods he bought, the sale not being one by description. See further E Jacobs 'The Pitfalls of Consumer Protection' (1985) 4 Tr L 297; R G Lawson 'Consumer Transactions (Restrictions on Statements) Order' (1986) 150 JPN 420; D Parry 'Criminal Controls over Exemption Clauses and Guarantees' (1990) 2 Law for Business 307.

19   *Disguised Business Sales*, HC Paper (1976) No 355. See further the discussion of the Fair Trading Act 1973 in ch 11.

20   SI 1977/1918; M, H & P pp 543–547; BSSCCL p 704. See also *Blakemore v Bellamy* [1983] RTR 303, QBD; M, H & P p 544; Harvey (1983) 127 Sol Jo 163 and 179; Edmondson (1983) 147 JPN 309; Bragg (1983) 91 ITSA MR 182.

b) any remedy available to another party to the contract by reason of such a misrepresentation,

that term shall be of no effect except in so far as it satisfies the requirement of reasonableness as stated in section 11(1) of the Unfair Contract Terms Act 1977; and it is for those claiming that the term satisfies that requirement to show that it does.

In the 1977 Act no guidelines for the interpretation of the substituted section 3 above are given except that the term must have been a fair and reasonable one to be included having regard to the circumstances which were, or ought reasonably to have been, known to or in the contemplation of the parties when the contract was made (s 11(1)). There now exists some judicial guidance as to the way these provisions (both pre and post the 1977 substitution) are to be construed. In *Overbrooke Estates Ltd v Glencombe Properties Ltd*[1] a clause, limiting the authority of auctioneers and the firm's employees to make or give representations or warranties, was held to fall outside the scope of the original version of section 3 since it was a limitation on the apparent authority of the auctioneers rather than an exemption clause. This case was followed in *Collins v Howell-Jones.*[2] In *Cremdean Properties Ltd v Nash*[3] and *Howard Marine and Dredging Co Ltd v A Ogden & Sons (Excavations) Ltd*[4] the court expressed the view that the clauses in question with respect to exemption from liability for misrepresentations were unreasonable.

Moving now to cases decided on section 3 as substituted by the 1977 Act, in a decision of great potential importance for conveyancers, *Walker v Boyle*,[5] Dillon J held that in the circumstances of this case a standard condition in the National Conditions of Sale (19th edn), which stated that 'without prejudice to any express right of either party or to any right of the purchaser in reliance on section 24 of the Law of Property Act 1969 to rescind the contract before completion, no error, misstatement or omission in any preliminary answer concerning the property . . . shall annul the sale' was ineffective to exempt from liability for a pre-contractual misstatement. The misstatement by the vendor was as to the absence of any boundary dispute, this being the subject matter of a specific preliminary enquiry by the purchaser. There was in fact a boundary dispute, the existence of which persuaded the purchaser not to proceed with the purchase after exchange of contracts. Dillon J said that the standard condition of sale in question did not meet the requirements of fairness and reasonableness required by

1 [1974] 3 All ER 511, [1974] 1 WLR 1335, Ch D.
2 [1981] 2 EGLR 108, CA; see Murdoch (1981) 97 LQR 522.
3 (1977) 244 Estates Gazette 547, CA; M, H & P p 360.
4 [1978] QB 574, [1978] 2 All ER 1134, CA.
5 [1982] 1 All ER 634, [1982] 1 WLR 495, Ch D. See Aldridge (1981) 125 Sol Jo 731.

section 11 of the 1977 Act. He ordered that the deposit paid by the purchaser should be returned with interest and the contract rescinded. Most conveyancing transactions were subject either to the National Conditions of Sale mentioned above or to the Law Society's Conditions of Sale. In March 1990 these were replaced by the Standard Conditions of Sale (1st edn). Condition 7.1.3 of the 3rd edition (1995) now entitles rescission of the contract only:

a) where the error or omission results from fraud or recklessness

or

b) where he would otherwise be obliged, to his prejudice, to transfer or accept property differing substantially (in quantity, quality or tenure) from what the error or omission had led him to expect.

It remains to be seen whether or not this satisfies the reasonableness test.

A further example of an exclusion clause failing to satisfy the reasonableness test of section 3 occurs in *South Western General Property Co Ltd v Marton*.[6] Here a clause which purported to exclude liability for a misrepresentation, that land sold at an auction could be used for building on providing a planning application was made, was not shown to be reasonable in a contract with a private purchaser of the land.

The above decisions show the willingness of the courts to interpret the wide guidelines laid down by the Act in a sensible manner and in the interests of the consumer. The policy embodied in the Act of 'leaving it to the courts' has, however, not always attracted judicial support. Lord Hailsham described some of the 1977 Act's provisions as 'ban-yan tree justice' when debating it as a Bill. The 1977 Act has forced sellers of goods to consumers to live without the exemption clauses which were almost automatically inserted in many standard form contracts before 1973, and this is a welcome development. The matter is not so straightforward as between two businessmen of equal economic power, since the allocation of deliberately assumed risks can be carefully costed and insured against. This is not an area where there is any obvious moral basis for interference by the legislature.

Unfair Terms in Consumer Contracts Regulations 1999[7]

Introduction

As indicated earlier, the 1999 Regulations were introduced, from 1 October 1999, to replace the Unfair Terms in Consumer Contracts Regulations 1994,[8]

---

6   [1982] 2 EGLR 19, QBD.
7   SI 1999/2083.
8   SI 1994/3159.

which had first implemented the EC Directive on unfair terms in consumer contracts.[9] Although the Directive was required to be implemented by 31 December 1994, the 1994 Regulations only came into force on 1 July 1995. Any disputes regarding the Regulations must be decided in accordance with the Directive on which they are based, with rulings from the European Court being used, where necessary.

The provisions are in addition to the pre-existing common law and statutory controls under the 1977 Act as discussed above; therefore often reference to three different aspects of the law will be needed to assess whether or not a particular clause is binding on both parties to a contract.

Although, for convenience, discussion of the 1999 Regulations is located here, in connection with exemption clauses, and particularly in relation to the supply of goods, it is important to realise that the 1999 Regulations are not confined to exclusion clauses, but may apply to the majority of terms in particular contracts. Further, the contracts concerned need not involve the supply of goods; the supply of services will suffice.

Required parties

The 1999 Regulations apply to 'consumers' who deal with 'sellers or suppliers', as defined in regulation 3(1). A 'consumer' is a 'natural person who, in contracts covered by these Regulations, is acting for purposes which are outside his trade, business or profession.' From this it can be seen that companies and partnerships cannot be 'consumers' under the 1999 Regulations, which is to be contrasted with the position under section 12 of the 1977 Act.[10] A 'seller or supplier' must, when making the contract in question, be 'acting for purposes relating to his trade, business or profession, whether publicly owned or privately owned.' Transactions by private sellers and suppliers and business sellers and suppliers, when acting in a private capacity, are, therefore, excluded.[11] It is interesting to note that the DTI Guide on the 1994 Regulations suggested[12] that a business which *buys* from a consumer, for example a second-hand car dealer, can be a 'seller.' Reference was made to the French version of the Directive, which refers to 'consumers and professionals.'

9 93/13/EEC, OJ No L 95, 21.4.93, p 29. The Commission has published a report: *On the Implementation of Council Directive 93/13/EEC of 5 April 1993 on Unfair Terms in Consumer Contracts*, 27/4/00, COM(2000)248 final. This includes consultation on proposed changes to the Directive.

10 See, in particular, *R & B Customs Brokers Co Ltd v United Dominions Trust Ltd (Saunders Abbott (1980) Ltd, third party)* [1988] 1 All ER 847, [1988] 1 WLR 321, CA, M, H & P p 357; discussed above p 129.

11 Compare with s 6(4) of the 1977 Act, above p 128.

12 *The Unfair Terms in Consumer Contracts Regulations 1994 Guidance Notes*, DTI, July 1995, para 4.8.

Included contracts

The contract concerned must involve the sale or supply of goods or the supply of a service and there must be a 'consumer' and a business 'seller or supplier'. Contracts of insurance are clearly included,[13] and transfers of land appear also to be covered.[14]

Qualifying terms

Rather than concentrating on looking at the whole of the contract, the 1999 Regulations focus on the individual terms in a contract. Only certain terms qualify for protection. By regulation 5(1), the Regulations apply to any 'contractual term which has not been individually negotiated.' The Regulations are not, therefore, confined to exemption clauses. Regulation 5(2) provides that a term is not individually negotiated 'where it has been drafted in advance and the consumer has therefore not been able to influence the substance of the term.' Clearly the terms in standard form contracts are covered, as will be standard terms used regularly by the seller or supplier and even any standard terms which are used occasionally. It is up to the seller or supplier to show the term was individually negotiated.[15] Even if specific terms or certain aspects of a particular term have been individually negotiated, the Regulations still apply to the remainder of the contract if 'an overall assessment of it indicates that it is a pre-formulated standard contract.'[16]

Exempted terms

Even where a term has not been individually negotiated and so is a qualifying term, there are two types of term which are exempted by regulation 4(2). First is where the term reflects mandatory statutory or regulatory provisions, including provisions under the law of any member state or in Community legislation which has effect in the United Kingdom without further enactment. The DTI, in its consultation on a review of the Directive,[17] suggests that there are three possible interpretations of this. First, only provisions *required* by legislation to be included in contracts would be

13 Compare with Sch 1, para 1(a) of the 1977 Act.
14 See DTI *1995 Guide* paras 3.19–3.20 and *Unfair Contracts Terms Bulletin Issue 8*, December 1999, OFT 291, para 1.6.
15 Reg 5(4).
16 Reg 5(3).
17 *European Commission Review of Directive 93/13/EEC on Unfair Terms in Consumer Contracts: A Consultation paper*, DTI, July 2000, paras 3.9–3.16.

excluded. A second interpretation would include all terms whose use is required or expressly permitted by law, to the extent that they do not exceed what is required or permitted. An example could be terms inserted to comply with the Package Travel, Package Holidays and Package Tours Regulations 1992.[18] Finally it could mean all terms which ultimately derive from a provision in a statute are excluded. Contract terms of commercial suppliers which have been approved by an administrative authority acting under statutory approval, for example Ofgem, Ofwat etc, or, possibly, rules of self-regulatory organisations, for example for financial services or insurance, could then fall within this exclusion. The Commission is currently considering removal of this exemption. The second exclusion is of terms which reflect provisions or principles of international conventions to which the member states or the Community are party.

Effects of the 1999 Regulations

The Regulations have two main effects: they regulate the *clarity of language used* in terms and the *fairness* of terms. By regulation 7 written terms of contracts (providing they are not exempted terms) must be 'expressed in plain, intelligible language.' There is no indication provided as to whose standards are to apply in testing the intelligibility of a term – ie is it the reasonable consumer, lawyer, seller etc? The Office of Fair Trading interprets this as 'within the understanding of ordinary consumers without legal advice'.[19] It might appear to be up to the consumer to challenge the clarity of the term, although this is not specified. A ruling from the European Court of Justice[20] suggests that national courts have the power to raise the *unfairness* of a jurisdiction clause on their own initiative, as consumers may often be ignorant of the protection afforded them. This principle may, in due course, be extended to permit the court's intervention for any ambiguous or unfair term. No direct sanctions are indicated. All regulation 7 states is that where there is doubt over the meaning of a written term 'the interpretation which is most favourable to the consumer shall prevail.' It will depend on case law developments to decide whether or not a totally obscure term may simply be ignored by the consumer.

18 SI 1992/3288, BSSCCL p 766. See further ch 7 p 206.
19 *Unfair Contracts Terms Bulletin No 2*, OFT, September 1996, para 2.13.
20 *Oceano Grupo Editorial SA v Quintero* C-240/98 (27 June 2000, unreported), ECJ; (2000) 23 Consumer Law Today, Issue 8, p 1.

Exemption clauses and unfair terms

Fairness

This is the most significant aspect of the Regulations as unfair terms in contracts between consumers and sellers or suppliers are not binding on consumers (reg 8). It is to be noted first that two types of otherwise 'qualifying' terms are excluded from the fairness test by regulation 6(2): any which relate to 'the definition of the main subject matter of the contract' or which concern 'the adequacy of the price or remuneration, as against the goods or services supplied in exchange'. These are often referred to as 'core terms or provisions'. [1] There are few complications regarding the pricing aspect but much more debate arises over core terms defining the subject matter of the contract.[2] For example in the insurance field deciding which terms are defining the insured risk and which are excluding liability or regulating the claims process may be difficult.

It is now necessary to examine closely the test of unfairness laid down in regulation 5. There are three requirements: a term is unfair if (1) contrary to the requirements of good faith, it (2) causes a significant imbalance in the parties' rights and obligations arising under the contract, (3) to the detriment of the consumer. All three requirements must be satisfied before a term is considered unfair. In applying the fairness test, regulation 6(1) requires consideration of the nature of the goods or services involved and, viewed at the time the contract was made, all the circumstances attending the making of the contract, all other terms of the contract (which may include the 'core provisions', such as price) and any other contract on which it is dependent (for example a guarantee contract).

Good faith

The 1994 Regulations included, in Schedule 2, guidance on the requirement of 'good faith', a concept which is not very familiar to English lawyers, unlike their continental counterparts.[3] This included the strength of the bargaining positions of the parties; any inducements to agree to the term; special orders of the consumer, and the extent to which the seller or supplier

1   For an unsuccessful argument that a term, regarding the interest to be paid by a borrower in default on a loan, was a core term see *Director General of Fair Trading v First National Bank plc* [2000] 2 All ER 759, CA, discussed below at p 144.

2   See, for example, regarding the 1994 Regulations: R Brownsword and G Howells 'Implementation of the EC Directive on Unfair Terms in Consumer Contracts – Some Unresolved Questions' [1995] JBL 243; E Macdonald 'Mapping the Unfair Contract Terms Act 1977 and the Directive on Unfair Terms in Consumer Contracts [1994] JBL 441.

3   See further Beatson and Friedmann (eds) *Good Faith and Fault in Contract Law*, M, H & P p 338; R Brownsword, N J Hurd and G Howells (eds) *Good Faith in Contract*.

had dealt fairly and equitably with the consumer. These provisions have not been re-enacted in the 1999 Regulations; no specific elaboration has been included. The Department of Trade and Industry previously indicated that it took the view that 'the key element of the test of fairness is that of good faith and that where a seller or supplier has dealt fairly and equitably with a consumer, that requirement will be satisfied.'[4] If a seller or supplier has dealt fairly with a consumer, then although there is a significant imbalance (even if detrimental to the consumer) in the parties' positions under the contract, it would appear that, nevertheless, the term in question would not be 'unfair'.

Schedule 2 of the Regulations (reproduced verbatim from the Directive) provides an extensive 'indicative and non-exhaustive' list of terms which 'may be regarded as unfair'. It is important to stress the fact that this list is for guidance only and the use of such terms may be judged to be fair in particular circumstances. Examples include unilateral alterations by the seller or supplier without valid reasons (paras 1(j) and (k)), excluding or limiting the seller's or supplier's liability in cases of death or personal injury caused by an act or omission of the seller or supplier (para 1(a)), and obliging the consumer to fulfil all his obligations where the seller or supplier does not perform his (para 1(o)).

Although the Regulations specify that an unfair term will not be binding upon the consumer, there is no indication of where the burden of proving or disproving the fairness lies. It would appear to be up to a consumer who wishes to challenge the fairness of a term to prove that it is unfair.[5] This is to be contrasted with section 11(5) of the 1977 Act. Providing the remainder of the contract can continue in the absence of a term proved to be unfair, the contract continues (reg 8(2)).

Director General's role

So far the 1999 Regulations have been considered from the point of view of a claim by a consumer in an individual contract. Regulation 10 provides another method of dealing with unfair terms, involving the Director General of Fair Trading. The Director is under a duty, very similar to that under the Control of Misleading Advertisements Regulations 1988,[6] to consider complaints made to him that a contract term drawn up for general use is unfair. If he considers it appropriate to do so, the Director may either accept undertakings about the use of such a term or may seek an injunction to prevent the use of that term (reg 12). In granting an injunction, the court

---

4   DTI *1995 Guide* para AI.4.
5   DTI *1995 Guide* para 5.3.
6   SI 1988/915, as amended by SI 2000/914; see further p 46.

has power to refer to any similar term or a term having like effect used or recommended by any person (reg 12(4)).

In the first application for an injunction, *Director General of Fair Trading v First National Bank plc*,[7] the Director was successful, on appeal, in establishing that the term was unfair and the court accepted an undertaking from the bank to incorporate amendments to their contract terms. The term in question concerned the payment of interest at a variable contractual rate on the outstanding capital of a loan and on accrued unpaid interest existing at the date of judgment for default. Peter Gibson LJ, in discussing the requirement of good faith said:

> 29. As aptly said in *Anson's Law of Contract* (27th edn, 1998) p 293, the 'good faith' element seeks to promote fair and open dealing, and to prevent unfair surprise and the absence of real choice. A term to which the consumer's attention is not specifically drawn but which may operate in a way in which the consumer might reasonably not expect and to his disadvantage may offend the requirement of good faith. Terms must be reasonably transparent and should not operate to defeat the reasonable expectations of the consumer. The consumer in choosing whether to enter into a contract should be put in the position where he can make an informed choice.
>
> 30. The element of significant imbalance would appear to overlap substantially with that of the absence of good faith. A term which gives a significant advantage to the seller or supplier without a countervailing benefit to the consumer (such as a price reduction) might fail to satisfy this part of the test of an unfair term.
>
> 31. Finally the element of detriment to the consumer must be present for the term to be found to be unfair. [at p 769]

The Director has power to obtain documents and information (reg 13), and to provide advice and information on the Regulations (reg 15). The Office of Fair Trading has issued guidance notes and regular bulletins on the contract terms it has investigated.[8] The latest figures[9] show that, to the end of June 1999, the OFT considered 4,140 complaints, of which 682

---

7   [2000] 2 All ER 759, CA, reversing [2000] 1 All ER 240, QBD. The case was brought under reg 8 of the 1994 Regulations, the predecessor of reg 12 of the 1999 Regulations.

8   *Unfair Standard Terms Briefing*, July 1995; *Unfair Contract Terms Bulletins: Issue 1*, May 1996, OFT 159; *Issue 2*, September 1996, OFT 170; *Issue 3*, March 1997, OFT 188; *Issue 4*, December 1997, OFT 202; *Issue 5*, October 1998, OFT 246; *Issue 6*, April 1999, OFT 262; *Issue 7*, July 1999, OFT 268; *Issue 8*, December 1999, OFT 291; *Unfair Contract Terms Guidance: Interest Variation Terms*, February 2000, OFT 297.

9   *Unfair Contract Terms Bulletins: Issue 8*, OFT 291, p 40.

were dealt with by advice or warnings, 361 were not considered unfair, 410 involved informal undertakings and eight involved formal undertakings. Others were not proceeded with because of duplication, defects in the complaints or were better dealt with under other legislation. 223 complaints rejected involved excluded terms and 185 'core' terms.

The bulletins indicate the considerable range of contracts examined by the OFT and the companies and organisations which have been involved, ranging from sole traders and small businesses to major companies such as Northern Rock Bank, British Telecommunications and BSkyB, universities and other educational establishments, societies and associations etc. The activities of the OFT have benefited many millions of consumers. Contracts by providers of satellite television services have undergone major changes. The National Audit Office estimated that investigations involving penalty clauses in loan and mortgage contracts and notice periods for mobile phones have saved consumers more than £100 million a year.[10] In addition the OFT has been active in approaching trade associations which provide model contracts for their members to ensure compliance.[11]

Qualifying bodies' role

Since the introduction of the 1999 Regulations, a number of other bodies are now able to seek injunctions, in addition to the Director. This was introduced, partly in response to an action commenced by the Consumers' Association in the European Court, challenging the implementation of the Directive and partly in anticipation of the Injunctions Directive[12] which includes the Unfair Terms in Consumer Contracts Directive as one requiring wider injunctive powers. Regulation 12(1) permits any 'qualifying body' to apply for an injunction, subject to notifying the Director at least 14 days previously or obtaining the Director's consent to an earlier application (reg 12(2)). Qualifying bodies are listed under Schedule 1 Part I as the Data Protection Registrar, the Director Generals of Electricity and Gas (including those for Northern Ireland), Telecommunications and Water Services, the

10 Reported by John Bridgeman 'Aiming True' (2000) 27 Fair Trading, p 11 at p 12.
11 These include the Glass and Glazing Federation – Northern Ireland, the Professional Photographic Laboratories Association, Association of British Travel Agents, the Kitchen Specialists' Association and the Federation of Recruitment and Employment Services.
12 98/27/EC, OJ No L 166, 11.6.98, p 51. See also *Injunctions Directive: Implementation in the UK*, DTI, February 2000; 'Widening the net', OFT (2000) 26 Fair Trading 13.

Rail Regulator, every weights and measures authority in Great Britain and the Department of Economic Development in Northern Ireland (now the Department of Enterprise, Trade and Investment). Schedule 1 Part II lists the Consumers' Association.

Qualifying bodies have an obligation to notify the Director of any undertakings given to them regarding unfair terms and the outcome of any injunction proceedings or applications to enforce previous court orders (reg 15). Those bodies listed under Schedule 1 Part I also have similar powers to the Director's to obtain documents and information (reg 13(2) and (3)). Agreements regarding joint enforcement of the regulations have been concluded between the Director and the Consumers' Association, OFTEL, local authorities and the Department of Enterprise, Trade and Investment in Northern Ireland.[13]

The 1994 Regulations, and their successor 1999 Regulations, have had a very considerable impact on the terms used in many contracts affecting large numbers of consumers. It is likely, with the increased number of bodies which can now be involved in enforcing the regulations, that in future an even greater impact will be observed. In the majority of consumer transactions now there is considerable opportunity for both individual consumers and consumer bodies to have a marked effect on the terms contained in such contracts.

13   See OFT Press Release PN 22/00, 22 June 2000; (2000) 27 Fair Trading 15 and 'Small-print watchdog set for big changes' (1999) 24 Fair Trading 26.

6 Product liability and tort-based remedies

I. NEGLIGENCE-BASED LIABILITY

The majority of consumer complaints concerning defective goods are made by purchasers whose expectations are disappointed and who are usually claiming for purely economic loss. The law is reasonably clear in this area and in practice the vast majority of complaints that would, if litigated, be under the Sale of Goods Act 1979 are settled. This is either because the result of any litigation is predictable and the cost of remedying the defect is comparatively small, or because, even if the complaint is doubtful or clearly unjustified – retailers often complain that customers damage their goods after purchase and bring trumped-up complaints – sellers wish to preserve their goodwill and avoid troublesome disputes. From the consumer's point of view, liability based on statutory implied terms in contract is, in practice, strict. Once the claimant has established unfitness or unsatisfactory quality, the claim cannot be defeated by a defence that all reasonable care was taken to prevent the defect.[1] It is perhaps surprising that English law should put liability for consequential loss and injury on the shoulders of the retailer when it might involve damages of many thousands of pounds[2] on a sale of a cheap article in these circumstances,[3] but there are undoubted advantages to the consumer. In addition, where there is no damage to persons or property and the complaint is that the goods are shoddy or inefficient, the consumer's remedies lie in contract and not in tort.

1 *Frost v Aylesbury Dairy Co* [1905] 1 KB 608, CA (typhoid in milk); *Wren v Holt* [1903] 1 KB 610, CA.
2 See *Godley v Perry* [1960] 1 All ER 36, [1960] 1 WLR 9, QBD, discussed in ch 5.
3 See Waddams 'Strict Liability, Warranties and the Sale of Goods' (1969) 19 Univ Toronto L Jo 157.

These contract-based remedies have been given a statutory basis since 1893 and had a common law one for many years before.[4] They suffer, as was mentioned above, from a defect fatal if the consumer does not happen to be the purchaser, or if the purchaser for some reason cannot or does not wish to sue the seller. Being contract-based, privity of contract is essential. The purchaser must be the person suffering the loss and who sues the seller under the 1979 Act. An exception would be if the purchaser can be shown to have been acting as agent for the injured consumer. Here, unless the purchaser was expressly authorised to contract for the principal, such a contract can only be ratified if the purchaser *at the time of making the contract* professed to contract on the principal's behalf.[5]

Contracts made on or after 11 May 2000, and falling under the provisions of the Contracts (Rights of Third Parties) Act 1999, also provide an exception to the privity requirements. Here, under section 1, a third party to a contract may enforce a term of the contract if the contract expressly so provides or if the term purports to confer a benefit on that person.[6] It is necessary for the third party expressly to be identified in the contract either by name, or as a member of a class or answering a particular description. An example of where this might apply is where gifts are purchased for specifically identified persons. The donees can legally act in their own right, instead of having to rely on the goodwill of the seller to deal directly with them or needing the donors to pursue breaches of statutory terms should the item prove defective. The Act does not, however, assist unidentified donees, non-contracting members of the household, guests, employees etc who may be injured by a defective product.

The case of *Daniels and Daniels v R White & Sons Ltd and Tarbard*[7] is often taken as an example of the problems of privity.[8] Mr Daniels purchased a bottle of lemonade from Mrs Tarbard, a publican. It had been manufactured by R White & Sons Ltd and contained a quantity of carbolic acid. Mr and Mrs Daniels both became ill as a result of drinking it. As between the buyer, Mr Daniels, and the seller, Mrs Tarbard, the conditions implied by the 1893 Act were capable of applying. It was found that, whilst

---

4   See eg *Gardiner v Gray* (1815) 4 Camp 144 for an early case holding that bags of silk must be 'saleable in the market under the denomination mentioned in the contract between them. The purchaser cannot be supposed to buy goods to lay them on a dunghill', per Lord Ellenborough.

5   *Keighley, Maxsted & Co v Durant* [1901] AC 240, HL. The injured person may be presumed to be the purchaser in such cases as where two or more people buy food together in a restaurant; see *Lockett v A & M Charles Ltd* [1938] 4 All ER 170, KBD; M, H & P p 40.

6   This does not apply if, on the proper construction of the contract, it appears the parties did not intend the term to be enforceable by the third party, s 1(2).

7   [1938] 4 All ER 258, KBD; M, H & P p 38.

8   See Law Com Working Paper No 64 *Liability for Defective Products* (1975), paras 8, 120.

there was no implied condition of fitness (since the buyer had not relied on the seller's skill or judgement), the implied condition of merchantability applied and had been broken. Mr Daniels was able to recover from Mrs Tarbard damages for personal injuries without proving that she had been negligent. Mrs Daniels could not sue Mrs Tarbard, but could properly sue the manufacturers, Whites, for the tort of negligence. On the facts she failed to prove breach of the necessary duty of care, though in this respect the decision would probably not be followed today.[9] Mr Daniels could also have sued the manufacturers successfully in tort had negligence been provable. Mrs Tarbard would not necessarily have borne the loss. Either by joining in her supplier (who would in turn join in his supplier and so on down the line of suppliers to the manufacturer in theory) or by separate proceedings, she could recover on an indemnity basis for the supplier's breach of the implied condition. Insolvency, inaccessibility or an effective exemption clause would break the chain at an intermediate stage.

Normally, tort-based remedies will be pursued in those circumstances where the consumer is debarred from using contractual remedies. In cases where the consumer, having suffered damage to person or property, has a choice of suing in either contract or tort, normally contract would be chosen because many implied terms impose strict liability. With the introduction of the Consumer Protection Act 1987, for products put into circulation after 1 March 1988, strict liability is also available in tort.[10] Other factors are unlikely to be decisive either way. The limitation period during which an action must be brought if personal injuries are involved, three years from the time the claimant knew or ought to have known of the damage, is the same whether suing in contract or tort[11] and is six years in other cases.[12] An action under Part I of the Consumer Protection Act 1987 cannot be commenced after 10 years from the product being put into circulation.[13] Although the tests for remoteness and measure of damages have detailed

9   See *Hill v James Crowe (Cases) Ltd* [1978] 1 All ER 812, QBD; M, H & P p 204. In addition, strict liability would now arise under the Consumer Protection Act 1987, s 2, see below.
10 See below pp 173–187.
11 Limitation Act 1980, s 11.
12 Limitation Act 1980, ss 2 and 5. This period might commence later in tort-based actions since the period commences at the moment the loss occurs, whereas in contract the period commences when the defective goods are delivered. The tort test gave rise to considerable problems in cases of latent damage – eg where the effects of negligence by a house builder, surveyor or solicitor do not become apparent for some time. Now under the Limitation Act 1980, s 14A as inserted by the Latent Damage Act 1986, s 1, in cases of latent damage not involving personal injuries, the period is the longer of six years or three years from the date of discovery or reasonable discoverability of significant damage. There is a cut-off point of 15 years from the last negligent act or omission (s 14B).
13 Limitation Act 1980, s 11A as inserted by the Consumer Protection Act 1987, s 6(6) and Sch 1, see p 185.

differences in contract and tort respectively, in practice whether the damages recovered are in respect of the defective goods themselves or consequential loss the amount recovered will be similar. If contributory negligence on the part of the victim is alleged, then the contractual action would be preferable as the defence is unavailable in cases of strict contractual liability,[14] whilst it is available in tort.[15]

Torts generally

Although the tort of negligence had, until the introduction of the strict liability tort under the Consumer Protection Act 1987, overshadowed most of the other torts in importance, as in contract-based remedies, the person advising a consumer contemplating legal action must do so with the whole of the law of tort in mind. This is not simply a question of bearing in mind such matters as the defences available generally in the law of tort. It may also be wise, for instance, to consider whether there might be liability for the tort of deceit,[16] or for supplying irresponsible persons with dangerous articles such as airguns or petrol to children[17] as well as, or as an alternative to, actions based on the breach of a duty of care.

Consideration should also be given to the possibility of action for the tort of breach of statutory duty,[18] particularly where the consumer has been injured by a defective article covered by regulations made under the Consumer Protection Act 1987, section 11. Section 41(1) of the 1987 Act gives a specific civil right of action in these circumstances. (A general duty is imposed upon manufacturers etc to ensure that articles used at work are, so far as reasonably practicable, designed and constructed so as to be safe when properly used, but no civil right of action lies for breach – see the Health and Safety at Work etc Act 1974, sections 6 (as amended) and 47, which is not strictly a consumer protection enactment since it pertains to the production process.)

14 *Barclays Bank plc v Fairclough Building Ltd* [1995] QB 214, [1995] 1 All ER 289, CA.
15 Law Reform (Contributory Negligence) Act 1945 and Consumer Protection Act 1987, s 6(4).
16 *Langridge v Levy* (1837) 2 M & W 519; affd sub nom *Levy v Langridge* (1838) 4 M & W 337 (false statement about dangerous gun which exploded).
17 See *Bebee v Sales* (1916) 32 TLR 413 (airgun); *Yachuk v Oliver Blais Co Ltd* [1949] AC 386, [1949] 2 All ER 150, PC (petrol).
18 The constituent elements of this tort are breach of the relevant statutory duty by the defendant resulting in damage to the claimant. See further p 263, below.

The *Donoghue v Stevenson* duty

This well-known decision of the House of Lords was something of a watershed in the law of tort since the wide dicta of the judges encouraged vigorous development of the use of the tort of negligence in a variety of situations. We are concerned here with the 'narrow' principle in the case defining the nature of the duty that manufacturers owe to the ultimate consumers of their products.

In *Donoghue v Stevenson*[19] the appellant and a friend went to a cafe where the friend bought some ice cream and ginger beer in a bottle made of dark opaque glass. After the appellant had consumed some of the ginger beer, the friend poured out the remainder of the bottle revealing a decomposed snail. The appellant suffered shock and gastro-enteritis due to the impure ginger beer. It will have been noted that the appellant was not the purchaser and could not therefore sue the cafe proprietor in contract. It was held that the manufacturer owed a duty of care to the ultimate consumer. Lord Atkin explained the nature of this duty in the following words:

> A manufacturer of products, which he sells in such a form as to show that he intends them to reach the ultimate consumer in the form in which they left him with no reasonable possibility of intermediate examination, and with the knowledge that the absence of reasonable care in the preparation or putting up of the products will result in an injury to the consumer's life or property, owes a duty to the consumer to take reasonable care.[20]

Bearing in mind that 'negligence means more than heedless or careless conduct … ; it properly connotes the complex concept of duty, breach, and damage thereby suffered by the person to whom the duty was owing,'[1] the following matters need some further elucidation when considering a consumer's possible cause of action against a manufacturer in negligence.

'The consumer'

Possible claimants, in an action against the manufacturer, extend beyond the purchaser to include, to adapt another of Lord Atkin's well-known dicta in *Donoghue v Stevenson*, anyone who is so closely and directly affected

19   [1932] AC 562, HL.
20   Ibid at 599.
1   Per Lord Wright in *Lochgelly Iron and Coal Co v M'Mullan* [1934] AC 1, HL, at 25.

by the manufacturer's act that he ought to have them in contemplation as being so affected when directing his mind to the acts or omissions called in question. As in *Donoghue v Stevenson* itself, friends of the purchaser are obviously included, as are members of the purchaser's family, persons to whom the purchaser has given or lent the product, employees who handle it,[2] and even bystanders who are injured by it.[3] The age of the consumer is immaterial. A child born disabled has a right of action in negligence in respect of pre-natal injuries under the Congenital Disabilities (Civil Liability) Act 1976, eg where the foetus is affected by drugs having a teratogenic effect. It is immaterial that the product was given away free.

The parties liable

The primary duty is the manufacturer's, but liability has been extended to cover almost anyone responsible for the marketing of goods who can be shown to be at fault including sub-contractors, assemblers, packers and bottlers, wholesalers, distributors, repairers, letters on hire and occasionally even retailers.[4]

Proving negligence

The burden of proving negligence is on the claimant. It must be established that the defendant owed the claimant a duty of care, that this was broken and, as a result, injury to person or property (and not purely economic loss)[5] has been caused. In an increasingly complex technological age this can be a difficult task and may involve an expensive investigation of the producer's system of work and testing, safety record with other goods and so forth. However, in product liability cases where the 'snail in the ginger beer bottle' type of situation exists, the courts will readily infer negligence on the manufacturer's behalf which will only be displaced by strong rebutting evidence.[6] The manufacturer may be able to shift the blame

---

2 *Vacwell Engineering Co Ltd v BDH Chemicals Ltd* [1971] 1 QB 88, [1969] 3 All ER 1681, QBD; M, H & P p 206.

3 *Stennett v Hancock and Peters* [1939] 2 All ER 578 (claimant injured in leg by piece flying off inefficiently repaired lorry).

4 See *Fisher v Harrods Ltd* [1966] 1 Lloyd's Rep 500, QBD; M, H & P p 213 (retailer responsible for loss resulting in selling unsafe and improperly tested or labelled jewellery cleaning fluid, which splashed into claimant's eye). See also *Devilez v Boots Pure Drug Co Ltd* (1962) 106 Sol Jo 552 (inadequately bottled corn solvent).

5 See below p 157.

6 See remarks of the Privy Council in *Grant v Australian Knitting Mills Ltd* [1936] AC 85. See also *Ward v Tesco Stores Ltd* [1976] 1 All ER 219, [1976] 1 WLR

by showing that the fault was caused by an independent contractor who was carefully chosen and whose work was checked,[7] or, perhaps because of the length of time the product has been used before the defect materialised. It is also a defence to show that an intermediate examination sufficient to reveal the defect was to be reasonably expected. Goods sold in opaque bottles or definitively pre-packaged cannot come within this defence.

The standard of safety

Almost any goods can be dangerous if abused. Tobacco is carcinogenic and can cause other health problems; alcohol taken to excess can be dangerous; a car driven too fast can be dangerous; materials used in commonly produced goods, particularly man-made fibres, can be inflammable and dangerous. So how would a court react when faced with a claim, for example, by the representatives of a deceased smoker who has died from cancer after smoking a large number of the defendant's cigarettes? In addition to problems of proving a defective product, claimants clearly face problems of proving the causal link especially if several brands have been smoked. There may also be the possibility of the defence of *volenti non fit injuria*, or the partial defence of contributory negligence because of misuse in smoking to excess.

In America many hundreds of law suits have been taken against tobacco manufacturers; until recently almost all have been rejected. A number of successful first instance cases, involving substantial punitive damages, have been reported during 2000. In March 2000 Leslie Whiteley, a 40-year-old ex-smoker dying of lung cancer, was awarded, by a Californian Court, punitive damages of $10 million each against Philip Morris and RJ Reynolds. In addition $1.7 million was awarded for medical care, lost wages and to compensate her husband for loss of companionship.[8] This was the first successful case brought by a smoker who commenced smoking in 1972 after the Surgeon-General's health warning, required by Federal

---

810, CA (customer slipped on supermarket floor owing to spilt yoghurt; held, that it was for the supermarket to *disprove* that this was due to lack of care on their part which, here, they could not do); and *Hill v James Crowe (Cases) Ltd* [1978] 1 All ER 812, QBD; M, H & P p 204 (lorry driver injured when defective wooden packing case on which he stood collapsed – perhaps an example of foreseeable misuse. Negligent manufacture was assumed.)

7   *Taylor v Rover Co Ltd* [1966] 2 All ER 181, [1966] 1 WLR 1491, Birmingham Assizes (chisel splintered through excessive hardening by independent contractor); *Evans v Triplex Safety Glass Co Ltd* [1936] 1 All ER 283, KBD; (manufacturer of windscreen not responsible for shattered windscreen possibly caused by defective assembly by car manufacturer).

8   See *Times* 29 March 2000; [2000] The Lawyer, April 3, p 72.

Cigarette Labelling and Advertising Act of 1965, had begun appearing on cigarette packets in 1969. In rejecting an argument that Mrs Whiteley had harmed herself in disregarding the warning, the jury found that the companies had negligently designed the cigarettes and had made false or misleading statements to the public. The Superior Court judge refused to overturn the jury's verdict in June 2000,[9] and Mrs Whiteley died of cancer in July 2000.

In July 2000 a law suit, lasting two years, was decided in Dade County, Florida.[10] The action was brought on behalf of an estimated 500,000 unidentified Florida smokers made ill with heart disease, lung cancer and 18 other ailments. Having earlier awarded awarded three smokers compensatory damages of $12.7 million, the jury ordered punitive damages of $145 billion (£96 billion). The companies involved were found to have misled consumers about the health risks and addictiveness of smoking. Two trade groups funded by the industry, the Council for Tobacco Research and the Tobacco Institute, were also found liable. Appeals will be lodged, in particular as the judge had instructed the jurors not to order damages that could bankrupt the companies, which instruction had been ignored. In an earlier case[11] brought in 1999 by 28 flight attendants, representing 60,000 colleagues, claiming passive smoking had made them ill, during the trial the tobacco companies settled by paying $349 million, $300 million of which was to fund a medical research foundation.

As a result of actions taken by state Attorney Generals to recover monies paid to Medicaid funds for the treatment of state citizens for smoking-related illnesses, an agreement, the Master Settlement Agreement, was announced on 16 November 1998.[12] Under the agreement 46 states and four major tobacco companies agreed a payment of $206 billion (£126 billion) over 25 years. Further companies subsequently joined the Agreement which, in addition to financial compensation, imposes restrictions on tobacco advertising[13] and marketing, requires industry funding for anti-smoking campaigns and the dissuasion of the public, especially young people, from buying tobacco products.

9   See *Whiteley v Raybestos-Manhatten Inc* No 303184 (Cal Super Ct, San Franscisco County, May 24, 2000); (2000) 16 Tobacco Industry Litigation Reporter, No 13, p 8 and *San Francisco Examiner*, 6 July 2000.

10   See *Howard A Engle v R J Reynolds Tobacco Co*, Case No 94-08273 CA-22; (2000) Times, 15 and 18 July, CNN transcript No 00071403V00.

11   *Brion v Philip Morris*, cited in the EC *Green Paper on Product Liability*, COM(99)396.

12   See J P Nehf 'The Advertising and Marketing Mandates of the Attorney General Tobacco Settlement' (1999) 7 Consum LJ 281, pp 281–295 for the background to the settlement.

13   See *Times* 3 March 1999, where the outlawing of the 'Marlboro Man' billboard advertisements by 23 April 1999 was reported.

To date in the United Kingdom there has not been successful litigation. In February 1999 a group action brought against two tobacco companies, Imperial Tobacco and the Gallagher Group, on behalf of 53 victims of cancer caused by cigarettes, was held by the High Court to be time barred for most claimants which led to a discontinuation of the action. The manufacturers agreed not to pursue the claimants for costs in exchange for an agreement by the claimants' solicitors not to take further action against any tobacco company for five years.[14]

The manufacturer is entitled to expect reasonable and proper use of the product by the consumer. Damage caused by a product which is safe when used by normal people, but which causes injury when used by an abnormally sensitive or allergic person, will not be compensated since no general duty of care has been broken.[15] But whether the claimant is sufficiently abnormal to be outside the class of consumers to whom the duty is owed is a matter of degree. A product is dangerous 'if it might affect normal users adversely, or even if it might adversely affect other users who had a higher degree of sensitivity than the normal, so long as they were not altogether exceptional'.[16]

If the product is known to be capable of causing danger if improperly used, and it is reasonable to anticipate that improper use might occur, then there is a probability that the manufacturer will be liable to damages for negligence unless a proper warning was given. The case of *Vacwell Engineering Co Ltd v BDH Chemicals Ltd*[17] is revealing on this and a number of other related points. The defendants began manufacturing and marketing for industrial use a chemical named boron tribromide. It was put up in glass ampoules with a warning label marked 'harmful vapour'. After discussion with the claimants and visits to their plant the claimants bought a supply of the chemical. In order to manufacture transistors the ampoules were put in a sink of water and detergent to wash off the labels. A visiting Russian physicist was engaged in doing this when there was a violent explosion that killed him and extensively damaged the claimant's property. The overwhelming probability was that an ampoule had been dropped into the sink, and then broken, and, as a result, the chemical came into contact with water. This caused a violent reaction that, in turn, broke the glass in the other ampoules in the sink, and the explosion occurred.

14   See *Times*, 27 February 1999, cited by Whincup, [1999] 7 Consum L J 240.
15   This seems to follow from the non-breach of the implied condition of fitness where eg dermatitis is caused to an allergic person, who gives no warning of it, by the use of hair dye as in *Ingham v Emes* [1955] 2 QB 366, [1955] 2 All ER 740, CA.
16   Per Denning LJ in *Board v Thomas Hedley & Co Ltd* [1951] 2 All ER 431, CA, at 432.
17   [1971] 1 QB 88, [1969] 3 All ER 1681, QBD; M, H & P p 206.

Negligence-based liability

The claimants successfully claimed damages for negligence and (inter alia) breach of the implied term of fitness for purpose under the Sale of Goods Act 1893. As regards the negligence action, the defendants were held to be in breach of their duty of care in not ascertaining that the chemical exploded when mixed with water. This was a fact that had been noted in French scientific journals in 1878 and again in 1899, though omitted from some more modern textbooks. Having ascertained the hazard the defendants should have at least put a warning such as, 'Warning – Harmful Vapour. Reacts violently with water and explodes'. Finally, the explosion and damage being foreseeable, the defendants were liable therefor, the magnitude and extent of the actual damage being irrelevant.[18] The Court of Appeal later upheld an agreed settlement of the appeal on the basis that the damages recoverable on the above basis should be reduced by 20 per cent in respect, presumably, of contributory negligence.[19] To this the caveat must be added that a manufacturer's warning which really amounts to an exemption clause, in that it imposes 'restrictive or onerous conditions' within the Unfair Contract Terms Act 1977, section 13, will be rendered nugatory (or subject to the reasonableness test imposed by section 2 of that Act).[20]

Damages

As will have been inferred from the *Vacwell* case considered above, a small degree of carelessness can result in an apparently disproportionate amount of damage. A crucial consideration is how much of the damage is recoverable from the defendant when claiming in tort. As in the *Vacwell* case, the test adopted is whether the damage is of a type or kind which ought reasonably to have been foreseen, though the extent of the damage need not have been foreseen. If an explosion should have been foreseen, the fact that its magnitude exceeded all expectation is immaterial.[1] Where property damage is sustained the measure of damages is normally the cost

18 Applying dicta in *Smith v Leech Brain & Co Ltd* [1962] 2 QB 405, [1961] 3 All ER 1159, QBD (foreseeable burn to claimant's husband followed by unforeseeable cancer; damages awarded in respect of husband's death to widow).
19 [1971] 1 QB 88 at 112. See also *Hurley v Dyke* [1979] RTR 265, HL, for the extent of a vendor's duty of care when an unroadworthy car which subsequently crashes and causes personal injuries is sold at auction 'as seen and with all its faults and without warranty' – a warning held adequate on the particular facts by the House of Lords.
20 See Macleod (1981) 97 LQR 550.
1   See in general, *The Wagon Mound* [1961] AC 388, [1961] 1 All ER 404, PC; *Hughes v Lord Advocate* [1963] AC 837, [1963] 1 All ER 705, HL.

of replacement.[2] For physical injuries the courts and insurance companies operate a rough tariff according to the nature and extent of the injury.[3] It still seems to be generally accepted in English tort law that pure economic loss cannot be compensated. There must be some preceding physical loss, even if minimal. This was established in *Spartan Steel and Alloys Ltd v Martin & Co (Contractors) Ltd*.[4] The House of Lords, in *Junior Books Ltd v Veitchi Co Ltd*,[5] did permit a claim for pure economic loss where the relationship between the parties was sufficiently close. However, in the majority of cases there will not be sufficient proximity between the parties and the necessary element of reliance will be missing, thus preventing successful claims for pure economic loss. This can be seen in *Muirhead v Industrial Tank Specialities Ltd*[6] where damages for pure economic loss were denied, although damages for physical loss to property and losses consequential on this were allowed. Here the claimant lobster farmer lost his stock of lobsters when the pumps, manufactured by the third defendant and used to oxygenate the water, failed. The court decided that the relationship between the claimant and defendant did not demonstrate the required degree of proximity and reliance to permit recovery for pure economic loss. The House of Lords in *Murphy v Brentwood District Council*[7] confined recovery for pure economic loss to cases where there is a special relationship of proximity, akin to contract, with an element of reliance present. Lord Bridge indicated:

> … if a manufacturer produces and sells a chattel which is merely defective in quality, even to the extent that it is valueless for the purpose for which it is intended, the manufacturer's liability at common law arises only under and by reference to the terms of any contract to which he is a party in relation to the chattel; the common

2   See eg *Harbutt's Plasticine Ltd v Wayne Tank and Pump Co Ltd* [1970] 1 QB 447, [1970] 1 All ER 225, CA (factory burnt down due to overheated plastic piping which was unsuitable for purpose. Damages of £146,000 awarded).
3   See eg Kemp and Kemp *The Quantum of Damages*.
4   [1973] QB 27, [1972] 3 All ER 557, CA.
5   [1983] 1 AC 520, [1982] 3 All ER 201, HL. Here the appellants (sub-contractors) laid a concrete floor in the respondents' factory. The floor was defective and the appellants were found liable for the cost of replacing it, although the floor was not dangerous to health or property and there was no contractual relationship between the appellants and the respondents.
6   [1986] QB 507, [1985] 3 All ER 705, CA. See also *Candlewood Navigation Corpn Ltd v Mitsui OSK Lines Ltd* [1986] AC 1, [1985] 2 All ER 935, PC; *Leigh and Sillivan Ltd v Aliakmon Shipping Co Ltd, The Aliakmon* [1986] AC 785, [1986] 2 All ER 145, HL; *D & F Estates Ltd v Church Comrs for England* [1989] AC 177, [1988] 2 All ER 992, HL; and *Simaan General Contracting Co v Pilkington Glass Ltd (No 2)* [1988] QB 758, [1988] 1 All ER 791, CA.
7   [1991] 1 AC 398, [1990] 2 All ER 908, HL; M, H & P p 216. See also pp 216–217.

law does not impose on him any liability in tort to persons to whom he owes no duty in contract but who, having acquired the chattel, suffer economic loss because the chattel is defective in quality. If a dangerous defect in a chattel is discovered before it causes any personal injury or damage to property, because the danger is now known and the chattel cannot safely be used unless the defect is repaired, the defect becomes merely a defect in quality. The chattel is either capable of repair at economic cost or it is worthless and must be scrapped. In either case the loss sustained by the owner or hirer of the chattel is purely economic. It is recoverable against any party who owes the loser a relevant contractual duty. But it is not recoverable in tort in the absence of a special relationship of proximity imposing on the tortfeasor a duty of care to safeguard the plaintiff from economic loss. There is no such special relationship between the manufacturer of a chattel and a remote owner or hirer [at pp 475, 926].

Exemption clauses and manufacturers' guarantees[8]

The type of exemption clause that was often contained in a document in the name of the manufacturer and purported to be a guarantee, but which in fact gave the buyer less rights than provided under the Sale of Goods Act 1893, is, as a result of the Supply of Goods (Implied Terms) Act 1973 and subsequent legislation, a thing of the past.[9] The manufacturer's objective was both to negative the consumer's rights against the retailer and to negative his own in respect of any liability in negligence. It is this aspect which must now be considered. Under current law, the enforceability of these guarantees is somewhat conjectural since this depends upon there being a contract between manufacturer and consumer. If construed as a unilateral contract, that is one where an offer is made to a range of possible offerees and is accepted by a particular offeree doing the contemplated act, the contract would probably be completed by purchase of the article. This would both operate as acceptance and furnish consideration by the purchaser, provided there was knowledge of the existence of the guarantee at the time of purchase. If the contract is construed as a bilateral one, involving a communicated acceptance by the buyer, 'registration' of the guarantee by filling it in and posting it would probably both constitute

---

8   See M, H & P pp 274–278.
9   Such 'guarantees' are not necessarily objectionable. They may, and modern ones often do, give the consumer valuable rights over and above those implied by the Sale of Goods Act 1979.

acceptance and furnish consideration by the buyer.[10] If a contract can be established between the parties, a manufacturer could seek to rely on a clause in the 'guarantee' to provide exemption from negligence actions. Alternatively the guarantee might operate as a non-contractual notice and, in exceptional cases, thereby exclude liability.

Exemption clauses in manufacturers' guarantees are regulated by the Unfair Contract Terms Act 1977, section 5.[11] This section applies only to cases where possession or ownership of the goods does not pass under the contract. So in contracts between seller and buyer, as opposed to manufacturer and buyer, exemption clauses relating to negligence will be avoided or regulated under section 2 (considered in detail in ch 7), rather than section 5.

Section 5 provides that, in the case of goods of a type ordinarily supplied for private use or consumption, where loss or damage a) arises from the goods proving defective while in consumer use, and b) results from the negligence of a person concerned in the manufacture or distribution of the goods, any exemption clause in the guarantee excluding or restricting liability for the loss or damage is void. For these purposes 'guarantee' and 'in consumer use' are defined. A guarantee is anything in writing if it contains or purports to contain some promise or assurance (however worded or presented) that defects will be made good by complete or partial replacement, or by repair, monetary compensation or otherwise. Goods are regarded as in consumer use when a person is using them, or has them in possession for use, otherwise than exclusively for the purpose of a business.[12]

It will be appreciated that section 5 operates only where a) it can be proved that loss or damage of any sort has occurred owing to the negligence of the manufacturer or distributor,[13] and b) there is what would, apart from section 5, have been a successful attempt to negative or restrict such liability by a contractually binding exemption clause or an effective non-contractual notice.

It would appear that the Unfair Terms in Consumer Contracts Regulations 1999[14] could apply to manufacturers' guarantees where they create a contractual relationship. A 'seller or supplier' is defined, in regulation 3(1), as 'any natural or legal person who, in contracts covered

---

10   *Chappell & Co Ltd v Nestlé Co Ltd* [1960] AC 87, [1959] 2 All ER 701, HL (useless chocolate wrappers accompanying money sent to Nestlé's for a copy of 'smash hit' record held to be part of the consideration).

11   See BSSCCL p 412.

12   See Macleod 'Instructions as to the Use of Consumer Goods' (1981) 97 LQR 550.

13   Note the strict liability arising under the Consumer Protection Act 1987, Part I cannot be excluded or restricted; see s 7, below at p 186.

14   SI 1999/2083, see further ch 5 at p 138.

by these regulations, is acting for purposes relating to his trade, business or profession, whether publicly owned or privately owned'. This would seem to apply to manufacturers in such circumstances and the contracts that involve non-negotiated terms would certainly be covered by the Regulations. Where a consumer seeks to enforce a guarantee, in deciding whether particular terms[15] are 'unfair' or not, a court might be inclined to look more favourably on terms inserted by the manufacturer. Although some terms may appear, prima facie, to be one-sided, the guarantee is given voluntarily and provides redress over and above that currently required by law.

There have been a number of consultation papers produced regarding guarantees, putting forward proposal for reform.[16] In addition, the European Directive on Certain Aspects of the Sale of Consumer Goods and Associated Guarantees[17] requires implementing measures to be passed by 1 January 2002. Article 6 concerns 'guarantees'. These are defined as:

> any undertaking by a seller or producer to the consumer, given without extra charge, to reimburse the price paid or to replace, repair or handle consumer goods in any way if they do not meet the specification set out in the guarantee statement or in the relevant advertising (art 1(2)(e)).

Free guarantees, when provided, are to be legally binding on the offerer under the conditions laid down in the guarantee statement and associated advertising (art 6(1)). Thus producers and sellers are free to decide whether or not they offer guarantees, but if they are provided then their provisions will be legally binding. Extended warranties, for which the consumer pays, are not affected by the Directive.

Certain requirements for what is to be included in guarantees are stipulated in Article 6(2):

> The guarantee shall:
> – state that the consumer has legal rights under applicable national

15 Other than those seeking to exclude liability which could be dealt with under the Unfair Contract Terms Act 1977 or the Consumer Protection Act 1987, see above.
16 *Consumer Guarantees: A Discussion Paper*, OFT, August 1984; *Consumer Guarantees: A report by the Director General of Fair Trading*, OFT, June 1986; *Competing in Quality*, NCC, April 1989; *Consumer Guarantees*, DTI, February 1992; also A Clark 'Product Liability and Economic Loss: a radical proposal' [1993] JBL 383.
17 99/44/EC, OJ No L 171, 7.7.99, p 12, discussed further in ch 5. See also C Twigg-Flesner 'The EC Directive on Certain Aspects of the Sale of Consumer Goods and Associated Guarantees' (1999) 7 Consum LJ 177.

legislation governing the sale of consumer goods and make it clear that those rights are not affected by the guarantee,[18]

- set out in plain intelligible language the contents of the guarantee and the essential particulars necessary for making claims under the guarantee, notably the duration and territorial scope of the guarantee as well as the name and address of the guarantor.

Consumers may request copies of guarantees in writing or some other durable medium (art 6(3)) and should be able to consider and compare the different guarantees offered prior to selecting goods. The validity of guarantees that infringe the requirements of the Directive is not affected; consumers are able to continue to rely on them and enforce them (art 6(5)). The Directive is included amongst those listed under Directive 98/27/EC on Injunctions for the Protection of Consumers' Interests[19] for which consumer organisations will be able to seek injunctions.

Two case studies on design defects

Introduction

In the field of product liability, design defects in products are regarded with particular horror by manufacturers. Manufacturing defects, which no doubt give rise to the largest number of claims based on defective products, can at least be prevented in future by tightening quality control processes. But design defects can affect a huge number of individual products that may be awaiting sale or already sold and, once the defect is identified, can involve the manufacturer in frightening financial liability in modifying the product, often after an expensive recall.[20] The reluctance of some manufacturers to recall suspect products in time is illustrated by the Thalidomide saga to which reference is made in chapter 8 and by the first

18 Similar to the requirements of arts 4 and 5 of the Consumer Transactions (Restrictions on Statements) Order 1976, SI 1976/1813, see further pp 135–136.
19 OJ No L 166, 11.6.98, p 51. See further *Injunctions Directive: Implementation in the UK*, DTI, February 2000 and 'Widening the net', OFT (2000) 26 Fair Trading 13.
20 Whilst there is no general duty to recall defective products in the UK, failure to do so when the defect has been identified can greatly increase the liability to pay damages. In the case of motor vehicles the Department of the Environment, Transport and the Regions is entitled to information on safety defects and to put its views to the manufacturer on remedial action under the Code of Practice on Action concerning Vehicle Safety Defects between the DETR and the Society of Motor Manufacturers and Traders Ltd. See Anthea Worsdall *Consumer Law for the Motor Trade* (4th edn).

of the two cases considered below, *Walton v British Leyland (UK) Ltd.*[1]

The second case selected for a more detailed analysis is *Lambert v Lewis*.[2] This case does not involve the, sometimes complex, question of whether a product *is* defective. (For an illustration of the standard of care laid down by the tort of negligence see *Vacwell Engineering Co Ltd v BDH Chemicals Ltd.*[3]) Both cases, however, provide graphic examples of the difficulty of apportioning blame (in terms of damages) 1) where a product is defectively designed; 2) this fact comes to light some time after its being marketed and 3) the product could perhaps have been prevented from causing damage had a third party taken proper action.

Walton v British Leyland (UK) Ltd, Dutton Forshaw (North East) Ltd and Blue House Lane Garage Ltd (1978) Times, 13 July), QBD[4]

Mr and Mrs Walton, the claimants, were travelling as passengers in an Austin Allegro car that was being driven along a motorway by Mr Walton's brother, Albert. As the vehicle was travelling at about 60 mph the rear nearside wheel came off. As a result the vehicle collided with the central crash barrier. Mr Walton escaped with minor injuries but his wife was thrown from the car and suffered injuries so catastrophic that she was left a quadriplegic.

The car had been bought by Albert in 1974. It was described, by Willis J, as a 'thoroughly bad car'. It had been in and out of Duttons, the second defendants, for repair throughout 1975; the clutch having been replaced four times. The first symptom of the ultimate disaster was in early 1975 when Albert noticed a noise in the rear offside wheel and Duttons then replaced the bearing and fitted the larger washer, recommended by the manufacturers, to that particular wheel only. The car was later taken to Blue House Lane Garage Ltd, the third defendants (who, unlike Duttons, were not franchised dealers for Leylands) and they gave it a 6,000 mile service and later a 12,000 mile service. At the latter service the brakes and bearings were adjusted and the wheels changed. The accident occurred some 1,400 miles later without warning.

The case revealed a great deal of detailed evidence as to the history of 'wheel adrift' problems in Allegro cars in the early 1970s. To summarise, by

---

1   (1978) Times, 13 July, QBD, M, H & P p 208.
2   [1979] RTR 61, QBD; on appeal sub nom *Lexmead (Basingstoke) Ltd v Lewis* [1982] AC 225, [1980] 1 All ER 978, CA; revsd [1982] AC 225, [1981] 1 All ER 1185, HL.
3   [1971] 1 QB 88, [1969] 3 All ER 1681, QBD; M, H & P p 206; above, p 155.
4   This case does not appear to have been officially reported but a transcript appears in Product Liability International, August 1980, 156, and the decision received some publicity in newspapers. For detailed extracts see M, H & P pp 208–213.

February 1975 some 104 cases of 'wheel adrift' problems had been reported to Leylands from the UK and abroad. The problem was regarded as serious. As the learned judge remarked, 'lives were plainly at risk, but so were sales, and a solution, or at least a palliative, had to be found urgently'.

At first the blame was put on servicing mechanics unfamiliar with the type of end float bearings used on this model (along with others, such as Marinas). If over-tightened it was considered that this would lead to overheating, bearing collapse and, in the worst cases, wheels coming off. In fact after September 1974 the cars were manufactured with large washers in the rear hub assembly 'to improve bearing security' and all dealers were both warned of the dangers of incorrect adjustment and urged to fit larger washers when servicing earlier models. The judge described this 'palliative' as 'a limited education programme directed to mechanics working in distributors' garages'. The effect of fitting a larger washer was admitted to be not to prevent bearing failure but to prevent the wheel coming off should bearing failure occur. A revealing memorandum from a chief engineer at Leylands in late 1974 stated: 'The design was introduced to satisfy performance demands at lower cost, and it is true to state that provided design requirements are adhered to no problem would be experienced. Unfortunately the design is not "idiot-proof" and will therefore continuously involve risk. The risk becomes greater as vehicles become older and ever more carelessly maintained. Had we incorporated the large washer from the commencement the risk would have been tolerable. ... Engineering have considered the possibility of recall action but do not favour it owing to the fact that it would damage the product' (ie adversely affect sales). In fact a recall campaign would have cost, in 1974, £300,000, and an education campaign to franchised outlets was chosen instead.

Expert evidence at the trial was to the effect that the outer bearing had collapsed and that the inner cone had been welded by excessive heat onto the stub axle. The probable, but not certain, cause of the accident was over-tightening of the retaining nut, exacerbated by lack of grease.

The case against Duttons was that they should have fitted the larger washer to both hubs, instead of just one, when the car was brought in to them. But the learned judge was not convinced that the instructions they had had from Leylands gave any indication of the real gravity of the problem and thought them ambiguous as to the need in all circumstances to change *both* hub washers following a complaint about only one. He went on to hold Duttons blameless.

The case against Blue House, and its allegedly negligent mechanic, was that the accident was caused by the over-tightening of the vulnerable wheel bearing. Again the judge held this garage, who were not Leyland dealers and had no knowledge of the desirability of fitting larger washers, not negligent even if over-tightening were the cause of the breakdown (which he did not regard as by any means established).

As to Leylands responsibility, this was held to be 'total'. Having become aware of the 'wheel adrift' problem on this model, what was Leyland's position?

The duty of care owed by Leyland to the public was to make a clean breast of the problem and recall all cars which they could, in order that the safety washers could be fitted. I accept, of course that manufacturers have to steer a course between alarming the public unnecessarily and so damaging the reputation of their products, and observing their duty of care towards those whom they are in a position to protect from dangers of which they and they alone are aware. The duty seems to me to be the higher when they can palliate the worst effects of a failure which, if Leyland's view is right, they could never decisively guard against. They seriously considered recall and made an estimate of the cost at a figure which seems to me to be in no way out of proportion to the risks involved. It was decided not to follow this course for commercial reasons. I think this involved a failure to observe their duty of care for the safety of the many who were bound to remain at risk, irrespective of the recommendations made to Leyland dealers and to them alone.[5]

By way of footnote to this decision it might first be noticed that no Sale of Goods Act claim could be made by the claimants since they were not the buyers. Subject to the possible problem of durability, there is little doubt that a breach of section 14 of that Act would otherwise have occurred. Second, the design problem was not clearly identified in the decision. The bearing in question was made by a respectable third party manufacturer, Timken, and was fitted to cars of various types world wide. It was clear that Leylands were not negligent in using this component. Third, it was clear that the critical breach of the duty of care was not to instigate a recall, apparently for commercial reasons, after a large number of similar faults had been reported. Fourth, it was clear that the limited warning system adopted by Leylands was not adequate to shift responsibility to third parties for improper servicing. It was not regarded as any excuse that unfranchised repairers were involved. This is presumably because no car owner is obliged to use franchised dealers for repair work.[6] If, therefore, a design is not 'idiot proof' manufacturers must anticipate that unfranchised garages, or even do-it-yourself owners, will fall into the trap that the design lays for them if it is not completely unreasonable for them to do so.

5   Per Willis J.
6   It is understood that warnings against over-tightening are now impressed on the hub itself.

Lambert v Lewis[7]

The facts of this case concerned a tragic motor accident in 1972. The claimants, a mother and daughter, were travelling in a Reliant car driven by the father in which the son was also a passenger. As their car approached an oncoming Land Rover, driven by a farmer's employee, a trailer being towed by the Land Rover became unhitched and slewed across the road into the path of the claimants' car. In the ensuing accident the father, who was driving the car perfectly properly, was killed together with his son, and the mother and daughter injured. The mother sued on her behalf and on behalf of her deceased husband and son under the provisions of the Fatal Accidents Acts 1846 to 1959 and the Law Reform (Miscellaneous Provisions) Act 1934. The daughter sued in her own right through her mother as next friend.

In an accident of this sort the claimants will be advised that it is highly likely that negligence will be involved on at least one person's behalf, since trailers should not become detached from towing vehicles. Assuming for the moment that the fundamental fault was in the design or manufacture of the hitch, though careless maintenance or driving might have exacerbated the problem, and bearing in mind the Sale of Goods Act 1979, section 14, the possible defendants can be illustrated diagrammatically as follows:

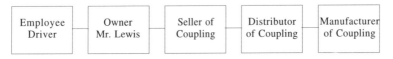

| Employee Driver | Owner Mr. Lewis | Seller of Coupling | Distributor of Coupling | Manufacturer of Coupling |

Unfortunately, there was one vital link missing from this chain. The sellers and suppliers of the coupling, Lexmead, could not identify the stockist or distributor who sold them the Dixon-Bate trailer coupling, thus preventing any possible indemnity to them under the Sale of Goods Act. In the event the claimants sued as joint defendants the employee-driver, the owner, the seller of the coupling and the manufacturer. By a process of third and fourth party notices, the driver and owner claimed indemnity from the seller of the coupling, should they be held liable to pay damages. The seller also claimed an indemnity or contribution from the manufacturers, in the event that the seller was held liable to pay damages. It can thus be seen that the manufacturer was under attack on two fronts. There was the direct claim by the injured claimants based on the consequences of failure to take care in the manufacture of the coupling. There was also the potential claim by

7   [1979] RTR 61, QBD; on appeal sub nom *Lexmead (Basingstoke) Ltd v Lewis* [1982] AC 225, [1980] 1 All ER 978, CA; revsd [1982] AC 225, [1981] 1 All ER 1185, HL.

Negligence-based liability

the driver and owner of the Land Rover for indemnity from the seller who, in turn, looked for indemnity from the manufacturers, under the principles of the Law Reform (Married Women and Tortfeasors) Act 1935. The law of *contract* was not available in this particular instance owing to the failure to identify the distributor, the missing link in the chain. However, whether there was any claim at all by the seller against the manufacturer depended, of course, on the seller first being made liable either to compensate the claimants for negligence or to indemnify the driver or owner in respect of any negligence attributed to them.

At first instance[8] Stocker J formulated three issues for decision. The first question was why did the trailer become detached from the Land Rover. The judge found this was because of the defective coupling. It was a dual purpose towing hitch which could be used either attached to a cup-type trailer attachment, as here, or to a ring-type trailer attachment. It consisted of a towing pin ending at the top in a ball, and locked at the bottom by a brass spindle and spiral pin with handle. What had happened was that the towing pin, securely locked at the top, rose out of the jaws of the towing assembly to which it should have been locked at the bottom. On subsequent examination, the brass spindle and handle were found to be missing, and the hitch dirty. In fact it was only dirt that was keeping the towing pin in position and it only needed a jolt to dislodge it.

The second issue was – who was primarily liable for the detachment of the trailer? The judge held the manufacturer responsible. He held the coupling unsafe for the use for which it was designed and that the designers ought to have realised that the adaptation of a dual purpose coupling of this sort from ring-type to cup-type attachments resulted in a fundamental change in its function. It became subject to vertical stresses to which it would not have been subject if coupled to a ring attachment. That made the handle, and through it the spindle on which the integrity of the lock depended, vulnerable. He therefore found the manufacturers liable in negligence for the claimants' loss and damage, and the finding was not challenged by the manufacturers.

The judge also considered the farmer-owner's liability, it having been established that the driver was not negligent. The owner had coupled the Land Rover to the trailer and moved it up and down to make sure it was secure. But 'he continued to use this coupling over a period of months in a state in which it was plainly damaged without taking steps to have it repaired or even to ascertain whether or not it was safe to continue to use it in such a condition'.[9] He was thus held to be negligent also, in that he had been insensitive to public safety and to the condition of the vehicle. The judge also went on to consider whether the seller of the coupling ('the

8 [1979] RTR 61.
9 At p 87.

suppliers') had been negligent, but held that this was not so since they had purchased the component from reputable manufacturers and the design defect could not have been identified by intermediate examination.

The judge therefore awarded the claimants a total of £45,000 attributable as to 75 per cent to the manufacturers and 25 per cent to the farmer-owner.

The third issue was whether the owner could claim indemnity from any other party along the line. The owner claimed against the suppliers on the basis that the implied conditions of fitness for purpose and merchantable quality under the Sale of Goods Act 1979, section 14 had been broken, and that the damage caused by the accident resulted from these breaches. The judge held that the sale of the badly designed coupling did break both conditions, but the owner could claim nominal damages only. This was because the damages for which the owner was held liable (25 per cent of £45,000) were caused by his own independent negligence in continuing to use the defective coupling, and the damage suffered was therefore too remote from the seller's breach.

It was this latter point on which the substance of the appellate litigation in this case depended. The Court of Appeal[10] held that the seller of goods was responsible for all damage which flowed naturally and directly from a breach of warranty or condition in a contract of sale.[11] This damage included the accident here because the suppliers should have foreseen that some such negligence might occur. The Court of Appeal therefore held the suppliers liable to indemnify the owner in respect of his liability for damages. The suppliers, however, were unable to establish that the manufacturers were, in turn, responsible to indemnify them because of their dangerous design (thus being 100 per cent liable). The reasons for this were a) no special relationship existed for a claim for negligent misrepresentation, and b) the loss to the suppliers caused by the manufacturers' negligence was purely financial loss, and 'pure economic loss' unaccompanied by physical damage is not recoverable.[12]

The House of Lords, in effect, restored the substance of the position following Stocker J's judgment by reversing the Court of Appeal and finding the suppliers not liable to indemnify the owner. Lord Diplock formulated the issue thus:[13]

> In what circumstances can a party ('A') to a contract who has been found liable for a breach of a duty of care owed by him to a stranger

10 [1982] AC 225, [1980] 1 All ER 978.

11 See 1979 Act, s 53(2) and *Hadley v Baxendale* (1854) 9 Exch 341.

12 See *SCM (UK) Ltd v W J Whittall & Son Ltd* [1971] 1 QB 337, [1970] 3 All ER 245, CA, and *Spartan Steel & Alloys Ltd v Martin & Co (Contractors) Ltd* [1973] QB 27, [1972] 3 All ER 557, CA, which were followed on this difficult and controversial point. See above at p 157.

13 [1982] AC 225 at 275, [1981] 1 All ER 1185 at 1190.

('X') to the contract, recover from the other party ('B') to the contract as damages for breach of warranty the amount of damages for negligence which 'A' himself has been ordered to pay to 'X'?

The answer to this was held to be in the ratio decidendi of *Mowbray v Merryweather*,[14] as restated by Winn LJ in *Hadley v Droitwich Construction Co Ltd*:[15]

> ... in a case where A has been held liable to X, a stranger, for negligent failure to take a certain precaution, he may recover over from someone with whom he has a contract only if by that contract the other contracting party has warranted that he *need not* – there is no necessity – take the very precautions for the failure to take which he has been held liable in law to [X].

Did any or all of the implied conditions under the Sale of Goods Act 1979 amount to such a warranty? The House of Lords held that they did not. They might have had continuing force for 'a reasonable time' which here might be some three to six months before the accident at which time the farmer should have become aware that the handle of the locking mechanism was missing. But if the accident had happened before then, the owner could not have been held to be negligent in the first place. After the owner should have noticed the defect in the coupling,

> the only implied warranty which could justify his failure to take the precaution either to get it mended or at least to find out whether it was safe to continue to use it in that condition, would be a warranty that the coupling would continue to be safely used to tow a trailer on the public highway notwithstanding that it was in an obviously damaged state. My Lords, any implication of a warranty in these terms needs only to be stated, to be rejected.

It therefore followed that there was no need to consider the suppliers' claim for indemnity against the manufacturers, since there was no liability imposed on the suppliers to indemnify the owners.

It has been suggested by some commentators[16] that the issue in *Lambert v Lewis* would have been more simply resolved if manufacturers' strict liability for defective products had then been part of English law, as it now is under the Consumer Protection Act 1987. This, it is submitted, is not necessarily true. To start with, the same preliminary work must be done

14   [1895] 2 QB 640, CA.
15   [1967] 3 All ER 911 at 914, [1968] 1 WLR 37 at 43, CA.
16   See eg *Which?* October 1980, p 596.

by the claimant's advisers to establish the cause of the accident. In *Lambert v Lewis* expert evidence had to be adduced that submission to a steady upward thrust of 1.05 tons would be enough to bring the towing pin out of the jaws if the pin had not been worn, and where it was worn (as here), a pressure of 0.87 tons would have been sufficient. The evidence of engineers would also be needed to establish that this degree of upward thrust, given the dual design of the coupling, rendered its design defective. Exactly the same investigation is needed successfully to sue the producer under the strict liability regime, since such liability depends on identifying a defect in the product. At that point a claimant would no doubt only bring proceedings against the producer, unless there are doubts about the producer's ability to pay. It is, however, the case that the existing law of negligence remains and applies in particular to the liability of 'producers' inter se and their rights of recourse against third parties.[17] Nor are rights under the Sale of Goods Act 1979 affected. Therefore a claimant in a similar situation to that arising in *Lambert v Lewis* will be primarily interested in redress from the manufacturer, though it is usual practice to rely on 'belt and braces' and sue anyone else who might be liable as well. It is quite likely that the owner, who will still be liable for any independent negligence, will be joined in as co-defendant. Even if not, the producer might well seek contribution from the owner in respect of any independent negligence, in which case the owner will be joined in as a third party.[18] It might be argued that the existence of strict liability makes litigation less probable, but it should be understood that insurers are likely to remain hidden parties behind the producer and probably the vehicle owner. Where large amounts of money are at stake – the actual amount depending on the chance consequence of the financial status of the party or parties killed, and, if injured rather than killed, the extent of those injuries – the insurers may insist on their right to have their insured's liability properly established.

It is also of interest to focus on the position of the 'consumer' in *Lambert v Lewis*. Here he was the defendant rather than the claimant, the vehicle owner who had bought a coupling hitch that was badly designed and caused a catastrophic accident. The damage resulting was primarily his own liability to pay damages for negligence as a result. The owner's attempt to transfer on this liability to the seller of the towing hitch was finally defeated in the House of Lords on the somewhat recondite grounds of causation described above. Perhaps the lesson is that whilst there is always scope for rationalisation of the law, it cannot be 'made simple' if

---

17   Consumer Protection Act 1987, s 2(6).
18   See Civil Liability (Contribution) Act 1978, s 1(1) of which states that 'any person liable in respect of any damage suffered by another person may recover contribution from any other person liable in respect of the same damage (whether jointly with him or otherwise)' and the Consumer Protection Act 1987, s 2(5).

justice is to be done as between the various parties involved in this type of accident.

The evolvement of strict liability for defective products

The object of this part of the chapter is to trace the proposals for reform made over the last 40 years or so; the developments which have taken place, culminating in the Consumer Protection Act 1987, which will be considered in detail later in the chapter; and to see what the future might hold. In North America in particular, but also in some parts of Europe, the idea of strict liability for defective products has to a greater or lesser extent taken root and is now established in the United Kingdom.

A regime of strict liability for defective products is one in which the claimant will succeed if it can be proved that 1) the product was defective, 2) that there was a causal link between that defect and any injuries, and 3) there are no defences available to the defendant.

Theories of strict product liability first gained acceptance in the USA, initially as an extension of implied sales warranties to others in the distributive chain[19] and then as part of the developed law of tort.[20] There has been considerable alarm in some quarters as to developments in the USA, and even reluctance by some non-USA manufacturers to export their products to North America. A current example concerns the potential extension of liability of gun manufacturers for accidental or deliberate misuse of guns. Some companies are disposing of their gun manufacturing subsidiaries or are leaving the American market.[1] An 'Inter-Agency Taskforce' was set up in the USA, in 1975, as a result of allegations that insurance cover was difficult to obtain, but the subsequent report found no problem of widespread unavailability. There were further concerns in the 1980s when a major pharmaceutical company filed for bankruptcy over product liability claims. Some states, for example Alabama, are now imposing limits on the amounts of punitive damages that can be awarded.[2] This is

19 See *Henningsen v Bloomfield Motors Inc* 161 A 2d 69 (NJ, 1960), M, H & P p 52.
20 See in particular *Greenman v Yuba Power Products Inc* 377 P 2d 897 (Cal, 1963); M, H & P p 255 (Traynor CJ). See also the formulae for strict tort liability stated in the American Law Institute's Restatement of Tort, 2d, s 402A and the Restatement (Third) of Torts: Products Liability, and generally M, H & P pp 255–272; Stapleton *Product Liability*; Howells *Comparative Product Liability*, ch 12.
1 Eg Tomkins, a UK manufacturing group is seeking to sell Smith & Wesson, the American gunmaker, which has already agreed, with the US Government and local authorities, to improve its safety measures to settle litigation and avert law suits: see *Times*, 25 July 2000.
2 See (1999) Consum LJ 363.

the greater of $1.5 million for bodily injury (or $500,000 for non-bodily injury) or three times the compensation awarded. Congress has, so far, resisted calls for a national limit. In contrast, in 1999 General Motors were ordered by the Los Angeles Superior Court, to pay $1.2 billion (£760 million) to six survivors of a car blaze blamed on the faulty design of the vehicle.[3] The jury's earlier award of $4.9 billion (£3.1 billion), of which $107 million was compensation, had been reduced by the court.

It should be borne in mind that, although there have been a number of spectacular decisions emanating from the USA in this area of law, there are important divergencies in the way the law is formulated and in the underlying legal system there compared with the system operating in the UK. These differences include the fact that, in the USA, verdicts and damages (including the possibility of punitive damages) are left to juries; in civil cases in the UK of the sort under discussion judges assess the damages. Also, in most American states liability extends beyond the producer to other commercial suppliers; under the Consumer Protection Act 1987 strict liability only attaches to the producer, 'own brander' or Community importer (with limited responsibility on suppliers), liability of others continuing to depend on the law of negligence.

In Europe theories of strict liability were developed in France and the Netherlands in the 1960s and by the German Supreme Court in 1968. The debate on reforming English tort law centred on proposals from Europe and from the English and Scottish Law Commissions.[4] The Commissions recommended amendment of the law of tort so that producers should bear the risk of, and be strictly liable for, death or personal injury caused by defects in their products irrespective of fault. In addition, the Royal Commission on Civil Liability and Compensation for Personal Injuries (Chairman, Lord Pearson) specifically considered compensation in respect of death or personal injury suffered 'through the manufacture, supply or use of goods or services'.[5] The Commission concluded that there was no justification, at that time, for introducing a 'no-fault' scheme for injuries caused by defective products. It did consider that a scheme involving strict liability (ie liability without proof of actual negligence), along the lines recommended by the Council of Europe Convention and the EC Directive discussed next, should be introduced.

A proposal for a Council Directive[6] (the 'EC Directive') was presented, by the Commission, to the Council of the EC in 1976. Revisions followed with lengthy discussions on areas of disagreement including a) whether

3   *Anderson v General Motors*; see *Times*, 28 August 1999 and (1999) 22 Consumer Law Today, issue 9, p 7.
4   *Liability for Defective Products*, 1977, Law Com No 82, Scot Law Com No 45, Cmnd 6831.
5   1978, Cmnd 7054.
6   OJ No C 241, 14.10.76, p 9.

Negligence-based liability

or not there should be a 'development risks' defence, b) the extension of liability to property damage, and c) the imposition of maximum limits of liability. The Directive was finally adopted on 25 July 1985.[7] The main feature of the Directive, under Article 1, is to make the producer strictly liable for damage caused by defects in a product. The Directive was introduced into English law in Part I of the Consumer Protection Act 1987, which is discussed fully below. The European Commission issued its first report on the implementation of the product liability Directive in 1995.[8] Subsequently, an amending Directive,[9] removing the permissible derogation for unprocessed agricultural products and game, was passed in 1999 and will be implemented into United Kingdom law on 4 December 2000. Following the adoption, by the Commission, of the *Green Paper on Liability for Defective Products*,[10] the Commission is preparing its second monitoring report, for the end of 2000, on the practical implementation of the Directive. If further amendment is considered necessary a draft directive will be published.

The economic assumption behind the 1985 Directive was, according to its accompanying memorandum of September 1976, that 'the compensation paid forms part of the general production costs of the product. This increase in cost is reflected in the pricing. The damage is thus, from an economic point of view, spread over all the products that are free from defects.' The Council has been accused of acting ultra vires, in that such matters as product liability fell outside the ambit of Article 2 of the EEC Treaty, which set out as an object 'a harmonious development of economic activities'. However, the preamble to the Directive reflects the EC view that: 'the approximation of the laws of the Member States concerning the liability of the producer for damage caused by the defectiveness of his products is necessary, because the existing divergencies may distort competition and affect the movement of goods within the common market and entail a differing degree of protection of the consumer against damage caused by a defective product to his health or property'.

Strict liability for death or personal injuries caused by defects in products also forms the basis of the European Convention on Products Liability in regard to Personal Injury and Death (the 'Strasbourg Convention'). The Convention was adopted by the Committee of Ministers of the Council of Europe, at Strasbourg, in September 1976 and opened for signature on 27

---

7   85/374/EEC, OJ No L 210, 7.8.85, p 29.
8   COM(95)617, 13.12.95.
9   1999/34/EC, OJ No L 141, 4.6.99, p 20; discussed below at p 177.
10   COM(99)396 of 28.7.99; see also J J I Peris 'Liability for Defective Products in the European Union: Developments Since 1995 – The European Commission's Green Paper' (1999) 7 Consum LJ 331.

January 1977. Although some Member States have signed the United Kingdom does not propose to sign in the light of the EC Directive.[11]

With regard to the future, a revolutionary proposal for reform was contained in *Consumer Guarantees*.[12] Here the question was raised of whether or not manufacturers should be jointly and severally liable, with retailers, for the *quality* of goods under sale of goods provisions. This, if adopted, would change entirely the manufacturer-retailer-consumer relationship. By establishing a form of vertical privity between manufacturers and consumers, this would enable many who, for some reason are prevented from suing in contract and are affected by the rules relating to pure economic loss in tort, to receive compensation under a form of strict contractual liability. Claims could then be directed against those responsible for producing defective goods rather than those who happen to sell them. As a consequence, much of the law of tort, both fault-based and strict, would become redundant where goods are involved, as contractual actions would be available.

The European Commission, in its Green Paper on *Guarantees for Consumer Goods and After-sales Services*,[13] mooted the idea of making producers and suppliers jointly liable to initial and subsequent purchasers of new, durable goods for failing to meet the consumer's legitimate expectations. The ensuing Directive[14] did not include such a provision, although Recital 23 does refer to the fact that 'it may by necessary to envisage more far-reaching harmonisation notably be providing for the producer's direct liability for defects for which he is responsible'. It is likely to be some time before any such changes are proposed.

2. CONSUMER PROTECTION ACT 1987

Part I of the Consumer Protection Act 1987 ('the 1987 Act') seeks to implement the EC Directive on Product Liability 85/374/EEC[15] (s 1(1)). The

11   *Implementation of EC Directive on Product Liability – An Explanatory and Consultative Note*, DTI, November 1985, Annex II.
12   Department of Trade and Industry, February 1992.
13   Com (93) 509, OJ C 388, 15.12.93, p 5.
14   Directive on Certain Aspects of the Sale of Consumer Goods and Associated Guarantees, 99/44/EC, OJ L 171, 7.7.99, p 12; discussed further in ch 5 and above at p 160.
15   For further reading on the 1987 Act see *Guide to the Consumer Protection Act 1987, Product liability and safety Provisions*, DTI, http://www.dti.gov.uk/access/consumer/contents.html; Cotter *Defective and Unsafe Products – Law and Practice;* Howells *Butterworths Common Law Series: Product Liability*; Kelly and Attree *European Product Liability*, 2nd edn; Miller *Product Liability and Consumer Safety Encyclopaedia*, Div III; Stapleton *Product Liability*; Whincup *Sales Law and Product Liability, a business guide* and tort textbooks. See also A Clark, 'The Consumer Protection Act 1987' (1990) 50 MLR 614.

effect of this is to impose strict tortious liability on producers of goods that prove to be defective and which cause damage to persons or, in some circumstances, property, subject to certain defences.

The Bill had its first reading in the House of Lords on 19 November 1986 and received Royal Assent on 15 May 1987. The Committee stage, Report stage and Third Reading in the House of Commons were all curtailed to enable the Bill to be completed before the recess of Parliament for the election in June 1987. There was, therefore, very little chance to debate amendments in the Commons.

Part I of the 1987 Act came into force on 1 March 1988 and, by section 50(7), liability for defects under the Act only arises as regards those products supplied to others by their producers after that date. The provisions of the 1987 Act are in addition to existing contractual and tortious rights (s 2(6)).

Before looking in detail at the liability created under the Act it is necessary to define two of the terms used.

Product. This is defined in section 1(2) as 'any goods or electricity'; goods being defined in section 45(1) as including substances (natural or artificial, in solid, liquid or gaseous form), growing crops, things comprised in land by virtue of being attached to it, ships, aircraft and vehicles.[16] In addition 'product' includes component parts and raw materials incorporated into finished products. Although buildings are included within the definition of goods, section 46(4) excludes from Part I 'supplying goods comprised in land where the supply is effected by the creation or disposal of an interest in land'. This means that if a building caused damage, for example by collapsing due to a design defect or defective construction, no claim can be made under the 1987 Act against the builder. However a claim may be made if any of the component parts of the building eg the brick, tiles, cement etc are defective and cause damage to persons or other property. This is the consequence of section 46(3), which establishes that, where goods are provided by their incorporation into buildings, this *is* a supply of goods. A detailed enquiry into issues of causation will therefore be needed where defects in a house cause claimable damage.

Producer. By section 1(2) a 'producer' of a product means:
a) the person who manufactured it;
b) in the case of a substance which has not been manufactured but has been won or abstracted, the person who won or abstracted it;
c) in the case of a product which has not been manufactured, won or abstracted but essential characteristics of which are attributable to an

16 Note that this is a different definition from that under the Sale of Goods Act 1979, s 61(1).

industrial or other process having been carried out (for example in relation to agricultural produce), the person who carried out that process.

This definition covers: under a), the manufacturer; under b), producers of products like minerals and natural gas; and, under c), those who, for example, refine petroleum or process food, activities which cannot be described as 'manufacturing' in the usual sense. With regard to the processing of food there is much debate over such activities as canning and freezing – do these processes have the effect of giving the product 'essential characteristics', or are they simply a method of preserving the food, without affecting its characteristics? If the former is the case, then the person responsible for the canning or freezing will be a 'producer' and liability will fall on that person for defects in the food, whether these are caused by the processing itself or are inherent in the food. If the latter applies then the processor will not acquire the status of a 'producer' and will not, therefore, be liable for the defective food, even if his or her handling of it caused the defect to arise. It is necessary to consider defective foodstuffs in conjunction with section 2(4), discussed below.

Who is liable?

Section 2(1) places the liability for damage caused by defective products on three classes of person identified in subsection (2). These are a) producers of products (as defined in section 1(2), see above); b) certain own branders; and c) importers of products into the Community. In the case of an own brander liability arises if he has put his name on or uses a trade mark or distinguishing mark in relation to the product where he 'has held himself out to be the producer of the product' (s 2(2)(b)). Thus if, for example, a supermarket chain sells its own branded goods, representing itself as the producer and without revealing the actual manufacturer's name, this will result in the supermarket being liable as producer.[17] If the actual manufacturer's name is indicated then the supermarket will simply be a 'supplier' (see below). One slightly more problematic case is where supermarket X has products labelled as 'made for X', without revealing by whom they have been produced. Here it could be argued that the supermarket has not 'held [it]self out as the producer' and is therefore only a 'supplier'.

17 This considerably extends its liability. The strict liability for the quality of goods implied under the Sale of Goods Act 1979 only applies to those privy to the contract of sale (see ch 5) and ordinary tortious actions require proof of negligence. Under the 1987 Act there is no privity requirement, anyone injured may sue, and without the need to prove negligence.

Where someone imports a defective product into the Community from outside the Community in order, in the course of business, to supply it to another, then that importer is liable for the product. If a non-Community product is imported into Great Britain via another member state (eg Germany) then the liability will fall upon the person who imported the product into Germany. The action will depend upon the rules of private international law to determine who has jurisdiction and what laws are applicable. It is, therefore, important to all Community citizens how each member state implements the Directive, in particular as regards the optional derogations.[18]

To deal with situations where the producer or importer may not readily be identifiable, section 2(3) places some responsibility on the supplier of goods. A supplier here is one who supplies[19] the defective goods to the person who suffers the damage, to the producer (in the case of component parts and raw materials) or any other person. The retailer of goods will clearly come under this definition. The supplier's liability only arises if: a) the person suffering damage asks the supplier to identify one or more persons falling under section 2(2) (ie producer, own brander or importer); b) that request is made within a reasonable period after the damage occurred and at a time when it is not reasonably practicable for the person making the request to identify all those persons; and c) the supplier fails, within a reasonable period of time after receiving the request, to comply with the request or identify the person who supplied the product to him. It can be seen that the supplier's liability will not arise very often. It will need a product which does not bear marks identifying a producer, own brander or importer and the supplier can completely discharge the liability either by identifying the person or persons requested or by identifying the person from whom the product was obtained. In the latter case the person suffering the damage would then have to repeat the process up the distribution chain until the person properly liable for the product is identified or no response is received to a request for information. It is easy to foresee practical difficulties arising over what is a reasonable period of time, both in terms of delays by the consumer as he or she slowly works back up the distribution chain and by the supplier on whom liability will rest if there is undue delay in providing the necessary information. Suppliers of goods from reputable manufacturers who clearly mark their goods have nothing to fear from section 2(3). It is only those who supply goods of undisclosed origin that may be affected by it.

---

18 Ie whether or not 'products' includes primary agricultural produce and game (until 4 December 2000), the development risk defence and a ceiling for total liability for a producer of identical products with the same defect. See Annex III *Implementation of the EC Directive on Product Liability*, DTI, November 1985 and Stapleton *Product Liability* pp 50–51.

19 Defined widely in s 46, including such things as sale, hire, hire-purchase, trading stamp redemption, work and materials contracts, prizes and gifts.

The discussion of section 2 has, so far, omitted to mention the exception to both subsections (2) and (3) currently contained in subsection (4). This is the controversial exclusion of persons who supplied game or agricultural produce to others when, at the time of supply, it had not 'undergone an industrial process'. The original wording of the Directive permitted Member States to include such products if wished (art 15(1)(a)) but the British Government chose not to. The amending Directive[20] deletes Article 15(1)(a) thereby bringing all agricultural produce and game within the scope of the Directive for all consumers in the European Economic Area. Implementation into United Kingdom law occurs on 4 December 2000 and repeal of section 2(4) is, therefore, imminent.[1]

For claims arising prior to the repeal, the Act defines 'agricultural produce' as 'any produce of the soil, of stockfarming or of fisheries' (s 1(2)) but provides no definitions of 'game' or 'industrial process'. It is not clear, for example, whether the shelling and freezing of peas or the filleting and freezing of fish would be industrial processes. The situation is further complicated by the problem of identifying a 'producer', as mentioned above. Even if the food had 'undergone an industrial process', unless that process changed the 'essential characteristics' of the item, the person processing it would not be classified as a 'producer' and no liability would be placed upon that person. It is interesting to note that the Act did not here followed the (original) wording of the Directive, where under Article 2 reference was made to products which 'have undergone initial processing'. This is, perhaps, a clearer concept than 'industrial processing'.[2]

Under section 2 it is possible for more than one person to be responsible for the liability imposed. In these cases subsection (5) stipulates that such liability is joint and several. This will give an injured consumer a better chance of obtaining full compensation, for if there are several possible defendants it will mitigate the effects of insolvency of one of them. However, since all potential defendants in the chain will, if they are prudent, insure against the risks, the costs of this insurance will inevitably be passed on to consumers generally. There are, of course, rights of recourse, contribution and relief between co-defendants such as assemblers and component part manufacturers.[3]

20   1999/34/EC, OJ No L 141, 4.6.99, p 20. See *Implementation of Directive 1999/ 34/EC extending product liability to primary agricultural products and game, consultation paper*, DTI, June 2000.
1   See Consumer Protection Act 1987 (Product Liability) (Modification) Order 2000, SI 2000/2771, operative from 4 December 2000, which repeals the definition of 'agricultural produce' in s 1(2) and s 2(4).
2   For a discussion of the arguments see *The Implementation of the EC Directive on Product Liability*, DTI, November 1985, paras 28–34.
3   See Civil Liability (Contribution) Act 1978, mentioned above p 169.

When is there a 'defect'?

In order to have a claim under the Act it must be shown that the product in question is defective. Under section 3(1) of the 1987 Act there is a defect in a product 'if the safety of the product is not such as persons generally are entitled to expect'. The meaning of 'safety' is further explained in that subsection. It includes safety in the context of risk of damage to property as well as risk of death and personal injury;[4] also it refers to safety with respect to component parts comprised in the product. It is important that the definition is not confined to products which are dangerous to health as many will prove only to be a risk to property but may cause considerable damage and inconvenience.

The test of the expected level of safety is clearly an objective one and guidance is given in section 3(2) as to what sort of factors should be taken into account. First, under a) 'the manner in which, and purposes for which, the product has been marketed, its get-up, the use of any mark in relation to the product and any instructions for, or warnings with respect to, doing or refraining from doing anything with or in relation to the product'. This covers a number of matters. It is obviously important to examine the purposes for which a product is marketed, how and where it is advertised, whom it is aimed at (children or adults, expert users or amateurs), packaging (including safety catches, child-proof features, etc), labels, instructions, warnings and the like.

Some of these factors have been considered in two recent cases. In *Richardson v LRC Products Ltd,*[5] a woman unsuccessfully sued for financial loss caused by the birth of her daughter. She claimed the pregnancy was caused by a faulty condom. Ozone damage to the surface of the rubber condom whilst at the factory was said to be the cause of its failure. The court decided fractures could happen by chance, there was no evidence of a weakness in the system of testing used by the producers, and the condom had been manufactured to the required standard.

The nature and extent of warnings were central in *Worsley v Tambrands.*[6] The claimant alleged that she had suffered from toxic shock syndrome (TSS) due to use of the defendant's tampon. In addition to issues of causation, a key aspect was the adequacy of warnings on the tampons box and in leaflets provided in the box. The warning leaflets had changed over the years that Mrs Worsley had used tampons and she had registered the risk of contracting TSS and some of the symptoms, but she had not read or retained the leaflet in the pack she was using when she became ill.

4   See below for a discussion of what types of damage are recoverable.
5   (2 February 2000, unreported), QBD, (2000) 23 Consumer Law Today, Issue 4, p 3.
6   (2000) 23 Consumer Law Today, Issue 5, p 1, QBD.

She failed to recognise the symptoms of TSS and, when taken ill, did not inform her doctor of her use of tampons. Treatment was, accordingly, delayed and she nearly died. The court rejected the argument that a full, detailed warning should be on the box; it was sufficient to provide a clearly legible general warning directing the reader to the detailed leaflet. It was found that the leaflet was legible, literate and unambiguous and contained suitable indications of warning signs and action to take if particular symptoms occurred. It was not necessary for the producers to take further steps to protect those who had lost their leaflets. The claim was, therefore, unsuccessful both in the tort of negligence and under the 1987 Act.

The second consideration, under section 3(2), is 'b) what might reasonably be expected to be done with or in relation to the product'. In addition to examining the normal uses to which a product may be put, this requires manufacturers to take into account foreseeable misuses of their products and perhaps guard against some of them by warnings, etc. A product causing harm whilst being misused in an unreasonable or unforeseeable way would not, however, be considered as defective. An example may help to illustrate the combined effects of a) and b).

Typewriter correction fluid is marketed to do the job its name suggests and it would presumably meet the safety requirements when being so used. It is, however, capable of causing accidental harm if swallowed or inhaled and so it has long been the practice of manufacturers to indicate such risks on the labels. The accuracy and clarity of such warnings in preventing accidental harm are further factors to be examined in determining the safety of the product as a whole. An additional problem arises with this type of product in that it may be deliberately misused by inhaling it, sometimes with fatal results. Providing no encouragement for such misuse is given in the advertising of the product and clear warnings are given on the labels, the product is likely to satisfy the safety requirement even if it did cause harm when being misused. It is interesting to note that Tipp-Ex was reported to be considering removing its solvent-based thinner (used with the correction fluid) from the market following reported deaths from inhalation in England and Belgium.[7]

The third consideration specified in section 3(2) is 'c) the time when the product was supplied by its producer to another'. It is further stipulated that a product is not defective simply because a safer product is later produced. These are obviously important provisions for manufacturers; otherwise there would be a reluctance to improve the safety levels of products, lest earlier versions were then branded as defective. It also recognises that standards do improve over the years and that, when judging the safety of a product it should be looked at, at least to some extent, in the light of expectations and standards current at its time of supply.

7   *Times*, 17 October 1991.

When considering the level of safety that people are entitled to expect from medicinal products particular problems arise. It is recognised that many drugs have side effects, some of which may be harmful in themselves. In deciding the safety issue a balance has to be drawn between the risks of harm from the illness compared to those from drugs. In the case of very serious illness a drug may satisfy the safety requirement despite its side effects whereas if used for minor illnesses it may not.[8] This cost-benefit analysis approach may well be relevant for other products also.[9]

'Damage'

Liability under Part I of the 1987 Act is for any 'damage' as defined in section 5. This covers death and personal injury and also loss or damage to any property including land (sub-s (1)). 'Personal injury' is defined in section 45(1) as 'including any disease and any other impairment of a person's physical or mental condition'. It would seem, therefore, that claims for nervous shock are permissible under the Act.[10] It is also important to note that there is no mention of being able to claim for pure economic loss, an important issue in many pre-Act negligence cases. The 1987 Act does not alter the law on this area in any way.

There are several restrictions on claims for property damage. First, under section 5(2), there is no liability for the loss of or damage to the defective product itself. Thus if the defective product self-destructs the only remedy available would be for the purchaser to sue in contract, there being no claim for such events under the tort of negligence either. In addition there is no liability for any loss or damage to the whole or part of any product supplied with the defective product 'comprised in it'. This means that if a car is supplied with a defective tyre, which causes the car to crash, there is no liability for the loss of or damage to the car, nor, of course, for the tyre. In contrast if the tyre were supplied separately as a replacement then there would be liability for the damage to the car under the Act, though still not for the tyre itself.

The second restriction on property claims is under section 5(3). If the property, at the time it is damaged, is not:

a) of a description of property ordinarily intended for private use, occupation or consumption; and

---

8   *Implementation of EC Directive on Product Liability*, DTI, paras 53–54.
9   See, for example, Miller *Product Liability and Consumer Safety Encyclopaedia* Div III [121]; C Newdick (1987) 103 LQR 288 at 300.
10 There is some doubt as to whether nervous shock is covered by the Directive. There were unsuccessful attempts to include a requirement to compensate for psychological damage during the passage of the amending Directive 99/34/EC, OJ No L 141, 4.6.99, p 20.

b) intended by the person suffering the loss or damage mainly for his own private use, occupation or consumption;

then there is no liability under the Act. It is necessary to look both at the nature of the property itself and the particular use to which it was being put at the time it suffered the damage in question.[11] Several significant product liability cases decided under the tort of negligence would therefore be outside the scope of the 1987 Act, for example *Aswan Engineering Establishment Co v Lupdine Ltd*[12] and *Muirhead v Industrial Tank Specialities Ltd.*[13] The third restriction on property claims is that under section 5(4). The damage suffered to the property must exceed £275. The reason for this minimum limit is to prevent numerous small claims being pursued. It will, however, produce anomalies: a defective television set which explodes only destroying a £276 video will enable a claim to be made under Part I for the video, whereas if the video was worth £274 it will not.

Section 5(5)-(7) assist in determining who has suffered property damage and when it occurred, an important consideration when limitation periods are involved (see below). Damage to property is deemed to occur at the earliest time that someone who has an interest in the property has knowledge of the material facts about the loss or damage.

Defences

The 1987 Act provides a number of defences in section 4. In all of them it is up to the person proceeded against to establish the defence. First, under section 4(1)(a), it is a defence to show that the defect is *attributable* to compliance with any statutory requirement or Community obligation. This does not mean that by complying with statutory requirements (such as safety regulations under s 11[14]) there is an automatic defence. The defence only arises if, in complying with the regulations, this causes the defect. It is going to be unusual for a producer to be able to show that the consequence of complying with a statutory requirement or Community obligation is to make a product defective, especially as most such provisions are designed to make products more not less safe.

The second defence, under section 4(1)(b), is that the person proceeded against did not at any time supply the product to another. This will cover cases of mistaken identity, where a wrong distributor or manufacturer is sued, and where products cause harm before they leave the producer, for

---

11 It is unfortunate that yet another 'consumer use' definition is provided. The wording of the subsection does not correspond with that used in the Unfair Contract Terms Act 1977, s 5 nor that in s 12 of that Act, see pp 159 and 128 respectively.

12 [1987] 1 All ER 135, [1987] 1 WLR 1, CA.

13 [1986] QB 507, [1985] 3 All ER 705, CA. See above p 157.

14 See ch 9, p 259.

example to the producer's employees. It would also apply if the goods were stolen from the producer and then distributed. The Department of Trade and Industry Consultation Document[15] suggests drugs used in trials before marketing would be covered here. They are not 'supplied' in terms of the definition in section 46.

Under section 4(1)(c) the third defence has two limbs. The only supply by the person proceeded against must be otherwise than in the course of a business of that person and either section 2(2) does not apply to that person (ie not a producer, own brander or Community importer, discussed above) or, if it does apply, that the activity was not done to make a profit. Put simply, it is a defence that the person supplied the goods privately, for example selling one's own goods second-hand or giving gifts to friends. Also, even if the person is a producer, etc of the goods, as long as they were not distributed to make a profit for that person, there is a defence. This provides a vital defence for, for example, people who make cakes and jams for charity stalls.

A fourth defence is that the defect did not exist in the product at the relevant time (s 4(1)(d)). The relevant time is explained under section 4(2). For electricity it is when it was generated, before transmission or distribution. Electricity companies will be able to use this defence to avoid liability under the Act for damage caused by voltage surges or falls caused by distribution faults. For defendants falling under section 2(2) (see above), the relevant time for all other products is when the person supplied the product to another. This means that a producer, own brander or Community importer will not be liable for defects caused by others further down the distribution chain. This could involve unauthorised removal of labels, warnings, etc by suppliers, alterations to or adaptation of the products causing them to become defective, subsequent deterioration of foodstuffs, etc. This is akin to a plea of *novus actus interveniens*.

For defendants who do not fall under section 2(2) such as retailers, the relevant time for seeing if a defect exists is when the product was last supplied by someone coming within section 2(2). A retailer will have no liability under the Act if, when the goods were last supplied by the producer, own brander or Community importer, they were not defective. If they were defective at that time the retailer will incur the liability of a supplier as discussed above. This will mean that where a product becomes defective by, for example, a retailer removing a warning label, the producer will have a defence under section 4(1)(d), as there was no defect when it left the producer. The retailer will also have the same defence for the same reason, the defect being absent at the relevant time (when the product left the producer). In such a case the victim of the defective product will be without

---

15 *Implementation of EC Directive on Product Liability*, para 56.

a remedy under the Act. It would still be open to the injured person to take a negligence action against the retailer.[16]

Perhaps the most important and certainly the most controversial[17] defence is that under section 4(1)(e). This states:

> that the state of scientific and technical knowledge at the relevant time was not such that a producer of products of the same description as the product in question might be expected to have discovered the defect if it had existed in his products while they were under his control.

The Directive made the adoption of this defence optional for member states (art 15) and, despite strenuous attempts by the consumer lobby to have it rejected, the Government included it in the Act. The European Commission believed that the wording of section 4(1)(e) did not correctly transpose the Directive into United Kingdom law and sought a declaration from the Court of Justice of the European Communities to this effect. In *EC Commission v United Kingdom*[18] the court dismissed the Commission's application. It indicated that the burden of proof was correctly placed on the producer and that there was 'no restriction on the state and degree of scientific and technical knowledge at the material time which is to be taken into account'. Further, the wording does not suggest, as alleged by the Commission, 'that the availability of the defence depends upon the subjective knowledge of a producer taking reasonable care in the light of the standard precautions taken in the industrial sector in question'. The Commission had not been able to refer to any national judicial decision demonstrating an interpretation inconsistent with the Directive. Finally, there was no evidence to indicate that the United Kingdom courts would fail to interpret the provision in a way consistent with the Directive, especially as this is required by section 1(1) of the Act.

The defence is sometimes referred to as the 'development risks' defence, on other occasions as the 'state of the art' defence. Both of these expressions can have several different meanings and this can lead to

---

16   See, for example, *Holmes v Ashford* [1950] 2 All ER 76, CA; *Kubach v Hollands* [1937] 3 All ER 907, QBD.

17   See M, H & P pp 245–251; C Newdick 'The Development Risk Defence of the Consumer Protection Act 1987' (1988) 47 CLJ 455; C Newdick 'Risk, Uncertainty and Knowledge in the Development Risks defence' (1991) 20 Anglo-Am LR 309; 482 HL Official Report (5th series) col 1003 et seq (2nd Reading, 8 December 1986); 483 HL Official Report (5th series) col 819 et seq (Committee, 20 January 1987). The suggestion of such a defence was rejected by both the Law Commission, Law Com No 82, Cmnd 6831, para 105 and the Pearson Commission, Cmnd 7054, para 1259.

18   Case C-300/95 [1997] All ER (EC) 481, ECJ; M, H & P p 246.

confusion. Here 'development risks' will be used to cover the defence under section 4(1)(e) as it more accurately reflects the nature of the defence.

The test is objective, based on a reasonable producer, so the resources and experience of the particular producer will not be relevant.[19] The words 'expected to have discovered the defect' may refer either to the issue of whether any producer ought to have been looking for the particular defect (such as the presence of the HIV virus in blood before much was known about it), or, alternatively, the problem of devising suitable tests to discover if a contemplated or known defect is present (eg tests for screening blood products for HIV virus). Just because a producer follows all the tests and procedures fellow producers use, this may not in itself be sufficient to establish the defence if further testing would be expected, given the state of scientific and technical knowledge at the time.

The 'relevant time' is that defined under section 4(2) (see above) and here it is the time when the product was *supplied* by the producer, not when it was manufactured. This means a producer has to keep abreast of developments until the product leaves the producer's control. As has been seen earlier, just because safer products are subsequently produced, this does not necessarily mean that a product was defective when put into circulation. In such cases there is no need for the producer to resort to the development risks defence; instead it can be argued that the claimant has failed to establish a defective product under section 3 or, if this is unsuccessful, section 4(1)(d) above can be raised. The main area of likely argument over the applicability of the development risks defence is that of new drugs with unexpected side effects. If all that is required by the courts to satisfy the defence is that producers perform the standard tests drug companies generally undertake then much of the anticipated benefit of the introduction of strict product liability will be lost. All that would be achieved would be, effectively, a reversal of the burden of proof, with the producer having to show the absence of negligence rather than the victim having to establish its presence. If, on the other hand, the defence is applied stringently as the Department of Trade and Industry assert will be the case[20] then it will be difficult for a producer to establish that a particular defect could not have been discovered.

The final defence under section 4(1)(f) concerns component parts. It is a defence if the defect is in a finished product in which the component part is incorporated and the defect is wholly attributable either to the design of the finished product or to compliance by the component producer with

---

19   See *EC Commission v United Kingdom*, n 18; at para 20; M, H & P at p 248. See also C Hodges 'Development Risks: Unanswered Questions' (1998) 61 MLR 560; M Mildred and G Howells 'Comment on "Development Risks: Unanswered Questions"' (1998) 61 MLR 570.

20   *Implementation of the EC Directive on Product Liability*, para 22. See also *EC Commission v United Kingdom*, n 18.

instructions provided by the producer of the finished product. To qualify for the defence the component producer must have no responsibility for the design of the finished product or be simply following specifications that prove to be unsuitable. The producer of the finished product will in such cases be liable for the defects.

Linked with the defences, provided under section 4, is the availability of a plea of contributory negligence on the part of the person injured. Section 6(4) applies the Law Reform (Contributory Negligence) Act 1945 and the Fatal Accidents Act 1976, section 5 (relating to contributory negligence) to claims under Part I. The claim of a person suffering damage as a result of a defective product can, therefore, be reduced (or even completely removed) if that person was in some way to blame for the harm suffered.[1]

Limitation periods

Section 6(6) and Schedule 1 operate to amend the Limitation Act 1980 and to introduce time limits for actions under Part I of the 1987 Act. There is an overall cut-off point for any proceedings to be brought which is 10 years after the 'relevant time' (Limitation Act 1980, s 11A(3) as inserted by Sch 1, para 1 of the 1987 Act). The 'relevant time' is defined in section 4 of the 1987 Act. For producers, own branders and importers it is the time when they supplied the product to another. For others, for example retailers, it is the time when the product was last supplied by a producer, own brander or importer (see above). A right of action is 'extinguished' after the 10 years, irrespective of whether or not it accrued and whether or not time had begun to run under section 11A(4) (see below). This fixed cut-off point assists producers to know the likely time period during which they can expect claims to be made and may assist in obtaining insurance against potential liability. It will mean that victims of defective products that may take many years to demonstrate their harmful effects, such as drugs and chemicals, may have lost their right of action long before they even realise that any harm has been suffered. In such cases there would, however, still be the possibility of an action in the tort of negligence.[2] It is clear that producers, importers and own branders will have to keep very careful and detailed records of when they supplied products if they are to take full advantage of the 10-year limitation on claims.

---

1   The risk of harm from a product may be so obvious (eg sharp knives) or the acts of the person harmed so unreasonable (eg solvent abusers) that the product is not found to be defective anyway. See above p 178.

2   See Limitation Act 1980, s 14 and, for example, *Wright v Dunlop Rubber Co Ltd* (1972) 13 KIR 255, CA (long-term carcinogenic properties of chemicals).

The second limitation on actions is contained in the Limitation Act 1980, section 11A(4) (as inserted by the 1987 Act, Sch 1). Claims for personal injuries or property damage cannot be brought more than three years after the later of:

a) the date on which the cause of action accrued; and
b) the date of knowledge of the injured party or, in the case of loss or damage to property, the date of knowledge of the claimant or (if earlier) of any person in whom his cause of action was previously vested.

The cause of action accrues when the damage or loss is suffered. In many cases this will be immediately appreciated by the victim and so time will begin to run from then. If, however, the victim is not immediately aware of the damage then the alternative starting date may apply. The 'date of knowledge' is defined in the Limitation Act 1980, section 14(1A) (inserted by the 1987 Act, Sch 1, para 3). This requires knowledge about the damage caused by the defect, the causal link between the damage and the alleged defect and the identity of the defendant. Special provisions are included in both the amendments to the Limitation Act 1980 and in section 6 of the 1987 Act to cover the position where the victim has died.

Exclusion of liability

Section 7 of the 1987 Act prevents the exclusion or limitation of the liability of a person under Part I of the Act, whether by any contract term, notice or any other provision. It would, however, be open to a producer to prevent any liability arising by providing detailed warnings and instructions so as to ensure that the product in question is not found to be defective (see above).

Conclusion

The implementation of the EC Directive on Product Liability in Part I of the Consumer Protection Act 1987 undoubtedly simplifies the claimant's task in establishing liability, since fault no longer has to be proved and often there will be several potential defendants to sue. By no means all the difficulties have disappeared however. In particular the allegation that a product is defective may be strongly contested with lengthy debate over the level of safety that persons generally are entitled to expect. This is demonstrated by the cases involving tampons and condoms discussed above. It is also still necessary to prove that the damage incurred was attributable to the defect, and problems over causation have in England and in other jurisdictions given rise to great difficulty in complex cases. Whilst it is reasonable to provide for a reduction in damages if the claimant has contributed to the accident, this also inevitably brings in the proof of fault and complicates the trial process. Above all in cases of new products with unexpected defects the availability of the development risks defence will raise the whole issue of fault and may result in the strict liability tort action being much less of a revolutionary development than expected. In keeping with the provisions of Article 15 of the EC Directive (which enables modification of the development risks defence under the Directive) section 8 of the 1987 Act provides a power to modify Part I of the Act by Order in Council.[3] It may be that some time in the future the defence will be removed.

The balance sheet reflected by the Consumer Protection Act 1987 nevertheless shows a clear gain by consumers and others injured by defective products. The cost of the measures is likely to have been an increase in the price of all products, safe or unsafe, approximately equivalent to the cost of insurance of the risks. The potential benefit to many injured consumers is, however, great.

To date there have been very few reported court decisions involving the 1987 Act, although several settlements have been noted. The National Consumer Council, in its Report,[4] was uncertain why, at the time of their investigation, there was little apparent use being made of the Act. Delays in the legal process, ignorance of the availability of the provisions and restrictions under the Act could all provide reasons. It could also be that many producers are settling claims, by providing compensation, without consumers resorting to court action or even legal advice.

An interesting application of the Act is for a person who, having had a hip replaced, experienced problems with the artificial hip, leading to two further operations and another hip replacement.[5] Another development is recognition of the potential to redirect claims by injured consumers away from suing a service provider, in the tort of negligence, to claiming from a manufacturer in strict liability, when a product breaks during use. A patient settled a claim[6] against the manufacturer of a surgical implement that broke during an operation and part of which was left behind in the patient. Prior to the Act a claim would have normally been made against the medical authorities in the tort of negligence.

As a result of the 1987 Act retailers should not be burdened with quite so many claims regarding damage done by products. However, it is interesting to note that the retailer's strict contractual liability will remain more onerous than the producer's strict tortious liability, since only the latter will be able, in some cases, to plead the development risks defence and/or contributory negligence.

3   This has been used to introduce the changes regarding agricultural produce, discussed above p 177.
4   *Unsafe Products – How the Consumer Protection Act works for consumers*, NCC, November 1995; M, H & P p 254.
5   *Times*, 12 September 1995; (1995) 18 Consumer Law Today, Issue 11, p 3.
6   See *Which?* February 1993, p 5.

7 The supply of services

Chapters 5 and 6 have been concerned with consumer transactions involving goods. Where the contract between consumer and supplier is one of services, the hallmark of which is that the consideration consists of value other than the primary (as opposed to incidental) supply of goods,[1] and the services are defective, the consumer's legal rights again depend on a) any express or implied terms applicable to the contract of services, and b) any right of action he or she might have in tort, particularly the tort of negligence.

I. IMPLIED TERMS

Prior to 1982, the implied terms in contracts for services depended largely on the common law. Following the recommendations of the National Consumer Council in its report *Service Please - Services and the law: a consumer view* (October 1981) to codify certain of the common law implied terms, a Private Member's Bill was introduced in January 1982. This received Royal Assent on 13 July 1982 as the Supply of Goods and Services Act 1982 ('the 1982 Act').[2] Part I of the Act is concerned with the implied terms in contracts for the supply of goods,[3] whilst Part II, which came into force on 4 July 1983,[4] involves the supply of services. Part IA, which was inserted by the Sale and Supply of Goods Act 1994 and came into force on 3 January 1995, concerns contracts for the supply of goods in Scotland. It is similar to Part I of the Act and will not be discussed further in this book.

1 Contracts for work and materials are mentioned above, ch 5.
2 See BSSCCL p 462.
3 See ch 5.
4 S 20(3) and the Supply of Goods and Services Act 1982 (Commencement) Order 1982, SI 1982/1770.

In July 1982 the Law Commission was asked by the Lord Chancellor to consider if any reforms were needed to the implied terms in contracts for the supply of a service, the exclusion of liability and the consequences of breach and to make recommendations. The Report (Law Com No 156) was published in April 1986 and concluded that no immediate amendment of the 1982 Act was called for and that it would be premature to consider changes to the law concerning exclusion clauses.

Contract for the supply of a service

Section 12 of the 1982 Act[5] defines a contract for the supply of a service as 'a contract under which a person ("the supplier") agrees to carry out a service'. Subsection (2) makes it clear that contracts of service or apprenticeships are not included in the definition. It does not matter that the contract may also involve the transfer or hire of goods, for example work and materials contracts, and any consideration will suffice, it need not be money (sub-s (3)). Power is given to the Secretary of State for Trade and Industry to exempt, by statutory instrument, specified services from all or any of the implied terms (sub-ss (4) and (5)).[6] It can be seen, therefore, that a very wide range of contracts for services are included within the definition, from hairdressers and shoe repairers to solicitors, architects and doctors providing private medical treatment, and from high-street consumer deals to industrial services such as cleaning and security.[7]

Reasonable care and skill

Where advice is given which falls below the standard of expertise reasonably to be expected, or in the common case where services are defectively performed, what remedy has the disappointed consumer in contract? It must be shown that there is an express or implied term that the service would be rendered with reasonable care and skill and that the supplier is in breach of this term. If the contract is one where the supplier is acting in the course of a business[8] then section 13 of the 1982 Act implies such a term. This reflects the common law position and there are many

5   See BSSCCL p 472.
6   See discussion re s 13 below for orders made to date. This power to exclude can be used to ensure that the legislation does not extend the existing law, merely codify it.
7   See Law Com No 156, paras 2.7–2.17; and generally M, H & P pp 151-164.
8   Defined in s 18(1) as including 'a profession and the activities of any government department or local or public authority'.

decisions to give guidance.[9] The standard of care in contract is the same as that in tort:

> the standard of the ordinary skilled man exercising and professing to have that special skill . . . It is well-established law that it is sufficient if he exercises the ordinary skill of an ordinary competent man exercising that particular art.[10]

The test is an objective one – the supplier of the service must come up to the standard of an ordinary supplier of that type; if special skills are claimed then the supplier is judged against someone possessing that special skill.[11]

Any attempt to exclude the implied term is permissible (s 16(1)), but may be subject to the Unfair Contract Terms Act 1977, section 2 and the Unfair Terms in Consumer Contracts Regulations 1999.[12] In addition, certain types of services have been excluded from the operation of section 13 by statutory instrument. These are:

1) the services of an advocate in court or before any tribunal, enquiry or arbitrator and in carrying out preliminary work directly affecting the conduct of the hearing;[13]
2) the services of directors of companies in their capacity as such;[14]
3) the services of directors of building societies;[15]
4) the services of members of the management committees of industrial and provident societies;[16] and
5) the services of an arbitrator (including an umpire).[17]

---

9 For an example using s 13 see *Wilson v Best Travel Ltd* [1993] 1 All ER 353, QBD; M, H & P p 168.

10 McNair J, *Bolam v Friern Hospital Management Committee* [1957] 2 All ER 118 at 121, [1957] 1 WLR 582 at 586, QBD; as approved in *Whitehouse v Jordan* [1981] 1 All ER 267, [1981] 1 WLR 246, HL.

11 See Law Com No 156 paras 2.19-2.27.

12 See below pp 198 and 202 respectively.

13 The Supply of Services (Exclusion of Implied Terms) Order 1982, SI 1982/1771, art 2(1), see below pp 210-211.

14 SI 1982/1771, art 2(2). For the common law liability of directors see *Re City Equitable Fire Insurance Co Ltd* [1925] Ch 407, [1924] All ER Rep 485, CA.

15 The Supply of Services (Exclusion of Implied Terms) Order 1983, SI 1983/902. For the common law position see *Sheffield and South Yorkshire Permanent Building Society v Aizlewood* (1889) 44 Ch D 412.

16 The Supply of Services (Exclusion of Implied Terms) Order 1983, SI 1983/902.

17 The Supply of Services (Exclusion of Implied Terms) Order 1985, SI 1985/1. The common law position is governed by *Sutcliffe v Thackrah* [1974] AC 727, [1974] 1 All ER 859, HL, and *Arenson v Casson Beckman Rutley & Co* [1977] AC 405, [1975] 3 All ER 901, HL. See also F Miller 'The Judicial Immunity of Arbitrators' (1991) 141 NLJ 633.

In many cases it is not material whether a professional or skilled contractor is sued in contract for breach of the implied term above or whether action is taken for breach of a duty of care, using the tort of negligence. It may be of significance, however, where limitation periods are involved since time starts to run from when the term is broken in contract and from when the damage is sustained in tort.[18] On many occasions the courts have considered whether or not to restrict claims against professional people privately engaged by a client to those in contract when there is the possibility of both contractual and tortious liability arising. The restrictive approach was favoured for many years, the argument being that 'where the complaint made is of failure by him to do the very thing which he contracted to do, there is no room for saying that any duty other than the contractual duty has been broken'.[19]

In contrast in *Midland Bank Trust Co Ltd v Hett, Stubbs and Kemp (a firm)*[20] Oliver J refused to follow the restrictive approach and held a firm of solicitors liable in tort (as well as contract) for neglecting to register an option to purchase land. This decision was applied regarding insurance contracts in *Forsikringsaktieselskapet Vesta v Butcher*,[1] medical treatment in *Thake v Maurice*[2] and solicitors in *Forster v Outred & Co (a firm)*[3] and *Bell v Peter Browne & Co.*[4]

The House of Lords examined the question of concurrent liability in some detail in *Henderson v Merrett Syndicates*,[5] a case concerning claims by Lloyd's names who were members of syndicates managed by the defendant underwriting agents. The court decided that, where a person

---

18 In the case of latent damage, in the tort of negligence a claimant may obtain the benefit of the Limitation Act 1980, s 14A which allows three years from the date of 'the knowledge required to bring an action' or six years from accrual. This is not permitted where the action is based in contract for breach of a negligence-based term: see *Iron Trade Mutual Insurance Co Ltd v J K Buckenham Ltd* [1990] 1 All ER 808, QBD.

19 Counsel *arguendo* in *Bagot v Stevens, Scanlan & Co Ltd* [1966] 1 QB 197, [1964] 3 All ER 577, QBD.

20 [1979] Ch 384, [1978] 3 All ER 571, Ch D.

1   [1986] 2 All ER 488 at 507, QBD; on appeal [1988] 2 All ER 43 at 47, CA.

2   [1986] QB 644, [1986] 1 All ER 497, CA (doctor liable in negligence for failing to warn of risks of reversal of a vasectomy, performed as a private operation).

3   [1982] 2 All ER 753, [1982] 1 WLR 86, CA.

4   [1990] 2 QB 495, [1990] 3 All ER 124, CA. Here the decision in *Midland Bank Trust Co Ltd v Hett, Stubbs and Kemp (a firm)* [1979] Ch 384, [1978] 3 All ER 571, Ch D, was not followed on the question of time limits. Damage accrued in both contract and tort at the time when a solicitor negligently failed to protect his client's equitable interest in a property, there being no continuing contractual relationship between the solicitor and client, unlike in the *Midland Bank* case. For further comment on limitation aspects and negligent solicitors see H Brayne and G Martin (1991) 88 LS Gaz No 11, p 25.

5   [1995] 2 AC 145, [1994] 3 All ER 506.

rendering professional services assumes responsibility, with a concurrent reliance by the person receiving the services, a tortious duty of care arose irrespective of whether or not there was also a contractual relationship. Lord Goff stated:

> there is no sound basis for a rule which automatically restricts the claimant to either a tortious or contractual remedy. The result may be untidy; but, given that the tortious duty is imposed by the general law, and the contractual duty is attributable to the will of the parties, I do not find it objectionable that the claimant may be entitled to take advantage of the remedy which is most advantageous to him, subject only to ascertaining whether the tortious duty is so inconsistent with the applicable contract that, in accordance with ordinary principle, the parties must be taken to have agreed that the tortious remedy is to be limited or excluded.[6]

Time for performance

Where the contract for the supply of a service is one where the supplier is acting in the course of a business then, if no time for carrying out the service has been fixed by the contract, nor any method for determining it stipulated, there is an implied term, under section 14(1) of the 1982 Act, that the service will be carried out within a reasonable time.[7] It is a question of fact what is a reasonable time (s 14(2)). A pre-Act example of this can be seen in *Charnock v Liverpool Corpn*.[8] Here a car, which should have been repaired in five weeks, took eight weeks. Damages were awarded for breach of the implied term of completing the work within a reasonable time.

Consideration

Section 15 of the 1982 Act implies a term, in any contract for the supply of a service, where the consideration has not been provided for by the contract or by a course of dealings, that the customer will pay the supplier a reasonable charge.[9] It is a question of fact as to what is a reasonable charge (s 15(2)). The section applies irrespective of whether or not the supplier is in the course of a business. Reference is made to 'consideration' and 'charge' as there is no requirement for payment to be in the form of

---

6   At pp 194, 532-533.
7   See M, H & P pp 156-158; BSSCCL p 472; Law Com No 156, paras 2.28-2.29.
8   [1968] 3 All ER 473, [1968] 1 WLR 1498, CA; M, H & P p 156.
9.   See M, H & P pp 158-160; BSSCCL p 473; Law Com No 156 paras 2.30-2.33.

money in such contracts.[10] Services may be provided for goods and/or other services, as well as money. Section 15 does not, however, deal with the situation where an exorbitant charge has been agreed under the contract.[11]

Stricter and additional obligations

The terms implied under Part II of the 1982 Act are not exhaustive.[12] Section 16(3) preserves any rule of law imposing a stricter duty than that under sections 13 and 14 and any additional implied terms that are not inconsistent with Part II. Also by section 16(4) it is 'subject to any other enactment which defines or restricts the rights, duties or liabilities arising in connection with a service of any description'. An area where liability has been extended, beyond that provided by the 1982 Act, is that involving the fitness of buildings.

Fitness of buildings

At common law 'it is quite clear . . . that when a purchaser buys a house from a builder who contracts to build it, there is a threefold implication: that the builder will do his work in a good and workmanlike manner; that he will supply good and proper materials; and that it will be reasonably fit for human habitation'.[13]

This common law duty was reinforced and expanded by the provisions of the Defective Premises Act 1972.[14] Under section 1, a person taking on work for, or in connection with, the provision of a dwelling (by erection, conversion or enlargement), owes a duty to the person ordering the work and to subsequent owners of a legal or equitable interest in the dwelling. The duty is to see that the work is done in a workmanlike or professional manner, with proper materials so that the dwelling will be fit for habitation when completed. Any cause of action in respect of a breach of this duty is deemed to accrue when the dwelling was completed (s 1(5)). The duty cannot validly be excluded or restricted by agreement (s 6(3)). Section 3 also abolished the common law rule that vendors, lessors and other

10   Section 12(3).
11   See below p 213 for the position re solicitor's charges.
12   See M, H & P pp 160-164; BSSCCL p 473; Law Com No 156 paras 2.3-2.6 and 2.34-2.36.
13   Per Denning MR in *Hancock v B W Brazier (Anerley) Ltd* [1966] 2 All ER 901 at 903, CA.
14   The Act substantially implemented proposals of the Law Commission's *Report on Civil Liability of Vendors Etc for Defective Premises* (Law Com No 40).

Implied terms

contractors were generally not liable in negligence if they carried out the work before the ownership of an interest in the land of a person subsequently injured by that negligence.

As to the question of 'fitness for habitation', in *Batty v Metropolitan Property Realisations Ltd*[15] developers acquired a site on a hill on which builders erected houses. The site appeared to be suitable, but there was evidence from surrounding land that land slips might occur. The claimants took a long lease of a house on a plateau from the developers, who expressly warranted that the house had been built in an efficient and workmanlike manner and of proper materials and so as to be fit for habitation. Three years later the garden of the house was affected by a severe land slip, and the evidence showed that the house would also be affected by further slippages within the next 10 years, rendering it valueless. It was held that the developers were liable under their warranty of fitness for habitation, which extended beyond the mere manner of building or materials used. The developers were liable in contract and in tort.

In the case of buildings for commercial purposes the courts have, on occasions, implied a term that the building should be fit for the purpose for which it was required.[16] This imposes on the builder 'a higher duty than is ordinarily implied in a contract for the design of a building by an architect. The latter, like the engineer, solicitor, doctor and other professionally qualified persons, has only to use reasonable care and skill'.[17]

Damages

The principles on which the courts assess damages, in cases of breach of contract for the supply of goods, have been discussed in chapter 5. Similar principles apply to breach of contract to provide services. The damages recoverable are in respect of consequences 'arising naturally, ie according to the usual course of things', from the breach, or 'such as may reasonably be supposed to have been in the contemplation of both parties, at the time they made the contract, as the probable result of the breach of it' under the rule in *Hadley v Baxendale*[18] referred to above. As an example, the late

---

15 [1978] QB 554, [1978] 2 All ER 445, CA. The builders were also liable in negligence for not having conducted sufficient tests on the site having regard to the defects in the surrounding area. Following *Murphy v Brentwood District Council* [1991] 1 AC 398, [1990] 2 All ER 908, HL, this aspect of the decision has been overruled as it involved pure economic loss, see below p 216.

16 *Greaves & Co (Contractors) Ltd v Baynham, Meikle & Partners* [1975] 3 All ER 99, [1975] 1 WLR 1095, CA; M, H & P p 160; *Basildon District Council v J E Lesser (Properties) Ltd* [1985] QB 839, [1985] 1 All ER 20, QBD.

17 Judge John Newey QC, *Basildon District Council v J E Lesser (Properties) Ltd* [1985] 1 All ER 20 at 26, QBD.

18 (1854) 9 Exch 341, Exchequer; see p 119.

arrival of a taxi, booked four months previously, to take a couple to their wedding, led to the award of £150 damages for disappointment and £100 expenses.[19] The couple planned to spend the money on a re-enactment of the wedding to enable photographs to be taken.

In many cases services may be provided, under a contract, for the benefit of more than one person, for example where a man books a package holiday on behalf of himself, his wife and children. Traditionally, the principles of privity of contract would limit the man's claim for damages for any breach of contract to a claim in respect of his own losses and disappointment. But the Court of Appeal held in *Jackson v Horizon Holidays Ltd* [20] that in these circumstances a husband could recover not only in respect of his own discomfort and disappointment, but also that of his wife and children. For contracts made on or after 11 May 2000, the Contracts (Rights of Third Parties) Act 1999 may also make claims by qualifying third parties sustainable.[1]

The Law Commission, in its Report *Implied Terms in Contracts for the Supply of Services*,[2] examined the existing remedies and canvassed the creation of new remedies. It concluded that any proposals for change would be premature and inappropriate.

2. NEGLIGENCE

The basis of this tort has already been discussed in connection with defective goods. As regards services, there are many cases where the provision of defective services may involve liability both for breach of a term of the contract between the consumer and provider and in tort. In some instances, since there is no contract between the parties, liability is in tort alone, usually the tort of negligence. For example, where there is breach of the limited duty of care, by persons giving advice or information to someone who they should have known would rely on it and without any effective disclaimer, under the principle formulated in *Hedley Byrne & Co Ltd v Heller & Partners Ltd*.[3] In cases of medical negligence, a National Health Service patient has no contract with the doctor. Alternatively, a person may contract privately with a doctor or surgeon for an operation on their child (the claimant being the child).

---

19 (2000) 23 Consumer Law Today Issue 6, p 6.
20 [1975] 3 All ER 92, [1975] 1 WLR 1468, CA; M, H & P p 42. But see also the criticism of the *Jackson* case in *Woodar Investment Development Ltd v Wimpey Construction (UK) Ltd* [1980] 1 All ER 571, [1980] 1 WLR 277, HL; M, H & P p 44.
1   See above p 148.
2   Law Com No 156, April 1986, Part IV.
3   [1964] AC 465, [1963] 2 All ER 575, HL.

Examples of situations where providers of services are liable to consumers, and indeed any 'neighbour' injured by their negligence under the *Donoghue v Stevenson* principle, are legion. A repairer of goods owes a duty of care to their users. In *Haseldine v C A Daw & Son Ltd*[4] breach of duty was expressed as involving i) a want of care on his part in the performance of the work he was employed to do, and ii) circumstances which show that the employer (ie the customer) will be left in ignorance of the danger which the lack of care has created. The latter stipulation seems appropriate only to the type of situation under review in this case - ie where the claimant was injured in a lift that fell down a shaft because of a defective repair by the landlord's agents. It is part of the general principle that 'a repairer of a chattel stands in no different position from that of a manufacturer, and does owe a duty to a person who, in the ordinary course, may be expected to make use of the thing repaired'.[5]

Another fertile source of difficulty arises where the customer's property is left with the provider of the service and is misappropriated. It is an advantage of suing in negligence that under the principle of vicarious liability an employer is liable in respect of the torts committed by his employees in the course of employment. There may, therefore, be a good case for suing the owner of a restaurant or other place where the customer's goods are left and from where the theft of them is known to have been effected by an employee. The nature of the duty of care, where goods left under a bailment are lost or damaged, was explained by Lord Denning MR in *Morris v C W Martin & Sons Ltd*.[6] Here the customer's mink coat had been left with a furrier for cleaning. He sent it, with her consent, to the defendants, where it was stolen by one of their employees. If the bailment is a gratuitous one, for example where a coat is left in a host's hall and stolen by a servant, the host is not liable because he is under no duty to prevent it being stolen, but only to 'keep it as his own'.[7] Somewhat similarly, if an actor's clothes are stolen from his theatre dressing room, owing to a negligent porter allowing a thief to enter, the employing theatre is not liable for the loss. This is because the relationship of master and servant gives rise to no duty to protect the actor's belongings from theft (nor is the theatre proprietor a bailee of the clothes).[8] But where the bailment is for reward, as it will be when a consumer enters into a contract for the cleaning of clothes,

4   [1941] 2 KB 343, [1941] 3 All ER 156, CA.
5   Ibid per Goddard LJ.
6   [1966] 1 QB 716, [1965] 2 All ER 725, CA.
7   See *Coggs v Bernard* (1703) 2 Ld Raym 909 at 914 per Holt CJ – 'so far is the law from being unreasonable as to charge a man for doing such a friendly act for his friend'.
8   See eg *Deyong v Shenburn* [1946] KB 227, [1946] 1 All ER 226, CA; *Edwards v West Herts Group Hospital Management Committee* [1957] 1 All ER 541, [1957] 1 WLR 415, CA.

it is the bailee's duty to take reasonable care to keep the bailed goods safe, and this duty cannot be delegated to a servant. The bailee's only defence is to show that the loss was without any fault on his or his servants' part. And in this particular case it has been held that a sub-bailee owes to the owner all the duties of a bailee for reward and could be sued successfully for the misappropriation by the servant to whom the master gave the duty of taking reasonable care (but not, apparently, if it had been by some other unconnected servant). In the case of thefts of the customers' goods from restaurants, it is not always certain that there has been sufficient delivery of possession to the restaurant proprietor to constitute a bailment, as opposed to a mere licence whereunder the owner is permitted to leave possessions on the premises. But if there is a bailment, the bailee may be held responsible for loss either because of the breach of the obligation to take reasonable care imposed by the law of bailment or for negligence.[9]

Vehicles left in car parks can also give rise to problems of whether there has been a bailment or a mere licence. In *Ashby v Tolhurst*[10] it was held that a car parked in the defendant's car park in return for a shilling fee and a 'Car Park Ticket' was not bailed to the defendant and that he was not liable for its theft. An exemption clause, in any event, absolved the defendant from liability for loss or damage to cars. Likewise in *Fred Chappell Ltd v National Car Parks*[11] the payment of £2, retention of the keys by the owner and no actual transfer of custody when parking in an open car park, without a barrier, did not result in the creation of a bailment. This was despite the inappropriate wording of the parking ticket which referred to 'misdelivery' and 'right to refuse to release any vehicle'. Handing over keys or putting a car in an hotel's covered garage will normally[12] give rise to a bailment and the bailee must then disprove negligence.

9   See *Ultzen v Nicols* [1894] 1 QB 92 (restaurant proprietor liable for loss of diner's coat hung on a hook behind him by a waiter). See also *Samuel v Westminster Wine Co Ltd* [1959] CLY 173.
10 [1937] 2 KB 242, [1937] 2 All ER 837, CA; M, H & P p 180, followed in *Tinsley v Dudley* [1951] 2 KB 18, [1951] 1 All ER 252, CA and *Becvar v Jarvis Norfolk Hotel Ltd* [1999] CLY 833, Brighton CC (no disclaimer notice evident). But see now the Unfair Contract Terms Act 1977, s 2(2) and the Unfair Terms in Consumer Contracts Regulations 1999, below.
11 (1987) Times, 22 May, QBD. Here, obiter, the judge decided that a term purporting to reverse the burden of proof in respect of any alleged breach of bailment would be reasonable under the Unfair Contract Terms Act 1977, s 2(2) (below) considering the small charge, the nature of facilities offered and the difficulties in protecting the vehicles.
12 See *B G Transport Service v Marston Motor Co Ltd* [1970] 1 Lloyd's Rep 371, QBD. See generally N E Palmer *Bailment*, ch 5.

Avoidance of liability for negligence

Finally on the topic of negligence, it is appropriate to draw attention to the statutory restrictions placed on the use of exemption clauses by the Unfair Contract Terms Act 1977 and the Unfair Terms in Consumer Contracts Regulations 1999, considering first the important reform effected by the 1977 Act, section 2.[13] This section was based on the recommendations of the Law Commission in their Second Report on Exemption Clauses (1975).

Section 2 provides that 1) a person cannot by reference to any contract term or notice exclude or restrict his liability for death or personal injury resulting from negligence, and 2) in the case of other loss or damage, a person cannot so exclude or restrict his liability for negligence except in so far as the contract term or notice satisfies the requirement of reasonableness. This means, by virtue of section 11(1), that the term must be regarded by the court as a fair and reasonable one to be included having regard to the circumstances which were, or ought reasonably to have been, known to or in the contemplation of the parties when the contract was made. In the case of a non-contractual notice, section 11(3) indicates that 'it should be fair and reasonable to allow reliance on it, having regard to all the circumstances obtaining when the liability arose or (but for the notice) would have arisen'. Section 2 also makes it clear that the defence of *volenti non fit injuria* (based on the voluntary assumption of risk) is not necessarily available to the supplier simply because the injured person has agreed to or is aware of a contract term or notice excluding or restricting liability for negligence.

The wide scope of this provision should be noted. Within the application of the Act any exemption clause in respect of negligence which results in death or personal injuries is void. Exemption clauses in respect of other loss or damage caused by negligence, such as 'goods accepted at owner's risk', must satisfy the reasonableness test, providing that the person causing the loss is under the general law liable in negligence for it. This may not necessarily be the case where, for example, the bailment is entirely gratuitous and for the benefit of the bailee alone. In this case it could well not be relevant to consider section 2, since there was never any pre-existing liability for negligence out of which to contract. Whilst such exemption clauses might normally have been found in contracts for services of one sort and another, the section also applies to such clauses in contracts for sale or other disposition of goods under which ownership or possession passes. The clause must relate to business liability as defined by section 1(3) - ie obligations or duties arising from things done or to be done in the course of a business, or from the occupation of business premises. The

---

13 See M, H & P pp 326 and 342-350; BSSCCL p 411 and Law Com No 156, paras 3.3-3.12.

contract must not be one of insurance (which industry has entered into a voluntary code of insurance practice) or otherwise within the isolated exceptions listed in Schedule 1 (contracts relating to land, intellectual property, companies and securities). Providing all requirements are satisfied, such exemption clauses are regulated by section 2. It matters not whether they are in respect of 'consumer transactions' or otherwise.

In respect of liability for 'negligence', negligence is defined (in s 1(1)) for the purposes of the Act as meaning the breach

a)   of any obligation, arising from the express or implied terms of a contract, to take reasonable care or exercise reasonable skill in the performance of the contract;

b)   of any common law duty to take reasonable care or exercise reasonable skill (but not any stricter duty);

c)   of the common duty of care (owed by occupiers of premises to their visitors) imposed by the Occupiers' Liability Act 1957 and equivalent legislation in Northern Ireland.

Judicial guidance indicates how the concept of reasonableness operates in the many contracts which consumers make for the supply of services on standard terms. In *Waldron-Kelly v British Railways Board*[14] the effect of the reasonableness test laid down by the 1977 Act on a standard form contract for carriage of goods by British Rail was discussed. The claimant had contracted with British Rail for his suitcase to be sent from Stockport to Haverfordwest by rail, at owner's risk, for a charge of £6.03. The standard form contract contained comprehensive exemption clauses in respect of loss, misdelivery, damage or delay unless the claimant could prove wilful misconduct by British Rail. If the goods failed to arrive at all, financial liability of British Rail was limited to a sum by reference to the weight of the goods (£27) as opposed to their value (£320.32). The suitcase never materialised and the claimant sued for the loss of the value of his goods and for compensation for distress and inconvenience. The judge held that in the case of non-delivery of goods, it was for the bailee to show that the loss was not his fault,[15] and this British Rail had failed to do. British Rail's exemption clause did not apply because it failed to satisfy the test of reasonableness set out in sections 2, 3 and 11 of the 1977 Act. In consumer cases the 1977 Act had supplanted the doctrine of fundamental breach, and the court should not look outside the terms of the 1977 Act. Accordingly the claimant was awarded the value of the suitcase and its contents (£320.32) but nothing for general damages. In contrast in *Wight v British Railways Board*[16] the court accepted the limitation by reference to weight clause as

14   [1981] CLY 303, Stockport County Court.
15   See *J Spurling Ltd v Bradshaw* [1956] 2 All ER 121, [1956] 1 WLR 461, CA; *Levison v Patent Steam Carpet Cleaning Co Ltd* [1978] QB 69, [1977] 3 All ER 498, CA; M, H & P p 179.
16   [1983] CLY 424, Bloomsbury and Marylebone County Court.

Negligence

reasonable. The reasons given included the fact that British Rail had no means of knowing the true value of the goods whereas the owner did and could insure them and competitors used similar, and often less generous, limitation clauses.

Exclusion clauses in film processors' contracts have been examined in *Woodman v Photo Trade Processing Ltd*[17] and *Warren v Truprint Ltd*.[18] In the *Woodman* case a clause limiting liability to the cost of a replacement film was held to be unreasonable. Reference was made to the fact that the clause offered no insurance facility, no advice was given to insure and the customer's attention was not specifically drawn to the clause. The court noted that the Code of Practice for the Photographic Industry[19] recommended a two-tier system of a normal service with total exclusion of liability and a special service at a higher charge with full acceptance of liability. No such special service was offered here. In the *Warren* case an alternative service *was* offered with the clause indicating 'We will undertake further liability at a supplementary charge. Written details on request.' Even this did not satisfy the reasonableness test as the alternatives were not plainly and clearly explained: the company could have set out the 'further liability' and the cost to the consumer.

An example of a non-consumer dispute concerning section 2(2) arose in *Phillips Products Ltd v Hyland*.[20] Here the negligent driver of a hired excavator damaged the hirer's factory. The clause, which purported to place responsibility for the driver's actions on the hirer, failed to satisfy the reasonableness test. The hirers did not regularly hire plant and drivers, had no control over the driver and had little opportunity to arrange insurance. The court supported the view of Lord Bridge in *George Mitchell (Chesterhall) Ltd v Finney Lock Seeds Ltd*[1] that in such cases appellate courts should be reluctant to overturn decisions at first instance and emphasised that the issue of reasonableness was specific to the particular contract involved. The subjective nature of the test was confirmed in *Stevenson v Nationwide Building Society*.[2] Here an exclusion clause in a mortgage application form, which accepted no liability for the value or condition of a property, was held to be reasonable using section 11(3). The building society was offering a valuation without liability or, if the purchaser wished, he could have a full survey at additional cost with

---

17   (7 May 1981, unreported) cited in (1981) 131 NLJ 935, Exeter County Court; see M, H & P p 343; *Which?* 1981 p 426 (lost wedding photographs).

18   [1986] BTLC 344, Luton County Court (lost photographs of silver wedding and an award presentation).

19   See ch 11, p 374.

20   [1987] 2 All ER 620, [1987] 1 WLR 659n, CA. See also (1985) 82 LS Gaz 2393.

1   [1983] 2 AC 803 at 816, [1983] 2 All ER 737 at 743, HL; M, H & P pp 319 and 365. See ch 5 at p 132.

2   (1984) 272 Estates Gazette 663, QBD.

acceptance of liability. The purchaser chose not to have the full survey and could not then sue for the negligent valuation.

The House of Lords has examined the operation of section 2(2) in two cases, heard together, concerning disclaimers of liability made by surveyors: *Smith v Eric S Bush,* and *Harris v Wyre Forest District Council.*[3] In the first case the claimant received a copy of the survey report prepared, by the defendants, for her building society prior to obtaining a mortgage. She relied on the report, having no further survey done. In assessing the reasonableness of provisions seeking to exclude liability for the negligence of surveyors, Lord Griffiths declared that certain factors should always be taken into account: 1) the bargaining powers of the parties, 2) in the case of advice, the practicality of consulting alternative sources, 3) the difficulty of the task undertaken and 4) the practical consequences of the decision on the question of reasonableness. This involves the sum of money potentially at stake and the availability of insurance. He indicated:

> We are dealing in this case with a loss which will be limited to the value of a modest house and against which it can be expected that the surveyor will be insured. Bearing the loss will be unlikely to cause significant hardship if it has to be borne by the surveyor but it is, on the other hand, quite possible that it will be a financial catastrophe for the purchaser who may be left with a valueless house and no money to buy another. . . . The result of denying a surveyor, in the circumstances of this case, the right to exclude liability will result in distributing the risk of his negligence among all house purchasers through an increase in his fees to cover insurance, rather than allowing the whole of the risk to fall on the one unfortunate purchaser. [at pp 858, 531]

Different considerations may operate regarding industrial properties, blocks of flats and very expensive houses, where purchasers may be expected to have their own surveys done, thus enabling surveyors acting for the providers of finance to exclude or limit their liability.

In the second case the appellants applied to a local authority for a mortgage. The local authority had the premises valued and, on the basis of this, offered to advance 90 per cent of the asking price for the house, conditional on some minor repair work. The appellants assumed the house was worth at least the amount of the valuation and purchased the house without their own survey. An unsuccessful attempt was made by the respondents to argue that liability never arose under *Hedley Byrne & Co Ltd v Heller & Partners Ltd*[4] because of the disclaimer of liability and that

3 [1990] 1 AC 831, [1989] 2 All ER 514, HL; M, H & P p 366. See below p 218.
4 [1964] AC 465, [1963] 2 All ER 575, HL.

therefore section 2(2) of the 1977 Act did not apply. Lord Templeman indicated: 'This construction would not give effect to the manifest intention of the 1977 Act but would emasculate the Act.' He referred to sections 11(3) and 13(1) and said that 'these provisions support the view that the 1977 Act requires that all exclusion notices which would in common law provide a defence to an action for negligence must satisfy the requirement of reasonableness.' The clause did not satisfy the reasonableness test and in the words of Lord Templeman:

> It is open to Parliament to provide that members of all professions or members of one profession providing services in the normal course of the exercise of their profession for reward shall be entitled to exclude or limit their liability for failure to exercise reasonable skill and care. In the absence of any such provision valuers are not, in my opinion, entitled to rely on a general exclusion of the common law duty of care owed to purchasers of houses by valuers to exercise reasonable skill and care in valuing houses for mortgage purposes. [at pp 853, 527]

In contrast, an estate agent was permitted to rely on a disclaimer of responsibility for the accuracy of details of a property in *McCullagh v Lane Fox & Partners Ltd*,[5] where land represented as 0.92 acre turned out to be 0.48 acre. In deciding that it would be fair and reasonable to allow reliance on the disclaimer, the Court of Appeal indicated that the purchaser was a sophisticated and experienced member of the public, who had the benefit of legal advice and representation. The disclaimer was commonly used in many agents' particulars and the purchaser expected its presence. Section 3 of the 1977 Act, discussed in chapter 5 in the context of the supply of goods, can be relevant also to contracts for services.

Unfair terms in contracts for services

Where a service is supplied under a contractual relationship, in addition to considering the 1977 Act in relation to exemption clauses, it is also often necessary to refer to the wider powers of the Unfair Terms in Consumer Contracts Regulations 1999.[6] The Regulations apply, subject to certain restrictions, where services are supplied in a business context to consumers, whether or not goods are also supplied. Most types of term, not just exemption clauses, may be affected. For detailed discussion of the Regulations, see chapter 5.

5   [1996]18 EG 104, CA.
6   SI 1999/2083, see pp 138-143.

3. EUROPEAN DEVELOPMENTS

In June 1994, in view of the opposition it had encountered, the Commission announced withdrawal of the proposed draft Directive on the liability of suppliers of services,[7] in favour of a changed approach.[8] This involves three features: 1) improved information for consumers centring on the development of voluntary standards and codes of conduct; 2) the preparation of specific texts concerning sectors in respect of which particular needs are established; and 3) support for the initiative regarding access to justice, the simplified settlement of disputes and guarantees and after-sales services. The Commission's Consumer Policy Action Plan 1999–2001[9] indicates that:

> [T]he Commission intends to examine the need to reinforce the safety of services. The Commission will identify the practical problems faced by consumers in different service sectors, especially those of a transnational nature. On the basis of an analysis of the results, the Commission will propose EU initiatives that will address both service safety and the liability of service providers. [para 4.3]

The European Parliament has called for mandatory regulations on the liability of service providers which would apply to certain services (installation and building services, medical services and information technology services).[10]

4. SPECIAL CONSIDERATIONS AFFECTING SPECIFIC SERVICES

As a tailpiece to this chapter, it is worth mentioning that a consumer with a complaint against a provider of a service must be prepared to consider remedies lying outside the law of contract and tort as so far discussed in this chapter. It must also be borne in mind that the provider of services may have specific rights against the customer's goods.

---

7   OJ No C 12, 18.1.91, p 8. This would have made suppliers of services subject to non-excludable liability for damage to people and movable or immovable property caused by fault on the part of the supplier. The burden of proving the absence of fault rested on the supplier.
8   COM (94) 260.
9   COM (98) 696.
10 OJ No C 279, 1.10.99, para 45.

Innkeepers

The ancient strict liability of the 'common innkeeper' for the safe-keeping of guests' property, the historical reason for which is the former tendency of some innkeepers to work in close association with highwaymen and footpads, is now modified by the Hotel Proprietors Act 1956. Establishments formerly styled common inns are now 'hotels', and are within the ambit of the statute if they hold themselves out as offering food, drink (alcoholic or otherwise) and, if required, sleeping accommodation to any traveller appearing to be able and willing to pay a reasonable sum for the services provided and in a fit state to be received (s 1(3)). ('Private hotels' may be outside this definition.) Failure to accept a traveller when there is sufficient room renders the hotelier liable for damages. If the traveller has engaged sleeping accommodation the hotelier is an 'insurer' of any luggage other than that left in a car or the car itself. The only defences are act of God, act of the Queen's enemies, or the guest's own negligence.[11] The hotel proprietor may limit liability by the prominent display of a notice, in accordance with the Act, which states that liability is limited to £50 for one article or £100 in total per guest unless either the hotel or its servants are guilty of neglect or wilful default, or the property has been deposited expressly for safe custody with the hotel proprietor. (Private hotels and boarding houses are within the ordinary law of negligence only.) The other side of the coin is that the innkeeper enjoys the right to detain, under a lien, the guest's goods brought to the hotel until the cost of food and lodging is met. If the goods are detained for six weeks the goods may be sold if the sale is advertised as specified by the Act at least a month beforehand (Innkeepers Act 1878).

Repairers

Again, a consumer whose goods are sold without agreement by a repairer may not have a valid complaint if the sale was within the terms of the Torts (Interference with Goods) Act 1977.[12] Repairers, in common with many other providers of services, may detain the goods until their charges are met (solicitors, bankers, factors and wharfingers also have rights of lien). But if the customer never returns at all - a common complaint of tailors and shoe repairers, for instance - the repairer needs to sell the goods to defray any charges. It is possible, and is perhaps advisable, to reserve the right

11   See *Shacklock v Ethorpe Ltd* [1939] 3 All ER 372, HL (hotel liable even though guest, whose jewellery was stolen from a locked dressing case, did not lock the door).
12   See BSSCCL p 396.

to do this on the terms stated in the contract. If goods are sold without such a contractual right the repairer will commit the tort of wrongful interference with goods[13] and must reimburse the owner on the basis of the value of the article when sued, less the value of any improvement. In an inflationary period this can be an open-ended commitment. The 1977 Act enables repairers or other persons providing treatment to sell the goods and account for the net proceeds to the owner after deducting charges and costs. The bailee has the right to sell the goods by the best method of sale reasonably available in the circumstances. To exercise this right the following factors must be present. Firstly, the bailor must be in breach of an obligation to take delivery of the goods, or the bailee must have taken reasonable steps to trace the bailor in order to impose such obligation on the bailor by the notice mentioned below, but without success. If such an obligation does not already exist by virtue of the terms of any contract, the bailee may impose such an obligation on the bailor by serving him with a notice stating (inter alia) that the goods are ready for delivery and specifying any amount due to the bailee. The requirements of such a notice are specified in more detail in Part I of Schedule 1 to the Act. Secondly, the bailee must serve a notice (concurrently with the notice mentioned above, if appropriate) that the bailee intends to sell the goods on or after a specified date. The date must be sufficient to afford the bailor a reasonable opportunity of taking delivery of the goods, and if an amount is owing to the bailee, the period must be not less than three months. The notice must also specify the name and address of the bailee and specify the amount due to the bailee by the bailor. The notice must be in writing and sent by registered letter or by the recorded delivery service (Sch 1, Part II). A sale duly made gives a good title to the purchaser as against the bailor.

The bailee is then liable to account to the bailor for the proceeds of sale less a) the costs of sale, and b) sums payable in respect of the goods by bailor to bailee before notice of sale was given (see generally s 12).

Package holidays

The ordinary law of contract and tort considered already can often deal with problems which arise from package holidays.[14] In addition, there is criminal liability under section 14 of the Trade Descriptions Act 1968 where services, facilities and holiday accommodation are misdescribed.[15] Many holidays are also protected by the Association of British Travel Agents Codes of Conduct.[16]

13 Under the Torts (Interference with Goods) Act 1977.
14 See M, H & P pp 165-171.
15 See further ch 12 at p 400.
16 See further ch 11 at p 373.

In the 1980s, however, there was growing concern about the protection afforded to holiday-makers within the European Community, culminating in the EC Directive on package travel, package holidays and package tours[17] being adopted in June 1990. This has been implemented in United Kingdom law by the Package Travel, Package Holidays and Package Tours Regulations 1992.[18] The Regulations apply to package holidays which involve an overnight stay or which last more than 24 hours, where at least two components out of the following are involved: a) transport, b) accommodation; and c) other tourist services (such as guided tours, excursions, sporting activities) if forming a significant part of the package. The package must be sold at an inclusive price and must be pre-arranged before the contract is made (reg 2(1)). A number of requirements are imposed on such holidays, enforceable by civil and/or criminal proceedings.

On the civil side compensation is payable if descriptive matter relating to the packages is misleading (reg 4); many particulars in brochures constitute implied warranties with strict, rather than fault-based liability (reg 6); the contents and form of contracts are specified in regulation 9 and Schedule 2; there are restrictions on price revisions (reg 11); and provisions are included covering transfers of bookings, alteration of essential terms, withdrawal by consumers and cancellation by organisers (regs 10, 12 and 13). Where a significant proportion of services are not provided, the organiser has to make suitable alternative arrangements where possible, and if not, make arrangements to return the consumer to the point of departure. Compensation is also payable where appropriate (reg 14).

Regulation 15 codifies the pre-existing British position on liability for proper performance:

> The other party to the contract is liable to the consumer for the proper performance of the obligations under the contract, irrespective of whether such obligations are to be performed by that other party or by other suppliers of services but this shall not affect any remedy or right of action which that other party may have against those other suppliers of services.

It also covers liability for damage caused to consumers by improper or non-performance. This liability will not arise if the damage is not due to the

---

17   90/314/EEC, OJ No L 158, 13.6.90, p 59.
18   SI 1992/3288, as amended by SI 1995/1648 and SI 1998/1208, see BSSCCL p 766; M, H & P pp 171-178 and 446-450. See *Looking into the Package Travel Regulations – A Guide for Organisers and Retailers*, DTI January 1995; *The Package Travel Regulations: Question and Answer Guidance on the Law Relating to Package Travel (Rev 1)*, DTI, http://www.dti.gov.uk/CACP/ca/package/index.htm; *Package Travel – Due Diligence Guidance*, LACOTS, November 1994.

fault of the organiser or retailer nor any other supplier of services but instead is due to the consumer (eg missing a train due to over-sleeping), an unconnected third party (eg bomb scares), unusual and unforeseeable circumstances which could not be avoided by taking all due care (eg unexpected severe weather) or an event which the organiser or retailer, even if careful, could not foresee or forestall (eg air traffic control delays). *Griffiths v Flying Colours Holidays Ltd (t/a Sunset Holidays)*[19] is an example of where there was liability for a family holiday spoilt by building work on the hotel premises, but not for sewerage replacement work being done in the resort. Limitations of liability are controlled and implied terms concerning the giving of prompt assistance to consumers in difficulty and the finding of appropriate solutions when complaints are made are included. Consumers are required to notify the supplier of services and organisers/retailers of deficient services.

Criminal measures focus on the information required to be provided in brochures (reg 5 and Sch 1);[20] specified information to be provided prior to contract (reg 7); information to be provided prior to commencement of the journey (reg 8); and the security to be provided in case of insolvency (regs 16-22). Enforcement provisions are contained in regulations 23-26 and Schedule 3, with a due diligence defence and by-pass provisions.[1] The Package Travel Directive is one of those listed in the Directive on injunctions for the protection of consumers' interests.[2] Implementation measures, permitting consumer protection bodies to seek injunctions, will be necessary by 1 January 2001.

Where the complaint against a provider of services does not arise out of a clear-cut breach of contract or a tort, and the objective is to obtain redress by other means, the point has already been made at various junctures in this book that it may be worthwhile considering a complaint to any professional association to which the provider of services belongs. This is particularly so if a) membership of such an association obliges the member to adopt a Code of Practice which has been infringed or b) a Code of Practice has been agreed with the Office of Fair Trading (considered in more detail in ch 11) and there are facilities for arbitration of disputes, or c) there is statutory or other machinery for handling of complaints against a particular profession.

19 7 January 1999, [1999] CLY 3820, St Helen's County Court.
20 See *Inspirations East Ltd v Dudley Metropolitan Borough Council* (1998) 106 ITSA 3 MR 24, DC, hotel falsely described as 'suitable for those with walking difficulties or using a wheelchair' and 'having ramps to all public access areas'.
1   For discussion of similar measures regarding consumer safety see ch 9 at p 261; also *Package Travel – Due Diligence Guidance*, LACOTS, November 1994.
2   98/27/EC, OJ No L 166, 11.6.98, p 51. See also *Injunctions Directive: Implementation in the UK*, DTI, February 2000 and 'Widening the Net', OFT, (2000) 26 Fair Trading 13.

Bankers

In the case of banker and customer the relationship may be governed both by common law and specific statutes dealing with obligations to as well as rights of the customer.[3] However, the bank's fundamental duty is the contractual one of obeying its customer's mandate (and thus not to pay out on a cheque bearing a forged signature). Correspondingly, the customer's fundamental duty is to exercise reasonable care not to facilitate fraud by the manner in which cheques are drawn, breach of which will result in the customer's being responsible for losses sustained by the bank.[4] The details of this complex relationship are properly within the sphere of commercial law.

With effect from March 1992 a new Code of Banking Practice became operational, with a revised version[5] issued in February 1994. The current, third edition (operative from 31 March 1999),[6] provides a minimum standard for banks, building societies and card issuers with many banks providing their own versions, giving additional rights to customers. The Code[7] covers such matters as putting a £50 limit on liability for losses from cash dispensers and the use of cards for electronic funds transfers (Switch cards and the like) unless the bank can establish 'fraud or gross negligence' on the part of the account holder; greater confidentiality of information on accounts, mailing lists etc; a 14-day cooling-off period for new accounts; protection for investors in superseded accounts and the publication of tariffs covering basic account services. The Code is monitored by the Banking Code Standards Board, which has criticised the banking industry for the standards of advice given.[8]

In addition to legal action, an aggrieved banking customer can refer a complaint to the Banking Ombudsman if the bank concerned is a member of the scheme. Currently 126 banks and subsidiaries are members. This option commenced in January 1986 and applies to complaints from individuals, sole traders, partnerships and unincorporated bodies. Companies with an annual turnover of less than £1 million are also covered. Compensation of up to £100,000 is possible. The Ombudsman's decisions are binding on the banks but not the customers. The 1998-99 Report of the Ombudsman shows 12,713 written complaints were received, with damages

---

3   Bills of Exchange Act 1882; Cheques Act 1957; Cheques Act 1992.
4   *London Joint Stock Bank v Macmillan and Arthur* [1918] AC 777, HL.
5   This was subject to criticism for not doing enough for customers by the Director General of Fair Trading, see OFT Press Release 11/94 and *Annual Report of the Director General of Fair Trading 1994* (1995) HCP 419, p 21.
6   A 4th edition was announced on 19 September 2000 to take effect from 1 January 2001: see http://www.bankfacts.org.uk.
7   BSSCCL p 1041.
8   *The Times*, 4 July 2000.

averaging £3,334 awarded in 47 per cent of cases.[9] The highest award was £86,243. The Banking Ombudsman Scheme is due to become part of the Financial Ombudsman Scheme[10] in 2001.

Medical profession[11]

With regard to complaints against members of a profession, the position of medical practitioners is particularly important. In the case of complaints against doctors for inadequate treatment under the National Health Service reference should be made to the complaints machinery under the National Health Service Act 1977 and the National Health Service (General Medical Service) Regulations 1992.[12]

Doctors have to establish a 'practice based complaints procedure', with an identified person to receive and investigate complaints. If there is an allegation that a doctor has failed to comply with his or her terms of service, the matter may be referred, by the health authority, to a discipline committee. These committees have a solicitor or barrister as chair, with no more than three lay members and no more than three professional members, appointed by the health authority. The discipline committee will investigate the matter at a private hearing and will report to the health authority with its findings of fact, inferences to be drawn from these and recommendations for action.

The health authority may, having regard to the recommendations, take no further action, limit or reduce the doctor's list of patients and/or impose a financial penalty. It may also make representations to the tribunal established under section 46 of the 1977 Act for removal of the doctor's name from the medical list. Somewhat similar provisions apply to complaints against dentists, chemists and opticians in respect of National Health Service work. In the case of serious professional misconduct by doctors, disciplinary action may be taken by the General Medical Council to whom complaints can also be made. It must be emphasised that this complaints machinery is in addition to the patient's common law rights as previously discussed.

---

9   See also http://www.obo.org.uk; *Consumer Redress Mechanisms*, OFT, 1991, paras 4.75-4.76 and Appendix 2, Table 4 which reviews complaints dealt with in 1986-90; M. Seneviratne, R James and C Graham 'The Banks, The Ombudsman and Complaints Procedures' (1994) 13 CJQ 253; R James and M Seneviratne 'The effect of complaints on banks and building societies' (1994) 4 Consumer Policy Review 66.

10 See G Cox 'Introducing the Financial Ombudsman Service' (2000) 108 ITSA 8 MR 20.

11 For comments and criticism see *Alternatives to State Regulation*, Better Regulation Task Force, July 2000, para 4.4.

12 SI 1992/635, as amended.

Legal profession

Complaints against lawyers pose slightly different problems. It was held by the House of Lords in *Rondel v Worsley*[13] that a barrister was not liable for negligence in the conduct of litigation or in advising in connection with it. The immunity, which was justified on grounds of public policy, also extended to solicitors in respect of advocacy work. The House of Lords has, however, now reconsidered the immunity of advocates in *Arthur J S Hall & Co (a firm) v Simons, Barratt v Ansell (t/a Woolf Seddon (a firm)), Harris v Scholfield Roberts & Hill (a firm)*.[14] All seven Law Lords declined to follow *Rondel v Worsley* with regards to immunity in civil cases and a majority of four to three would not now permit the immunity in criminal cases. Each case concerned actions against solicitors but the court, in deciding them, considered primarily the position of barristers, before deciding that the same conclusions would apply to solicitors.

In deciding that barristers' immunity from action was no longer necessary, issues such as the 'cab rank' principle,[15] the public policy against re-litigating a decision of a court of competent jurisdiction (collateral attack), the barrister's duty to the court (divided loyalty), the position of other professionals and in other jurisdictions were examined. It was held that, although the decision in *Rondel* had been correct at the time, the situation today no longer merited the granting of immunity to advocates. Lord Steyn indicated[16] that 'it would be right to say that while standards at the Bar are generally high, in some respects there is room for improvement. An exposure of isolated acts of incompetence at the Bar will strengthen rather than weaken the legal system.' He also considered that 'public confidence in the legal system is not enhanced by the existence of the immunity. . . It tends to erode confidence in the legal system if advocates, alone among professional men, are immune from liability for negligence.' It is likely to be rare that an advocate would be found to be negligent in conducting court proceedings and various procedural safeguards exist to prevent vexatious litigants etc.

For legal services unconnected with advocacy, barristers are liable[17] in respect of negligent work or advice. It is also well established that solicitors are so liable (for breach of contract, as discussed above). The immunity of advocates is currently recognised in connection with the Supply of Goods and Services Act 1982. A contract for the services of 'an advocate in court

13   [1969] 1 AC 191, [1967] 3 All ER 993, HL.
14   [2000] 3 All ER 673, HL.
15   Whereby barristers are not able to reject to act for clients on the grounds of disapproval of the clients or their cases.
16   At p 683.
17   *Saif Ali v Sidney Mitchell & Co (a firm)* [1980] AC 198, [1978] 3 All ER 1033, HL.

or before any tribunal, inquiry or arbitrator and in carrying out preliminary work directly affecting the conduct of the hearing'[18] does not include the implied term of reasonable care and skill under section 13.[19] This is likely to be changed in the light of the *Arthur J S Hall & Co* case. In addition, a consumer may wish to use other avenues of complaint, either because negligence is not necessarily involved or if there are easier or cheaper alternatives to litigation.

In the case of barristers, complaints concerning professional misconduct and inadequate professional service may be made in writing to the Bar Council.[20] The complaint is, initially, considered by the Complaints Commissioner and, if not dismissed, is referred to and investigated by the Professional Conduct and Complaints Committee which has both barristers and lay members. The Committee can dismiss the complaint, issue a written warning, refer the matter to the relevant Inn, deal with the matter in an informal hearing or by a summary procedure. If there is sufficient evidence for a prosecution for professional misconduct the complaint is taken to a Disciplinary Tribunal, appointed by the President of the Bar Council and chaired by a judge. If the complaint, of professional misconduct, is upheld, a barrister may be given advice as to future conduct, admonished, reprimanded, fined up to £5,000, suspended or, in serious cases, disbarred by his or her Inn of Court (and thus disentitled to practise). Any fees may be ordered to be returned or to be foregone but there is no power to award compensation where a client has suffered financial loss. If a charge of inadequate professional service is proved the Disciplinary Tribunal may require a formal apology to the complainant, repayment or remission of all or part of any fee or payment of compensation of up to £5,000. Where there is no evidence of professional misconduct, complaints of inadequate professional service may be brought before an Adjudication Panel,[1] which has similar powers to those of the Disciplinary Tribunal. Provision is made for appeals by barristers against decisions. Approximately 400 complaints are made each year, with about 35 tribunals held.

Complaints against solicitors are much more common than against barristers, which is to be expected since all clients' work must go through solicitors and they undertake responsibility for a far wider spectrum of work. Complaints about professional misconduct (for example, undue delay in the transaction of business or misappropriation of funds) or unsatisfactory service should be made in the first instance to the solicitors' firm involved.

18 Supply of Services (Exclusion of Implied Terms) Order 1982, SI 1982/1771, art 2(1).
19 See above p 190.
20 See the Bar Council's *Code of Conduct* (7th edn) and *Complaints Rules*, operative from 15 May 2000; http://www.barcouncil.org.uk.
1   Consisting of the Complaints Commissioner, one lay member and two barrister members of the Professional Conduct and Complaints Committee.

Since May 1991, each firm must establish an internal complaints handling process, with a complaints-handling partner.[2] If the complaint is unresolved it may then be directed to the solicitors' governing body, the Law Society. In respect of defalcations, a Compensation Fund is maintained by the Society out of which it may compensate clients who have been unable to recover money owed to them by their solicitor. As regards professional conduct generally, the Society has power to make rules for the regulation of discipline.[3]

The Report of the Royal Commission on Legal Services (1979, Cmnd 7648) recommended that The Law Society should investigate not only allegations of professional misconduct but also allegations of bad professional work, irrespective of whether or not the client may be entitled to pursue a claim in the courts.[4] This was introduced in the Solicitors Act 1974, section 44A[5] and has been replaced by the Solicitors Act 1974, section 37A and Schedule 1A.[6] The Law Society Council may, if the services provided by solicitors are 'not of the quality which it is reasonable to expect of them' (s 37A), impose sanctions on the solicitors. The sanctions include remission of the solicitor's costs, rectification by the solicitor of any error or omission, payment of compensation of up to £5,000 and taking specified actions in the interest of the client.[7]

All complaints to The Law Society about solicitors are directed to the Office of Supervision of Solicitors (OSS) which was set up in 1996.[8] A complaint is first referred to the firm concerned when either the client has not first approached the firm or where the firm has not complied with the spirit of Practice Rule 15, which requires firms to have an internal complaints procedure. If the complaint is satisfactorily resolved or if the OSS, having seen the firm's complaint file, decides the complaint has been properly handled no further action will be taken. If an investigation is necessary, the matter might be referred to a local conciliation officer (a solicitor or retired solicitor) to help resolve it. The OSS aims to carry out 90 per cent of

---

2 Solicitors' Practice Rules 1990, r 15.
3 Solicitors Act 1974, s 31 and see Solicitors' Practice Rules 1990. The Law Society is currently revising the Rules.
4 Para 25.24.
5 As inserted by the Administration of Justice Act 1985, s 1, operative from 1 January 1987, SI 1986/2260.
6 As inserted by the Courts and Legal Services Act 1990, s 93 and Sch 15 as of 1 April 1991.
7 Solicitors Act 1974, Sch 1A as inserted by the Courts and Legal Services Act 1990, s 93(3) and Sch 15 and amended by SI 2000/644.
8 The Law Society is considering proposals for reform with an independent lay commissioner to supervise consumer-related complaints, see (2000) 97/28 Law Soc Gaz 4. For discussion of the regulation of solicitors see *Models of Self-regulation*, NCC, October 1999, pp 39-41.

its investigations into cases of poor service and professional misconduct within three months and the other 10 per cent within five months.

Cases of serious misconduct are referred by the OSS to the Solicitors Disciplinary Tribunal. This Tribunal is constituted by the Master of the Rolls from experienced solicitors and lay members. The Tribunal is a judicial body independent of The Law Society, and if the Tribunal finds the complaint proved it may strike the solicitor off the Roll (thus removing the right to practise) or suspend or fine the solicitor up to £5,000.[9] Either party may appeal to a divisional court of the Queen's Bench Division.[10] Similarly a solicitor or barrister may be excluded from undertaking work under the Community Legal Service or Criminal Defence Service for misconduct,[11] and the solicitor or barrister has a final right of appeal to the High Court against such exclusion.[12]

Complaints involving alleged professional negligence may enable a client to seek damages through the courts. All solicitors are required to be insured against 'claims in respect of any description of civil liability'.[13] To assist, the OSS may refer a complainant to its negligence panel scheme, where up to one hour of free advice is given by the solicitor panel member.

Complaints about solicitors' bills are governed by different procedures. The client has two methods of safeguarding against excessive charges. Firstly there is the right to have the bill assessed by the court. The bill will be assessed on a 'solicitor and own client' basis so that all costs are allowed except so far as they are unreasonable in amount or have been unreasonably incurred. In contentious bills many items are fixed in accordance with scales laid down by the Civil Procedure Rules. Thus unless the bill is reduced by at least 20 per cent the client must pay the costs as a contractual debt. Alternatively, and without prejudice to the right to have the bill assessed, the client may ask the solicitor to apply to the Law Society to certify that the sum is fair and reasonable. This procedure is more apt for bills in respect of non-contentious business where the solicitor's remuneration is such sum as may be fair and reasonable having regard to all the circumstances of the case. The Solicitors' (Non-Contentious Business) Remuneration Order 1994[14] lays down a number of guidelines which must be considered. These include the complexity of the matter, the skill involved, the time spent on business and (very often the most important) the amount or value of the property involved and the importance of the matter to the client. A solicitor cannot bring proceedings to recover

9   Solicitors Act 1974, s 47 as amended by the Courts and Legal Services Act 1990, s 92.
10   Solicitors Act 1974, s 49.
11   See Administration of Justice Act 1985, ss 40-44 as amended.
12   Administration of Justice Act 1985, ss 42(3) and 43(5).
13   Solicitors Act 1974, s 37 and Solicitors' Indemnity Insurance Rules 2000.
14   SI 1994/2616.

costs on a bill for non-contentious business unless the client has been informed of the right to obtain a certificate from the Society or to have the bill assessed by the court. The client must require the solicitor to apply for a remuneration certificate within one month of being informed of the right to do so.

Legal Services Ombudsman[15]

The White Paper *Legal Services: A Framework for the Future* proposed[16] the creation of a new statutory office of Legal Services Ombudsman to cover solicitors, barristers and licensed conveyancers. This was brought about by the Courts and Legal Services Act 1990, section 21, the first English ombudsman, Michael Barnes, taking up office in January 1991. Appointment is made by the Lord Chancellor for a renewable three-year period. The current ombudsman is Ann Abraham.

The functions of the ombudsman are specified in section 22 and involve investigation of any allegation relating 'to the manner in which a complaint made to a professional body' regarding authorised advocates and litigators, licensed conveyancers, registered foreign lawyers, recognised bodies or duly certified notary publics, members of the professional body and any employee of such a person, has been dealt with by the professional body (sub-s (1)). The ombudsman, thus, has power to investigate both the matter which gave rise to the original complaint and also how that matter has been dealt with by the professional body. Any ombudsman enquiry cannot proceed whilst the matter is still under investigation by the professional body, pending any appeal against a determination by that body or until expiry of the appeal period (sub-s (5)). She may, however, investigate if the complaint concerns failures by the body to investigate or delays in completion of an investigation. Certain matters are excluded from the ambit of the ombudsman to prevent 'retrials': issues which are being or have been determined by a court, the Solicitors Disciplinary Tribunal, the Disciplinary Tribunal of the Council of the Inns of Court or other specified tribunal (sub-s (7)).

On completion of an investigation, the ombudsman produces a written report of her conclusions under section 23. She may recommend reconsideration by the professional body, that the body considers exercising its powers with regard to the person with respect to whom the complaint was made or anyone connected with him, that specified

---

15   See R James and M Seneviratne 'The Legal Services Ombudsman: Form versus Function?' (1995) 58 MLR 187; M Barnes 'The Role of the Legal Services Ombudsman' (1995) 145 NLJ 930.

16   Cm 740, 1989, para 10.13.

compensation be paid by the person complained against or the body to the complainant for 'loss suffered by him, or inconvenience or distress caused to him', and reimbursement by the person or body of the cost or part of the cost of making the allegation (sub-s (2)). The recipients of any such recommendations must indicate to the ombudsman, within three months, what action they propose to take to comply with the recommendation (sub-s (7)). Failure to comply with a recommendation must be publicised, with reasons given, in a manner specified by the ombudsman (sub-s (8)). Since September 1999, to strengthen the role, the ombudsman has also had powers to order compensation payments under subsection (2A).[17] In addition to investigating complaints the ombudsman also has an advisory function concerning investigation procedures of the professional bodies (s 24).

Legal Services Complaints Commissioner

In the light of growing public concerns about the need for independence in the supervision of complaints about legal professionals a new body is to be created. Section 51 of, and Schedule 8 to, the Courts and Legal Services Act 1999, when in force, will enable the Lord Chancellor to appoint a Legal Services Complaints Commissioner; an independent person who may not be a professional lawyer. The Lord Chancellor, under section 52, may direct the Commissioner to consider exercising specified powers where a legal professional body is not handling complaints about its members 'effectively and efficiently'. The powers concern aspects of complaints handling and include requiring the provision of information, conducting investigations, making recommendations, target setting and requiring plans to be submitted. If a plan for handling complaints is required and the plan provided is not considered adequate or if complaints are subsequently not handled in accordance with the plan, the Commissioner may impose a penalty, up to a maximum specified in a statutory instrument, on the body concerned. To avoid conflict between the Legal Services Ombudsman and the Commissioner, the Ombudsman's powers will cease when a matter has been referred to the Commissioner.

Surveyors[18]

It is well established that a surveyor who, for a fee, surveys a client's building and does so negligently is liable for the consequent loss to the

---

17 As inserted by the Courts and Legal Services Act 1999, s 49.
18 See generally K Richards 'Surveying the judges' (1995) 5 Consumer Policy Review 2.

client along the same lines as apply to other professional people (discussed above). If the surveyor negligently fails to identify defects in a property problems concerning quantification of damages may arise if the cost of repairing those undisclosed defects exceeds the diminution in value of the property (ie value with known defects compared with the price actually paid for the property). The current position is that the purchaser can only recover the diminution in value. This was decided by the Court of Appeal in *Watts v Morrow*.[19] In addition damages for distress and inconvenience were only recoverable when caused by the physical consequences of the breach; claims for general disappointment, anxiety etc would not be allowed.

The purchase of a house is likely to be the most expensive transaction the ordinary consumer undertakes. In the comparatively uncommon case where the purchase is not financed by a mortgage from a building society or bank the house buyer is entirely free to choose whether to have a preliminary survey or not before entering into a binding contract. In an effort to encourage surveys the Royal Institution of Chartered Surveyors (RICS) introduced in 1981 a 'Homebuyer's Survey and Valuation' scheme. This provides house buyers with a truncated standard survey report following a limited inspection by the surveyor, plus some indication of the value of the house. The fee for the service is usually considerably less than that for a full structural survey. The RICS scheme seeks to limit the potential liability to negligence of surveyors offering this service, since there may be some defects that only a more detailed survey would have revealed. It is uncertain whether this type of exemption clause would be upheld as reasonable within the Unfair Contract Terms Act 1977, section 2(2) and would satisfy the requirements of the Unfair Terms in Consumer Contracts Regulations 1999 discussed above in this chapter.

Since September 1998 the RICS has operated a Surveyor's and Valuer's Arbitration Scheme, administered by the Chartered Institute of Arbitrators. Claims for financial loss by clients and certain third parties, against RICS members and Incorporated Valuers and Auctioneers, up to a maximum of £50,000, are permitted.

The position of surveyors vis-a-vis third parties affected by their surveys has changed considerably in recent years. The first situation to consider is when a surveyor is acting for a local authority under statutory powers to ensure that local byelaws are complied with during the construction of houses. In 1990 the House of Lords in *Murphy v Brentwood District Council*[20] overruled its earlier decision of *Anns v Merton London Borough Council*[1] and denied the owner of a house affected by defective foundations a claim for compensation against the local authority whose negligent consulting engineers had approved the plans for the house. The house had been purchased in 1970 having been constructed on a concrete raft foundation to prevent settlement damage. The raft foundation proved to be defective and the house settled, causing cracks that were visible by 1981. Repairs to the foundations would have cost £45,000 but the claimant did not undertake these. Instead he sold the house for £35,000 below the market value if in sound condition in 1986. In the absence of actual damage to the owner's property (other than the house itself) or personal injury no claim for what is effectively pure economic loss could be made. The *Anns* case had allowed a claim on the basis that there was an imminent danger to the health or safety of the occupiers and that the cost of averting such danger was claimable against the local authority. In the light of subsequent cases, which had considerably restricted the scope of the *Anns* decision,[2] it was not surprising that the House of Lords in *Murphy* declared the damage suffered as pure economic loss and denied the existence of a duty of care to prevent such damage.

The other situation in which a house buyer is vitally concerned with a survey of the house, undertaken for another, is where the house purchase is financed by a mortgage. By the Building Societies Act 1986, section 13, a building society is under a duty to make arrangements for the valuation of properties offered as securities for advances. Their practice is to appoint a surveyor in the locality who makes a survey and valuation to the building society. The building society makes its decision on whether or not to lend on this basis. The borrower, as a term of the loan, must normally repay to the society the cost of such valuation. In *Yianni v Edwin Evans & Sons*[3] a firm of surveyors and valuers who made a survey and valuation of a London house for the Halifax Building Society in connection with a loan application by the claimants, Mr and Mrs Yianni, negligently reported to

2   See eg *Governors of the Peabody Donation Fund v Sir Lindsay Parkinson & Co Ltd* [1985] AC 210, [1984] 3 All ER 529, HL; *Investors in Industry Commercial Properties Ltd v South Bedfordshire District Council* [1986] QB 1034, [1986] 1 All ER 787, CA; and *D & F Estates Ltd v Church Comrs for England* [1989] AC 177, [1988] 2 All ER 992, HL.

3   [1982] QB 438, [1981] 3 All ER 592; M, H & P p 198. According to *Secretary of State for the Environment v Essex, Goodman & Suggitt* [1986] 2 All ER 69, [1986] 1 WLR 1432, QBD, in the case of a surveyor the cause of action accrues when the person relying on the survey acts on the report, thus distinguishing *Pirelli General Cable Works Ltd v Oscar Faber & Partners* [1983] 2 AC 1, [1983] 1 All ER 65, HL, where actual occurrence of damage was the significant date for engineers, builders and architects. Cases governed by the Limitation Act 1980, s 4A (as inserted by the Latent Damage Act 1986, s 1) may benefit from the new provisions whereby the limitation period runs from the later of six years from accrual of the cause of action or three years from the earliest date on which the claimant had the 'knowledge required for bringing an action for damages in respect of the relevant damage and the right to bring such an action' (s 14A(4)-(10)). Note, however, the 15-year long stop provision of s 14B.

the building society that the property was suitable security for a loan of £12,000. In fact the property was subject to serious defects and the report of the surveyors was described by the judge as 'grossly incompetent and negligent'. The claimants were sent a statutory notice by the building society saying that the making of the advance would not imply any warranty by the society that the purchase price was reasonable. The claimants had not purchased a house before, nor did they requisition an independent survey. The surveyor's report to the building society was not shown to them. Nevertheless, it was held that the surveyors in this case knew the purpose of the report and that the claimants would know, if the building society made an advance, that the surveyors must have recommended that their house was suitable for a mortgage of £12,000, being 80 per cent of its price. The defendants therefore owed a duty of care to the claimants since they should have foreseen that carelessness on their part might be likely to cause damage to the claimants. The damages obtainable would be related to the £8,000 worth of remedial work that was required.

The House of Lords confirmed the existence of a duty of care owed by valuers to purchasers when valuing for local authority or building society mortgages in *Smith v Eric S Bush,* and *Harris v Wyre Forest District Council.*[4] In the words of Lord Templeman:

> ... in my opinion the valuer assumes responsibility to both mortgagee and purchaser by agreeing to carry out a valuation for mortgage purposes knowing that the valuation fee has been paid by the purchaser and knowing that the valuation will probably be relied on by the purchaser in order to decide whether or not to enter into a contract to purchase the house. The valuer can escape the responsibility to exercise reasonable care and skill by an express exclusion clause, provided the exclusion clause does not fall foul of the Unfair Contract Terms Act 1977.[5]

Lord Griffiths indicated that it matters not whether the valuer is employed by the mortgagee, acting on his own account or is employed by a firm of independent surveyors, the duty as a professional person remains the same. The duty would, however, be limited to the purchaser of the house; there would be no duty to subsequent purchasers. It is interesting to note that here liability is imposed for economic loss suffered by the purchaser. Lord Griffiths explains that the necessary proximity between the valuer and purchaser 'arises from the surveyor's knowledge that the overwhelming probability is that the purchaser will rely on his valuation, the evidence

---

4   [1990] 1 AC 831, [1989] 2 All ER 514, HL; M, H & P p 348. See above p 201.
5   At pp 847, 524. For discussion of the exclusion of liability see above p 198.

was that surveyors knew that approximately 90 per cent of purchasers did so, and the fact that the surveyor only obtains the work because the purchaser is willing to pay his fee' (at pp 865, 536).

In some cases the vendor commissions a survey prior to sale, for the use of prospective purchasers, as is recommended in recent proposals to speed up and simplify house-buying. Here the idea of a duty being owed to prospective purchasers must be in contemplation when the survey is commissioned and the Contracts (Rights of Third Parties) Act 1999 could also assist.[6] The terms of the contract between the vendor and surveyor would need to be examined closely to determine the extent of liability.

Estate agents

For many years concern has been felt regarding the inadequacies of controls over the activities of estate agents.[7] There is no prohibition on anyone setting up as an estate agent, whatever his or her qualifications or lack of them, and in the course of that business receiving deposits from potential purchasers. Of course, it would be an offence under the Trade Descriptions Act 1968 for such a person wrongly to be described as, for instance, an Associate of the Royal Institution of Chartered Surveyors. However, there is nothing to prevent an unqualified person freely engaging in most of the activities of a professionally qualified auctioneer and estate agent. The Estate Agents Act 1979, which contains the main statutory controls over the activities of estate agents, falls far short of ensuring that estate agents must have followed a standard course of education and training (as is the case with medical practitioners, barristers, solicitors etc). There is, however, provision in section 22(1)[8] for making regulations prescribing minimum standards of competence for those engaged in estate agency work.

---

6   See p 148.
7   See, for example, *The Regulation of Estate Agency: A Consultative Document,* Dept of Prices and Consumer Protection, 1975; *Estate Agents Act 1979: A Review by the Director General of Fair Trading,* OFT, December 1988; *Review of Estate Agency,* DTI, June 1989; *Estate Agency: A consultation document by the Director General of Fair Trading,* OFT, September 1989; *Estate Agency: A report by the Director General of Fair Trading,* OFT, March 1990; R Bragg 'Regulation of Estate Agents, A Series of Half-hearted Measures?' (1992) 55 MLR 368; OFT Press Release PN 34/99, 20.9.99; *Annual Report of the Director General of Fair Trading 1999,* 2000 HCP 576, p 30.
8   This section is not yet in force. The Director General did not believe implementation of these provisions would assist consumers as most are affected by unethical practices rather than incompetence; see *Estate Agency,* OFT, March 1990, para 2.3.

The 1979 Act indicates that the profession of estate agency is open to any person until such time as that person is declared by the Director General of Fair Trading to be unfit to practise under section 3. Lessons having been learned from the huge expense of the licensing system under the Consumer Credit Act 1974, this Act in effect imposes a system of negative licensing – ie a person can practise until forbidden to do so or restricted in so doing.[9] Initially, the grounds in section 3 which could be used to declare a person unfit to carry out estate agency work centred on convictions for offences such as fraud, dishonesty or violence, certain offences under the 1979 Act itself, discriminatory practices (as detailed in Sch 1) and failures to comply with obligations imposed under sections 15, 18, 20 and 21 of the 1979 Act (see below). In response to the Director's report *Estate Agency* (March 1990), regulations have been made under section 3 to extend these grounds. Convictions for a number of specified offences, for example unlawful harassment of debtors, licensing, canvassing and advertising offences under the Consumer Credit Act 1974 and pricing offences under the Consumer Protection Act 1987, now enable prohibition proceedings to be taken.[10] Furthermore certain practices have been declared undesirable and thus grounds for prohibition or restriction.[11] These include failure to disclose a personal interest in the property, promptly and in writing, discriminating against prospective purchasers who do not desire other services from the estate agent and failing to give clients prompt, written notification of offers received from prospective purchasers. Failure to comply, without reasonable excuse, with a prohibition or restriction order is an offence under section 3(8). Provision is also made, under section 4, for warnings to be issued in cases of failure to comply with obligations under the Act or for engaging in undesirable practices; future misbehaviour could then lead to a banning order being made.

The Act also imposes certain duties on practising estate agents. These are contained in sections 12 to 21 and include the following duties or obligations:

a) The duty to give certain information about charges and the point of time when these charges become payable (it having been for many years controversial as to whether estate agents earn their fee on

9   For details of people prohibited from practising or restricted in their activities see Annual Reports of Director General of Fair Trading. Up to the end of 1999 262 estate agents had been banned, 13 restricted and 11 warned. 84 had given undertakings not to work as estate agents.

10 Section 3(1)(a)(iii) and the Estate Agents (Specified Offences) (No 2) Order 1991, SI 1991/1091, as amended.

11 Section 3(1)(d) and the Estate Agents (Undesirable Practices) (No 2) Order 1991, SI 1991/1032. See OFT booklet *The Estate Agency Guide* (OFT031) and *Using an estate agent* (England, Wales and Northern Ireland OFT 157, Scotland OFT 167).

'introducing a person ready and willing to buy' or on actual exchange of binding contracts), additional services offered and explanations of certain terms used (s 18 and regulations made thereunder).[12]

b) A duty to declare any conflict of interest, actual or potential, or any personal interest of the estate agent with respect to the transaction (s 21).

c) No estate agent may seek from a purchaser a pre-contract deposit in excess of a prescribed limit (s 19).[13]

d) Where a deposit is taken from a purchaser, either as a pre-contractual deposit or as a deposit on exchange of contracts, there are duties relating to the keeping of such money in separate 'client accounts' in a manner comparable to that applicable to solicitors (ss 12-17).[14]

These duties are designed to encourage fairness and openness in dealings with vendors and purchasers and to avoid a number of well-publicised incidents where estate agents have decamped with purchasers' deposits, there being no compulsory compensation scheme applicable in this type of case. Failure to comply with provisions concerning the keeping of clients' accounts is an offence (s 14(8)) and failure to provide information under section 18 makes any contract unenforceable without a court order (s 18(5)).

The enforcement of the Act is under the overall supervision of the Director. Local weights and measures authorities in Great Britain and the Department of Enterprise Trade and Investment in Northern Ireland are also enforcement authorities. They are given powers, under section 11,[15] of entry and inspection. They may use these powers to require production of books or documents and to seize and detain any books or documents which may be required as evidence in proceedings, provided that the authorised officer has reasonable cause to suspect that an offence has been committed under the Act. Most of the Act came into force on 3 May 1982 although, as already noted, some sections are still awaiting commencement regulations.

---

12 Estate Agents (Provision of Information) Regulations 1991, SI 1991/859.

13 This section is not yet in force.

14 See Estate Agents (Accounts) Regulations 1981, SI 1981/1520. For comment on the practical aspects see C Sweeting 'Little Ado About Something' (1985) 93 ITSA MR 216 and 'Estate Agents' (1993) 101 ITSA MR 18. Provisions relating to insurance cover for clients' money under ss 16 and 17 are not yet in force. In *Estate Agents Act 1979: A review by the Director General of Fair Trading*, OFT, 1988, it was felt that implementation of these provisions would be too costly for both government (local and national) and estate agents' customers in view of the few problems which arise (see paras 16.1-16.3).

15 See also the Estate Agents (Entry and Inspection) Regulations 1981, SI 1981/1519.

Two additional developments affect estate agents. First the Property Misdescriptions Act 1991[16] created criminal liability for misdescriptions of property. This is discussed further in chapter 12. Second, the Director, in his report *Estate Agency*, advocated a voluntary code of practice for estate agents to supplement the legal framework, with a redress procedure incorporated. In 1990 the Ombudsman for Corporate Estate Agents (OCEA) was set up by the 15 largest corporate residential agencies. From 1 January 1998 it became the Ombudsman for Estate Agents Scheme (OEA) which in May 2000 covered 2560 offices of 10 corporate estate agencies and 1046 offices from independent firms. There is a code of practice[17] and the ombudsman may award up to £25,000 compensation. If not satisfied with the decision, the consumer can still take legal action.

Insurance

A review of insurance law is outside the scope of this book but the conduct of insurance business and of claims made by consumers of the services of insurers has for some years been the subject of various criticisms.[18] In particular, the following two matters give rise to difficulties.

Duty of disclosure

Since the insurance contract is one 'of the utmost good faith' it has long been established 'in connection with insurance of all sorts, marine, fire, life, guarantee and every kind of policy that, as the underwriter knows nothing and the man who comes to him to insure knows everything, it is the duty of the assured . . . to make a full disclosure to the underwriters without being asked of all the material circumstances'.[19] The failure to disclose material facts by the insured entitles the insurance company to refuse to honour claims. A rather dramatic application of this principle occurred in *Woolcott v Sun Alliance and London Insurance Ltd*.[20] There the insured had been sentenced to 12 years' imprisonment for robbery and had other criminal convictions. In 1972 he had applied for a loan of £12,000 through his building society towards the purchase of a house. Under the

16 See BSSCCL p 579.
17 See p 375.
18 See M, H & P pp 182-198; *Which?* March 1991, p 133.
19 *Rozanes v Bowen* (1928) 32 Ll L Rep 98 at 102, CA. See Law Com No 104, Pt 3, Cmnd 8064; H Y Yeo 'Of reciprocity and remedies – duty of disclosure in insurance contracts' (1991) 11 Legal Studies 131; S Kilcommins 'Materiality in Insurance Law: an Appraisal' (1997) 16 Trad L 2.
20 [1978] 1 All ER 1253, [1978] 1 WLR 493; M, H & P p 183.

terms of the mortgage the building society insured in the joint names of themselves and the insured. The insured never completed a proposal form but filled in an application form for a loan in which he was asked to state the amount for which he wished his house to be covered. No mention was made of his previous convictions. Having purchased the house, some two years later the house was totally destroyed by fire. The insurance company indemnified the building society to the extent of the advance but refused to meet a claim for the balance by the insured on the grounds that he had failed to disclose his previous robbery conviction. The High Court upheld the insurers on the principle that the insured was under a duty to disclose such facts as a reasonable and prudent insurer might have treated as material. A previous conviction for such a serious offence as robbery was clearly a fact which came within this category. The insurance company was therefore within its rights in refusing to honour the insured's part of the claim. The insured here was not assisted by the Rehabilitation of Offenders Act 1974 which makes provision for convictions to be regarded as 'spent' after a certain period has elapsed, the maximum period being 10 years. This does not apply to serious sentences including imprisonment for a term exceeding 30 months.

The Law Commission in its report on Non-Disclosure and Breach of Warranty[1] stated that 'the present law as to non-disclosure is defective. The mischiefs in the present law cannot be cured by voluntary measures of self-regulation by the insurance industry such as Statements of Insurance Practice. In the absence of effective administrative control of underwriting, reform of the law is therefore required' (para 10.5). The Law Commission went on to propose that the duty of disclosure should be modified along the lines suggested in the Fifth Report of the Law Reform Committee. Under these proposals a fact should be disclosed to the insurer by an applicant if:

a) it is material in the sense that it would influence a prudent insurer in deciding whether to offer cover against the proposed risk and, if so, at what premium and on what terms; and

b) it is either known to the applicant or it is one which he can be assumed to know; for this purpose he should be assumed to know a material fact if it would have been ascertainable by reasonable enquiry and if a reasonable man applying for the insurance in question would have ascertained it; and

c) it is one which a reasonable man in the position of the applicant would disclose to his insurers, having regard to the nature and extent of the insurance cover which is sought and the circumstances in which it is

1 Law Com No 104, October 1980.

sought.[2] (NB it should be particularly noted that the duty to disclose material facts, both under the existing law and under the proposed reforms, continues to apply in the case of annual renewals of policies. Most insurance policies in England, other than policies of life insurance, are contracts for a term of one year and are renewable annually.)

Warranties

A second feature of insurance contracts which has given rise to concern relates to 'warranties'. Warranties are those statements actually made by the insured in the course of filling in the proposal form which are incorporated into the insurance contract. If any answer to a question asked is untrue the insurers may refuse to pay out on a claim on the ground of 'breach of warranty'.

Again the Law Commission regarded the present law in regard to warranties as defective and recommended statutory reform. In particular, it is proposed that a term of a contract of insurance should only be capable of constituting a warranty if it is material to the risk. This proposal is designed to negate the harsh result of the House of Lords' decision in *Dawsons Ltd v Bonnin*[3] where it was held that a wrong answer in the proposal form relating to the address at which a motor vehicle was to be garaged, though admittedly immaterial, nevertheless entitled the insurers to avoid liability under the policy.

The Unfair Contract Terms Act 1977, section 1(2) and Schedule 1 state that sections 2 to 4 of that Act (relating to the avoidance of liability for negligence, breach of contract and indemnity clauses) do not apply to any contract of insurance. However, the Unfair Terms in Consumer Contracts Regulations 1999[4] do not contain any such limitation and apply to terms in insurance contracts which were not individually negotiated and which do not define the subject matter of the contract, ie which do not define or circumscribe the insured risk and the insurer's liability.

It is clear that in the light of the Law Commission's Report above referred to, there is now considerable impetus towards reform on a number of

---

2   Law Com No 104, paras 4-47 et seq, para 10-5, and see also draft Bill attached to that Report. See NCC response *Insurance law – non-disclosure and breach of warranty* (1981); M, H & P p 185.

3   [1922] 2 AC 413; M, H & P p 190. In some cases the court will determine a case in a way more favourable to the consumer, see, eg, *Economides v Commercial Union Assurance Co plc* [1997] 3 All ER 636, CA; M, H & P p 192; [1998] JBL 279 (N Hurd).

4   SI 1999/2083. See further ch 5 at p 138.

aspects of insurance law in the consumer interest. To date no legislation has been forthcoming; instead the insurance industry modified its Statements of General Insurance Practice[5] to require disclosure of facts one could reasonably be expected to disclose.

Meanwhile a welcome development relating to the treatment of claims by insurance companies was the launching, in 1981, of the Insurance Ombudsman Bureau to deal, without charge, with complaints as to the handling of claims by consumers.[6] Over 220 insurers are members of the scheme. The Bureau investigates disputes concerning general insurance policies,[7] made with individuals resident in the United Kingdom. In 1999 the Insurance Ombudsman received 7,063 new cases; of 4,645 completed investigations he upheld the policyholder's complaint in 33 per cent of them. Awards of up to £100,000 may be made by the Ombudsman (£20,000 a year for permanent health insurance). His decision is binding on the member companies but a complainant may still take court action if the complaint is rejected or the complainant is dissatisfied.

Another method of deciding insurance disputes involves the Personal Insurance Arbitration Service (PIAS) to which a number of insurance companies belong. Here disputes are, with the consent of the member insurance company, resolved by arbitrators from the Chartered Institute of Arbitrators. The decision is binding on both parties and the service is free.

The work of the Insurance Ombudsman and PIAS is to transfer to the Financial Ombudsman Service[8] in 2001; the Insurance Division is to be headed by Tony Boorman.

5   January 1996.
6   See M, H & P pp 425-428; *Consumer Redress Mechanisms*, OFT, November 1991, paras 4.73-4.74 and Appendix 2, Table 2; *Ombudsmen*, Consumers' Association, 1997; *Review of the Insurance Ombudsman Bureau Scheme*, NCC, 1997; http://www.theiob.org.uk.
7   Household, motor, travel, loan protection, personal accident, pets, medical and legal expenses insurance are common areas examined.
8   See G Cox 'Introducing the Financial Ombudsman Service' (2000) 108 ITSA 8 MR 20.

8 The enforcement of consumer rights – civil and criminal proceedings

I. CIVIL PROCEEDINGS

Introduction

The object of this chapter is first to describe and assess the formal machinery for recovery of compensation by a consumer where a claim lies, as it is likely to, in contract or in tort. Legal aid and advice is also explained. The second part of the chapter describes the criminal process which may be involved where a crime is committed against the consumer and in particular describes how compensation may now be obtained in criminal cases without the necessity of separate civil proceedings.

Courts exercising the relevant civil jurisdiction

If a consumer wishes to pursue a complaint about the defective quality of goods or services provided or about personal injury or loss caused by defective goods or services the cause of action will lie in contract or tort. The accompanying diagram on p 229 indicates the relevant courts and avenues of appeal available in a typical consumer complaint case. The action will originate in either the Queen's Bench Division of the High Court or in the county court.

The relationship and division of business between the High Court and the county court have frequently been debated, as had the possibility of integration of the two courts, with their differences in practice and procedure so perplexing to the layperson.[1] The first major reform reflected

---

1 See for example the Gorell Committee on County Court Procedure 1908-09, H C 71; Beeching Commission on Assizes and Quarter Sessions, Cmnd 4153,

the deliberations of the Civil Justice Review Body.[2] The former mechanical criteria were almost entirely dependent on whether or not the debt, demand or damage did not exceed £5,000, in which case the county court took jurisdiction. Then, by virtue of the High Court and County Courts Jurisdiction Order 1991, (made under the Courts and Legal Services Act 1990) from 1 July 1991 county courts had unlimited jurisdiction for general list cases. Criteria for trial allocation depended upon substance, importance and complexity.

Post-Woolf procedural reforms

The current position reflects the reforms recommended in Lord Woolf's Final Report 1996 (see above) which found that the civil justice system was still too slow, too costly and too complex. People were deterred from using the courts and those that did found that the length of the process was uncertain and the costs incurred often disproportionate. At the heart of the problem was the traditional role of the judge in common law jurisdictions as passive umpire leaving the parties largely to make the running. Lord Woolf concluded that there was no alternative but to take case progress out of the hands of the parties and to make judicial case management a crucial part of the reforms.

One consequence has been that new Civil Procedure Rules (CPR) have been introduced to govern all proceedings commenced on or after 26 April 1999. They provide a complete and self-contained procedural code for both the High Court and the county court. They are set out in Parts (formerly Orders); are written in plainer language; contain 'signposts' cross-referring to other relevant rules; contain a 'glossary'; and contain a number of new, more self-explanatory expressions. 'Signposts' cross-refer to other relevant rules. The CPR are much less detailed than the old rules but are supplemented by an extensive array of Practice Directions. One of the consequences of all this is that most actions are commenced, under CPR Part 7, by using a 'claim form' whether this is in the High Court or the county court, and the term 'claimant' therefore replaces 'plaintiff'. (The term 'defendant' remains.) The form is accompanied by notes for guidance on its completion and there are separate notes for the defendant on the options available.

1969, p 73. Lord Woolf conducted an Inquiry into the civil justice system in England and Wales and an interim report was produced in June 1995. Lord Woolf identified some 60 previous reports therein. His Final Report followed – see Lord Woolf MR, *Final Report to the Lord Chancellor on the Civil Justice System in England and Wales* (London, HMSO 1996).

2   See Cm 394, 1988, Ch 3.

House of Lords

Court of Appeal
Civil Division

High Court of Justice
Queen's Bench
Division

County Courts

Small Claims
Arbitrations

(*'Leapfrog' appeals
under Administration of
Justice Act 1969, Part II)

*   Appeals may, exceptionally, go from the Queen's Bench Division direct to the
    House of Lords if the trial judge, the parties and the House of Lords agree and a
    point of law of general public importance is involved relating to statutory
    interpretation or if the judge was bound by a previous decision of the Court of
    Appeal or House of Lords.

'Pre-action protocols' have been and will be issued giving guidance to
the parties on the steps which should be taken before issuing proceedings.
They are designed to achieve early identification of the issues and evidence
and to encourage parties to settle disputes out of court where possible –
'ADR' (alternative dispute resolution) being a concept much encouraged
in the Woolf report. There is a general requirement that there should be a
reasonable exchange of information and documents in all claims, including
'small claims'. The existing protocols are also designed to enable the parties
to cope with court-imposed timetables.

In terms of jurisdiction the county court retains its unlimited jurisdiction
for handling contract and tort claims. Issue in the High Court is limited to
personal injury claims with a value of at least £50,000 (as before), other
claims exceeding £15,000, and claims required by statute to be in the High
Court or within one of its special lists such as the Commercial List.

It should be noted in the context of venue that if the claim is for a fixed
amount and an individual defendant defends, the claim is transferred to
the defendant's 'home court', ie the court or district registry of the area in
which he or, if represented, his solicitor is situated.

Civil proceedings

An important feature of the Woolf reforms is the allocation of the case to the appropriate 'track' so that it can get the appropriate judicial management to deal with the case justly and expeditiously. When a defence is filed an 'allocation questionnaire' is issued by the court to all parties with a deadline for its return. The file is then passed to a procedural judge for directions as to what needs to be done to prepare for the hearing and allocation to track. Under CPR, Part 26, allocation is to one of three tracks: the small claims track, the fast track and the multi-track. Of these, cases with a value of more than £5,000 but not more than £15,000 will normally be allocated to the fast track, which is designed to ensure that costs remain proportionate to the amount in dispute. Those up to £5,000 will normally be allocated to the small claims track, dealt with in more detail below, and those with a value over £15,000 (likely to be more complex) will be allocated to the more flexible multi-track.

The county court

Civil judicial statistics show that over 90 per cent of all civil proceedings have, over recent years, been commenced in the county court. These include the vast majority of claims by or against buyers of goods and services. The total not only applies to claims brought under the court's general jurisdiction in contract and tort mentioned above but also under its special jurisdiction given by some 150 statutes dealing with specific areas – hire-purchase and landlord and tenant being two very prevalent examples. County courts were created by the County Courts Act 1846 to try, on a local basis, cases involving smaller sums of money. They are not in any way based on geographical counties. The county court operates in about 300 towns and cities, and these are grouped into over 60 districts to each of which is allocated at least one circuit judge. On the passing of the Courts Act 1971 existing county court judges became circuit judges. New appointments are made by the Crown on the recommendation of the Lord Chancellor from amongst barristers or solicitors who have enjoyed general rights of audience in the Crown Court or in county courts for 10 years. A District Judge of at least three years' standing is also eligible. Each district must also have a District Judge, formerly known as a Registrar, assisted by Deputy District Judges (usually local solicitors in practice). The Courts and Legal Services Act 1990 took away the administrative functions of the former Registrars and District Judges, who are required (in effect) to be barristers or solicitors of at least seven years' standing, are responsible for the procedural steps in county court litigation and, of particular importance to consumer claims, the trying of 'small claims' (discussed later). In this connection it should be noted that after 26 April 1999 any proceedings in which the sum claimed or amount involved does not exceed

£5,000 will normally be allocated to the small claims track and be heard by a District Judge.[3]

Arbitration

In commercial dealings in particular, the solution of disputes by referring them to arbitration as an alternative to proceedings in the ordinary courts has long been commonplace in the UK and abroad. Many commercial contracts, including insurance contracts, contain provisions whereunder parties must refer a dispute to arbitration before court proceedings are started, and in *Scott v Avery*[4] it was established that court proceedings could be stayed if this step had not first been taken. In these circumstances the agreement to refer to arbitration is contractual. A party to an arbitration agreement against whom court proceedings are brought in respect of a relevant matter may apply to the court to have the proceedings stayed. Procedure is governed by the Arbitration Act 1996 which restated and revamped the law to ensure user-friendliness and a fair and economic disposal of the dispute. There is considerable latitude for the parties to agree their own procedure. Appeals are very limited. Broadly an arbitral award may be set aside by the court if there is found to have been a 'serious irregularity' (s 68) or, with the agreement of all other parties or leave of the court, on a point of law arising out of the award. The court's power to give leave is substantially restricted (s 69). This now very limited power of the court to intervene should be borne in mind by the consumer who decides to make use of arbitration procedures under the provisions of a contract or Code of Practice.

The development of 'small claims' procedures

A systematic attempt to deal with consumer small claims on a voluntary arbitration basis was made in 1971 in Manchester by the formation of an Arbitration Scheme for Small Claims, and a Small Claims 'Court' was established in Westminster in 1973. Much good work was done by these arbitration panels and their organisers claimed that since there were no pleadings and no pre-trial review they were speedier and simpler than county court proceedings. Arbitrators, usually solicitors, were appointed from a rota of those willing to do the work for a nominal fee. However, the preliminary difficulty of securing the consent of *both* parties, since the

---

3   Personal injury claims over £1,000 are excluded from the new regime.
4   (1856) 5 HL Cas 811. Note, however, the Arbitration Act 1996, ss 89–91 discussed in chapter 11 at p 363.

schemes were voluntary, the lack of any easily operated enforcement procedure and, most critically of all, the lack of any public or charitable funding to continue the schemes led to their demise by 1980. Interestingly, in the early 1990s there was a movement to introduce alternative dispute resolution (ADR), where, essentially, a skilled conciliator guides the parties towards an agreed settlement of the dispute outside the court system altogether, but has no power to act further if agreement cannot be reached.[5] This is mentioned again below.

At the same time a parallel development was taking place in the county court itself, no doubt in response to the criticism of over-formal, slow and expensive court procedures mentioned below. The Administration of Justice Acts 1973 and 1977, amending the County Courts Act 1959, gave power for County Court Rules to prescribe cases in which proceedings may be referred to arbitration, either automatically or by order of the court, and enacted that the order of the arbitrator shall be as binding and effectual as if given by the judge. The scheme, which provided the basis of the new 'small claims track', had the following main features:

a) Most proceedings involving an amount of £3,000 or less stood referred automatically to the District Judge as soon as a defence to the claim was received.

b) At the hearing the proceedings were directed to be informal and the strict rules of evidence were inapplicable. Since representation by lawyers was normally absent, the arbitrator was required to give each party a fair and equal opportunity to present their case.

c) Generally no legal costs were allowed in respect of arbitrated claims of £3,000 or below.[6] The exceptions were the costs stated on the summons, any costs of enforcing the award and costs certified by the arbitrator as having been incurred by the unreasonable conduct of the other party.

d) The arbitrator could proceed at a hearing despite the other party's absence, but there was a discretion to set aside such an award.

e) An award could be enforced as a judgment of the court. Accordingly all the machinery of the county court for enforcement of judgments, particularly warrants of execution against the debtor's property and attachment of earnings orders, were available.

f) The procedure could, of course, be used *against* consumers as well as by them, a point sometimes overlooked.

As mentioned above, this procedure involved an arbitration not a trial and the possibility of appeal was very limited. For all practical purposes the arbitrator's decision was final on the facts.

---

5   The process is distinct from arbitration because no adjudicated decision is imposed on the parties.
6   Ord 19, r 1(11).

It will also be noted that because no legal costs were normally awarded in respect of the hearing legal representation was discouraged, but not forbidden. However, consumers and other litigants were, of course, entitled to avail themselves, if eligible, of the 'green form' scheme of legal advice from a solicitor in preparing a claim or defence.

The current position reflects the post-Woolf reforms which are superimposed on the old system. This was regarded as sufficiently successful to have its jurisdiction raised again, as mentioned below. The small claims track is dealt with by CPR Part 27 and the following are the main changes:

1. Jurisdiction is increased to a maximum of £5,000, with the exception of claims for personal injury (limited to £1,000) and similarly limited claims in respect of housing repairs. Parties may consent to this track even if their claim exceeds the limit, subject, however, to the court's consent. In this case the limited costs regime does not apply but parties are limited to costs allowed under the fast track procedure and hearings are limited to one day.

2. There is no automatic reference to the small claims track. Defended claims are allocated to this track in the same way as to the other two in the light of answers to the allocation questionnaire (Form N150). The concept of an arbitration disappears and is replaced by 'a small claims hearing' with a simplified procedure. Most of the former aspects of the scheme are retained, including their informality, the encouragement of an interventionist approach by the judge and limited costs and rights of appeal (see below).

3. Hearings will generally be in public – see CPR Part 39. Representatives are allowed and these may be lay if the party is also present or the court gives leave. No expert evidence is allowed without the court's permission. The allocation questionnaire seeks details of any proposed expert's contribution. Exceptionally a maximum of £200 may be ordered as a contribution to the cost of an expert if the case is won.

4. Judges may propose to the parties adjudication on the basis of the written documentation (paper adjudications). If a party objects there is then a normal hearing.

5. A party not wishing to attend may give at least seven days' notice accordingly. The judgment must then give reasons for the decision.

6. Costs are limited to court fees, an amount, presently a maximum of £260, for legal advice if the action is for an injunction or specific performance, a maximum of £50 per day for the claimant or a witness for loss of earnings due to attendance at court (and any additional travelling and overnight expenses), enforcement costs and costs incurred through the unreasonable conduct of the other party. Apart from this, the winning party cannot get his costs paid by the losing party.

7. Appeals must set out the grounds with particulars of the serious irregularity or mistake of law alleged, within 14 days of the order. A circuit judge may dismiss the appeal without a hearing or list it for hearing.

Critique – access to civil justice by consumers

Mainly thanks to the far-reaching suggestions for reform of the Civil Justice Review and Lord Woolf's Report, change is occurring and the idea that courts are there for the benefit of litigants as consumers of the services of lawyers and judges is no longer heretical. From the courts' point of view, the requirement that they should take on an increased volume of work has not always been accompanied by the necessary resources in trained administrators. But until, for example, small claims in particular are able to be heard on Saturdays and one or two late evenings, so that litigants do not need to take so much time off work, many consumers will continue to find the legal process 'user unfriendly', however co-operative the staff of the courts actually try to be.

An underlying difficulty, however, is that the applicable substantive law is not necessarily 'simple' just because the amount of money in issue is 'small'. District Judges are mitigating the problems by being prepared to take a more 'interventionist' or 'inquisitorial' role and those concerned with further reform might usefully compare the modus operandi of such tribunals as Social Security Appeal Tribunals.

A penetrating survey into what actually happened at small claims proceedings in the county courts was concluded in 1995 by the Institute of Judicial Administration at the University of Birmingham under the auspices of Professor John Baldwin. A significant number of district judges, court officials and litigants were interviewed and courts attended. Although in many respects the system was found to be working quite well, the survey revealed some disturbing features. These included (1) fundamental disagreements amongst the judges as to whether they were obliged to apply the substantive law strictly or whether a 'commonsense' solution without regard to legal niceties was permissible; (2) a reluctance amongst the majority of judges to read the papers in advance of the hearing; (3) a lack of systematic training and peer review, as compared to that offered, for instance, to Chairmen of statutory tribunals. On the other hand judges were found to be courteous if, sometimes, necessarily brisk, with litigants, prepared to assist them with presentation of their cases and prepared to adjudicate on what was before them, even if evidence was less than adequately presented.

The survey also came to two other important conclusions. Firstly, a consumer-litigant very much increases chances of success if he or she turns up to the hearing. Secondly, consumer-litigants often come to grief despite a decision in their favour by a failure effectively to enforce the judgment. 'Sending the bailiffs in' under a warrant of execution is the more often tried remedy, little use being made of garnishee or attachment of earnings orders – and courts seemingly being much less helpful to litigants on enforcement procedures. A sizeable proportion of litigants simply abandon the unequal struggle at this late stage.

This conclusion was echoed by a survey carried out by the National Audit Office in 1996.[7] Reviewing 3,000 small claims there was a high level of satisfaction. But although 94% of claimants obtained a favourable judgment, only 54% recovered all or part of their claim and 36% nothing. The small claims procedure is popular. In 1998 there were nearly 99,000 such hearings, a figure accounting for nearly 88% of all county court trials.

Litigants in person

Particularly with the advent of the small claims arbitration procedure in the county court, there has been a move to reduce the cost of litigation by litigants dispensing with solicitors, and acting and appearing for themselves. At the same time county courts have tried to change their rather forbidding image and become more accessible and helpful to such litigants. In particular the Court Service has produced a number of leaflets intended to explain every step taken by claimants and to give practical advice on what to do next. Every litigant in person unused to court procedures should study these leaflets, available free from the courts and some Citizens' Advice Bureaux and Advice Centres, which perform a valuable service in the administration of justice at ground level.

With regard to costs in actions when the claim involved exceeds the financial limit below which solicitors' costs, other than those shown on the claim form, are not allowed, the successful litigant in person was formerly not entitled to remuneration in respect of time and labour involved. Mainly as a result of pressure from the Consumers' Association the Litigants in Person (Costs and Expenses) Act 1975 abrogated this rule as from 1 April 1976. The lay litigant may now recover up to two-thirds of the sum which would have been allowed to his solicitor in accordance with an hourly rate.

The trend towards official encouragement, or at least absence of positive discouragement, to litigants in person continues with the setting up of an office in the Royal Courts of Justice in London whose staff are available with advice on procedures for the common forms of action. There have

7   *Handling small claims in the county courts* (1996), HCP 271, (1996) 93 LS Gaz, Issue 10, p 5.

Civil proceedings

long been personal application facilities for obtaining grants of probate and letters of administration, and divorce procedure in undefended cases has also been simplified to enable parties to act for themselves.

Alternative dispute resolution

Reaction, particularly by businessmen, against the costs and delays of traditional adjudication by judges or arbitrators has led to a growing interest in alternative dispute resolution (ADR). This has received judicial blessing not least by a Practice Statement in the Commercial Court encouraging parties to disputes to consider ADR as an alternative means of resolving issues or disputes. The Clerk to the Commercial Court accordingly keeps a list of individuals and bodies offering mediation, conciliation and other ADR services.

As stated above, the basic principle here is encouraging, through a neutral mediator, the parties to come to a sensible compromise on the issues in dispute. The compromise will impose a contractual settlement on the parties. Varieties of ADR have been in operation for many years in the United States, Canada, Australia and New Zealand.

The advantages to industry are that if the process works at all it is comparatively cheap and quick. Subsequent litigation is not debarred if the process fails to work, though it is possible that disclosures against a party's interest subsequently regretted might be made, though these will normally be made 'without prejudice' and hence not usable as formal evidence. Even so, experience suggests that they can have an important psychological effect.

Although ADR has an obvious role in such non-business disputes as, for example, occur between neighbouring house owners, use of the process in practice is predominantly in commercial disputes between businesses. If the procedure is to be tried, there must be a clear preliminary agreement between the parties on the procedure to be adopted since ADR processes vary and are not subject to any statutory rules. Post-Woolf procedures specifically draw litigants' attention, via a questionnaire, to the possibility of ADR. But ADR is not a panacea and Article 6 of the European Convention on Human Rights states that everyone is entitled, in the determination of their civil rights and obligations, to a fair and public hearing within a reasonable time by an independent and impartial tribunal established by law. Judgment shall be pronounced publicly. ADR arrangements do not fit this prescription, so care must be taken not to inhibit legitimate recourse to the courts.[8]

8   See generally R C A White *The English Legal System in Action* (3rd edn) 1999.

Class actions[9]

In the UK the remedies available to a consumer must generally be obtained by personal initiative, often accompanied by the expenditure of time and money. This factor no doubt accounts for the comparative paucity of reported cases in the UK on sale of goods problems where one party is a consumer as opposed to where both parties are in business. In the UK there is no real equivalent to the 'class action' for ordinary civil claims as understood in the USA. In England and Wales claimants must normally take action personally. Admittedly Order 15, rule 12 of the Rules of the Supreme Court made provision for representative actions where numerous persons had the same interest in any proceedings, and judgments and orders were binding on all the persons as representing whom the claimant sued. This procedure is now laid down in the Civil Procedure Rules 1998 (r 19.6). However, the phrase 'same interest' was narrowly interpreted in *Markt & Co Ltd v Knight Steamship Co Ltd*[10] on the basis that where an identical term in separate contracts made with a number of shippers was broken there were nevertheless distinct contracts giving rise to quantifiably different claims for damages.

More recently, in three cases the court appears to have taken a more liberal view of the scope of representative actions. In *Prudential Assurance Co Ltd v Newman Industries Ltd*[11] the claimant company was a shareholder in Newman Industries Ltd. In connection with a takeover bid the claimant brought an action claiming damages for conspiracy against the defendants, the chairman and the vice-chairman alleging (inter alia) that a circular issued was misleading. The claimant proposed to bring a representative action on behalf of the shareholders of Newman seeking a declaration that all such shareholders who had suffered damage as a result of Newman's conduct should be entitled to damages for conspiracy. Vinelott J held that the court had jurisdiction to entertain a representative action by a claimant suing on behalf of a class where the cause of action of the claimant and each member of the class was alleged to be a separate cause of action in tort. However, there were certain conditions which must be present. These included a condition that the court must be satisfied that no member of the class would, by virtue of the representative action, be able to claim a right which he could not have claimed in a separate action and, therefore, a claimant in his representative capacity would normally be able to obtain only declaratory relief (as opposed to damages). Further conditions were that the members of the class shared an interest which was common to all

9   See generally C Hodges *Multi-Party Actions* (OUP 2000), a detailed study of Group Litigation Orders and M, H & P pp 472–481.
10 [1910] 2 KB 1021. See generally M, H & P ch 9.
11 [1981] Ch 229, [1979] 3 All ER 507.

of them; and that the court was satisfied that it was for the benefit of the class that the claimant be permitted to sue in a representative capacity. In this particular case permission was given for the claimant to sue in a representative capacity. In *EMI Records Ltd v Riley*[12] Dillon J came to a somewhat similar conclusion in allowing a member of the British Phonographic Industry Ltd (BPI) to sue, on its own behalf and on behalf of all other members of BPI, a market trader who was alleged to be manufacturing, selling and distributing 'pirate records'. Furthermore, in the particular circumstances of this case, the judge held that it was appropriate that damages should be recoverable by the claimant in its representative capacity since this would avoid the procedural complication that, for the purpose of the enquiry into damages which the court had to make, either all the members of BPI would have to be joined as co-claimants or they would have to issue separate writs. *Prudential Assurance Co Ltd v Newman Industries Ltd* (above) was distinguished in this respect. Representative actions are subject to the drawback that the representative may unilaterally decide to withdraw or settle privately before judgment and is, in any event, solely liable for costs – so even if others benefit by the representative's action, no contribution can be compelled.

Where there was a multiplicity of claimants, Order 15 rule 4 allowed joinder of these claimants where 'some common question of law or fact would arise in all the actions' and all rights to relief claimed arose out of the same transactions or series of transactions. This is a 'group action' rather than a representative action. A detailed 'Guide for Use in Group Actions' was issued by the Supreme Court Procedure Committee[13] covering the procedural technicalities, explaining how economies in time and documentation might be made. In particular it was possible to have one master statement of claim setting out all the general allegations with the addition of a schedule from each claimant specifying which of the general allegations were relied on and setting out the specific facts relevant to that claimant.[14] As to legal aid, the Board was of the view that funding should be concentrated in one co-ordinating solicitor or a small group of firms, who would have conduct of the case. The solicitor first instructed by the client would deal with the client on a day-to-day basis.[15]

12   [1981] 2 All ER 838, [1981] 1 WLR 923. See also *Foskett v McKeown* [1997] 3 All ER 392.
13   See M, H & P p 459.
14   For litigation arising out of claims for personal injuries based on the use of the tranquillisers Ativan and Valium – 'a group pharmaceutical action' involving well over 900 plaintiffs – see *B v John Wyeth & Brother Ltd* [1992] 1 All ER 443, [1992] 1 WLR 168, CA
15   See Legal Aid Board Report, Cm 688, 1989; and subsequently *Handling of Group Actions and Other High Cost Civil Cases* (June 1997).

Before considering the third case, *Davies v Eli Lilly & Co*,[16] the problem of dealing with a large number of claimants individually, particularly as to quantum, needs discussion in the light of the history of Thalidomide. Even though representative or group actions are now becoming better recognised, they cannot be regarded in practice as a simple panacea for all the ills of the consumer, even in what might be thought of as a fairly obvious case, such as the circumstances arising out of the use of the drug Thalidomide. There, 62 actions for damages for negligence were initially brought against the manufacturers of the drug, Distillers Ltd, who had always denied negligence. Negotiations for settlement proceeded on the basis that 40 per cent of what a court would have awarded for a successful negligence claim would be paid to the affected children, and this was approved by the court (as is required where a minor settles a civil action). However, the notional amount that a court would have awarded could not be agreed[17] and two test cases were brought. As a result a total of £1 million was paid by Distillers, apportioned according to disability. Other parents were dissatisfied with this amount and the Court of Appeal upheld the right of dissident parents to have their children's interests considered separately.[18] Public opinion had also gathered in force, and following public discussion and adverse criticism of Distillers a greatly increased sum, involving an estimated total of £20 million, was paid partly in lump sum compensation and partly to a trust fund into which the government also paid £5 million to offset the effects of taxation of the income of the fund. The point of this saga, for present purposes, is that even where there is a mass tragedy on this scale it is essential that the interests of each affected claimant should be separately considered. Furthermore, judges may feel that they should be properly satisfied as to proof of injury in each case, particularly where alleged drug reactions may in fact be symptoms wholly or partially attributable to some other cause. Economies can be made in England where the same firm of solicitors and the same counsel can be appointed to represent all claimants.

16   (1987) 131 Sol Jo 807; affd [1987] 3 All ER 94, [1987] 1 WLR 1136, CA (concerning the sharing of costs).
17   A difficulty compounded by the uncertainty of whether a claimant could recover in respect of ante-natal injuries – see now Congenital Disabilities (Civil Liability) Act 1976.
18   See *Re Taylor's Application* [1972] 2 QB 369, [1972] 2 All ER 873. The Thalidomide affair is briefly outlined in ch 26 of the Pearson Royal Commission's Report on Civil Liability and Compensation for Personal Injury (1978), Cmnd 7054.

The drug Opren

Owing to widespread concern about the alleged side-effects of the anti-arthritis drug Opren, the Opren Action Group was formed in 1982. The Law Society, in view of the very considerable number of potential claimants, agreed to liaise with all those solicitors contemplating the issue of proceedings for their clients. By 1986 a very large number of actions for personal injuries allegedly caused by this drug were instituted both against the manufacturers of Opren, the Eli Lilly group, and against the Committee on Safety of Medicines and the Department of Health and Social Security who were involved in licensing Opren for use in this country. Negligence was alleged on the footing that the Lilly defendants were negligent in the testing and marketing of the drug, and that the government defendants were negligent in its licensing. Since the great majority of Opren cases were legally aided so that the expense of conducting this huge volume of litigation on the claimants' side predominantly fell to the public purse, Hirst J in *Davies v Eli Lilly & Co*[19] laid down the procedure which he wished to be followed. He explained that a very substantial proportion of the actions were being conducted by six firms who in close co-operation advised and acted for members of the Opren Action Group. They represented 679 individual claimants or potential claimants. There were known to be a significant number of actual or potential claimants outside this organisation. The learned judge drew attention to the following cost saving measures:

1) Making use of short two-page specimen pleadings or schedules, cross-referenced to the very long and complicated master statement of claim and the two master defences of the respective groups of the defendants.

2) Organising one single discovery process to cover as many actions as possible.

3) In the light of the very complex technical and scientific questions arising, for the purpose of the trial on liability it was feasible and necessary to select an appropriate group of 'lead claimants' who were suitably representative of the various categories into which Opren claimants could be divided, having regard to the claimants' medical history, to represent the various different aspects relevant to the issues of liability.

4) Meanwhile all other Opren actions should be stayed pending the conclusion of the main trial on liability. (The case was eventually settled with agreed awards of compensation.)

5) A timetable should be agreed for issuing the writ (if not yet issued), for delivery of the details of the claim, for notification to the defendants

---

19   (1987) 131 Sol Jo 807. See O Hansen (1986) NLJ 883. Rvsd on issues of disclosure [1987] 1 All ER 801, [1987] 1 WLR 428, CA.

of the wish to join in the 'Opren scheme' outlined by the judge above, and notification by all concerned of the proposed lead actions. The judge concluded:

> It will be appreciated that this is a most unusual procedure devised to fit the special needs of this litigation. The intention is to be fair to all interested parties, including the present claimants, serious claimants, and all the defendants, and to strike a fair balance between their interests.

Group actions of this sort nevertheless lacked clear ground rules and attracted the reforming eye of Lord Woolf. Meanwhile the Law Society in its 1995 Report 'Group Actions Made Easier' recommended a new rule of court flexible enough to deal with one-off disasters and 'rolling claims' such as those involving defective products. A 'lead firm' should be appointed, claimants would not need to issue writs but simply join a register, representative test cases should be selected to define and try common issues and should be settled or continued only with leave of the court, and any global offer of settlement should have a three-month (rather than 28-day) acceptance limit.

In his Final Report 'Access to Justice',[20] Lord Woolf looked in some detail at multi-party actions, building on the experience outlined above and the Law Society's report, 'Group Actions Made Easier' (1995). It was recognised that any scheme under the new rules should (a) benefit those large numbers of people affected by another's conduct but whose individual loss is too small to make litigation a viable proposition; (b) provide effective methods of resolving cases where there are a number of claimants who could justify individual action but where it is not possible to manage the litigation under normal procedures; achieve balance between the rights of claimants and defendants to litigate individually and the interests of a group of parties to litigate as a whole and in an effective manner. The focus was on the central role of a pro-active managing judge appointed to control and hear the case.

Another problem concerned the vexed question of whether there should be an 'opt-out' approach, whereunder a person's rights may be established in multi-party litigation without his or her express consent (as per procedure in the USA, rule 23, and parts of the Commonwealth). Group members could however opt out and lose any group benefits but have the right to bring a separate action. This could be unfair to defendants in personal injury litigation who would not know the size of the group and the number of claims and their nature. An opt-in basis was preferred by the Law Society, with the establishment of a register at the initial stage of certification, and with provision for varying the joining criteria as the case developed, for

20 See M, H & P pp 477–480.

cut-off dates and for costs sharing. This was the preferred approach where there was a well defined or identifiable group of claimants.

Lord Woolf's eventual principal recommendations were that in appropriate proceedings the parties or the Legal Aid Board should apply for a multi-party situation (MPS) to be established. This would suspend the operation of the Limitation Act. Claimants could join the MPS at the application stage or subsequently by entering their names on a register. The court would certify an MPS if satisfied that that was appropriate. A High Court or Circuit Court judge could be appointed managing judge as soon as possible and handle the case throughout. The court should have power to approve the lead lawyer if a difficulty arose in appointing one. The court should then progress the case on an opt-out or opt-in basis as appropriate. The court should decide whether the case has merit and should proceed and the criteria to be satisfied by those wishing to join the action. The court should determine the arrangements for costs and cost sharing at the outset.

A complication not foreseen was the replacement of the legal aid scheme on 1 April 2000 by the Community Legal Service run by the Legal Services Commission, under the Access to Justice Act 1999. Personal injury cases are normally excluded from the scheme, parties having to rely instead on private conditional fee agreements. There is an exception where 'Support Funding' is available in cases with high investigative costs.

Currently the new Civil Procedure Rules make provision for a Group Litigation Order (r 19.11) allowing a claim on behalf of a group with one statement of claim but with a separate schedule setting out the facts specific to an individual claimant. A register of claimants is established for the case management of claims which give rise to common or related issues of fact or law. Any judgment on these 'GLO issues' is binding on the parties to all the other claims on the group register, unless the court orders otherwise (r 19.12). The court also has power to order that group litigation proceeds via a test claim (CPR 1998 r 19.15) though normally here there should first be an undertaking by the defendant to treat the result as binding in regard to all identified similar cases. There can, too, be problems with costs which in principle cannot be shared with non-litigants and also as to whether the test claim is truly typical. In summary, progress is being made in thinking out the most effective procedures for group actions, but the rules need to be fleshed out with more practice directions and the whole mechanism tested when a suitable live issue emerges.

Community Legal Service

Since 1949 litigants who have satisfied certain financial tests have been able to sue or be sued and to have their legal costs in whole or in part met from public funds. Initially the scheme for free or subsidised legal aid or advice was administered by the Law Society but in 1989 the Legal Aid Act 1988 created a new administrative body, the Legal Aid Board, which took over the administration of the scheme. Then, by virtue of the Access of Justice Act 1999, as from 1 April 2000 the civil legal aid scheme was replaced by the Community Legal Service (CLS) run by the new Legal Services Commission, under the 'general guidance' of the Lord Chancellor. Part of the claimed advantages of the new scheme is that public funds are used to best effect so that people have access to legal services which best meet their needs. There are various ways in which the budget for the scheme can be better controlled than under the old scheme which appeared to successive governments like a 'black hole' of expenditure, demand-led by impecunious litigants. CLS has the following key features:

1) To receive services from the CLS, clients have to satisfy criteria set out in the Funding Code and be financially eligible to receive the services in question. The Code replaces the old 'merits test' under the Legal Aid Scheme and is designed to identify meritorious cases where it is economic to litigate on the non-small claim basis. The Commission may direct funding to priority areas such as housing and cases with a wider public interest.

2) The provision is divided into a number of different 'levels of service', each having its own definition, criteria and procedures. The two most important ones are probably Legal Help, which enable firms and agencies operating under one of the Commission's general contracts to give 'first aid' legal advice corresponding to the old 'Green Form' scheme (but with a controlled budget), and Legal Representation, corresponding to the old civil legal aid, which can extend to cover the full litigation process.

3) The aim is that all services funded from the CLS will be delivered through contracts between the Legal Services Commission and solicitors in private practice and the advice sector – eg not-for-profit law centres. Contracts are awarded after a quality control audit. Thus for example, clinical negligence cases were limited to some 230 solicitors' firms. Previously any of the 11,000 firms doing legal aid work could have taken on clinical negligence cases. The Commission has claimed that there has been an identifiable rise in standards. 'Controlled work' contracts now govern Legal Help services. Family and immigration work is also limited to those with contracts.

4) As under the old scheme, eligibility is subject to means tests designed to identify a claimant's disposable income and disposable capital as stipulated by regulations made under the Act. The limits are not generous. Many claimants in work will find themselves either disqualified or liable to make a significant contribution. It is worth noticing that, in computing disposable capital, the value of the

claimant's residence is only partially ignored; the equity over £10,000 after allowing for a maximum mortgage of £100,000 is included. (Government proposals in 2000 were to reduce the disregarded sum to an equity of £3,000 above which a contribution would be required.)

5) Legal representation is available for cases in county courts, the High Court and Court of Appeal, the House of Lords, Family Proceedings Courts (part of the magistrates' court), the Employment Appeal Tribunal, the Mental Health Review Tribunal, Immigration Adjudicator and Appeal Tribunal.

6) Certain categories of case are excluded altogether, particularly most personal injury cases, now normally pursued under private conditional fee agreements (no win, no fee), business, partnership, company or trust cases, boundary disputes and libel and slander.

Conclusions

The Legal Aid and Advice Schemes have played a major part in making the administration of justice available to some of those who would otherwise not be able to afford the cost of professional representation or advice. Being means-tested and geared to the recovery of some of the expense by way of contributions from assisted persons and payment of costs by unsuccessful unassisted opponents, it has also been administered comparatively economically. But the schemes are subject to some serious criticisms.[1] In brief these are:

i) CLS funding is not at present available in most tribunals, but it is fair to add that there is little agreement amongst chairmen of tribunals on whether legal representation is necessarily desirable.

ii) There is a disparity in bargaining power as between an assisted litigant and an unassisted opponent. The former may tend to resist a settlement and prolong the proceedings in the knowledge that they are at public expense and that, if the claimant loses, costs will not be likely to be granted out of public funds to the unassisted opponent. This is discussed in more detail above. Completely unmeritorious claims may be pursued in the knowledge that the other party will find it cheaper to settle than contest.

iii) The financial limits are arbitrary and cause substantial injustice to many litigants. In particular, a) the middle socio-economic groups are likely to be disqualified on both income and capital grounds and yet often cannot without hardship afford to litigate, particularly in the High

1   See also M McAteer 'Access for all? challenges for the new civil justice system' (2000) 10 Consumer Policy Review 133 and *Community Legal Services: Access for All?*, NCC, May 2000.

Court or above, unless they are assured of success and of the opponent's ability to pay damages and costs; b) the capital limit causes injustice to all groups, particularly the lower socio-economic groups, where the applicant has been provident enough (and unwise enough?) to make savings. These have often involved considerable self-sacrifice in the past and the disqualification of such people is a highly objectionable feature of the scheme.

As Lord Borrie has stated:

> We are still far from the ideal of Magna Carta: 'To none will we sell, deny or delay right or justice ...' For people in the upper working or middle classes, litigation is an uncertain and costly venture and the risk of ruinous financial loss is the greater because of the general rule that the loser pays the winner's costs.[2]

Reform in this vital area inevitably comes up against government restraints on public expenditure. The volume of litigation is increasing and likely to continue to do so as the citizen, influenced perhaps by what is seen to be happening in the USA, becomes more aware of his or her 'rights'. Demand for legal services is not easily 'capped'. Government budgets are therefore easily overrun. On the other hand there has been abundant evidence from practitioners of costs thrown away by wasted attendances at abortive hearings, and that many court proceedings are over-elaborate and unduly dependent on the adversarial process. It is in this area that reform priorities have been duly identified by Lord Woolf, as outlined above, though the tangible results of the streamlining of the management by the court of the progress of civil litigation are likely to take some time to show.

Meanwhile the civil legal aid scheme, costing approximately £800 million per annum, is being refashioned in the radical way described above. The most significant change reported by practitioners a year after Lord Woolf's reforms were implemented is that there have been fewer and quicker cases, and much more emphasis on earlier settlement and the need to try mediation. But a MORI poll published in *The Times* (25 August 2000) revealed increased public dissatisfaction with 'the courts' (47% dissatisfied). The expense of civil justice is thought to have been one factor. Dissuading potential litigants from using the courts in the first place on grounds of affordability can hardly be claimed as a structural improvement to what is an important human right – the right to a fair trial by a properly established and independent court, whether criminal or civil.

2   Borrie 'Law Reform: A Damp Squib' University of Birmingham, 1970.

2.   CRIMINAL PROCEEDINGS

Introduction

The consumer will not usually be a direct party to criminal proceedings in the common case of a trader committing a trade descriptions, weights and measures, or food and drugs offence. The prosecution here will be undertaken by a solicitor or an officer of the responsible authority and in the former two cases usually by a trading standards or weights and measures inspector.[3] It is not therefore proposed to deal with the details of criminal procedure and evidence. A large number of offences by traders involving the consumer are treated as summary offences triable in the magistrates' court. Thus section 84 of the Weights and Measures Act 1985 provides penalties under the Act 'on summary conviction'. Where the offence is tried on indictment the case will have started at the magistrates' court whose magistrates sit as examining justices and remit the case for trial by the Crown Court before judge and jury. At the time of writing the government has introduced controversial legislation to reduce the number of offences where the accused can opt for trial by jury as of right.

Classification of offences

Before the coming into force of Part III of the Criminal Law Act 1977 the determination of the mode of trial, whether summary or on indictment, was beset by complexities. In some cases summary offences could be tried on indictment and in others indictable offences could be tried summarily. 'Hybrid' offences could be taken either summarily or on indictment according to elections made by the prosecutor or accused.

As a result of the implementation of many of the recommendations of the James Committee on the Distribution of Criminal Business Between the Crown Court and Magistrates' Courts (1975, Cmnd 6323), Part III of the Criminal Law Act 1977 ('the 1977 Act') creates three categories of offence, namely:

a)   offences triable only on indictment;
b)   offences triable only summarily;
c)   offences triable either way.

At common law all offences are indictable and it follows, therefore, that where there is no express statutory provision an offence is triable only on indictment. In addition an offence can be made triable only on indictment

---

3   By s 223 of the Local Government Act 1972 a local authority may authorise any member or officer to prosecute, defend or appear on its behalf in a magistrates' court whether or not he is a solicitor.

by statute – a classification in practice restricted to offences of an especially serious character. It also follows that an offence triable only summarily must be so designated by statute – see in particular Criminal Law Act 1977, Schedule 1. Most of the offences dealt with in this book are within the third category above, that is triable either way. This is because this third category includes not only the offences formerly listed in Schedule 3 to the 1977 Act and now in Schedule 1 to the Magistrates' Courts Act 1980 ('the 1980 Act') but also those offences which the statute creating them expressly makes triable either summarily or on indictment (1977 Act, s 16(4)). An example is section 14 of the Trade Descriptions Act 1968 (considered in ch 12).

Procedure with 'either way' offences

Where a person aged at least 17 is charged with an offence triable either way, the procedure to be adopted is laid down by sections 17 to 28 of the 1980 Act (as amended). The main steps involved where the prosecutor is not the Attorney-General, the Solicitor-General or the Director of Public Prosecutions, and where the accused has not declared an intention to plead guilty (in which case the magistrates' court will deal with the matter) are as follows:

1) The court must cause the charge to be written down, if this has not already been done, and read to the accused (s 19(2)).

2) The court must afford first the prosecutor and then the accused an opportunity to make representations as to which mode of trial would be more suitable (s 19(2)).

3) The court then considers which mode of trial is the more suitable in the light of these representations and in the light of the following matters: whether the circumstances make the offence one of serious character; whether the punishment which a magistrates' court has power to inflict would be adequate (see below); any other circumstance which appears to the court to make it more suitable for trial one way rather than the other (s 19(3)).

4) If the court regards summary trial as appropriate it must then be explained to the accused in ordinary language that he can either consent to such trial or, if he wishes, be tried by jury. It must also be explained to him that if he is convicted and, in the light of his character and antecedents, the court is of the opinion that greater punishment should be given than the magistrates' court has a general power to inflict, the court may commit him for sentence to the Crown Court under section 38 of the 1980 Act. If the accused elects for jury trial by the Crown Court the court must proceed as examining justices, but the accused's decision if he is later convicted may both involve him in

heavier costs and, in the case of 'either way' offences such as those under the Trade Descriptions Act 1968, make him liable to the higher penalties (unlimited fine or imprisonment for a term not exceeding two years or both in this case) applicable to a conviction on indictment.

5) If, on the other hand, the court decides that the offence is more suitable for trial on indictment, the court so informs the accused and proceeds as examining justices (s 20(3)). Neither the prosecutor nor the accused can object to this course of action.

6) The court may change from summary trial to committal proceedings at any time before the conclusion of the evidence for the prosecution, and may change from committal proceedings to summary trial at any time during the enquiry into the information as examining justices, with the consent of the accused in the latter case (s 25).

7) Section 23 of the 1980 Act states that where the accused is represented by counsel or a solicitor who in his absence signifies the accused's consent to the proceedings for the determination of the mode of trial, and the court is satisfied that there is good reason for proceeding in the accused's absence, the court may proceed in his absence. Any necessary consents to summary trial may be given by the accused's counsel or solicitor.

As referred to above, the power of a magistrates' court to sentence is limited. In particular, a magistrates' court has no power to impose imprisonment for more than six months in respect of any one offence (s 31(1)) or in aggregate except in the case of either way offences when the total of consecutive sentences must not exceed 12 months (s 133). But where an adult is tried for an either way offence and convicted by a magistrates' court and the court considers that because of the defendant's character and antecedents greater punishment should be inflicted than the justices have power to impose, they may commit the defendant to the Crown Court for sentence (s 38).

Penalty

Section 32 of the 1980 Act makes specific provision for penalties on summary conviction for offences triable either way. In the case of such offences which are not listed in Schedule 1 to that Act, that is, inter alia, offences under the Trade Descriptions Act 1968, the maximum fine is the 'prescribed sum' unless a particular statute specifically imposes a larger fine. With few exceptions, the maximum punishment for an 'either way' offence tried summarily is six months' imprisonment and/or a fine of £5,000 (Criminal Justice Act 1991, s 17).

Territorial jurisdiction

As a general rule a British subject cannot be tried under English law for what would have been offences eg under the Trade Descriptions Act 1968 if they had not been committed abroad. There are, however, exceptional cases where a domestic criminal court can take jurisdiction in such circumstances. These include:

a) offences under statutes which, exceptionally, confer such jurisdiction – eg Offences against the Person Act 1861, section 9 (murder by a British subject abroad);

b) offences committed by anyone on board British ships whether or not on the high seas and even if a foreign court has concurrent jurisdiction;

c) offences committed on foreign ships within British territorial waters – see Territorial Waters Jurisdiction Act 1878; or on foreign ships not in territorial waters by British subjects not 'belonging' to the ship – see generally Merchant Shipping Act 1995, section 281, considered by the House of Lords in *R v Kelly*;[4]

d) offences committed on installations or designated parts of the continental shelf adjacent to the United Kingdom – see Oil and Gas (Enterprises) Act 1982, section 22;

e) offences committed on British controlled aircraft whilst in flight – see Civil Aviation Act 1982, section 92 and *Air-India v Wiggins*.[5]

In addition, specific statutes may make it an offence to assist or induce the commission abroad of what would be an offence in the United Kingdom – see, for example, Trade Descriptions Act 1968, section 21 (accessories to offences committed abroad).

With regard to jurisdiction over offences committed within England and Wales, a magistrates' court for a county has jurisdiction to try all summary offences committed within the county (Magistrates' Courts Act 1980, s 2(1)). A magistrates' court also has jurisdiction over a person charged jointly with another person who is in custody or is to be proceeded against within the county (MCA 1980, ss 1(2)(b) and 2(2)). Similarly, a magistrates' court by which any person is tried for any offence has jurisdiction to try him for any other summary offence, wherever committed (MCA 1980, s 2(6)).

With regard to indictable offences, a magistrates' court has jurisdiction as examining justices over a person whether the offence was committed in the county or not, and the same applies with regard to its power to try summarily an offence triable either way (MCA 1980, ss 2(3) and 2(4)).

---

4   [1982] AC 665, [1981] 2 All ER 1098 (referring to the former Merchant Shipping Act 1894, s 686).
5   [1980] 2 All ER 593, [1980] 1 WLR 815, HL.

Time limits and procedure

In summary proceedings section 127 of the Magistrates Courts Act 1980 imposes a general time limit on trying an information within six months from the time when the offence was committed. This does not apply to indictable offences including offences triable either way (see further Trade Descriptions Act 1968, s 19, discussed later). Taking a weights and measures offence by way of example, the genesis of the case may well be a complaint by a member of the public to a trading standards officer who will take down particulars on a form designed for the purpose. If an offence appears to have been committed and the time limit, in this case 12 months from the time of the commission of the offence or three months from when the prosecutor has sufficient evidence to prosecute (whichever first occurs)[6] has not expired, the complainant may be asked to give a written and signed statement which may be given in evidence in court.[7] An inspector will then interview the trader and, if appropriate, make tests. The relevant Code of Practice under the Police and Criminal Evidence Act 1984 applies in these circumstances and if there are reasonable grounds for suspecting that a person has committed an offence he or she should be cautioned thus: 'You do not have to say anything. But it may harm your defence if you do not mention when questioned something which you later rely on in court. Anything you do say may be given in evidence.' A record is then made of questions asked and statements made (normally tape recorded).

A policy decision is then made as to whether or not to prosecute. This may turn on whether the trader has been warned or prosecuted on previous occasions. If prosecution is decided upon it is commenced by an information being laid before a justice of the peace (in the jurisdiction where the offence was committed[8]) to the effect that a stipulated person has committed or is suspected of committing an offence. In this case it will be in writing and signed by an officer authorised by the local weights and measures authority. Otherwise, only a chief police officer (now via the Crown Prosecution Service (see Prosecution of Offences Act 1985)) may lay an information in respect of a weights and measures offence – it is not open to a member of the public to do so. (This is in contrast with the Trade Descriptions Act 1968, under which a lay person may lay an information.[9]) A summons, specifying the defendant, the alleged offence and the date and place of the hearing, and signed by a justice, is then served on the

---

6   Weights and Measures Act 1985, s 83.
7   Under Criminal Justice Act 1967, s 9; Magistrates' Courts Act 1980, s 102. The witness must attend personally if there is an objection to written evidence.
8   Magistrates' Courts Act 1980, s 1.
9   This is because the Act contains no limitation on the common law right of any person, whether aggrieved or not, to prosecute privately.

defendant. Had the offence been serious, or the address insufficient for service of the summons, a warrant for the defendant's arrest would have been issued instead.

At the hearing, summary trial having been decided upon, if there is a plea of guilty (the clerk to the justices having first read out the offence with which he is charged and asked him to plead) the prosecutor outlines the circumstances in which the offence was committed and informs the bench of any previous convictions. The defendant may then plead in mitigation of sentence, after which the magistrates pronounce the appropriate sentence. Penalties on summary conviction for offences triable either way are limited to a maximum of six months' imprisonment or the presently prescribed sum of £5,000 (s 32 as amended), though in serious cases the magistrates' court may commit the defendant to the Crown Court for sentence under section 38 of the Magistrates' Courts Act 1980. If the actual offence is giving short weight contrary to section 28 of the 1985 Act, the court must refer to the Act to ascertain the correct penalty. Under section 84 this is a fine of up to £5,000.

If the accused pleads not guilty the prosecutor is required to prove his case beyond reasonable doubt. The prosecutor will outline his case and call his witnesses who will give evidence on oath. They are examined (avoiding leading questions) by the prosecutor and may be cross-examined by the accused or his advocate. The questioning of witnesses in accordance with the complex rules of evidence is a skilled art, but where the accused is unrepresented he may in practice be assisted a little by the justices' clerk. The accused then calls any witnesses of his own, who go through the same process of examination-in-chief, cross-examination and, if necessary, re-examination, and finally may address the court summarising in what ways the prosecutor's case is not proved. Only if the bench then convicts may evidence of previous convictions be given.

Appeals

The defendant may appeal against either sentence or conviction to the Crown Court and against sentence only if he pleaded guilty. On an appeal against conviction the case is completely reheard, though sentencing powers are limited to those available to magistrates' courts (from which it follows that the Crown Court can increase the severity of sentence within these limits). Alternatively, appeals may lie on a point of law by way of case stated to the Divisional Court of the Queen's Bench Division of the High Court. It will be observed that most of the decisions on trade descriptions discussed in chapter 12 arose in this way. The appeal may be by defendant or prosecutor. The Crown Court in its appellate jurisdiction may also state a case for the opinion of the Divisional Court. If a point of law of general public importance is involved and the Divisional Court gives its certificate to this effect and either it or the House of Lords gives leave to appeal, there may be further appeal to the House of Lords. If the trial was on indictment, appeal against conviction and/or sentence goes from the Crown Court to the Court of Appeal (Criminal Division) and from thence by either party to the House of Lords provided a) a certificate is given by the Court of Appeal that a point of law of general importance is involved and b) leave to appeal by either the Court of Appeal or the House of Lords is given (Criminal Appeal Act 1968, s 33).

Compensation orders

A development of great importance to the consumer is the power of magistrates' courts and the Crown Court to make compensation orders in favour of victims of offences. Such a power was introduced in 1972 and is now to be found in the Powers of Criminal Courts Act 1973 (ss 35 to 38 as amended by ss 104 and 105 of the Criminal Justice Act 1988). Although there was power to award compensation for loss of property under section 4 of the Forfeiture Act 1870 in the case of indictable offences, the power was held to be inapplicable in a case arising under the Trade Descriptions Act 1968 because, inter alia, there was no loss of property in the particular case.[10] The aggrieved consumer's only remedy was therefore to bring a civil action in which, under section 11 of the Civil Evidence Act 1968, the criminal conviction may be pleaded to prove that the defendant committed the offence. There was criticism of this too cumbersome procedure in the House of Commons during debate on the Criminal Justice Bill in 1971, particularly as the Trade Descriptions Act was intended to protect the consumer and this could be better achieved if a magistrates' court could award compensation. The Bill was eventually amended to embody what now appears in the Powers of Criminal Courts Act 1973.

Section 35 of the 1973 Act (as amended) states that the court after convicting for any offence may, instead of or in addition to its sentencing power, and on application or otherwise, make a compensation order requiring the defendant to pay compensation for any personal injury, loss or damage resulting from the offence or any other offence taken into consideration by the court in determining sentence. The question of whether to make an order and, if so, of what amount, must be judged with regard to the means of the defendant. If there is a choice, the court should give preference to a compensation order. At present a magistrates' court may not make an order for more than £5,000[11] in respect of each offence of

10 *Lieske v Blakemore* (1971) 135 JP Jo 826, Croydon Quarter Sessions.
11 The amount was raised from £2,000 by s 17(3) of and Sch 4 to the Criminal Justice Act 1991 from October 1992.

which the offender is convicted. Compensation orders in respect of offences taken into consideration may not exceed any balance of each £5,000 in respect of offences which have led to the conviction after deducting compensation orders actually made (see Magistrates' Courts Act 1980, s 40). This provision can result in injustice. If the prosecutor charges a number of offences separately a compensation order can be made in respect of each 'victim' adversely affected by the offence. But if a number of offences are taken into consideration, the amount of compensation available is arbitrarily lowered. This can be serious in the case, for instance, of a large tour operator whose holidays brochure contains material misdescriptions affecting a number of different consumers.[12] If subsequent civil proceedings are brought, damages are assessed without regard to the compensation, but credit is given in the amount actually awarded for the amount of any compensation order. The compensation order is enforced in the same way as a fine.[13]

A number of decisions[14] have indicated that compensation orders should only be made in clear and simple cases where the defendant has the means to satisfy the order. Magistrates' courts in particular are ill-equipped to measure disputed problems of causation and loss, and such matters are as a general rule left to the civil courts to assess.

As regards the consumer, the power to make compensation orders is particularly valuable in trade descriptions cases where the prosecuting officer of the trading standards authority should in appropriate cases ask for a compensation order on the consumer's behalf, thus saving the trouble and expense of bringing subsequent civil proceedings. The raising of the maximum in magistrates' courts to £5,000 gave the power added importance.[15] Since the Criminal Justice Act 1988 the court must give reasons if it fails to make an order.

12 It is conceivable that if offences so taken into consideration were subsequently prosecuted a plea of autrefois convict would be unsuccessful. See generally H Street 'Compensation Orders and the Trade Descriptions Act' [1974] Crim LR 345.
13 Magistrates' Courts Act 1980, s 76.
14 *R v Kneeshaw* [1975] QB 57 at 60; *R v Daly* [1974] 1 All ER 290, [1974] 1 WLR 133; *R v Vivian* [1979] 1 All ER 48, [1979] 1 WLR 291 – but see the author's criticism of this decision in (1979) Local Government Chronicle 75. See also J Vennard 'Magistrates' Assessments of Compensation for Injury' [1979] Crim LR 510. See also *R v Boardman* (1987) 9 Cr App Rep (S) 74, (following *R v Vivian* (above)) and *R v Horsham Justices, ex p Richards* [1985] 2 All ER 1114, [1985] 1 WLR 986. (Where the question of whether there had been loss, and if so what loss, is raised, evidence should be produced in support of representations made by the parties.)
15 See generally Home Office Report No 102, 1988, by T Newburn *The Use and Enforcement of Compensation Orders in Magistrates' Courts*; M, H & P pp 429–433.

The Annual Reports of the Director General of Fair Trading always present an invaluable compilation of statistical data on the volume of both consumer complaints and of convictions under specific legislation, broken down under sectors of trade. Amounts awarded under compensation orders are now given and for 1999 £119,796 was granted in respect of compensation for false descriptions of goods alone. Of this sum, £103,002 related to offences concerning second-hand cars.[16]

16 *Annual Report of the Director General of Fair Trading 1999*, 2000 HCP 576, p 90.

9 A survey of the protective legislation including safety

I. INTRODUCTION

This chapter surveys the umbrella of protection given to the consumer by a considerable number of statutes creating various criminal offences. Some also give certain civil rights in England and Wales to the consumer, and where appropriate these are mentioned too. It will be seen from the tables in chapters 12 and 13 that certain of these, namely the Weights and Measures Act 1985, the Trade Descriptions Act 1968, Part III of the Consumer Protection Act 1987 and the Food Safety Act 1990, give rise to the largest number of consumer complaints and cases reported to the Office of Fair Trading. These, together with the Fair Trading Act 1973, will be dealt with in greater detail in subsequent chapters.

The following table gives an idea of the ambit of the main statutes affecting the consumer. The size and complexity of the legislation merely outlined in this chapter, much of it enforceable by local authorities, are better appreciated when it is realised that a number of these statutes have spawned subsidiary legislation which is both highly technical and extremely voluminous. There are, for example, over 130 regulations made under the food legislation alone and a substantial percentage of this activity is pursuant to EC Directives.

The main criminal statutes affecting consumers

Subject matter	Legislation
Inaccurate quantities	Weights and Measures Act 1985.
Statement of and control of prices	Consumer Protection Act 1987; Mock Auctions Act 1961; Prices Acts 1974, 1975.

Subject matter	*Legislation*
Food quality and hygiene	Food Act 1984; Food Safety Act 1990; Food Standards Act 1999.
False descriptions	Trade Descriptions Act 1968; Trading Representations (Disabled Persons) Act 1958; Food Safety Act 1990; Property Misdescriptions Act 1991; Copyright, Designs and Patents Act 1988; Trade Marks Act 1994; Package Travel, Package Holidays and Package Tours Regulations 1994.
Unsolicited goods and services	Unsolicited Goods and Services Acts 1971 and 1975; the Consumer Protection (Distance Selling) Regulations 2000.
Consumer credit	Consumer Credit Act 1974.
Consumer safety; Licensing; Labelling of dangerous products	Consumer Protection Act 1987; General Product Safety Regulations 1994; Animal Health Act 1981; Petroleum (Consolidation) Act 1928; Explosives Acts 1875 and 1923; Poisons Act 1972; Medicines Act 1968; Farm and Garden Chemicals Act 1967.
Road safety	Road Traffic Act 1988 (selling defective motor cycle crash helmets (s 17) and offences relating to the condition of vehicles).
Insurance policy holders' protection	Insurance Companies Act 1982; Policyholders Protection Act 1975 (as amended); Financial Services Act 1986.
Pressurised selling	Consumer Credit Act 1974; Timeshare Act 1992; Consumer Protection (Cancellation of Contracts Concluded away from Business Premises) Regulations 1987.
Trading stamps	Trading Stamps Act 1964.
Hallmarking of precious metals	Hallmarking Act 1973.
Handling stolen goods/ obtaining money by deception	Theft Act 1968 (ss 22, 15).

2. LOCAL AND CENTRAL GOVERNMENT

Enforcement and Administration

It is broadly true that the Departments of State are responsible for legislative policy and administration of consumer protection statute law creating criminal penalties, and local government trading standards and environmental health departments are charged with the enforcement of the legislation. This not only involves the prosecution of offenders but also the prevention of offences by warnings to and education of traders affected by the legislation. There is, in addition, some central government responsibility for enforcement of particular statutes. For instance, the Director General of Fair Trading has various enforcement powers (jointly with local authorities) under the Consumer Credit Act 1974 in respect of (inter alia) those who trade without obtaining the appropriate credit licence.

The department primarily involved with consumer protection is the Department of Trade and Industry which administers the Weights and Measures Act 1985, the Consumer Protection Act 1987, the Prices Acts 1974 and 1975, the Consumer Credit Act 1974, the Fair Trading Act 1973, the Hallmarking Act 1973, the Trade Descriptions Act 1968, the Unsolicited Goods and Services Acts 1971 and 1975, the Estate Agents Act 1979, the Timeshare Act 1992, the Package Travel Package Holidays and Package Tours Regulations 1994, the Consumer Protection (Cancellation of Contracts Concluded away from Business Premises) Regulations 1987 and all aspects of competition policy including the European Community competition rules.

The Secretary of State for Health and the Food Standards Agency are concerned with food supplies and food hygiene. The Agency is primarily responsible for administering matters relating to food standards covering such matters as composition, labelling, marking, presenting and advertising of food, food safety including the monitoring of enforcement authorities and the Meat Hygiene Service covering slaughterhouses and meat inspection. The Home Office has a general responsibility for the administration of criminal justice and supervises the control of explosives, firearms and dangerous drugs.[1]

---

1   The institutional framework of consumer protection is further discussed in ch 3.

3.   SUMMARY OF SPECIFIC CRIMINAL LEGISLATION

Consumer safety and licensing

Introduction

A number of statutes seek to use the criminal law to ensure that consumers are protected from unsafe goods. Before examining the relevant provisions it may be helpful to outline the developments which have taken place since the 1960s.

In 1961 the Consumer Protection Act was passed. It was inspired by the need for preventive legislation in respect of dangerous goods identified by the Molony Committee.[2] The 1961 Act was subsequently amended by the Consumer Protection Act 1971 and then in 1976 the government published a Green Paper entitled *Consumer Safety – A Consultative Document*.[3] This considered such issues as the possibility of recalls, seizure and destruction of unsafe goods, problems encountered over making regulations, compliance with recognised standards and enforcement procedures.

The then government was unable to introduce the necessary reforming legislation because of pressures on parliamentary time but it supported a private member's Bill which became the Consumer Safety Act 1978. The 1978 Act was designed to strengthen and consolidate consumer safety legislation other than in the field of food and drugs. It came into force on 1 November 1978 except for those provisions repealing the Consumer Protection Acts 1961-1971, the Regulations under which also continued in force. It was intended that the Regulations made under the 1961 Act would eventually be re-made as safety regulations under the 1978 Act. The delays in this process were recognised[4] and the enforcement powers under the 1961 Act were improved by being made the same as those under the 1978 Act.[5]

The effectiveness of the 1978 Act, coupled with the Acts of 1961-1971, was reviewed in the White Paper *The Safety of Goods* published in July 1984.[6] Several of the recommendations of the White Paper were then incorporated in a private member's Bill which became the Consumer Safety (Amendment) Act 1986.

In the autumn of 1986 the government introduced the Consumer Protection Bill in the House of Lords. As well as dealing with product

---

2   Cmnd 1011 (Interim Report).
3   Cmnd 6398.
4   *The Safety of Goods* Cmnd 9302, para 54.
5   Consumer Safety (Amendment) Act 1986, s 16 and Sch 1.
6   Cmnd 9302 (1984).

liability[7] and the pricing of goods and services,[8] it sought to consolidate existing laws on consumer safety and to introduce a general safety duty as proposed in the White Paper *The Safety of Goods*.[9] The Bill received Royal Assent on 15 May 1987 and Part II (dealing with safety matters) came into force on 1 October 1987. The 1961-71 Acts, the 1978 Act and the 1986 Act were all repealed although Regulations made under them were continued, with some modifications.[10]

In 1992 the European Council passed the General Product Safety Directive[11] with a requirement that this be incorporated into national laws by 29 June 1994. Following consultations on draft regulations by the Department of Trade and Industry, the General Product Safety Regulations 1994[12] were made in September 1994 and came into force on 3 October 1994. These Regulations are in addition to the existing framework of protection under the Consumer Protection Act 1987, Part II, although section 10 of the 1987 Act is largely replaced by them.[13]

It is proposed to examine the Consumer Protection Act 1987 ('the 1987 Act') first, followed by the General Product Safety Regulations 1994 ('the 1994 Regulations') and finally other statutes affecting safety.

Consumer Protection Act 1987[14]

Discussion of the 1987 Act will begin with those aspects that consolidate and improve on earlier legislation and then move to a brief discussion of the general safety duty which was introduced in the 1987 Act.

Section 11 enables the Secretary of State to make 'safety regulations' to secure that goods are 'safe', that unsafe goods are not made available

7 See further ch 6.
8 See further ch 12.
9 Cmnd 9302, paras 33-48; M, H & P pp 593.
10 Section 50(4) and (5) and Consumer Protection Act 1987 (Commencement No 1) Order 1987, SI 1987/1680. For details of the regulations still remaining in force now, see Appendix I at pp 461-471.
11 92/59/EEC, OJ No L 228, 11.8.92, p 24. The Commission is reviewing the Directive, see COM (2000) 139 final; internet discussion paper: DG XXIV site:http://europa.eu.int/comm/dg24, *Proposal for revision of the EC General Product Safety Directive: Consultation Document*, DTI, July 2000 and F Maniet (1999) 7 Consum LJ 376.
12 SI 1994/2328, as amended by SI 1994/3142 and SI 1994/3144, BSSCCL p 800, M, H & P p 595.
13 For further discussion see p 266.
14 BSSCCL p 524. See also Askham and Stoneham *European Community Consumer Safety*; Cotter *Defective and Unsafe Products – Law and Practice*; Hodges *Product Safety*; Howells *Consumer Product Safety*; Micklitz, Roethe and Weatherill *Federalism and Responsibility*, ch 10; D Parry 'Criminal Liability for the Safety of Goods' (1989) 1 Law for Business 219.

either generally or to particular classes of person and that appropriate information is, and inappropriate information is not, provided (sub-s (1)). 'Safe' is defined in section 19(1) and (2). It means 'such that there is no risk or no risk apart from one reduced to a minimum' that death or personal injury will be caused by the goods, their keeping, use or consumption, assembly, any emission or leakage from the goods or reliance on the accuracy of any measurement, calculation or other reading made by or by means of the goods. Safety is, therefore, not only concerned with the use of the goods but also their storage. Goods excluded from consideration for safety regulations include food, controlled drugs and licensed medicinal products (s 11(7)). Section 11(2) lists the types of provisions which the safety regulations may contain eg with respect to composition, design, construction, finish or packing, approval schemes, testing, inspections, disposals, instructions and prohibitions on supplying etc the goods. Further provisions concerning prosecution aspects such as time limits are detailed in subsection (3).

The requirement of consultations by the Secretary of State prior to laying a draft safety regulation before Parliament and procedures for parliamentary approval are specified in section 11(5) and (6). In *R v Secretary of State for Health, ex p United States Tobacco International Inc*[15] an application for judicial review was granted against the decision by the Minister to make the Oral Snuff (Safety) Regulations 1989.[16] The applicant company was the sole manufacturer and packager of oral snuff in the United Kingdom. Because of the company's special position, the fact that it had been encouraged, by the government, to set up business in Scotland and the catastrophic effect on its business of any ban, the Secretary of State, when proposing new Regulations, should have given the company a full opportunity to know and respond to the proposals. The court decided that there had been unfairness in the way these Regulations had been made and they would therefore be quashed. Taylor LJ indicated that draconian measures require procedural propriety to be observed and fair treatment for those concerned. New Regulations were subsequently made following the correct procedures.[17]

15   [1992] QB 353, [1992] 1 All ER 212, QBD, M, H & P p 586. For other litigation concerning these Regulations, see *R v Secretary of State for Social Security, ex p United States Tobacco International Inc* (21 July 1988, unreported), CA, re disclosure of representations by other interested parties and *United States Tobacco International Inc v Secretary of State for Health* (1990) 155 JP 144, QBD, re territorial extent of the Regulations.

16   SI 1989/2347.

17   SI 1992/3134; see Appendix I at p 464.

Unlike the 1978 Act, the 1987 Act does not contain special provisions for making prohibition orders[18] to deal quickly with dangerous goods as they come on to the market. Instead, section 11(5) enables the consultation process to be by-passed if a safety regulation is not to last more than 12 months and the Secretary of State specifies that it appears to him that 'the need to protect the public requires that the regulations should be made without delay'. Such an 'emergency' safety regulation can be replaced, on its expiry, by a permanent safety regulation introduced after full consultation.

Appendix I contains a summary of current regulations made under section 11 of the 1987 Act, the Consumer Protection Act 1961 and the Consumer Safety Act 1978; also listed are regulations made under the European Communities Act 1972.

Breach of safety regulations is not an offence in itself (s 11(4)). However it is an offence to supply[19] where the regulations prohibit such a supply (s 12(1)). There are also offences connected with the testing of goods, provision of prohibited information and failure to supply correct information (s 12(2)-(4)). There is a penalty of six months' imprisonment and/or a fine of up to level 5 on the standard scale for these offences.[20] It is a defence to show that all reasonable steps have been taken and all due diligence exercised (s 39(1)).[1] Seven days' notice to the prosecutor is required for an allegation of act or default of another or reliance on information given by another (s 39(2)). In addition, a defence based on reliance on information supplied by another will not be accepted unless the defendant shows it was reasonable, in all the circumstances, to rely on the information, having regard to the steps he took or might reasonably have taken to verify the information and whether he had any reason to disbelieve the information (s 39(4)).[2]

18 These were designed to prevent anyone from supplying etc particular goods that were considered unsafe. They involve a 28-day consultation procedure or, in emergency, could be made at once. The Order lasted for one year and could be renewed or replaced with a safety regulation. Examples covered children's nightwear, toy tear-gas capsules, toy water snakes, gas catalytic heaters, expanding novelties and scented erasers.

19 A wide definition of supply is provided in s 46, including selling, hiring, hire-purchase, trading stamps and giving as prizes and gifts. The supply must be in the course of a business (s 46(5)). Equipment provided in a holiday flat is 'supplied', see *Drummond-Rees v Dorset County Council* (1996) 162 JP 651, DC.

20 For enforcement details from 1 April 1993-31 March 1998 see *Consumer Safety – Report of the Secretary of State for Trade and Industry*, 1998 HCP 9.

1   See generally B Cotter 'Due Diligence: the Disappearing Defence' (1992) 142 NLJ 133 and 170; D Parry 'Judicial Approaches to Due Diligence' [1995] Crim LR 695.

2   This re-acts the provisions of s 12 of the 1986 Act which were introduced following the recommendations in para 20 of *The Safety of Goods* Cmnd 9302 (1984).

In *Rotherham Metropolitan Borough Council v Raysun (UK) Ltd*[3] the court confirmed the need for positive and sufficient steps to be taken to satisfy the reasonable precautions and due diligence defence under section 12 of the 1986 Act, now replaced by section 39(1) of the 1987 Act. Here agents of the respondents in Hong Kong did partially supervise the producer of crayons and one packet out of 10,000 dozen packets was tested in the UK. Subsequently, in *P & M Supplies (Essex) Ltd v Devon County Council*,[4] where a company had operated a sampling and testing system for toys (378 (0.49 per cent) of 76,960 toys imported sampled, 18 sent to public analyst), the court emphasised that it was up to the defendant to establish that there had been sufficient sampling to satisfy the defence requirements. The need for assistance to be given to magistrates by the defendant, preferably in the form of independent statistical evidence as to what should be done by a reasonable trader in the circumstances, was highlighted. Subsequently in *Sutton London Borough v David Halsall plc*[5] the court emphasised that any sampling undertaken should be 'properly organised random sampling with a sufficient number of samples being properly tested to indicate compliance with the specifications'.[6] Here on each occasion five Halloween capes, from batches of several thousand, were tested for flammability in-house, with one sent to an independent testing house. The test used did not comply with British Standards and there was no evidence produced as to whether it was an equivalent test or not. The company was convicted.

Cases concerning reliance on documentary evidence have proved unsuccessful for defendants. In *Bury Metropolitan Borough Council v United Norwest Co-Operatives Ltd*[7] a general letter from the manufacturers confirming that warranties were supplied with all goods was insufficient to satisfy the defence. Reliance on Cenelec and IMQ Certificates, which demonstrated compliance with certain safety standards, also was inadequate when Italian-made cooker hoods melted when used with gas cookers.[8] Finally, in *Balding v Lew-Ways Ltd*[9] compliance with British Standards, which did not cover all areas covered by safety regulations,

3   (1988) 153 JP 37, DC. See also S Weatherill 'Unsafe Goods: Protecting the Consumer and Protecting the Diligent Trader' [1990] JBL 36.
4   (1991) 156 JP 328, DC.
5   (1994) 159 JP 431, DC.
6   Kennedy LJ at p 435.
7   Unreported, 14 November 1994, LEXIS Transcript, DC.
8   *Whirlpool (UK) Ltd and Magnet Ltd v Gloucester County Council* (1993) 159 JP 123, DC. The case here concerned a breach of s 10 of the 1987 Act, see below p 267, to which the s 39 defence applies also.
9   (1995) 159 JP 541, DC.

did not provide a defence for failure to comply with the Toys (Safety) Regulations 1989.[10]

A by-pass provision is included in section 40 to enable the prosecution of the person, in the course of any business of his,[11] whose act or default caused another to commit an offence, eg manufacturers or importers.

In addition to criminal proceedings being taken for certain breaches of obligations under safety regulations, section 41(1) provides (unless excluded in regulations) for a civil action for breach of statutory duty for anyone who has been 'affected by a contravention of the obligation'.[12] The constituents of this tort are that the claimant must prove that a) a statutory duty existed, b) this was broken by the defendant, c) damage was suffered. The liability cannot be limited or excluded by contract terms or notices (s 41(4)) but contributory negligence by the claimant is a partial defence.

Section 13 of the 1987 Act re-enacts the provisions, first introduced in section 3 of the 1978 Act, relating to prohibition notices and notices to warn. A prohibition notice is directed at a named trader to prevent that trader from supplying dangerous goods. It may be used against, for example, the sole manufacturer, importer or retailer of a particular item. A retailer who creates risks by selling certain goods to a particular class of person, for example children, or by the way goods are sold, for example without assembling them properly or carrying out the necessary safety checks, would also be an appropriate target. The procedures for making prohibition notices are laid down in Schedule 2, Part I and involve at least a 21-day consultation process. An example of a prohibition notice under section 3 of the 1978 Act illustrates its use. In March 1983 the then Minister for Consumer Affairs, Dr Gerard Vaughan, issued a warning about gas catalytic heaters, some of which contained asbestos. The main suppliers were asked to stop supplying them and all voluntarily did so except for Impact Heaters (UK). On 26 September 1983 a prohibition notice was issued against Impact Heaters (UK) prohibiting sales. This was then followed by a Prohibition Order, the Gas Catalytic Heaters (Safety) Order 1983,[13] which in turn was replaced by the Gas Catalytic Heaters (Safety) Regulations 1984,[14] thus permanently banning the dangerous heaters. Each step taken

10   SI 1989/1275.
11   See *R v Warwickshire County Council, ex p Johnson* [1993] AC 583, [1993] 1 All ER 299, HL, ch 12 at p 421.
12   In many other criminal statutes no such express stipulation is made and a litigant may have to establish the right to sue for breach of statutory duty in the courts. This is unnecessarily unhelpful and has often been criticised. There is a presumption against the availability of an action for breach of statutory duty when the statute is silent. However, proof of a criminal conviction in a subsequent civil case affords prima facie evidence of the facts on which it was based (Civil Evidence Act 1968).
13   SI 1983/1696; see also DTI Press Notice, 21 November 1983.
14   SI 1984/1802; see Appendix I at p 469.

helped to deal with the immediate problem and gave time for the necessary consultations before the next stage. Similar steps are used under the 1987 Act, with the emergency procedure for Safety Regulations being used in place of the Prohibition Order (see above).

The provisions for notices to warn require a person to publish at his own expense warnings about specified goods considered by the Secretary of State to be unsafe. The procedures for issuing such notices are contained in Schedule 2, Part II and involve a 28-day consultation process. To date no notices to warn have been issued and the Secretary of State has given evidence[15] that the procedures are 'relatively cumbersome and slow and difficult to apply effectively' in some cases. The Department of Trade and Industry does, however, regularly issue general warning notices about the safety of goods.

Contraventions of prohibition notices or notices to warn are offences under section 13(4) with the same penalties, defences and by-pass provisions as for breaches of safety regulations. There is no action for breach of statutory duty for harm resulting from either prohibition notices or notices to warn (s 41(2)). This can be contrasted with the previous position under section 6 of the 1978 Act where there was such an action in the case of prohibition notices.

Section 14 of the 1987 Act re-enacts, with minor alterations, the provisions of section 3 of the 1986 Act relating to 'suspension notices'. It enables the stopping of the supply of goods believed to be dangerous whilst they are tested or a prosecution brought.[16] If an enforcement authority has reasonable grounds to suspect that any safety provision[17] has been contravened in relation to any goods, it may serve a suspension notice on a person. The notice prohibits that person from supplying etc those goods without the consent of the authority, for a specified period of up to six months (s 14(1)). Breach of a suspension notice is (subject to the defence provisions of s 39) an offence with up to six months' imprisonment and/or a fine of up to level 5 on the standard scale (s 14(6)). To enable the enforcement authority to keep track of suspended goods the notice may require their whereabouts to be notified to the authority throughout the suspension period (s 14(3)). An appeal procedure is laid down in section

---

15 See *R v Liverpool City Council, ex p Baby Products Association* (2000) 108 ITSA 2 MR 26 at p 29, QBD (Crown Office List), see below.
16 See Cmnd 9302, paras 23-25.
17 Defined in s 45(1) as the general safety requirement in s 10 (see below) or any provision of safety regulations, a prohibition notice or suspension notice. The requirements of the General Product Safety Regulations 1994, SI 1994/2328 are also included within the definition by virtue of reg 14(b) of those Regulations; see below p 273.

15 and compensation may be payable if the goods in fact conform to safety requirements (s 14(7) and (8)).[18]

The case of *R v Birmingham City Council, ex p Ferrero Ltd*[19] examined the provisions of section 14 and considered the methods of appeal available to a producer who wished to challenge a suspension order. The judgment of the Queen's Bench Division,[20] which had granted judicial review of the decision by Birmingham City Council to suspend the supply of 'Kinder Surprise Eggs', was overturned by the Court of Appeal. Producers aggrieved by the issue of a suspension order against their products have to use the appeal process laid down in section 15 to seek removal of the order by establishing that the goods in question are safe. The case concerned small toys depicting the Pink Panther, contained in the chocolate eggs. A child had died from swallowing part of one of the toys and, as a result, supply of the eggs was suspended for six months under section 14. In rejecting the use of judicial review in such circumstances Taylor LJ stated:

> The real issue was whether the goods contravened a safety provision and the section 15 appeal was geared exactly to deciding that issue. If the goods did contravene the safety provision and were dangerous to children then, surely, procedural impropriety or unfairness in the decision-making process should not persuade a court to quash the order. The determining factors are the paramount need to safeguard consumers and the emergency nature of the s 14 powers.[1]

In contrast, in *R v Liverpool City Council, ex p Baby Products Association*,[2] the local authority had not, in fact, initiated proceedings under section 14, but had issued a press release concerning certain models of babywalker which were said to fail standard tests of safety. The purpose was said to give a public warning so as to cause a recall of the identified products and to cause a suspension of supply. The legality of the press notice was challenged and the court ruled that its issue was contrary to law. In the words of Lord Bingham CJ: 'By acting as it did the Council purported to exercise a power it did not have and in so doing deprived the companies of rights and safeguards which Parliament had enacted that they should enjoy [under s 13 of the Act]' (at p 29).

As under section 6 of the 1986 Act, section 16 of the 1987 Act allows enforcement authorities to apply for an order forfeiting goods that

---

18   See Cardwell and Kay 'The Consumer Protection Act 1987: Liability of the Enforcement Authorities' (1988) 6 Trad Law 212.
19   [1993] 1 All ER 530, CA; M, H & P p 591.
20   (1990) 154 JP 661, QBD.
1   [1993] 1 All ER 530 at pp 538-9.
2   (2000) 108 ITSA 2 MR 26, QBD (Crown Office List).

Summary of specific criminal legislation

contravene safety provisions. The court, if satisfied of the contravention, may order the destruction of the goods or their release to a specified person for possible repair or as scrap (s 16(6) and (7)). An appeal process is provided under section 16(5) with power to delay the destruction of the goods pending the appeal.

The enforcement provisions, under Part IV of the 1987 Act (ss 27-35),[3] reflect the recommendations in the White Paper *The Safety of Goods*,[4] which were subsequently introduced in the 1986 Act. Enforcement officers can inspect and seize goods for testing, inspect documents etc at the point of first supply ie before they have been supplied to consumers in the United Kingdom (s 29). It is thus possible to check goods for compliance with relevant safety provisions both at the retail stage and at the manufacture/ import stage. There is an appeal procedure against any seizure of goods, together with the possibility of compensation if there has been no breach of safety provisions (ss 33 and 34). The Commissioners of Customs and Excise may, under section 37, disclose to trading standards officers, information on goods imported into the United Kingdom (subject to confidentiality restrictions contained in s 38). In addition, customs officers are given powers to seize and detain goods for up to two working days to enable trading standards officers to inspect the goods (s 31).[5]

The provisions of the 1987 Act discussed so far have been those covering areas already dealt with under previous legislation. The 1987 Act also created a new general safety duty. The idea of such a duty was mooted in the White Paper *The Safety of Goods*[6] because of the problem with existing safety legislation that 'only a limited number of categories and aspects of consumer goods' are covered (para 33). The White Paper proposed 'to place a general obligation on the suppliers of consumer goods to achieve an acceptable standard of safety where it is reasonable to expect them to anticipate and reduce the risks arising from those goods' (para 34). This was enacted in section 10 of the 1987 Act. Since implementation of the General Product Safety Directive[7] in the General Product Safety Regulations 1994,[8] section 10 has been 'disapplied' in cases where the safety of a product is covered by the 1994 Regulations (see below). Brief discussion of section 10 is included as there are a few remaining situations

---

3   See further K Cardwell 'The Consumer Protection Act 1987: Enforcement of Provisions Governing the Safety of Consumer Goods' (1987) 50 MLR 622.
4   See Cmnd 9302 paras 21-22.
5   See Cmnd 9302 paras 27-32.
6   Cmnd 9302 paras 33-48; M, H & P p 593; see also *Implementation of EC Directive on Product Liability*, DTI, November 1985, pp 8-10.
7   92/59/EEC.
8   SI 1994/2328, BSSCCL p 800; M, H & P p 595.

where section 10 still survives[9] and, in order to assess the impact of the 1994 Regulations, some knowledge of the pre-existing provisions is necessary.

Section 10 makes it a criminal offence for a person to supply,[10] offer or agree to supply or expose or possess any consumer goods 'which fail to comply with the general safety requirement'. 'Consumer goods' are defined, in subsection (7), as goods ordinarily intended for private use and consumption, but excluding such things as water, food, feeding stuff, controlled drugs, licensed medicinal products, aircraft (other than hanggliders) and motor vehicles. These areas were, according to the White Paper, excluded from existing safety legislation or were 'already adequately covered by other statutes' (para 44). Also excluded is tobacco as the application of a general duty 'could raise particular problems' (para 44).

Consumer goods will fail to comply with the general safety requirement if they are not reasonably safe having regard to all the circumstances including the manner in which and purposes for which they are marketed, their get-up, use of marks, instructions and warnings,[11] any published standards of safety for such goods and the existence of reasonable means (considering cost, likelihood and extent of any improvement) for making the goods safer (s 10(2)). This is quite wide in its scope and is not limited to situations where published standards and regulations exist. The main difficulty with such a safety requirement is that, in imposing strict criminal liability, there is a need for certainty – to know what is and is not permitted by law – and yet the definition of what fails to satisfy the requirement is very general and flexible. Where there is no clear and straightforward breach of a published standard or regulation, defendants can argue strenuously that their goods are not in breach of the safety duty. Compliance with statutory requirements or Community obligations will not be regarded as a failure to comply with the safety requirement, nor will failure to do more than is required by safety regulations or legislation (sub-s (3) as amended).

A conviction under section 10(1) may lead to imprisonment for up to six months and/or a fine of level 5 on the standard scale (s 10(6)). In addition to the standard defence of reasonable steps and due diligence under section 39, section 10(4) provides further defences. These are a) reasonable belief that the goods would not be used or consumed in the United

---

9 See eg the DTI in *The General Product Safety Regulations 1994 – Guidance for Businesses, Consumers and Enforcement Authorities*, para 8 states: 'Section 10 will continue to apply to suppliers of products which are subject to specific product directives where the UK implementing regulations only impose obligations on the person who first places the product on the market (for example, regulations implementing the Personal Protective Equipment Directive).'

10 S 46(5) makes it clear that any such supply etc must be in the course of a business.

11 See similar wording re the meaning of a defect in Pt I of the 1987 Act (s 3) in ch 6 at p 178.

Kingdom, or b) that the supply etc was in the course of a retail[12] business and at the time of supply etc the supplier neither knew nor had reasonable grounds to believe that the goods failed to comply with the general safety requirement, or c) that the terms of supply etc indicated that the goods to be acquired[13] were second-hand. The exclusion of second-hand goods and goods for export was suggested in the White Paper (para 41) but attracted much criticism from consumer organisations.

Contrary to the recommendations of the White Paper (para 48), there is no action for breach of statutory duty available for breach of the general safety requirement (s 41(2)).

European Developments – The General Product Safety Regulations 1994[14]

The European Community has been active in the area of consumer safety and the effects of numerous Directives can be seen in the regulations, detailed in Appendix I. In particular, as part of the progression towards free movement of goods and services between member states, there has been harmonisation of many safety provisions. This is usually achieved by a general standard being imposed, which can be satisfied by compliance with national standards or with European standards devised by the private standards organisations CEN (European Committee for Standardization) and Cenelec (European Committee for Electrotechnical Standardization).

To achieve greater harmonisation and market integration, the General Product Safety Directive was adopted in 1992. It largely reflects the general product safety requirements of section 10 of the 1987 Act, discussed above, in establishing a general safety requirement for all products available within the Community. It requires enforcement provisions for the control of, and, where necessary, the banning of, unsafe goods (arts 5 and 6) and the establishment of information exchange procedures to ensure that the existence of dangerous products is known throughout the Community (art 7).[15] It creates a new system for dealing with emergency situations

12   As defined in s 10(5).

13   S 10(4)(c)(ii) refers to 'the acquisition of an interest' in the goods so cases of hire would be excluded from the special defence.

14   SI 1994/2238, as amended by SI 1994/3142 and SI 1994/3144, BSSCCL p 800, M, H & P p 595. See generally P Cartwright 'Product Safety and Consumer Protection' (1995) 58 MLR 222; D Clarke 'General Product Safety Regulations' (1995) 103 Trading Standards Review No 2, p 16; D Parry 'Product Safety: European Style – an Appraisal' [1995] JBL 268; *The General Product Safety Regulations 1994 – Guidance for Businesses, Consumers and Enforcement Authorities*, DTI, (http://www.dti.gov.uk/access/safreg94/foreword.html); Howells *Consumer Product Safety*.

15   The Rapid Information Exchange System (RAPEX) was first introduced in 1984, 84/133/EEC, OJ No L 70, 13.3.84, p 13.

(arts 8, 9 and 11) and establishes a new body, the Committee on Product Safety Emergencies, to assist the Commission to deal with products which pose a 'serious and immediate risk' to the health and safety of consumers (art 10). Those parts of the Directive requiring implementation in the United Kingdom were brought into force from 3 October 1994 in the form of the General Product Safety Regulations 1994, made under section 2(2) of the European Communities Act 1972. It is to be noted that the 1994 Regulations are largely in addition to the pre-existing regime under Part II of the 1987 Act, although, as mentioned above, section 10 of the 1987 Act is now largely superseded. It is necessary to consider both measures together as they inter-relate closely.

To understand the 1994 Regulations it is first necessary to examine their scope. They apply to 'products' as defined in regulation 2(1). The key features are that all goods 'intended for consumers or likely to be used by consumers'[16] for their private use are covered, whether new, second-hand or reconditioned, irrespective of whether any consideration is given for them, when supplied in the course of commercial activity.[17] Where goods are used exclusively in a commercial context, even when used by or for consumers, for example escalators in department stores and washing machines in launderettes, these are not affected by the 1994 Regulations. Products aimed at consumer use are clearly covered but so also are those which are intended for business use but which are subsequently supplied to consumers, for example building and decorating equipment like cement mixers and wallpaper strippers. The range of products covered by the 1994 Regulations is clearly much more extensive than that caught by section 10 of the 1987 Act. There is no list of excluded goods as in section 10(7), and second-hand goods are covered (although antiques are excluded under reg 3, as are goods supplied for repair or reconditioning if the person supplied is clearly informed to that effect). Where a product is covered by specific Community provisions, dealing with *all* aspects of its safety, then those provisions will apply and not the 1994 Regulations (reg 3(c)), for example toys under the Toys Safety Directive.[18] If the safety of a product is only partially covered by Community measures, the 1994 Regulations will apply to those aspects not already regulated (reg 4).

The 1994 Regulations place differing responsibilities on 'producers' and 'distributors' and the definitions of these terms do not correspond exactly with the traditional meanings ascribed to them. Regulation 2(1) provides three meanings of 'producer'. First there is the manufacturer or reconditioner of a product, if established in the Community, including those 'presenting'

16   Defined in reg 2(1) as 'a consumer acting otherwise than in the course of commercial activity'.
17. Including a business or trade: reg 2(1).
18   88/378/EEC, 1988 OJ No L 187 p 1; see Toys (Safety) Regulations 1995, SI 1995/204, Appendix I at p 466.

themselves as manufacturers by affixing names, trade marks or other distinctive marks to the goods. Second, where the manufacturer is not established in the Community, his representative, if established in the Community, or the importer of the goods into the Community is a 'producer'. Finally 'other professionals in the supply chain, in so far as their activities may affect the safety properties of a product placed on the market' are 'producers'. It is here that those who are traditionally thought of as suppliers may, on occasion, become 'producers'. For example, if a shop-keeper removes instructions and labels from a product or incorrectly assembles a product, then his actions may 'affect the safety properties of the product' and thereby cause him to become a 'producer'. A 'distributor' is defined as 'any professional in the supply chain whose activity *does not* affect the safety of the product' (reg 2(1), italics added). Interesting issues also arise over 'inactivity' that affects the safety of a product – a shop-keeper or wholesaler who stores, at room temperature, foodstuffs requiring refrigeration, for example.

Having established who is the 'producer' of a product, it is necessary to examine the obligations placed on producers. The primary requirement is that under regulation 7 which states:

> No producer shall place a product on the market unless the product is a safe product.

Contravention of this is an offence under regulation 12.[19] Under regulation 13 producers are also strictly liable for preparatory offences: if they offer or agree to place on the market or supply any dangerous[20] product or expose or possess such a product for placing on the market or supply.

Clearly, of crucial importance is the definition of a 'safe product'. Regulation 2(1) indicates that a product is safe when, under normal or reasonably foreseeable conditions of use (including foreseeable misuses), including duration, it does not present any risk or only the minimum risks compatible with its use,[1] 'considered as acceptable and consistent with a high level of protection for the safety and health of persons'. Strictly a product which causes property damage could be said to be 'safe', but often property damage, for example fire, also puts personal safety at risk, thereby making the product 'unsafe'. The definition further makes it clear that just because a higher level of safety may be obtainable, or there are other products available which present a lesser degree of risk, this alone does not make a product unsafe. Issues of cost arise here – the incorporation of additional safety features, for example air-bags in cars, may occur with

---

19   For discussion of defences, penalties etc, see below at p 273.
20   Defined in reg 2(1) as 'any product other than a safe product'.
1   For example sharp knives, chemicals used for removing rust etc.

prestige models but not with basic models, but the basic models should not automatically be considered unsafe. Also the 'price' of making a product safe may not be acceptable; cars limited to travelling at 20 mph would be much safer!

A number of specific factors are required to be considered in judging safety. These are:

(a) the characteristics of the product, including its composition, packaging, instructions for assembly and maintenance;

(b) the effect on other products, where it is reasonably foreseeable that it will be used with other products;

(c) the presentation of the product, the labelling, any instructions for its use and disposal and any other indication or information provided by the producer; and

(d) the categories of consumers at serious risk when using the product, in particular children.

These factors largely reflect the pre-existing British civil and criminal requirements regarding defective products, under Parts I and II of the 1987 Act. The difficulty a producer faces is in not knowing, in advance, whether a strict liability criminal offence is committed when a product is placed on the market.

Some further guidance is given to producers, under regulation 10, in that where products comply with specific United Kingdom laws detailing health and safety requirements which *must* be complied with for a product to be marketed, there is a rebuttable presumption that the general safety requirement has been satisfied.[2] Where no mandatory rules exist, then conformity of a product to the general safety requirement is assessed by considering voluntary United Kingdom standards giving effect to a European standard, for example some BSI standards; or European technical specifications, for example CEN standards. In the absence of these, standards drawn up in the United Kingdom or codes of good practice regarding health and safety in the product sector concerned or the state of art and technology are considered. Although compliance with these various standards may assist arguments that a product meets the general safety requirement, the other major consideration is 'the safety which consumers may reasonably expect'. The interpretation given to this will be significant. It could be taken to mean that where cheap goods are marketed, consumers do not 'reasonably expect' very high safety levels, in comparison with more expensive models. Poorer consumers buying inferior goods would, in these circumstances, receive less protection than wealthier consumers buying more expensive goods.

---

2   Eg a pushchair supplied under the Wheeled Child Conveyances (Safety) Regulations 1997, SI 1997/2866; see p 467.

Producers are under further obligations, imposed by regulation 8. 'Within the limits of his activity'[3] a producer has to provide consumers with relevant information to enable them to assess the non-obvious risks in using a product throughout its expected life and to take precautions against those risks, for example by the use of protective clothing. Producers must also adopt suitable measures to enable them to learn of potential risks from their products and to take appropriate action, including product withdrawal/recall to avoid those risks. Such measures may include batch marking, sample testing, complaint investigation and informing distributors of monitoring activities. The steps taken will vary with the nature of the product; the type and degree of risk a product poses; and the market it is aimed at, for example more activity may be needed where children are concerned. No specific sanctions are specified for failure to comply with regulation 8.[4] Some aspects may link with the general safety requirement under regulation 7, for example the giving of instructions and warnings. Otherwise the most likely consequence would be that a producer facing prosecution under regulation 12 or 13 would be unable to satisfy the 'due diligence' requirements of a defence (see below). Contrary to the wishes of the consumer lobby,[5] there is no compulsory product recall provision. The Department of Trade and Industry has, however, published detailed guidance on product recall.[6]

Distributors also have specific responsibilities. Under regulation 9(a) they are required to act with 'due care' to help ensure compliance with the general safety requirement; in particular a distributor must not supply products which 'he knows, or should have presumed, on the basis of information in his possession and as a professional' are dangerous. Breach of this is an offence under regulation 12. The offence requires mens rea: either actual knowledge or fault-based imputed knowledge. This can be contrasted with section 10 of the 1987 Act where the retailer's liability is strict, subject to a due diligence defence. It is interesting to note the reference to 'as a professional', which requires an objective assessment

---

3   According to the DTI in its Guidance booklet, op cit p 267, n 9, this is 'considered to refer to the capacity of a person, given his position in the supply chain, to influence the safety of a product' at para 32.

4   The DTI in its Guidance booklet, op cit p 267, n 9, para 53 states such failures 'may constitute offences under those parts of the 1987 Act applied by the Regulations'. Presumably this refers to prohibition orders, notices to warn, suspension notices, etc (see pp 263 and 264), although it is not clear how any offences would arise.

5   See P Locke, Policy Director, Consumers' Association, (1994) 91 L S Gaz pt 18, p 7; T Watt 'Improving Recalls of Unsafe Products' (1993) 3 Consumer Policy Review 204.

6   *Consumer Product Recall – A Good Practice Guide*, DTI, CBI and BRC, December 1999.

of imputed knowledge, not an assessment based on the capabilities of the individual distributor who may, for example, be illiterate in English.[7]

Regulation 9(b) requires distributors to act with due care and, within the limits of their activities, to participate in monitoring the safety of products placed on the market. This covers, particularly, passing on information about product risks (between producers and consumers) and co-operating in the action taken to avoid those risks, such as product recalls and distribution of information. This links with the producer's obligations under regulation 8 and, similarly, there is no direct enforcement mechanism. Distributors who fail to comply with regulation 9(b), are, however, prevented from relying on the 'due diligence' defences under regulation 14 (discussed below) or section 39 of the 1987 Act, if they are prosecuted under either measure (reg 14(5)).

The most significant impact on distributors' activities will be the possibility of prosecution under regulation 13 for preparatory offences: offering or agreeing to place on the market dangerous goods or exposing or possessing such products for placing on the market or supply. These are strict liability offences, which are much more likely to be used in preference to the more complex, mens rea offence contained in regulation 9(a).

The penalties for conviction for offences under regulations 12 and 13 are a fine not exceeding level 5 and/or imprisonment for three months.[8] There is a by-pass provision to enable the prosecution of another person whose act or default committed 'in the course of a commercial activity' has caused the offence (reg 15).[9] Regulation 13 extends section 13 of the 1987 Act (concerning prohibition notices and notices to warn) to products covered by these Regulations. The requirements of the 1994 Regulations constitute 'safety provisions' for the purposes of sections 14 and 15 (suspension notices), 16 and 17 (forfeiture) and 18 (power to obtain information) of the 1987 Act, with three months' imprisonment, instead of six, under sections 13(4) and 14(6) substituted. A 'reasonable steps and due diligence' defence is provided for in regulation 14. The wording of the defence is the same as that under section 39 of the 1987 Act.[10]

Petroleum (Consolidation) Act 1928

Petroleum spirit may not be kept without a licence issued by a local authority, and it is an offence to do so, or to contravene a condition of a

---

7   As in *Denard v Abbas* [1987] Crim LR 424, a case concerning s 24(3) of the Trade Descriptions Act 1968.
8   Reg 17. Compare 6 months' imprisonment under the 1987 Act.
9   Note similarity to s 40 of the 1987 Act and see *Padgett Bros (A-Z) Ltd v Coventry City Council* (1998) 106 ITSA 5 MR 24, DC.
10 See above p 261.

licence. There are exceptions in favour of the storage of small quantities for private use, and storage without a licence in well-ventilated places of up to 10 litres in one metal vessel is permitted for certain engines such as lawn mowers by the Petroleum Spirit (Motor Vehicles etc) Regulations 1929 (as amended).[11] Since 1982 storage in plastic containers, not exceeding five litres' capacity, which comply with the Petroleum Spirit (Plastic Containers) Regulations 1982[12] has also been permissible.

Explosives Acts 1875 to 1976 (as amended)

This legislation mainly concerns the manufacture in licensed factories of gunpowder, nitro-glycerine, dynamite and other explosives. It is an offence to keep explosives in an unauthorised place, except small quantities for private use. Licences are granted by the Health and Safety Executive and local authorities. It is an offence to hawk explosives in public places (1875 Act, s 30) to sell them to children under 16 (1875 Act, s 31 as amended by Explosives (Age of Purchase &c) Act 1976 and the Consumer Protection Act 1987)), or to sell explosives except in properly labelled and constructed packages (1875 Act, s 32 as amended). The Act also makes it an offence to throw a firework in a public place (1875 Act, s 80 as amended) and the manufacture of fireworks is controlled by the Fireworks Act 1951.

Pharmacy and Poisons Act 1933; Poisons Act 1972; Medicines Acts etc

This legislation forms part of a series of Acts which, amongst other matters, control, under the criminal law, the sale of poisons and medicines. For example, retail chemist shops must be under the personal control of a registered pharmacist and the name and certificate of registration of the person having control of the business must be conspicuously exhibited on the premises (Medicines Act 1968). The Poisons Act 1972 prohibits the sale of specified poisons in Part I of the Poisons List other than by authorised sellers; and poisons may not be sold by automatic machine. Certain other persons as listed by local authorities may sell poisons in Part II of the Poisons List. Enforcement is by the Pharmaceutical Society and by local authorities.

Regulations made under the Medicines Act 1968 provide, inter alia, that all pre-packed medicines shall have written on a label or container so as to be clearly legible the appropriate designation of the substance or its active

---

11 S R & O 1929/952 as amended by SI 1979/427, SI 1982/630, SI 1992/1811 and SI 1999/743.

12 SI 1982/630 as amended by SI 1999/743.

constituents. In addition certain medicines may only be sold by authorised sellers, but there is an elaborately described class of proprietary medicines outside this prohibition.

The Medicines Act 1968 makes it an offence to sell any medicinal product which is not of the nature or quality demanded by the purchaser to his prejudice (s 64) and it is also an offence to adulterate medicinal products (s 63). Some classes of medicine may be sold only on prescriptions by doctors, dentists, vets, registered nurses, midwives and health visitors (s 58 as amended). Part VI of the Act contains an elaborate code prohibiting false or misleading advertisements relating to medicinal products. Also relating to advertisements, the Cancer Act 1939 makes it an offence to take part in the publication of an advertisement offering to treat a person for cancer, prescribing remedies or giving advice in connection with such treatment. There are exceptions in respect of advertisements not aimed at the general public.[13]

The Farm and Garden Chemicals Act 1967 gives power to make regulations as to the labelling and marking of substances including insecticides and weedkillers commonly used in farming and gardening. It is an offence to sell or consign for sale an unlabelled product required by the regulations to be labelled (see the Farm and Garden Chemicals Regulations 1971).[14]

Road safety

Road Traffic Act 1988

The Road Traffic Act 1988 contains numerous provisions as to the construction, use and safe loading of vehicles which benefit consumers directly or indirectly, but this topic must be left to works of a specialist nature.

With regard to sales of vehicles or accessories, section 75 (as amended)[15] contains a general prohibition of the supply of motor vehicles or trailers which are unroadworthy by reason of defective brakes, steering gear or tyres and generally as to construction, weight, or equipment or

13 See also the Medicines (Labelling and Advertising to the Public) Regulations 1978, SI 1978/41 as amended and the Medicines (Advertising) Regulations 1994, SI 1994/1932, as amended by SI 1996/1552, which, inter alia, prohibit advertisements for medical products available on prescription only and also advertisements relating to medical products for the treatment of specified diseases; these include VD, tuberculosis, cancer, diabetes, cataracts and glaucoma. Advertisements of spermicidal contraceptives are stringently controlled.
14 SI 1971/729.
15 As amended by the Road Traffic Act 1991, ss 16, 83 and Sch 8.

where their condition would involve a danger of injury to any person if used on the road. Nor may vehicles be altered so as to render them unroadworthy or so that they would involve a danger of injury to any person. Subject to the defence that the vehicle was supplied or believed to be for use abroad, any person who sells, offers to sell or supply or exposes for sale or alters a vehicle in contravention of these provisions is guilty of an offence punishable on summary conviction with a fine up to level 5 on the standard scale.[16] It is also an offence to fit or sell defective or unsuitable vehicle parts (s 76).

Section 15A[17] enables regulations to be made prescribing safety equipment for use by children in vehicles; selling or offering to sell items not of a prescribed type or in contravention of the regulations is an offence. By section 17 it is an offence to sell or offer for sale for use in Great Britain a motor cycle crash helmet other than one conforming to regulations designed to afford protection to motor cyclists in the event of accident. Section 18(4) makes it an offence to sell or offer for sale unauthorised head-worn appliances for use on motor cycles, for example visors, eye protectors[18] and earphones. The penalty for each offence is a fine up to level 3 on the standard scale on summary conviction, and local authorities are empowered to institute proceedings.[19]

Prices

Mock Auctions Act 1961

It is an offence, punishable by maximum sentences of a fine of level 5 and/ or imprisonment of three months on summary conviction (unlimited fine/ two years on conviction on indictment), to promote or conduct or assist in the conduct of a mock auction. A sale of goods by way of competitive bidding is a mock auction if during the course of sale i) a lot is sold to a person bidding for it at a price lower than the amount of his highest bid for that lot, or part of the price is repaid or credited to him or stated to be so

16 Road Traffic Offenders Act 1988, s 9 and Sch 2.
17 As inserted by the Motor Vehicle (Safety Equipment for Children) Act 1991, s 1.
18 Motor Cycles (Eye Protectors) Regulations 1999, SI 1999/535.
19 Road Traffic Offenders Act 1988, s 9 and Sch 2 and s 4 respectively. It is also an offence for a person wilfully to apply to equipment, information, a helmet or head-worn appliance a warranty not given in relation to it (Road Traffic Act 1988, Sch 1, para. 6 as substituted by the Motor Vehicles (Safety Equipment for Children) Act 1991, s 2(4)) or to give to a purchaser a false warranty in writing (ibid). See also s 80 – applying false approval marks to vehicles (indicating conformity with EC or international standards) is an offence under the Trade Descriptions Act 1968.

(unless the goods are found to be defective), or ii) the right to bid is or is stated to be restricted to persons who have bought or agreed to buy one or more articles, or iii) any articles are given away or offered as gifts (s 1). 'Competitive bidding' is defined as including 'any mode of sale whereby prospective purchasers may be enabled to compete for the purchase of articles whether by way of increasing bids or by the offer of articles to be bid for at successively decreasing prices or otherwise' (s 3(1)). In *Lomas v Rydeheard*[20] it was held by the Divisional Court (on appeal from the Crown Court) that where the defendant offered articles for sale to customers assembled in his salerooms, calling out a series of progressively decreasing prices, but not asking for bids until his final price when he offered the item to an individual in the crowd who bought it without bargaining, this was still 'competitive bidding' since it could be inferred that prices would have been reduced further if people had been unwilling to buy. The Act applies to lots comprising plate, linen, china, glass, books, pictures, prints, furniture, jewellery, articles of household or personal use or ornament or any musical or scientific instruments or apparatus (s 3). In *Clements v Rydeheard*[1] the defendant held sales at which he offered, at a fixed price, a number of boxes with undisclosed contents and selected the purchasers from those who put up their hands. Purchasers of later lots were similarly selected but only from those who had purchased boxes. The Divisional Court held that this was a sale by competitive bidding.

Competitive bidding includes any mode of sale whereby persons can compete for the purchase of articles in any way, whether or not by reference to price. In *Allen v Simmons*[2] the audience was asked, by the respondent, who would pay him 30p for a set of glasses. Hands were raised. There was only one set of glasses. The successful 'bidder' was sold the glasses for 1p and a similar performance took place relating to an offer for sale of an undisclosed item for 50p.

In the view of Melford Stevenson J it was difficult to form a precise view of the meaning of the word 'otherwise' in section 3(1), but the subsection did contemplate bidding in what was or appeared to be competition with other bidders. The mere fact that the effect of the bid depended on the whim of the person conducting the so-called auction did not matter. Following *Clements v Rydeheard* above, the court in effect construed section 3(1) set out above as stopping at the words 'may be enabled to compete for the purchase of articles', and the offence had accordingly been committed. As has been pointed out[3] there seems to be no point, and indeed no justification in law, in construing section 3(1) in

20 (1975) 119 Sol Jo 233, DC.
1   [1978] 3 All ER 658, DC.
2   [1978] 3 All ER 662, [1978] 1 WLR 879, DC.
3   [1978] Crim LR 362 at 363.

this curtailed way. Either decision could be justified by simply relying on the words 'or otherwise'.

The Court of Appeal in *R v Pollard*[4] agreed with the decisions in *Clements v Rydeheard* and *Allen v Simmons* above. It refused to apply the *ejusdem generis* rule to the words 'or otherwise' and require the competitive bidding to be on a financial scale. The fastest hand up was a competitive bid. May LJ drew attention to the words 'includes any mode of sale' which widened the ambit of the subsection.

The Act is designed to prevent fraudulent practices at auctions covering the lots as specified above. It was introduced as a Private Member's Bill and, as will be inferred from the above litigation, doubts have arisen as to its precise ambit. Its existence has certainly not prevented the fairly common practice of 'one day sales' with all the problems of enforcing civil remedies for defective goods that they bring. The OFT in 1979 wrote to all chief trading standards officers suggesting local codes of practice to protect consumers. The assumption is that all those who hire out public halls in a particular area can guard against abuses by incorporating appropriate conditions in the letting contract.[5] A number of such codes have been adopted and hirers of halls have been asked to notify Trading Standards Departments in advance of all proposed sales.

Auctions (Bidding Agreements) Acts

Other legislation exists to prohibit dealers' bidding rings. By the Auctions (Bidding Agreements) Act 1927 (as amended), if a dealer induces another person to abstain from bidding, both commit an offence carrying a maximum fine of level 5 and/or six months' imprisonment. Persons convicted may be ordered by the court not to participate in auctions for up to three years (Auctions (Bidding Agreements) Act 1969).[6] (Here the consumer is the seller who is a consumer of the auctioneer's services.)

4   (1983) 148 JP 679, CA.
5   For a helpful account of the objectives of the Act, see (1981) 131 NLJ 49 (A T H Smith). Trading Standards Departments' experience with many mock auctions is that the proceedings often involve the commission of other offences, eg under the Trade Descriptions Act 1968, as well as under the 1961 Act. North Yorkshire County Council have devised an interesting method of controlling such sales under their own private Act of Parliament: see S Pudney 'North Yorkshire County Council Act 1991' (1991) 99 Trading Standards Review, Pt 12, p 8. Similar legislation, ie private bills, is currently being proposed by Kent and Medway County Councils.
6   It can often be difficult to distinguish between bidders acting as partners as opposed to forming an illegal bidding ring. For a review of the law see A T H Smith 'Auction Rings' [1981] Crim LR 86. See also *R v Jordan* [1981] CLY 131, Swansea Crown Court. See for further detailed discussion of this legislation, Harvey & Meisel *Auctions Law and Practice* (2nd edn).

Prices Acts 1974 and 1975

These Acts provide for the regulation of prices of food and other commodities by the Secretary of State. By section 2 of the 1974 Act (as amended by s 2 of the 1975 Act) the Secretary of State may make orders regulating prices and orders were formerly made relating to (inter alia) bread, butter, cheese, flour, and tea.[7] By section 4 (as amended) orders may be made regulating the way prices are marked and indicated, including unit pricing (price per unit of measurement or other unit). One order, the Price Marking (Food and Drink on Premises) Order 1979, relates to food and drinks offered for retail sale for consumption on the premises.[8] As to the display of prices in restaurants (a matter on which the law seems in some areas to be more honoured in the breach than in the observance) the Order requires (inter alia) prices to be easily legible to an intending purchaser (normally near the entrance to the eating area) and prices must include VAT in all cases and also cover charges etc unless the contrary is clearly indicated in the same way as the price of the food is required to be displayed. The Order does not apply to bona fide clubs, staff canteens and the like. Also controlled are price displays at hotels for sleeping accommodation (maximum and minimum charges).[9]

Of considerable significance is the Price Marking Order 1999[10] which seeks to implement the EC Directive on indicating prices of products offered to consumers.[11] The object of the Directive is that consumers should know the selling price and the price per unit of measurement of the items they wish to buy prior to purchase, to improve consumer information and to enable comparisons to be made. The scope of the 1999 Order is indicated in article 3, with certain items (products supplied in the course of providing a service, sales by auction and sales of works of art or antiques), being excluded. The Order applies to traders, ie those selling or offering or exposing products for sale which fall within the trader's commercial or professional activity. Article 4 stipulates that, where a trader indicates that a product is for sale to a consumer, the selling price must be provided in accordance with the regulations, except regarding products sold from bulk or in an advertisement. The price must include VAT and all other taxes and it must be the price of a single item or a specified quantity (art 1(2)). Article 9 makes provision for changes in VAT or other taxes. The price indicated must be in sterling (art 6) and be unambiguous, easily identified and clearly

---

7   There are no orders currently in force.
8   SI 1979/361.
9   See Tourism (Sleeping Accommodation Price Display) Order 1977, SI 1977/1877 (made under the Development of Tourism Act 1969, s 18).
10 SI 1999/3042. The DTI has consulted on amendments – see *Price Marking Order 1999*, DTI, May 2000.
11 Council Directive 98/6/EC, OJ No L 80, 18.3.98, p 27, BSSCCL p 883.

Summary of specific criminal legislation

legible (art 7(1)(a)). Prices should be displayed 'in proximity to the product' (art 7(1)(b)) so traders are not required to price each item. This does nothing to assist consumers to keep a check on shelf prices compared with the prices they are charged where barcodes are used to record prices at the till. One new feature of the 1999 Order is that customers must be able to see the price without needing assistance from the trader (art 7(1)(c)). This removes the problem created by the decision in *Allen v Redbridge London Borough Council*[12] where perfumes, with individual price tickets on their back or underside and stored in a locked cabinet, were held to comply with an earlier order, even though customers could not view their prices without assistance from a member of staff.

Unit pricing for products sold from bulk and pre-packaged goods required, under Weights and Measures legislation, to be marked with a quantity or sold in prescribed quantities, is required by article 5. A system of exemptions, for example for pre-packaged goods sold in small shops, by itinerant traders and from vending machines, (art 5 and Sch 1) and restrictions on permissible units of measurement (art 1(2) and Sch 2) is provided.

Section 5 of the 1974 Act relates to the information to be displayed by 'price range notices'.[13] The Schedule to the 1974 Act relates to the enforcement of the Act and orders made thereunder. A duty is placed on local weights and measures authorities, which have sole responsibility for prosecutions. Persons contravening orders made under sections 2, 4 and 5 are liable to an unlimited fine on conviction on indictment and a fine not exceeding £5,000 on summary conviction.

Trade representations

Trading Representations (Disabled Persons) Acts 1958 and 1972

The 1958 Act (as amended) makes it an offence to represent when selling, exchanging or soliciting orders for goods by house-to-house visits, by post or by telephone, that blind or otherwise disabled persons are employed in the production of the goods. There are exceptions in favour of local authorities, institutions and associations registered under various Acts or by the Government and persons carrying on a business who are substantially disabled. In England and Wales a local authority may institute proceedings. Offenders are punishable by a fine not exceeding £5,000 on

12   [1994] 1 All ER 728, DC.
13   Retailers may be ordered to display information as to the range of prices within which specified goods are commonly sold by retail in the UK at a particular date or period. No such orders apply currently.

summary conviction, or an unlimited fine and/or up to two years' imprisonment on conviction on indictment (s 1 of the 1958 Act as amended).

Trading stamps

Trading Stamps Act 1964

This Act originated as a Private Member's Bill. It is designed to regulate the promotion of trading stamps and the conditions under which retailers may use them. 'Trading stamps' are widely defined to include coupons, vouchers and tokens whether adhesive or not.

The Act makes it an offence for any person other than a company (ie a registered limited company) or an industrial and provident society to carry on business as a promoter of trading stamps (s 1). It is also an offence to issue any trading stamp on any sale or credit transaction unless it bears on its face in clear and legible characters a value expressed in or by reference to current coins of the realm.[14]

Trading stamps and stamp books must also bear the promoter's name and catalogues must indicate the number of stamps needed to obtain anything described in the catalogue. It is an offence to contravene these provisions (ss 2, 5). It is also an offence to advertise the cash value of trading stamps by associating the worth of any trading stamps with what the holder pays or may pay (for goods) to obtain them, or in misleading or deceptive terms. The offences carry varying fines.

Shops are required to post notices showing the cash value of trading stamps and giving sufficient particulars to enable customers to ascertain the number of trading stamps to which they are entitled on a purchase, and a copy of any current catalogue must be kept where customers may conveniently consult it. If these provisions are contravened without reasonable excuse, the occupier or person having control of the shop is liable on summary conviction to a fine up to level 1 on the standard scale. A person pulling down such a notice is also liable to a similar penalty.[15]

The Act also incorporates two useful civil rights in favour of the consumer. By section 3 the holder of trading stamps having an aggregate cash value of not less than 25p may insist on their being redeemed for cash. Where the stamps are redeemed for goods, section 4[16] implies terms by the trader that he has the right to give the goods in exchange, for quiet possession and freedom from encumbrances and that the goods shall be of satisfactory quality.

14 Trading Stamps Act 1964, s 2(1), as substituted by the Consumer Credit Act 1974, Sch 4, para 24.
15 Trading Stamps Act 1964, s 7 as amended by the Criminal Damage Act 1971.
16 As amended by the Sale and Supply of Goods Act 1994, s 7 and Sch 2 para 1.

The government has proposed[17] repealing the Trading Stamps Act 1964, as it is considered redundant in the light of changes in technology and retailing practices. It is claimed to be costly to comply with, whilst providing no worthwhile protection for consumers. The criminal measures would be withdrawn but the civil protection, incorporating implied terms regarding goods supplied, would be continued, using the Supply of Goods and Services Act 1982.[18]

Unsolicited goods and services

Unsolicited Goods and Services Acts 1971 and 1975

The 1971 Act was designed to meet problems caused by 'inertia-selling'. Goods were sent to the potential customer without his or her prior knowledge or request and then various techniques, from the sending of an invoice to demands for payment and threats, were used to extract the notional price of the goods from the customer. The Act makes no specific provision for enforcement by public authorities. Amendments have recently been enacted regarding inertia selling (see below), and further simplification is proposed.[19]

Section 2 (as amended) makes it an offence (maximum fine of level 4 on the standard scale on summary conviction) for someone in the course of business to demand payment or assert a present or prospective right to payment in respect of goods, known to be unsolicited goods, sent with a view to someone acquiring them in the course of a business.[20] Similarly, threatening legal proceedings or the placing of the name of a person on a debtors' or defaulters' list or invoking or threatening any other collection procedure is an offence (maximum fine level 5 on the standard scale on summary conviction).

Section 3 makes it an offence (maximum fine level 5 on the standard scale on summary conviction) to demand payment for unsolicited entries in respect of a directory relating to that person or his trade or business. There is no right to charge for such entries unless there has been signed by the directory entrant an order or note in the form specified by the Act. There are currently proposals[1] to amend section 3 to enable electronic

---

17   See *Consultation on repeal of the provisions of the Trading Stamps Act 1964 and associated provisions*, DTI, http://www.dti.gov.uk/consumer/law/3a.html.

18   See further ch 5 at p 91.

19   *Simplification of the Unsolicited Goods and Services Act 1971*, DTI, December 1999.

20   For an unusual case on the area see *Eiman v London Borough of Waltham Forest* (1982) 90 ITSA MR 204, DC; M, H & P p 613.

1   *Simplification of the Unsolicited Goods and Services Act 1971*, DTI, December 1999, sections 3 and 4.

signatures and electronic or e-mail, in addition to paper, notes to be used. The documentary requirements for repeat entries (renewals) would also be relaxed.

Section 4 makes it an offence to send published material or advertisements which the sender knows or ought reasonably to know are unsolicited, and which describe or illustrate human sexual techniques. A prosecution under this section needs the consent of the Director of Public Prosecutions. The maximum penalty is level 5 on the standard scale.

The Act also (in common with many other criminal laws affecting the consumer) makes provision for offences by corporations. A director, manager or other officer of a company who consents to, connives at or has been neglectful with regard to the commission of the offence, as well as the company, is liable to be proceeded against and punished (s 5).

Consumer Protection (Distance Selling) Regulations 2000 [2]

These Regulations, which implement the Distance Selling Directive,[3] repealed that part of the Unsolicited Goods and Services Act 1971 relating to civil remedies for sending unsolicited goods and introduced new measures in regulation 24, effective for goods and services supplied after 31 October 2000. A consumer is able to treat unsolicited goods as an unconditional gift if sent without the recipient's agreement or knowledge, by someone with no reasonable cause to believe the goods would be acquired for business purposes. The sender loses all rights to the goods (reg 24(1)-(3)).

Two criminal offences may also arise. First, where someone, without reasonable cause to believe in a right to payment, demands payment or asserts a right to payment, with knowledge that unsolicited goods or services have been supplied otherwise than for business purposes of the recipient. A summary conviction may lead to a level 4 fine (reg 24(4)). Second, a person without reasonable cause to believe there is a right to payment for unsolicited goods or services, who threatens to bring legal proceedings, places the name of any person on a defaulters list or invokes any other collection procedure, is guilty of a summary offence (reg 24(5)). A fine of level 5 on the standard scale may be imposed.

---

2   SI 2000/2334.
3   Directive 97/7/EC on the protection of consumers in respect of distance contracts (OJ No L 144, 4.6.97, p 19); BSSCCL p 858.

Hallmarking

Hallmarking Act 1973 as amended

Hallmarking is one of the oldest, most important and most taken for granted forms of consumer protection. The fundamental need for protection arises because gold, silver and platinum are too soft to be of much practical use and normally need to be alloyed with other metals. But this lowers the intrinsic value of the article, and it is therefore essential to establish by chemical analysis what proportion the precious metal content bears to the whole. Accurate analyses are therefore carried out by Assay Offices on small samples removed from the article before polishing prior to the article being certified as containing metal conforming to one of the legal standards of fineness and purity. There are now four Assay Offices (Birmingham, London, Sheffield and Edinburgh) which are incorporated by Royal Charter or statute and are independent of trade organisations.

With regard to gold, a gold carat is 1/24, so an article of 22 carats consists of 22 parts gold and 2 parts alloy. Legal standards have varied since 1300 when hallmarking was introduced. In 1575 22 carats was the legal standard, and in 1798, 1854 and 1932 the current 9 carat, 14 carat and 18 carat standards were established. Standards of silver are a minimum of 800 parts in 1,000, 'Sterling' (925 parts silver in 1,000) and 'Britannia' (958.4 parts silver in 1,000). The standards for platinum, which was first covered by legislation from 1 January 1975, are a minimum of 850 parts in 1,000, 950 and 999 parts in 1,000. The, now optional, standard mark for gold is a crown and the standard of fineness in figures (916 for 22 carats, 750 for 18 carats, 585 for 14 carats and 375 for 9 carats). The standard mark, since ancient times, for Sterling silver is a lion and for Britannia silver the figure of Britannia. For platinum the standard mark is an orb surmounted by a cross (Hallmarking Act 1973, Sch 2). Also permitted are marks struck in a European Economic Area State, by an independent body, in accordance with the law of that State, which provide information equivalent to approved hallmarks, and which is intelligible to United Kingdom consumers (s 2(1)(d)). Foreign hallmarks may be approved by order of the Secretary of State pursuant to an international convention or treaty (s 2(1)(c)). These powers are being used to implement the International Convention on the Control and Marking of Articles of Precious Metals.

The illustration on page 285 of a hallmark shows first the sponsor's (or maker's) mark, then the mark for sterling silver, then the mark of the London Assay Office and finally the date letter for 1975.[4]

The main offence, under section 1 of the Act, is for any person, in the course of a trade or business, to apply to an unhallmarked article, a

4   See generally *British Hallmarks on Gold, Silver and Platinum*, published by the Assay Offices of Great Britain and reproduced in Butterworths Trading and Consumer Law.

description indicating that it is wholly or partly made of gold, silver or platinum, or to supply or offer to supply an unhallmarked article to which such a description is applied. This is subject to certain exemptions in favour of articles such as coins, articles manufactured before 1920, articles of a minimum fineness and of a very light weight (gold less than 1 gram, silver less than 7.78 grams, platinum less than 0.5 gram).[5] Certain descriptions are exempted from this. These are 'plated' or 'rolled' gold, 'plated' silver and 'plated' platinum, provided the words 'plated' or 'rolled' are as large as any other lettering in the description. In addition the description must not be false or applied to an article of which the description is inappropriate. A description is also permissible if confined to the colour of an article (s 1 and Sch 1).[6] Subject to exceptions, it is also an offence to make any addition, alteration or repair to a hallmarked article, or to alter or deface any mark (except by battering an article to make it fit only for remanufacture) without the written consent of an assay office (s 5). The exceptions permit additions to an 'old' article, if its character remains unaltered, where the addition is of the same precious metal and fineness as the article and its weight does not exceed the specified standards or thin coatings of the article, with permitted metals of a specified fineness (s 5 (4) and (5)).

Section 6 lays down offences in connection with the counterfeiting of dies and marks and section 9 states that it is the duty of every local weights and measures authority to enforce the Act within their area. Penalties for offences are on summary conviction a maximum fine of £5,000 or on indictment an unlimited fine and/or imprisonment for up to two years, or in the case of counterfeiting, 10 years.

Insurance policyholders' protection

Policyholders Protection Act 1975; Insurance Companies Act 1982; Financial Services Act 1986

The Policyholders Protection Act 1975[7] imposes a scheme, funded by a levy on insurance companies and friendly societies to which the Act applies, to ensure that, if a company is unable to meet its liabilities, policyholders

---

5   Exempted articles as listed in the Hallmarking Act 1973, Sch I, Pt II (as amended) may be hallmarked voluntarily.
6   These provisions apply equally to imported articles. It is the importer's responsibility to send the articles for hallmarking.
7   As amended by the Friendly Societies Act 1992, the Damages Act 1996, the Policyholders Protection Act 1997 and SI 1997/2781.

nevertheless receive at least 90 per cent of the benefits that they would otherwise have received. It is an offence for such a company knowingly or recklessly to give false information in a statement required to be made to the Policyholders Protection Board or to the Secretary of State or to make default in giving such information or statements (Schs 2 and 3).

The Insurance Companies Act 1982, Part I, restricts the carrying on of insurance business to authorised insurers. It is an offence to carry on business without authorisation or knowingly or recklessly to furnish false information in order to obtain authorisation (s 14). Part II of the Act lays down detailed regulations for companies to deposit accounts and statements of their business with the Secretary of State, to apply assets relating to long-term business alone thereto, and a number of other matters designed to prevent or give warning of insolvency. It is an offence not to comply with the various requirements (s 71). Part III (s 72) empowers the Secretary of State to make regulations controlling insurance advertisements. Section 133 of the Financial Services Act 1986 makes it an offence for any person to make false, deceptive, dishonest or reckless promises or forecasts to induce another person to enter into a contract of insurance. Prosecutions must have the consent of the Secretary of State, the Industrial Assurance Commissioner or the Director of Public Prosecutions (s 201(2) of the 1986 Act).

Theft and deception

The Theft Act 1968 is an important part of the general criminal law. Consumers are not, as such, more directly concerned with the Act than members of the public in any other capacity, but in the course of buying goods several sections could be material. The problem of buying goods which turn out to have been stolen has already been discussed.[8] The Act states that a person handles stolen goods if knowing or believing them to be stolen goods he dishonestly receives the goods, or dishonestly undertakes or assists in their retention, removal, disposal or realisation by or for the benefit of another person. A person buying goods that he knows to be stolen 'receives the goods'. The penalty for 'handling' is a maximum of 14 years' imprisonment on conviction on indictment (s 22).

Cheating of various kinds is covered by section 15. This states that a person who by any deception dishonestly obtains property (defined in s 4 as including money) belonging to another with the intention of permanently depriving the other of it shall on conviction on indictment be liable to a maximum of 10 years' imprisonment. 'Deception' is any deception, whether deliberate or reckless by words or conduct as to fact or as to law,

8   See above, p 92 and also below, p 341.

including a deception as to the present intentions of the person using the deception or any other person. This section accordingly covers a large number of situations where money or property is obtained by deception. These range from the alteration of a car's mileage to obtain a higher selling price, falsely claiming expensive repairs are necessary[9] or have been done, to the doorstep seller of goods and services taking money in advance with no intention of fulfilling the obligation. The Theft Act 1978 makes additional provision for dishonestly obtaining services by deception, evasion of liability by deception and making off without payment where payment on the spot is required or expected. The 1968 Act also makes clear that where property has been stolen or obtained by fraud or other wrongful means, the title to that or any other property shall not be affected by reason only of the conviction of the offenders (s 31). Questions of title to goods which have been stolen are therefore left to the civil law. The general principle involved is that the property in goods remains in the person from whom they were stolen.[10] Formerly the true owner had to sue for their return within six years but this rule was abrogated by the Limitation Amendment Act 1980, section 2 (now the Limitation Act 1980, s 4).

---

9   See *R v King* [1987] QB 547, [1987] 1 All ER 547, CA and (1999) 22 Consumer Law Today Issue 12, p 7 (prison sentences for two bogus builders who overcharged elderly customers for shoddy work).

10   See above, p 92.

10 Consumer credit

Something has already been said of the economic background to consumer credit in chapter 1 and we commence this chapter with a description of the genesis of the present legislation governing this field, the Consumer Credit Act 1974 ('the Act').[1]

1. CONSUMER CREDIT – THE BACKGROUND

The Crowther Committee was appointed in September 1968 by the Secretary of State for Trade and Industry to carry out a wide-ranging review of consumer credit. The Committee's terms of reference were:

i)   to enquire into the present law and practice governing the provision of credit to individuals for financing purchases of goods and services for personal consumption;
ii) to consider the advantages and disadvantages of existing and possible alternative arrangements for providing such credit, having regard to the interests of consumers, traders and suppliers of credit including depositors;
iii) to consider in particular whether any amendment of the Moneylenders Acts was desirable; and
iv) to make recommendations.

---

1   See also M, H & P ch 6; BSSCCL p 255 ff; Bennion *Consumer Credit Control*; R M Goode et al *Consumer Credit Law and Practice*; Guest and Lloyd *Encyclopaedia of Consumer Credit Law*; *Butterworths Trading and Consumer Law* (the latter four works being looseleaf encyclopaedias). Textbooks on the subject include Goode *Consumer Credit Law and Practice*; Harding *Consumer Credit and Consumer Hire Law: A Practical Guide*; and Rosenthal *Guide to Consumer Credit Law and Practice* (2nd edn).

The Committee's two volume report appeared in March 1971 (Cmnd 4596). The Report made serious and far-reaching criticisms of the then existing law and in particular criticised the regulation of transactions on the basis of legal abstractions rather than on the basis of commercial reality:

> The greatest weakness of the present law of credit, and that from which most of the other defects stem, is the failure to look behind the form of a transaction and deal with the substance. [para 4.2.2.]

The Report also contains a full historical, economic and social critique of consumer credit and proposed a new legal framework. This involved repeal of the Moneylenders Acts, Bills of Sale Acts, Pawnbrokers Acts and Hire-Purchase Acts. The proposed legislation was to cover sums advanced of up to £2,000. On the basis that there should be 'truth in lending', it would enable debtors to 'shop around' for credit on the most favourable terms (para 3.8.2 et seq) by requiring that the effective cost of borrowing in terms of an annual percentage rate should be disclosed (para 6.5.16). The Report also recommended introduction of a comprehensive licensing system administered by a single agency.

The Report was followed by a White Paper *The Report of the Law on Consumer Credit* (1973, Cmnd 5427) which, after much consultation, affirmed the Government's intention to implement the Report with a few modifications. The Government did not accept the need for a Lending and Security Act as recommended by the Report and proposed raising the financial limits for statutory protection of credit from £2,000 to £5,000.

The Act was passed on 31 July 1974 and is designed to provide the framework for the implementation of the above proposals, the details being left to regulations. As a result, the supply to individuals of credit not exceeding £25,000[2] is comprehensively regulated throughout the United Kingdom by this Act.

Subsequently the EC Directive on Consumer Credit was agreed on 22 December 1986.[3] Based largely on the Consumer Credit Act 1974, it is not, however, as extensive. It aims to ensure that annual percentage rates of charge (APRs) are indicated in certain advertisements, to control the form and content of credit agreements, to provide information about credit charges, to make provisions concerning repossessions and early settlements, to provide connected-lender liability and to control credit grantors by means of a licensing or similar system. The Directive left the

---

2   The original limit of £5,000 was raised to £15,000, as of 20 May 1985 (SI 1983/1878). The subsequent increase to £25,000, as of 1 May 1998, was introduced by the Consumer Credit (Increase of Monetary Limits) (Amendment) Order 1998, SI 1998/996.

3   87/102/EEC, OJ No L 42, 12.2.87, p 48.

details of implementation to the member states, requiring provisions to be operative by 1 January 1990. The Directive does not apply to certain agreements, in particular those of less than 200 ECU (approximately £164) or more than 20,000 ECU (approximately £16,400). Only a few minor modifications to regulations were necessary in order to implement the Directive in the United Kingdom. An amendment to the Directive was passed on 22 February 1990,[4] with the ultimate aim of introducing a common Community method of calculating the annual percentage rate of charge. The new provisions specified the matters to be included and excluded from the calculations of APRs, required additional information to be given in writing to consumers and extended the exemption for loans guaranteed by a mortgage secured on immovable property. Implementation took place through amendments to regulations. A further amending Directive was passed on 16 February 1998,[5] to establish one single method of calculating the APR and to remove certain transitional provisions. The necessary amendments to United Kingdom law became effective from 14 April 2000.[6]

The Directive on Consumer Credit is included in the Directive on injunctions for the protection of consumers' interests.[7] Implementation of the Directive is required by 1 January 2001 and it is proposed that the Director be the lead body, with enforcement, trade and consumer bodies being able to seek injunctions to enforce the Directive.

Different British Governments have, for many years, been examining the impact of consumer credit legislation on businesses. Consideration has been given to ways of removing some controls from certain sectors of the business community, initially as part of the Conservative Government's Deregulation Initiative and now, under the Labour Government, the Better Regulation Initiative.

The 1988 White Paper, '*Releasing Enterprise*',[8] recommended the removal of all business lending and hiring from the scope of the Act, simplification of several aspects of the Act and its regulations and outlined proposals for removing the necessity to possess a licence for many sectors of the credit industry. The then Director General of Fair Trading, Sir Gordon Borrie, expressed serious reservations about the proposed licensing changes.[9]

4   90/88/EEC, OJ No L 61, 22.2.90, p 14.
5   98/7/EC, OJ No L101, 1.4.98, p 17.
6   See below pp 305–306.
7   98/27/EC, OJ No L 166, 11.6.98, p 51. See also *Injunctions Directive: Implementation in the UK*, DTI, February 2000, and 'Widening the net', OFT, Issue 26 Fair Trading, p 13.
8   Cm 512.
9   *Annual Report of the Director General of Fair Trading 1988* (1989 HCP 440), p 27; OFT Press Release 65/88.

In 1993, Sir Bryan Carsberg, as Director, was asked by Ministers to review several aspects of the working and enforcement of the Consumer Credit Act 1974 from a deregulation perspective. In particular, he considered proposals to change ancillary credit and hire traders from a system of positive licensing to negative licensing;[10] whether the Government's proposals on credit marketing[11] should be implemented; and whether or not there was a good case for removing all business lending and hiring from the scope of the Act or for extending coverage to small incorporated businesses. The Director advised against licensing changes and the implementation of the credit marketing proposals[12] and decided to consult further before giving a view on the extension or contraction of coverage for business lending and hiring. In the light of these earlier proposals and the Deregulation Initiative, consultation papers were issued by the Director on *The Working and Enforcement of the Consumer Credit Act 1974* (August 1994), *The Treatment of Business Consumers under the Consumer Credit Act 1974* (September 1994) and *The Use of Group Licensing* (January 1995). Public hearings were also held to debate the issues raised.

In January 1994 the Department of Trade and Industry published *Deregulation Task Force's Proposals for Reform* which included a number of recommendations concerning consumer credit.[13] These were followed, in June 1994, by the Director's report, *Consumer Credit Deregulation*, which supported some of these recommendations and considered a number of other proposals for reform, the Government was minded to accept the Director's proposals, but to enable other proposals to be made and to assess the cost implications of reform, the Department of Trade and Industry issued a Consultation Document *Deregulation of United Kingdom Consumer Credit Legislation* in August 1995. Some changes, concerning quotations and monetary limits, including the upper limit for regulated agreements, followed. The Department of Trade and Industry subsequently published *Deregulation of Lending and Hiring to Unincorporated Businesses: A Further Consultation* in November 1996.

With the election of a Labour Government, in 1997, consumer credit controls were reassessed. A consultation paper was published by the Department of Trade and Industry in February 1998: *Clarification and Simplification of United Kingdom Credit Law*. This focussed on the advertising of low-start mortgages, wealth warnings on advertisements,

---

10   See p 310 below.
11   *Revised Proposals for Legislation on Credit Marketing*, Department of Trade and Industry, December 1991.
12   OFT Press Release 35/93 and *Consumer Credit Deregulation*, OFT, June 1994, paras 1.2–1.3.
13   Recommendations 381–395, summarised in *Consumer Credit Deregulation*, OFT, June 1994, Annex C.

warnings on equity release schemes, short-term hire agreements and unsigned mail order credit agreements.

In place of the Conservatives' Deregulation Task Force, the Better Regulation Task Force was created. In its *Consumer Affairs Report*, published in May 1998, it concluded that the Consumer Credit Act needed updating 'to make it more transparent and effective both for business and consumers'. The Government was encouraged to continue to pursue its commitment to an overall simplification and updating of the legislation. The 1999 White Paper *Modern Markets: Confident Consumers*[14] examined the protection given by the Act to consumers. Amendments regarding the calculation of annual percentage rates, wealth warnings and low-start mortgage advertising followed. The system of licensing was also identified as an area to investigate and an online consultation: *A Review of Consumer Credit Licensing*[15] took place in the Spring of 2000. The various reform proposals are discussed, where relevant, below.

2. FEATURES OF THE CONSUMER CREDIT ACT 1974

The draftsman of the Act, Mr F A R Bennion (who is well known for his criticisms of the usually unhelpful and obscure presentation of statute law) set new standards of comprehensibility in this particular measure. It does, of course, deal with a difficult area; perhaps too complex to be dealt with satisfactorily in one Act, however well drafted, but those who have to study it in detail will find the following novel and helpful features:

a)   Examples illustrating the application of the most important terms in the Act are set out in Schedule 2. Some of these are referred to later. In case of conflict, the provisions of the Act prevail over the examples (s 188).

b)   The 35 offences created by the Act, and the penalties that they attract, are set out in tabular form in Schedule 1 (as amended). The onus of proof in various court proceedings is summarised in section 171.

c)   In addition to a comprehensive definition section (s 189), Schedule 2 lists the new terminology used in the Act and refers the reader to the section and example where a definition and explanation are respectively to be found.

d)   Schedule 3 deals with the commencement provisions in a comprehensible way.

A note makes it clear that 'except as otherwise mentioned in this Schedule, the provisions of this Act come into force on its passing, that is on 31 July 1974'. Provisions awaiting commencement orders were listed and section

14   Cm 4410, July 1999.
15   http://www.gov.uk/consumer /law/1.htm.

192 required the relevant provision in Schedule 3 to be amended when an order was made. Those with a fully updated text therefore do not need to delve into volumes of statutory instruments to find commencement dates. The Act became fully in force on 19 May 1985.[16]

The Act is laid out in 12 Parts. Part I deals with the duties of the Director General of Fair Trading ('the Director'). In particular it mentions a duty to 'keep under review and from time to time advise' the Secretary of State for Trade and Industry about social and commercial developments in the United Kingdom and elsewhere relating to the provision of credit and the working of the Act. Part I also deals with the powers of the Secretary of State and gave the Council on Tribunals a supervisory function over the adjudicating functions of the Director.[17] Part II deals with the basic concepts relating to the provision of credit in its various forms, with particular reference to credit agreements, hire agreements and linked transactions. Part III deals with the licensing system administered by the Director, since all businesses which carry on a consumer credit (or hire) business where the agreements are regulated require a licence (s 21). Part IV relates to the advertising of such businesses. Parts V to X regulate the various types of individual credit and hire agreements. Part XI deals with enforcement of the Act and, in particular, lays down the powers of the Director, the powers relating to entry, inspection and the making of test purchases by local weights and measures authorities, and related provisions. Part XII ('Supplemental') deals with definitions and other residual matters.

Although the Act is fully in force, it is occasionally necessary when advising on particular credit transactions to check the commencement dates of relevant sections as many only apply to agreements *made* on or after the commencement date. Commencement dates are not generally included in the text.

3. THE LAW OUTSIDE THE ACT

It must be borne in mind that the Act is not a comprehensive code relating to all aspects of contracts for consumer credit. The ordinary law of contract governs the formation of such contracts and such vitiating factors as misrepresentation or illegality. Furthermore the Act normally only applies

16 An extension of licensing requirements for certain agreements under £30 came into force on 31 July 1989: Consumer Credit Act 1974 (Commencement No 10) Order 1989, SI 1989/1128.
17 See now the Tribunals and Inquiries Act 1992, s 1 and Sch 1, para 17.

where the credit does not exceed £25,000 or where the debtor is not a body corporate.[18]

Where mortgages of personal property (ie property other than land) occur these are still governed by the Bills of Sale Acts 1878–82 as slightly amended by section 192 of the Act and Schedule 4. A bill of sale is a document by which the property in goods is transferred by one person to another, either absolutely or by way of security. Absolute bills, under which a person disposes of goods but remains in possession of them, are required to be registered under the 1878 Act in order to warn the public that the possessor is not the true owner. Bills of sale by way of security are governed by the 1878 and 1882 Acts. The latter Act is designed to safeguard the grantor of the bill against oppressive terms. If the provisions of the 1882 Act, which lay down a form for such bills, are not complied with the security may be void.

The hire-purchase terms in the Supply of Goods (Implied Terms) Act 1973[19] remain. There are accordingly implied terms of title, correspondence with description, and satisfactory quality, (except regarding defects a) specifically drawn to the attention of the bailee or hirer before the agreement is made, b) which any examination made ought to have revealed and, c) where goods are hired or bailed by sample, which would have been apparent on reasonable examination of the sample). There is also an implied term of fitness for purpose, where that purpose has been expressly or impliedly made known either to the creditor or credit-broker, and the circumstances do not show that the recipient of the goods either did not rely, or that it was unreasonable to rely, on the other party's skill or judgement. These implied undertakings relating to quality and fitness also apply where a hire-purchase agreement is made by a person who, in the course of a business, is acting as agent for the creditor, thus embracing the common tripartite dealer-finance company-consumer relationship which usually occurs under a hire-purchase agreement.

The Hire-Purchase Act 1965 was repealed and the Hire-Purchase Act 1964 was repealed except as to section 37 and Part III dealing with the title to motor vehicles dealt with below. Part III of this Act is conveniently reproduced, as amended by the new terminology introduced thereby, in Schedule 4, paragraph 22 of the 1974 Act.

---

18   There have been proposals that business lending and hiring (for sole traders, partnerships and unincorporated bodies) should be removed from the Act, save for licensing requirements: see *Deregulation of United Kingdom Consumer Credit Legislation*, DTI, August 1995, ch 2 and *Deregulation of Lending and Hiring to Unincorporated Businesses: A Further Consultation*, DTI, November 1996.

19   As amended by Sch 4 to the 1974 Act, the Unfair Contract Terms Act 1977 and the Sale and Supply of Goods Act 1994.

4. DEFINITIONS AND SCOPE OF THE ACT

The meaning of credit

Although credit is purportedly defined in section 9, this section does not actually provide a full definition but merely states (inter alia) that 'credit' includes a cash loan, and any other form of financial accommodation. A clue to the concept of 'credit' in the Act lies, if anywhere, in the expression 'financial accommodation'. It is the presence or absence of this factor which dictates whether a simple case such as the payment of newspaper or milk bills monthly brings those transactions within the Act as 'credit' or whether there is some other element in the transaction which must be present before the Act applies. There is evidence of some misunderstanding on this fundamental point. As Goode points out[20] there must be a contractual deferment of the time when the debt would ordinarily be paid. For instance, in the common cases of newspapers or milk bills being paid monthly, there is no contractual deferment of the time at which the debt would have been paid under the contract to supply these commodities. Only when an extra-contractual provision expressly defers the time for payment of the debt does 'credit', for the purposes of the Act, become a factor. In some cases it is necessary to make a sophisticated analysis under the ordinary law relating to the supply of goods and services as to when the debt would ordinarily become payable, but in everyday cases the principle is clear enough. The main subject matter of the Act is, in fact, agreements whereunder the debt in question is not only postponed but repayable by set instalments.

Regulated agreements

Comprehension of the structure of the Act can only be achieved by understanding the meaning of the terms used to describe various types of agreement. An approximate picture can be obtained by studying the tabular illustration in Appendix II.

A concept central to the working of the Act is that of the 'regulated agreement'. Only regulated agreements are governed by the requirements of the Act (including the licensing provisions, but this is not so with regard to advertising and the reopening of extortionate credit bargains which are governed by provisions of far wider scope; see ss 43 and 137 respectively). Section 189 defines a regulated agreement as 'a consumer credit agreement,

20   Goode *Consumer Credit Legislation 1999*, Vol 1, para 443, as cited, with approval, in *Dimond v Lovell* [1999] 3 All ER 1, CA at p 11; see also [2000] 2 All ER 897, HL at p 903 (Lord Hoffman) and p 913 (Lord Hobhouse).

or consumer hire agreement, other than an exempt agreement'. The agreement must also not have been made before 1 April 1977.[1] Each of the above expressions must therefore be examined separately.

Consumer credit agreements

A consumer credit agreement is a personal credit agreement by which the creditor provides the debtor with credit not exceeding £25,000 (s 8(2)[2]). A 'personal credit agreement' is also defined as an agreement between an individual ('the debtor') and any other person ('the creditor') by which the creditor provides the debtor with credit of any amount (s 8(1)). 'Individual' is defined as including a partnership or other unincorporated body of persons (not consisting entirely of bodies corporate) (s 189)[3] and 'credit' includes a cash loan, and any other form of financial accommodation (s 9(1)). Consequently, the Act applies not only to the common form of instalment credit relating to goods, such as hire-purchase and credit sale agreements. A hire-purchase agreement is defined, at some length, in section 189. In essence it is an agreement under which goods are bailed, by the bailor, in return for periodical payments by the bailee, and the property in the goods will pass to the bailee a) on fulfilment of the terms of the agreement, and b) on the bailee exercising thereafter an option to purchase them. A conditional sale agreement is an agreement for the sale of goods or land under which the price is payable by instalments and the property is to remain in the seller until the specified conditions are fulfilled. A credit sale agreement is similar except that the property passes to the buyer without any preconditions (s 189). The Act applies also to any other agreement to which credit is extended, such as budget and option accounts, credit cards, loans and overdrafts. It currently[4] matters not that the debtor is a partnership and the transaction concerns goods required for their business. There is no concept of a 'consumer' as opposed to 'business' transaction such as is to be found in the Unfair Contract Terms Act 1977, section 6. The Act regulates all non-exempt credit agreements where the debtor is not a body corporate.

1   Consumer Credit Act 1974 (Commencement No 2) Order 1977, SI 1977/325, art 2(1).
2   As amended by the Consumer Credit (Increase of Monetary Limits) Order 1998, SI 1998/996.
3   It has been proposed by both the Director: *Consumer Credit Deregulation*, OFT, June 1994, ch 4, and the DTI: *Deregulation of United Kingdom Consumer Credit Legislation*, DTI, August 1995, ch 2 and *Deregulation of Lending and Hiring to Unincorporated Businesses: A Further Consultation*, DTI, November 1996, that all business lending and hiring be exempt agreements, save that licensing requirements should still apply.
4   Ibid.

Definitions and scope of the Act

Consumer hire agreements

A consumer hire agreement is, by section 15,[5] declared to be an agreement
made by a person with a hirer for the bailment of goods to the hirer, which
a)   is not a hire-purchase agreement, and
b)   is capable of subsisting for more than three months, and
c)   does not require the hirer to make payments exceeding £25,000.
Unless it is an exempt agreement a consumer hire agreement is a regulated
agreement[6] (see below).

Exempt agreements

By section 16(1) (as amended) outside the scope of the Act are consumer
credit agreements where the creditor is a local authority or some other body
specified by Order being
a)   an insurance company,
b)   a friendly society,
c)   an organisation of employers or of workers,
d)   a charity,
e)   a land improvement company,
f)   a body corporate specifically referred to in any public general Act,
ff)   a body corporate specifically referred to in orders made under certain
      sections of the Housing Act 1985, the Housing (Scotland) Act 1987,
      the Housing (Northern Ireland) Order 1981 or the Housing (Northern
      Ireland) Order 1983,
g)   a building society, or
h)   an authorised institution or wholly-owned subsidiary of such an
      institution,
provided the agreement also falls within section 16(2) which, broadly,
relates to agreements concerned with the financing of land or dwellings
on any land. Also exempt are consumer credit agreements where the creditor
is a housing authority and the agreement is secured by a land mortgage
(s 16(6A)). Thus, whilst mortgages granted by building societies, banks
and local authorities are exempt, those made by non-approved credit
organisations, together with many second mortgages will not be exempt,
and, indeed, will be regulated, if the loan does not exceed £25,000.

---

5   As amended by the Consumer Credit (Increase of Monetary Limits) Order 1998,
     SI 1998/996.
6   See further Palmer and Yates 'The Application of Consumer Credit Act 1974 to
     Consumer Hire Agreements' (1979) 38 CLJ 180; J Macleod 'Credit Hire' [1999]
     JBL 452. See also OFT booklet 'Hire Agreements' (OFT 017) for details of the
     provisions of the Act relating to hire contracts.

Section 16(5) gives the Secretary of State power to make orders exempting agreements in various circumstances, eg where the number of payments does not exceed a number specified or the total charge for credit does not exceed a stipulated percentage. An Order has been made exempting fixed-sum debtor-creditor-supplier agreements (see below for definition), where there are not more than four instalment repayments payable in not more than 12 months and which are not hire-purchase, conditional sale or pledge agreements, or agreements financing the purchase of land, thus exempting many ordinary credit accounts.[7] Also exempted are running-account debtor-creditor-supplier agreements where one repayment by the debtor is due for each regular period. Thus, for example, weekly or monthly trade credits are exempt, as are such credit card agreements as Diners Club and American Express where the entire debt must be discharged monthly (distinguish Visa and Mastercard).

Some debtor-creditor agreements at a comparatively modest rate of interest are similarly exempted. If the credit is offered to a particular class or particular classes of individuals (and not the public generally), it will be exempt if the rate cannot, at any time, exceed 1 per cent above the highest of the base rates of a number of specified banks, being the rate prevailing 28 days before the agreement is made. Similarly, where there is a restricted offer, with no increase permitted in the rate or amount of any item included in the total charge for credit, and the rate does not exceed 1 per cent above the specified bank base rates. Finally, if the creditor is a credit union, where the rate does not exceed 12.7 per cent (see generally Consumer Credit (Exempt Agreements) Order 1989).[8] In addition certain credit transactions concerning the import into or export out of the United Kingdom of goods and services are exempt if the credit is provided in the course of a business carried on by the debtor.

Consumer *hire* agreements are not exempt unless an Order is made exempting consumer hire agreements a) relating to the supply of electricity, gas or water by meter or b) where the owner of the thing hired is a specified public telecommunications operator[9] (to cover telephones). The 1989 Order mentioned above exempts hiring agreements within category a).

---

7   Contracts for the hire of replacement vehicles after accidents have often been worded in a way which makes them capable of lasting more than 12 months, thereby not being exempt. This can then lead to enforcement problems if the documentation does not contain all relevant details, see *Dimond v Lovell* [2000] 2 All ER 897, HL and below p 317. There have been numerous first instance car hire cases, noted in Current Law, concerning this exemption.

8   SI 1989/869 as amended by SI 1989/1841, SI 1989/2337, SI 1991/1393, SI 1991/1949, SI 1991/2844, SI 1993/346, SI 1993/2922, SI 1994/2420, SI 1995/1250, SI 1995/2914, SI 1996/1445, SI 1996/3081, SI 1998/1944 and SI 1999/1956. See BSSCCL p 744. For further guidance see OFT booklet 'Regulated and Exempt Agreements' (OFT 140).

9   Section 16(6) as amended by the Telecommunications Act 1984, s 109 and Sch 4, para 60(1).

Definitions and scope of the Act

Whilst exempt agreements are outside the regulation provisions of the Act, such agreements are still subject to control by the courts if they fall within the description of extortionate credit bargains laid down by section 138.

Computing the £25,000 limit

The principle behind the regulation provisions of the Act is to fix control by reference to the credit loaned to the borrower. To cover cases where interest rates fluctuate, interest or finance charges are excluded from the calculation of the loan. For instance, in hire-purchase cases the measure of the fixed sum credit supplied is 'an amount equal to the total price of the goods less the aggregate of the deposit (if any) and the total charge for credit' (s 9(3)).

Example (see Sch 2, example 10)[10]

Facts. C (in England) agrees to bail goods to D (an individual) in return for periodical payments. The agreement provides for the property in the goods to pass to D on payment of a total of £27,500 and the exercise by D of an option to purchase. The sum of £27,500 includes a down-payment of £1,000. It also includes an amount which, according to regulations made under section 20(1), constitutes a total charge for credit of £1,500.

Analysis. This is a hire-purchase agreement with a deposit of £1,000 and a total price of £27,500 (see definitions of 'hire-purchase agreement', 'deposit' and 'total price' in s 189(1)). By section 9(3), it is taken to provide credit amounting to £27,500 − (£1,500 + £1,000), which equals £25,000. Under section 8(2), the agreement is therefore a consumer credit agreement, and under sections 9(3) and 11(1) it is a restricted-use credit agreement for fixed-sum credit. A similar result would follow if the agreement by C had been a hiring agreement in Scotland.

Running account, or revolving credit, is credit which fluctuates, as, for example in the case of a bank overdraft, or credit card or an option account. Running account credit is regulated by the Act if the credit limit as defined by section 10(2) does not exceed £25,000. Section 10(2) defines the credit limit as the maximum debit balance which is allowed to stand on the account during any agreed period, disregarding permitted temporary loans exceeding the maximum.

The credit limit is taken not to exceed £25,000, even if the agreement indicates a limit in excess of £25,000 if: i) the debtor cannot draw *at any*

10   Modified to take into account the increased financial limit of £25,000.

one time more than £25,000; or ii) the rate of the total charge for credit increases or some other condition favouring the creditor comes into operation at a figure below £25,000; or iii) at the time the agreement is made it is probable that the amount of credit will not rise above £25,000 (s 10(3)(b)). These rules are designed to prevent artificially high credit limits being used to avoid an agreement being classified as a 'regulated agreement'.

Fixed sum credit is any other facility whereunder a debtor is enabled to receive credit, whether in one amount or by instalments (s 10(1)(b)). Examples would be a fixed sum bank loan, hire-purchase, credit sale or conditional sale agreements, check or voucher trading.

'Restricted-use' and 'unrestricted-use' credit

Section 11 defines restricted-use credit as, essentially, a regulated consumer credit agreement whereunder the credit supplied is to finance a *particular* transaction. This may be a transaction between the debtor and the creditor, for example hire-purchase, conditional sale, or a shop providing its own credit card scheme or budget account (s 11(1)(a)). Second, the credit may be to finance a transaction between the debtor and a supplier (someone other than the creditor), for example a loan from a finance company paid directly to a garage to purchase a car from that garage, credit card agreements such as Mastercard and Visa and check and voucher trading agreements (s 11(1)(b)). Finally, if the finance is to refinance any existing indebtedness of the debtor, either to the creditor or to a third party, this is also a restricted-use agreement, for example the consolidation of several separate credit agreements into one agreement (s 11(1)(c)). Unrestricted-use credit, under section 11(2), is credit supplied under any other regulated agreement not falling under subsection (1). The hallmark of this is that the credit is at the disposal of the debtor, as where he has overdraft facilities or a personal loan, even though certain uses would contravene the agreement (s 11(3)).

Debtor-creditor-supplier agreements and debtor-creditor agreements

These mind-boggling terms are the shorthand way in which the draftsman has subdivided the structure of regulated credit agreements. The distinction is simply between those where the creditor is also the supplier of the goods, or has a pre-existing business connection with the supplier (a debtor-creditor-supplier agreement under s 12), and those where the creditor is not also the supplier and has no pre-existing business connection with the supplier (a debtor-creditor agreement under s 13). Perhaps the first expression might have been better written as a 'debtor and creditor-supplier agreement'. Examples of debtor-creditor-supplier agreements are 1) any arrangement where the supplier of goods also provides the buyer with credit within the financial limits or, 2) the arrangement under a hire-purchase transaction where a finance house agrees to buy goods from the dealer and let them on hire-purchase terms to the customer, and 3) credit card transactions, since there is a pre-existing connection between supplier and creditor. Examples of debtor-creditor agreements are agreements to re-finance existing debts of the debtor and personal bank loans or overdrafts not tied to any particular transaction. The expression is in fact defined to catch all regulated agreements that are not debtor-creditor-supplier agreements.

The distinction is important to understand not only because these terms are used throughout the Act but also because, for instance, whilst debtor-creditor-supplier agreements may be canvassed off trade premises by specifically licensed lenders, it is an offence so to canvass debtor-creditor agreements (s 49). The object here is to prohibit 'doorstep' cash loan facilities and merely to regulate such activities as doorstep sale of goods transactions on credit terms.

Credit token agreements

Section 14(2) states that a credit token agreement is a regulated agreement for the provision of credit in connection with the use of a 'credit-token'. 'Credit-token' is defined by section 14(1) as a card, check, voucher, coupon, stamp, form, booklet, or other document or thing given to an individual by a person carrying on a consumer credit business who undertakes that on production of it (whether or not some other action is also required) the debtor is entitled to receive cash, goods or services from the creditor or a third party.[11] Examples are credit cards issued by individual stores, credit cards such as Mastercard and Visa, checks and vouchers, and cash cards used to obtain cash from banks' computerised cash machines. Cheque cards guaranteeing cheques up to a stated amount are issued under a 'consumer credit agreement' but are not credit tokens since the bank is merely paying the cheques drawn on it pursuant to the guarantee, not paying for goods or services. Example 21 in Schedule 2 of the Act elaborates this point.

Amongst the specific provisions in the Act relating to credit tokens is section 51(1) making it an offence to supply unsolicited credit tokens. In

11 See generally M, H & P pp 294–297.

Elliott v Director General of Fair Trading[12] shoe retailers circulated past customers with a cardboard replica credit card which stated, inter alia, that credit was 'immediately available if you have a bank account'. On a charge brought under section 51 the defence argued that the card was merely a promotion of sales and the real credit card would be issued only after an application form had been filled in. The Divisional Court, upholding the magistrates' conviction of the defendant retailers, held that the cardboard replica fell within the wording of the definition of a credit token in section 14(1) (see above). The defendant had *undertaken* that on the production of a card he would supply credit (whether or not some other action was also required). Section 84 limits the debtor's liability arising out of accidental loss of a credit token to £50[13] though there is no such limit if the misuse is by a person acquiring possession with the debtor's consent. Liability for subsequent misuse ceases altogether after giving notice of loss to the creditor. Agreements for the issue of credit tokens are subject to Part V of the Act. This relates to entry into, withdrawal from and formalities governing regulated agreements, and section 85 requires the creditor to give the debtor a copy of any executed agreement on issuing a new credit token (other than the first).

Small agreements

A small agreement is a regulated consumer credit agreement or consumer hire agreement for credit or hire payments not exceeding £50,[14] being an agreement which is either unsecured or secured by a guarantee or indemnity only (s 17[15]). Hire-purchase and conditional sale agreements are specifically excluded, but a credit-sale agreement where credit not exceeding £50 is repayable by instalments and the property in the goods passes to the buyer immediately would be a 'small agreement'. Whilst being generally subject to the Act as regards default, termination and control by the courts, there

---

12 [1980] 1 WLR 977, [1980] ICR 629, QBD; M, H & P p 295. See also Fairest (1980) 130 NLJ 1194; reply, Lister (1981) 131 NLJ 73; West (1981) 145 JPN 113.
13 Increased from £30 to £50 by the Consumer Credit (Increase of Monetary Amounts) Order 1983, SI 1983/1571, as of 20 May 1985. For contracts negotiated at a distance, there is no liability at all for fraudulent use of lost or stolen cards, see Consumer Protection (Distance Selling) Regulations 2000, SI 2000/2334, reg 21(5) which amends s 84 as of 31 October 2000. Section 84 is disapplied in such cases.
14 It has been proposed to increase this to £150: see *Deregulation of United Kingdom Consumer Credit Legislation*, DTI, August 1995, ch 3.
15 As amended by the Consumer Credit (Increase of Monetary Limits) Order 1983, SI 1983/1878.

is relaxation of the requirements relating to form and content, withdrawal and cancellation under Part V of the Act if the agreement is a small debtor-creditor-supplier agreement for restricted-use credit.

Non-commercial agreements

A 'non-commercial agreement' is not subject to various provisions of the Act – eg the formal requirements of Part V of the Act relating to entry into agreements (s 74), connected lender liability (s 75) or the giving of certain information to the debtor or hirer under sections 77–79 or sections 107–110. A 'non-commercial agreement' is defined as a consumer credit agreement or consumer hire agreement not made by the creditor or owner in the course of a business carried on by him (s 189(1)) and occasional transactions belonging to a business of that type are ignored (s 189(2)). If A, a private person, lends B £20 as a friendly act or a solicitor makes a temporary and isolated loan to a client in respect of a conveyancing transaction, these would be non-commercial agreements.[16]

Multiple agreements

If a single agreement falls into more than one category each part is to be treated as a separate agreement and that separate agreement is then regulated by the appropriate part of the Act (s 18). As a result of difficulties in interpreting section 18, both the Director[17] and the Deregulation Task Forces[18] have proposed reforms. To date no amendments have been made.

Linked agreements

These are defined in section 19. The object of the complex definition and provisions relating to linked agreements is to provide that a subsidiary agreement linked to a regulated agreement stands or falls with that regulated agreement. The section provides three criteria which, if any one of them fits the preliminary transaction (except if it is a provision of security such

---

16 For an example under the former legislation (the Moneylenders Act 1900) see *Wills v Wood* (1984) 128 Sol Jo 222, [1984] LS Gaz R 1211, CA; M, H & P p 284; where a solicitor's client lending money to other clients, making seven loans over four years, was held not to be in the business of being a moneylender. For discussion of 'occasional' transactions see *R v Marshall* (1989) 90 Cr App Rep 73, CA; M, H & P p 285.

17 *Multiple Agreements and section 18 of the Consumer Credit Act – A Discussion Paper*, OFT, June 1995.

18 *Deregulation Task Forces Proposals for Reform*, DTI, January 1994, para 382.

as a guarantee), results in that preliminary transaction being classified as a linked transaction. It is then automatically cancelled or terminated if the principal credit agreement is cancelled or terminated.

The three criteria are, summarised:

a) the transaction is entered into in compliance with a term of the principal agreement – eg a contract that the supplier of goods on credit shall also maintain them at the debtor's expense, or for insurance of the goods; or

b) the principal agreement is a debtor-creditor-supplier agreement and the transaction is financed by the principal agreement – eg under a tripartite credit-sale agreement between customer, dealer and finance house (by pre-existing arrangement) the purchase of the goods by the customer from the dealer will be linked to the loan to the customer from the finance house; or

c) a creditor (or other person similarly placed) initiates the preliminary transaction by suggesting it to the debtor so as to induce the creditor to enter into the principal agreement or for a purpose related to it – eg a contract of life insurance is entered into by D at the suggestion of C and C then enters into a regulated agreement with D.

There is provision, in section 19, for coupling an agreement made by a debtor's 'relative' (as defined by ss 184 and 189) with the debtor's principal agreement.

Total charge for credit

As was mentioned above, the Crowther Committee recommended that debtors should have means of determining the true cost of credit provided or to be provided – the 'truth in lending' principle. Rates of interest can often be deceptively stated, either by a reference to an amount of money rather than a true percentage rate per annum or, for example, by not allowing for the effect of repaying a capital sum on which an interest rate is based by instalments, the interest being charged on the full amount borrowed. Section 20 empowers the Secretary of State to make regulations to achieve this principle. This is an immensely complex exercise, for not only must the total charge be calculated by including certain charges payable under the transaction, but statutory assumptions must be made relating to the effect of the time element in which the credit is advanced, when it is to be repaid, and whether repayments are index-linked. These matters are dealt with in detail in the Consumer Credit (Total Charge for Credit) Regulations 1980 (as amended),[19] that reflect the requirements of Directive 98/7/EC.[20]

19   SI 1980/51 as amended by SI 1985/1192, SI 1989/596 and SI 1999/3177.
20   OJ No L101, 1.4.98, p 17, amending Directive 87/102/EEC, OJ No L 42, 12.2.87, at p 48.

Although the details of the Regulations cannot be dealt with here, it is important to understand the basis of the cost of credit as shown by many advertisements for credit (see the Consumer Credit (Advertisements) Regulations 1989[1]). The central idea is first to calculate the total charge for credit taking into account all relevant additional charges as indicated above, and then to express this as an annual percentage rate of charge ('APR'). The APR then becomes a reliable yardstick to measure the cost of credit when comparing alternative sources. Further information on this can be found in the OFT's booklet on Credit Charges and APR.[2] In connection with the regulations referred to above controlling advertisements for credit or hire facilities, the OFT's booklet on Credit Advertisements should also be consulted (see below).

Licensing

The Act introduced a potentially powerful regulatory weapon by requiring all proprietors of consumer credit or hire businesses to be licensed by the Director General of Fair Trading (s 21). Section 21 exempts from this requirement a) local authorities and b) bodies corporate empowered by a public general Act to carry on a business, and section 189 makes it clear that only businesses concerned with *regulated* agreements are within the licensing provisions. Ancillary credit businesses as defined by section 145 (credit brokers, debt adjusters, debt counsellors, debt collectors and credit reference agencies) also require licences (s 147). The scope of the licensing requirement is therefore very wide – far wider, for instance, than the old system requiring moneylenders to be licensed. Now almost all businesses dealing with consumer credit or hire agreements as defined must be licensed. It was estimated that some 90,000 businesses would be affected. In fact, from 1976 to December 1999, 481,055 applications for new licences had been made and 461,078 licences granted.[3]

The original timetable for licensing in stages comprised the period from February 1976 over the following 12 months. This was later extended to 1978 because of a flood of last-minute applications, many of which were defective.[4] In 1989 a further category of traders was brought within the licensing system: those only making regulated agreements not exceeding £30.[5] It is of the essence of the scheme that the Director must be satisfied

1   SI 1989/1125 as amended by SI 1999/2725, SI 1999/3177 and SI 2000/1797.
2   OFT 144, p 6.
3   Appendix C 8, *Annual Report of the Director General of Fair Trading 1999* (2000 HCP 576).
4   See (1976) 95 Law Notes 226.
5   Consumer Credit Act (Commencement No 10) Order 1989, SI 1989/1128.

that the applicant is a fit person to hold the licence. There can, therefore, be no unauthorised short cuts in this process.

The detailed provisions regarding licensing[6] are to be found in Part III of the Act and these provisions are supplemented by Regulations.

Types of licence

Under section 22 these are of two types, namely standard licences issued by the Director to individuals, partnerships, incorporated or unincorporated bodies, and group licences. A group licence has been granted, for example, to the Law Society in respect of ancillary credit businesses carried on by solicitors.[7]

Period of licence

Originally the standard period of licence was three years. This was extended, in 1979, to 10 years and then to 15 years in 1986. As of 1 June 1991, the licence period is five years.[8]

Authorisation of specific activities

A licence to carry on a business covers all lawful activities done in the course of that business, though the licence may limit the activities it covers. In particular a licence covers the canvassing off trade premises of debtor-creditor-supplier or regulated consumer hire agreements only if it so provides (s 23).

Administration

The applicant having applied for a licence on the specified form (s 6) and paid a fee, the Director must be satisfied that the applicant is a fit person

6   See generally M, H & P pp 283–293; G Borrie 'Licensing Practice Under the Consumer Credit Act' [1982] JBL 91; and OFT booklet 'Do You Need a Credit Licence?' (OFT 147).

7   Renewal has been granted for only one year, instead of five, and is subject to quarterly reviews, due to concerns over the handling of consumer complaints by the Law Society: see OFT Press Release 30/00, 20 July 2000.

8   Consumer Credit (Period of Standard Licence) Regulations 1975, SI 1975/2124 as amended by SI 1991/817. The reason for the extension was to enable the licensing system to be computerised prior to requests for renewals being received (see *Bee Line* No 42 p 8). Once achieved, a reduced licence period was introduced.

trading under a name which is not misleading or undesirable (s 25).[9] Relevant factors listed in section 25 to be considered are whether the applicant or, in the case of a body corporate, anyone controlling it, has committed offences involving fraud or dishonesty, or unfair business practices. Before determining not to issue a licence he must allow the applicant to make representations after having explained the reasons why he is minded to refuse the application. (Directors have shown themselves willing to use this machinery in the case of eg photocopier leasing firms with unfair selling practices and estate agents who fail to meet their legal obligations and who are involved in undesirable practices.[10]) There are provisions for renewal, variation, suspension and revocation of licences again accompanied by a duty to consider representations. Persons prejudiced by a refusal or compulsory variation have a right of appeal to the Secretary of State as specified more particularly in section 41.[11]

The sanctions for engaging in activities for which a licence is required whilst unlicensed are both criminal and civil. Section 39(1) makes it an offence to do so, the offence carrying a fine of up to £5,000 if the case is tried summarily, and up to two years' imprisonment[12] and/or a fine if tried on indictment (see ss 39, 167 and Sch 1 (as amended)).[13] Similarly, it is an offence for a licensee, under a standard licence, to carry on a business under a name not specified in the licence (s 39(2)) or to fail, within 21 working days, to notify the Director of changes in particulars[14] entered in the register, which the Director maintains, of all licences and applications under section 35. The register is open to public inspection at a fee (s 35(3)).

---

9   See *Fair Trading* No 9, Winter 94/95, p 11.

10   For further details see OFT Press Releases 2/92 and 34/94, *Bee Line* 91/4, *Photocopier Selling Practices*, OFT Report March 1994, *Annual Report of the Director General of Fair Trading 1994* (1995 HCP 419) at p 21 and *Annual Report of the Director General of Fair Trading 1997* (1998 HCP 762) at p 19 re photocopier leasing and OFT Press Release 34/99, *Annual Report of the Director General of Fair Trading 1999* (2000 HCP 576) at p 30 and *Fair Trading* Issue 25, Feb 2000, p 3 re estate agents.

11   See Consumer Credit (Licensing Appeals) Regulations 1998, SI 1998/1203; *North Wales Motor Auctions Ltd v Secretary of State for Trade* [1981] CCLR 1, QBD and *Credit Default Register Ltd v Secretary of State for Trade and Industry* [1993] CCLR 59, QBD.

12   See eg *R v Curr* (1980) 2 Cr App Rep (S) 153, CA (12 months' prison, £2,400 fine).

13   By the Magistrates' Courts Act 1980, s 32 as amended (increased from £2,000 by the Criminal Justice Act 1991, s 17(2) from October 1992).

14   Some simplification and streamlining of these requirements have been proposed by the Director General: *Consumer Credit Deregulation*, OFT, June 1994, paras 9.27–9.31, and the DTI: *Deregulation of United Kingdom Consumer Credit Legislation*, DTI, August 1995, ch 4 and *Review of Consumer Credit Licensing*, DTI, Spring 2000, http://www.dti.gov.uk/consumer/law/1.htm.

By section 147 the criminal sanctions which apply to unlicensed consumer credit businesses also apply to unlicensed ancillary credit businesses. Three criminal cases have examined the need for licences for credit brokerage, which under section 145(2) is, inter alia, the 'effecting of introductions' of people desiring credit to persons carrying on a consumer credit business or other credit-brokers. In *Brookes v Retail Credit Card Ltd*[15] it was held that, on its own, the provision of display boxes and application forms, belonging to the respondent company, in an unlicensed retail shop did not amount to 'introducing' persons seeking credit to a consumer credit business under section 145(2). The respondent company was thus not guilty of aiding, abetting, counselling or procuring an offence by the shop. In *Hicks v Walker and Frank Reynolds Ltd*[16] the court held that a car dealer who, having been refused a credit licence, introduced customers to a licensed credit-broker with a view to introductions to a licensed credit business, did effect introductions of credit brokerage facilities to a credit-broker and thus committed an offence under section 39. The number of transactions which can be involved before a credit-broking 'business' is established, thus requiring a licence to be obtained, was examined in *R v Marshall*.[17] As mentioned above in connection with non-commercial agreements,[18] section 189(2) recognises that 'occasional' entry into particular transactions does not amount to carrying on that type of business. The court decided that it was a question of fact for the jury to decide whether the activity was occasional or regular and, due to a misdirection on this point, the appeal against conviction for unlicensed trading was allowed.

The civil consequence of not obtaining a licence is that any regulated agreement not being a non-commercial agreement is unenforceable against the debtor or hirer (s 40). Section 40(2) gives power to the Director to remedy the position by making an order treating regulated agreements made during the unlicensed period as if they had been licensed. The Director must act judicially and consider representations by the trader as well as how far debtors have been prejudiced. There is, again, an appeal against refusal by the trader to the Secretary of State (s 41).[19] There are similar civil sanctions against agreements for the services of persons running ancillary credit businesses (no fees or commission can be claimed without an order from the Director) and regulated agreements made on introductions by unlicensed credit-brokers (ss 148, 149). It should be noted that the effect of the Act on the agreements mentioned above is to make them

15   (1985) 150 JP 131, [1986] BTLC 56, QBD.
16   (1984) 148 JP 636, QBD; M, H & P p 286.
17   (1989) 90 Cr App Rep 73, CA; M, H & P p 285.
18   See above p 304.
19   See D Foulkes (1983) 113 NLJ 135.

unenforceable against the debtor or hirer, not void. The debtor or hirer can exercise rights under the agreement against the creditor or owner.

In October 1988, coinciding with the publication of the White Paper *Releasing Enterprise* (Cm 512), the Department of Trade and Industry announced a review of consumer credit licensing.[20] Some proposals, for example the extension of licensing requirements to those only making agreements under £30 and the shortening of the period of licences, were implemented. The major suggestion, that, in general, ancillary credit businesses should no longer be required to apply for a licence, was not implemented. Reaction from consumer organisations and successive Directors to the proposal of negative licensing for ancillary credit businesses was unfavourable.[1] As an alternative, Sir Bryan Carsberg, as Director, proposed, in *Consumer Credit Deregulation*,[2] a simplification of licensing requirements, to replace the six existing categories with a licence covering all categories, save for situations where a Director had reasons to refuse to grant a licence for a particular category of business to a particular trader or where a trader requested a restricted licence. A number of other licensing proposals made in the Director's report,[3] await implementation. In response to the 1999 White Paper *Modern Markets: Confident Consumers*,[4] in Spring 2000 an online consultation, *A Review of Consumer Credit Licensing*,[5] canvassed options ranging from scrapping the licensing system to making the application process stricter and more onerous.

5. SEEKING BUSINESS

Part IV of the Act and sections 151–154 are aimed at protecting the consumer from two mischiefs, namely uncontrolled advertising of credit or rental facilities and canvassing off trade premises of certain regulated agreements. As in many other Parts of the Act, a number of details are contained in Orders made by the Secretary of State.

20 (1988) 11 Consumer Law Today, No 12, pp 1–3.
1   See, for example, *Consumer Credit Licensing*, NCC Policy Paper, December 1988; *Review of Consumer Credit Licensing: Comments by the Director General of Fair Trading on the Proposals of the Department of Trade and Industry*, OFT, December 1988; OFT Press Release 35/93; *Consumer Credit Deregulation*, OFT, June 1994, paras 9.9–9.21.
2   OFT, June 1994, paras 9.25–9.26. This proposal was also supported by the Deregulation Task Forces: *Deregulation Task Force's Proposals for Reform*, January 1994, para 384.
3   Op cit, ch 9.
4   Cm 4410, July 1999.
5   http://www.gov.uk/consumer/law/1.htm.

The ambit of Part IV is delineated by section 43. An advertiser is within the scope of Part IV if an advertisement for the purposes of his business indicates that he is willing a) to provide credit, or b) to enter into agreements of bailment or hire. But this does not apply if the advertiser does not carry on a consumer credit or consumer hire business, or does not supply credit to individuals secured on land, or where the agreement is unregulated because the law applicable to the agreement is that of a foreign land. Nor does the advertisement come within the controls if it indicates that the credit must exceed £25,000 and that no security is required or that the security is to consist of property other than land, or that credit is available only to a body corporate (s 43(3)[6]). The categories exempted have been extended by Order.[7] The meaning of 'indicating' in section 43(1) has been discussed in *Jenkins v Lombard North Central plc*,[8] where the court held that price stickers with the credit company's name and logo on them did not 'indicate' a willingness to provide credit. To be an advertisement covered by the Regulations it must state that the company is willing to provide credit. Suggestions that it is willing, based on the reputation of the company, are not sufficient.

The effect of this provision is to make Part IV apply to all consumer credit businesses, consumer hire businesses and any sort of agreement to provide credit to individuals secured on land *unless* the agreement falls within subsection (3) because, for example, the advertisement makes it clear that credit is available to a body corporate only.

The following are the main provisions regulating advertisements within the ambit of Part IV:

a) An advertiser advertising credit under restricted-use credit agreements relating to goods or services who does not also hold himself out as prepared to sell the goods or services for cash commits an offence (s 45).

b) If an advertisement is in a material respect false or misleading the advertiser commits an offence. This includes falsely stating or implying an intention on the advertiser's part that he has not got (s 46).[9]

c) Advertisements contravening the above may also render others knowingly involved in the illegal advertisement criminally liable – eg the publisher or deviser of it (s 47).

---

6 As amended by the Consumer Credit (Increase of Monetary Limits) (Amendment) Order 1998, SI 1998/996 and the Contracts (Applicable Law) Act 1990, s 5 and Sch 4, para 2.

7 See Consumer Credit (Exempt Advertisements) Order 1985, SI 1985/621.

8 [1984] 1 All ER 828, [1984] 1 WLR 307, QBD.

9 See eg *Home Insulation Ltd v Wadsley* [1988] BTLC 279, QBD; *Metsoja v H Norman Pitt & Co Ltd* (1989) 153 JP 485, QBD; and *Rover Group Ltd and Rover Finance Ltd v Sumner* [1995] CCLR 1.

The form and content of advertisements are governed by the Consumer Credit (Advertisements) Regulations 1989[10] made under powers contained in section 44. The section lays down that the framework of any provision made under it must be designed so that an advertisement conveys a fair and reasonably comprehensive indication of the nature of the credit or hire facilities offered by the advertiser and of their true cost to persons using them. The Regulations apply to all forms of advertising, including by radio, television and film. Advertisements are divided according to the amount of information given, into 'simple', intermediate', and 'full'. Simple credit advertisements may only give the name of the person providing credit, a postal address, telephone number, logo, occupation – eg 'moneylender' – and any other information other than that the person is willing to provide credit or the cash or other price of goods, services, land or other things. Intermediate credit advertisements must consist of the advertiser's name and postal address or telephone number (except in certain circumstances), warning notices for loans secured on land[11] and foreign currency mortgages, any other security requirements, insurance and deposit requirements, credit broker's fee, information about terms of business, cash price for debtor-creditor-supplier agreements, the APR where a cash price is given, if no APR is given, a statement that the total amount payable is no greater than the cash price and if the APR is not fixed, a statement that it is variable. Certain additional information is permitted, eg logo, restrictions on credit availability and advance payments requirements. Full credit advertisements must include the same compulsory information as intermediate advertisements, together with additional compulsory matters such as the frequency, number and amount of advance payments and of repayments, the total amount payable and details of other payments or charges. Certain other additional matters may also be included, eg logos, occupation and rates of interest charged. The requirements for simple, intermediate and full hire advertisements are similar. In all cases the form of the advertisement must be given clearly, together as a whole, and the APR be given the required prominence.

The Regulations are lucidly explained, with examples, in the OFT's explanatory guide 'Credit Advertising'. Quotations must contain warnings, similar to those in advertisements, where the agreement is secured on homes or land.[12]

---

10   SI 1989/1125, as amended by SI 1999/2725, SI 1999/3177 and SI 2000/1797.
11   The inclusion of such requirements for secured loans in the absence of similar warnings for unsecured loans was unsuccessfully challenged in *First National Bank plc v Secretary of State for Trade and Industry* (1990) 154 JP 571, CA.
12   See the Consumer Credit (Content of Quotations) and Consumer Credit (Advertisements) (Amendment) Regulations 1999, SI 1999/2725 as amended by SI 2000/1797.

Section 167 and Schedule 1 (as amended) lay down penalties for the above offences. Section 168 provides general defences to criminal proceedings brought under the Act. It states that it is a defence to prove that the act or omission was due to a mistake, or to reliance on information supplied to the defendant,[13] or to an act or omission by another person or to an accident *and* that the defendant took all reasonable precautions and exercised all due diligence to avoid the act or omission in question. There are provisions requiring notice of the defence that it was a third party's fault and identification of the third party. There is a similar defence in the Trade Descriptions Act 1968, section 24(1) (and also the Fair Trading Act 1973, s 25(1)). There has been considerable litigation on the defence under the Trade Descriptions Act 1968 – see eg *Tesco Supermarkets Ltd v Nattrass*,[14] as to the meaning of an 'act or omission by another person'.

Sections 48–51 deal with canvassing offences. Canvassing regulated agreements off trade premises is defined as where an individual ('the canvasser') solicits the entry of another individual ('the consumer') into the agreement by making oral representations to the consumer, or any other individual, at a place which is not the place of business of either of the parties or that of the creditor, owner or supplier, being a visit which is a) carried out for the purpose of making such oral representations and b) not carried out in response to a request made on a previous occasion (s 48). Note that the representations may be made eg to a member of the consumer's family, that the visit in question must be made *for the purpose of* making oral representations and a previous request legitimates the canvassing. Physical presence of the canvasser is required – a telephone call is not enough.

The offences are:

a) canvassing debtor-creditor agreements off trade premises (without a request);

b) canvassing debtor-creditor agreements off trade premises in response to a request unless the request was in writing and signed by or on behalf of the person making it (s 49);[15]

c) sending circulars to minors containing invitations to borrow money or obtain goods or services on credit or to apply for information about these matters. It is a defence that the minor was not known or suspected to be a minor (s 50(2));

d) giving persons credit-tokens who have not asked for them, the request being in a signed document, unless it is a small debtor-creditor-supplier agreement (s 51).

13 This can include advice on the legality of advertisements from a trade organisation: see *Coventry City Council v Lazarus* (1994) 160 JP 188, QBD.

14 [1972] AC 153, [1971] 2 All ER 127, HL, see ch 12.

15 See, for example, *R v Chadda* [1984] CCLR 1, 91 ITSA MR 43, Newcastle Crown Court.

In connection with a) and b) it should be noted that only debtor-creditor agreements are within the ambit of the offence. A typical transaction would be a personal loan. Debtor-creditor-supplier agreements may be canvassed by specifically licensed suppliers, but in these circumstances the consumer may have rights of cancellation (see s 67). A request must be in writing and signed to take a debtor-creditor agreement out of the offence provisions. Under section 49(3) the Director can authorise[16] the soliciting of agreements to overdraw current accounts of existing customers.

In connection with credit-tokens, unsolicited credit-tokens such as credit cards are not permitted,[17] but excepted from this are tokens issued under an existing agreement or renewals or replacements of tokens (s 51(3)). A request for a credit-token must be in a signed document unless it is a small debtor-creditor-supplier agreement. The definition of a credit-token in section 14 has been mentioned above.

A number of aspects of Part IV of the Act have been the subject of review and reform proposals. Credit marketing was reviewed by the Department of Trade and Industry, with a consultative document[18] published in December 1990, followed, in December 1991, by a further consultative document.[19] Both the Director[20] and the Deregulation Task Forces[1] recommended abandonment of these proposals. The Task Forces also recommended repeal of the regulations relating to advertisements and quotations.[2] Whilst supporting the latter suggestion,[3] the Director recommended[4] replacing the Consumer Credit (Advertisements) Regulations 1989[5] with much simpler requirements for credit, hire agreements and credit-brokerage. The 'simple', 'intermediate' and 'full' categories would be abandoned. Instead, for credit agreements, information should be clear and legible; when interest rates or figures relating to the

---

16   See Determination of Director General, 1 June 1977, *Annual Report of Director General of Fair Trading 1977* (1978 HCP 228) p 66.

17   See, for example, *Elliott v Director General of Fair Trading* [1980] 1 WLR 977, [1980] ICR 629, QBD; M, H & P p 295.

18   *Proposals for New Legislation on Credit Marketing, A Consultative Document* DTI, December 1990.

19   *Revised Proposals for Legislation on Credit Marketing, A Consultative Document* DTI, December 1991.

20   OFT Press Release 35/93; *Consumer Credit Deregulation*, OFT, June 1994, para 1.3.

1   *Deregulation Task Forces Proposals for Reform*, January 1994, para 395.

2   Op cit, paras 389 and 387 respectively. Repeal of the Quotations Regulations is also recommended by the DTI – *Deregulation of United Kingdom Consumer Credit Legislation*, DTI, August 1995, ch 6.

3   *Consumer Credit Deregulation*, OFT, June 1994, paras 5.20–5.28.

4   Ibid, paras 5.5–5.19.

5   SI 1989/1125.

cost of credit are stated, the APR should be stated with equal prominence; general advertising by traders should be permitted, but where terms are quoted sufficient information[6] of cost and cash flows should be given; and warnings where credit is secured on a borrower's home should continue for printed advertisements only. For hire advertisements all information should be clear and legible, when specific facilities are offered details of deposits, the timing and amount of hire payments and any other charges and fees payable would have to be stated and where illustrative examples are given these should clearly state that it involves the hire or bailment of goods, not credit.

The Director's proposals found favour with the Better Regulation Task Force in its report *Consumer Affairs*,[7] which encouraged simplification of advertisement requirements. Meanwhile the new Government was consulting on aspects of advertising in *Clarification and Simplification of United Kingdom Consumer Credit Law*.[8] During 1999, at the request of the Government, the OFT consulted on advertising changes, including whether the 1994 proposals are still appropriate and researched consumers' information needs and understanding. The OFT's findings and recommendations are due to be presented to the Government in 2000.[9] Meanwhile, changes have been made to the advertising of low-start mortgages, to the requirements of 'wealth warnings' on radio, television and film broadcasts and to the disclosure of the annual percentage rate. The original Quotations Regulations[10] were revoked[11] from March 1997, subsequently being replaced by simplified requirements from February 2000.[12]

6. FORMING AND CANCELLING AGREEMENTS

These matters are governed by Part V of the Act and regulations made thereunder.

---

6 Ie the amount of credit offered, the number, timing and amount of repayments, the interest and APR and any other charges or fees payable.
7 May 1998.
8 DTI, February 1998.
9 *Annual Report of the Director General of Fair Trading 1999*, 2000 HCP 576, pp 23–24.
10 Consumer Credit (Quotations) Regulations 1989, SI 1989/1126.
11 Consumer Credit (Quotations) (Revocation) Regulations 1997, SI 1997/221.
12 Consumer Credit (Content of Quotations) and Consumer Credit (Advertisements) (Amendment) Regulations 1999, SI 1999/2725 as amended by SI 2000/1797.

Disclosure

Section 55 contains a preliminary requirement for disclosure of information to the debtor or hirer as specified by regulation. Failure to do this results in the agreement being 'not properly executed', which means that the agreement is enforceable against the debtor or hirer on an order of the court only (s 65). There are no current plans for regulations to be made under this section.

Negotiator as agent of financier

Section 56 deals with 'antecedent negotiations', ie negotiations with the debtor or hirer a) by the creditor or owner in relation to the making of any regulated agreement, b) a credit-broker in relation to goods to be sold under a debtor-creditor-supplier agreement under section 12(a),[13] and c) a supplier in relation to a transaction to be financed by a debtor-creditor-supplier agreement under section 12(b) or (c). Typically a dealer will negotiate with a 'customer' with a view to the formation of a hire-purchase agreement whereunder a finance company buys the goods from the dealer and then as creditor lets them on hire (with an option to purchase) to the debtor. Section 56(2) states that in the case of any debtor-creditor-supplier agreement negotiations with the debtor shall be deemed to be conducted by the negotiator in the capacity of agent of the creditor as well as in his actual capacity. Antecedent negotiations include any representations made by the negotiator to the debtor or hirer (s 56(4)), and agreements are void in so far as they purport to exclude liability for the acts or omissions of the negotiator (s 56(3)). The effect of this is therefore to give non-excludable rights to the debtor or hirer against the negotiator in respect of breaches of express conditions and warranties or of actionable misrepresentations. These rights under section 56 do not, however, apply to implied terms; nor do they apply to contracts of hire where no credit is provided. In *Moorgate Mercantile Leasing Ltd v Gell and Ugolini Dispensers (UK) Ltd*[14] an attempt to make a hire company liable for the misrepresentations of the supplier of an ice shake dispenser failed as the contract was not a consumer credit agreement and the supplier was not a negotiator under section 56.

13 See, for example, *Forthright Finance Ltd v Ingate (Carlyle Finance Ltd, third party)* [1997] 4 All ER 99, CA.
14 [1986] CLY 371, Grays Thurrock County Court. See also Dobson [1983] JBL 312.

In some situations there is an overlap between sections 56 and 75[15] and one case decided under section 75 should, in fact, have been decided using section 56.[16]

Making the agreement

The provisions relating to formalities are somewhat similar to those laid down by the former hire-purchase legislation. The formalities apply to all regulated agreements including hire-purchase and conditional sale agreements, but not to small[17] debtor-creditor-supplier agreements for restricted-use credit or non-commercial agreements (s 74).

By section 60 the Secretary of State must make regulations as to the form and content of documents embodying regulated agreements. The current regulations are the Consumer Credit (Agreements) Regulations 1983.[18] These are designed to ensure that the debtor or hirer is made aware of a) the rights and duties conferred or imposed upon him by the agreement, b) the amount and rate of the total charge for credit, c) the protection and remedies available under the Act, and d) any other matters which it is desirable for the debtor to know about.[19]

A properly formed document must be signed by the debtor or hirer and by or on behalf of the creditor or owner (s 61). An interesting example of failure to comply with this requirement arose in *Dimond v Lovell*.[20] Here an agreement for a hire vehicle as a replacement whilst the hirer's car was repaired following an accident was believed not to be a 'credit agreement' and thus not regulated.[1] It did not, therefore, contain full details of the hire charges etc and, as such, was improperly executed.

The debtor or hirer is entitled to at least one copy of the completed agreement, delivered there and then if the document is 'an executed agreement' because the creditor or owner has also signed it. If the agreement has not yet been signed by the creditor or owner, the debtor or

---

15 See post p 322; also Fairest and Rudkin (1978) 128 NLJ 243, Hill-Smith (1983) 133 NLJ 1012 and 1063.
16 See *Porter v General Guarantee Corpn Ltd* [1982] RTR 384, QBD, below p 324.
17 For the purposes of Part V, if the agreement is one to which the Consumer Protection (Cancellation of Contracts Concluded away from Business Premises) Regulations 1987, SI 1987/2117, apply a small agreement is one not exceeding £35, see post at p 321.
18 See SI 1983/1553 as amended by SI 1984/1600, SI 1985/666, SI 1988/2047 and SI 1999/3177.
19 For guidance see OFT booklets 'Cancellable agreements' (OFT 018) and 'Non-Cancellable agreements' (OFT 019).
20 [2000] 2 All ER 897, [2000] 2 WLR 1121, HL.
1 See above p 299.

hirer is entitled to both a copy when he signs and a further copy within seven days of its being made (s 63). If the unexecuted agreement is, instead, sent to the debtor or hirer, a copy must accompany it. If when the debtor or hirer signs it has not been signed by the other party, a further copy must be given within seven days of its being made (ss 62, 63).

There are special provisions for cancellable agreements and regulated agreements secured on land. In the case of the former, section 64 imposes a duty[2] to include on every copy of such an agreement (see below) a notice of how and when it is cancellable.[3] In addition, if a second copy of the agreement is required under section 63, in the case of a cancellable agreement this must be sent by post (s 63(3)). The same provisions do not apply to second mortgages because of the conveyancing difficulties that would arise. Instead, the unexecuted mortgage agreement must contain a notice in a prescribed form[4] indicating the right to withdraw from the agreement (s 58, and see s 61(2)).

An improperly executed regulated agreement may be enforced, for example, by the retaking of goods or land, on an order of the court only (s 65).[5] In the case of a cancellable agreement, if the requirement to give a cancellation notice under section 64(1) has not been complied with then, by section 127(4), the court cannot make an enforcement order.

The Deregulation Task Forces proposed the repeal of section 58 relating to loan agreements.[6] As an alternative the Director proposed[7] that agreements falling within section 58 be exempted from the requirement under section 62(2) to provide a second copy of the unexecuted agreement, thereby reducing the copies given in such cases from three to two.

Withdrawal

The Act, under section 57, includes and extends the common law right to withdraw from an agreement before it has been accepted. The provisions apply to any regulated agreement save those exempted under section 74. A written or oral notice of withdrawal, however expressed, may, as at common law, be given to the creditor or owner. In addition, by section 57(3), notice may be given to a credit-broker or supplier who acted as a

---

2   Subject to the Director General being empowered to make a determination exempting this requirement, see Consumer Credit (Notice of Cancellation Rights) (Exemptions) Regulations 1983, SI 1983/1558.
3   See Consumer Credit (Cancellation Notices and Copies of Documents) Regulations 1983, SI 1983/1557 as amended by SI 1984/1108, SI 1985/666, SI 1988/2047 and SI 1989/591.
4   SI 1983/1557 as amended and SI 1983/1553 as amended.
5   The agreement is not, however, void, see *R v Modupe* [1991] Crim LR 530, CA.
6   *Deregulation Task Forces Proposals for Reform*, January 1994, para 388.
7   *Consumer Credit Deregulation*, OFT, June 1994, para 6.29.

'negotiator' or any person, who in the course of a business, acted on behalf of the debtor in negotiating the agreement. The effect of withdrawal is the same as cancellation, bringing to an end both the prospective regulated agreement and any linked transaction, subject to certain exceptions (see below).

Cancelling agreements

The Consumer Credit Act 1974 is based on similar, but not identical, provisions in the Hire-Purchase Act 1965 designed to curtail over-enthusiasm by 'doorstep' salesmen. The provisions apply to all regulated agreements (save those exempted by s 74) subject to the following points:

1) They only apply where oral representations[8] are made in the presence of the debtor by or on behalf of the negotiator (s 67);
2) They do not apply where the agreement is signed at the business premises of the creditor, a party linked to the transaction or the negotiator (s 67);
3) They do not apply to agreements secured on land, restricted use credit agreements to finance the purchase of land or agreements for bridging loans in connection with the purchase of land (s 67).

Special 'cooling-off' arrangements apply to agreements involving land mortgages, primarily because of the extra dimension which the proprietary rights acquired involve and the difficulties of 'cancelling' mortgages. If the various requirements in sections 58 and 61 are not observed, such an agreement is 'improperly executed' and unenforceable except by court order.

If the agreement is a 'cancellable' one, the debtor enjoys a cooling-off period. This is to the end of the fifth day following the day on which he receives the statutory copy of the agreement under section 63(2) or a notice under section 64(1), or where regulations dispense with the need for a copy, 14 days following the day on which he signed the unexecuted agreement. Under section 63(2) the second copy must be given to the debtor within seven days of the making of the agreement. Accordingly, where an agreement is made on 1 July, the second copy received on 7 July, the agreement is cancellable until 12 July expires.

If within the cooling-off period the debtor serves a written cancellation notice on the creditor or his agent, 'however expressed', indicating his intention to withdraw from the agreement, the notice operates to cancel the agreement and any linked transaction (or promise to enter into a linked

---

8   Ie statements of fact or opinion or an undertaking as to the future which is capable of inducing the proposed borrower to enter the agreement – see Straughton LJ in *Moorgate Property Services Ltd v Kabir* [1995] CCLR 74, CA.

transaction) (s 69). Only three types of linked transactions continue despite cancellation: contracts of insurance, guarantees of goods and current and deposit accounts opened in pursuance of the agreement.[9] If the post is used to serve the notice of cancellation, it takes effect on posting, even if never received by the creditor or his agent (s 69(7)).

The effect of cancellation is to entitle the debtor to repayment of any sums paid and he has a lien on any goods in his possession pending repayment. Despite cancellation, there are provisions favourable to the debtor concerning the repayment by instalments of any credit and interest (see s 71). This is to discourage the making of advances of money during the cooling-off period, a factor which might otherwise discourage the debtor from exercising his cancellation rights. Goods acquired under a restricted-use debtor-creditor-supplier agreement must be restored to the person from whom the debtor obtained them (s 72). The debtor is not obliged to do so other than at his own premises and in pursuance of a written request by the creditor, but while the goods are in his possession he is under a duty to retain possession of them and to take reasonable care of them (ibid). Any breach of his duty is actionable as the tort of breach of statutory duty (ibid) and damages can thus be awarded. It is worth noting that the obligation to restore the goods does not apply in certain cases, for example if they are perishable goods or consumables that are consumed prior to cancellation (s 72(9)).[10]

There are proposals to amend the cancellation provisions. In *Consumer Credit Deregulation,*[11] the Director recommended that cancellation rights should cease for fixed sum and running account agreements where face-to-face negotiations have occurred on trade premises but where the document is subsequently signed off trade premises. In addition he proposed further consideration be given as to whether the cancellation period should be changed to seven days from signature by the debtor to bring it into line with the EC Directive on Doorstep Selling.[12]

As a result of this Directive, the Consumer Protection (Cancellation of Contracts Concluded away from Business Premises) Regulations 1987[13]

---

9   See Consumer Credit (Linked Transactions) (Exemptions) Regulations 1983, SI 1983/1560. See also Bone & Rutherford [1985] JBL 209.

10 See Dobson (1978) 128 NLJ 56 for possible abuses by consumers. On cancellation generally see OFT booklet 'Cancellable Agreements' (OFT 018).

11 OFT, June 1994, ch 6.

12 Directive to protect the consumer in respect of contracts negotiated away from business premises, 85/577/EEC, OJ No L 372, 20.12.85, p 31. This proposal had the support of the DTI, see *Revised Proposals for Legislation on Credit Marketing, A Consultative Document*, DTI, December 1991, and the Deregulation Task Forces, see *Deregulation Task Force's Proposals for Reform*, January 1994, para 391.

13 SI 1987/2117 as amended by SI 1988/958 and SI 1998/3050; BSSCCL p 705.

were brought into force on 1 July 1988. The effect of these Regulations is to give protection, initially only in civil law and subsequently, from 31 December 1998, also in criminal law, to many non-credit consumers who make contracts away from business premises in a similar way to that given to those buying on credit. Certain contracts are excluded, for example food and drink supplied by regular roundsmen and where payments will not exceed £35. A seven-day cancellation provision is included, with the contract being unenforceable if the customer is not informed of the right to cancel. A criminal offence also arises, under section 4A, for failure to provide the necessary notice of cancellation rights. In due course an injunction procedure will be introduced, with the Director as the lead body, to implement the Injunctions Directive.[14]

The Regulations[15] implementing the Distance Selling Directive[16] involve contracts for the supply of goods and/or services, concluded at a distance, between a business supplier and a consumer (natural persons acting outside their trade business or profession). Specified information is required to be provided prior to the conclusion of contracts made at a distance, with written confirmation thereof and notification of withdrawal rights. Withdrawal will be permitted, subject to certain exceptions, within seven working days, the commencement of the period of cancellation depending upon whether goods or services are involved. An extended period of three months will be permitted, in the absence of notification of withdrawal rights. The Regulations also provide that, subject to agreement between the parties, contracts must be performed within 30 days. Arrangements are made for the cancellation of related credit agreements where the credit is provided by either the supplier or a third party, on the basis of an agreement with the supplier. The Directive was due to be implemented by 4 June 2000 but was not implemented until 31 October 2000.

Problems encountered by consumers over the selling of timeshares led to the Timeshare Act 1992,[17] modelled, in part, on the cancellation provisions of the Consumer Credit Act 1974. Both cash and credit purchasers are covered, with a minimum 14-day cooling-off period. The timeshare agreements covered are: i) those made under the law of the United Kingdom or part of the United Kingdom; ii) when the agreement is made

---

14 Directive 98/27/EC, OJ No L 166, 11.6.98, p 51; see *Injunctions Directive: Implementation in the UK*, DTI, January 2000; 'Widening the net', OFT (2000) 26 Fair Trading 13.
15 Consumer Protection (Distance Selling) Regulations 2000, SI 2000/2334.
16 OJ No L 144, 4.6.97, p 19, BSSCCL p 858.
17 As amended by the Timeshare Regulations 1997, SI 1997/1081, which implement Directive 94/47/EC on the protection of purchasers in respect of certain aspects of contracts relating to the purchase of the right to use immovable properties on a timeshare basis.

one or both of the parties are in the United Kingdom; iii) where the accommodation is situated in the United Kingdom; or iv) where the offeree is ordinarily resident in the United Kingdom and the accommodation is situated in another European Economic Area state. Failure to inform consumers of the cancellation rights is a criminal offence where a business is selling timeshare, although this does not apply to timeshare credit agreements (to maintain consistency with the provisions of the 1974 Act). Other criminal provisions include offences relating to the provision of specified information, advertising, forms of agreement, translation requirements and for requesting or accepting an advance payment prior to the end of the cooling-off period. A due diligence defence and the ability to prosecute employees are included. The civil consequences of cancellation are similar to those under section 71 of the Consumer Credit Act 1974 and, where there is a failure to provide certain specified information, the cancellation period is extended to three months and ten days. A Consultation Paper: *Timeshare Sales*,[18] includes proposals for reform in this area and an injunction procedure should be introduced by January 2001, with the Director as lead body, to implement the injunctions Directive.[19]

7. DURING THE AGREEMENT

There are a number of matters which, if they arise during the currency of the agreement, are regulated by Part VI of the Act. The main provisions are now summarised.

Liability of creditor for breaches by supplier[20]

The object of section 75 is to make it clear that, where there is a debtor-creditor-supplier agreement and the supplier is not also the creditor (such as where the debtor buys goods by using Mastercard or Visa), the creditor is jointly and severally liable with the seller to the debtor for damages in respect of any misrepresentation or breach of contract – an apparent

18 DTI, April 2000.
19 See n 14 above.
20 See M, H & P pp 300–305; *Connected Lender Liability – A Review by the Director General of Fair Trading*, OFT March 1994; *Connected Lender Liability – A second report by the Director General of Fair Trading*, OFT May 1995; *Connected Lender Liability in United Kingdom Consumer Credit Law, A Consultation Document*, DTI, December 1995 and OFT leaflet 'Equal Liability' (OFT 303).

exception to the basic principle of privity of contract. In *United Dominions Trust v Taylor*,[1] a debtor, under an agreement within the ambit of section 75, was sold an unsatisfactory car in reliance on the supplier's misrepresentation. He purported to rescind both the 'sale' contract and the loan agreement (although the finance company had made no misrepresentation itself). The debtor was held entitled to do this on the basis of the statement in section 75 that a debtor with a claim in respect of misrepresentation or breach of contract against the supplier 'shall have a like claim' against the creditor. The approach of section 75 'leaves no room for the idea of privity of contract which is fundamental to the common law of contract'.[2] It is, perhaps, unfortunate that the 'like claim' was interpreted as one of rescission instead of one for damages. Under the purchase contract, following rescission, the debtor would be entitled to payment of money sufficient to enable termination of the credit agreement. It would seem preferable to consider the creditor jointly liable to 'pay' this and thereby discharge the credit agreement, rather than suggesting that the credit agreement is rescinded following the rescission of the purchase agreement. A 'like claim' of rescission of the credit agreement would clearly not operate in cases where a credit card is used to fund the purchase of goods. Here, although the purchase contract for the goods might be rescinded by reason of a misrepresentation, the credit card agreement continues. By interpreting the 'like claim' as one for damages, confusion is less likely to arise in future cases, whilst still enabling the same result to be achieved.

Although the creditor has a right of indemnity from the supplier, if the supplier is insolvent the additional right will prove valuable to customers, as for example, with the collapse of the airline Debonair in 1999.[3] This provision does not apply to non-commercial agreements or to agreements with a cash price of £100 or less or more than £30,000.[4] By virtue of the

---

1   1980 SLT 28, Sh Ct, Scotland; M, H & P p 302.
2   See also (1980) 130 NLJ 924; (1980) 96 LQR 343; (1981) 97 LQR 532; [1980] JBL 277; [1981] JBL 179; M, H & P pp 302–304. For the possible interrelationship between s 56 (in antecedent negotiations the negotiator is deemed to be the agent of the creditor) and s 75, see (1978) 128 NLJ 243; also (1983) 133 NLJ 1012 and 1063; [1979] JBL 331.
3   See OFT Press Release 36/99, 12 October 1999.
4   Section 75(3) as amended by the Consumer Credit (Increase of Monetary Limits) Order 1983, SI 1983/1878. It was proposed to change these limits to a minimum of £100 and a maximum of £25,000 *of credit granted:* see *Deregulation of United Kingdom Consumer Credit Legislation*, DTI, August 1995, ch 3; but subsequently the DTI recommended no change pending the European Commission's review of the Consumer Credit Directive: see *Connected Lender Liability in United Kingdom Consumer Credit Law, A Consultation Document*, DTI, December 1995, ch 7.

Consumer Credit Act 1974 (Commencement No 3) Order 1977[5] this 'connected lender' liability applies to tripartite debtor-creditor-supplier agreements (under s 12(b) or (c)) made after 30 June 1977. Section 75 should not, however, apply to two party debtor-creditor-supplier agreements such as hire-purchase as section 12(a) is not mentioned in that section. Such agreements do not need the special protection granted by section 75 as with them the creditor is also the supplier of the goods or services. The debtor, therefore, has contractual rights against the creditor for defective goods etc and by section 56(2) any representations by a negotiator are deemed to be made by the negotiator as agent for the creditor. However, in *Porter v General Guarantee Corpn Ltd*,[6] the court applied section 75 to a hire-purchase agreement to make the finance company responsible for the misrepresentations of the car dealer who had negotiated the deal. It is submitted that section 56 would provide a more appropriate basis for the decision (see above). A similar mis-classification was made at first instance in *Renton v Hendersons Garage (Nairn) and United Dominions Trust*,[7] but on appeal the Sheriff Principal correctly classified a conditional sale agreement as falling under section 12(a) and therefore section 75 did not apply to it.

Problems have arisen following the collapse of some major companies in that credit card companies sought to limit their liability under section 75 to those contracts made by traders with whom they have a merchant acquirer agreement. For example, Barclaycard sought to deny responsibility for their Visa cardholders dealing with Lowndes Queensway because the company had been recruited into the Visa system by another bank. The Office of Fair Trading and the Department of Trade and Industry disagree with this policy and take the view that, where cards are issued to customers by one member of a network and the trader is recruited to the network by another, connected lender liability provisions apply fully. Currently, liability is accepted by some banks on a voluntary basis.[8]

Another disputed aspect is where overseas purchases are made using credit cards issued in the United Kingdom. The Office of Fair Trading considers the position is the same where a creditor issues a credit card to a United Kingdom-based cardholder, whether purchases are made in the

5   SI 1973/802.
6   [1982] RTR 384, QBD. See also Thornley [1983] CLJ 201.
7   [1994] CCLR 29, Sh Ct.
8   See 'Equal Liability and Credit Cards', *Bee Line* No 91/2 pp 25–26; *Connected Lender Liability – A Review by the Director General of Fair Trading*, OFT March 1994, pp 25–6 and *Connected Lender Liability in United Kingdom Consumer Credit Law, A Consultation Document*, DTI, December 1995, ch 2.

United Kingdom or abroad.[9] Card issuers agreed, on an ex gratia basis, to meet fully claims on overseas transactions.[10]

Connected lender liability was examined, in detail, by the Director in a report issued in March 1994.[11] This was followed, in May 1995, with a second report,[12] which proposed reform in the case of credit cards only. In response, the Department of Trade and Industry issued a Consultation Paper in December 1995: *Connected Lender Liability in United Kingdom Consumer Credit Law*. The Director recommended that the liability of card issuers should be limited to the amount charged to the card account. This proposal was not endorsed by the Department of Trade and Industry.[13] Also the Director supported card issuers being given a right of subrogation where insurance or bonding schemes exist for suppliers who go out of business. The view of the Department of Trade was to maintain the status quo.[14] Although the Director sought early implementation of his proposals, the Department of Trade and Industry advocated no change.[15]

Duty to give notice before taking certain action

If the regulated agreement allows the creditor to demand earlier payment, recover possession of goods or land or treat any of the rights of the debtor as terminated, restricted or deferred, section 76 states that the creditor must give to the debtor at least seven days' notice of his intention to exercise such rights. The form such a notice must take is contained in the Consumer Credit (Enforcement, Default and Terminations Notices) Regulations 1983.[16]

9   *Connected Lender Liability – A Review by the Director General of Fair Trading*, OFT March 1994, pp 26–8. This view is supported by the DTI, see *Connected Lender Liability in United Kingdom Consumer Credit Law, A Consultation Document*, DTI, December 1995, ch 3.

10 *Connected Lender Liability – A second report by the Director General of Fair Trading*, OFT May 1995, p 9 and *Fair Trading* No. 10 Summer 1995, p 5. See *Jarrett v Barclays Bank plc, Jones v First National Bank plc, Peacock v First National Bank plc* [1999] QB 1, [1997] 2 All ER 484, CA, for s 75 claims concerning timeshare purchases in Spain and Portugal, using UK-issued loans.

11 *Connected Lender Liability – A Review by the Director General of Fair Trading*, OFT March 1994.

12 *Connected Lender Liability – A second report by the Director General of Fair Trading*, OFT May 1995.

13 Op cit ch 5.

14 Op cit ch 6.

15 Annual R*eport of Director General of Fair Trading 1996* (1997 HCP 104), p 24.

16 SI 1983/1561 as amended by SI 1984/1109.

Rights to information

Sections 77 and 78 confer upon the debtor the right to obtain information from the creditor as to such matters as the amount already paid and the amount owing. In addition section 97 supplements the debtor's right to complete payments ahead of time at a discount (see ss 94 and 95) by requiring the creditor to indicate the amount needed to settle the account.

The debtor is also under a liability to tell the creditor where the goods are when the agreement requires the debtor to keep the goods in his possession or control (s 80).

Appropriation of payments

If a debtor has two or more agreements with the same creditor, one payment may be made which is insufficient to discharge the total due on each. If a particular sum is not specifically appropriated to a particular agreement, the payment is to be appropriated towards the satisfaction of the sums due under the several agreements respectively in the proportions which those sums bear to one another (s 81). For example if £60 is due under one regulated agreement and £40 under another, the debtor's payment of £60 is appropriated as to £36 to the first agreement and £24 to the second.

Variation of agreements

There is, of course, no power to vary agreements unilaterally, but if the agreement itself permits this the effect, when exercised, is to revoke the inconsistent parts of the earlier agreement. Section 82 provides (inter alia) that this shall not be effective before notice of the variation is given to the debtor in the prescribed manner. The Consumer Credit (Notice of Variation of Agreements) Regulations 1977[17] require seven days' written notice to be given personally to the debtor or hirer. Problems have been encountered in practice over modifying agreements where the original agreement contains no power to modify and the procedures under section 82(2) have to be followed. A simplification of these procedures has been proposed.[18]

---

17 SI 1977/328 as amended by SIs 1979/661 and 667.
18 See *Deregulation Task Forces Proposals for Reform*, January 1994, para 393; *Consumer Credit Deregulation*, OFT, June 1994, paras 6.40–6.42.

8. TERMINATION OF THE AGREEMENT

Hiring agreements

If the agreement is a regulated consumer hire agreement,[19] section 101 confers the right for the hirer to terminate it after at least 18 months has expired, even if the hiring was for a fixed term of longer duration. The hirer must give notice equivalent to the shortest period between two payments, or of three months, whichever is less. In the case of some commercial agreements such a statutory licence to terminate prematurely would not be justified by public policy, so section 101 incorporates some exceptions. These relate to agreements involving 1) hiring rentals of more than £1,500 per annum (an amount which has been raised by Order[20] under s 181(1)), 2) goods hired for the purpose of the hirer's business, and including the business of hiring them to other persons in the course of business and persons carrying on consumer hire businesses in favour of whom 3) the Director directs (on their application) that section 101 shall not apply.

Where the agreement is terminated under the above, all liabilities accrued under the agreement up to termination must be discharged (section 101(2)).

Early settlement – consumer credit agreements

At any time during the lifetime of a regulated consumer credit agreement the debtor may give notice to the creditor that he wishes to complete his payments ahead of time (s 94). On payment of the required amount his indebtedness is then discharged. As the creditor is receiving his payment early, section 95 provides for regulations to be made to calculate the rebate of charges for credit that the debtor is allowed. The current Regulations are the Consumer Credit (Rebate on Early Settlement) Regulations 1983.[1] A number of formulae are provided to calculate the *minimum* rebate permitted.[2] To enable the debtor to make an informed decision whether or

---

19 See OFT booklet 'Hire agreements' (OFT 017).

20 Originally £300, increased to £900, from 20 May 1985, by SI 1983/1571, and to the present level of £1,500, as of 1 May 1998 by the Consumer Credit (Further Increase of Monetary Amounts) Order 1998, SI 1998/997.

1 SI 1983/1562 as amended by SI 1989/596. For discussion of rebates allowable on judgment debts, see *Forward Trust Ltd v Robinson* [1987] BTLC 12, Birmingham County Court; and *Forward Trust Ltd v Whymark* [1990] 2 QB 670, [1989] 3 All ER 915, CA.

2 See *Home Insulation Ltd v Wadsley* [1988] CCLR 25, QBD, for a case where the credit company literature indicated a higher rebate allowable, in error. Company obliged to allow the higher sum.

not to settle early section 97 imposes a duty on the creditor to provide the required information within 12 days of receipt of a written request.[3]

The Director, in *Consumer Credit Deregulation*,[4] concluded that the formula commonly used for calculating the rebate, the 'Rule of 78', was unsatisfactory and unfair to consumers. He proposed that 1) the method of calculating the rebates should be made more equitable, with the replacement of the 'Rule of 78' by an actual reducing balance formula, 2) a fixed fee for compensation for administrative costs should be introduced, and 3) there should be more transparency of the system to ensure consumers are made aware of early settlement terms. The Department of Trade and Industry initially supported[5] the first and last proposal but favoured lenders stating if they charge a settlement fee, and using licensing powers to ensure that such fees are reasonable. Subsequently a Parliamentary Statement[6] indicated that the regulations would not be changed.

The Director pursued the issue with the new Government[7] and the OFT have been working with the Department of Trade and Industry to produce revised proposals, which are still awaited. Meanwhile the Director has issued guidelines for lenders and brokers[8] advising lenders to discontinue the use of the Rule of 78 for unregulated non-status (ie those outside section 95 of the 1974 Act) and has used his powers under the Unfair Terms in Consumer Contracts Regulations[9] to prevent their use.[10]

3   See Consumer Credit (Settlement Information) Regulations 1983, SI 1983/1564 and Consumer Credit (Prescribed Periods for Giving Information) Regulations 1983, SI 1983/1569. See generally OFT booklet 'Matters arising during the lifetime of an agreement'(OFT 020). Note also *Home Insulation Ltd v Wadsley* above.

4   OFT, June 1994, ch 8.

5   *Deregulation of United Kingdom Consumer Credit Legislation*, DTI, August 1995, ch 5.

6   No 5719 on 21 November 1996.

7   *Annual Report of the Director General of Fair Trading 1997* (1998 HCP 762) at p 24 and *Annual Report of the Director General of Fair Trading 1998* (1999 HCP 524) at p 24.

8   Currently *Non-status Lending: Guidelines for lenders and brokers*, OFT, November 1997. See also 'Crackdown on unscrupulous lenders', OFT, Issue 18 Fair Trading, 15.

9   SI 1999/2083, replacing SI 1994/3159, see further pp 143–145.

10   See OFT Press Release 6/98, 12 February 1998 and *Unfair Contract Terms* Issue No 5, October 1998, pp 8–9 for an example concerning City Mortgage Corporation, which undertook not to apply the rule of 78 calculation, plus a charge of six months' interest when unregulated loans were repaid before their full term. A less onerous formula would be applied.

Termination by debtor – consumer credit agreements

As under the old law (see Hire-Purchase Act 1965, s 27) the debtor under a regulated hire-purchase or conditional sale agreement may terminate it. The debtor can do so at any time before his final payment is due by giving, to the creditor or owner, notice (s 99). (The creditor may also terminate where there has been no default on giving the debtor at least seven days' notice (s 98).) The right to terminate does not apply to conditional sale agreements relating to land which has become vested in the debtor, but it does apply to conditional sale agreements for goods unless the property in the goods is transferred from the debtor to a third party. On such termination, the property in the goods reverts to the original owner if it is not already in him (s 99(3)–(5)).

The position following termination by the debtor is as follows (s 100):

1) He must discharge all accrued liabilities (s 99(2)).
2) Unless the agreement provides for a smaller payment or makes no provision, the debtor must pay to the creditor the amount (if any) by which one-half of the total price exceeds the aggregate of a) the sums paid and b) the sums due in respect of the total price at date of termination (section 100). This '50 per cent rule' is a long-standing one in hire-purchase law (see Hire-Purchase Act 1965, section 28). Where an installation charge is specified as part of the total price the debtor must pay this in full plus half the remainder of the total purchase price.
3) The court has discretion to order payment of a lesser fraction of the total price if it considers such a sum would adequately compensate the creditor for the depreciation that inevitably occurs.
4) The debtor must pay compensation for any failure to take reasonable care of the goods or land.
5) If the debtor wrongfully retains the goods the court must order their redelivery to the creditor, without giving the debtor an option to pay the value of the goods, unless it is satisfied that this would be unjust.

Termination of regulated agreements by the creditor on debtor's default

Where the debtor is in breach of his agreement, the creditor will probably wish to terminate the agreement and recover the goods. In the past there was abuse of the contractual position leading to situations where, for instance, a debtor had almost completed his instalments when, as a result of a minor delay in payment, the creditor 'snatched back' the hired goods. There has been legislation for many years protecting the debtor in these circumstances and this is repeated in an extended form in the 1974 Act.

A precondition of termination is the service on the debtor of a default notice. Section 87 states that this is necessary before the creditor can become entitled, by reason of any breach of the regulated agreement, a) to terminate the agreement, or b) to demand earlier payment of any sum, or c) to recover possession of any goods or land, or d) to treat any of the debtor's rights as terminated, restricted or deferred, or e) to enforce any security. The form of the notice is as prescribed by regulation (s 88 and the Consumer Credit (Enforcement, Default and Termination Notices) Regulations 1983[11]) and must correctly specify[12] the breach, what action is required to remedy the breach if capable of being remedied, or the notice may require compensation. In effect, seven days' notice to remedy is required, and the notice may state that the creditor will take one of the courses of action specified in section 87, eg demand repossession of the goods, unless the breach is duly remedied or compensation paid. If the debtor takes the action specified within the time limit the breach is treated as not having occurred (s 89). (See also s 76 – duty to give notice in other cases.)

Repossession of goods

In order to protect debtors from the risk of the 'snatch-back' of goods by creditors from debtors in circumstances where a considerable proportion of the total price of the goods has been paid, the concept of 'protected goods' is used. These provisions, in section 90, apply to regulated hire-purchase and conditional sale agreements only. The section provides that where the property in the goods remains in the creditor and the debtor has paid to the creditor one-third[13] or more of the total price of the goods, the creditor is not entitled to recover possession of the goods without a court order. It is now also a precondition that the debtor is in breach of the agreement. Any installation charge included in the total purchase price must, in effect, first be paid and the one-third fraction applied to the balance (s 90(2)).

The consequences of contravening section 90 are serious. The regulated agreement, if not already terminated, terminates and the debtor is both released from all further liability and is entitled to recover from the creditor all sums paid under the agreement (s 91).

In the following cases there is no infringement of this provision:

---

11 SI 1983/1561 as amended by SI 1984/1109.
12 A notice failed in *Woodchester Lease Management Services Ltd v Swain & Co (a firm)* [1999] 1 WLR 263, CA, when the incorrect amount of arrears was indicated in a default notice.
13 See *Julian Hodge Bank Ltd v Hall* [1998] CCLR 14, CA re calculation of one-third of the total price.

i) Where the debtor consents to repossession (s 173(3)). Thus, in *Mercantile Credit Co Ltd v Cross*[14] a finance company obtained repossession of the debtor's motor cycle combination after he had paid more than one-third of the price, having first written him a letter terminating the agreement because of arrears. The hirer voluntarily returned the motor cycle to the shop from which he had obtained it. It was held by the Court of Appeal that this was not enforcing 'any right to recover possession – other than by action' contrary to the then legislation (Hire-Purchase Act 1938). Although the hirer's consent to repossession must be voluntary, in this case he was deemed to be aware of his statutory rights.

ii) The section envisages recovery 'from the debtor' and does not therefore cover repossession from a person other than the debtor as defined by section 189(1) (a definition which includes a person to whom the debtor's rights and duties have passed by assignment or operation of law). Thus if the goods are in the wrongful possession of a third party, or have been abandoned (see *Bentinck Ltd v Cromwell Engineering Co*[15] – debtor abandoned damaged vehicle at garage) the restrictions on repossession do not apply.

iii) The restrictions do not apply if the debtor terminates the agreement (s 90(5)).

Even if the goods are not 'protected goods' the creditor is not entitled to enter any premises to take repossession of goods under a regulated hire, hire-purchase or conditional sale agreement, or to recover possession of land under a conditional sale agreement relating to land, except under an order of the court (s 92), or unless the debtor consents (s 173(3)). Contravention of section 92 is actionable as a breach of statutory duty (s 92(3)). In addition, section 93 prevents the debtor from being charged an increased rate of interest when in breach of the agreement.[16]

Death of the debtor or hirer

In the event of the death of the debtor or hirer before the completion of a regulated agreement, other than an agreement of unspecified duration, if the agreement is fully secured the creditor is not entitled to do any act for which a default notice is required, for example terminate the agreement, demand earlier repayment or recover possession of the goods (s 86). If the agreement is partly secured or unsecured the creditor may only do any of

14 [1965] 2 QB 205, [1965] 1 All ER 577, CA.
15 [1971] 1 QB 324, [1971] 1 All ER 33, CA.
16 See generally OFT booklet 'Matters arising during the lifetime of an agreement' (OFT 020).

those acts on the order of the court. The creditor may, however, restrict or refuse any further credit.

9. POWERS OF THE COURT

Litigation concerning hire-purchase and similar regulated agreements is within the jurisdiction of the county court (see definition in s 189). In Part IX of the Act wide discretionary powers are conferred on the court to control regulated agreements and securities, to grant relief to debtors and protection to the goods of creditors, and to reopen extortionate bargains, whether regulated or not.

Time orders (s 129) and enforcement orders (s 127)

Time orders made by the court are designed either to adjust the rate and time of payments of instalments if the sum is owed under regulated agreements (the most common type in practice) or to specify the period by which a breach of the agreement must be remedied, other than a breach relating to a non-payment of money.

The court can make such an order if it thinks it just to do so 1) on an application for an 'enforcement order' (an order to enforce an improperly-executed agreement under eg s 65(1), see s 127), 2) on an application by a debtor after being served with a default notice, a creditor's notice of calling-in under section 76, or a notice of termination in non-default cases under section 98, or 3) on a creditor's action to enforce any security or recover possession of any goods or land the subject-matter of a regulated agreement.

The time order must be made 'having regard to the means of the debtor' (s 129(2)(a)), unless the debtor makes an acceptable offer (s 130(1)) and the section also applies to hirers and sureties. In the case of hire-purchase and conditional sale agreements the order may relate to sums not yet due (s 130(2)).

One situation where the use of such orders is appropriate is where mortgagees seek repossession of houses. In *First National Bank plc v Syed*[17] the Court of Appeal gave guidance on the factors to be considered in deciding whether or not to make a time order. The creditor's position must be considered as well as the debtor's. Here, in view of the history of default, sporadic repayments and the unlikelihood of improvement in the debtors' finances, a time order was refused and enforcement of a possession order permitted.

17 [1991] 2 All ER 250, CA; M, H & P pp 305–306.

A number of conflicting decisions were reported[18] on the question of whether the court had powers to examine the total sum outstanding (ie the loan, the interest on the loan and any default interest) and make adjustments to the term of the loan and/or the rate of interest, or whether it was confined to examining and adjusting the arrears. The Court of Appeal has clarified the position in *Southern and District Finance plc v Barnes*; *J & J Securities Ltd v Ewart; Equity Home Loans Ltd v Lewis*.[19] Leggatt LJ provided a number of guiding principles including: that a time order should normally be made for a stipulated period to cover temporary financial difficulty (it was not suitable where there was no prospect of resumption of payment of at least the contractual instalments); the 'sum owed' meant every sum which was due and owing under the agreement, not just the arrears; the court must consider what instalments would be reasonable as regards amount and timing, having regard to the debtor's means; any amendments to the agreement which were just to both parties could be made (including varying the interest rate under s 136, see below); and possession orders should be suspended whilst the terms of a time order are complied with.

Enforcement orders under section 127 may be sought in cases of: a) improperly executed agreements (s 65), b) improperly executed security instruments (s 105), c) failure to serve a copy of a notice on a surety (s 111), or d) taking of a negotiable instrument in contravention of section 123 (s 124). The court must refuse to make an enforcement order under section 65 if the debtor has not signed a copy of the agreement (s 127(3))[20] or, in the case of a cancellable agreement, if the copies rules under sections 62 and 63 were not complied with and were not rectified before commencement of proceedings or if the provisions relating to cancellation notices under section 64(1) were not complied with (s 127(4)). In other cases it is discretionary whether or not the court enforces an agreement. It may, in granting an enforcement order, reduce or discharge any sum payable by the debtor, hirer, or surety to compensate for any prejudice suffered as a result of the contravention in question (s 127(2)).

Protection orders (s 131)

In order to protect the goods of the creditor 'pending the determination of proceedings under this Act', the court, on the application of a creditor under a regulated agreement, may make an order protecting the goods

18 Eg *Ashbroom Facilities Ltd v Bodley* [1992] CCLR 31; *Cedar Holdings Ltd v Thompson* [1993] CCLR 7.
19 [1996] 1 FCR 679.
20 See, for example, *Dimond v Lovell* [2000] 2 All ER 897, [2000] 2 WLR 1121, HL.

against damage or depreciation. This may include orders restricting or prohibiting their use or as to their custody. Such an order can be made in respect of any goods under a regulated agreement whether or not they are 'protected'.

Financial relief for hirer (s 132)

If, under a consumer hire agreement, the owner has repossessed the goods other than by action, the court may make an order for repayment of the whole or any part of the sum paid by the hirer and that the obligation to pay any sum owed by the hirer shall cease. The court makes such order as it thinks just having regard to the extent of the enjoyment of the goods by the hirer. The object of the section is to give some protection to the hirer, who is without the benefit of the protected goods' concept applicable to hire-purchase and conditional sale agreements only (see above, p 330).

Special powers relating to hire-purchase and conditional sale agreements (s 133)

The court has power to make a variety of orders as regards the above agreements in addition to time and protection orders. Section 133 provides that on an application for an enforcement order or time order or in an action by the creditor for recovery of possession of goods the court may if it appears just make a 'return' order or a 'transfer' order. A 'return order' is an order for the return of the goods to the creditor. Such an order may be suspended under the general power to make conditional or suspended orders in section 135.

A transfer order is the modern equivalent of a 'Solomon's judgment'. The order will be for transfer of the title to some of the goods to the debtor and the return of some to the creditor (though obviously the goods must be capable of division in this way unlike Solomon's child). The section lays down a condition that must be fulfilled before a transfer order can be made. This is that the 'paid-up sum' exceeds the part of the total price referable to the transferred goods by an amount equal to at least one-third of the unpaid balance of the total price (s 133(3)). Thus the debtor must have paid the value of the transferred goods plus at least one-third of the total price of all the goods before a transfer order can be made. The 'paid-up sum' is normally the sum paid by the debtor to the creditor to date, but adjustments are made for sums owed by the creditor to the debtor, or vice versa, in respect of the goods (s 133(2)). Subject to this, 'the transferred goods shall be such of the goods to which the agreement relates as the court thinks just' (s 133(3)).

After a return order or transfer order has been made, if the debtor pays the balance of the purchase price and fulfils 'any other necessary conditions', then provided the goods are not in the possession of the creditor the debtor may claim the goods back. If the debtor fails to comply with a transfer order the court, on the creditor's application, may revoke the order and instead order the debtor to pay the balance of the total price as is referable to the goods. Conditional and suspended orders may also be made (s 135).

Variation of agreements (s 136)

The court has a general power to make an order to amend any agreement or security. It is generally thought that this power would be used only in connection with the making of the orders discussed above.

Extortionate credit bargains (ss 137, 138, 139)

The court has power to re-open a credit agreement so as to do justice between the parties if it finds a credit bargain extortionate.[1] This applies to all credit agreements, whether or not regulated, provided they are made with an 'individual', and not a body corporate. It does not apply to hire agreements. The credit 'bargains' may be examined generally. The power resembles provisions formerly in the Moneylenders Acts, and a similar equitable power has been exercised in land mortgage cases (see *Cityland and Property (Holdings) Ltd v Dabrah*).[2]

Some guidance is given by section 138 on when bargains are extortionate. A bargain is extortionate if the payments to be made by the debtor are grossly exorbitant or otherwise grossly contravene ordinary principles of fair dealing. There is a helpful list of factors to be taken into account in deciding whether a bargain is extortionate. These include interest rates prevailing at the time (there is now no presumption against interest rates exceeding 48 per cent), the age, experience, business capacity and state of health of the debtor and the degree of risk accepted by the creditor (see s 138(2), (3) and (4)). The burden of disproving that the bargain is extortionate is on the creditor once the debtor has made such an allegation

---

1   See M, H & P pp 306–313; Wilkinson (1979) 8 Anglo-Am 240; Hill-Smith (1982) 126 Sol Jo 530; Wilkinson (1986) 136 NLJ 796; Bently & Howells [1989] Conv 164 and 234; OFT leaflet 'Extortionate Credit' (OFT 014); *Unjust Credit Transactions*, Report by Director General, OFT, September 1991; *Extortionate Credit in the UK, A Report to the Department of Trade and Industry*, E Kempson and Claire Whyley, June 1999.

2   [1968] Ch 166, [1967] 2 All ER 639.

under section 139 (s 171(7)). The court should require the debtor to support his allegation with prima facie evidence. Under section 139 the court in re-opening extortionate bargains has wide powers including those to rewrite the agreement, set aside the debtor's obligations or order repayments to be made. The draftsman of the Act, when writing on this topic, expressed the view that 'it is likely that the courts will be sparing with relief. The bargain must after all be grossly exorbitant or unfair.'[3] This view has been borne out by the decisions of the courts, with very few cases being re-opened.

In *A Ketley Ltd v Scott*[4] the defendants contracted to buy a flat but were unable to complete (because of lack of funds) on the due date. Mr Scott, therefore, obtained a loan from the claimants of £20,500 to enable him and his wife to complete. The interest was expressed as being 12 per cent over three months, this being equal to 48 per cent per annum. He did not declare to the claimants that he had given a legal charge on the property to his bank to cover an overdraft and was liable under certain further guarantees to third parties. The loan not having been repaid the claimants sued for payment due and possession and obtained judgment, but an enquiry was ordered into the question of whether the interest was 'extortionate'. The court held that material considerations were that the claimants had lent 82 per cent of the value of the property without time for enquiry, the risk being highly speculative. Furthermore Mr Scott had failed to disclose his overdraft at the bank and other financial commitments and these were deceitful acts. Having regard to the degree of risk the interest charged was not disproportionately high and it was therefore not just to re-open the credit bargain. This was followed, in 1984, by *Wills v Wood*[5] where a retired hotelier loaned money on security of mortgages to other clients of his solicitor. In deciding that an agreement with the defendant did not 'grossly contravene the principles of fair dealing' the court indicated that although the defendant may have been unwise in borrowing the money, the claimant had not dealt in any unfair or improper way. As Sir John Donaldson indicated 'the word is "extortionate" not "unwise"'. The same conclusion was reached in *Coldunell Ltd v Gallon*.[6]

The provisions of section 138 received detailed study in *Davies v Directloans Ltd*[7] where Edward Nugee QC (sitting as Deputy Judge of

3   F A R Bennion (1979) 121 Sol Jo 485.
4   [1981] ICR 241, QBD; M, H & P p 308. See (1980) 130 NLJ 749. Jurisdiction is now given to the county court in the case of applications by a debtor or surety for all regulated agreements and also all other agreements for fixed-sum or running-account credit (s 139(5) as amended by the High Court and County Courts Jurisdiction Order 1991, SI 1991/724, art 2(1)(h),(8) and Sch, Pt. I).
5   (1984) 128 Sol Jo 222, [1984] LS Gaz R 1211, CA; M, H & P p 309. See also (1984) 134 NLJ 355.
6   [1986] QB 1184, [1986] 1 All ER 429, CA.
7   [1986] 2 All ER 783, [1986] 1 WLR 823, Ch D. See also (1986) 136 NLJ 796.

the High Court) indicated that it was unnecessary and not permissible to look outside the Act at earlier authorities to ascertain its meaning. He indicated that:

> Under the 1974 Act the test is not whether the creditor has acted in a morally reprehensible manner, but whether one or other of the conditions of section 138(1) is fulfilled, and, although it may be thought that if either condition is fulfilled there is likely to be something morally reprehensible about the creditor's conduct, the starting and ending point in determining whether the credit bargain is extortionate must be the words of section 138(1). [at pp 789, 831]

In deciding that the mortgage agreement in question was not extortionate, the court noted that the borrowers had received independent advice from a solicitor, were not under greater than normal financial pressure, the degree of risk to the lender justified a significantly higher rate of interest than a building society would charge and the true rate of interest was not grossly exorbitant when compared with prevailing interest rates.

The following cases involve a credit agreement being re-opened and the amount of interest charged altered. In *Barcabe Ltd v Edwards*[8] the court was influenced by the fact that a flat interest rate of 100 per cent, APR 319 per cent, was extortionate in comparison with other companies charging 18–20 per cent. The court reduced the interest rate charged to 40 per cent. An APR was reduced from 39 per cent to 30 per cent for a well-secured loan of £10,000 in *Devogate v Jarvis*.[9] In *Prestonwell Ltd v Capon*[10] a flat rate of 42 per cent was halved to 21 per cent for an £18,000 mortgage. The comparative rates for loans elsewhere, the debtors' lack of business capacity, financial pressure and lack of access to legal advice all contributed to the decision. In *Shahabinia v Giyahchi*[11] the creditor appealed to the Court of Appeal over the interest rate of 15 per cent imposed by the Queen's Bench Division when it re-opened three agreements. A rate of 30 per cent was substituted so as to do justice between the parties, 15 per cent having been even less than bank rate for some of the relevant time. Finally, in *Castle Phillips & Co Ltd v Wilkinson and Wilkinson*[12] a bridging loan, with interest at 4 per cent per month (three and one third times the building society rate), was reduced to 20 per cent per annum (one and one third times the building society rate) to reflect the short length of

---

8   [1983] CCLR 11, Birmingham County Court.
9   (16 November 1987, unreported), Lexis transcript, Sevenoaks County Court.
10 (1988) unreported, Corby County Court.
11 (5 July 1989, unreported), Lexis transcript, CA.
12 [1992] CCLR 83, County Court.

the loan. In this case the security for the £21,000 loan exceeded the nominal amount advanced to the borrowers, who had acted honestly and openly.

An example of an agreement grossly contravening ordinary principles of fair dealing can be seen in *Falco Finance Ltd v Michael Gough*.[13] Here a term permitting a finance company to have a dual rate of interest, the lower 'discounted' rate being permanently lost if any single payment during the life of the mortgage was delayed or deficient, was considered unacceptable. It was also ruled to be unfair under the Unfair Terms in Consumer Contracts Regulations 1994.[14]

In 1990 Mr Edward Leigh, Parliamentary Under Secretary of State for Industry and Consumer Affairs, requested that the Director review the effectiveness of the extortionate credit provisions. Consultations took place during 1991 and his report was published in September 1991.[15] The Director proposed reform of the provisions of sections 137–140 by replacing the idea of an 'extortionate credit bargain' with that of an 'unjust credit transaction'. To determine whether or not a transaction was 'unjust', account could be taken of 'excessive' payments, the current factors under section 138(2), (3) and (4) and 'the lender's care and responsibility in making the loan, including steps taken to find out and check the borrower's credit-worthiness and ability to meet the full terms of the agreement' (para 1.9, sub-para 4). In addition, it was recommended that, instead of 'otherwise grossly contravenes the ordinary principles of fair dealing' in section 138(1), the transaction be examined to see if it involved business activity which was deceitful or oppressive or otherwise unfair or improper, using the same terms as those for licensing decisions under section 25(2)(d). In addition to application by the debtor, the court should have power to re-open a credit transaction itself.[16] It was further proposed that the Director and Trading Standards Departments should, in the public interest, be able to initiate proceedings for a declaration that particular credit transactions, or parts of them, are unjust. Government support was given to these proposals, with some modifications.[17] Payments should be 'grossly excessive' to qualify and it was proposed to detail the factors to be considered in deciding whether or not there is an unjust credit transaction in regulations to allow for greater flexibility.

Further reforms concerning extortionate credit bargains were advocated by the Law Commission in its report *Transfer of Land – Land Mortgages*.[18] Here it was proposed that all control over the form, content and enforcement

---

13   (1999) 17 Tr LR 526, Macclesfield County Court.
14   SI 1994/3159, now replaced by SI 1999/2083; see further pp 138–146.
15   *Unjust Credit Transactions*, OFT, September 1991. See also Stephenson 'Unjust Credit Transactions' (1992) 9 Tr. Law 130.
16   See also *Releasing Enterprise*, Cm 512, para 6.8.8.
17   See (1992) 15 Consumer Law Today, Issue 4, p 6 and *Bee Line* 91/4, p 9.
18   Law Com No 204, see especially Pts VIII and IX.

of land mortgages should be removed from the 1974 Act. In particular this would remove land mortgages from the provisions of sections 137–140 and replace these controls with similar, but more extensive, ones addressed specifically to the land mortgage contract.

In the absence of any progress on reform, in 1997 the Director General re-examined the 1991 proposals of a previous Director General and, after consultation, found them still to be appropriate.[19] He wrote to the Minister in February 1999, urging reform. The Government is now examining the issue, having commissioned research on the extent to which extortionate credit is a problem.[20] One of the recommendations arising from the research; that the courts should have power to re-open a credit agreement on their own initiative, is the subject of specific consultation,[1] and developments are awaited.

10. CREDIT STATUS ENQUIRIES

There has been a great deal of concern by consumer organisations about the means used to assess a consumer's credit rating[2] and the accuracy of information obtained by potential creditors from credit reference agencies operating on a commercial basis. The term 'credit reference agency' is defined as a person carrying on a business comprising the furnishing of persons with information relevant to the financial standing of individuals, being information collected by the agency for that purpose (s 145(8)). Banks' status enquiries and solicitors' enquiries about eg the status of a potential tenant of their client landlord, do not bring them within the definition of a credit reference agency. The Act, together with the Data Protection Act 1998, contains a number of provisions to remedy the main problems that can arise.

Since 1 March 2000, depending upon the identity of the seeker of information, different legislative provisions apply. Where the applicant is a partnership or other unincorporated body of persons not consisting

---

19 See *Annual Reports of the Director General of Fair Trading 1997, 1998 and 1999*, 1997 HCP 762 at p 23; 1998 HCP 524 at p 24 and 2000 HCP 576 at p 23 respectively.

20 *Extortionate Credit in the UK, A report to the Department of Trade and Industry*, E Kempson and C Whyley, June 1999; Modern *Markets: Confident Consumers*, Cm 4410, July 1999, para 5.21.

1 *Discussion Paper on the Extortionate Credit Provisions in the Consumer Credit Act 1974*, DTI, 2000.

2 See also *Credit Scoring: A Report by the Director General of Fair Trading*, OFT, May 1992, 'Keeping score on lenders', OFT, Issue 22 Fair Trading 6. A new edition of the credit industry's *Guide to Credit Scoring* is anticipated in 2000, see *Annual Report of the Director General of Fair Trading 1999* 2000 HCP 576, p 24.

entirely of bodies corporate (a 'consumer'),[3] then the situation is governed by the Consumer Credit Act 1974 and the Director. For 'individuals', who are not partnerships or unincorporated bodies (ie ordinary people), the 1974 Act, the Data Protection Act 1998 and the Data Protection Commissioner apply.

Section 157 puts any creditor, owner or negotiator under a duty to disclose to the debtor or hirer on request the name and address of any credit reference agency to which the creditor applied for information about his financial standing. The duty ceases after 28 days from the end of the antecedent negotiations. For 'consumers' section 158 puts credit reference agencies under a duty to give, within seven working days, a copy of the file relating to the 'consumer' kept by the agency, rendered if necessary into 'plain English'. This is provided the 'consumer' has a) requested it in writing, b) given sufficient particulars to enable the agency to identify the file, and c) paid a fee of £2.[4] For 'individuals' a similar requirement for credit reference agencies to provide information lies under sections 7 and 9 of the 1998 Act and is subject to the same conditions.[5]

The agency must also (under s 158(2) of the 1974 Act and s 9(3) of the 1998 Act respectively) send applicants a statement[6] of their rights to have erroneous entries removed or corrected under section 159. This latter section enables any objector (whether an 'individual' or 'consumer') to have wrong and prejudicial information removed or amended from the file by giving notice to the agency that this is required to be done. If the agency complies, it must give the objector a notice stating that it has done so and send a copy of any amended entry. Section 159 also lays down the procedure to be followed if agreement cannot be reached. Either the objector or the agency may apply to the relevant authority,[7] who may make such order as he thinks fit. If the 'consumer' is a business consumer (eg a partnership or firm), rights to receive information may be restricted in the interests of the effective operation of the credit reference agency, by revealing confidential sources of information. Here the Director may call for a copy of the file and disclose, to the 'consumer', such information as he thinks fit (s 160).

Breach of any of the above duties under the 1974 Act involves the commission of a criminal offence, triable summarily with maximum penalty of level 4 on the standard scale (Sch 1).[8] Failure to comply with a request

---

3   Section 158(1)(a) as amended.
4   Increased from £1 by the Consumer Credit (Further Increase of Monetary Amounts) Order 1998, SI 1998/997.
5   Data Protection (Subject Access) (Fees and Miscellaneous Provisions) Regulations 2000, SI 2000/191.
6   As prescribed in the Consumer Credit (Credit Reference Agency) Regulations 2000, SI 2000/290.
7   The Director for partnerships and unincorporated bodies, the Data Protection Commissioner for individuals.
8   As amended by the Criminal Justice Act 1982, s 38.

made under section 7 of the 1998 Act may lead to a court order requiring compliance, breach of which would be contempt of court (s 7(9)). The Consumer Credit (Conduct of Business) (Credit References) Regulations 1977[9] also lay down a general duty by credit traders and hire traders to disclose to the credit-broker the particulars of any agency consulted, whether or not any request is made, if (inter alia) the introduction is made through a credit-broker and the prospective creditor or owner decides not to proceed with the agreement, informing only the credit-broker of this. Failure of duty is controlled through the licensing system in this case.

11. PROBLEMS OF TITLE

It is an important general rule in commercial law that one person cannot pass a good title in goods 'sold' to another person unless the seller at the time of the sale owns those goods – *nemo dat quod non habet*. To this rule there are a number of exceptions that are explained in full in books on commercial law. A material exception in the case of transactions involving a buyer who pays for the goods by instalments, and to whom by agreement the property in the goods has not passed,[10] is contained in the Sale of Goods Act 1979, section 25.[11] This states, in short, that where a person having bought or agreed to buy goods obtains possession of them, the delivery or transfer of them to any person receiving them in good faith is as good as if he were validly authorised by the owner of the goods to sell them.

In early litigation it was held that where a customer was obliged to pay two instalments of 'rent' for furniture delivered under what purported to be a hiring agreement, and on payment of the second instalment but not before, the property should pass to the customer (who enjoyed no right to terminate the agreement) the transaction was a contract of sale and the customer had agreed to buy. So when the customer sold the goods to the defendant before having paid the full instalments, the defendant having taken in good faith, the defendant obtained a good title to the goods.[12] The blossoming piano and furniture industries needed a safer system to protect their interests where goods which had been delivered were to be paid for by instalments, and the concept of hire-purchase was first

9   SI 1977/330 as amended by SI 2000/291.
10 Under the Sale of Goods Act 1979, s 18, r 1, where there is an unconditional contract for the sale of specific goods in a deliverable state, the property in the goods passes to the buyer when the contract is made, whether or not the time of payment and/or delivery is postponed. This is subject to a contrary intention.
11 BSSCCL p 443. See also Factors Act 1889, s 9, BSSCCL p 68, in similar terms.
12 *Lee v Butler* [1893] 2 QB 318, CA.

successfully tested in *Helby v Matthews*.[13] Here the subject matter of the hiring agreement was a piano, and the customer was obliged to pay a monthly rental over three years unless he terminated the agreement and redelivered to the owner possession of the piano. The agreement included two clauses the effect of which was to state that the property was to remain in the owner until all instalments had been paid, but if and when all instalments had been paid the piano should 'become the sole and absolute property of the hirer'. On a premature transfer by way of pledge by the hirer it was held, perhaps rather beneficently, that this was a hiring agreement with a mere option either to return the piano or to purchase it at the end. The hirer had not therefore agreed to buy and could not transfer title to the pawnbroker to whom he had pledged it. The piano accordingly had to be redelivered to the owner. Thereafter the hire-purchase agreement, defined as we have seen as essentially a hiring agreement containing an option in favour of the customer to purchase the subject matter after payment of the last instalment (and often for a further nominal consideration) became an established and well-understood commercial agreement. It remains true that the hirer under a hire-purchase agreement cannot validly transfer title to a purchaser from him under this part of the sale of goods legislation. Recent confirmation of this can be seen in *Close Asset Finance Ltd v Care Graphics Machinery Ltd*,[14] where instalments of about £2.5 million were required, with an option to purchase at a fee of £50. It was held there was no agreement to buy, despite the insignificant price of the option.[15]

Credit sale agreements, under which the goods normally become the purchaser's as soon as the agreement is made, and conditional sale agreements, under which the property was expressed to pass on payment of the last instalment, were both vulnerable to premature sales by the purchaser. In the first case the purchaser was in fact the owner and, in the second case, had 'agreed to buy' and could therefore pass a good title as described above. In the latter case, conditional sales, the 1974 Act made a significant change in the form of common law provision. It was stated, formerly in Schedule 4 to the Act, and now restated in the Sale of Goods Act 1979, section 25(2) that, for the purposes of the Sale of Goods Act 1979, section 25(1) considered above, the buyer under a conditional sale agreement which is a consumer credit agreement shall be deemed not to be

13 [1895] AC 471, HL.
14 [2000] 12 LS Gaz R 42, QBD.
15 Cf *Forthright Finance Ltd v Carlyle Finance Ltd* [1997] 4 All ER 90, CA, where, under the agreement, the property passed after the instalments were paid *unless the hirer elected not to exercise the option to purchase*. This was held to be a conditional sale agreement and accordingly an agreement to buy. It fell outside the provisions of s 25(2), discussed below, because the purchase price of the car in question was above the then current financial limits of the 1974 Act.

a person who has bought or agreed to buy goods.[16] Estoppel by conduct under section 21(1) can also arise. It now makes no difference to questions of title whether a purported sale has taken place under such a conditional sale agreement or a hire-purchase agreement. In either case the original owner remains the true owner and can normally recover the goods from an innocent third party, subject to the exception next considered.

As a matter of policy the Hire-Purchase Act 1964 reversed the above position in the case of a purported sale of a motor car by a hirer under an undischarged hire-purchase agreement. The relevant provisions of the 1964 Act are reproduced in slightly amended form in the Consumer Credit Act 1974, Schedule 4. This states that where under a hire-purchase or conditional sale agreement a motor vehicle is disposed of to a private purchaser who takes in good faith and without notice of the relevant undischarged agreement, 'that disposition shall have effect as if the creditor's title to the vehicle has been vested in the debtor immediately before that disposition' (s 27(2)). The same result occurs when the debtor sells the vehicle to a trade or finance purchaser, who in turn passes the vehicle on to a private purchaser. The latter obtains a good title. The original debtor retains full criminal and civil liability for his actions.

The ascertainment of whether a buyer is a 'private purchaser' is often obvious but can cause difficulties. In *Stevenson v Beverley Bentinck Ltd*[17] a purchaser bought a car which was subject to an undischarged hire-purchase agreement, but the purchaser took in good faith and without notice. In the spare time after his full-time employment in a manufacturing company he carried on a part-time business of purchasing motor vehicles for resale. He bought this particular car for his private use. The finance company under the original hire-purchase agreement repossessed the car and resold it. The claimant purchaser claimed that he was the true owner by reason of the provisions discussed above in the Hire-Purchase Act 1964, but the defendant finance company denied that he was a private purchaser. This expression is elucidated in section 29 of the 1964 Act. This defines a trade or finance purchaser as 'a purchaser who ... carries on a business which consists, wholly or partly, (a) of purchasing motor vehicles for the purpose of offering or exposing them for sale' and a 'private purchaser' as one who, at the time of the disposition to him, does not do so. It was held that the claimant was not a private purchaser because when he bought the car he was carrying on, in part, the business of a motor dealer. It was the status of the purchaser that mattered, not whether he happened to buy a car for his private use or for resale.

---

16 See also Sch 4 to the 1974 Act amending the Factors Act 1889, s 9 to similar effect.
17 [1976] 2 All ER 606, [1976] 1 WLR 483, CA.

Problems of title

Trade purchasers are treated more severely than private purchasers because it is easier for them to check that cars are unencumbered. It was revealed in *Moorgate Mercantile Co Ltd v Twitchings*[18] that all the major finance companies were members of HP Information Ltd ('HPI') and about 8,000 motor dealers were affiliated to it. About 98 per cent of hire-purchase agreements relating to cars are registered with HPI by reference to the cars' registration numbers. Affiliated dealers can enquire by telephone whether a particular vehicle is registered with HPI. In this case a car was subject to a hire-purchase agreement with the claimants, a finance company, who for some inexplicable reason failed to follow their usual practice of registering the hire-purchase agreement with HPI. The car was 'sold' by the hirer to the defendant motor dealers who enquired from HPI whether there was any hire-purchase agreement registered or recorded against the car and received a negative answer. The House of Lords held, by a majority, that HPI were not agents, in a general sense, of the finance companies, which were members of it. Nor did the answers given by HPI amount to a representation that none of the finance house members of the HPI had any interests in the car in question. Furthermore, the claimants, in not registering the hire-purchase agreement with HPI, were not in breach of any duty of care to persons such as the defendants who might in future buy it, notwithstanding that both were members of HPI.[19]

---

18 [1977] AC 890, [1976] 2 All ER 641, HL.

19 Citizens' Advice Bureaux and the Automobile Association are equipped to make enquiries from HPI with regard to the status of second-hand cars on behalf of private purchasers. It is also possible to contact HPI on the internet. From November 1995 a compensation scheme of up to £10,000 has been provided for anyone receiving an 'all clear' from HPI who subsequently has to hand over a vehicle found to have been stolen or subject to a finance or leasing deal.

11 Fair trading

The Fair Trading Act 1973[1] has been called 'potentially the most comprehensive measure ever passed' to protect the economic interests of the consumer.[2] It has undergone quite substantial amendment, in particular in relation to competition matters, since enactment. The importance and scope of the Act, as amended, are indicated by this brief summary of its 12 parts:

- *Part I* provides for appointment of the Director General of Fair Trading and establishment of the Consumer Protection Advisory Committee;
- *Part II* deals with references to the Consumer Protection Advisory Committee and power of Secretary of State to make orders by statutory instrument imposing criminal sanctions in respect of conduct adversely affecting the economic interests of consumers.
- *Part III* empowers the Director to obtain undertakings from businessmen persisting in conduct detrimental to the interests of consumers and to take proceedings before the High Court or other appropriate court if necessary.
- *Part IV* deals with the functions of the Director and the Competition Commission in relation to monopoly situations.
- *Part V* deals in a similar way with mergers.
- *Part VI* deals with other references to the Competition Commission, such as restrictive labour practices relating to the employment of workers in commercial activities in the United Kingdom.
- *Part VII* deals with procedural matters relating to references to the Consumer Protection Advisory Committee and the Competition Commission.

1   See BSSCCL p 206.
2   Fair Trading and Consumer Protection in Britain, HMSO, p 6.

- *Part VIII* contains supplemental and procedural matters relating to references to the Competition Commission, including the criteria for determining the public interest.
- *Part IX* has been superseded by subsequent legislation.
- *Part X* was repealed by the Restrictive Trade Practices Act 1976.
- *Part XI* deals with trading schemes like 'pyramid selling' whereunder, typically, an escalating number of participants not operating from business premises are enrolled by the promoter of a business in the expectation of receiving benefits. This Part gives the Secretary of State power to prescribe regulations to prevent participants in such schemes from being unfairly treated and spelling out their rights and obligations. The current provisions are the Trading Schemes Regulations 1997,[3] contravention of which involves a criminal offence (s 120(2)).
- *Part XII* deals with miscellaneous and supplemental matters including the duty of the Director General to make an annual report of the Director's, the Advisory Committee's and the Competition Commission's activities for each calendar year.

This chapter is concerned with the office of Director and the organisation of and functions of the Office of Fair Trading, combined with a discussion of unfair trading practices and voluntary codes of conduct. The control of monopolies and mergers and the competition aspects of the work of the Director have already been mentioned in chapter 1.

I.   THE FUNCTIONS OF THE DIRECTOR AND THE OFFICE OF FAIR TRADING

Genesis

The Fair Trading Bill was introduced into the Commons in November 1972, without being preceded by any sort of published enquiry, Green or White Paper.[4] Speaking of the Bill on its second reading, and explaining its objects, Sir Geoffrey Howe, Minister for Trade and Consumer Affairs, remarked that the Bill had two complementary purposes; firstly the promotion of increased economic efficiency and secondly protection of the consumer against unfair trading practices. He continued,

> Just as fair trading is good business, so consumer protection is in itself an integral part of the market economy. That is why competition policy needs to be considered, as it is in the Bill, as a whole. It is this

---

3   SI 1997/30, BSSCCL p 821.
4   This feature attracted critical comment in debate – see 848 HC Official Report (5th series) col 469 (13 December 1972).

integrated view of competition policy that leads to the first institutional innovation proposed in the Bill – the appointment of a Director General of Fair Trading – The Government have concluded that given the specialist and detailed nature of the work and the need for continuity in its performance, it would best be done by an independent official body.[5]

The Bill with a number of amendments (about 125 of approximately 4,000 proposed) became law on 25 July 1973.

The Director General of Fair Trading

Section 1 provides for the appointment of an officer known as the Director General of Fair Trading (and referred to in the Act itself and here as 'the Director') by the Secretary of State for a renewable term of five years. The Director has power to appoint such staff as he thinks fit subject to the approval of the Minister for the Civil Service as regards numbers and conditions. The Director may not be an MP.[6] The first Director was appointed on 1 November 1973 (M J Methven). He was succeeded on 14 June 1976 by Gordon Borrie[7] who served three five-year and one one-year terms as Director. The third Director, appointed from June 1992, was Sir Bryan Carsberg, who moved from being Director General of Telecommunications. He resigned after only three years and was replaced, for a few months, by Jeffrey Preston, the Deputy Director General. The fourth Director, Mr John Bridgeman, was in office from October 1995 to September 2000. His background was that of a company managing director and member of the Monopolies and Mergers Commission. He did not seek re-appointment and his successor is Professor John Vickers, a former Professor of Political Economy at Oxford and, subsequently, Chief Economist and Executive Director of the Bank of England.

The Director's functions[8] are specified in section 2 and in various other sections of the Act. Additional functions have been added by subsequent legislation, for example, the Consumer Credit Act 1974. They may be summarised as follows:

1) There are various functions in relation to monopolies, mergers, restrictive practices and uncompetitive practices which have been considered in chapter 1.

5   848 HC Official Report (5th series) col 454 (13 December 1972).
6   House of Commons Disqualification Act 1975, s 1(1)(f) and Sch 1, Pt III.
7   Now Lord Borrie.
8   For a discussion of the powers and position of the Director see Sir Gordon Borrie *The Development of Consumer Law and Policy – Bold Spirits and Timorous Souls (The Hamlyn Lectures)* 1984, Stevens & Sons.

2) The carrying on of commercial activities in the UK relating to the supply to consumers in the UK of goods and services must be kept under review, and the collection of information with a view to ascertaining practices which may adversely affect the economic interests of such consumers.

3) The receipt and collation of available evidence with respect to the activities in 2) above which appear to be evidence of practices which may adversely affect the interests (whether economic, or relating to health, safety or other matters) of UK consumers. Such practices may be referred to the Consumer Protection Advisory Committee ('the Advisory Committee'), which may lead to the Secretary of State making an Order prohibiting or regulating the practice under Part II of the Act. Since there is some overlap here with the primary responsibilities of other Ministries the duty is phrased as being 'to receive and collate evidence' which would then be passed on.

4) Action may be taken against persons carrying on business who persist in conduct detrimental to the consumer, under Part III of the Act.

5) The publication of information and advice for UK consumers and encouragement of relevant associations to prepare and disseminate to their members codes of practice for guidance in safeguarding and promoting the interests of UK consumers, and the submission to the Secretary of State of Annual Reports (Pt XII).

6) The Consumer Credit Act 1974 imposes on the Director the duties relating to consumer credit originally envisaged as being those of an independent 'Commissioner for Consumer Credit'. These duties involve supervision of consumer credit activity generally, supervision of the enforcement of the Act and administration of the licensing system. Consumer credit is discussed in chapter 10.

7) The Estate Agents Act 1979, section 25, imposes a general duty upon the Director to superintend the working and enforcement of the Act.

8) The Control of Misleading Advertisements Regulations 1988[9] enable the Director to seek an injunction prohibiting misleading advertising and comparative advertising that contains prohibited material.

9) The Unfair Terms in Consumer Contracts Regulations 1999[10] enable the Director to seek assurances and injunctions to prohibit contract terms drawn up for general use which are unfair.

10) The Director is also proposed as the lead body for the seeking of injunctions relating to consumer credit, distance selling,[11] doorstep

---

9   SI 1988/915, as amended by the Broadcasting Act 1990, s 203(1) and Sch 20, para 51 and SI 2000/914. See further ch 2 at p 46.

10   SI 1999/2083, replacing SI 1994/3159. See further ch 5 at p 143.

11   Implemented by the Consumer Protection (Distance Selling) Regulations 2000, SI 2000/2334, regs 27 and 28 as of 31 October 2000.

selling, package travel and timeshare under the proposals for implementation of the Injunctions Directive,[12] from January 2001.

The Office of Fair Trading

The functions of the Director are performed from and through the Office of Fair Trading ('OFT') at Fleetbank House, 2-6 Salisbury Square, London EC4Y 8JX. The OFT is financed by the Department of Trade and Industry and is described as a 'non-ministerial department of government', there being no statutory recognition of its existence in the 1973 Act.

The office is staffed by over 400 people headed by the Director, with Directors of Divisions dealing with Consumer Affairs, Competition Policy and Legal matters. It also has an Information Branch and a Resources and Services Branch. It is important to note that the OFT does not formally deal with complaints received direct from the public other than as mentioned in section 34 (conduct by a person detrimental to consumers) and regarding misleading advertising and unfair contract terms. Its information comes primarily from its own investigations and information supplied by trading standards departments of local authorities, the courts, who are authorised to inform the Director of material convictions, and the news media. Individual complaints should not normally, therefore, be sent to the OFT, since as can be seen, in most respects the Director is a 'watchdog' not a 'bloodhound'.

It is proposed[13] to create a new Authority for the OFT to give it corporate status. Under the chairmanship of the Director there will be a Board of at least five members to provide greater transparency and accountability. Primary legislation will be needed to achieve this.

References to the Consumer Protection Advisory Committee

Part II of the Act deals with references to the Advisory Committee. Its membership must consist of not less than 10 and not more than 15 members appointed by the Secretary of State for Trade and Industry, having regard to their experience in consumer protection work. Membership of the Advisory Committee is currently suspended as, in 1982, the then Minister of Consumer Affairs, Dr Gerard Vaughan, announced[14] that he would not

---

12   Directive 98/27/EC, OJ No L 166, 11.6.98, p 51; see also OFT 'Widening the net' (2000) 26 Fair Trading 13.
13   See DTI Press Notice P/2000/337, OFT Press Notice PN 20/00, 18 May 2000. See also ch 3.
14   DTI Press Notice, 24 September 1982; *Annual Report of the Director General of Fair Trading 1982*, 1994 HCP 20, p 45.

be re-appointing existing members nor appointing any new members to the Committee as there were no current or proposed references. The Advisory Committee will be re-established should a reference be made. The possibility of reviving Part II and the CPAC has been mooted,[15] but to date no developments have occurred.

References may be made by the Secretary of State, any other minister, or the Director on the question of whether a consumer trade practice adversely affects the economic interests of UK consumers (s 14).[16] 'Consumer trade practice' is defined by section 13. The term means any practice carried on in connection with the supply of goods or services to consumers and which relates a) to the terms and conditions (whether as to price or otherwise) on which goods and services are to be supplied; b) to the manner in which those terms and conditions are communicated to persons to whom goods or services are supplied (eg misleading 'small print' in documents); c) to all forms of promotion of the supply of goods or services; d) to methods of salesmanship employed in dealing with consumers; e) to the way in which goods are packed or otherwise got up for the purpose of being supplied; or f) to methods of demanding or securing payment for goods or services supplied. Section 15 excludes practices relating to services as specified in Schedule 4 which are subject to investigation by the Competition Commission, and section 16 restricts references relating to specified supplies of goods and services, mainly by public services, by requiring the consent of the appropriate minister.

References may be 'general' or purely investigative under section 14, but by section 17, where it appears to the Director that a consumer trade practice does or may:

a) mislead customers as to, or withhold from them adequate information as to, their rights and obligations, or

b) otherwise mislead or confuse with respect to any matter in connection with relevant consumer transactions, or

c) subject consumers to undue pressure to enter into relevant consumer transactions, or

d) cause the relevant terms or conditions to be so adverse as to be inequitable to them,

the Director's reference may then include proposals that the Secretary of State should exercise his order making powers to prohibit or modify the practice. A 'relevant consumer transaction' is any transaction to which a

---

15   *The Better Regulation Task Force: Response to Consumer Affairs Review*, 17 September 1998, Kim Howells, Parliamentary Under-Secretary of State for Competition and Consumer Affairs; *Annual Report of the Director General of Fair Trading 1998*, 1999 HCP 524, pp 23-4; *Reform of Part II of the Fair Trading Act 1973: Draft Regulatory Impact Statement*, http://www.dti.gov.uk/consumer/law/7a.htm.

16   See M, H & P pp 538-547.

person is, or may be invited to become, a party in his capacity as consumer (s 17(5)). The word 'consumer' is also defined and its meaning may be summarised as a person to whom goods or services are supplied by a commercial supplier who does not receive the goods or services in the course of his business (s 137(2)).

Any such reference must specify which particular effect the Director considers the trade practice has and the reference is published in the London, Edinburgh and Belfast Gazettes (s 17).

The Advisory Committee must then report to the Secretary of State, normally within three months of the reference, stating whether or not it agrees with the Director's proposals (assuming it finds that there is an adverse consumer trade practice), or whether it would agree to modified proposals. The Advisory Committee itself, which consists partly of members experienced in consumer affairs and has a maximum of 15 members, in the case of section 17 references must take into consideration representations by interested bodies who are normally also permitted to give to them oral evidence (s 81). Their report must, as far as practicable, exclude the private affairs of individuals or the affairs of a body of persons in so far as any such matter might, if published, seriously prejudice their interests (s 82). The report is then laid before Parliament in the manner specified by section 83.

Orders in pursuance of the report

In cases where the Advisory Committee agrees with the Director's proposals or agrees with specified modifications, the Secretary of State may, 'if he thinks fit', make an order under the powers in section 22. A draft of any such order must be laid before Parliament and approved by resolution of each House of Parliament (s 22(4)). Contravention of a prohibition in any such order confers no civil right of action (s 26), but constitutes a criminal offence punishable on summary conviction by a maximum fine of £5,000 and on conviction on indictment to a fine or imprisonment for a maximum of two years, or both (s 23 as amended). There are the defences familiar in trade descriptions law (inter alia) of mistake, act or default of another, accident, or cause beyond the defendant's control, provided in each case reasonable precautions were taken and due diligence shown (s 25).

The enforcement of any orders made is the responsibility of local weights and measures authorities. They are given power to make test purchases (s 28) and to enter premises and seize goods and documents, subject to some limitations (s 29). It is also an offence to obstruct an officer exercising these powers (s 30). In order to promote liaison with the Director, authorities are required to notify intended prosecutions under section 23 of the Act; the Trade Descriptions Act 1968; Part III of the Consumer Protection Act 1987; the Property Misdescriptions Act 1991 and the Timeshare Act 1992 (s 130, as amended).

References and orders made

Two references were made to the Advisory Committee in 1974. The first reference[17] covered the practice of some shops of informing the customer that no money would be refunded or otherwise misleading the customer, by a notice displayed or otherwise, as to his rights under the sale of goods legislation. This in due course resulted in the Consumer Transactions (Restrictions on Statements) Order 1976[18] which implements the proposed banning of these practices and has already been discussed in chapter 5. The second reference[19] covered practices connected with seeking to induce consumers to enter into mail order transactions with payment in advance without undertaking to return the money if the goods are not sent within a specified period, or without giving the seller's name and address. It was also the Director's view that any trader, who took a prepayment of £10 or more, should give the consumer a written commitment that, if the goods were not supplied within a specified period, the money would be refunded within seven days of a request for it and the transaction annulled. These recommendations were partially adopted in the Mail Order Transactions (Information) Order 1976[20] which applied to written advertisements, circulars etc, in which persons in the course of business invited orders from consumers by post for goods for which payment in advance was required. Such advertisements had to contain a legible description of the name and business address of the person inviting orders (and not, for example, purely a box number). The Order has been revoked, as of 31 October 2000, as part of the implementation of the Distance Selling Directive.[1]

A reference[2] was made to the Advisory Committee in 1975 relating to the practice of seeking to sell goods to consumers without revealing (whether deliberately or not) that the goods are being sold in the course of

---

17 OFT Dossier 17/1 'The Purported Exclusion of Inalienable Rights and Failure to Explain their Existence'; CPAC Report: 'Rights of Consumers' 1975 HCP 6.

18 SI 1976/1813 as amended by SI 1978/27, see BSSCCL p 701.

19 OFT Dossier 17/2 'Prepayment in Mail Order Transactions and in Shops'; CPAC Report: 'Prepayment for Goods' 1976 HCP 285.

20 SI 1976/1812.

1 Directive 97/7/EC, OJ No L 144, 4.6.97, p 19, see the Consumer Protection (Distance Selling) Regulations 2000, SI 2000/2334, reg 2.

2 OFT Dossier 17/3 'Seeking To Sell Goods Without Revealing That They Are Being Sold In The Course Of A Business'; CPAC Report: 'Disguised Business Sales' 1976 HCP 355. For extracts of the Dossier and the CPAC Report see M, H & P pp 540-543.

a business – 'disguised business sales'. Advertisements in the classified columns of newspapers are the usual vehicles of communication used. The danger is that consumers may not realise that many of the rights given to them only arise when buying from someone selling in the course of a business. This resulted in the promulgation of the Business Advertisements (Disclosure) Order 1977[3] under which a person seeking to sell goods in the course of a business[4] must make this fact clear in any advertisement.

In January 1977 a reference was made[5] to the Advisory Committee affecting the display of prices and quotations without a clear statement that VAT is included. The recommendation was that failure to show the VAT-inclusive price should be a criminal offence. The Advisory Committee agreed[6] with the Director's view that advertising, displaying or otherwise quoting to consumers VAT-exclusive prices or charges was economically detrimental to consumers and agreed the Director's proposals for control subject to two general modifications. For some four years no action followed this recommendation, but on 23 July 1981 the Minister of State for Consumer Affairs announced, in a written reply in the House of Commons, that she proposed to make an order under the Prices Act 1974 on the price marking of VAT and ancillary charges. Consultations followed but no Order was made and on 29 July 1982 the new Minister for Consumer Affairs, Dr Gerard Vaughan, announced, in reply to a Parliamentary question,[7] that the proposed Order had been dropped and that a comprehensive review of the controls over price comparisons, bargain offers, etc would be undertaken.[8]

The rather slow reaction to the recommendations of the Director and comments of the Advisory Committee by the government caused disappointment in some circles. In his Second Report the Director commented, however, that whilst being disappointed, the references had had the beneficial effect of publicising and causing widespread discussion of the suspect trading practices in question. This itself tends to lead to a

---

3   SI 1977/1918, see M, H & P p 543 and BSSCCL p 704. For some information and statistics on the use of this Order in penalising disguised business sales of used cars, electrical goods, carpets and bicycles being goods commonly sold in classified columns of newspapers by businesses masquerading as private sellers, see (1981) 89 ITSA Monthly Review 147. There are usually about 50 convictions per annum under this Order.

4   The meaning of 'in the course of a business' in this Order has been discussed in *Blakemore v Bellamy* (1982) 147 JP 89, [1983] RTR 303, QBD; see M, H & P pp 544-546.

5   OFT Dossier 17/4 'VAT-Exclusive Prices'.

6   See CPAC Report 'VAT-Exclusive Prices' 1977 HCP 416.

7   DTI Press Notice 29 July 1982, 28 HC Official Report (6th Series) cols 628-9 (29 July 1982).

8   See further ch 12.

voluntary reduction in the operation of the practice.[9] It may also be supposed that the government showed understandable caution in implementing proposals which, however efficiently handled by the criminal courts, converted what were primarily breaches of the letter or spirit of the civil law into criminal offences.

If one looks at the operation of Part II, it is not the CPAC consultation process which causes difficulties or delays. The CPAC worked quickly and effectively, and generally supported the Director's proposals. There are, however, three major hurdles with the process. The first hurdle is that the practice in question must fall within the definition of a 'consumer trade practice' (s 13) and must affect the 'economic interests of consumers' (s 14). Sir Gordon Borrie cited the example of misdescriptions of house property as falling outside these provisions.[10]

The second hurdle is that the Director has to initiate the procedure. If he chooses not to do so then no further steps may be taken under Part II. From time to time the OFT issues consultation papers with a view to a possible CPAC reference, for example prepayments in non-mail order transactions,[11] but these are not always pursued as a section 17 reference. It is not always appropriate to seek new criminal offences as successive Directors have indicated.[12]

The third, and perhaps most important, hurdle is that the decision to act ultimately rests with the Minister. There is need for the Minister to support the proposals of the CPAC and no mechanism exists to prevent delays or to ensure that a draft statutory instrument is in fact laid before Parliament. Sir Gordon Borrie summed up Part II as:

> an example of a bold idea smothered by an excess of nervous caution so that the resulting provisions have inevitably been a disappointment.[13]

Abolition of the Advisory Committee has been discussed[14] but this would need primary legislation, since Part II powers can only be fully exercised

9   *The Second Report of the Director General 1975*, 1976 HCP 288 at p 9.
10 Borrie *The Development of Consumer Law and Policy* p 127.
11 See *Annual Reports of the Director General for 1978 and 1979*, 1979 HCP 79 at p 21; 1980 HCP 624, p 21.
12 Borrie *The Development of Consumer Law and Policy* p 126; *1975 Director General's Report*, 1976 HCP 288, p 9; *1977 Report of the Director General*, 1978 HCP 228, p 7; *Annual Report of the Director General of Fair Trading 1993*, 1994 HCP 551 pp 8-11. Voluntary changes in practice have been made regarding unfair contract terms and notices, using licensing powers under the Consumer Credit Act 1974, (see further ch 10 at p 307), and the Unfair Terms in Consumer Contracts Regulations 1994 and 1999 (SI 1994/3159 and SI 1999/2083) (see further ch 5 at p 143).
13 *The Development of Consumer Law and Policy* p 127.
14 *Report on Non-Departmental Public Bodies* (Cmnd 7797, January 1980).

by and with the involvement of the Advisory Committee. In April 2000 the Department of Trade and Industry proposed[15] an amended order-making power for the Secretary of State to prohibit or modify specified trade practices that are unfair but not otherwise illegal, which cause detriment to consumers. Developments are awaited.

Undertakings from and action against traders

Part III of the Act gives the Director a 'bloodhound' as well as 'watchdog' function with regard to persons carrying on a business who persist in a course of conduct which a) is detrimental to the interests of UK consumers, whether economic or relating to health, safety or otherwise, and b) is to be regarded on the criteria stated as unfair to consumers (s 34). These criteria involve either contraventions of duties, prohibitions or restrictions imposed by the criminal law, whether or not the conduct has resulted in a conviction, and also breaches of contract or other breaches of duty enforceable by civil proceedings, whether or not proceedings have actually been brought (s 34(2) and (3)). The Director may take into account complaints received by him, whether from consumers or from other persons, as well as any other information collected by or furnished to him, to judge whether detrimental conduct has been persisted in. Guidance has been issued by the OFT[16] to Trading Standards Officers and others as to whether complaints about problem traders are sufficiently serious for the Director to pursue.

The Director's first line of attack is to obtain a satisfactory written assurance that the trader will refrain from continuing that course of conduct and from carrying on any similar course of conduct in the course of that business. A number of these assurances are obtained each year from traders individually or from traders who consent to or connive at the course of conduct of a company. The texts of the undertakings are often publicised and details appear in the Annual Report. In many cases the traders in question have been convicted of criminal offences, particularly offences under the Trade Descriptions Act 1968, or have been unsuccessful defendants in more than one civil action arising out of their business conduct.

A case involving repeated offences and subsequent undertakings which were given publicity was *R v Director General of Fair Trading,*

---

15 *Reform of Part II of the Fair Trading Act 1973: Draft Regulatory Impact Statement,* http://www.dti.gov.uk/consumer/law/7a.htm.

16 *Bee Line* No 23 at p 3. See also *Assurances by Traders – an Introduction to the Operation of Part III of the Act*; *Assurances by Traders – Guidance on the Operation of Part III of the Act,* OFT, October 1985 and *Part III Assurances – a new approach,* OFT, March 1993.

ex p F H Taylor & Co Ltd.[17] T Ltd were the importers of toys and electrical equipment and had been convicted on 13 occasions under the Consumer Protection Act 1961. They gave a written assurance to the Director that they would 'refrain from continuing a course of conduct and from carrying on a similar course of conduct in the course of a business'. The Director issued a press release which recorded, inter alia, that T Ltd had only given the assurances after being warned that proceedings would be begun, and the number and nature of the convictions including the fines and costs ordered to be paid. T Ltd complained that, when asked to give the assurances, they were not warned that the Director would make their compliance the subject of a press release, and the press release involved an abuse of the Director's powers under section 124 (publication of information and advice) and a breach of section 133 (general restrictions on disclosure of information). It was held that the complaint must be dismissed, for if a press release was justifiable there was no reason why the Director should have warned T Ltd. In order to make good the complaint, T Ltd should have alleged that they were in some way misled into giving assurances. T Ltd had been given an opportunity to make amendments to the draft press release, but had not done so, nor did they suggest limiting its circulation. The court did, however, raise some questions which the Director might wish to consider in framing press releases on assurances. There followed a period when little publicity was given to assurances but then, in January 1989, press announcements, usually in local newspapers and relevant trade journals, were introduced.[18]

Should the Director be unsuccessful in receiving a satisfactory assurance, or if such an assurance is broken, the Director may bring proceedings either in the High Court (or Court of Session in Scotland) under section 35 (as amended), or in smaller cases, in the county court for the district in which the practice is carried on (or sheriff's court in Scotland) (s 41). The first case was in fact brought in the Cardiff County Court, in respect of a broken undertaking, in February 1977. The trader in question, a gas central heating supplier, had not observed his undertaking to refrain from installing central heating equipment not in accordance with the contract with his customer and to refrain from committing offences under the Gas Safety Regulations 1972 by installing gas pipes which leaked gas.[19]

The powers of the courts specified include a) the obtaining of an undertaking to refrain from the specified course of conduct or b) to make

17   [1981] ICR 292, QBD; M, H & P pp 551-552
18   For examples see M, H & P pp 549-551.
19   *Director General's Annual Report for 1977*, 1978 HCP 228, p 51. For a case taken before the Restrictive Practices Court in respect of traders with a large number of convictions under the Food and Drugs Act 1955, see *Director General of Fair Trading v Smiths Bakeries (Westfield) Ltd* (1978) *Times*, 12 May, Restrictive Practices Court. See generally M, H & P pp 547-552.

an order in similar terms. The court also has power to obtain undertakings from or make orders against accessories, directors or officers of companies and other members of a group of interconnected bodies corporate. Appeal lies to the Court of Appeal,[20] or from the sheriff court to the Court of Session in Scotland (ss 35-41A). Breach of any undertaking given or order made would put the defendant in contempt of court, punishable by imprisonment in the case of individuals, or a fine. Examples of contempt proceedings can be seen in the cases of Mr Gilliam,[1] where imprisonment of 14 days was ordered, and Saray Electronics (London) Ltd, where a fine of £1,950 was imposed for the initial contempt, followed by a further fine of £50,000 for the company and £10,000 for each director, with three months' imprisonment, suspended for two years, for a second contempt.[2] Finally, a prison sentence of 15½ months was imposed for contempt of court against a car mechanic, Mr France, for breaching an assurance given in 1986 regarding poor workmanship. A court order made against him had previously been broken in 1994 (with a £500 fine) and 1997 (with a 9½ month suspended sentence).[3]

Up to the end of 1999, 887 assurances, undertakings or orders have been obtained, the most common trading activities involved being cars and motoring, electrical goods, and home improvements. In recent years between four to 30 assurances have been given each year, with 3-4 per annum necessitating court action under sections 35 and 38. A total of 16 actions for contempt of court have also been taken. It is, however, difficult to evaluate the effectiveness of the assurance process. Despite the large number of people engaged in business activities and the large number of recorded complaints by consumers, comparatively few assurances have been given. The comparatively small number of court cases for breaches of assurances or court orders may be because, having given an assurance, traders modify their behaviour to comply with the law or even decide to cease trading altogether. In some cases, however, subsequent breaches have not been detected, especially where the trader has set up a new company, possibly involving different goods or services, often in another part of the country. It is particularly difficult to keep track of such traders.[4]

20   For an unsuccessful appeal by the Director see *Director General of Fair Trading v Jamshid Diwan* 30 October 1996, unreported, (1998) 21 Consumer Law Today, Issue 10, p 1, CA; *Director General's Annual Report 1996*, 1997 HCP 104, p 29; M, H & P p 549.

1   See *Director General's Report for 1983*, 1984 HCP 493, p 57; M, H & P p 551; (1982) 90 ITSA MR 190; (1983) 91 ITSA MR 202.

2   See *Bee Line* No 39 p 17; OFT Press Release No 26/89 and *Director General's Annual Report for 1989*, 1990 HCP 502, p 65.

3   OFT, (1999) 24 *Fair Trading* 3; *Director General's Annual Report for 1999*, 2000 HCP 576, p 27.

4   For a discussion and analysis of assurances given up to 1980 see Hope (1981) 89 ITSA MR 96 and 180. See also Crossley (1986) 94 ITSA MR 139 for a critical

Reform of Part III

Sir Gordon Borrie, when Director, put forward proposals for 'a complete overhaul of Part III'[5] as a result of reviewing the operation of assurances. The definition of 'unfair' conduct, required before an assurance could be sought,[6] would be expanded to encompass 'deceptive or misleading' business practices (with a non-exhaustive list of illustrative acts or practices) and 'unconscionable' practices.[7] New enforcement procedures were also proposed, involving both local trading standards authorities and the OFT. Government support was given to the need for reform in principle. On appointment as Director, Sir Bryan Carsberg re-appraised his predecessor's proposals and reported to the President of the Board of Trade in November 1993.[8] He agreed that the powers of the Director under Part III were inadequate and proposed a widening of the definition of 'unfair' business conduct to include 'deceptive, misleading or oppressive' actions which might not be breaches of the civil or criminal law. Also recommended were a reduction in the 'persistence' requirement and a speedier process with a power to issue warning notices requiring unfair conduct detrimental to consumers to be discontinued, subject to court review, instead of the need to seek an assurance. The concept of 'unconscionable conduct' as a separate category of unfair conduct was rejected, as was the inclusion of an illustrative list of unacceptable practices. Enforcement powers would not be extended to trading standards officers but would be retained by the OFT.

In response to these amended proposals, the Department of Trade and Industry issued a Consultation Paper[9] in December 1994, aiming to increase the strength and effectiveness of the Director's powers. In the absence of any published report on the 1994 consultation, John Bridgeman, as Director, issued a press release[10] in September 1997, making eight recommendations to the Minister for Consumer and Corporate Affairs in the new Labour administration. He advocated enforcement powers for trading standards departments, in addition to the OFT, with a new procedure

---

review of assurances; *Trading Malpractices,* OFT Report, 1990, paras 4.8-4.18 for Sir Gordon Borrie's assessment and *Reform of Part III of the Fair Trading Act 1973 – A Consultation Paper*, DTI, December 1994, for the views of the previous Government and Sir Bryan Carsberg.

5   *Trading Malpractices*, OFT Report, 1990, para 1.8, M, H & P p 559.
6   See above p 355.
7   See op cit paras 5.18-5.28, M, H & P pp 561-563.
8   For the text of Sir Bryan's proposals see *Reform of Part III of the Fair Trading Act 1973 – A Consultation Paper*, DTI, December 1994, Annex B.
9   *Reform of Part III of the Fair Trading Act 1973 - A Consultation Paper*, DTI, December 1994.
10   OFT Press Release No 39/97, M, H & P p 564. See also A Wilson and R McArthur 'Fair Trading' (1998) 8 Consumer Policy Review 138.

to be followed. Prior to issuing an order to discontinue a course of conduct, the enforcer would warn the trader, allowing representations to be made. An order, once made, could be challenged in court. Breach of an order would lead to a fine or a ban from carrying on the trading activity in question, with criminal sanctions available for breach of court orders. A new statutory test of unfairness would be used to determine unfair practices.

The Better Regulation Task Force considered[11] the current Part III provisions to be 'cumbersome and ineffective' and encouraged reform. The Government has now promised[12] reform of Part III, when parliamentary time permits. It will seek to provide:

[A] power for the courts to grant injunctions against specific practices carried out by specific traders;

a power for the courts to ban from trading for a period traders with a history of disregarding their legal obligations;

a power for the Secretary of State to make orders by secondary legislation to specify that certain unfair practices (for instance those associated with so-called 'one day sales') should become criminal offences, so ensuring they are not carried out by traders in general. (para 7.6)

Trading standards departments would join the OFT in enforcing the powers, with local courts being used. Consultation on proposals for reform closed in April 2000.[13] The proposed new injunctions procedure would not require assurances to be sought before an application could be made. Evidence of engagement in a 'course of unfair conduct' would be all that was needed.[14] Banning orders could be sought for those breaching injunctions, committing offences involving fraud, other dishonesty or violence, or engaging in conduct unfair or detrimental to consumers 'of such frequency or over such a period of time or over such a wide geographical area as to demonstrate that the [person] is not a fit person to engage in business with consumers'(para 43). Orders could last for up to 15 years and might be restricted to particular kinds of business or geographical areas. A public register of injunctions and banning orders is also proposed.

11   *Better Regulation Task Force Review: Consumer Affairs*, May 1998, p 10.
12   *Modern markets: confident consumers*, Cm 4410, July 1999.
13   *Reform of Part III of the Fair Trading Act 1973*, DTI, http://www.dti.gov.uk/consumer/law/8.htm.
14   Described as 'a number of connected unfair acts or omissions of the same or a similar kind, but not that the conduct extend over a period of time or that there be any element of intention or recklessness' (para 17).

2.   VOLUNTARY CODES OF PRACTICE[15]

In his Second Report the then Director wrote:

> I believe that proposals to change the law should be made only when
> absolutely necessary because I have increasingly realised that
> extension of the law is no automatic panacea for consumer problems.
> It is all too easy to suggest measures for consumer protection which
> are either impractical or prohibitively costly. . . . I have always
> considered that one of my most important functions is the duty to
> encourage voluntary codes of practice. . . . Codes, to be effective,
> must be carefully constructed and precise. General expressions of
> goodwill towards the customer, or declarations of good intent, are
> not nearly enough. Once a code has been negotiated and publicised
> it cannot stop there. It must be kept up to date in the light of changing
> expectations and events, and it must be monitored to see if it is
> working effectively.[16]

The duty to which the Director was referring is contained in section
124(3). This states that it shall be the duty of the Director to encourage
relevant associations to prepare, and to disseminate to their members, codes
of practice for guidance in safeguarding and promoting the interests of
UK consumers.

Creation of a new code or modification of an existing one should be
quicker than legislation. No parliamentary time is needed, only the
endorsement of the Director. In some cases, for example changes to the
Association of British Travel Agents' (ABTA) Codes, this may occur
regularly and quickly, whereas in other areas, for example car auctions,
negotiations were conducted over several years without an OFT approved
code materialising. The advantage of the voluntary or self-regulating code
is that it is tailor-made for the problems commonly met in a particular
industry, and can thus be more detailed and specific than is practicable in
legislation.

On the other hand a code, being voluntary, lacks any direct way of
enforcing it. A trade association may reprimand erring members, fine them
or ultimately expel them. Expelled members can, of course, still trade freely
as there is no legal requirement of membership and unless there is publicity
for expulsions, members of the public will not know of misdeeds. Some
trade organisations are reluctant to publicise miscreants lest their industry

15   See M, H & P ch 10; *Models of Self-regulation*, NCC, October 1999; *Self-
     regulation: Interm report*, Better .Regulation Task Force, October 1999;
     Alternatives to State Regulation, Better Regulation Task Force, July 2000.
16   1976 HCP 288, pp 9-10.

is tainted. Others wish to draw attention to their 'strict' control of members. Expulsion from a trade association or adverse notice from the OFT can be powerful indirect sanctions. This is particularly so if breaches are not widespread among members, if valuable benefits accrue from membership and if public awareness of the trade association and the benefits derived from the code is high, for example with the ABTA codes. One major disadvantage is that a voluntary code drawn up with an association can only be 'binding' on members of that association. Rogue operators are much less likely to join trade associations than honest and experienced traders.

In 1980 the OFT engaged Professor Pickering to investigate whether OFT sponsored codes had been beneficial to consumers. He concluded that 'the net effects of the Codes of Practice investigated are likely to have been beneficial on balance.'[17] He did, however, believe they had only a slight impact on consumer and trader behaviour and he made recommendations for future consideration by the OFT. Over a period of time many commentators have voiced criticisms of these codes. Some criticisms centre on the modest nature of the 'guarantees' given to the customer,[18] others with more general criticisms of the ineffectiveness of the codes.[19]

By 1982 the Director conceded that:

some measures of self-regulation may prove to be less effective than was hoped ... self-regulatory codes have two principal weaknesses. First, they cannot be enforced against non-members – this may be felt to put member-firms, who are likely to be the more responsible

17 See *Voluntary Codes of Practice: A consultation paper*, OFT, December 1996, para 2.4; *Raising Standards of Consumer Care: Progressing Beyond Codes of Practice*, OFT, February 1998, para 2.5; J F Pickering and D C Cousins 'The Benefits and Costs of Voluntary Codes of Practice' (1982) (No 6) European Journal of Marketing, 31; M, H & P pp 509-511.

18 See S E Marsh 'Voluntary Codes of Practice' (1977) 127 NLJ 419, G Borrie 'Laws and Codes for Consumers' [1980] JBL 315; R G Lawson (1977) 121 Sol Jo 4; A G Page [1980] JBL 24; *A general duty to trade fairly, A discussion paper*, OFT, 1986, ch 3; R B Ferguson 'Legal Status of Non-statutory Codes of Practice' [1988] JBL 15; G Borrie 'Consumer Protection Laws for the 1990's' [1988] JBL 116.

19 See, for example, problems identified by OFT in 1987: *Voluntary Codes of Practice: A consultation paper*, OFT, December 1996, para 2.7; *Raising Standards of Consumer Care: Progressing Beyond Codes of Practice*, OFT, February 1998, para 2.6. For the pros and cons of codes see also *A general duty to trade fairly, A discussion paper*, OFT, August 1986, ch 3, paras 3.8-3.18; Borrie *The Development of Consumer Law and Policy* pp 74-75; *Models of self-regulation*, NCC, October 1999, ch 3; *Self-regulation: Interim report*, Better Regulation Task Force, October 1999, pp 4-5 and M, H & P pp 499-500 and 507-511.

Voluntary codes of practice

traders, at a competitive disadvantage. Secondly, codes are difficult to enforce, even against members.[20]

He gave, as an example, difficulties encountered with the Motor Agents' Association Code and the requirement of displaying a pre-sales information report on used cars.

In 1991 the Director and the OFT announced[1] the adoption of a new approach regarding codes. Instead of becoming involved in detailed negotiations over the wording of codes, endorsement is now given for those codes which meet a series of criteria, setting out what the OFT regards as 'best practice'. The guidelines provided require the trade association to have a significant influence on the sector concerned, with compliance with the code as mandatory on members. Consultation with, inter alia, consumer organisations and enforcement bodies is needed in preparing the code and the OFT must be consulted on competition aspects. The code must give genuine benefits to consumers beyond legal requirements, setting high standards and seeking to remove undesirable practices. There are requirements concerning provision of information to customers, publicity for the code and those complying with it, and availability of copies of the code. Adequate complaints handling machinery is needed, with a conciliation service and a low-cost independent scheme of redress as an alternative to court action. Monitoring of the code by the trade association is required, with annual reports provided. Penalties for non-compliance must be instituted and, where appropriate, mechanisms established to ensure that judgments against members are met, in the event of members defaulting. From 1993, an element of independence in both redress and disciplinary procedures has been added.

In December 1996 the OFT commenced a major consultation on the operation of codes of practice,[2] which led to a report in 1998[3] and a conference later that year.[4] Consideration of the OFT proposals for a new initiative regarding codes of practice and the latest Government responses are discussed below.[5]

The main features of the OFT supported codes, which vary in some details, can be gathered from a short summary of those at present in existence. The conciliation and arbitration provisions require further explanation. Initially, under some of the trade association arbitration

20   *Director General's Report for 1982*, 1983 HCP 20, p 11. See also *The Motor Code – A Report on a Monitoring Survey*, OFT, September 1986, paras 7.8 and 7.19.

1   See *Bee Line* No 91/1, pp 3 and 24-25 and M, H & P pp 500-503.

2   *Voluntary Codes of Practice: A consultation paper*, OFT, December 1996.

3   *Raising Standards of Consumer Care: Progressing Beyond Codes of Practice*, OFT, February 1998.

4   *Raising Standards of Consumer Care: Conference Report*, OFT, February 1999.

5   See p 377.

schemes, attended hearings before an arbitrator were offered, instead of the case being heard on a 'documents only' basis. This led to difficulties.[6] In some cases the costs of the hearing considerably exceeded any damages awarded. As a result of adverse publicity, the Director asked the trade associations offering attended hearings to inform consumers of the potential expense involved and that it could be more expensive than taking action in the courts. In September 1980 a consultation document entitled *Redress Procedures under Codes of Practice* was issued by the OFT and this was followed, in December 1981, by a report of the same name. These both proposed a documents-only arbitration scheme. A new model arbitration scheme, based on the OFT proposals, was introduced by the Chartered Institute of Arbitrators in 1983. Most of the schemes are administered by the Chartered Institute, although some use independent panels of arbitrators.[7]

The use of the trade association arbitration schemes is at the option of the customer with the complaint. There may, however, be a contractual agreement to submit a dispute to arbitration. If a customer signs a contract with an individual supplier of goods or services, and this contract contains a '*Scott v Avery* clause' stipulating that no right of action shall accrue until the amount of damages has been ascertained by arbitration, this could bar a court action, since it is a defence to court proceedings that arbitration has not taken place as agreed.[8] The Arbitration Act 1996, sections 89-91, prevent compulsory arbitration for consumers in certain circumstances. Section 91 provides that a term which constitutes an arbitration agreement is 'unfair', under the Unfair Terms in Consumer Contracts Regulations 1999,[9] if the dispute concerns a claim for compensation which does not exceed the specified limit. The current specified limit for England, Scotland and Wales is £5,000;[10] for Northern Ireland it is £3,000.[11] Although the 1999 Regulations are limited to consumers who are natural persons,[12] the Arbitration Act 1996 extends protection regarding arbitration agreements to consumers who are legal persons also (s 90). An option to go to arbitration under a voluntary code obviously involves no contract to do

---

6   For an assessment of consumer satisfaction with the trade association arbitration schemes see *Simple Justice*, NCC, 1979, ch 10; *Out of Court*, NCC, 1991; *Consumer Redress Mechanisms*, OFT, 1991, paras 4.47-4.57.

7   See E Brennan 'Data from Consumers' Association: Arbitration v the Small Claims Court' (1993) 2 Consumer Policy Review 79.

8   *Scott v Avery* (1856) 5 HL Cas 811. See above p 231.

9   SI 1999/2083, see further pp 138-143.

10   Unfair Arbitration Agreements (Specified Amount) Order 1999, SI 1999/2167.

11   Unfair Arbitration Agreements (Specified Amount) Order (Northern Ireland) 1996, SI 1996/598.

12   See Unfair Terms in Consumer Contracts Regulations 1999, SI 1999/2083, reg 3(1) discussed at p 139.

so, but once arbitration is in fact agreed to in writing then this can be enforced.[13]

Two reports, published in 1991, examined the operation of consumer arbitration schemes and made proposals for improvements. First the National Consumer Council, in *Out of Court*, examined three low-cost arbitration schemes: those of the Association of British Travel Agents,[14] the Glass and Glazing Federation[15] and British Telecom. The report, which involved surveys and questionnaires, produced a number of recommendations for improvements.[16] These included greater publicity for and commitment to arbitration, annual reports for each scheme, the option of personal hearings, some improvements in the information provided about the schemes, a speeding up of the process and specific recommendations for each of the three schemes studied. It was also felt that more research into the operation of conciliation was needed. Second, the OFT, in *Consumer Redress Mechanisms*,[17] also advocated greater publicity for the schemes and the production of annual reports. Consideration should be given to the idea of trade organisations providing independent conciliation services and the possibility of a common redress scheme was mooted. The suggestion of personal hearings being reintroduced was not supported.

3.   INFORMATION ABOUT CODES

Included below are brief details[18] of the OFT-approved codes of practice currently in operation. The OFT publishes explanatory leaflets on some of the codes; these are indicated where relevant.

Cars

There are two Codes concerning the sale and repair of cars: the Code of Practice for the Motor Industry and the Vehicle Builders and Repairers Association's Code of Practice. Some information about these Codes can be found in the OFT leaflet 'Buying a Used Car'.

---

13   Arbitration Act 1996, s 5. See also the discussion of arbitration in ch 8.
14   See below p 373. See also R Fernihough 'The Holidays from Hell' (1997) 105 ITSA 10 MR 10.
15   See below p 370.
16   See *Out of Court*, NCC, 1991, pp 72-73.
17   See paras 4.36-4.57 and ch 6.
18   For the full texts of a number of these codes see *Butterworths Trading and Consumer Law* Div 4 and 5.

Joint Code of the Society of Motor Manufacturers and Traders, the Retail Motor Industry Federation Ltd and the Scottish Motor Trade Association

This Joint Code (as revised in 1981) covers the advertising, sale, repair and servicing of new and used cars. Advertising controls include prohibition of misleading comparisons of models and pricing must make clear what is included and excluded. New car sales are governed by testing schedules and pre-delivery inspection checklists should be given to the customer, order forms and warranties must be clear, unexpired warranties must be transferable, and rectification work on a warranty must be capable of being done by any franchised dealer, not just the vendor dealer. Used cars are also subject to pre-sales inspections, mileage must be verified (or the customer told that the mileage is not verified) and where possible a signed statement from the previous owner as to mileage should be obtained and all relevant information such as service records, repair invoices, handbooks and warranties handed to the purchaser. Members must reveal any defects on an approved checklist which must be prominently displayed in the car and given to the customer before any sale. Repairs and servicing are governed by stipulations including the requirements of specifying minimum periods for the availability of spare parts by manufacturers, of giving where possible firm quotations for the cost of major repairs (with estimates also for major servicing) and of guarantees of workmanship for a specified mileage or period. With regard to complaints, if conciliation fails, 'low-cost' arbitration can be provided as an alternative to court proceedings. The arbitrator's award is binding not only as between manufacturer or dealer and customer, but also, where appropriate, between manufacturer and dealer.

This Code had been the subject of monitoring exercises by the OFT and three reports (in 1978, 1980 and 1986) have been produced.[19]

Vehicle Builders and Repairers Association (VBRA)

This Code, which has been periodically updated, governs the conduct of VBRA members carrying out vehicle body repairs and includes a comprehensive complaints and arbitration procedure. Written estimates must be offered, detailed invoices supplied, a minimum of 24 months' or 24,000 miles guarantee of materials and workmanship provided, and reasonable care of vehicles in the charge of members exercised.

An early version of this Code was monitored by the OFT in 1986.[20]

19 See *Bee Line* Special Edition Research Papers Nos 4 and 7 and *The Motor Code: A Report on a Monitoring Survey*, September 1986.
20 See *The Code of Practice for Vehicle Body Repair: A Report on a Monitoring Survey*, OFT, November 1986.

Credit

To date six codes relating to the credit industry have been negotiated.

Consumer Credit Association of the United Kingdom

The Consumer Credit Association (CCA(UK)) was the first organisation in the consumer credit market to launch a Code in 1984. The updated version of 1989 achieved OFT approval. The CCA has over 600 member businesses in six main areas of the unsecured credit market namely personal loans, credit sales, hire purchase, checks/vouchers, running account and hire/rental. The Code covers such matters as credit brokerage, checking the creditworthiness of consumers, debt collection and default procedures and complaint handling. An arbitration scheme is included.

Consumer Credit Trade Association (CCTA)

A Code was launched in 1988 and was derived originally from the Finance Houses Association Code of Practice (see below) with modifications to suit CCTA members, involving hire purchase, store credit cards and personal loans. In 1995 a revised Code was issued, based on the Finance and Leasing Association Code of Practice (see below). The CCTA has approximately 650 members, including finance houses, retailers and building societies. To avoid conflict with the work of the Building Societies Ombudsman, the Code does not apply to building societies who are members of CCTA. Conciliation and arbitration schemes operate.

Credit Services Association (CSA)

This Code was agreed in January 1991 and has since been updated. The CSA represents debt-collecting agencies and the Code sets out guidelines of good business conduct in the collection of debts. In consumer transactions the Code requires the use of plain English, headed notepaper and clear identification of staff. Consumers must be given prior written notification of any collection charges, which must be fair and reasonable. Guidelines are provided on collection procedures. There is a complaints procedure and a conciliation scheme.

Finance and Leasing Association

The Finance Houses Association (FHA), which represented providers of instalment credit, launched its Code in 1987. In 1992 the FHA merged with the Equipment Leasing Association to form the Finance and Leasing Association and together they launched a revised Code in March 1993. The latest version of the Code came into operation on 1 September 2000. The Code encourages responsible attitudes in granting credit, and leasing and hiring goods. It covers the terms and conditions of contracts, payment protection insurance, the marketing and provision of credit, the use of credit-brokers and credit-scoring techniques and requires monitoring of credit-granting practices and debt-collecting procedures. Conciliation and arbitration schemes operate.

London Personal Finance Association Ltd (LPFA)

Introduced in 1989, this Code is based on the original FHA Code (see above). The LPFA has approximately 120 members representing both individuals and companies. Both conciliation and arbitration schemes operate.

National Consumer Credit Federation

In 1989 the Federation adopted the original FHA Code (see above) on behalf of its members who are concerned with short-term shopping check business and companies who collect repayments of loans from customers' homes. A revised code commenced in 1995. The code requires care to be taken in the granting of credit, confidentiality in dealings, and the monitoring of credit-brokers and debt-collecting procedures. Conciliation and arbitration schemes operate.

Direct selling

This Code of Practice, commenced in February 1980, with the latest revision in 1997, is aimed particularly at the practice of selling goods at parties and by door-to-door salesmen.

The main points of the Code are: a) invitations to meetings will make the purpose of the meeting clear to customers; b) invitees will be informed that there is no obligation to purchase and will be provided with contact details; c) provision for cancellation of orders within a minimum of 14 days, and the consequential refund of deposits; d) when placing orders, customers will be given a copy of the order which must indicate where queries or complaints should be referred; e) the Association provides a conciliation service on disputes referred to it, f) copies of the Code of Practice will be made available to customers. The Code Administrator can adjudicate in cases of dispute.

The DSA publish consumer information leaflets and operate a web site which contains the main points of this Code.

Electrical goods and servicing

There are three Codes concerned with the sale and servicing of electrical goods. These are: the Association of Manufacturers of Domestic Electrical Appliances (AMDEA) Code, the Radio, Electrical and Television Retailers' Association (RETRA) Code and the Code on Extended Warranties on Electrical Goods.

The electrical Codes were the subject of OFT monitoring in 1979[1]. As a result of this changes were made to the AMDEA Code.

Association of Manufacturers of Domestic Electrical Appliances

The AMDEA Code was launched in 1975, the latest revision being 1999. It requires members to provide an appointment for servicing equipment at a user's home within two working days and complete at least 80 per cent of all service jobs on the first visit, and the remaining 20 per cent within 9 working days. Service appointments when made should be kept. Repair work and parts are provided with guarantees and detailed invoices have to be provided. On the important matter of spare parts, the Code requires manufacturers to stock sufficient parts to service current models and to maintain them for a minimum period after production ceases (eg 10 years for washing machines). AMDEA assists with conciliation and an independent system of arbitration is also available.

Radio Electrical and Television Retailers' Association (RETRA)

This Association represents more than 4,000 firms including the majority of companies with multiple outlets. The Code was launched in 1976. All members are required to give a comprehensive 12-month guarantee, covering parts and labour, when selling new electrical appliances, radios and television sets. This is in addition to any manufacturer's guarantee. Members unable to repair appliances under guarantee within 15 days must supply a replacement or, if impractical, extend the period of the guarantee by the number of days over which the customer is deprived of his use of the appliance. Repairs are to be guaranteed for three months and completed within 15 days of any visit made. Deposits must be refunded for goods not

1   *Bee Line* Special Edition Research Paper No 8 (1980).

available on time and receipts, detailed invoices and other information given to customers. Disputes may be referred by customer or member to the Secretary of RETRA and from there, if still unresolved, to the RETRA Customer Conciliation Panel.

Code on Extended Warranties on Electrical Goods

In response to the OFT Report on Extended Warranties on Electrical Goods[2] the Retail Consortium, the Association of British Insurers and RETRA (see above) introduced a Code of Practice on Extended Warranties for Electrical Goods. The Code, which was amended in 1998, concerns information to be provided at point of sale, including prices, terms and conditions, cancellation rights etc, contractual documentation, and insured and uninsured warranties. A monitoring system for compliance is also included.

Footwear

There are two Codes concerned with the sale and repair of footwear. The OFT has published an explanatory leaflet 'Buying and Repairing Shoes' referring to the Codes.

National Association of Multiple Shoe Repairers and British Shoe Repair Council

Members of the above two Associations are responsible for about 85 per cent of shoe repairs in the UK. The Code includes a prohibition on members' limiting their liability for repairs carried out, a stipulation that prices for repairs inclusive of VAT will be displayed and customers should be issued with a ticket showing the cost and estimated date for collection. 'Worth', 'value' and 'price elsewhere' claims will not be made (and will in any event usually be contrary to pricing provisions), and where disputes cannot be resolved a test report will be obtained and honoured.

Footwear Distributors' Federation

This Code was introduced in 1976 and is designed to improve customer relations and to ensure that more information is provided about shoes.

2   December 1994.

Adherence to the Code is not obligatory on members of the FDF – only those members displaying the Code symbol must comply with it. This aspect has been criticised by the OFT. A Footwear Testing Centre has been set up, and customers may send shoes which are the subject matter of a dispute between them and the retailer to the Centre for testing and a report. If this is favourable, the customer's contribution to the test fee will be refunded. The Code also provides that all retailers of children's footwear will provide facilities for measuring children's feet, all prices shown will include VAT, footwear will be labelled to show the material from which uppers and soles are made (leather or some other material), though this does not apply to wellington boots, plimsolls and most slippers. The Code has been monitored three times, in 1978, 1980 and 1985.[3]

Glass and glazing

The Glass and Glazing Federation's (GGF) Code of Ethical Practice was introduced in November 1981. Following the publication of *The Glass and Glazing Code: A Report on Monitoring Surveys* by the OFT in 1987, a revised Code was issued in 1988. Under the Code both the products and the installations are required to comply with the relevant BSI Codes of Practice and GGF Standards. Delivery periods and completion dates have to be provided and if the customer has made time of the essence, work uncompleted after six weeks may be cancelled without penalty. The Code also provides a right of cancellation for both cash and credit contracts which have been negotiated away from business premises. A Deposit Indemnity Fund is available to ensure the return of deposits or the completion of work in the event of a member going out of business. A conciliation and arbitration scheme is provided.[4]

Holiday caravans

Following a Monopolies and Mergers Commission Report on holiday caravans in Northern Ireland (in July 1983) the Director began negotiations with the National Caravan Council and the British Holiday and Home Parks Association Ltd with a view to introducing a national Code. Two such Codes were finally introduced in January 1987, both of which offer conciliation and arbitration services. A revised version of the Selling and Siting Holiday Caravans Code was agreed in 1997.

---

3   *Bee Line* Special Edition Research Papers Nos 5 (1978) and 9 (1980).
4   For a detailed examination of the operation of the arbitration scheme see *Out of Court*, NCC, 1991.

Code of Practice for Letting Holiday Caravans

The Code requires caravan park owners to ensure that park facilities function correctly, site licence conditions are satisfied and staff are available during all reasonable hours. The condition of the caravans to be let is specified under the letting obligations and detailed information concerning the sites and the caravans must be sent to enquirers.

Code of Practice for Selling and Siting Holiday Caravans

The 1997 Code is concerned with the sale and siting of permanently sited caravans. It lays down terms as to tenure of pitches, the length of notice required to remove a caravan and to increase pitch fees. Details of the information to be included in written agreements for pitches are stipulated and rights regarding the resale of caravans and the substantial alteration of park arrangements are also included.

Introduction agencies

The Association of British Introduction Agencies had their Code of Practice approved by the Director in March 1995. The Code lays down standards of practice for introduction and dating agencies and marriage bureaux, concerning the matching of clients, the number of introductions, fees and refunds. Advertising is also regulated. There is a complaint handling procedure, a conciliation service and an arbitration scheme administered by the Chartered Institute of Arbitrators.

Laundry

The Textile Services Association Ltd (formerly ABLC)

This 1991 Code prohibits members from excluding liability for negligence by 'small print clauses',[5] and requiring them to pay fair compensation for loss or damage to property for which they are responsible. Members are also required to display current prices and to give customers a receipt showing the charge and the date for collection. Complaints about the quality of the work should be met by reprocessing the article free of charge.

5   For examples of written exemption clauses rendered ineffective by verbal misrepresentation see *Curtis v Chemical Cleaning and Dyeing Co Ltd* [1951] 1 KB 805, [1951] 1 All ER 631, CA (dry cleaning) and *J Evans & Son (Portsmouth) Ltd v Andrea Merzario Ltd* [1976] 2 All ER 930, [1976] 1 WLR 1078, CA (carriage of goods).

Disputes may be settled through the Association's Customer Advisory Service which will provide a free technical report if the TSA considers it necessary.

Mail order trading

There are two Codes involved with mail order trading: the Direct Marketing Association Code of Practice, covering direct marketing activities, and the Mail Order Traders' Association Code, covering catalogue sales. An OFT leaflet entitled 'Buying by Post' covers the Codes.

The Direct Marketing Association Code of Practice

In 1993 the British Direct Marketing Association merged with, inter alia, the Association of Mail Order Publishers to form the Direct Marketing Association and launched a new Code, incorporating many features from the organisations' previous Codes. The second edition of the Code (1997) covers all forms of direct marketing including advertisers, agencies, database practitioners and mailing houses and suppliers. It deals with such matters as telephone marketing, direct or door-step selling, prize draws and competitions, collectibles and client service. There is a conciliation service provided by the Direct Marketing Authority, which has been established to provide independent adjudication of complaints.

Mail Order Traders' Association (MOTA)

This Code was launched in 1978 by MOTA which represents the leading firms selling goods through catalogues with part-time agents as intermediaries between the companies and their customers. The 1999 version of the Code requires that the catalogues must contain the trading name of the advertiser and an address for enquiries and complaints, full information about the size, colour, materials, price including VAT and non-optional extras and restrictions on use for goods advertised. The goods must be dispatched 'on approval' without prior payment unless otherwise stated and customers have a minimum of 14 days in which to change their minds. A conciliation scheme is provided and if this does not satisfactorily resolve the dispute then there is also an arbitration scheme.

Mechanical breakdown insurance schemes

Operated by the Society of Motor Manufacturers and Traders (SMMT), a Code of Practice was adopted in 1989 covering what are often referred to as extended warranties. The Code provides that such schemes must be underwritten either by an insurance company or by a Lloyd's syndicate. It requires documentation in the form of booklets or certificates, written as a direct contract between the motorist and the insurer. If a dispute arises this can be referred to the Personal Insurance Arbitration Scheme or the Insurance Ombudsman, depending upon membership. There are also conciliation procedures with SMMT, Lloyd's Consumer Enquiries Department and the Association of British Insurers.

Motorcycles

A Code of Practice for the motorcycle industry was drawn up in 1984 by four organisations representing motorcycle manufacturers (the Motor Cycle Association) and retailers (the Motor Agents' Association, now the Retail Motor Industry Federation Ltd, the Scottish Motor Trade Association and the Motorcycle Retailers' Association, now the Motorcycle Association of Great Britain). The Code covers the supply of new and used motorcycles, parts and accessories, servicing and repairs. It requires the transfer of manufacturers' warranties on new motorcycles to subsequent owners and the inspection of used motorcycles, with a checklist to be made available to purchasers. In connection with repairs and servicing, quotations or estimates are to be provided, with repairs guaranteed for a specific time period or mileage. The Code provides a conciliation and arbitration service.

Package holidays

Association of British Travel Agents

ABTA operates a Code of Conduct for travel agents and tour operators. It is regularly updated to take into account new situations and problems. The Code (May 2000) specifies the standards of service to be provided. There are provisions relating to brochures, advertising and promotion, and booking conditions and procedures, including on-line transactions. Measures deal with significant alterations to travel arrangements, including compensation requirements, overbooking and building work. Principals (tour operators) must accept responsibility for the proper performance of the contract, subject to certain exceptions and for the acts and/or omissions of their employees, agents, sub-contractors and suppliers. They may not exclude liability for misrepresentations or for failure to exercise reasonable care and skill in making the holiday arrangements. Also prohibited are clauses barring claims if not made within a fixed period if this is unreasonably short. The Code also covers relations between tour operators and travel agents. Travel agents are required to give accurate information and keep clients fully informed. There are provisions relating to insurance, passports, visa and health requirements.

ABTA ceased operating its conciliation service in 1991[6] as it was suggested this delayed dispute resolution. Instead it has replaced it with a Consumer Affairs Department to monitor complaints against members, determine whether or not breaches have occurred and advise complainants on pursuing a remedy. In the case of disputes with a tour operator, the holidaymaker may either choose to go to arbitration under a scheme administered by the Institute of Arbitrators[7] or to court. This choice may be made after the extent of the loss has been calculated. The arbitration scheme does not apply to claims for more than £1,500 per person or £7,500 per booking form, nor does it apply to claims which are solely or mainly in respect of physical injury or illness. Alleged breaches of the Code are considered by the Code of Conduct Committee.

Earlier versions of the ABTA Code has been monitored by the OFT in 1978 and 1988.[8]

Photographic industry

A Code of Practice for the photographic industry came into operation in May 1979 and was revised in 1986. It is supported by eight trade associations representing all sectors of the industry. The main provisions for retailers are: a) retailers must provide informed information about the products which they sell; b) the manufacturer's guarantee will be available for inspection before purchase; c) delivery dates must be quoted in writing when a deposit is taken and refunds offered when those dates cannot be met; d) price lists for developing films will be displayed and customers given a receipt stating the estimated collection date; e) repairs are normally to be carried out within 21 days and customers to be warned if there is unforeseen delay or substantially more cost involved than was originally estimated; f) retailers will carry out detailed inspection of all second-hand equipment before sale and will guarantee second-hand items whenever possible.

6   See *Bee Line* 91/2, p 6.
7   For a detailed examination of the operation of the arbitration scheme see *Out of Court*, NCC, 1991 and E Brennan 'Data from Consumers' Association: Arbitration v The Small Claims Court' (1993) 2 Consumer Policy Review 79. See also R Fernihough 'Holidays from Hell' (1997) ITSA 10 MR 10.
8   *Bee Line* Special Edition Research Paper No 3 (1978) and *The Package Holiday Codes: A Report on Monitoring Surveys*, OFT, July 1988.

Manufacturers have complementary duties to the above and must maintain stocks of spare parts for at least five years following the last sale to the trade. There are also provisions relating to professional photographers concerning information about fee structures and the quality of work produced. A conciliation and arbitration scheme is provided.

Residential estate agency

The 1997 Code of Practice for Residential Estate Agents applies to members of the Ombudsman for Estate Agents Scheme and has also been adopted by the Incorporated Society of Valuers and Auctioneers, the National Association of Estate Agents and the Royal Institution of Chartered Surveyors. It regulates the terms on which the agent acts, including when fees become due and withdrawal of instructions, controls the erection of 'For Sale' boards, publicity material, the handling of offers, access to premises, clients' money, conflicts of interest and the supply of financial services. The Ombudsman for Estate Agents Scheme[9] provides opportunities for conciliation and redress.

Tickets

The Society of Ticket Agents and Retailers (STAR) was formed in 1997, with the support of the OFT, the British Tourist Authority, the London Tourist Board and the Society of London Theatres. Its membership includes companies and organisations in the business of reselling tickets and operating entertainment venues selling tickets directly to the public. The Code of Practice requires that enquiries and bookings should be handled courteously. The face value of tickets and any service charges or booking fees must be disclosed and terms and conditions must be fully explained, including any restrictions on transferability. There are provisions for telephone bookings and dispatching tickets and documentation. A complaint handling procedure is specified and conciliation services are provided.

Tyre and fast fit industry

The National Tyre Distributors Association, which represents 65% of the tyre and fast fit industry, agreed a Code in November 1995.[10] It regulates

9   See further p 222.
10   See M, H & P p 503.

advertising, the provision of replacement tyres and fast fit motor components, requires detailed invoices to be provided, and prevents disclaimers avoiding legal liability for loss of or damage to property. A conciliation and arbitration service is provided.

Vehicle rental and leasing

The British Vehicle Rental and Leasing Association, whose members deal with over 85 per cent of vehicles operated in the rental leasing and fleet management industry, introduced a Code of Practice in April 1995. The Code establishes standards of good practice with rental and leasing and fleet management charters. Provisions relating to vehicle suitability, safety, insurance, pre-rental checks, refuelling charges and methods of payment are included. There is a complaint-handling mechanism and a conciliation procedure.

Criminal enforcement of voluntary codes of practice

It is, of course, a weakness of voluntary or self-enforcing codes of practice that they, by definition, bind only those traders who are members of an appropriate association. But, as regards trade association members, are the sanctions sufficient? Disciplinary action by the trade association may be taken but this does not always result in justice being seen to be done. It has been argued that a representation that a trader is adhering to a particular code of practice is akin to a statement that certain known services or facilities are provided. The provisions of the codes contain statements of fact, and therefore if the requisite 'statement' as to adherence to the facilities which go with the Code is made falsely or recklessly, an offence under the Trade Descriptions Act 1968, section 14 has been committed.[11] In one case adjudicated upon by a magistrates' court the defendant car traders had misdescribed the car mileage on a used model and were charged that they 'in the course of trade or business recklessly made a statement which was false as to the provision of a service in the course of trade or business by a notice which read' that they subscribed to the Motor Agents' Association Code of Practice. The court convicted.[12]

---

11   See A J Street (1979) 87 ITSA Monthly Review 63.
12   See *Re V G Vehicles (Telford) Ltd* (1981) 89 ITSA Monthly Review 91. See also *R v Piper* (1996) 160 JP 116 re false claim of membership of the Guild of Master Craftsmen, offence under s 14(1) Trade Descriptions Act 1968.

4. TRADING MALPRACTICES

It has been accepted for many years that Codes of Practice, in their present form, do not always provide consumers with adequate protection from rogue traders. Lord Borrie, when Director, therefore, on a number of occasions[13] mooted the idea of introducing a general duty to trade fairly linked to the codes of practice. Following consultations, in August 1986, the OFT published *A general duty to trade fairly – A discussion paper.* The document made provisional recommendations that the existing civil and criminal laws could be supplemented by the introduction of a broad statutory duty to trade fairly. This would be supported by Codes of Practice, both vertical (by trading practice) and horizontal (by sector), which set out the trading practices regarded as acceptable or unacceptable. Resulting from the comments received and further consideration of the proposals, the Director published *Trading Malpractices* in July 1990. The arguments for and against a general duty to trade fairly were presented[14] and, on balance, the Director decided against pursuing the idea of a general duty.

Sir Gordon recognised that it was not possible within one measure both to raise trading standards generally and to assist in providing redress for consumers. The report, therefore, favoured concentrating 'directly on tackling unlawful, deceptive or objectionable trading practices which have not been, or cannot be, controlled effectively by existing legislation' (para 1.6). To achieve this a radical overhaul of Part III of the Fair Trading Act 1973 (discussed above) was proposed.

In 1996, John Bridgeman, as Director, returned to the question of codes with the publication of *Voluntary Codes of Practice: A consultation paper.*[15] This identified a number of problems with codes (see para 2.7) and set out policy options ranging from ceasing to give OFT support to codes to introducing codes with statutory force. The Report, *Raising Standards of Consumer Care: Progressing beyond codes of practice,*[16] advocated the creation of a new regime for codes. A core standard was proposed, with a number of sector-specific standards, based on the principles of the core standard. An independent body, assisted by

13   See, for example, G Borrie 'Laws and Codes for Consumers' [1980] JBL 315; *Home Improvements – A Discussion Paper*, OFT, March 1982, ch 6; *Home Improvements: A Report by the Director General of Fair Trading*, June 1983, ch 12; M, H & P pp 507-508; G Borrie *The Development of Consumer Law and Policy*, pp 75-78.

14   *Trading Malpractices*, OFT, 1990, pp 20-22.

15   OFT, December 1996.

16   OFT, February 1998. See also *Raising Standards of Consumer Care: Report on a conference at new Hall College, Cambridge by the Office of Fair Trading, 22 September 1998*, OFT February 1999; 'Raising the standard', OFT, (1998) 18 Fair Trading 8; A Wilson and R McArthur 'Fair Trading' (1998) 8 Consumer Policy Review, 138.

consumers and traders, would be required to draw up the standards, these being made under the auspices of the British Standards Institution. A new approvals body would be needed to organise accreditation schemes, the use of logos, the maintenance of a directory of approved firms, a redress scheme and disciplinary procedures.

The government, in the White Paper *Modern markets: confident consumers*,[17] sought to 'create a climate where consumers' natural choice is to seek out a business that meets the terms of a good code or has its own reputation for equal or higher standards' (para 4.5). It proposed the establishment of core principles for effective codes, with the OFT having responsibility for the operation of the scheme. The Better Regulation Task Force, meanwhile, gave encouragement to the use of alternatives to state regulation and advised the government to develop and publish guidance for policy makers on them.[18] Most recently, the DTI has published a *Policy Paper on Codes of Practice*,[19] which proposes giving the Director an enhanced role regarding codes and provides some details of how this might operate. Further developments are awaited.

It can be seen that, having initially centred on codes of practice as a starting point for improving trading standards, this approach fell out of favour for a while. More recently codes have experienced somewhat of a renaissance and now feature quite prominently in government proposals, albeit in conjunction with enhanced procedures and powers under Part III of the Fair Trading Act 1973. Any major changes are likely to be dependent upon statutory modification and thus will have to wait for parliamentary time to be available.

5.   BRIEF ASSESSMENT

This chapter has, it is hoped, given an impression which does not purport to be comprehensive, of the functions, powers and activities of the Director and the OFT outside the duties relating to competition policy, consumer credit, advertising and unfair contract terms. It has concentrated on activities under Parts II and III of the Fair Trading Act 1973 and with codes of practice. This does not, however, fully reflect the Director's activities in the field of consumer protection. The Directors and the OFT have been very active both in informing consumers and traders of their rights and obligations via leaflets, posters, booklets, etc and also in proposing, introducing and supporting moves to improve the protection afforded to consumers. This has been done often by examining the practices of

17   DTI, July 1999, Cm 4410, ch 4.
18   *Alternatives to State Regulation*, July 2000, ch 6.
19   March 2000, http://www.dti.gov.uk/consumer/law/2.htm.

reputable traders and encouraging wider adoption of such practices, to the benefit of both traders and consumers. A glance at any annual report of the Director and *Fair Trading* illustrates the range of activities. Areas covered include financial services, insurance, marriage bureaux, prepayments for goods and services, guarantees and extended warranties, cars (selling and repairing), one-day sales, home improvements, mail order protection schemes, telephone selling, care-homes for the elderly, pre-paid funerals and timeshare. The OFT has published its strategy on consumer affairs,[20] works to performance targets set out in its Code of Practice on Enforcement Activities[1] and reports annually.[2]

The Directors and the OFT have been, and no doubt will be, criticised by both consumer and trade interests for too little or too much activity, but on balance it must be said that there has been a beneficial impact on the field of consumer protection. In the words of Sir Gordon Borrie:

> As one man's keen business practice is another man's unfair trading, it is never easy to be the referee.[3]

---

20   *Consumer Affairs: the way forward*, October 1998; see also 'Taking aim', OFT, (1998) 21 Fair Trading 26.
1   See the OFT booklet *Helping You*, OFT107.
2   See *Annual Report of the Director General of Fair Trading 1999*, 2000 HCP 576, Appendix A.
3   *Annual Report for 1985* (HC Papers (1985-1986) No 403) at p 13.

Brief assessment

12 Trade descriptions, property misdescriptions and price indications

1. INTRODUCTION

Earlier chapters in this book have dealt with various examples of legislation aimed at the prohibition of false descriptions, hallmarking being an important and long standing example. Before the Trade Descriptions Act 1968 repealed them, the Merchandise Marks Acts 1887–1953 were the main body of legislation dealing specifically with the false or deceptive description of goods and the wrongful application of trade marks.

The Molony Committee received a considerable volume of evidence critical of the protection provided both to traders and consumers by the Merchandise Marks Acts.[1] Evidence was also given, inter alia, of misleading price claims, especially at times of seasonal or 'special' sales. It was doubtful if the Acts applied to these practices and, if they did, the penalties were by modern standards absurdly low.[2] The Committee also noted the widespread view that the Acts were laxly enforced, particularly by the Board of Trade.

The Report recommended reform under five heads:
a) removal of defects in the Acts making the meaning of the Acts obscure, their application unfair or their administration difficult;
b) extension and amendment of the definition of trade description;
c) incorporation in the Acts of a power to define imprecise or corrupt terms used in trade descriptions;
d) extension and amendment of the definition of applying a trade description;
e) improvement in the enforcement of the Acts.[3]

---

1   See Final Report, (1962) Cmnd 1781, Part V.
2   Ibid, paras 588, 589.
3   Ibid, para 575.

Introduction

Reform was implemented by the Trade Descriptions Act 1968.[4] It applies to Scotland, and with the modification necessary for a different legal and administrative system, to Northern Ireland (s 40). Since the Crown is not 'named' in the Act, it does not bind the Crown, HM Forces or Visiting Forces. State industries and public corporations are controlled and 'owned' by ad hoc bodies, which do not act for the Crown and they consequently cannot claim immunity.[5] The 1968 Act was extended in 1972 to require an indication of origin on certain imported goods but the 1972 Act was repealed in 1987 since its policy was regarded as in conflict with the Treaty of Rome.

A few general points can usefully be noted about the 1968 Act before its more important provisions are examined. First, it is necessary to appreciate that though its primary purpose is to protect the public, it extends to transactions between traders. Second, the 1968 Act widened the law that it replaced. The provisions relating to misdescription of goods are a modern adaptation of the law contained in the Merchandise Marks Acts, but section 11, which concerned false price indications, and section 14, covering false statements as to services, accommodation and facilities, were both new provisions. Third, under section 1, false trade descriptions of goods, there is no need to prove an intention to deceive or, indeed, any mens rea.[6] The Act does, however, lay down a number of defences in sections 24 and 25, which mitigate the rigour of what is, otherwise, strict liability. Section 14, on the other hand, applies only to statements as to services etc *known* to be false or made *recklessly*. Here mens rea is required; the reason perhaps being that, unlike section 1 offences, there was no precedent for this particular provision and caution in introducing it was desirable. In view of the difficulties surrounding this provision it is perhaps not without significance that it was omitted from the otherwise very similar Hong Kong Trade Descriptions Ordinance (1980). Fourth, the right to prosecute for an offence is not limited to local authorities.[7] Accordingly, as the common law right for any person, whether aggrieved or not, to prosecute in respect of an offence is not abrogated, private prosecutions may be brought. Finally, section 23 contains a provision familiar in consumer law statutes to the effect that if a person commits an offence due to the act or default of some other party, that other person is guilty of the offence whether or not the first mentioned is proceeded against.

---

4   See BSSCCL p 154.
5   See generally *Butterworths Trading and Consumer Law* (Butterworths Looseleaf Encyclopaedia). It is proposed to remove Crown Immunity, see DTI Consultation on Amendments to the Trade Descriptions Act 1968 (2000) para 24.
6   This was confirmed by the Divisional Court in *Alex Norman Garages Ltd v Phillips* (1984) 148 JP 741, [1985] RTR 164, DC. But the defendant must know that there *is* a trade description attached to the goods: see *Cottee v Douglas Seaton (Used Cars) Ltd* [1972] 3 All ER 750, [1972] 1 WLR 1408, DC, M, H & P p 615.
7   See *Snodgrass v Topping* (1952) 116 JP 332.

2. PENALTY FOR OFFENCES AND TIME LIMITS

Offences under the Act generally attract a penalty on summary conviction of a fine not exceeding £5,000[8] and on conviction on indictment of a fine without specific limit or imprisonment for up to two years or both. No prosecution may be commenced after the expiration of three years from the commission of the offence or one year from its discovery[9] by the prosecutor, whichever is the earlier (s 19). A magistrates' court may try an information laid at any time within twelve months from the commission of the offence. This is notwithstanding section 127 of the Magistrates' Courts Act 1980, which requires informations normally to be laid within six months from the time when the offence was committed (s 19(2)), unless the offence is triable 'either way', when the longer time limits specified above apply.

3. ENFORCEMENT

It is the duty of every weights and measures authority to enforce within its area the Act and orders made under it. An authority may be required to report to the Secretary of State who also has power to investigate complaints of non-enforcement by ordering a local enquiry. Authorities and their duly authorised officers have wide powers to make test purchases, enter premises and seize goods and documents (ss 27, 28). Obstruction of an officer acting in pursuance of the Act is an offence (s 29).

Under sections 222 and 223 of the Local Government Act 1972, a local authority may prosecute, defend or appear in any legal proceedings where it is expedient for the promotion or protection of the interests of the inhabitants of their area, and may authorise any member or officer to prosecute, defend or appear on its behalf in proceedings before a magistrates' court, whether or not the member or officer is a solicitor with a current practising certificate.

In practice proceedings are normally conducted by a solicitor employed by a local authority[10] or a senior member of staff of the Council's Trading

---

8   Section 18 as amended by the Criminal Law Act 1977, the Criminal Justice Act 1982, s 37 and the Criminal Justice Act 1991, s 17. The only purely summary offence in the 1968 Act is obstructing an authorised officer, which under s 29 attracts a maximum fine of £1,000 (being level 3 on the standard scale).

9   What 'discovery' involves was elucidated in *R v Beaconsfield Justices, ex p Johnson & Sons Ltd* (1985) 149 JP 535, DC where it was held, in effect, that 'discovery' occurs where the prosecuting authority becomes aware of the relevant facts even though admissible evidence to support those facts still needs to be obtained. The time limit in s 19(1) also applies to conspiracy to contravene s 1 of the 1968 Act (*R v Pain* [1986] BTLC 142, CA).

10   Normally the county council or metropolitan district (or 'unitary') council for the relevant area, or a London Borough Council: see redefinition of local weights and measures authorities in Weights and Measures Act 1985, s 69.

Standards Department. Local authorities are required to inform the Office of Fair Trading of the results of prosecutions brought, and results of convictions reported in 1998–99 were as follows:

False descriptions of goods (s 1 TDA 1968)	635
False or reckless statements as to services etc (s 14 TDA 1968)	154
False price claims (s 20 CPA 1987)	59
TOTAL	848

Total fines	£715,520
Total compensation	£129,923

Various terms of imprisonment were also imposed. (*Source*: Annual Report of Director of Fair Trading 1999.)

It may be noted that the Office of Fair Trading's Review of the Trade Descriptions Act 1968 (1976, Cmnd 6628), referred to throughout this chapter, recommended that the Director General of Fair Trading be given a national role as enforcer of the Act (para 224).

4. PROHIBITION OF FALSE TRADE DESCRIPTIONS

Section 1(1) states that:

Any person who, in the course of a trade or business–
a) applies a false trade description to any goods; or
b) supplies or offers to supply any goods to which a false trade description is applied;
shall, subject to the provisions of this Act, be guilty of an offence.

This subsection, which is the core of the Act, must be read in conjunction with sections 2 to 6 of the Act, which sections interpret and expand the expressions used in section 1(1) (s 1(2)).

To understand subsection (1) it is necessary to analyse a number of points in order, making reference to the first six sections where appropriate.

'Any person'

This includes a limited company.[11] Section 20 contains special provisions dealing with offences by corporations, making any director, manager,

11 Interpretation Act 1978, Sch 1.

secretary or other similar officer jointly liable if the offence is proved to have been committed with their consent or connivance. Although 'any person' will normally be the seller of goods, it is also possible for a buyer to apply a false description. In *Fletcher v Budgen*[12] a car dealer told a private customer that his car was irreparable and fit only for scrap. The dealer then bought it for £2, carried out repairs costing £56, obtained a test certificate and advertised it for sale at £135. The Divisional Court held that an offence could be committed by a buyer who applied a false trade description to the goods (eg 'fit only for scrap') where buying them in the course of his trade or business.

'In the course of a trade or business'

The Act is intended to penalise the dishonest business person rather than imposing strict criminal liability on private sellers who may or may not be strictly honest, though it appears that there may be an exception where section 23, considered below, can be used. (However, a dishonest private seller who, for instance, sells a car having tampered with the odometer, a factor affecting the price obtained, may well have obtained property by deception contrary to s 15 of the Theft Act 1968.) This expression is familiar in other areas of law such as income tax[13] and value added tax, and there have been a number of decisions on its meaning in the present context, there being no definition in the Act. In *John v Matthews*[14] it was held, by the Divisional Court, that it was not possible to commit an offence under section 11 (now repealed, but formerly catching misleading indications of price of goods), where the supply of goods was by a working men's club to a member, since the Act was designed to protect the public, not a husband from his wife or a club and its members. Its primary charging provisions relate only to transactions of a commercial nature, notwithstanding that under this particular section the requirement of the supply being in the course of a trade or business was not expressed. In *Havering London Borough v Stevenson*[15] a car sold by a car hire firm had a false trade description as to mileage. Though not car dealers, the firm regularly sold its cars after a period of use. It was held by the Divisional Court that the sale was in the course of its trade or business as a car hire firm. And in

---

12 [1974] 2 All ER 1243, [1974] 1 WLR 1056, DC; M, H & P p 605. See also *Fletcher v Sledmore* [1973] RTR 371, DC (the false statement may be made by someone not privy to the contract of supply). The case is mentioned below.
13 See as to income tax, Sch D Cases 1 and 2, Income and Corporation Taxes Act 1988, and the many tax cases on the meaning of 'trade'. The expression is also relevant (inter alia) in bankruptcy and landlord and tenant law.
14 [1970] 2 QB 443, [1970] 2 All ER 643, DC.
15 [1970] 3 All ER 609, [1970] 1 WLR 1375, DC.

Fletcher v Sledmore[16] the defendant was a panel beater who bought, repaired and sold old cars. A dealer and his prospective customer visited him and he falsely stated that the car had a 'good little engine'. The panel beater sold the repaired car to the dealer and he resold to the customer who was influenced by the panel beater's remark. Despite the lack of any contractual relationship between the eventual buyer and the panel beater, the latter was directed to be convicted of applying a false trade description in the course of his trade or business contrary to section 1(1)(a).

In *Davies v Sumner*[17] the activities of a self-employed courier, whose car's odometer had gone right round the clock, thus presenting a false reading, were reviewed on his sale of that car. Here, he owned the car but in the past he had hired his vehicles. The House of Lords held that a normal business practice of buying and disposing of cars had not been established and the relevant sale was therefore not caught by section 1(1)(a).

In the civil context, the Court of Appeal held in *R & B Customs Brokers Co Ltd v United Dominions Trust Ltd*[18] that a corporate purchaser had not bought a car 'in the course of a business' for the purposes of the Unfair Contract Terms Act 1977, section 12(1)(a). This decision has been criticised for introducing a potential loophole in the ambit of protection of the criminal law in over-emphasising the need for regularity and trying vainly to equate the tests for buying in the course of a business and selling in the course of a business.[19]

'Applies'

The word 'applies' is amplified in section 4. A person applies a trade description to goods if he–

a) affixes or annexes it to or in any manner marks it on or incorporates it with–
   i)   the goods themselves, or
   ii) anything in, on or with which the goods are supplied; or
b) places the goods in, on or with anything which the trade description has been affixed or annexed to, marked on or incorporated with, or places any such thing with the goods; or
c) uses the trade description in any manner likely to be taken as referring to the goods.

16   [1973] RTR 371, DC.
17   [1984] 3 All ER 831, [1984] 1 WLR 1301, HL; M, H & P p 611. See also *Devlin v Hall* (1990) 155 JP 20, DC.
18   [1988] 1 All ER 847, [1988] 1 WLR 321, CA.
19   D Parry 'Business or Consumer: A Trap for the Unwary' (1988) 6 Trading Law 270. Contrast also the decision reached in *Stevenson v Rogers* [1999] QB 1028, [1999] 1 All ER 613, CA under the Sale of Goods Act 1979, s 14, see p 98.

This subsection is similar to section 5 of the Merchandise Marks Act 1887 as amended and there is a quantity of case law on the interpretation of the former provision which the draftsman no doubt had in mind in drafting section 4. An interesting illustrative case in which that part of section 4 referring to where a person 'affixes or annexes or in any manner marks it', with 'anything in, on or with which the goods are supplied' was relevant was *Donnelly v Rowlands*.[20] There a milk retailer sold milk in bottles the foil caps of which read 'Untreated milk Produced from TT Cows', followed by his name and address. The bottles themselves were marked with the name of various well-known suppliers, such as CWS, to whom the actual bottles belonged. The prosecutor's appeal from the magistrate's dismissal of the informations alleging that he had sold bottles of milk to which false trade descriptions had been applied was also dismissed by the Divisional Court. It was held that the words on the cap were an accurate trade description. The words on the milk bottles, which could have been a false trade description had the public been misled into thinking that the names thereon had something to do with the production of milk, could only reasonably apply to the ownership of the bottles. The defendant was therefore saved by the wording on the cap which was required by the Milk (Special Designation) Regulations 1963.[1]

Section 4(2) states that an oral statement may amount to the use of a trade description. Although there are similar provisions in food and drugs and weights and measures law,[2] this was a controversial innovation in trade descriptions law. The Molony Committee recognised that oral misstatements were a widespread problem, but considered that to make an oral misdescription an offence would 'put a very powerful weapon into the hands of a disappointed shopper'.[3] However, the government took the view that this provision was essential if a comprehensive system of protection was to be provided. No doubt because of the increasing fallibility of a witness's memory of alleged oral misdescriptions, section 19(4) attempted to disapply the normal time limits of three years from the commission of the offence or one year from its discovery by the prosecutor, whichever is the earlier, and by implication substitute the shorter one of six months. It is now apparently the case that, though unrepealed, section 19(4) is negated by section 127(2) of the Magistrates' Courts Act 1980 and

---

20 [1971] 1 All ER 9, [1970] 1 WLR 1600, DC. See also *Roberts v Severn Petroleum and Trading Co Ltd* [1981] RTR 312, DC, M, H & P p 614, where the respondents were held to have infringed s 1(1)(a) where they had falsely displayed Esso signs in the vicinity of petrol tanks not containing Esso petrol.
1 SI 1963/1571 (now superseded).
2 See Food Safety Act 1990, s 14 (misrepresentations as to nature, substance or quality of food) and Weights and Measures Act 1985, s 28 (short quantity).
3 Cmnd 1791, para 659.

the time limit is the same as for other either way offences.[4] The point was important where a prosecution was brought more than six months after the alleged offence was committed. In *Rees v Munday*[5] it was unsuccessfully argued that where a vehicle was falsely described ('first class condition, 12-yard capacity') in a trade journal, the operative misdescription occurred when the vendor stated to the purchaser orally that the vehicle he was buying was the one advertised. Some importance was attached by Lord Widgery CJ to the fact that there was only one lorry in the vendor's possession answering the relevant description. The description was therefore 'applied' when the advertisement was published. Section 4(3) also makes it clear that when goods are supplied in pursuance of a request in which a trade description is used, the supplier is deemed to have applied that trade description to the goods where the circumstances make it reasonable for that to be inferred.

For a conviction under section 1(1)(a), the courts have established that the description applied to the goods must be associated, in some way, with the sale or supply of goods. This is illustrated by *Wycombe Marsh Garage Ltd v Fowler*,[6] *Wickens Motors (Gloucester) Ltd v Hall*[7] and *Fletcher v Sledmore*,[8] and accepted in *Formula One Autocentres Ltd v Birmingham City Council*.[9]

Even though a trade description can be deemed to have been applied to goods in accordance with the Act, it is a necessary ingredient of the offence that the offender should have knowledge, at the time of the supply or offer to supply goods, that a trade description is applied to them.[10]

---

4   See the extensive discussion in BTCL, 3[196].
5   [1974] 3 All ER 506, [1974] 1 WLR 1284, DC, M, H & P p 734. In *Louis C Edwards & Sons (Manchester) Ltd v Miller* (19 January 1981, unreported), DC (but see (1981) Monthly Rev 240), suppliers of meat to a local education authority were convicted under s 1(1)(b) for failing to supply meat which complied with the specification in the tender. Since there was a standing contract which only required goods to be supplied when there was a request, s 1(1)(b) applied by virtue of s 4(3) considered below. But the court took care to stress that it was not every breach of contract of sale of goods which also contravened the Trade Descriptions Act.
6   [1972] 3 All ER 248, [1972] 1 WLR 1156, DC; false description applied to car tyres during MOT test, no offence.
7   [1972] 3 All ER 759, sub nom *Hall v Wickens Motors (Gloucester) Ltd* [1972] 1 WLR 1418, DC; false statement made some weeks after purchase of car, no offence.
8   [1973] RTR 371, DC; see above p 386, panel beater who had retained the car after selling it had sufficient interest in subsequent sale to be convicted.
9   [1999] RTR 195, DC; discussed below at p 392.
10   See *Cottee v Douglas Seaton (Used Cars) Ltd* [1972] 3 All ER 750, [1972] 1 WLR 1408, DC; M, H & P p 615.

'A false trade description to any goods'

The definition of 'false trade description' is contained in sections 2 and 3 in particular. Section 3 states that a *false* trade description is a trade description which is false to a material degree, and also includes within the expression 'false' descriptions which, though not false, are misleading. Anything likely to be taken for an indication of the matters specified in section 2 (discussed below), though not a 'trade description' will, if false, be deemed a false trade description (s 3(3)), and a similar provision applies to false indications of specified or recognised standards.

Again, this section is somewhat similar to section 3 of the Merchandise Marks Act 1887, as amended, on which repealed section there are a number of still relevant reported cases. For instance in *Sandeman v Gold*[11] it was held to be a false trade description to describe as 'port' what was in fact Tarragona wine, and in *Kat v Diment*[12] the term 'non-brewed vinegar' was held to be false when applied to a solution of acetic acid and caramel. A number of other examples are mentioned in the discussion of 'trade description' under section 2 below.

The term 'trade description' is defined comprehensively in section 2 (as amended). The section is a greatly extended version of the previous law. Subsection (1) states that a trade description is an indication, direct or indirect, and by whatever means given of any of the matters specified thereby with respect to any goods. Included in the list, lettered in paragraphs (a) to (j), are (a) quantity, size or gauge, (b) method of manufacture or production, (c) composition, (d) fitness for purpose, strength, performance, behaviour or accuracy, (e) any other physical characteristics, (f) testing by any person and the results thereof, (g) approval by any person or conformity with an approved type, (h) place or date of manufacture, production etc, (i) person by whom manufactured or processed, and (j) other history, including previous ownership or use.

In relation to '(a) quantity, size or gauge', quantity includes length, width, height, area, volume, capacity, weight and number (s 2(3)). There is some overlap here between this provision and the 'short weight' etc offences contained in the Weights and Measures Act 1985 and discussed in chapter 13 but technically it would be an offence under the Trade Descriptions Act to supply greater quantities than indicated.

In relation to '(c) composition', examples under the old law include misdescriptions such as 'natural mineral water', a mixture of cotton and linen described as 'linen' and artificial silk stockings described as 'silk'.[13] A case under the 1968 Act illustrates that 'composition' includes

---

11   [1924] 1 KB 107.
12   [1951] 1 KB 34, [1950] 2 All ER 657.
13   See *Allard v Selfridge & Co Ltd* [1925] 1 KB 129.

component parts. In *British Gas Corpn v Lubbock*[14] a Gas Board brochure stated, with regard to gas cookers for sale, 'Ignition is by hand-held battery torch supplied with the cooker'. This was held to be (inter alia) a trade description relating to composition of goods and an offence was committed when a cooker was sold without a torch, despite a notice that specifications might be changed without notice. The description could also be regarded as coming within '(e) any physical characteristics not included in the preceding paragraphs'.

Linked with '(d) fitness for purpose' are 'strength, performance, behaviour or accuracy'. Thus for example, a 'diver's watch' described as 'waterproof' is not one which fills with water after being immersed in a bowl of water for an hour.[15] Second-hand car sales have often fallen foul of this paragraph. The courts have been willing to hold that such expressions as 'beautiful car' and 'immaculate condition' are either actually false descriptions within this paragraph, where the car though good externally was internally in poor condition, or at least capable of being false, depending on the impact of the description on the ordinary person.[16] It was noted in *Shropshire County Council (David Walker) v Simon Dudley Ltd*[17] that many breaches of contract under the fitness for purpose provisions of section 14 of the Sale of Goods Act 1979[18] would also be technical breaches of the Trade Descriptions Act 1968. Prosecutors would need to use their discretion to decide whether the case warrants intervention of the criminal law, instead of only seeking a civil remedy.

The paragraph dealing with 'approval by any person' etc, lettered (g), was introduced to catch false claims such as that certain encyclopaedias were 'approved' by a well-known educational institution. Falsely stating that an article complies with a British Standard will also be caught here.

Paragraph (i) deals with statements as to 'by whom manufactured, produced, processed or reconditioned'. Section 36 of the 1968 Act deems goods to have been manufactured in the country in which they last

14 [1974] 1 All ER 188, [1974] 1 WLR 37, DC. See also *Denard v Smith and Dixons Ltd* [1991] Crim LR 63, DC, where a placard advertised a computer with a software package including a number of games. The package sold was known to be incomplete. This was held to be a supply of goods to which a false trade description as to composition had been applied.
15 *Sherratt v Geralds the American Jewellers Ltd* (1970) 114 Sol Jo 147, DC; M, H & P p 721.
16 Compare *Robertson v Dicicco* [1972] RTR 431, DC, and *Kensington and Chelsea Royal London Borough Council v Riley* [1973] RTR 122, DC. See also *Hawkins v Smith* [1978] Crim LR 578, Portsmouth Crown Court, when it was held that a dealer's advertisement that a car was in 'showroom condition throughout' contravened s 1(1)(b), and (obiter) that 'showroom condition' referred to exterior, interior and mechanical condition.
17 (1996) Tr LR 69, DC.
18 See p 105.

underwent a treatment or process resulting in a substantial change. Guidance notes have been issued by the Department of Trade and Industry regarding origin marking.[19] Prosecutions founded on section 2(1)(i) could also be brought by or on behalf of manufacturers in respect of the 'passing off' of their goods by rival manufacturers. An example would be *Horner v Kingsley Clothing Co Ltd*,[20] where sweatshirts bore a 'Marc O Polo' name across the front but were not genuine Marc O Polo garments made by the Cotton Company in Denmark, which had registered the trade mark.

Paragraph (j) deals with 'other history, including previous ownership or use'. This covers such descriptions as 'Railway Lost Property', 'Army Surplus', 'one lady owner' and the like. An indication of a vehicle's age by reference to its date of registration or its suffix letter on a number plate is caught.[1] Also covered is the common case of a car's odometer registering a lower mileage than the true one, this being capable of being a trade description applied by the seller at the time of the offer for sale – a point discussed later in this chapter.

Section 2 goes on to state that the above matters in relation to animals include sex, breed or cross, fertility and soundness, and in relation to semen, the identity and characteristics of the animal from which it was taken and measure of dilution (s 2(2)). Descriptions and marks applied in pursuance of a number of statutes dealing with horticulture and agriculture are deemed not to be trade descriptions (s 2(4)), nor are descriptions applied pursuant to the food and drugs legislation (s 2(5)). References in the Act to 'goods' include ships and aircraft, things attached to land and growing crops (s 39(1)).

Falsely indicating that goods or services are as supplied to the Royal Family or simulating the Queen's Award to Industry device are separate offences under section 12. Similar false indications of supply to 'any person' are caught by section 13.

19 See BTCL 3[846]. For an exploration of the law relating to the frequent mislabelling of valuable musical instruments, see Harvey and Shapreau, *Violin Fraud* (2nd edn OUP 1997), see also Harvey *Buying and Selling Art and Antiques* (LAPADA, 1998).

20 [1989] Crim LR 911, DC. See also *J Bollinger v Costa Brava Wine Co Ltd* [1960] Ch 262, [1959] 3 All ER 800, (calling wine made in Spain 'Spanish Champagne' infringed the exclusive right of the wine producers of the Champagne district of France to that description).

1 See *R v Haesler* [1973] RTR 486, CA. See also *Routledge v Ansa Motors (Chester-le-Street) Ltd* [1980] Crim LR 65, DC (car manufactured in 1972 but first registered in 1975 capable of being falsely described as 'one used 1975 Ford Escort').

'Supplies or offers to supply any goods to which a false trade description is applied'

Section 6 elucidates the first part of the above by stating that a person exposing goods for supply or having goods in his possession for supply shall be deemed to offer to supply them. The section is deliberately widely drafted. It avoids the type of difficulty found in such cases as *Fisher v Bell*[2] where flick knives were displayed in a shop window, this being an invitation to treat rather than an 'offer for sale' contrary to section 1(1) of the Restriction of Offensive Weapons Act 1959. Such goods would have been 'exposed' for sale. Even if the goods to which a false trade description is applied belong to someone else so that it could not be said that the seller has them 'in his possession for supply', he still 'exposes them for supply'. The Trade Descriptions Act thus catches a variety of operations provided 'possession for supply' is proved, whether or not the supplier is eg a warehouseman selling to traders or a mail order firm selling to the public. The word 'supply' is wider than 'sale', and would seem to cover free gifts if the supply is made in the course of trade or business, as well as hire and hire-purchase transactions, goods for gift tokens and the like.[3] It is clear from the expression 'is applied' that a sale etc of goods already bearing a false description put on by a third party is caught.

One judicial decision that appears to have extended the application of section 1(1) is *Formula One Autocentres Ltd v Birmingham City Council*.[4] A car, which had previously been inspected by a consultant automobile engineer, was put in for a Formula One 'Master Service'. It was subsequently collected and an invoice, indicating that a Master Service had been carried out, was paid. When the car was re-checked it was shown that many items included in the Master Service had not been done. On appeal, convictions under section 1(1)(a) and (b) were upheld. The appellants, unsuccessfully, tried to argue that the prosecution should have been brought under section 14.[5] Mitchell J indicated that sections 1 and 14 were not mutually exclusive. Using authorities on the meaning of 'supply' in connection with the Misuse of Drugs Act 1971, in particular *R v Maginnis*,[6] it was held that 'supply' meant more than the mere transfer of physical control of some chattel. When a car was returned to its owner after a service:

2 [1961] 1 QB 394, [1960] 3 All ER 731, DC.
3 For a decision illustrating the breadth of this concept see *Stainthorpe v Bailey* [1980] RTR 7, DC; M, H & P p 620, considered below.
4 [1999] RTR 195, DC.
5 False and misleading statements relating to services etc, requiring proof of mens rea: see below pp 400 and 405.
6 [1987] AC 303, [1987] 1 All ER 907, HL.

the company, by virtue of the transfer of physical control were 'enabling the recipient to apply the thing handed over to the purposes for which he desires or has a duty to apply it.' It therefore follows that the appellant was supplying the car on that occasion within the meaning of both sections 1(1)(a) and 1(1)(b) of the Trade Descriptions Act 1968. (Mitchell J at pp 32–33)

This decision greatly assists trading standards officers in dealing with problems of inadequate car servicing in permitting the use of strict liability offences in addition to the, well-established, use of section 14. The reasoning is, however, open to criticism as unduly straining the language of section 1 and removing the distinction between section 1 and section 14 in a wide variety of service contracts where property of the customer is temporarily bailed to the service provider for repair or maintenance. In this particular case there seems no reason why a successful prosecution should not have been brought under section 14 despite the mens rea requirement (see below).

Trade descriptions used in advertisements

Advertisements tend to generalise, so it is necessary to provide a fair test to enable the courts to identify whether a particular advertisement applicable to a class of goods has applied a trade description to particular goods. Section 5(2) states that the trade description shall be taken as referring to all goods of the class, whether or not in existence at the time the advertisement is published, for the purpose of determining whether an offence under section 1(1)(a) (applying a false trade description to goods) has been committed. The same applies to offences under section 1(1)(b) where goods of the class are supplied or offered to be supplied by a person publishing or displaying the advertisement – thus catching mail order sales for example.

Section 5(3) states that, when determining whether goods are of a class to which an advertised trade description relates, regard shall be had not only to the form and content of the advertisement but also to the time, place, manner and frequency of its publication and all other matters making it likely or unlikely that a person to whom the goods are supplied would think of the goods belonging to the class in question. This is an attempt to ensure that the advertised trade description can fairly be regarded as current and applicable to the goods in question.

'Advertisement' is widely defined to include a catalogue, a circular and a price list (s 39(1)); but a printed, filmed, or broadcast trade description is not deemed to be made in the course of a trade or business unless it forms part of an advertisement (s 39(2)). This provision is designed to prevent prosecutions founded on descriptions contained in genuine news items.

Disclaimers

Offences arising out of the sale of cars with false odometer readings are the most prevalent offence dealt with by enforcement authorities. The question of disclaimers frequently arises in this context since an offence under section 1(1)(b) is committed if the odometer reading is false and has not been disclaimed, whether or not the seller is aware that the trade description is false. In *Norman v Bennett*[7] a purchaser looked at a second-hand car not yet prepared for sale in a sale-room. The exposed odometer reading was some 23,000 miles though the true mileage was about 68,000 miles. The purchaser questioned the low mileage and was told by a salesman that they had been told it was a director's car (apparently regarded as a sufficient explanation for low mileages). The purchaser agreed to buy it, knowing from previous dealings that he would have to sign an agreement. A little later he read and signed an agreement containing the words 'speedometer reading not guaranteed'. He had read and signed similar agreements before.

On appeal to the Divisional Court against dismissal of the information by the magistrates' court, the Lord Chief Justice stated that, to be effective, a disclaimer

> must be as bold, precise and compelling as the trade description itself and must be as effectively brought to the notice of any person to whom the goods may be supplied. In other words, the disclaimer must equal the trade description in the extent to which it is likely to get home to anyone interested in receiving the goods.[8]

This was not the case here, though on the particular facts since the buyer and seller were both experienced dealers in cars, a trade description had not been effectively applied.

The Court of Appeal in *R v Southwood* [9] confirmed the proposition that it was not open to a person who had actively applied a false trade

---

7   [1974] 3 All ER 351, [1974] 1 WLR 1229, DC.
8   Ibid at 354, 1232. The Lord Chief Justice also thought that 'applied' in s 1(1)(b) meant applied at the time of supply or having been so applied in the course of negotiations leading to such supply. This decision was followed in *Zawadski v Sleigh* [1975] RTR 113, DC.
9   [1987] 3 All ER 556, [1987] 1 WLR 1361, CA; M, H & P p 636. See also, as to the problems caused when a replacement odometer is innocently fitted, *R v Crown Court at Shrewsbury, ex p Venables* [1994] Crim LR 61; (1993) 101 ITSA MR

description by deliberately altering the mileage of a car to purport to disclaim it by stickers or notices. If a disclaimer were to be effective at all it could only be appropriate to a charge laid under section 1(1)(b) where the false trade description had already been applied by somebody other than the supplier in question of the vehicle. Once the trade description has been made, a casual remark or 'small print' in a document is not enough to disclaim it. The true effect of an operative disclaimer is to negative the making of a trade description; it is not a defence once one has been made.[10]

The same point was reiterated in a case of importance to auctioneers, amongst some of whom there was thought to be a myth that the Act did not apply to those operating in the 'Art World'![11] An auction catalogue described a painting as being by J M W Turner when the auctioneer knew that it was not. The catalogue contained a clear and comprehensive disclaimer. The Divisional Court allowed an appeal against the justices' acquittal on a charge of applying a false trade description to a painting. The disclaimer could not prevent the application of a false trade description. (The point also arises in the context of clocking cars considered below.)

In contrast, in *R v Carl Bull*[12] an incorrect car mileage was written in a box on an invoice. An asterix next to the mileage explained that the garage had been unable to confirm its correctness and that it should be regarded as incorrect. The garage was charged under section 1(1)(a) for recording the mileage on the invoice (there was no suggestion the garage had tampered with the mileage). The court decided that the prosecution had failed to establish that, at the time the description was applied (ie the mileage was written on the invoice), it was 'false', because of the presence of the qualifying words. The court gave a clear indication that this was not to be seen as a means of evading liability. It appears that, if an offence arises because of the creation of a false description by the defendant, any disclaimer could not help avoid a section 1(1)(a) conviction. On the other hand, if the 'application' of a false trade description is merely repeating an incorrect description, created by someone else, then, depending upon the circumstances, a disclaimer may prevent an offence arising.

24, DC, and the critical analysis of this decision in BTCL 3[267]; also *Southend Borough Council v White* (1991) 156 JP 463, DC; M, H & P p 640.

10 See further on these points *R v Hammertons Cars Ltd* [1976] 3 All ER 758, [1976] 1 WLR 1243, CA (Criminal Division). The defence under Trade Descriptions Act 1968, s 24 that the seller, by making enquiries of his own seller etc has exercised all due diligence, held to be insufficient unless accompanied by a disclaimer; see *Simmons v Potter* [1975] RTR 347, DC. However, in *Ealing London Borough v Taylor* (1994) 159 JP 460 the DC held that if a disclaimer is effective there is no need to invoke s 24 at all. Nor is it as a matter of law necessary in all cases to make enquiries of previous owners.

11 *May v Vincent* (1990) 154 JP 997, [1991] 1 EGLR 27, DC.

12 (1995) 160 JP 240, CA; M, H & P p 641.

A disclaimer was perhaps undeservedly successful in the controversial decision of the Divisional Court in *Kent County Council v Price*.[13] A market trader sold cheap T-shirts marked on the front 'Adidas', 'Reebok' etc (and being unauthorised copies) and was convicted by the magistrates. He successfully appealed against conviction to the Crown Court, whose decision was upheld by the Divisional Court. The reason for this was because (inter alia) cards were put by the shirts saying 'brand copy', and indicating the price and it was decided that it was a question of fact for the Crown Court to decide on the overall impression. But this should not be taken as a 'pirate's licence', nor should it be forgotten that section 92 of the Trade Marks Act 1994 makes unauthorised use of *trade marks*, with a view to gain, an offence.

The concept of the disclaimer has been criticised as not clearly being permitted by section 1. The consultative document published by the Office of Fair Trading entitled 'Review of the Trade Descriptions Act 1968'[14] discussed the problem and recommended (inter alia) that disclaimers should be allowed to continue except in respect of descriptions applied by the trader to goods in his possession at the time. One reason given was that traders might otherwise cease to check second-hand goods and simply seek to repudiate all responsibility for the accuracy of descriptions. This conclusion by the Review Committee has also been strongly criticised on the grounds that the supposed difficulties of disallowing disclaimers are not 'insuperable' and that the decision in *Norman v Bennett* may encourage 'blanket' disclaimers as a substitute for checking descriptions already applied to goods properly before sale.[15] In April 1990 a consultative document was issued by the Department of Trade and Industry suggesting only that a new order-making power might be introduced controlling the use of disclaimers in specific areas of difficulty, such as descriptions of land and houses.[16] Following consultations in 1996,[17] the Office of Fair Trading recommended[18] that consideration should be given to make disclaimers ineffective if reasonable checks on the mileage had not been made. In addition a reformed Part III of the Fair Trading Act 1973[19] could be of assistance, together with licensing action under the Consumer Credit Act 1974.[20]

13 (1993) 157 JP 1161, DC.
14 Cmnd 6628 (1976), M, H & P pp 633–635, discussed further below.
15 G Borrie [1975] Crim LR 662, 667–669.
16 The text of the DTI's published consultative letter appeared in (1990) 7 Trading Law 115–124. See also P Cartwright (1991) 141 NLJ 888. The proposals are further considered at p 416.
17 *The purchase of used cars*, OFT, December 1996.
18 *Selling Second-Hand Cars*, OFT, October 1997, para 2.31. See generally 'Putting consumers back in the driving seat', OFT, (1998) 18 Fair Trading 8.
19 See further pp 358–359.
20 See further pp 306–310.

Specific areas of difficulty

'Clocking' cars

Reducing the mileage shown on the odometer of a used car is probably the most persistent offence under the Trade Descriptions Act and reference has already been made to it under 'Disclaimers' above. The Institute of Trading Standards Administration has calculated[1] that each year the 'clocking' of vehicles costs purchasers an estimated £100 million.

There have been various initiatives taken over the years to try and reduce the problems caused by clocked cars. In March 1981 a revised Motor Industry Code of Practice was promulgated making it compulsory for members to verify odometer readings or to warn the customer that this has not been done – as mentioned in chapter 11. In practice this is often not complied with.[2] The Office of Fair Trading has used licensing powers to withhold, suspend or revoke dealers' consumer credit licences and has sought assurances under Part III of the Fair Trading Act 1973 where dealers were found to be indulging in this practice. Their latest proposals,[3] in addition to the reforms mentioned regarding disclaimers, above, advocate a mandatory entry of vehicle mileages on vehicle registration documents on change of ownership etc; the computerisation of MOT test mileage data and its availability to all motor database companies; and certification of checks made by dealers on database files. In February 1999 the Government announced support for introducing mandatory recording of mileage recordings on vehicle documents.

In the context of 'clocking', the strict attitude of the courts to the sale of cars bearing false odometer readings is illustrated by the following cases. In *Holloway v Cross*[4] a motor trader had been convicted by Chatham Justices on charges of applying a false trade description contrary to section 1(1)(a) and (b) of the Act. The dealer had bought a Triumph car, first registered in 1973, of which the mileage was in fact in excess of 70,000. However, when he bought it, the odometer read only 716 miles. When a buyer saw the car and asked the defendant about the mileage it was made clear that the defendant did not know the true mileage but promised to

1   *Car Clocking – the invisible crime*, ITSA, June 1996, cited in *The purchase of used cars*, OFT, December 1996, ch 3.
2   An OFT survey, in 1994, found that, of 1000 dealers, 48% attempted to verify the mileage, 34% usually did and 18% never did. 30% put a disclaimer on all used cars, 28% used a disclaimer on cars with unverified mileages and 40% did not use disclaimers: *The purchase of used cars*, OFT, December 1996, paras 3.31–3.32.
3   *Selling Second-Hand Cars*, OFT, October 1997. See also 'Putting consumers back in the driving seat', OFT (1998) 18 Fair Trading 8; 'A driving force for change' OFT, (1999) 23 Fair Trading 10; *Annual Report of the Director General of Fair Trading 1999* 2000 HCP 576 at p 21.
4   [1981] 1 All ER 1012, DC; M, H & P p 630. Section 3(3) is discussed above.

make enquiries. He subsequently gave an opinion that the mileage was probably about 45,000 and the defendant wrote on the used-car invoice 'recorded mileage 716, estimated mileage 45,000 miles'. The justices had concluded that such an estimate was an opinion, and it therefore did not fall within section 2(1)(j) which provides that a trade description is an indication, whether direct or indirect and by whatever means, of any matter with respect to goods, including their history, previous ownership and use. However, they held that it was within the extension to the concept of a false trade description provided by section 3(3) and the disparity between the estimate and the actual mileage was sufficiently large to render the estimate false to a material degree. Donaldson LJ considered that it was debatable whether or not section 2 applied to the situation bearing in mind that section 2(1) relates to an indication 'direct or indirect'. In any event it was clear that the defendant's estimate was likely to be taken by the buyer as an indication of the history of the vehicle and, if that was so, it was one which was false to a material degree. The defendant's opinion was only relevant in so far as the buyer wished for an indication as to what the mileage was. The words complained of therefore amounted to a false description within section 3(3). The appeal was dismissed.

Another 'clocking' case of particular interest to Trading Standards Officers is *Stainthorpe v Bailey*.[5] In this case the defendant motor dealer advertised a van for sale knowing that the odometer incorrectly recorded a mileage of 36,000 miles, the true mileage being more than 97,000 miles. A Trading Standards officer visited the firm's premises and was re-directed to the home of the defendant. The van was parked outside the house. The officer asked 'Is that van for sale?'; the defendant said 'Yes, the keys are in it if you want to have a look round', and dealt with a telephone call at his house. When the defendant went outside the officer had gone. The Divisional Court directed the magistrates to convict on the basis (inter alia) that the defendant had exposed goods for supply and having them in his possession for supply, he was deemed to offer to supply them by virtue of section 6 of the Act. Nor had the defendant taken reasonable precautions and exercised all due diligence to avoid the commission of the offence, such as making a disclaimer as to the accuracy of the recorded mileage.

Corfield v Starr[6] involved a purported disclaimer which the Divisional Court considered illustrated the point that some disclaimers could themselves give rise to a false trade description.[7] Here the disclaimer placed

5   [1980] RTR 7, DC; M, H & P p 620.
6   [1981] RTR 380, DC.
7   This point is emphasised in *Newman v Hackney London Borough Council* [1982] RTR 296, DC; M, H & P p 638 where a car with an odometer reading of 46,000 miles had had the reading reduced deliberately by the defendants to 21,000 miles, which lower reading could still be seen despite a disclaimer stuck over it. The court held that it is not possible to disclaim the effect of one's own deliberate fraud.

on a dashboard reading of 35,000 miles known by the defendant to be incorrect read: 'With deep regret due to Customer's Protection Act we can no longer verify that the mileage shown on this vehicle is correct.' As Bingham J pointed out, 'the notice here referred to an Act of Parliament which does not exist and gives to it an effect which no Act of Parliament in fact has ... In my judgment, to counteract the statement (of mileage) on this odometer some statement would be needed clearly conveying to a customer or prospective customer that no reliance could be placed on the mileage reading for any purpose whatever, or that the reading was meaningless.' It was held that the justices should accordingly have convicted.

Some car dealers cover over odometer readings on dashboards to prevent a trade description being displayed, it being established beyond doubt that a reading on the car's odometer is an indication of the use that it has had within section 2(1)(j). Another practice had been to 'zero' the odometer, which seemed to meet with the approval of the Divisional Court in *K Lill (Holdings) v White*.[8] In that case Lord Widgery said that he could see a great deal of merit in this practice because it seemed that, for the time being at all events, it put the problem of a false odometer out of the reckoning because no one would be misled by such a record. However the Court of Appeal in *R v Southwood*[9] firmly stated that a person who zeroed the odometer was applying a false trade description just as much as a person who reduced it to, say, 15,000 miles. The Court of Appeal has since emphasised that the deliberate turning back of an odometer was in direct conflict with Parliament's intention that goods should be honestly described and convicted defendants should expect a term of imprisonment.[10]

Goods described as 'new'

The Molony Committee recommended that there should be added to the definition of 'trade description' formerly contained in the Merchandise Marks Acts, descriptions 'as to any goods being new in the sense of being unused' (para 636), but this does not appear explicitly in the Act. The problem has arisen particularly in the context of sales of cars and components.

In *R v Ford Motor Co Ltd*[11] a dealer ordered from Ford a Cortina car and later sold it to a customer describing it in the invoice as 'one new Ford

8   [1979] RTR 120, (1979) JP 534, DC; M, H & P p 637 (cited in *R v Southwood*, see below).
9   [1987] 3 All ER 556, [1987] 1 WLR 1361, CA; M, H & P p 636.
10   *R v Hewitt* [1991] RTR 357, CA.
11   [1974] 3 All ER 489, [1974] 1 WLR 1220, CA; M, H & P p 625.

Cortina'. Unknown to dealer and customer the car had been damaged in process of delivery and repaired under insurance for about £50. Ford appealed against its conviction in the Crown Court for applying the false trade description 'new' contrary to section 1(1)(b) and causing the dealer to do the same, contrary to section 23. The Court of Appeal quashed the convictions because 1) the repairs were not intended to conceal defects but to restore the car to sound condition, and could not therefore themselves amount to a false description, and 2) although it could be deemed to have applied a trade description under section 4(3), a car was not necessarily falsely described as 'new' if such damage as occurs is 'perfectly repaired so that it can in truth be said after repairs have been effected that the car is as good as new'. The court added that there must nevertheless come a point when damage is so serious that a car could not be repaired so as to qualify it as 'new'. There are obvious difficulties if this decision is taken too far. Buyers can surely assume in the normal way that 'new' goods travel from production line to retail outlet in pristine condition. Any repair, however skilful, can affect the durability of goods.[12] However, it will be noted that even had the Molony Committee's suggestion been implemented the car in this case would still presumably have been 'unused'.

A similar problem can arise where a car manufactured in one year, say 1972, is first registered in a later one, say 1975, and then advertised as a 'used 1975 Ford' – see *Routledge v Ansa Motors (Chester-le-Street) Ltd*.[13] The Divisional Court held that this could lead customers to think 1975 the year of manufacture and, in that event, the statement was false to a material degree. The practice of calling 'new' a car which is bought new from the manufacturer and then registered in the retail garage's name before a retail sale takes place (so that the purchaser is actually the second registered owner) was disapproved of in *R v Anderson*.[14] Although the cars here were undeniably mint, the description 'new' implied that there had been no previous registered owners.

5.   FALSE OR MISLEADING STATEMENTS AS TO SERVICES, ETC

Section 14 of the 1968 Act goes beyond the recommendations of the Molony Committee in laying down novel provisions to control statements about

---

12   See discussion *obiter* in *Cottee v Douglas Seaton (Used Cars) Ltd* [1972] 3 All ER 750, [1972] 1 WLR 1408, DC as to whether a car which has been cleverly repaired so as to conceal corrosion 'tells a lie about itself' so as to apply a false trade description within Trade Descriptions Act 1968, s 2 (indication of strength).

13   [1980] RTR 1, DC, and for used goods marked 'Display Stock Clearance' see (1985) 4 Trading Law 32.

14   (1987) 152 JP 373, CA.

services, accommodation and facilities. As has already been noted, this is not an absolute or strict liability offence, as can be seen from its wording:

(1) It shall be an offence for any person in the course of any trade or business–
a) to make a statement which he knows to be false; or
b) recklessly to make a statement which is false:
as to any of the following matters,

there then follow five provisions as to (i) the provision of, (ii) the nature of, (iii) the time at which, manner in which, or persons by whom services, accommodation or facilities are provided, or (iv) their examination, approval or evaluation by any person, or (v) the location or amenities of accommodation.

'Any person in the course of any trade or business'

This is discussed in relation to section 1, above,[15] but one issue which has arisen specifically in connection with section 14 is whether or not professions are included. In *R v Breeze*[16] an unqualified architect sought to argue that section 14 did not apply to professions, but only to businesses. The court, having pointing out that the defendant was not qualified and therefore not a professional, declined to decide the point. It was subsequently confirmed in *Roberts v Leonard*[17] that section 14 does apply to professions, this being included in dictionary definitions of 'business'.

'Make a statement'

Usually it is a simple matter to determine when a statement is 'made'. However, where statements are published and distributed to the public in the form of brochures, catalogues etc and may be in circulation for months or even years problems may arise as to exactly when a statement is 'made'. This issue was discussed in *Wings Ltd v Ellis*.[18] Here Lord Brandon

15 See pp 385–386.
16 [1973] 2 All ER 1141, [1973] 1 WLR 994, CA; M, H & P pp 643 and 653. See also below p 404.
17 (1995) 14 Tr LR 536, DC; M, H & P p 644, services of vets. In *R v Bow Street Magistrates' Court, ex p Joseph* (1986) 150 JP 650, DC it was held that the Law Society did not carry on any trade or business and so could not commit any offence under this section.
18 [1985] AC 272, [1984] 3 All ER 577, HL; M, H & P p 622, discussed in detail below at p 405.

indicated that he would regard a false statement contained in the respondent's brochures as having been a continuing false statement, that is to say a false statement which continued to be made so long as such brochures remained in circulation without effective correction. An advertisement exhibited on a street hoarding would be regarded in the same way. Lord Scarman endorsed this: 'I have no doubt that a statement as to the air-conditioning in the hotel was made when the brochure was published. But further statements to the same effect were made whenever persons did business with the respondents on the strength of the uncorrected brochure ...'. Statements in brochures etc are therefore 'made' when published and continue to be 'made' whilst the documents continue to be available.

'A false statement'

A major problem under this section is deciding where the line should be drawn in distinguishing what is merely a breach of contract not within the mischief of the Act, and statements which are false or misleading within section 14 as well, in many cases, as being breaches of warranty. This point is illustrated by *R v Sunair Holidays Ltd*.[19] Tour operators had published a brochure in 1969 for the 1970 season relating to a Spanish hotel in the course of which they made a number of glowing references to hotel facilities, including a swimming pool, push-chairs for hire at the hotel and special dishes for children. When the customer arrived the swimming pool was empty and could not be filled, push-chairs were not available at the hotel, and there were no special dishes for children. The Court of Appeal allowed the appeal against conviction on the grounds that section 14 dealt with statements of which it could be said that they were false at the time they were made – ie statements of fact, past or present, but not promises or forecasts about the future, as such. Although in some cases a promise might imply a statement about the present, in this case the statements referred to the future.[20] Similarly in *Beckett v Cohen*[1] where a builder agreed to build for a customer a garage like his neighbour's 'within 10 days', and did not do so, the Divisional Court upheld the magistrates' court's dismissal of the information. This was a statement made in regard to the future. The Act could not be used to make a breach of contract into a criminal offence.

19   [1973] 2 All ER 1233, [1973] 1 WLR 1105, CA; M, H & P p 646.
20   Cf *R v Clarksons Holidays Ltd* (1972) 116 Sol Jo 728, CA, where a number of statements about a hotel not yet built and illustrated by an 'artist's impression' were construed by the jury as being a representation of existing facts, and the ensuing conviction was upheld as being proper by the Court of Appeal.
1   [1973] 1 All ER 120, [1972] 1 WLR 1593, DC.

As the law now stands careful analysis is, therefore, required of the relevant statements to ascertain whether they are promises in the nature of a fallible forecast or whether the statement, although relating to services to be performed in the future, also contains a statement of existing fact. The point is further illustrated by the House of Lords decision in *British Airways Board v Taylor*.[2] A prospective passenger was booked, by BOAC, on a flight to Bermuda and a letter 'confirming the following reservation London/Bermuda BA 679 Economy Class – 28 August' had been received. BOAC, in common with many other airlines, operated an 'overbooking' policy on the usually correct assumption that some passengers would fail to arrive at the airport. At the time of the letter the flight was not overbooked, but it subsequently became so and no seat was available for the passenger. The House of Lords held that the justices had been entitled to find as a fact that the statement in the letter was false within section 14. Lord Edmund Davies, in particular, stated that the facts illustrated that an assertion of existing fact and a promise of future conduct may both be found in one and the same statement. The factual statement here was that a booking could be confirmed when the overbooking policy made it impossible to do this. The appeal was in fact allowed in the airline's favour on the technical ground that British Airways were not criminally liable for the acts of the former BOAC. (Consumers may be surprised to find overbooking policies continue to operate on many scheduled airline services. Airlines, when occasionally caught out by overestimating 'no shows', may attempt appeasement by an offer of compensation plus a seat on an alternative flight.)

It is important to note that, even where there is a statement of fact present, it is only if it is false *at the time it was made* that an offence can arise. In *Sunair Holidays Ltd v Dodd*[3] an error made in allocating customers to hotel rooms shortly before their arrival at the hotel did not create an offence. Here the description in the brochure correctly reflected the arrangements the tour operator had made with the hotel and so was not a false statement when the customer made the booking.

2   [1975] 3 All ER 307, [1975] 1 WLR 1197; M, H & P p 651. However, a pre- or post-contractual statement relating to services (as opposed to goods) may be caught by s 14 as in *Breed v Cluett* [1970] 2 QB 459, [1970] 2 All ER 662, DC; M, H & P p 645 – statement after exchange of contracts that bungalow covered by National Housebuilders' Registration Council scheme made by builder-owner was false and builder convicted under s 14. See also *Cowburn v Focus Television Rentals Ltd* (1983) 147 JP 201, DC (free hire of videos when postage chargeable) and *R v Bevelectric Ltd* (1992) 157 JP 323, CA (broken washing machines falsely assessed as needing new motors). See also *Formula One Autocentres Ltd v Birmingham City Council* [1999] RTR 195, DC, discussed above at p 392, for the overlapping use of s 1 offences in connection with services.

3   [1970] 2 All ER 410, [1970] 1 WLR 1037, DC.

False or misleading statements as to services, etc

'Services, accommodation or facilities'

Making a false statement about 'services' includes a person stating falsely, in the course of trade or business, that he has certain professional qualifications since this affects the likely quality of the services,[4] though employees with a tendency to overstatement are outside the ambit of the Act as regards their employers, since 'services' does not include anything done under a contract of service (s 14(4)).

It was also made clear by the Divisional Court in *Newell v Hicks*[5] that where an advertisement offered 'a video cassette recorder absolutely free with every X registration Renault' this was not a false statement as to the provision of services, accommodation or facilities within the meaning of section 14. This was because the word 'provision' could only be read as being concerned with the fact of providing services, accommodation or facilities and not as relating to the terms upon which they are provided. In other words section 14 does not comprehend statements as to price in relation to services, accommodation or facilities. Similarly, it was held in *Dixons Ltd v Roberts*[6] that the statement, 'refund the difference if you buy Dixon's Deal products cheaper locally at time of purchase and call within seven days' was not capable of giving rise to liability under section 14. 'It is impossible to accept that the offer of a refund on part of the price of goods could be taken as an offer to provide services' (per Forbes J).

---

4   *R v Breeze* [1973] 2 All ER 1141, [1973] 1 WLR 994, CA; M, H & P pp 643 and 653 (person who had passed only the intermediate stage of an architect's qualification falsely described himself as an architect). See also above p 401.

5   (1983) 148 JP 308, 128 Sol Jo 63, DC; M, H & P p 654. Facts of this sort should be assessed instead in the light of the pricing provisions of Part III of the Consumer Protection Act 1987, below. The reluctance here to include the provision of goods within s 14 can be contrasted with the inclusion of what would normally be considered as the provision of services under s 1 in *Formula One Autocentres Ltd v Birmingham City Council* [1999] RTR 195, DC, see above p 392.

6   (1984) 148 JP 513, DC. Para 1.5.2 of the Code of Practice on Pricing (see below) states 'Do not make statements like "if you can buy this product elsewhere for less we will refund the difference" about your "own brand" products which other traders do not stock, unless your offer will also apply to other traders' equivalent goods.' Contrast *Ashley v London Borough of Sutton* (1994) 159 JP 631, DC, where a book on how to succeed in gambling was accompanied by a 90-day money back guarantee which was not honoured. It was held that both goods (the book) and services (the information in the book) were provided and that the guarantee was a statement as to the nature of the provision of the service and s 14 was therefore infringed on a failure to honour it. Query, though, whether this should not be categorised as a simple breach of contract. Compare *R v Warwickshire County Council, ex p Johnson* [1993] AC 583, sub nom *Warwickshire County Council v Johnson* [1993] 1 All ER 299, HL, below.

In *Westminster City Council v Ray Alan (Manshops) Ltd* [7] it was held that a suspect 'closing down sale' was not offering a 'facility' within the meaning of section 14. The section applied to facilities *ejusdem generis* with services or accommodation, not, for instance, to shopping facilities.

Knowledge or recklessness

A statement is deemed to be made recklessly if it is made regardless of whether it is true or false, whether or not the person making it had reasons for believing that it might be false (s 14(2)(b)). It was held in *MFI Warehouses Ltd v Nattrass* [8] that 'recklessly' does not imply dishonesty. The prosecution need only show that the defendant did not have regard to the truth or falsity of his statement, even though it cannot be proved he deliberately closed his eyes to the truth. This rather diminishes the force of the *mens rea* requirement.

The *mens rea* aspects of section 14 were further and exhaustively analysed by the House of Lords in *Wings Ltd v Ellis* [9] where, as stated by Lord Scarman, 'the basic issue between the parties is whether on its proper construction section 14(1)(a) of the 1968 Act creates an offence of strict, or more accurately semi-strict, liability or is one requiring the existence of full *mens rea*'. The actual point certified by the Divisional Court as being of general public importance was whether a defendant may properly be convicted of an offence under section 14(1)(a) of the Trade Descriptions Act 1968 where he had no knowledge of the falsity of the statement at the time of its publication but knew of the falsity at the time when the statement was read by the complainant. The facts, briefly, were that for the 1981/82 winter season the appellant tour operator had distributed to travel agents a brochure giving details of accommodation provided for customers. Shortly after the brochure was distributed the tour operator discovered that the brochure contained a statement which was false to a material degree, namely that the accommodation provided at a hotel in Sri Lanka was furnished with air conditioning. In May 1981 the mistake was discovered and steps were taken to mitigate its effects but W had booked a holiday in January 1982 depending on an unamended brochure. At the time W read the unamended brochure the tour operators were aware that the statement was false. The House of Lords unanimously upheld the prosecutor's appeal

---

7   [1982] 1 All ER 771, [1982] 1 WLR 383, DC.
8   [1973] 1 All ER 762, [1973] 1 WLR 307, DC; M, H & P p 659 (misleading advertisement for 'folding door gear (carriage free)' not intended by advertisers to mislead).
9   [1985] AC 272, [1984] 3 All ER 577, HL; M, H & P p 662. See also *Yugotours Ltd v Wadsley* [1988] BTLC 300, DC. (Failure to correct a statement known to be false can be reckless within s 14(1)(b).)

against the Divisional Court which had quashed the original conviction of the tour operators. 'The brochure was inaccurate, the respondent knew that it was inaccurate and W was misled. The ingredients for an offence under section 14 were compounded. To hold otherwise would be to emasculate section 14 and to place a premium on carelessness by the respondents' (per Lord Templeman). It was pointed out that, although the tour operators never intended to make a false statement to W, an offence had been committed under section 14. The respondent tour operators had not attempted to put forward a defence under section 24, which might otherwise have been available, that the commission of the offence was due to a mistake etc and all reasonable precautions and all due diligence had been exercised to prevent the commission of the offence.

Property misdescriptions

Although section 14 of the Trade Descriptions Act 1968 applies to false or misleading statements as to any 'services, accommodation or facilities', it has been clear for many years that neither this section, nor the Act generally, applies to sales of interests in land (as opposed to the provision of short-term holiday accommodation). In March 1990 the Director General of Fair Trading, in his Report on Estate Agency, recommended new legislation to give more protection to consumers. Later that year a Private Member's Bill was introduced, sponsored by the Consumers' Association, to deal with property misdescriptions. The ambit of the Bill was widened considerably during its passage through Parliament to take account of statements made by builders, property developers and solicitors (when engaged in estate agency work), though the main target of the legislation is clearly an estate agency business. Its short title indicates its ambit – the Property Misdescriptions Act 1991.[10]

The Act makes it an offence to make a false or misleading statement about a prescribed matter in the course of an estate agency business or a property development business, otherwise than in providing conveyancing services (s 1). Where the making of a statement is attributable to the fault of an employee, the employee is guilty of an offence whether or not proceedings are also taken against the employer (s 1(2)). The offence carries, on summary conviction, a fine of the statutory maximum and on conviction on indictment, an unlimited fine. The making of such a false statement does not affect the validity of the underlying contract, and no right of action in civil proceedings in respect of any loss arises by reason only of the commission of such an offence (s 1(4)).

---

10   BSSCCL p 579. See R Bragg 'Regulation of Estate Agents' (1992) 55 MLR 368.

The terms 'false' and 'misleading' are defined in a similar way to that applicable to false trade descriptions generally and a 'prescribed matter' is any matter relating to land specified in the Property Misdescriptions (Specified Matters) Order 1992.[11] This Order specifies a wide range of matters including location, aspect, view, proximity to facilities, accommodation, measurements, survey, guarantees, history, length of time for sale, price (present or former), tenure or estate, council tax band and existence of planning permissions.

The statements in question must be made in the course of an estate agency business or a property development business. The latter means that the statement must be made 1) in the course of a business concerned wholly or substantially with the development of land, and 2) for the purpose of, or with a view to, disposing of an interest in land consisting of or including a building, or a part of a building, constructed or renovated in the course of the business. An estate agency business involves 'estate agency work' as defined by section 1 of the Estate Agents Act 1979 – broadly, disposing of or acquiring an interest in land on the instructions of a client with a view to the introduction of a third party who wishes to acquire or dispose of the relevant interest in land. The ambit of section 1 is therefore wide.

There is a 'due diligence defence' whereby the defendant must show 'that he took all reasonable steps and exercised all due diligence to avoid committing the offence' (s 2). Where this involves reliance on information given by another it must be shown to have been reasonable to have relied on the information in the light of steps which had been taken to verify it and consideration of whether he had any reason to disbelieve the information (s 2(2)). What, then, is the agent's position when repeating wrong information given by the vendor? A decision hailed as a landmark case[12] goes some way to clarify matters. There, the prosecuted agents advertised a four-bedroomed semi-detached house 'with one-bedroomed bungalow'. The bungalow turned out to have no planning permission (though 30 to 40 years old). The magistrates firstly held that the details were misleading – section 1(5)(b) states that a statement is misleading if (though not false) what a reasonable person may be expected to infer from it or from any omission from it, is false. The omission of the absence of planning permission was therefore prima facie culpable. However the Divisional Court confirmed that the defence of due diligence, under section 2, was available because in these circumstances, where there was no reasonable ground for suspicion, the agents were entitled to rely on the

11 SI 1992/2834; BSSCCL p 750.
12 *Enfield London Borough Council v Castles Estate Agents Ltd* [1996] 2 EGLR 21, 160 JP 618, DC.

vendor's assertion. The status of a new extension should, however, be checked.

There is a requirement, common in trading law statutes, that if third parties are to be joined in, seven clear days' notice must be given to the prosecutor to identify the person who committed the act or default (s 2(3)).

6. DEFENCES

The 1968 Act includes defences which are similar to defences provided by other penal consumer law statutes, eg weights and measures and food and drugs laws,[13] and mitigate the rigour of the strict liability imposed by sections 1 and (the former) 11 (though s 24(1) applies to 'any proceedings for an offence under this Act' and may be important also where services are in issue under the 'non-strict' s 14). The defences are primarily in section 24, but section 25 provides a defence that an advertisement committing an offence under the Act was published in the course of such a business and that the publisher 'did not know and had no reason to suspect that its publication would amount to an offence'. Section 23, dealing with offences due to the fault of some other person, is not strictly a defence provision, but it is convenient to examine section 23 along with section 24.

Section 24(1) states that, subject to the procedure laid down in section 24(2), it shall be a defence for the accused to prove (on the balance of probabilities) that he comes within *both* the following paragraphs:

a) that the commission of the offence was due to a mistake or to reliance on information supplied to him or to the act or default of another person, an accident or some other cause beyond his control; and

b) that he took all reasonable precautions and exercised all due diligence to avoid the commission of such an offence by himself or any person under his control.

Subsection (2) provides, in effect, that an accused relying on the act or default of or on information supplied by another person must give, at least seven days before the hearing, written notice to the prosecution giving such information to identify the other person as was then in his possession.

Subsection (3) provides a further defence to charges of supplying or offering to supply goods to which a false trade description is applied. The accused must prove 'that he did not know, and could not with reasonable diligence have ascertained, that the goods did not conform to the description or that the description had been applied to the goods'.

These provisions have been the subject of considerable litigation and the main points of interpretation must be separately discussed.

---

13 See generally M, H & P ch 15 – general statutory defences in consumer protection legislation.

Act or default of another person (s 24(1)(a))

Where the defendant is an individual, the expression 'another person' means any person other than himself. More difficulty arises where the defendant is a company and the offence arises out of the act or default of one of its servants. The crucial issue is whether the person alleged for the purposes of the defence to be another person is really the 'ego' or 'alter ego' of the company. The point arose in *Beckett v Kingston Bros (Butchers) Ltd*[14] where a turkey labelled 'Norfolk King Turkey' in fact came from Denmark. The mistake had been identified in the case of the consignment of which this was one, and all area managers had been warned by the managing director to alter the labels. One shop manager failed to comply with these instructions in respect of this turkey. The defendant company successfully established that the manager was 'another person', the Divisional Court stating that it would stultify the defence under section 24 if it were the law that because the person truly responsible for the offence was an employee the employer, provided he had taken reasonable precautions and shown due diligence, was still debarred from using the defence.

The same question arose in the House of Lords' decision in *Tesco Supermarkets Ltd v Nattrass*.[15] One of the chain of supermarkets, whose staff had been efficiently trained, displayed a 'flash' offer on a poster relating to money off the usual price of washing powder. The shop had run out of the packets to which they intended to apply the reduced price, being packets bearing a special indication of reduced price, and a shopper failed to get the price of an ordinary packet reduced. This had occurred because the shop manager had failed to supervise the actions of his assistant who had put out on display only the remaining full price packets. The company was summonsed under the provisions of section 11(2) (giving an indication that goods are being offered at a price less than that at which they are in fact being offered). It was held that the shop manager was 'another person' from his employing company. He could not be identified with the company itself or its *alter ego*. Lord Reid said that managers to whom functions are delegated by the company's board of directors are capable of being part of the embodiment of the company (and see s 20), but here the board had set up a chain of command through regional and district supervisors, but they remained in control. The shop managers had to obey their general directions and also take orders from

14 [1970] 1 QB 606, [1970] 1 All ER 715, DC.
15 [1972] AC 153, [1971] 2 All ER 127, HL; M, H & P p 711. See also *Lewin v Rothersthorpe Road Garage Ltd* (1983) 148 JP 87, DC; M, H & P p 511, to the same effect.

their superiors. The acts or omissions of shop managers were not acts of the company itself.[16]

As regards the identification of the other person, it has since been held that, to avoid the administration of the Act becoming slipshod, the company must show that it has done all that could reasonably be expected in enquiring and investigating into the matter of who was responsible for the act or default, and identify him or them as far as possible.[17]

Mistake

It was held in *Birkenhead and District Co-operative Society Ltd v Roberts*[18] that where the alleged offence arose out of the mis-labelling by the defendant's servant of a joint of beef, a 'mistake' by any person other than the one charged did not come within 'mistake'. Where it is someone else's mistake, 'act or default of another person' had to be pleaded and the procedure as to seven days' notice (under s 24(2)) would have to be followed.

'Reliance on information supplied to him'

Where reliance on information is raised, notice has to be given under section 24(2). Although it is not stated, it is assumed that the source of the information would have to be a reliable source. In *Naish v Gore*[19] a car originally sold with a recorded mileage of 83,060 ended up after several further sales with a recorded mileage of 35,000. A charge was brought against the last car dealer involved, in respect of applying a false trade description as to the history of the car by means of an incorrect odometer reading. The defendant was able to establish a defence under section 24(1) when he showed that an independent opinion from an Automobile Association expert had been obtained that the car's appearance and performance were consistent with the lower mileage.

Accident or cause beyond accused's control

There are a number of reported decisions on the similar weights and measures legislation as to the meaning of these words. For instance, a

16   Ibid at 175. See the criticism of this decision by Sir Gordon Borrie in *The Development of Consumer Law and Policy* pp 52–53, M, H & P p 717.
17   *McGuire v Sittingbourne Co-operative Society Ltd* [1976] Crim LR 268, DC.
18   [1970] 3 All ER 391, [1970] 1 WLR 1497, DC.
19   [1971] 3 All ER 737, DC.

manufacturer successfully established that a bag of crisps bore a wrong indication of its weight owing to an unforeseen fault in a well maintained and normally accurate machine, and this was a cause beyond the manufacturer's control.[20]

Reasonable precautions and due diligence (s 24(1)(b))

In addition to identifying grounds under section 24(1)(a), the requirements of section 24(1)(b) must also be satisfied for a defence to succeed. In the context of the meaning of reasonable precautions, O'Keefe states that the expression involves 'setting up a system to ensure that things will not go wrong: "due diligence" means seeing that the system works properly'.[1] An illustration of this can be seen in *Tesco Supermarkets Ltd v Nattrass*.[2] The company's duty as to 'reasonable precautions' and 'due diligence' was to set up an efficient system of training and show due diligence in subsequent inspections to see that the law was complied with, which it had done.

The concept of showing 'due diligence' is to be found in parallel defence sections of many other trading law statutes – and is mentioned again in this book in the context (for instance) of food offences. A full survey of the cases, some unreported, will be found in the standard trading law encyclopaedias. Suffice it to say here that the defendant will normally have to prove that 1) any staff responsible for the mischief in question were sensibly selected and properly trained, 2) a proper system exists for checking potentially offending stock, and if this is by sample, a reasonably comprehensive sample should be taken, and 3) any defect eg in a misdescribed car is truly latent. In summary, a positive and effective screening system must be shown to exist.

Section 24(3)

This involves what might be called a defence of 'innocent supply of goods' to a charge under section 1(1)(b) and is therefore more limited in its scope than the defence under section 24(1), which applies to any offence under the Act. It would be appropriate, for example, to the trader supplied with

20 *Bibby-Cheshire v Golden Wonder Ltd* [1972] 3 All ER 738, [1972] 1 WLR 1487, DC; M, H & P p 719.
1   O'Keefe *Law of Weights and Measures* (2nd edn) 1(281).
2   [1972] AC 153, [1971] 2 All ER 127, HL; M, H & P p 720.
3   The test was held to be an objective test in *Denard v Abbas* [1987] Crim LR 424, DC; M, H & P p 726. This does not appear to be consistent with the wording of s 24(3), which implies a subjective test.

Defences

offending goods where the trader did not know and had no cause to suspect[3] that the goods did not conform to the description, or that a description had ever been applied to them.[4] In *Barker v Hargreaves*[5] a second-hand car dealer advertised a car as being 'in good condition throughout' and sold it on that basis. The dealer had submitted it successfully for an MOT test and obtained the usual certificate containing printed warnings that the certificate should not be accepted as evidence of the car's condition. The car was in fact badly corroded on the underside, though this was partially hidden by under-sealing and other factors. On a charge under section 1(1)(b) of applying a false trade description by advertisement the defendant relied on section 24(3) – ie that he had relied on the information in the test certificate. The Divisional Court upheld the justices' conviction of the defendant. With reasonable diligence some of the corrosion could have been discovered. Nor could the defence under section 24(1) be prayed in aid. The defendant had relied solely on the certificate, which contained warnings and he had no system of his own for ascertaining the car's condition.

Section 23

This section allows the prosecution of a person other than the person actually committing the offence where 'the commission by any person of an offence' is due to the act or default of that other person. That other person may be charged and convicted whether or not the person actually committing the offence is prosecuted. Concurrent proceedings are, therefore, permitted and the position is similar (though not identical) to that under section 40 of the Consumer Protection Act 1987.

There is some difficulty with the meaning of 'commission by any person of an offence'. Strictly it might be argued that the first person would not have 'committed an offence' if it could shown that the situation could be brought within section 24(1)(a) and (b) by proving that it was due to the act or default of another and due diligence etc. However, Lord Widgery CJ explained in *Coupe v Guyett*[6] that where the first person referred to in

---

4   The overlap between ss 24(1)(a) and 24(3) was discussed in *Naish v Gore*, above, where it was suggested that s 24(3) was more apt where the goods were defective than where there was a representation about them. See also for an unsuccessful attempt to use s 24(3) where a car's false odometer reading could have been discovered with reasonable diligence, *Lewis v Maloney* [1977] Crim LR 436, DC.

5   (1980) 125 Sol Jo 165, [1981] RTR 197, DC; M, H & P p 725.

6   [1973] 2 All ER 1058, [1973] 1 WLR 669, DC; M, H & P p 729 following dicta of Lord Diplock in *Tesco Supermarkets Ltd v Nattrass*, above. In this case a lady 'sleeping' proprietor of a garage was entirely unaware of a false statement made by her repair workshop manager and was acquitted of an offence under s 14(1)(b) on this general ground. Accordingly, the 'other person', namely the manager, also had to be acquitted under s 23.

section 23 had a defence on the merits and without reference to section 24, it is not possible to operate section 23 so as to render guilty the person whose act or default gave rise to the matter in complaint. Conversely, if the first person would have been convicted of an offence but for section 24(1), he or she can be properly regarded as having 'committed an offence' for the purposes of prosecuting the other person under section 23. (Section 24 would be clearer on the same point if s 24(1)(a) were to refer to 'the commission of the *alleged* offence'.)

It is essential to show a direct causal connection between the offence by the first person and the act or default to which it is due of the other person. Section 23 cannot be used where there are two separate offences or possible offences not causally connected. This point is particularly relevant in the case of the sale of a car with a false odometer reading where the seller thus prima facie commits an offence under section 1(1)(b) in offering to supply goods to which a false trade description is applied. What is the position where a previous owner of the car has, for instance, sold it by auction at which the accused bought it some time before? It was held on similar facts found by the magistrates' court in *Tarleton Engineering Co Ltd v Nattrass*[7] that there was no causal connection between the events, the two sales being separated by a period of about three weeks, and even if the 'other person', ie the previous owner, had been separately charged under section 1, the 'other person' might have had a defence (eg a disclaimer, or act of a further third party under s 24). If a third party were actually found not guilty if separately charged under section 1(1)(b), it would indeed be strange to be convicted by using section 23 in respect of a later event.

A further controversial point is whether a third party, due to whose act or default an offence has been committed, may be prosecuted by virtue of section 23 if acting as a private individual. It is no objection, of course, to the section 24(1)(a) defence that the third party in question was a private individual (who, for example, turned back an odometer), but may that person also be prosecuted if not acting in the course of trade or business? Section 23 refers to 'an offence under this Act' being due to another person's default. The offences in sections 1, 9, 12, 13 and 14 all expressly state that the accused must act in the course of a trade or business, and the courts have implied this into the actus reus of the former prices offence under section 11.[8] On the face of it this procedure is improper since the section, in stating that the 'other person shall be guilty of *the* offence' clearly refers back to the commission by any person of 'an offence *under this Act*'. The section also refers to the third party's being charged with 'the offence',

---

7   [1973] 3 All ER 699, [1973] 1 WLR 1261, DC, followed in *Taylor v Smith* [1974] RTR 190, DC.
8   *John v Matthews* [1970] 2 QB 443, [1970] 2 All ER 643, DC.

similarly interpreted.[9] However the Divisional Court in *Olgeirsson v Kitching*[10] seemed to find little difficulty in extending criminal liability under section 23 to a private person who had falsely represented to a garage salesman that his vehicle had a true mileage of some 36,000 miles less than the reality. Stating that the words of section 23 must be given 'their plain and ordinary meaning', the court went on to decide that criminality was not confined to someone who is engaged in the same trade as the principal offender. The court did, however, query whether that was so only if his act or default was done with full knowledge that what he was doing was false or whether the result may be otherwise if the act or default is neither reckless nor careless. Although some comfort was found by the court in the previous decision in *Meah v Roberts*[11] the decision results in the illogical situation that section 23 can apparently be used to prosecute a private individual misdescribing goods which happen to reach the hands of a trader, whereas no prosecution would lie where the goods remain subject to private sales.

It is interesting to note that the Department of Trade and Industry appeared to share the concern about this extension in scope of section 23 by judicial decision. The 1990 consultative letter (referred to in more detail below) states (in Annexe A) that judicial decisions have confirmed 'that a private individual, ie a person not acting in the course of a trade or business, can be convicted by this means. There is a particular case for requiring knowledge or intention to be shown in such cases as an appropriate safeguard to protect persons who are otherwise generally outside the scope of the Act'. It was pointed out that the Consumer Protection Act 1987 explicitly requires the relevant third party's acts or defaults to be done 'in the course of a business of his' thus exempting employees (as opposed to proprietors). A similar approach to that in the 1987 Act (above) could be adopted as an alternative to requiring *mens rea*.

On the question of defences generally, the point which seems to have given rise to the most disquiet is the refusal of the courts to hold companies in effect vicariously liable for the acts of their employees in such circumstances as arose in the *Tesco Supermarkets Ltd v Nattrass* case.[12] The OFT's Review suggested that this decision distorts the operation of the Act and encourages some companies to shoulder all the blame for

---

9   The private person may have committed an offence under some other statute, eg obtaining property by deception under Theft Act 1968, s 15.

10 [1986] 1 All ER 746, [1986] 1 WLR 304, DC; M, H & P p 731.

11 [1978] 1 All ER 97, [1977] 1 WLR 1187, DC; discussed in the Food and Drugs context at p 436.

12 See p 409, above. See also G Borrie [1975] Crim LR 663–5, who is critical of the Committee's reluctance to impose vicarious responsibility which he considers would promote better trading standards. See also Borrie *The Development of Consumer Law and Policy*, pp 52–53.

offences within their organisation, whatever the circumstances, and others to establish due diligence and blame the staff responsible. In the latter case enforcement officers are reluctant to prosecute more lowly employees. There is, however, the 'potent argument' of Lord Reid in the *Tesco* case to the effect that since, to escape, the employer must show that he has done all that he could do to prevent an offence, 'how can he do more?' The Committee therefore reached no decision as to recommendations on this point. The 1990 consultation document suggested that a more modern version of the 'due diligence' defence might avoid these problems.

7. SENTENCING AND COMPENSATION ORDERS

As was noticed above, trials of Trade Descriptions Act offences may either be summary or on indictment and alternative penalties are laid down.[13] Whilst the maximum penalty on summary trial is £5,000 under section 18 (as amended), the same section provides for the penalties on conviction on indictment to be a fine (unlimited) or imprisonment for a term not exceeding two years or both. The Court in *R v Haesler*[14] said that offences under the Trade Descriptions Act, unless accompanied by dishonesty, would not normally be regarded as prison offences. But fines where the defendant has the ability to pay can be substantial. For instance the head of a firm selling flavoured water as a slimming aid was fined £10,000 by Teeside Crown Court[15] and Innovations (Mail Order) was fined £4,000 by Winchester Crown Court for a £7.99 electronic mosquito repeller which was so ineffective it put lives at risk.[16] Where dishonesty *is* involved, such as where a car has been deliberately clocked, the Court of Appeal has stated that a custodial sentence should be expected: see eg *R v Nash*.[17]

Since a false trade description can be proliferated by advertisements or holiday brochures, for example, the possibility of multiple prosecutions in different parts of the country, and correspondingly varying penalties, exists. In *R v Thomson Holidays Ltd*[18] the Court of Appeal, in a reserved judgment, held that false statements in a travel brochure contrary to section 14 are made when communicated to someone, so that each time a false statement

13　Above, ch 8. The offences are thus 'either way' and the procedure under the Magistrates' Courts Act 1980, s 18 applies. The great majority of offences under the Act are tried summarily.
14　[1973] Crim LR 586, CA.
15　(2000) Times, 2 June.
16　(1998) Times, 30 June.
17　[1990] RTR 343, CA – written-off car cosmetically and inadequately repaired and described as 'in excellent condition'. In fact it was a potential death trap; *R v Hewitt* [1991] RTR 357, CA – turning back odometer; *R v Adam (Rafiq Ahmed)* [1998] 2 Cr App Rep (S) 403, counterfeit clothing.
18　[1974] QB 592, [1974] 1 All ER 823, CA.

was communicated to a reader a fresh offence was committed. It followed that a plea of *autrefois convict* in respect of a similar previous conviction was invalid, nor would the court stay the proceedings as being oppressive. Nevertheless, it was agreed by the OFT Review Committee that multiple prosecutions (though thought to be very rare) could be unduly burdensome to both the courts and the trader.

One complication is the problem of compensation orders. Under the Powers of Criminal Courts Act 1973 (s 35) the court has a discretionary power to impose a compensation order on persons convicted of an offence, or any other offence which is taken into consideration by the court in determining sentence. This provision applies generally, but is used notably in trade descriptions cases. The limit of such an order in the magistrates' courts is £5,000 for each offence of which the offender is convicted.[19] It is therefore natural for consumers to wish to encourage the bringing of what are collectively multiple prosecutions in the circumstances outlined above in order to obtain the benefit of a compensation order, without incurring the trouble and expense of a separate civil action. The Review Committee stated that 'there is clearly a conflict between the public interest in avoiding multiple prosecutions and the private interest in not losing the benefits of compensation which a successful prosecution might bring' (para 231). They tentatively suggested that the best solution would be to make it a defence for a trader to prove a) a conviction (or presumably acquittal) for an 'identical' offence (ie arising out of the same chain of events) before the offence charged and subsequently the taking of all reasonable steps to avoid the further commission of an offence, and b) that ex gratia compensation has been given to all aggrieved persons who gave written notification that they had been injured by this or any 'identical' offence. The Committee drew a parallel with procedures under the Defamation Act 1952, but nevertheless realised that there were many unsolved difficulties in applying the proposed solution.

Compensation orders are discussed in more detail in chapter 8.

8. FUTURE OF THE 1968 ACT

As mentioned in the course of this chapter, the Department of Trade and Industry issued a consultative letter in 1990[20] regarding a general review of the Act. The document suggested that areas where reform might be considered were i) scope of the Act and section 23 (considered above); ii) possibly introducing strict liability for misstatements as to services etc;

19 Magistrates' Court Act 1980, s 40 as amended.
20 Reproduced in (1990) 7 Tr Law 115–124. See also the NCC's Review, November 1990.

iii) defences generally, which could be reformed by adopting a 'modern defence' regime involving all reasonable steps and exercising all due diligence to avoid committing the offence – which would encompass the need to show that sufficient had been done to guard against the inefficiency, incompetence etc of employees; iv) extension of the Act to catch certain activities associated with services such as timeshare promotions, newspaper bingo and homework schemes; v) a minor clarification of disclaimers (considered above); vi) the removal of possible conflicts with EC law on certificates of origin; and vii) a possible reformulation of the existing order-making powers. No amendments to the 1968 Act were, however, enacted.

Timeshare schemes have since become regulated by the Timeshare Act 1992,[1] which both prescribes formalities with which timeshare agreements must apply and a 14-day cooling-off period. The Act applies to leisure living accommodation anywhere provided that the agreement is i) governed by UK law; ii) at least one party is in the UK when the agreement is entered into; iii) the accommodation is situated in the United Kingdom or iv) when the agreement was made the offeree was ordinarily resident in the United Kingdom and the accommodation was in another European Area State. A person in the course of a business contravening the Act commits an offence. The Department of Trade and Industry is reviewing the legislation and considering reform.[2] In addition, the Timeshare Directive[3] is included in the Directive on injunctions for the protection of consumers' interests,[4] which requires implementation by 1 January 2001. It is proposed that the Director should be the lead enforcement body, with consumer organisations being able, also, to seek injunctions to enforce the Timeshare measures.

The White Paper *Modern Markets: Confident Consumers*[5] proposed the alignment of provisions relating to services, facilities and accommodation with those relating to goods. In Spring 2000 the DTI issued a consultation paper on this and related matters.[6] The key proposals are the amendment of section 14 to make the supplier of services under the same obligations as the supplier of goods, with strict liability; new provisions regarding the future supply of services and statements by experts; an expansion of the matters listed in section 14 about which false

1   As amended by the Timeshare Regulations 1997, SI 1997/1081: see BSSCCL p 582.
2   *Timeshare Sales, Consultation Paper*, DTI, April 2000.
3   94/47/EC, OJ No L 280 29.10.94, p 83.
4   98/27/EC OJ No L 166, 11.6.98, p 51; see also *Injunctions Directive: Implementation in the UK*, DTI, February 2000 and 'Widening the net', OFT (2000) 26 Fair Trading 13.
5   Cm 4410, July 1999, para 3.19.
6   *Amendments to the Trade Descriptions Act 1968*, www.dti.gov/consumer/law/4.htm.

statements may give rise to liability; improvements regarding enforcement matters and the disapplication of section 16 for goods imported from member states.

9. PRICE INDICATIONS[7]

Legislation to curb abuses in the statement of prices was a novelty when introduced by the 1968 Act. The Molony Committee was unfashionably unsympathetic to complaints about deceptive pricing methods:

> Our reaction ... is that consumers must be expected to go shopping with their eyes open and their wits reasonably alert. If it should happen to their cost that they fail to notice that the price on the bacon is quoted per ½ lb and not per lb ... they will have had a valuable lesson which might help them more than anything we could recommend.
> [para 813]

But in fact the Committee had included in its revised form of definition of a 'trade description' statements as to the 'former or usual price of any goods' (para 636). This was not the preferred option when finally enacted. Section 11 of the Trade Descriptions Act 1968 contained two offences relating to the pricing of goods. Subsection (1) concerned false indications that the price of goods equalled or was less than a recommended price or a previous price. Subsection (2) made it an offence to give an indication that goods were being offered at a price less than the price at which they were in fact being offered. Section 11 received some critical comment in the Review of the Trade Descriptions Act 1968 by the OFT's inter-departmental committee[8] and proposals for reform were made.

Bargain offers

'Bargain offers' have proved singularly intractable to legislate against. The mischief involves the misleading advertisement of price comparisons – that is misleading in the sense that the comparison is meaningless, not capable of substantiation or simply false. Following an Office of Fair Trading consultative document issued in 1975, a Bargain Offers Order was introduced in 1979, hastily followed by two amending Orders.[9] The Order

---

7 See M, H & P ch 14.
8 Review of the Trade Descriptions Act 1968, Cmnd 6628 (1976), ch viii. See also R G Lawson (1977) 141 JP 66.
9 Price Marking (Bargain Offers) Order 1979, SI 1979/364; as amended by SI 1979/633 and SI 1979/1124.

was widely condemned as obscure, difficult to apply and to enforce, and arguably ambiguous in intent in some respects.[10] The Office of Fair Trading was asked, by the Secretary of State, to review the Bargain Offers Order, paying particular attention to the increasing use of meaningless price comparisons technically complying with the Order. Examples included comparisons with 'after sales prices' quoted during 'sales' by certain furniture outlets, discounts off 'special order prices' where almost all goods on sale were available other than by 'special orders'[11] and comparisons with 'RAP' – ready assembled price, when furniture was, in practice, normally sold unassembled.

In October 1981 the Director reported that although the criticism of the Bargain Offers Orders had been in some respects exaggerated, it was conceded that the wording contained substantial ambiguities which caused difficulties in both interpretation and enforcement. There was, therefore, a case for amendment.

These proposals for review culminated in a Report of an Inter-Departmental Working Party on the review of legislation on false and misleading price information (1984).[12] This laid out a blueprint for what was to become the legislation now contained in Part III of the Consumer Protection Act 1987. Amongst the recommendations were that there should be a general legislative prohibition on traders providing consumers with false or misleading information about prices. It was also recommended that a statutory Code of Practice containing practical guidance would be the best means of providing much of the necessary detailed support for a general prohibition on false or misleading price information. The report pointed out that a number of other Acts had contained provisions for such a statutory code which is not legally binding – so that failure to observe any provision of the code does not itself render a person liable to any proceedings – but which is given a status which enables it to be admissible in evidence. It was also recommended that the primary legislation should contain provision for the Secretary of State to have power to make subordinate legislation. Enforcement should continue to be the responsibility of Trading Standards Authorities.

Both these recommendations were adopted in the 1987 Act. In particular a Code of Practice explains what is and what is not regarded as permitted by way of the sort of bargain offer mentioned above.

---

10 See 'Practical Problems arising from the Price Marking (Bargain Offers) Order 1979', M Carlisle (1979) 129 NLJ 815.
11 See T R French 'More than was bargained for' (1981) 89 Monthly Rev 80.
12 See M, H & P p 673.

Consumer Protection Act 1987[13]

Part III of this Act deals with misleading price indications. It replaced section 11 of the Trade Descriptions Act 1968 and the Price Marking (Bargain Offers) Orders 1979. The provisions create a general offence of giving a misleading price indication and empower the Secretary of State to approve a Code of Practice. Unlike the former section 11 of the 1968 Act, the provisions apply not only to goods but also to services, accommodation or facilities.

Section 20

The offence created by section 20(1) is that a person is guilty of an offence if, in the course of any business of his, he gives (by any means whatever) to any consumers an indication which is misleading as to the price at which any goods, services, accommodation or facilities are available (whether generally or from particular persons). Section 20(2) adds that a person is also guilty of an offence if:

a)   in the course of any business of his, he has given an indication to any consumers which, after it was given, has become misleading as mentioned in subsection (1); and

b)   consumers might reasonably be expected to rely on the indication at a time after it has become misleading; and

c)   he fails to take all such steps as are reasonable to prevent those consumers from relying on the indication. (Examples of price indications which become misleading are provided in the statutory Code of Practice,[14] Part 3.) It is to be noted that there are two separate offences and section 20(1) is not appropriate for indications which are correct when given but which subsequently become misleading.[15]

It is immaterial, by section 20(3):

a)   whether the person who gives or gave the indication is or was acting on his own behalf or on behalf of another;

b)   whether or not that person is the person from whom the goods, services, accommodation or facilities are available (eg travel agents indicating the price of holidays offered by tour operators); and

c)   whether the indication is or has become misleading in relation to all the consumers to whom it is or was given or only in relation to some of them (eg for pensioners or students).

---

13   See BSSCCL p 537.
14   Consumer Protection (Code of Practice for Traders on Price Indications) Approval Order 1988, SI 1988/2078; M, H & P p 695, BSSCCL 727.
15   See *Thomson Tour Operations Ltd v Birch* (1999) 163 JP 465, DC.

Section 20(6) defines both the terms 'consumer' and 'price'. As far as 'consumer' is concerned this term is defined as follows:

a) in relation to any goods, it means any person who might wish to be supplied with the goods for his own private use or consumption;

b) in relation to any services or facilities, it means any person who might wish to be provided with the services or facilities otherwise than for the purposes of any business of his; and

c) in relation to any accommodation, it means any person who might wish to occupy the accommodation otherwise than for the purposes of any business of his.

It will be noted that, unlike under the Trade Descriptions Act 1968, this offence does not apply in a business-to-business situation; it applies *only* to a business-to-consumer one. Furthermore, the expression 'in the course of a business of his' has now been held by the House of Lords[16] not appropriate to convict a branch manager – the words must mean any business of which the defendant is either the owner or has a controlling interest in.

So far as 'price' is concerned, in relation to any goods, services, accommodation or facilities, 'price' is defined as follows:

a) the aggregate of the sums required to be paid by a consumer for or otherwise in respect of the supply of the goods or the provision of the services, accommodation or facilities; or

b) except in section 21 (regarding the meaning of 'misleading') any method which will be or has been applied for the purpose of determining that aggregate.

The meaning of 'required to be paid by a consumer' has been considered by the courts in the context of the commonly met problem of the individual price mark on goods (usually marking a price reduction) being less than the bar code scanned by the cashier on computerised tills. In *Toys 'R' Us v Gloucestershire County Council*[17] the Divisional Court decided that, provided that the cashier in fact charged the ticket price (despite having rung up the bar code), there was no offence under section 20(1) – the ticket price was the price 'required to be paid by a consumer'. This would not be so, of course, if the higher bar code price had been demanded.

Misleading – section 21

The meaning of 'misleading' is of crucial importance in defining the scope of the offences under section 20(1) and (2). Section 21 is devoted to the

16   *R v Warwickshire County Council, ex p Johnson* [1993] AC 583, sub nom *Warwickshire County Council v Johnson* [1993] 1 All ER 299, HL; M, H & P p 675. See the extensive analysis of this case in BTCL 2 [3081].

17   (1994) 158 JP 338, DC; M, H & P p 683.

meaning of 'misleading'. Subsection (1) can be summarised by saying that a price is misleading if a (notional)[18] consumer might reasonably be expected to infer any of the following from the price indication:

a) The price is less than in fact it is. This covers the all too common situation in some shops where goods purportedly reduced are charged for at full price at the cash till.[19]

b) In effect, the price purports to be unconditional whereas in fact it is conditional – eg the advertised price of furniture is in fact applicable to that in one colour, anything else being more.[20]

c) The price covers matters in respect of which an extra charge is in fact made.[1] An example would be a charge for VAT at the retail till when a customer assumed that the displayed price is inclusive. Additionally, the Price Marking Order 1999[2] requires that in sales to consumers, where a 'selling price' has to be indicated, this must be inclusive of VAT (arts 1(2) and 4) – see chapter 9. Where the price differs when different methods of payment are made, for example by a credit card, the Price Indications (Method of Payment) Regulations 1991[3] prescribe that the differential pricing policy must be made clear, either by displaying the two prices or by expressing the one as a percentage of the indicated price of the other.

d) The price is to be increased or reduced or maintained (whether or not at a particular time or by a particular amount) when the person giving the indication has no such expectation.[4] For example, 'Prices now reduced by 10%. Hurry and buy now before prices return to normal' or 'Buy now to beat Budget price increases', when neither event is expected to occur, infringe this subsection.

e) The price is linked to factual information by reference to which consumers might reasonably be expected to judge the validity of relevant comparison with the price indication, and these facts or circumstances are not in fact what they are. This is a very wide, catch-all, provision designed to prohibit all other false or misleading price comparisons. *Genuine* comparisons are to be encouraged, but if comparisons such as 'Our price £9, £12 in X's supermarket', or 'Now reduced to £9, formerly £10', or 'Our price £9, mrp (manufacturer's

---

18 See *MFI Furniture Centres Ltd v Hibbert* (1995) 160 JP 178, DC – prosecution need not produce an actual customer to whom a misleading pride was indicated.

19 See Code para 2.1 and *Toys 'R' Us v Gloucestershire County Council* (1994) 158 JP 338, DC; M, H & P p 683.

20 See *Sweeting v Northern Upholstery Ltd* (1982) 2 Tr L 5, DC and Code paras 1.4 and 2.2.

1 See Code, Part 2.

2 SI 1999/3042.

3 SI 1991/199, see below re s 26.

4 See Code paras 1.3 and 1.9 and *A G Stanley Ltd (t/a Fads) v Surrey County Council Trading Standards Office* (1994) 159 JP 691, DC, discussed below.

recommended price) £10', are *falsely* made, an offence is committed. (Note that s 21(3) defines more closely what a 'relevant comparison' is (and includes by inference the above examples).)

An example of section 21(1)(e) can be seen in *A G Stanley Ltd (t/a Fads) v Surrey County Council Trading Standards Office*[5] where a table was reduced from £7.99 to £4.99 in October 1992 as part of a 'Style and Value' promotion. It continued at this price until March 1993 when it reverted to £7.99. Meanwhile, in November 1992, a 13-day 'super savers' event was advertised, with the table marked as 'was £7.99 now £4.99'. The 'Style and Value' promotion ended on 15 December, with the price of the table remaining at £4.99. In the Christmas sale, commencing 21 December, the table was advertised as 'now £4.99 was £7.99'. The court concluded that an offence had been committed. A particular issue raised concerned the '28-day rule' for comparisons with prices previously charged in the same business (Code para 1.2.2, formerly in s 11(3) of the 1968 Act). The crucial requirement is that the previous price with which comparison is made should be the *last* price at which the product was available in the previous six months for at least 28 consecutive days and in the same shop. The court rejected a suggestion that 'the last price' was the last numerically different price and not the price charged immediately before the particular offer in question.

In summary it will be seen that the test of 'a misleading price indication' under section 21(1) is whether the information as to a price conveyed to a consumer includes any of the five misleading factors listed. In some instances more than one factor may be applicable. Section 21(2) explains what is misleading as to a *method* of determining a price, so as to catch price comparisons expressed less directly. With regard to section 21(1)(a) – an indication 'that the price is less than in fact it is' – this is a similar test to that formerly contained in section 11(2) of the 1968 Act. The implication continues to be that the well-known contractual principle that the indication of a price displayed with goods in, for example, a shop window has no contractual effect because it is merely an invitation to treat[6] is nevertheless likely to be a criminal offence under section 20. Section 21(1)(a) and (c) appear to apply to the facts of certain cases previously decided under the former section 11 of the 1968 Act.[7]

5 (1994) 159 JP 691, DC.
6 See eg *Pharmaceutical Society of Great Britain v Boots Cash Chemists (Southern) Ltd* [1952] 2 QB 795, [1952] 2 All ER 456; *Fisher v Bell* [1961] 1 QB 394, [1960] 3 All ER 731, DC.
7 See in particular *Richards v Westminster Motors Ltd* (1975) 119 Sol Jo 626, DC – the price quoted for a vehicle did not indicate that VAT must be added and this was misleading to the ordinary consumer; *North Western Gas Board v Aspden* [1970] Crim LR 301, DC – Gas Board's displayed notice indicating that there was a '£3 allowance when you buy any two gas fires at the same time', which was intended to apply only to 'fixed' hearth gas fires, not all gas fires, was an indication

Services and facilities

It had previously been held by the Divisional Court in *Newell v Hicks*[8] that section 14 of the 1968 Act did not catch a false statement as to the terms, including the price, at which services, accommodation or facilities were being offered. Equally the old section 11 clearly only applied to the supply of *goods*. There was therefore a lacuna which the 1987 Act now fills. Section 22 of the Act explains the application of the section 20 offences to the provision of services and facilities in the following way:

> 22(1) Subject to the following provisions of this section, references in this Part to services or facilities are references to any services or facilities whatever including, in particular–
>
> a) the provision of credit or of banking or insurance services and the provision of facilities incidental to the provision of such services;
> b) the purchase or sale of foreign currency;
> c) the supply of electricity;
> d) the provision of a place, other than on a highway, for the parking of a motor vehicle;
> e) the making of arrangements for a person to put or keep a caravan on any land other than arrangements by virtue of which that person may occupy the caravan as his only or main residence.

The section goes on in subsection (2) specifically to exclude from the ambit of the Act services provided to an employer under a contract of employment, and by subsection (3), the services of an investment business (which is separately dealt with in the Financial Services Act 1986). It is possible for offences to arise under both Part III of the 1987 Act and other legislation, for example the Consumer Credit Act 1974.[9]

Accommodation

The application of Part III of the 1987 Act to the provision of 'accommodation or facilities' is severely circumscribed by section 23. The section in effect limits the ambit of the offence to *business* creations or disposals of major interests (fees simple or leaseholds of more than 21 years)

---

that the goods were being offered at a price £3 less than they were actually being offered, contrary to s 11(2). See also *Sweeting v Northern Upholstery Ltd* (1982) 2 Tr L 5, DC.

8   (1983) 148 JP 308, DC; M, H & P p 654.
9   See ch 10 and *R v Kettering Justices, ex p MRB Insurance Brokers Ltd* [2000] 20 LS Gaz R 43, DC.

in new dwellings – ie residences not previously occupied as such. Misleading price indications given in the ordinary disposals of privately owned residences are therefore not within the ambit of this legislation.[10]

Defences

Section 24 contains a collection of defences for Part III of the Act. When charges are laid under section 20(1) or (2) these specific defences are as follows:

1) The defendant's acts or omissions were authorised by a regulation made under section 26 of the 1987 Act;
2) If the price indication is published in a book, newspaper, magazine, film or in a programme included in a programme service (within the meaning of the Broadcasting Act 1990), that the indication was not contained in an advertisement;
3) If the price indication is published in an advertisement there is the familiar defence of innocent publication available to the person who carries on a business of publishing such advertisements;
4) Section 24(4) attempts to deal with the situation where eg a manufacturer's published 'recommended' price is not adhered to by those supplying consumers. It states that it is a defence, for section 20(1) offences only, for the accused to show that–
   a) the indication did not relate to the availability from him of any goods, services, accommodation or facilities;
   b) a price had been recommended to every person from whom the goods, services, accommodation or facilities were indicated as being available;
   c) the indication related to that price and was misleading as to that price only by reason of a failure by any person to follow the recommendation; and
   d) it was reasonable for the person who gave the indication to assume that the recommendation was for the most part being followed.

In addition to these specific defences, there is the general defence, contained in section 39, that in proceedings against any person for, inter alia, a section 20(1) offence, it is a defence for that person to show that he took all reasonable steps and exercised all due diligence to avoid committing the offence (s 39(1)). If the due diligence defence involves implicating a third party whose act or default is allegedly to blame, it is necessary to serve the prosecution with a notice to enable that third party to be identified,

10 They will, however, be covered under the Property Misdescriptions Act 1991: see pp 406–408.

normally not less than seven clear days before the proceedings (s 39(2) and (3)).

The due diligence defence includes a refinement supplied by section 39(4). This states as follows:

> (4) It is hereby declared that a person shall not be entitled to rely on the defence provided by subsection (1) above by reason of his reliance on information supplied by another, unless he shows that it was reasonable in all the circumstances for him to have relied on the information, having regard in particular–
> a) to the steps which he took, and those which might reasonably have been taken, for the purpose of verifying the information; and
> b) to whether he had any reason to disbelieve the information.

These defences apply also to those sections of the Act dealing with consumer safety and are discussed further in chapter 9.[11]

Code of Practice

In the light of the recommendations of the Inter-Departmental Committee mentioned above, the legislative text of the 1987 Act has been supplemented by a code of practice approved by order of the Secretary of State: the Code of Practice for Traders on Price Indications.[12] Its purposes are declared to be a) to give practical guidance and b) to promote desirable practices as to price indications of goods, services, accommodation or facilities (s 25(1)).

Section 25(2) further clarifies the status of such codes by stating that:

> A contravention of a code of practice approved under this section shall not of itself give rise to any criminal or civil liability, but in any proceedings against any person for an offence under section 20(1) or (2) above–
> a) any contravention by that person of such a code may be relied on in relation to any matter for the purpose of establishing that that person committed the offence or of negativing any defence; and
> b) compliance by that person with such a code may be relied on in relation to any matter for the purpose of showing that the

---

11 See also D Parry 'Judicial Approaches to Due Diligence' [1995] Crim LR 695.
12 SI 1988/2078; M, H & P p 695, BSSCCL p 727.

commission of the offence by that person has not been established or that that person has a defence.

If the Secretary of State approves a code of practice under section 25, the code may, after consultation, subsequently be modified or withdrawn. The order making powers are exercisable by statutory instrument subject to a negative resolution of either House of Parliament (s 25(3) and (4)).

There was much debate in the consultation over the precise terms of a possible code of practice and, as eventually promulgated, the Code contains detailed guidance as to legitimate and illegitimate price comparisons and guidance as to statements of the actual price of goods and services to the customer. It should be particularly noted that contravention of the Code does not itself give rise to any criminal or civil liability, but it may be relied upon by the prosecutor for the purpose of establishing that the defendant has committed the offence or to negative any defence. Similarly, the defendant may rely on compliance with the Code to show that the commission of the offence by that person has not been established, or that the person has a defence. The purpose of containing such provisions in a code is that it should provide greater flexibility to deal with a constantly changing market situation, though requests to modify it have, to date, been rejected.

The Code is widely relied on by retailers and gives important examples of some of the legitimate and illegitimate practices most often encountered. It covers price comparisons: generally, with the trader's own previous price and in particular circumstances; the presentation of actual prices to consumers, covering two different prices and incomplete information and non-optional extras; price indications which become misleading after having been given and the sale of new homes.

The White Paper *Modern Markets: Confident Consumers*[13] indicated that a revised version of the guidance given to traders on how to avoid misleading prices would be published early in 2000. This is awaited.

Regulations

As noted above, the Secretary of State, after consulting the Director General of Fair Trading and other appropriate persons, may make regulations for the purpose of regulating the circumstances and manner in which any person 1) gives any indication as to the price at which any goods, services, accommodation or facilities will be or are available or have been supplied or provided; or 2) indicates any other matter in respect of which any such indication may be misleading. Regulations may also be

---

13   Cm 4410, DTI, July 1999, para 3.13.

made for the purpose of facilitating the enforcement of the provisions of section 20 or of relevant subsidiary legislation (s 26). Three Regulations have been made under these provisions: the Price Indications (Method of Payment) Regulations 1991,[14] the Price Indications (Bureaux de Change) (No 2) Regulations 1992[15] and the Price Indications (Resale of Tickets) Regulations 1994.[16]

Penalties

Persons contravening section 20(1) or (2) are liable on conviction on indictment to a fine or on summary conviction to a fine not exceeding the statutory maximum (s 20(4)). Enforcement duties are imposed on every weights and measures authority in Great Britain. Enforcement authorities are given the usual power to make test purchases (s 28) and powers of search etc (s 29). It is a separate offence to obstruct an authorised officer (s 32). Prosecutions under section 20(1) or (2) must be brought either by the end of the period of three years from the day that the offence was committed or within one year of its discovery by the prosecutor, whichever is the earlier (s 20(5)).

By-pass

Section 40 contains a provision, familiar in trading law, enabling a third party whose act or default led to the offence being committed to be prosecuted instead of, or along with, the principal offender – though here the misleading price offence must have been committed by the third party *in the course of any business of his*. This contrasts with the position under section 23 of the 1968 Act and makes it impossible to prosecute an erring employee of the employer-principal.[17]

---

14   SI 1991/199, covering situations where different prices are charged depending upon the method of payment used by the customer.
15   SI 1992/737, governing the clarity with which exchange rate information must be given to consumers.
16   SI 1994/3248, governing the manner in which price indications must be given when tickets for places of entertainment are resold in the course of a business to a consumer.
17   See *R v Warwickshire County Council, ex p Johnson* [1993] AC 583, sub nom *Warwickshire County Council v Johnson* [1993] 1 All ER 299, HL; M, H & P p 675, discussed above.

13 Food; weights and measures

Introduction – enforcement

The legislation relating to food contained in the Food Safety Act 1990 and the Food Standards Act 1999 is massive and complex. The same is true of weights and measures. In both cases EC requirements have complicated the law still further. These areas differ from most of the others discussed in this book because they depend for their effective enforcement on the high degree of technical training given to the local government officers responsible for enforcing them. The United Kingdom's unusual (by EU standards) system of local authority, rather than central government, enforcement, will be noted.

Food authorities charged with enforcement were, from 1991 until 1995/6 county councils, district councils and London borough councils (with special arrangements for the City of London, the Inner and Middle Temple and the Scilly Isles, and Scotland). The reorganisation of local authorities discussed in chapter 3 has now resulted in the creation of a number of unitary authorities in England, Wales and Scotland undertaking the full range of responsibilities.

Accordingly, outside the unitary authorities both the county councils and the district councils are food authorities. Under powers given in the Act, the Food Safety Enforcement Authority (England and Wales) Order 1990 specifies that non-metropolitan district councils shall be responsible for the issue of emergency prohibition notices (where there is a health risk) under section 12 and county councils deal with offences involving the false description or presentation of food under section 15, this dovetailing in with the latter's powers under the Trade Descriptions Act 1968. All other duties of local food authorities are exercisable concurrently but in order to prevent consumers having to go from one district to another to get their complaints dealt with, a code of practice has been issued setting out a sensible division of labour. So, cases involving contamination by micro-organisms should be dealt with by district councils whereas county councils deal with cases of chemical contamination which pose no immediate risk to health. Cases of foreign bodies and mould affecting food should be dealt with by district councils under section 8 (the food safety requirement) or section 14 (food not of the nature or substance or quality demanded) – the appropriate officers in practice normally being environmental health officers and trading standards officers for districts and counties respectively. The code goes on to recommend liaison arrangements to avoid duplication of effort or omission.[1] In the case of food offences private prosecutions are possible.[2] But in the case of weights and measures offences the prosecution must be brought by a weights and measures authority or a chief officer of police.[3] In most cases the private consumer will be concerned only with the recognition of the offences created by these Acts, and then usually only a small number of the possible ones, and the reporting of the matter to the appropriate local environmental health department or to the local trading standards (weights and measures) department. It should be noted that enforcement of food laws in the UK is primarily at retail level.

In March 1998 the Cabinet Office Access Business Group, a partnership between central and local government and business, introduced an Enforcement Concordat. It contains provisions of considerable relevance to the administration of regulatory trading laws and seeks to set out the clear standards of service and performance the public and business people can expect to receive. It recognises that the main object of enforcement work is to protect the public, the environment and groups such as consumers and workers. At the same time, carrying out enforcement functions in an equitable, practical and consistent manner helps to promote a thriving national and local economy. The effectiveness of the legislation depends crucially on the compliance of those regulated. It is recognised that most businesses want to comply with the law. Enforcement officers will therefore take care to help business and others (eg voluntary and community organisations) to meet their legal obligations without unnecessary expense, while taking firm action, including prosecution where appropriate, against those who flout the law or act irresponsibly. The Concordat goes on to set out standards of openness, helpfulness, complaints about service,

1   Statutory Code of Practice No 1: Responsibility for Enforcement of the Food Safety Act 1990. LACOTS (see ch 3) is now renamed the Local Authorities Coordinating Body of Food and Trading Standards and involves Environmental Health Officers.
2   *Snodgrass v Topping* (1952) 116 JP 312 (the decision suggests that the private prosecutor should be a purchaser prejudiced by the food).
3   Weights and Measures Act 1985, s 83. In Scotland the Procurator Fiscal will prosecute.

proportionality in relation to the costs of compliance and the size of the business, consistency, including effective inter-authority liaison arrangements, and procedures prior to enforcement action.[4]

In order to fulfil their duties the officers responsible for the enforcement of the law in these two areas must have knowledge of, or at least access to, a forbidding mass of subsidiary legislation as well as the main Acts. Encyclopaedias exist for this purpose[5] and it would be both impractical and undesirable in a book of this nature to attempt to cover the whole ground. But it is important for the consumer and his adviser to be able to recognise the main offences under these Acts, which as collated statistically by the Director General in the OFT Annual Report of 1999 were as follows:

Food Safety Act 1990	*Number of convictions*
Not nature, substance of quality demanded	60
Unfit food	44
Labelling Regulations and others	62
Improvement notices	6

Weights and Measures Acts	*Number of convictions*
False or unjust equipment	3
Short weight or measure	32
Average weight and quantity offences	7
Packaged goods	6
Other offences	21

This chapter accordingly outlines the structure of the main Acts in the areas in question and examines in more detail the law relating to the more common offences.

I. FOOD

Food safety legislation – background

There has been legislation against impure food since Henry III's Assize of Bread and Ale in 1266, though legislative policy was directed at particular commodities, such as tea, coffee and bread. The first law against adulterated food generally was the Adulteration of Food or Drink Act 1860, and

---

4   For the full text, see *Butterworths Law of Food and Drugs*, A(17.1).
5   See *Butterworth's Law of Food and Drugs* and O'Keefe *Law of Weights and Measures* (2nd edn) which are essential tools for those working in the field.

adulterated drugs were dealt with by the Pharmacy Act 1868. The parentage of the 1990 Act can be traced from the Sale of Food and Drugs Act 1875. There then appeared a number of consolidations of this and several ad hoc laws dealing with composition, labelling, the addition of preservatives and the like. By virtue of the Medicines Act 1968 (Commencement No 7) Order 1977, references to 'drugs' in the former consolidating statute, the Food and Drugs Act 1955, were largely removed. Drugs are now dealt with by the Medicines Act 1968. The Food Act 1984 is largely replaced by the Food Safety Act 1990 which, despite its short title, deals not only with food safety but composition, labelling, advertising and other matters. This important Act, to which references in this Part relate unless the contrary is stated, was preceded by a White Paper *Food Safety – Protecting the Consumer* in July 1989. It should also be noted that Regulations made under the 1984 Act continue in force as if made by the 1990 Act (s 59(3)).

Food law can be very controversial, particularly in respect of additives which may be profitable to the manufacturer but are suspected to be less than healthy to the consumer. Furthermore there are considerations as to whether a food article such as a sausage can truly be described as such if there is very little meat in its actual composition. The government clearly requires expert advice on these topics and a Food Standards Committee was set up in 1947 to advise the appropriate ministers and was normally required to be consulted before regulations relating to composition of food and Codes of Practice were issued. This Committee, together with the Food Additives and Contaminants Committee, issued a number of valuable reports which led to legislative changes of importance such as the Labelling of Food Regulations 1970. Compositional standards exist for many foods, for instance 'extra jam' must be at least 45% of the relevant fruit (with certain exceptions) and 'jam' must be similarly 35% fruit (see Jam and Similar Products Regulations 1981 (as amended)). There is still debate as to whether existing compositional standards are extensive enough. Attention has been drawn to the use by unscrupulous producers of excessive water as a make-weight in food, and to machines called 'yield improvers' at one time advertised with the revealing adage – 'why sell meat when you could sell water?'[6]

On 1 November 1983 these two committees were merged and became the Food Advisory Committee. The terms of reference of this committee were to advise the Minister of Agriculture, Fisheries and Food and other relevant Secretaries of State on matters referred to it by the ministers relating to the composition, labelling and advertising of food; and additives, contaminants and other substances which are, or may be, present in food

6   See now the Meat Products and Spreadable Fish Products Regulations 1984 (SI 1984/1566 as amended) which besides laying down detailed compositional standards required a declaration of added water content – see reg 9. See also Food Labelling Regulations 1996, discussed below.

or used in preparation. The enabling power to make regulations as to composition of food appears in section 16 of the Act and section 17 empowers ministers to make regulations with respect to food as called for by any Community obligation – typically an EC Directive (see chapter 2). There are, for instance, detailed regulations concerning preservatives and colouring matter in food.

The closing decade of the 20th century saw considerable public concern over food safety and criticism of the way policy was administered by the Ministry of Agriculture, Fisheries and Food (MAFF). There were allegations that policy was affected by conflicts of interest as between farmers and the food industry on the one hand and consumers on the other. An independent central government body for food control was called for. This led to the setting up of the Food Standards Agency, as discussed in chapter 3, with the powers and duties laid down by the Food Standards Act 1999.[7] As a result MAFF lost many of its former functions relating to food safety and standards. It is charged with the development of food policy and the provision of advice to public authorities.

The sheer volume and complexity of the subsidiary legislation made under the Food Acts, much of it prompted by the EC Directives, can be gauged by the fact that *Butterworth's Law of Food and Drugs* devotes some one and a half of the six looseleaf volumes to setting out their accumulated texts. Some, if by no means all, yield readily appreciated benefits to consumers.

The main offences

Rendering food injurious to health

Adulterating food is one of the most ancient of the offences encompassed by food legislation and this particular section can be traced to legislation of 1872. Adulteration of food by eg the addition of water to milk (as those who play 'Happy Families' may remember) used to be widespread. Nowadays there are detailed controls over the use of additives or treatments and the presence of contaminants and so there is little use in practice of this section, section 7, which makes it an offence to render food injurious to health by the addition or abstraction of articles or constituents with the intent that the food shall be sold for human consumption. The court is directed to have regard to the probable cumulative effect of food of substantially the same composition on the health of a person consuming it in ordinary quantities. The section forms a useful bench mark for food

7   See the White Paper *The Food Standards Agency – A Force for Change* (1998, Cm 3830).

control. Civil 'product liability' may arise on the facts if injury is caused, by virtue of Part I, Consumer Protection Act 1987 (see ch 6).

Selling food not complying with food safety requirements

Section 8 introduces an important new concept to food law – the food safety requirement – which is not dissimilar to the 'general safety requirement' in the General Product Safety Regulations 1994 affecting non-food products and discussed in chapter 9. Food is deemed to have failed to comply with the safety requirement if it has been rendered injurious to health by means of the operations mentioned in section 7 (above) or if it is unfit for human consumption or unreasonably contaminated. Authorised officers of the Food Authority may at all reasonable times inspect food intended for human consumption and if necessary seize and remove it (section 9). The ambit of the offence in section 8 is, typically, very widely drafted and affects any person who sells for human consumption, or offers, exposes, or advertises for sale for such consumption, or has in his possession for the purpose of such sale or of preparation for such sale, or has consigned it to any other person for the purpose of such sale, any food which fails to comply with the food safety requirements.

There are a number of sections conferring regulation-making powers on the Minister, including section 16 which is concerned with securing adequate standards of food safety and consumer protection.

Selling food not of the nature etc demanded

It is possible to trace the genesis of this offence back to the Sale of Food and Drugs Act of 1875. The offence (under s 14) involves any person selling to the purchaser's prejudice any food which is not of the nature or substance or quality demanded by the purchaser. The sale must be for human consumption.

The following summarises the main points on the interpretation of the section (in a similar form to which it appeared in former legislation).

'A person ...' The defendant may be an individual or limited company. This is well established by case law and Schedule 1 to the Interpretation Act 1978 which states that unless the contrary intention appears, the expression 'person' includes a body of persons corporate or unincorporate.

It was held in *Pearks, Gunston and Tee Ltd v Ward*[8] that there was no 'contrary intention' in this provision. In many cases the sale will be actually

---

8   [1902] 2 KB 1.

conducted by an employee of the proprietor of the business. In *Goodfellow v Johnson*[9] the Divisional Court considered the legal position arising out of a sale of watered gin in a public house by a barmaid to a duly authorised sampling officer. As Lord Parker CJ explained, this:

> constitutes an absolute offence ... The forbidden act is the selling to the prejudice of the purchaser, and it has long been held that a person who has done the forbidden thing through somebody else like a servant or agent is himself liable ... The forbidden act in a provision such as this is not the parting with the title by the owner but is the physical handling and handing over of the goods by way of sale: in other words the shop assistant, or in this case the barmaid, is liable, and accordingly, in view of the general principle to which I have referred, any person on whose behalf that act of handling and handing over is done is also liable.[10]

'Sells to the purchaser's prejudice' It is specifically provided by subsection (2) that it shall not be a defence that the purchaser was not prejudiced because he bought for analysis or examination. Even where a servant buys on behalf of his employer, with the employer's money, it is open to the court to hold that the employer has been prejudiced.[11]

In most cases a purchaser of adulterated food or drugs is clearly 'prejudiced'. It has been long established, in addition, that he is prejudiced if he 'gets an article inferior to that which he demands and pays for', an unusual example of attaching criminal liability to a transaction which, in the absence of danger to health, would otherwise give rise only to civil liability in respect of breach of warranty. Difficulties can be caused by notices disclaiming that the food is pure. In a number of cases it has been held that a notice, eg stating that spirits have been diluted, is capable of taking effect so that a purchaser therefore cannot be said to be prejudiced. In the Scottish case of *Brander v Kinnear*[12] it was held that such a notice must be clear and unambiguous and acquaint the purchaser with the prejudice that he is asked to accept. The courts tend to construe such notices strictly in the interests of purchasers.[13] In *Thomas Robinson, Sons & Co Ltd v Allardice*[14] the Divisional Court held that the standard of quality which a purchaser can expect is that applicable to an ordinary purchaser.

---

9 [1966] 1 QB 83, [1965] 1 All ER 941.
10 Ibid, at 88, 89, and 944 respectively.
11 See *Garforth v Esam* (1892) 56 JP 521 (inspector bought through his servant).
12 1923 JC 42.
13 See *Rodbourn v Hudson* [1925] 1 KB 225.
14 (1944) 170 LT 297.

The opinion of a public analyst that, for instance, a cordial must contain sugar to answer that description, is not necessarily by itself conclusive.[15]

'Not of the nature or substance or quality demanded by the purchaser' It was emphasised in *Bastin v Davies*[16] that there are three distinct offences here relating to a) nature, b) substance and c) quality, of food demanded. An information alleging that a certain sale of food was 'not of the nature or not of the substance or not of the quality ...' was held bad for uncertainty, the Divisional Court being influenced by a long-standing statement to this effect in the then leading textbook, *Bell's Sale of Food and Drugs*.[17]

As to 'nature' it was held in *Knight v Bowers*,[18] where a purchaser had asked for the drug 'Saffron' and had been supplied with pure 'Savin', an abortifacient, that it was no defence to show that the article supplied was pure in itself if it was not also the one demanded.

This decision was followed in the instructive case of *Meah v Roberts*[19] where a brewery employee visited a restaurant and cleaned a beer dispensing machine with caustic soda. He placed the residue of this fluid in an empty lemonade bottle, marking it 'cleaner', and left it for use by the restaurant. A customer's children were by mistake supplied with caustic soda from this bottle, having ordered lemonade. One of the children became seriously ill as a result. The restaurant proprietors and the brewery employee, joined in under the former Act's section 100 (see below), were convicted by the justices under the former Act's sections 2 (in that the food was not of the 'nature demanded') and 8 (in that the food was unfit for human consumption). The defendants appealed on the basis that there had been no food supplied and no sale. It was held by the Divisional Court that there had been a sale of lemonade although caustic soda had been supplied. The expression 'sells any food' means 'sells something as a food'. Furthermore, the third party employee's acts or omissions had caused the breaches of the sections and he was guilty of the offence whether he personally sold the food or not. The magistrates' decision was upheld in every respect.

15   Contrast *Collins Arden Products Ltd v Barking Corpn* [1943] KB 419, [1943] 2 All ER 249 and *Broughton v Whittaker* [1944] KB 269, [1944] 2 All ER 544; see also (1944) 108 JP 303. 'To the prejudice of the purchaser'.

16   [1950] 2 KB 579, [1950] 1 All ER 1095. The redrafted version appearing in the 1984 Act made this point clearer still. The 1990 Act has unfortunately telescoped the wording again.

17   Such an information would not now comply with Magistrates' Courts Rules 1981, SI 1981/552, r 12. Earlier cases must be treated with caution because in s 6 of the 1875 Act the phrase was drafted conjunctively. This was changed to its present disjunctive meaning in 1928. See Butterworths *Law of Food and Drugs*, B(124).

18   (1885) 14 QBD 845. Section 14 in its previous form also applied to drugs. 'Nature' would also cover such matters as cod being sold after a demand for haddock.

19   [1978] 1 All ER 97.

As to 'substance', it has been held that milk is of the substance demanded if it is as it came from the cow, even if the milk supplied has a lesser fat content than specified by contract.[20] But if a significant foreign substance is found in the milk (eg penicillin) and this ought not to have been in the milk at the time of milking, an offence is committed.[1] Designated products may by usage develop a wider, generic, significance. Thus 'Demerara sugar', though originally referring to a certain type of brown sugar coming from the West Indies, is apt to describe the same type of sugar coming from Mauritius.[2] A prescribed standard for a food or drug, such as those of the British Pharmacopoeia, is prima facie the standard below which the article must not fall, unless there is evidence of a lower acceptable commercial standard.[3] In other cases the courts must apply such standards as are reasonable.[4] But this concept can cause apparent difficulties. Thus in both *T W Lawrence & Sons Ltd v Burleigh*[5]. and *Goldup v John Manson Ltd*,[6] butchers were charged with contravening section 2 of the 1984 Act in respect of excess fat in minced meat. In the *Lawrence* case the selling company's conviction was upheld in respect of selling mince with 30.8 per cent of fat when it had been ordered by telephone. The purchaser gave impressive evidence that she was 'prejudiced' and the analyst gave evidence to show that the fat content of the sample was at the top of the range of samples analysed in a survey of the fat content of mince. But in the *Goldup* case, where the meat contained 33 per cent fat, the magistrates' dismissal of the information was also upheld, partly, it seems, because minced meat was available both at a cheaper and more expensive price and partly because a notice in the shop stated that minced beef sold in the shop contained up to 30 per cent fat – the difference being dismissed as de minimis. It should be borne in mind, in this connection, that similar facts could give rise to an offence against section 1 of the Trade Descriptions Act 1968 (applying a false trade description to any goods in the course of a business, including orally).

As to 'quality', it was held in *Anness v Grivell*,[7] a case concerning what was alleged to be an unduly insubstantial butter fat content in a butter and margarine mixture, that 'quality' meant commercial quality of the article sold and not merely its description. Extraneous matter, such as a dead fly found

20 *Few v Robinson* [1921] 3 KB 504.
1   *Hall v Owen-Jones and Jones* [1967] 3 All ER 209.
2   *Anderson v Britcher* (1913) 78 JP 65.
3   *Boots Cash Chemists (Southern) Ltd v Cowling* (1903) 88 LT 539 (liniment of soap); *Dickins v Randerson* [1901] 1 KB 437 (mercury ointment).
4   See *Tonkin v Victor Value Ltd* [1962] 1 All ER 821, [1962] 1 WLR 339 – 'mock salmon cutlette' containing only 33 per cent fish held to be below any reasonable standard.
5   (1981) 146 JP 134.
6   [1982] QB 161, [1981] 3 All ER 257.
7   [1915] 3 KB 685.

Food

floating in an unopened bottle of milk,[8] or a nail in sweets[9] can make the food not of the quality demanded. In *Barber v Co-operative Wholesale Society Ltd*[10] a bottle of milk containing a green straw was delivered to a school and it was alleged that the food was not of the quality demanded by the purchaser. It was agreed by both parties that the presence of extraneous matter in the food could be evidence that it was not of the quality demanded and it was held, in addition, that it was unnecessary for the prosecution to prove that the matter was deleterious. The test was whether the purchaser could, in the context of the particular transaction, reasonably object to the presence of the matter.

The cases cited above as to the meaning of 'nature', 'substance' and 'quality' involve a degree of overlap. This was recognised in *Preston v Greenclose Ltd*[11] where the respondents were charged with selling to the prejudice of the purchaser a food, namely scampi, which was not of the substance demanded, being in part white fish and not scampi. The magistrates accepted the defence that the offence related to 'nature' and not 'substance of the food'. The Divisional Court allowed the prosecutor's appeal, holding that there was an area of common ground between the three words 'nature', 'substance' and 'quality'. They were not normally exclusive, and always to be precise in the selection of one or another could present difficult problems. In the present case it was impossible as a matter of law to pronounce as between the relevant appositeness of 'substance' or 'nature'. The overwhelming probability was that the case fell within both terms, in which event it was right for the prosecutor to choose that one of the two terms he thought the more appropriate.

The significance of the 'demand' by the 'purchaser' is that it identifies the food in question, and it must then be shown that the particular article fails one of the tests for nature, substance or quality as charged.[12]

Subject to the general defence below, the section imposes absolute liability. It is not a defence to show absence of any negligence.[13]

It will be apparent from the above litigation that many prosecutions were brought under the predecessors of section 14. The scene was further enlivened by specific defences to those so prosecuted. For instance, if food contained some extraneous matter it was a defence to show that the presence of that matter was an unavoidable consequence of the process of collection or preparation. So, when (for instance) a hawk moth caterpillar

8   *Newton v West Vale Creamery Co Ltd* (1956) 120 JP 318.
9   *Lindley v George W Horner & Co Ltd* [1950] 1 All ER 234.
10   (1983) 147 JP 296, 127 Sol Jo 424.
11   (1975) 139 JP Jo 245. See also *Shearer v Rowe* (1985) 149 JP 698.
12   See *Collins Arden Products Ltd v Barking Corpn* [1943] KB 419, [1943] 2 All ER 249. See also *McDonald's Hamburgers Ltd v Windle* (1986) 151 JP 333, DC – sale of liquid in response for demand for 'diet cola' not of quality demanded.
13   *Lindley v George W Horner & Co Ltd*, above.

was found in a tin of Smedleys' peas and the appellants were charged with supplying food 'not of the substance demanded by the purchaser', the appellant argued that since the chances of this happening were 874,999 to 1 against and there was a highly sophisticated mechanical screening process plus visual inspection, the incident was an 'unavoidable consequence'. This gave the then members of the House of Lords some innocent amusement in commenting on whether by the time 'the immolated insect had at length plodded its way to the highest court in the land', and whose protein content might, perhaps, be beneficial, any good was served by bringing such a prosecution. In the event, the court convicted.[14] Under the 1990 Act the defendant must rely on the general defence of due diligence set out in section 21 (below).

It should also be borne in mind that there may be some overlap between section 14 and section 8 – selling food not complying with food safety requirements. Section 8, as has been mentioned above, covers 'contaminated' food and would certainly seem more appropriate to cover food affected by mould, or which is rancid or stale – these offences formerly being prosecuted under the predecessor of section 14. Also, the statistics seem to reveal a declining number of prosecutions under this once popular section. It is possible that informations involving the seller's description are laid instead under section 1 of the Trade Descriptions Act 1968.

Falsely describing or presenting food

The offence here was formerly to be found in section 6 of the Food Act 1984 and has now been re-enacted with some important changes. Section 15 creates an offence of giving with any food sold or displaying with any food offered or exposed for sale or in possession for the purpose of sale, a label, whether or not attached to or printed on the wrapper or container which a) falsely describes the food; or b) is likely to mislead as to the nature or substance or quality of the food. (It can be seen that there is a considerable overlap with the Trade Descriptions Act 1968, section 1, which is frequently used as an alternative to this section.)

With regard to whether the label is misleading, this is a matter not for an expert witness, but for the court, which must decide whether the ordinary man is misled by it.[15]

The section also makes it an offence to publish or be a party to the publication of an advertisement which is false or calculated to mislead as above.

14   *Smedleys Ltd v Breed* [1974] AC 839, [1974] 2 All ER 21, HL.
15   *Concentrated Foods Ltd v Champ* [1944] KB 342 at 350 per Wrottesley J.

Section 15 is supplemented in particular by the Labelling of Food Regulations 1996[16] made under the power conferred on Ministers to make regulations as to the labelling and description of food formerly under section 7 of the 1955 Act and sections 4, 7 and 118 of the 1984 Act and now under sections 16 and 17 of the 1990 Act.[17] The main features of these intricate and voluminous regulations (which replace earlier regulations) are as follows:

a)   they require all food, subject to certain exceptions, to be marked or labelled with the name of the food, a list of ingredients, the quantity of certain ingredients, an indication of appropriate durability, any special storage conditions or conditions of use and the name and address of the manufacturer or packer or of the seller. Certain foods are required to be marked with a 'use by' date. This is appropriate to foods which are microbiologically highly perishable, and it is an offence to sell food after the 'use by' date shown (regs 21 and 44(1)(d)); in the case of other foods, a 'best before' indication is stipulated which indicates the period for which a food can reasonably be expected to stay in optimum condition (eg it will not be stale). It should be noted that it is not, as such, an offence to sell food after a 'best before' date. It is an offence, though, for any person other than the originator, to alter an appropriate durability indication (reg 44(1)(e)). Various foods require no durability indication (eg fresh fruit and vegetables, wine and bread normally consumed within 24 hours of its preparation);

b)   they specify additional labelling requirements for food sold from vending machines and for prepacked alcoholic drinks ('% vol.' or '% mas');

c)   they specify requirements as to the manner of marking or labelling of food including as to visibility and intelligibility (regs 35–39);

d)   they prohibit claims in the labelling or advertising of the food that it has tonic properties or can cure a human disease, and impose conditions for the making of a number of claims such as vitamin claims, energy claims and cholesterol claims;

The controversial question of the sale of genetically modified ingredients has been primarily dealt with by EC Regulations requiring the labelling of 'GMO particulars' (see 1139/98 and 1813/97). The Food Labelling (Amendment) Regulations 1999 give effect to the labelling requirements concerning genetically modified soya or maize.

The regulations are enforced by local Food Authorities. The labelling of medicines is also tightly controlled under regulations made under section 85 of the Medicines Act 1968. Labels must show, inter alia, the name of the

16   SI 1996/1499 as amended.
17   The regulations continue to implement Council Directive No 79/112/EEC and amending Directives. They supersede the Labelling of Food Regulations 1984.

product, the quantity in the container, directions for use and the expiry date if within three years of manufacture.

Defences

The 1990 Act completely redesigns defences available for those charged with food offences under its provisions. This replaces the former system where there are a number of miscellaneous defences, including the 'warranty' defence (where retailers relied on their suppliers who gave them a 'warranty' involving a contractual description). Now the defences are as follows.

Third parties There is the common form 'offence due to the fault of another person' provision to be found in section 20. This differs substantially from the old section 100 of the Food Act 1984 which enabled a person charged directly to bring in a third party. The current provision simply states that where the commission by any person of the relevant offence is due to an act or default of some other person, that other person shall be guilty of the offence. The third party may be charged with and convicted of the offence whether or not proceedings are taken against the original person. Although this section comes within the general heading of 'Defences' in the Act, it will be seen that it is not really a defence at all. Much will depend upon the discretion of the prosecutor. This may be exercised in the light of the availability of the section 21 'due diligence' defence discussed immediately below.

Defence of due diligence The defence of due diligence is familiar in trading law statutes. Section 21 establishes a single-limbed defence of 'all reasonable precautions and all due diligence'. (The word 'all' is important.) It is, in this form, in what is now its preferred version in trading law. In addition a person charged with an offence under section 8 (selling food not complying with the food safety requirements), section 14 (selling food not of the nature or substance or quality demanded) or section 15 (falsely describing or presenting food) has a specific defence. This is that if he has neither a) prepared the food in respect of which the offence is alleged to have been committed; nor b) imported it into Great Britain, the defendant is taken to have established the 'due diligence' defence provided certain other requirements are satisfied (s 21(2)). These are, in brief, that the defendant is able to prove that the commission of the offence was due to an act or default of another person not under his control, or to reliance on information supplied by such a person, and that he carried out all such checks of the food in question as were reasonable in all the circumstances (or reasonably relied on the checks carried out by a supplier); and that the

Food

defendant did not know and had no reason to suspect at the time of the commission of the alleged offence that his act or omission would amount to an offence under the relevant provision (s 21(3)). Section 21(4) contains a somewhat similar defence where the offence is due to the act or default of a third party not under the defendant's control and the sale is not under his name or mark – eg in typical non-own brand retailing situations.

It will be seen that the primary defence in section 21(1) is simply of showing all due diligence – there is no need to prove the fault of a third party under that subsection. A 'due diligence' system for the proper checking of food standards must be shown by the defendant. Section 21(2) then goes on to state that the due diligence shall be taken to have been established if the offence falls under section 8, 14 or 15 *and* the other requirements outlined above (involving the act or default of the third party) are present.[18] Section 21(5) requires a defendant bringing in a third party to give the prosecution at least seven clear days' warning before the hearing. Otherwise that defence may not, without leave, be relied on.

Defence of innocent publication Since there are offences involving the publication of advertisements for food, section 22 states that it is a defence for the person charged to prove that the advertisement was published in the course of a business of publishing or arranging for publication of advertisements and that the publisher had no reason to suspect that its publication would amount to an offence under the Act.

Enforcement powers

Food Authorities and authorised officers are given a range of enforcement powers in the Act. Some of these have already been mentioned. In particular powers are given of inspection and seizure (s 9), of giving an 'improvement notice' requiring that a proprietor comply with food hygiene conditions and practices (s 10), and of issuing prohibition orders prohibiting the use of processes, treatments or equipment or persons from being the proprietor of a food business, if convicted of a relevant food offence (s 11).

Registration of food premises

The 1990 Act contains a section, section 19, which empowers regulations to be made requiring food premises to be registered. The object of this is

18 For a comprehensive analysis of 'due diligence' and the many illustrative cases on it, see *A Guide to the Food Safety Act 1990* (ed Painter) (Butterworths) and *Butterworths Law of Food and Drugs*. See also *Food Safety Act 1990 – Guidelines on the Statutory Defence of Due Diligence* prepared by a consortium including LACOTS, the NCC and the Institute of Environmental Health Officers.

to give local authorities responsible for enforcing food law a complete picture of all the food businesses in their area, so that they can target their enforcement resources effectively. Inspections of premises which represent a high risk to health can therefore be expected. Accordingly, the Food Premises (Registration) Regulations 1991 (SI 1991/2825) have been made covering England, Wales and Scotland and are in force from 1 May 1992 since when it has been an offence to operate a food business from unregistered premises. Registration is with local Environmental Health Departments which have no discretion to refuse registration.

It will be noted that the registration will not make premises subject to the Food Safety Act 1990, since the Act *already* applies to all such premises and authorised officers have powers of entry to all premises whether registered or not. There are exceptions from the requirement to register, including premises used on less than five days in five consecutive weeks, domestic premises providing bed and breakfast in not more than three bedrooms, and premises, not storing food, used by voluntary organisations.

Code of Practice No 11, issued under the Food Safety Act 1990, section 40, gives guidance on the enforcement of these regulations.

2. WEIGHTS AND MEASURES

Weights and Measures Act 1985

The history of this complex subject has been outlined in chapter 1 (and see also the Introduction to this chapter for further background). Part 2 of this chapter concentrates on the structure of the 1985 Act (which consolidated previous legislation), the main offences of direct concern to the consumer created by it, and, to start with, an outline of the work of the weights and measures service.

The weights and measures service – central and local government functions

Weights and measures functions are shared between central and local government. Section 2 of the Weights and Measures Act 1985 ('the Act') now states that it is the duty of the Secretary of State (currently for Trade and Industry by virtue of the Secretary of State for Trade Order 1979, and formerly the Board of Trade) to maintain standards of the yard, pound, metre and kilogramme. These standards are known as 'United Kingdom primary standards'. All other standards of those units and of any other unit of measurement derived wholly or partly from any of those units are maintained by reference to these primary standards. A 'unit of measurement' is not defined, but means (to adopt the definition used by the Hodgson Committee on Weights and Measures (1951), Cmd 8219) 'a precisely defined and ideally invariable quantity of some particular kind, in terms of which the magnitudes of all other quantities of the same kind can be stated.' The scientifically minded might be interested to know that the true primary standards are the International Metre and International Kilogramme in the custody of the International Bureau of Weights and Measures at Sèvres. The International Metre is defined as 'the length of the path travelled by light in vacuum during a time interval of 1/299 792 458 of a second' (see Sch I, Pt I of the Act). The yard is defined as 0.9144 of a metre. For United Kingdom purposes the primary standards are defined by reference to the imperial standard bar of Baily's bronze metal for the yard, the imperial standard platinum cylinder for the pound, and British copies of the prototype metre and kilogramme (see Sch 2). The Department of Trade and Industry is responsible for secondary and tertiary standards of weights and measures, these being the measures of length and capacity set out in Parts I and IV of Schedule 3, and the weights set out in Part V of that Schedule. The Department is also responsible for the standards of weight of each coin of the realm for the time being authorised by the Coinage Act 1971. This duty is fulfilled annually by 'the trial of the Pyx' at which the Chancellor of the Exchequer is notionally on trial before a jury in order to establish that the quality of the country's coinage is maintained. By sample weighing and testing it is ascertained whether the minted coins are of the prescribed quality in terms of weight, size and material content.

The central government function is, then, to maintain the primary and other standards mentioned above, though the actual enforcement of the legislation is left to local weights and measures authorities. The premise behind the hugely complex technology which goes into the testing of these standards is simply that since the consumer is normally unable to test the petrol pump with which he fills his car's fuel tank, the pint pot in which the landlord measures his beer, the price-computing and weighing machine with which the grocer and butcher weigh and price the food that he is buying, the baggage weighing equipment at the airport, the factory machine which measures the quantity of sugar or crisps in their packets, and so on, he is entitled to assume that these weights and measures are tolerably accurate. When the central government has established the standards and exhaustively tested any new pattern of equipment used in the trade for weighing and measuring and given to the machine 'pattern approval', the details are published. The local inspector, now usually known as the Trading Standards Officer, who is responsible for passing items of weighing and measuring equipment in his area, then knows that the design has been given the DTI's approval and can confidently proceed with the necessary testing and stamping of the equipment. The local standards used by local authorities are also periodically tested by the central government service by reference to the tertiary standards kept by the Department.

At the local level, section 69 of the Act states that the local weights and measures authority shall be in England and Wales the relevant non-metropolitan county, metropolitan district or London Borough Council,[19] the Common Council for the City and the Temples, and the Council of the Isles of Scilly.

Section 4 of the Act requires local authorities to keep local standards. These are kept at a particular place and there must be a certificate of fitness for the purpose in respect of them issued by the DTI. 'Working standards', ie those actually used by inspectors in testing traders' weighing and measuring equipment, must also be provided by the local authorities. These standards must be tested periodically by reference to the local standards (s 5). It can be seen, therefore, that there is a chain of uniformity from national standards, through local and working standards to the traders' equipment.

Local authorities are also required to appoint and reasonably remunerate a chief inspector of weights and measures and sufficient inspectors for the efficient discharge of the functions imposed on them by law (s 72). Inspectors are required to be properly qualified by examination (ss 72, 73). The present examination is the Diploma in Trading Standards conducted by the Local Government Training Board, though this is likely to change shortly. The examination is designed to test not only a detailed knowledge of consumer protection law, but also ability in economics, materials technology and technical drawing, and statistics. The object is to ensure that inspectors have both the breadth and depth of knowledge to discharge their increasingly complex duties efficiently.

It is a feature of the office of inspector that he is himself criminally liable for falsely stamping equipment, deriving profit in connection with the marketing of weighing or measuring equipment, knowingly committing a breach of duty or otherwise misconducting himself in the execution of his office (s 75). Inspectors also have wide powers under section 79 of inspection and entry of premises within the inspector's area, subject to the production of credentials if requested. The inspector must have reasonable cause to believe that the equipment that he is to test is used for trade, and the premises must not be exclusively a private house.[20] He also

19 In England this means the 20 non-metropolitan counties and those metropolitan district councils which took over functions from the former metropolitan county councils pursuant to the Local Government Act 1985. A number of new 'unitary authorities' were created under the Local Government Act 1992. These are also weights and measures authorities for the purposes of the Act.

20 See *Brunner v Williams* [1975] Crim LR 250, where the defendant coal merchants were acquitted of obstructing an inspector who unsuccessfully tried to stop them emptying coal bags, before weighing them, in the curtilage of a private dwellinghouse.

has the power to seize and detain equipment liable to be forfeited under the Act. Forcible entry is only permitted under a written warrant by a justice on a sworn information that there is reasonable ground to believe that there are relevant equipment, goods, articles, or documents on any premises or that an offence under the Act is being or is about to be committed on the premises, and that entry has been refused, or (inter alia) that an application for entry would defeat the object of the entry. When an entry has been made, it is a criminal offence for the inspector or anyone accompanying him to disclose the proprietor's trade secrets otherwise than in the performance of his duty (s 79(7)). It is an offence wilfully to obstruct an inspector acting in the course of his duties (s 80). An offence is prima facie committed in any case where an inspector is refused entry after showing his credentials if required.

In the context of the functions of the trading standards inspectorate, its enforcement function under the Act must be differentiated from any consumer advisory services offered by councils to consumers in their area. The enforcement function must operate entirely impartially in the interests of both consumer and trader. 'It must be non-partisan and identified neither with buyer nor seller ... assessment of fault must regard the trade and the public equally. Trade secrets officially gained cannot be used for purposes other than enforcement.'[1] Other bodies giving advice to aggrieved consumers may be free to be partisan.

The main offences

Weighing and measuring for trade

Part I having prescribed the various units of measurements and the various national and local standards described above, Part II goes on to deal with weighing and measuring for trade. In particular section 7 defines the expression 'use for trade' in the context of which only those weights and measures prescribed by the Act may be used. The core of the definition of 'use for trade' is 'the transferring or rendering of money or money's worth in consideration of money or money's worth', provided the transaction is by reference to quantity and the use is for the purpose of the determination or statement of that quantity (s 7(1)). An exchange of value by reference to quantity is therefore the essence of the test.

With the object of standardising weights and measures used for trade and so as not to confuse the consumer with weird and wonderful measurements which are difficult to understand and compare, the units of

---

1   See the comprehensive review in *O'Keefe's Law of Weights and Measures* (2nd edn) (Butterworths), particularly Vol 1, 0(132) et seq.

measurement now lawful for use for trade are those specified in section 8. The prevalence of metric units reflects the metrication policy discussed further in this chapter. Permissible units of measurement in which quantities may be expressed are set out in Schedule 1 (which may be amended by order of the Secretary of State). These are the measures of length, area, volume, capacity and mass or weight specified there now primarily in metric units. The prescribed imperial units are now confined to the pint and fluid ounce (for the sale of draught beer or cider and of other specified liquids in returnable containers). This list should be compared with the thirty-two permitted metric units. Familiar measurements such as the square mile are no longer lawful for use in trade. It is an offence to use for trade any unit of measurement not in the Schedule, except that only precious metals and stones may be measured in troy ounces and carats (metric) and non-metric units of quantity may be used as supplementary indications provided they accompany metric indications which are more prominent (s 8(5A)).

Schedule 3 (which may also be amended by order – see s 8(6)) specifies the actual physical weights and measures which are lawful for use in trade when weighing or measuring quantities, the list being limited because it is necessary to keep these uniform as used in trade. These are the linear measures, the square measures, the cubic measures, the capacity measures, and the weights of primarily the metric system as specified. A linear measure may be marked in subdivisions. Whilst this Schedule lists the *physical* measures and weights lawful for use in trade, trade may lawfully be conducted by multiplying permitted *units* of measure and weight – see Schedule 1 and section 8(1).

It is an offence to contravene section 8 and any unlawful measure or weight used is liable to forfeiture. The Secretary of State has power to add to, remove or vary the items listed in these Schedules.

In order to simplify the process of metrication, the Secretary of State is empowered to make regulations to require or authorise persons using metric units to afford information (by conversion charts, etc) of the imperial equivalent (s 9).

Section 11 in Part II lays down the vital scheme for ensuring that the weights and measures used in everyday trade are accurate. It is an offence for any person to use for trade any such equipment as may be prescribed by regulation unless the equipment has been passed by an inspector as fit for such use, and bears a stamp that it has been so passed which remains undefaced except by reason of fair wear and tear. The trader must submit the equipment for testing by the inspector by means of such local or working standards as he considers appropriate. A weight or measure must be marked with its purported value before stamping. There are in force numerous regulations prescribing classes or descriptions of equipment and regulating their material, principles of construction, how they should be tested, and permissible margins of error. Some adaptation of UK law was made by the Measuring Instruments (EEC Requirements) Regulations 1988, implementing EEC Council Directive No 71/316 as amended. One of the consequences of these Regulations is that measuring instruments bearing the sign of EC pattern approval and exemption from EC initial verification or the mark of EC initial verification are exempted from the prohibition against use for trade in section 11.

Sections 16 and 17 create two further offences, one of which is commonly met. Section 16 relates to forging, counterfeiting, altering or defacing stamps and altering equipment so as to make it unjust after it has been stamped. Section 17 makes it an offence for a person to use for trade, or to have in his possession for use for trade, any weighing or measuring equipment which is false or unjust, and such equipment is liable to be forfeited (s 17(1)). In *Makinson v J K Dewhurst Ltd*[2] the Divisional Court dismissed the prosecutor's appeal against dismissal of a summons against the defendant butchers for having in their possession for use for trade unjust weighing equipment. They had a self-indicating and price-computing machine which had a built in tendency to give short weight unless a simple zeroing adjustment was made after a period of about two hours. Their employee failed to zero this when test purchases were made. The question was whether the machine was 'unjust'. The Divisional Court dismissed the prosecution appeal on the basis that as constructed the machine was a just one, even if as used without the recommended adjustment it was giving short weight. The result might have been different if the prosecution had been brought under section 28 in respect of short weight.

Statistics collated by the Office of Fair Trading indicate that using false or unjust equipment is one of the more common weights and measures offences. This provision is construed strictly. The equipment must be just, both loaded and unloaded, showing neither too much nor too little. Absence of fraud or acquiescence by the purchaser is irrelevant.

It is a defence under section 17 for the person charged to prove that he used the equipment in the course of employment by some other person and that he neither knew, nor might reasonably have been expected to know, nor had any reason to suspect, the equipment to be false or unjust.

Section 17(3) makes it an offence to commit fraud in the use of any weighing or measuring equipment or to be a party to such fraud. This offence is concerned with tricks such as tilting the scales or other

---

2   (1981) unreported, QBD, but see transcript in (1981) 89 Monthly Rev 87. See also the helpful discussion in *O'Keefe's Law of Weights and Measures* (2nd edn) para 1 (160). For a decision on the meaning here of 'in possession', see *Bellerby v Carle* [1983] 2 AC 101, [1983] 1 All ER 1031, HL, where it was held that two licensees were not in possession of unjust beer measuring equipment owned, supplied and maintained by Watney's Brewery pursuant to a contract with the licensees' company.

manipulation of the equipment. It was held in *Harris v Allwood*[3] that no offence is committed here where goods such as tea, sugar or raisins are weighed in their wrapping paper in the customer's presence, or where it is customary in the trade to include wrappings.[4]

There is a presumption that where equipment is found in a person's possession who carries on trade, or on premises used for trade, that person or the occupier of the premises is presumed to have the equipment in his possession for use for trade until the contrary is proved (s 7(5)).

Public weighing or measuring equipment

This equipment is regulated by Part III. Keepers of public weighing or measuring equipment for the use of which a fee is charged must hold a certificate issued by the Chief Inspector of Weights and Measures. Local authorities are empowered to provide and maintain such equipment, and there are various offences connected with misuse of it.

Regulation of certain transactions in goods

Part IV of the Act contains a number of provisions of considerable importance to the consumer. In particular, Schedules 4 to 7 prescribe that certain commodities may be sold by quantity only whether expressed in net or gross weight, capacity measurement, or volume – rather than by 'tins' or 'packets'.[5] This Part also contains the offence of giving short weight, now further considered.

Short weight

The offence contained in section 28, giving short weight, measure or number, applies to any goods whether or not they are listed in the Schedules mentioned under the previous heading. It also applies to sales at any point, not merely to retail sales.

The section states that any person who, in selling or purporting to sell any goods by weight or other measurement or by number, delivers or causes to be delivered to the buyer a lesser quantity than that purported

---

3 (1892) 57 JP 7; but in many cases now net weight or wrapper allowances are prescribed.
4 *King v Spencer* (1904) 68 JP 530.
5 The detail is too complex to be dealt with in this book. Students involved in working in this area should refer to *O'Keefe's Law of Weights and Measures* (2nd edn), where text and commentary will be found.

to be sold or than corresponds with the price charged shall be guilty of an offence (s 28(1)). Under section 28(2)(a) the indicated quantity on a pre-package within that Act is to be taken as the 'nominal' quantity, a concept explained later.

Sections 29 and 30 create a number of other offences. In summarised form they are:

a)   Misrepresenting by word of mouth or otherwise the quantity of the goods, or otherwise doing anything calculated to mislead another person as to the quantity, in connection with the sale *or purchase* of any goods (s 29(1));

b)   Overstating the quantity of goods pre-packed in or on a container by means of a written statement of quantity (s 30(1));

c)   Overstating the quantity of non pre-packed goods which are made up for sale or for delivery after sale in a container marked with a statement in writing of the quantity of the goods (s 30(2)). Subsections 30(3) and (4) modify the offences in section 30(1) and (2) by stating that an offence is committed notwithstanding that the quantity stated is expressed to be the quantity of the goods at a specified time falling before the time in question, except in specified circumstances. One of these is where the quantity is so expressed in pursuance of an express requirement of the Act;

d)   Making false statements in documents associated with goods (eg coal) (s 31(1)).

It should be noted that the facts giving rise to a prosecution for short measure contrary to section 28 may also involve using false or unjust equipment contrary to section 17 and may also amount to applying a false trade description to goods contrary to section 1(1) of the Trade Descriptions Act 1968.[6]

Although it is usually obvious when short weight has been delivered contrary to section 28(1), it is occasionally debatable what is meant by 'lesser quantity' in a particular context. Thus in *Marshall v Searles*[7] an inspector went to the defendant's public house and bought two pints of draught Guinness. Each pint glass that he was given included a head of froth. The total liquid content of each glass was about 6 per cent below a standard pint. The prosecution appealed against the justices' finding that no offence of selling less than a pint had been committed. The Divisional Court dismissed the appeal and held that reference to Guinness advertisements suggested that a general member of the public would expect to be served with a pint consisting of a composite mixture of liquid and

6   See, for example, *Kinchin v Haines* [1979] Crim LR 329, DC, mentioned below.
7   [1964] Crim LR 667. In late 1977 the Scottish High Court of Justiciary came to a similar conclusion with regard to ordinary beer, see *Dean v Scottish and Newcastle Breweries Ltd* 1978 SLT 24. These cases were followed in *Bennett v Markham* [1982] 3 All ER 641, [1982] 1 WLR 1230.

gas. That was what was being sold and purported to be sold. In fact, section 43(1) stated that gas comprised in any foam on beer or cider should be disregarded in ascertaining quantity, but the section needed a commencement order. In 1992 the Secretary of State announced his intention of implementing the section. This was in response to public complaints of short measure and checks by trading standards officers tending to support these complaints. Accordingly, a commencement order[8] for section 43 was made with a view to bringing the section into force on 1 April 1994. However, a sudden volte face occurred and the order was revoked before it could operate. Section 43 was then repealed by the Deregulation and Contracting Out Act 1994, section 14. An attempt was made to reinstate it by a Private Member's Bill in 1997 which, despite government support, was unsuccessful. The position appears, therefore, to depend on the cited case law interpretation.

The offence of misrepresenting quantities must be read in the light of section 28(2)(b), which states that any statement, whether oral or in writing, as to the weight of any goods shall be deemed, unless otherwise expressed, to be a statement of the net weight of the goods. A misrepresentation may also give rise to an offence under the Trade Descriptions Act 1968 (s 1), and give rise to civil remedies in tort and contract as discussed in previous chapters. But here the operative misrepresentation is not confined to one made by one party to a contract to the other. It is within the subsection if the statement is made by an interested third party to the buyer or seller and is likely to mislead him.[9]

Offences under section 28 (short weight) are of strict liability.[10] For instance, when considering misrepresentations, a representation is false if at the material time it was a false statement of fact, irrespective of the knowledge or belief of the person making the statement. In addition, the words 'calculated to mislead' which might be thought to imply mens rea, are construed as meaning 'likely to mislead' rather than 'intended to mislead'.[11]

8   Weights and Measures (Commencement) Order 1992, SI 1992/770.
9   *Collett v Co-operative Wholesale Society Ltd* [1970] 1 All ER 274, DC (farmers sold milk to Milk Marketing Board but consigned it direct to respondent dairies, although no contract with them existed. The respondents were convicted of misrepresenting alleged deficiencies in quantity of milk received from the farmers, as a consequence of which they would feel obliged to accept less money for the milk).
10 *Winter v Hinckley and District Co-operative Society Ltd* [1959] 1 All ER 403 (servant in charge of vehicle delivering Society's coal had caused short weight of 112 lb coal sacks by stealing some of their contents after leaving Society's premises. Held: no defence by Society that they did not know coal sacks were light, since no *mens rea* needed).
11 See *McDowell v Standard Oil Co (New Jersey)* [1927] AC 632 at 637, a case on similar wording in the Trade Marks Act 1905 and O'Keefe, op cit 1 (244).

During 2000 publicity was given to the fact that in internet-based supermarket shopping many customers were still expressing their orders in the old imperial weights 'eg a pound of sugar'. Although section 8 prohibits the use of such weights for trade the professional view is that there is nothing in the Act preventing this type of buyer's request. However, care should be taken by the seller not to commit an offence under sections 28 or 29 by ascertaining whether the exact metric equivalent is being ordered or whether the appropriate equivalent is really being intended (as is usually the case). Otherwise if, for example, a 1/4 lb of sweets is ordered, the metric equivalent to which is 113g, delivering 100g would be short measure.

General defence

Warranty (s 33) As was formerly the case with food it is a defence to an offence relating to the quantity or prepacking of goods that they were bought from some other person as being of a quantity represented by that person and with a *written* warranty that they were of the relevant quantity. The defendant must also show that he had no reason to believe the warranty inaccurate, that he did in fact believe it accurate, and if the warranty was given by a seller outside Great Britain that the defendant had taken reasonable steps to check its accuracy. Where the alleged offence relates to the quantity of goods, he must also show a) that he took all reasonable steps to ensure that the quantity remained unchanged while in his possession, and b) apart from any change in their quantity the goods remained in the same state as when he bought them. As with food and drugs, this latter provision is aimed against subtractions from the article, or breaking bulk.

The person by whom the warranty is alleged to be given is entitled to appear and give evidence (s 33(4)).

Additional defences and safeguards (s 34) Section 34, which originates from the former 1979 Act (amending s 26 of the 1963 Act), lists a number of other defences, some of which are similar to those in trade descriptions or food and drug cases.

a) It is a defence for the person charged to prove that he took all reasonable precautions and exercised all due diligence to avoid the commission of such an offence (s 34).

Before the amendments made to this defence by the Weights and Measures Act 1979 a 'mistake' or 'accident' also had to be proved, and the duty was for the defendant to have used all due diligence to avoid the commission of an offence by himself or any person under his control. The radically shortened version of the defence now substituted makes the other cases on the former section 26 not entirely reliable. The new version also makes it more likely that a defence will involve an employer 'passing the buck' to an employee. The employee may then often be prosecuted under section 34(2) (act or default of another person).[12]

Although less onerous than formerly, it may not be easy to convince a court that all reasonable precautions have been taken and all due diligence exercised. These two duties have been described as 'first, the setting up of an efficient system for the avoidance of offences under the Act, and second, the proper operation of that system'.[13] It was held in *Kinchin v Haines*[14] that a self-employed coal-merchant charged under section 1(1)(a) of the Trade Descriptions Act 1968 with falsely describing sacks of fuel marked as '1 cwt' but which were lighter than this because of foreseeable evaporation of moisture caused by heavy rain, had not exercised reasonable precautions when weighing the wet coal and not allowing for the effects of evaporation.

The defence has in its previous, more onerous, form been held to be applicable where an underweight packet of crisps was produced by an efficient and well maintained machine with an anticipated error of six underweight bags in every 10,000 of the weekly output or 0.0006 per cent of weekly production of 20 million bags.[15] The reasoning seems to be that if a normally reliable machine causes the error for no anticipated reason, the defence is available.[16]

The requirements of reasonable precautions and due diligence have been extensively considered in trade description cases and the similar defence in section 24 of the Trade Descriptions Act 1968 is discussed above.[17] It is important to note, too, that this defence cannot be relied on unless notice to the prosecutor is given in accordance with section 34(2), discussed below.

b) It is a defence in proceedings involving goods in containers marked with wrong quantities, or goods having associated with them documents stating wrong quantities, that the deficiency arose after the marking of the container or completion of the document, *and* was attributable to factors for which reasonable allowance was made in stating the quantity of the goods in the marking or document (s 35(2)). A similar defence applies to retail sales of non-prepacked food where

12 See particularly *Tesco Supermarkets Ltd v Nattrass* [1972] AC 153, [1971] 2 All ER 127, HL, discussed further in this book in the context of trade descriptions.
13 Per Fisher J in *Tesco Supermarkets v Nattrass* [1971] 1 QB 133, [1970] 3 All ER 357.
14 [1979] Crim LR 329, DC.
15 *Bibby-Cheshire v Golden Wonder Ltd* [1972] 3 All ER 738, DC, M, H & P p 719.
16 Contrast the decision of the House of Lords in the food case of *Smedleys Ltd v Breed* [1974] AC 839, [1974] 2 All ER 21, above.
17 See above, p 408. There is also a comprehensive discussion of how manufacturers can set up 'due diligence' systems in *O'Keefe*, op cit 1(281).

the deficiency is due wholly to unavoidable evaporation or drainage.[18] The defence under section 35(2) is available to the retailer as well as the person responsible for the marking, usually the manufacturer.[19]

c) Where the quantity of the foods is inaccurate because there is an excess, it is a defence to prove that the excess was attributable to the taking of measures reasonably necessary in order to avoid committing an offence in respect of a deficiency in those or other goods (s 36).[20]

d) There is a *de minimis* defence, the effect of which is that where one of a number of articles is tested and found deficient, the defendant shall not be convicted unless 'a reasonable number of those articles was also tested'. Where the proceedings concern one or more of a number of articles tested on the same occasion, the court must have regard to the average quantity in all the articles tested; and if the proceedings are in respect of a single article, the court 'shall disregard any inconsiderable deficiency or excess'; and the court must 'have regard generally to all the circumstances of the case' (s 37). The effect of this important section is to emphasise that an inspector should check a reasonable quantity of similar articles in these circumstances. But it was held in *Sears v Smiths Food Group Ltd*[1] where a private purchaser had two bags of crisps tested by an inspector, one of the bags being in fact underweight, that the inspector was under no obligation to test other packets available at the 'time and place' in question – ie when and where the bag or bags were brought to the inspector for testing.

Average quantities – EEC developments A development of great importance bearing on the question of how far it is permissible for manufactured pre-packed goods to conform *on average* to a stated weight was contained in two Directives of the EEC Council (75/106/EEC and 76/211/EEC). These Directives refer, inter alia, to an earlier Directive (71/316/EEC) on the approximation of the laws of the member states relating to common provisions for both measuring instruments and methods of metrological control, and providing that there should be harmonisation of the requirements for marketing certain products and in particular as regards the measuring and marking of pre-packed quantities. The Directives relate to pre-packaged goods (called 'pre-packages'), which are intended for sale in constant unit nominal quantities equal to values predetermined by the

18 See s 35(3).
19 *F W Woolworth & Co Ltd v Gray* [1970] 1 All ER 953. Here the retailer could not rely on the manufacturer's warranty because they had not taken steps to ensure that the quantity of the goods remained unchanged as required by Weights and Measures Act 1963, s 25(1) (but the appeal succeeded under s 26(2)).
20 See the facts of *Bibby-Chester v Golden Wonder Ltd*, above, where the machine was set to deliver bags of 17.5 drams instead of the 15 drams marked.
1 [1968] 2 QB 288, [1968] 2 All ER 721.

packer, expressed in units of weight or volume, and not less than 5g or 5ml and not more than 10kg or 10 litres.

The Directive requires that all pre-packages must bear an indication of the weight or volume of the product which they are required to contain, known as 'nominal weight' or 'nominal volume'. They must also bear the EC sign ('e') which guarantees that the requirements have been met by the packer or importer. Annex I of the Directive amplifies these provisions. The 'nominal quantity' of a pre-package refers to the quantity of product which the package is *deemed to contain*. The 'actual contents' are the quantity of product which it in fact contains. The 'negative error' of a pre-package is the quantity by which the actual contents of the pre-package are less than the nominal quantity. The core of the Directive is the statement that completed pre-packages must satisfy the following requirements:

1) the actual contents shall not be less, on average, than the nominal quantity;

2) the proportion of pre-packages having a negative error greater than the tolerable negative error laid down shall be sufficiently small to comply with the tests specified in Annex II of the Directive. Thus the tolerable negative error is first ascertained, and this factor is ignored for the purposes of the statistical checking of batches of pre-packages. The checking of the pre-packages is then done by sampling in two parts – a check covering the actual contents of each pre-package in the sample – and another check on the average of the actual content of the pre-packages in the sample. A batch of pre-packages shall be considered acceptable if the results of both these checks satisfy the criteria laid down. Plans in Annex II indicate how samples should be tested (destructive or non-destructive testing) and the number in the sample according to the size of the batch. Criteria for acceptance or rejection according to the number of defective units found in the sample are then laid down. Thus, in the case of the single sampling non-destructive testing plan, if the batch contains between 501 and 1,200 pre-packages, 80 must be sampled. The whole batch of pre-packages is acceptable if the number of defective units in the sample does not exceed 5; otherwise it is rejected.

These Directives were implemented by the Weights and Measures Act 1979, an Act whose policy attracted opposition from consumer organisations in that for the first time in many centuries the consumer had no guarantee that a purchased pre-package had at least the quantities indicated. However, at the date of entry of the UK to the Community (1 January 1973) a system of average weights and measures was well established in most other member states. The UK was unusual in having a 'minimum system' enforced at the local, rather than central level. Since by sophisticated quality control techniques it is possible to fill pre-packages with lesser quantities than under the minimum system, a factor significant in large-scale production, to maintain the UK's competitiveness in overseas markets it was thought necessary to accept this change. It is still perfectly legal, however, for packers to pack to the minimum system (since the test for average compliance will inevitably be satisfied) but a packer must still keep the records required by the legislation.

The 1979 Act, now consolidated in Part V of the 1985 Act, had introduced the following innovative features:

i)   A Metrological Co-ordinating Unit was established to ensure uniform enforcement of the Act in every local authority's jurisdiction. Its existence reflected the unusual character of the UK's weights and measures enforcement machinery, based on weights and measures authorities in the UK but normally enforced centrally on the Continent. The body was set up experimentally and the Act confers power on the Secretary of State to abolish it (ss 55 to 62). It was duly abolished (by the National Metrological Co-ordinating Unit (Transfer of Functions and Abolition) Order 1987) from 1 January 1988 and its functions transferred to the Secretary of State.

ii)   The main thrust of enforcement moves from the traditional retail level to the packaging plant or point of importation. The 'reference test' referred to below can usually only be carried out if statistically acceptable samples are available, which will not be the case on retail premises. Tests on non-prepacked goods or exempted and catch-weight goods continue to be made at retail level.

iii) Persons other than the packer or importer, who have in their possession for sale, or agree to sell or sell a relevant package which is inadequate (ie has a negative error larger than twice the tolerable negative error) only incur criminal liability if they know that the package is inadequate – ie mens rea is necessary (s 50(5)).

iv)   The Act makes provision for 'e' marked packages. Those bearing the EC's 'e' mark are guaranteed to meet the requirements of the Directives and can circulate freely within the Community without further checks. There is therefore a special responsibility on packers and inspectors as regards goods so marked (s 54).

v)   Special powers are given to inspectors to issue written instructions that suspect packages shall be kept at the disposal of the inspector with a view to their subsequent testing. No court order is necessary (s 63).

vi)   The Act must be read in conjunction with the Weights and Measures (Packaged Goods) Regulations 1986, which in turn incorporate the Code of Practical Guidance for Packers and Importers and the Manual of Practical Guidance for Inspectors.

The Act establishes the 'three rules for packers and importers'. These are:

1)   The actual contents of the packages shall not be less, on average,

than the nominal quantity (ie the statement of quantity marked on the container).

2) Not more than $2^1/_2$ per cent of the packages may be non-standard, ie have negative errors larger than the tolerable negative error (TNE) specified for the nominal quantity.

3) No package may be 'inadequate', ie have a negative error larger than twice the specified TNE (s 47).

Details of the statistical test, known as the 'reference test', to be carried out by inspectors are contained in the 1986 Regulations referred to above. The packer's duty is to ensure that his tested goods pass the reference test. It is then statistically probable, but not inevitable, that he has complied with the three rules above.

The Act creates a number of offences, the main ones being failure by a packer or importer to fulfil his statutory duties or failure to keep proper records (or falsification thereof). The primary duties are specified in section 47 and relate to the three rules already discussed. The DTI in 1997 announced its intention to review this area of the law with a view to adopting a common approach to 'e' marked packages, non-'e' marked packages, catch-weight products and products sold loose from bulk. Emphasis where prepackages are concerned is likely to be on the 'three rules for packers' rather than a reference test.

The only comprehensive, annotated, source of all relevant primary and secondary legislation, some of which is of great technical complexity to the layman, is *O'Keefe's Law of Weights and Measures* (2nd edn) (Butterworths). The Packers' Code contains a glossary of technical terms.

Offences due to third party (s 32) It is a condition of relying on the defence under section 34(1) of the Act (reasonable precautions taken and all due diligence exercised – see above) that the defendant give appropriate notice of this to the prosecutor at least seven days before the date of the hearing (s 34(2)). The person whose act or default caused the commission of the offence may then be convicted of the offence, under section 32, whether or not the original person is proceeded against. This procedure can be used against employees, suppliers and by and against a whole chain of distributors and sellers.

Metrication

The UK response to EC metrication policy has already been mentioned in chapter 1.[2] The Metrication Board had been established before the UK's

2   For the recent history of this in the UK, see Norman Stone 'Metrication and the Consumer' in Morris (ed) *Economics and Consumer Protection*. See also *O'Keefe*, op cit 0(23).

accession to the EEC in 1969 in order to simplify overseas trade processes. The Board was purely advisory, and responsible to the Secretary of State for Prices and Consumer Protection. Its main function was, obviously, to help acquaint the consumer with the significance of metric quantities and to ease the transition from imperial to metric units. The price control system under the Prices Acts is the mandatory element in this process, and can be used as a safeguard against unwarranted price increases. The Metrication Board itself was dissolved shortly after the return of the Conservative Government in 1979. In the light of the government's policy of slowing down the metrication process its continued existence as a 'quango' was thought to be unjustified.

The Weights and Measures, &c Act 1976 (now repealed and replaced by the 1985 Act) empowered the Secretary of State to:

a) set dates not before 21 April 1978 from which only metric packs of prescribed quantities would be permitted;

b) set dates ending the use of imperial units for other pre-packed goods or goods weighed or measured in front of customers. In the case of weighed-out meat, fish, fruit and vegetables sold retail, such dates not being before 1 January 1980;

c) generally prohibit the use in trade of all imperial units except the mile, foot, inch, gallon and pint;

d) restrict the use in trade of any imperial unit, sector by sector.

The Secretary of State may, under section 9 of the 1985 Act, require that where metric units are used for trade they are to be accompanied, for explanatory purposes, with information as to the equivalent imperial units. Conversion tables may also be required to be displayed. These powers are exercisable by statutory instrument subject to annulment in pursuance of a resolution of either House of Parliament. By the end of 1981 the majority of goods, particularly those pre-packed, could be sold in SI units. The major exceptions are draught beer, cider, and milk in returnable containers. Goods sold loose from bulk became subject to the regime from 1 January 2000. Concern about confusion has proved largely unfounded and little use has been made of section 9 above.

In the light of the fact that metrication is the norm in almost all the developed countries within and without the EC with which the UK trades (the USA being the main exception) continued progress towards full metrication was inevitable. Countries such as New Zealand which have pursued a full metrication policy more vigorously do not appear to have found the oft-quoted 'confusion of the elderly' argument to have been a major obstacle, particularly if the policy is accompanied for a time by a dual marking system in metric units with imperial equivalents. Accordingly, it was not surprising in July 1991 that the Secretary of State made a statement that the government would take maximum advantage of the transitional arrangements in the Units of Measurement Directives (80/181/ EEC and 71/617/EEC) and accordingly would:

a) cease to authorise, after 31 December 1994, imperial units used for economic, public health, public safety and administrative purposes except for the units used for the purposes set out in b) and c) below;

b) cease to authorise after 31 December 1999:

    I   the pound and ounce for goods sold loose from bulk;

    II   the pint and fluid ounce for beer, cider, waters, lemonades and fruit juices in returnable containers;

    III the fathom for marine navigation;

    IV   the therm for gas supply;

c) authorise the continued use without limit of:

    I   the mile, yard, foot and inch for road traffic signs and related distance and speed measurements;

    II   the pint for dispensing draft beer and cider and for milk in returnable containers;

    III the troy ounce for transactions in precious metals;

    IV   the acre for land registration purposes.

These changes were duly implemented by the Units of Measurements Regulations 1995[3] exactly as stated, except the commencement date slipped to 1 October 1995. From 1 January 2000, therefore, the only remains of the imperial system are distances on road traffic signs, the pub pint, the doorstep milk bottle, the troy ounce and the acre in conveyancing transactions involving the Land Registry. Otherwise metric units must be used for economic, public health, public safety and administrative purposes. The DTI Guidance Note on these changes reassuringly tells businesses that they may continue to use imperial units as supplementary indications and display conversion charts. 'Traders will also be free to serve (though in metric units) customers who ask for goods in imperial units.' The European Commission has published a proposal to permit imperial weights and measures as supplementary indicators until 31 December 2009. This allows the metric quantity to be accompanied by a 'no more prominent' indicator of the imperial equivalent. This is in recognition of the American market's requirement for imperial measures and would otherwise result in dual packaging requirements, one for the EU and the other for America.

3   SI 1995/1804.

Weights and measures

Appendix I
Safety regulations

a) Regulations made under the Consumer Protection Act 1987

As discussed in chapter 9 (pp 259–261) safety regulations can be made under the Consumer Protection Act 1987, section 11. Listed below are all such current Regulations.

The Furniture and Furnishings (Fire) (Safety) Regulations 1988, SI 1988/1324 (amended by SI 1989/2358 and SI 1993/207).[1] These regulations replace earlier provisions and are concerned with new and, in some cases, second-hand domestic furniture including garden furniture for use indoors and caravan furniture. There is a requirement for upholstery to pass a cigarette test (reg 5), for filling materials to pass ignitability tests (regs 6 and 7), for permanent and loose covers to pass match tests (regs 8 and 9) and for display and permanent labels to be attached to furniture (regs 10 and 11).

The Ceramic Ware (Safety) Regulations 1988, SI 1988/1647. These regulations replace earlier regulations and require ceramic ware to satisfy the requirements of BS 6748:1986 concerning the permissible release of lead and cadmium from ceramic ware for use with food.

The Gas Cooking Appliances (Safety) Regulations 1989, SI 1989/149. These regulations are now applicable only for second-hand gas cookers (following the introduction of subsequent regulations, see the Gas

1   The DTI reports a saving of 700 lives and 6,000 serious injuries as a result of these regulations, see (2000) 23 Consumer Law Today Issue 8, p 8 and Press Release P/2000/425, 20 June 2000.

Appliances (Safety) Regulations 1995, SI 1995/1629, below). The supply of cookers which do not comply with the specifications in the regulations, European Standard EN 30 or BSS 5386: Part 3: 1980 or Part 4: 1983 is prohibited.

The Low Voltage Electrical Equipment (Safety) Regulations 1989, SI 1989/728. These regulations, made in conjunction with the European Communities Act 1972, section 2(2), apply to any electrical equipment designed or adapted for use with voltages of 50-1,000 (AC) and 75-1,500 (DC), unless excluded by Schedule 1 or for export outside the EC. Electrical equipment is required to be safe and to be made in accordance with engineering practice generally accepted as good within the EC (reg 5). Compliance with certain harmonised standards, specified international safety provisions or, in the absence of these, with national safety provisions of a member state will suffice (reg 7). There is provision for the marking and certification of goods (reg 10). Enforcement duties and time limits for prosecution are also included. These regulations are revoked by the Electrical Equipment (Safety) Regulations 1994,[2] but continue to apply to electrical equipment placed on the market before 1 January 1997.

The Food Imitations (Safety) Regulations 1989, SI 1989/1291. These regulations replace earlier provisions and prohibit the supply etc of manufactured goods ordinarily intended for private use and which, although not food, have a form, odour, colour, appearance, packaging, labelling, volume or size which makes them likely to be mistaken for food especially by children, and thereby being put into mouths or sucked or swallowed with a risk of death or injury. Excluded are all items excluded from section 11 of the Consumer Protection Act 1987 by section 11(7), marbles, products representing food for dolls, houses, model scenes etc and items entirely made from food ingredients.

The Cosmetic Products (Safety) Regulations 1989, SI 1989/2233 (amended by SI 1990/1812, SI 1991/447, SI 1992/1525, SI 1993/1539, SI 1994/1529, SI 1995/1478 and SI 1996/1446). These regulations replaced the Cosmetic Products (Safety) Regulations 1984.[3] They were made in conjunction with the European Communities Act 1972, section 2(2) and were designed to implement a number of European Directives. Regulation 3 seeks to ensure that cosmetic products do not cause damage to human health when used under normal conditions. Products are prohibited from containing some 710 specified substances or may only contain other specified substances in specified circumstances (reg 4). Substances may

2   SI 1994/3260, reg 2(1), see below.
3   SI 1984/1260, as amended.

be authorised for use by the Secretary of State (reg 5) and there are requirements of marking products with specified information (regs 6 and 6A). Enforcement matters are also included. The regulations now apply only to products supplied before 16 December 1996, having been replaced by the Cosmetic Products (Safety) Regulations 1996.[4]

The All-Terrain Motor Vehicles (Safety) Regulations 1989, SI 1989/2288. Introduced to supersede earlier regulations which had been made under the emergency procedure in section 11(5) of the Consumer Protection Act 1987,[5] these regulations prohibit the supply of regulated vehicles with three wheels (reg 3). This encompasses vehicles propelled by internal combustion engines for leisure activities on all types of land but not those for disabled people nor two-wheeled motor-cycles with side cars. Four-wheeled vehicles designed or intended for use by children under 12 and for those aged between 12 and 16 are also prohibited unless they have maximum speeds within the specified limits and regulators to reduce the speed at which they can travel (regs 4 and 5). Warnings are also required on the vehicles for use by older children (reg 5).

Tobacco Products Labelling (Safety) Regulations 1991, SI 1991/1530 (amended by SI 1993/1947). These regulations have been made in conjunction with the European Communities Act 1972, section 2(2), to implement a Council Directive. The regulations require producers of tobacco products to ensure that packets carry the specified general warning (reg 3). Cigarettes and rolling tobacco are required to carry one of six additional health warnings as specified in Schedule 1 (regs 4 and 4A). Cigars, cigarillos and pipe tobacco are required to carry one of four health warnings specified in Schedule 1, Part II (reg 4B) and smokeless tobacco products have to carry a set warning (reg 4C). There are also requirements to display tar and nicotine yields of cigarettes (reg 6) with a testing system instituted (regs 9 and 10). Compliance with equivalent measures from another Community State will suffice (reg 8).

Heating Appliances (Fireguards) (Safety) Regulations 1991, SI 1991/2693. These regulations revoked earlier regulations and imposed requirements relating to gas fires and oil heaters. Fireguards could either comply with BS 1945:1971 or with standards published in EC member states of an equivalent level of safety. They were revoked as of 1 January 1996, in so far as they applied to gas appliances, by the Gas Appliances (Safety)

---

4 SI 1996/2925, see below.
5 The Three-Wheeled All-Terrain Motor Vehicles (Safety) Regulations 1988, SI 1988/2122.

Regulations 1992,[6] and were disapplied for new gas appliances as of that date by the Gas Appliances (Safety) Regulations 1995.[7] They are, therefore, only applicable now for second-hand gas appliances.

The Cigarettes (Maximum Tar Yield) (Safety) Regulations 1992, SI 1992/ 2783. These regulations were made in conjunction with the European Communities Act 1972, section 2(2), to implement an EC Directive. They prohibit the supply etc, for consumption in the United Kingdom, of cigarettes with tar yields exceeding the permitted maximum (15 milligrams up to 1 January 1998, 12 milligrams on or after 1 January 1998). There are provisions for determining the tar yield and for representations to be made by producers.

The Tobacco for Oral Use (Safety) Regulations 1992, SI 1992/3134. These replace the earlier Oral Snuff Regulations 1989,[8] and implement an EC Directive, as amended. They prohibit the supply, exposure for supply etc of oral snuff.

The Active Implantable Medical Devices Regulations 1992, SI 1992/3146 (amended by SI 1995/1671). These regulations are made in conjunction with the European Communities Act 1972, section 2(2), and implement a Council Directive. Under regulation 3 devices placed on the market must comply with essential safety requirements specified in Schedule 2. CE marks must be used for devices which are not custom-made or intended for clinical investigation (reg 4). Requirements for custom-made devices and clinical investigations are contained in regulations 6 and 7.

The Imitation Dummies (Safety) Regulations 1993, SI 1993/2923. These regulations prohibit the supply etc of imitation dummies which may cause death or personal injury. Exemptions are permitted for items which comply with BS 5239:1988 or equivalent and for toys which are covered by toy safety regulations.

The Plugs and Sockets etc (Safety) Regulations 1994, SI 1994/1768. These regulations revoke and largely re-enact earlier regulations, requiring electrical devices, such as plugs, sockets and adaptors, to meet approved standards and that most domestic appliances operating on a voltage of not less than 200 volts be supplied with a correctly fused and approved standard plug. There are provisions for approval of standard plugs and devices and information requirements are also included.

6   SI 1992/711, now revoked.
7   SI 1995/1629, see below.
8   SI 1989/2347, see ch 9 at p 260.

The Dangerous Substances and Preparations (Safety) (Consolidation) Regulations 1994, SI 1994/2844 (as amended by SI 1994/3247, SI 1996/ 2635, SI 1999/2084 and SI 1999/3193). As the name suggests, these regulations consolidate a number of previous regulations, which have thereby been revoked. They also implement EC Directives. They are concerned with preventing the supply of: ornamental objects, tricks, jokes and games containing dangerous liquids or preparations (reg 3); substances used as fuel in decorative lamps (reg 3A); children's dressing-gowns which have been treated with certain chemicals (reg 4); novelties which contain tear-gas, more than 1.5 ml of 'stink-bomb' substances or sneezing powder (reg 5); products containing benzene (with exceptions for motor fuels, industrial use and waste), and particularly balloon-making kits (reg 6) and carcinogens, mutagens and substances toxic for reproduction (regs 6A, 6B and 6C).

The Medical Devices Regulations 1994, SI 1994/3017. These regulations are made in conjunction with the European Communities Act 1972, section 2(2), and implement Council Directive 93/42/EEC. The regulations apply to certain medical devices which are classified into four classes (reg 4). Devices placed on the market must comply with the specified essential safety requirements, detailed in Annexes to the Directive. There are detailed provisions for CE marking for each class of device (regs 6-11), for registration of persons placing devices on the market (reg 14) and for custom-made devices (reg 15) and clinical investigations (reg 16). Enforcement provisions and prohibitions on supply in breach of requirements are also included.

The Motor Vehicles Tyres (Safety) Regulations 1994, SI 1994/3117 (as amended by SI 1996/3227 and SI 1997/815). Made in conjunction with the European Communities Act 1972, section 2(2), these regulations revoke earlier regulations and implement a Council Directive and EC Regulations. They prohibit the supply of new tyres for passenger cars, light trailers and motor-cycles that do not bear a mark indicating compliance with specified standards and the supply of tyres with false marks (regs 4-6). There are also provisions for the supply of part-worn tyres in regulation 7.

The Electrical Equipment (Safety) Regulations 1994, SI 1994/3260. These regulations are made in conjunction with the European Communities Act 1972, section 2(2), and implement a Council Directive and consolidate with amendments the Low Voltage Electrical Equipment (Safety) Regulations 1989.[9] The regulations apply to electrical equipment designed or adapted for use, with alternating current of 50–1,000 volts, and for direct current

9   SI 1989/728, see above.

75-1,500 volts, subject to certain exceptions. Such equipment must be safe and constructed in accordance with principles recognised in Member States as constituting good engineering practice. Compliance with harmonised standards, international safety provisions or national safety provisions is permitted. There are requirements for CE marking, second-hand and hired equipment and enforcement provisions included. Transitional provisions allow compliance with the 1989 Regulations for products placed on the market before 1 January 1997.

Toys (Safety) Regulations 1995, SI 1995/204.[10] These are made in conjunction with the European Community Act 1972, section 2(2), and implement Council Directives on toy safety. They consolidate, with amendments, earlier regulations. Toys to which the regulations apply have to satisfy the essential safety requirements (reg 4) as specified in Schedule 2. Toys supplied on or after 1 January 1995, which bear the CE marking, are presumed to comply (reg 5) as are those which comply with relevant national standards (reg 6) or which have an EC type-examination certificate (reg 7). There are detailed provisions regarding CE marking, EC type-examination certificates, information requirements and enforcement aspects.

N-Nitrosamines and N-Nitrosatable Substances in Elastomer or Rubber Teats and Dummies (Safety) Regulations 1995, SI 1995/1012. These regulations implement a Commission Directive and apply to teats and dummies which are intended to come into contact with foodstuffs. Supply of any teat or dummy which passes on to a saliva test solution N-Nitrosamines in excess of 0.01 mg or N-Nitrosatable substances in excess of 0.1 mg is prohibited. Test conditions are specified.

The Gas Appliances (Safety) Regulations 1995, SI 1995/1629. These regulations implement Commission Directives and consolidate, with amendments, earlier regulations. The regulations specify the essential safety requirements which gas appliances must attain and regulate the supply of appliances. There are provisions relating to EC type-examinations, CE marking, certification, testing and enforcement measures. Only new appliances are covered, earlier regulations continue to cover second-hand items.

---

10   For cases concerning earlier regulations see *Taylor v Lawrence Fraser (Bristol) Ltd* (1977) 121 Sol Jo 757, DC (seller of dangerous toys cannot rely on manufacturer's assurances); *P & M Supplies (Essex) Ltd v Devon County Council* (1991) 156 JP 328, DC (standard of sampling required for reasonable precautions defence).

The Cosmetic Products (Safety) Regulations 1996, SI 1996/2925 (as amended by SI 1997/2914, SI 1998/1727, SI 1999/1552 and SI 2000/1679). These regulations consolidate, with amendments, the earlier Cosmetic Products (Safety) Regulations 1989,[11] as amended. They were made in conjunction with the European Communities Act 1972, section 2(2) and are designed to implement a number of European Directives. There is a prohibition on the supply of cosmetic products liable to cause damage to human health under normal or reasonably foreseeable conditions of use (reg 3) and prohibitions or restrictions on the substances permitted to be included in cosmetic products (reg 4(2) – 767 chemicals, and (2A) – specified animal organs). Regulation 2(3) prohibits the use of ingredients which have been tested on animals after 30 June 2000 in order to satisfy any requirements of the regulations. Labelling referring to animal testing must indicate whether the tests involve the product or its ingredients (reg 2(4)). Marking requirements are specified (reg 6) and specific product information must be available for inspection by enforcement authorities (reg 8). There are also measures concerning enforcement, confidentiality, imported goods etc.

Fireworks (Safety) Regulations 1997, SI 1997/2294.[12] These regulations revoke and re-enact, with amendments, the Firework (Safety) Regulations 1996.[13] The supply of fireworks and assemblies classified as categories 1, 2 and 3 under BS 7114 is prohibited unless in compliance with BS 7114 requirements (reg 3(1)). There are also restrictions on the size and weights of fireworks and assemblies which may be supplied (reg 3(2)). Certain types of fireworks and assemblies, such as aerial shells and certain bangers, may only be supplied to professional operators, special effects businesses, local authorities, government departments etc and not to the general public (regs 4 and 5). The supply of fireworks and assemblies to persons apparently under the age of 18 is prohibited (reg 6). Marking requirements are specified (reg 7) and the splitting of primary packs and selection packs is prohibited (reg 8).

Wheeled Child Conveyances (Safety) Regulations 1997, SI 1997/2866. These regulations consolidate and amend earlier regulations relating to perambulators and pushchairs. Regulation 3 requires wheeled child conveyances to conform to BS 7409:1996. This will be satisfied if the item conforms to standards or specifications recognised for use in other member

11 SI 1989/2233, see above.
12 See *R v Secretary of State for Trade and Industry, ex p Garman (t/a Celebration Fireworks)* [1998] CLY 94 for an unsuccessful attempt to obtain judicial review of the regulations.
13 SI 1996/3200, which were of only one year duration.

states of the EC or the European Economic Area which provide an equivalent level of safety (reg 2(4)).

Pencil and Graphic Instruments (Safety) Regulations 1998, SI 1988/2406. These regulations revoke and replace earlier safety regulations. The supply etc of pencils and other graphic instruments is prohibited if they fail to satisfy certain requirements. The coatings of paint on pencils, pens and brushes must not contain more than a specified concentration of soluble arsenic, cadmium, hexavalent chromium, mercury, antimony, lead or barium (reg 4). Similarly, pencils, crayons, chalk and similar items have restrictions on the concentrations of these chemicals within them (reg 5). There are provisions regarding the method to be used to dissolve substances (reg 3 and the Schedule) and provision is made to permit compliance with standards or specifications from other EC or European Economic Area member states of equivalent standard (reg 3(4).

Cigarette Lighter Refill (Safety) Regulations 1999, SI 1999/1844. These regulations prohibit the supply etc of cigarette lighter refills containing butane to anyone under 18.

Road Vehicles (Brake Linings Safety) Regulations 1999, SI 1999/2978. In giving effect to an EC Directive, these regulations restrict the supply of brake linings containing asbestos. There is a general prohibition, under regulation 3, with exceptions for older vehicles and certain military vehicles. Brake linings supplied for 'relevant' vehicles must comply with specified standards (reg 5) and there is a prohibition on the supply of linings for fitting to 'other' vehicles, which would contravene the Braking Devices Directive (reg 6).

The Dangerous Substances and Preparations (Nickel) (Safety) Regulations 2000, SI 2000/1668. These regulations prohibit the supply of post assemblies to be inserted into pierced parts of the human body during epithelisation of the wound, which contain nickel or nickel compounds, unless the concentration of nickel is less than 0.5% (reg 3). Products containing nickel or nickel compounds, which will be in direct and prolonged contact with skin, are also prohibited unless the rate of nickel release does not exceed $0.5\mu g/cm^2$ per week (reg 3(2)). There are also similar restrictions on nickel products with non-nickel coatings (reg 3(3)).

b)   Summary of current regulations made under the Consumer Protection Act 1961

As mentioned in chapter 9, regulations made under the Consumer Protection Act 1961 which were still in force on 1 October 1987 continued to apply as if made under section 11 of the 1987 Act. Those still remaining are as follows.

Cooking Utensils (Safety) Regulations 1972, SI 1972/1957. Cooking utensils designed to come into contact with food must not have a metallic coating containing more than 20 parts in 10,000 of lead content.

Children's Clothing (Hood Cords) Regulations 1976, SI 1976/2. These regulations prohibit the hood of a child's outer garment, defined to include raincoats, overcoats and anoraks, being designed to be secured by means of a cord drawn through the material.

Oil Heaters (Safety) Regulations 1977, SI 1977/167. These regulations impose controls (based on a re-draft of British Standard 3300) on domestic oil heaters as regards the amount of carbon monoxide emitted, the amount of fuel escaping from overturned heaters, the control of the flame, draught resistance, the performance of the heater when tilted and other matters relating to design, construction and performance. A warning must be affixed to the heater in respect of possible misuses. Tests must be carried out by organisations authorised by the Secretary of State.

c) Regulations made under the Consumer Safety Act 1978

The regulations below were made under the 1978 Act and continue in force, with prosecutions being brought under section 12 of the 1987 Act.

The Filament Lamps for Vehicles (Safety) Regulations 1982, SI 1982/444. These regulations prohibit the supply etc of filament lamps to which certain EC regulations apply without being marked in accordance with the Motor Vehicles (Designation of Approval Marks) Regulations 1979.[14]

The Pedal Bicycles (Safety) Regulations 1984, SI 1984/145 (amended by SI 1984/1057). These regulations prohibit the supply etc of two-wheeled pedal cycles which are not constructed or adapted for mechanical propulsion unless they comply with BS 6102 Parts 1 and 2 or are of an equivalent standard. Parts for use in two-wheeled pedal cycles must also comply with the British Standard or be of an equivalent standard.

Gas Catalytic Heaters (Safety) Regulations 1984, SI 1984/1802 (amended by SI 1987/1979). These regulations prohibit the supply etc of any liquid

14 SI 1979/1088.

petroleum gas heater or catalytic unit or insulation device for gas catalytic heaters containing any asbestos.

The Asbestos Products (Safety) Regulations 1985, SI 1985/2042 (amended by SI 1987/1979). These regulations prohibit the supply etc of crocidolite asbestos minerals (blue asbestos) or amosite minerals (brown asbestos) or products containing such minerals other than for research and development or analysis (reg 2). Certain exceptions are made for torque convertors and brake bands for cars containing crocidolite providing warning labels are attached. By regulation 3 the supply of further specified asbestos minerals is prohibited unless labelled in accordance with the Schedule to the regulations and, in the case of products specified in regulation 4 (eg toys, paints and varnishes), any supply of those specified minerals is prohibited.

Nightwear (Safety) Regulations 1985, SI 1985/2043 (amended by SI 1987/286). These regulations revoked and replaced the Nightwear (Safety) Regulations 1967.[15] They prohibit the supply of children's nightwear (except pyjamas, babies' garments and cotton terry towelling bath-robes) made out of fabrics which do not satisfy the flammability performance requirements of BS 5722 (regs 4 and 5). Babies' garments, children's pyjamas, bath robes and adults' nightwear must be labelled in compliance with Schedule 2 and indicate 'KEEP AWAY FROM FIRE' and/or 'LOW FLAMMABILITY TO BS 5722' (regs 4 and 6).

There are further labelling requirements for nightwear which has been treated with flame retardant chemicals (reg 7 and Sch 3) and certain advertisements must contain warning notices (reg 9 and Sch 4).

Bunk Beds (Entrapment Hazards) (Safety) Regulations 1987, SI 1987/1337. These regulations prohibit the supply etc of bunk beds where there is a risk of a child under 6 becoming trapped in any part of it, thereby risking strangulation or injury. The regulations specify permissible gaps between sleeping surfaces and parts of the structure, the Schedule detailing how such gaps are to be measured.

d) Further regulations

Further regulations relating to safety have been made under other legislation. The table below indicates those which have been made under the European Communities Act 1972, section 2(2) without involving either the Consumer Protection Act 1987 or earlier safety statutes.

15 SI 1967/839.

Title	Number
Aerosol Dispensers (EEC Requirements)	SI 1977/1140
Regulations 1977 (as amended)	SI 1980/136
	SI 1985/1279
	SI 1996/2421
Gas Cylinders (Pattern Approval) Regulations 1987	SI 1987/116
Materials and Articles in Contact with	SI 1987/1523
Food Regulations 1987 (as amended)	SI 1990/2487
	SI 1991/1476
	SI 1994/979
Pressure Vessels (Verification) Regulations 1988	SI 1988/896
(as amended)	SI 1999/2001
Construction Products Regulations 1991	SI 1991/1620
(as amended)	SI 1994/3051
Simple Pressure Vessels (Safety) Regulations 1991	SI 1991/2749
(as amended)	SI 1994/3098
Supply of Machinery (Safety) Regulations 1992	SI 1992/3073
(as amended)	SI 1994/2063
Personal Protective Equipment (EC Directive)	SI 1992/3139
Regulations 1992 (as amended)	SI 1993/3074
	SI 1994/2362
	SI 1996/3039
Environmental Protection (Controls on Injurious	SI 1993/1643
Substances) (No 2) Regulations 1993	
Chemicals (Hazard Information and Packaging)	SI 1993/1746
Regulations 1993 (as amended)	SI 1993/3050
Notification of New Substances Regulations 1993	SI 1993/3050
(as amended)	SI 1994/3247
Notification of Existing Substances (Enforcement)	SI 1994/1806
Regulations 1994	
The Equipment and Protective Systems Intended	SI 1996/192
for Use in Potentially Explosive Atmospheres	
Regulations 1996	
Recreational Craft Regulations 1996 (as amended)	SI 1996/1353
	SI 1998/116
Lifts Regulations 1997	SI 1997/831
Environmental Protection (Controls on	SI 1998/545
Hexachloroethane) Regulations 1998 (as amended)	SI 1999/3244
Packaging (Essential Requirements) Regulations 1998	SI 1998/1165
Pressure Equipment Regulations 1999	SI 1999/2001
The Environmental Protection (Controls on Injurious	SI 1999/3244
Substances) Regulations 1999	

The annotated text of all safety regulations is conveniently set out in Miller *Product Liability and Safety Encyclopaedia.*

Safety regulations

Appendix II
Varieties of consumer credit transactions in tabular form

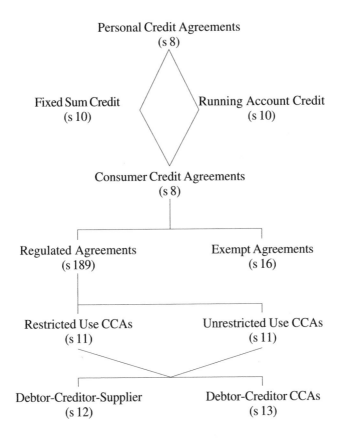

Personal Credit Agreements
(s 8)

Fixed Sum Credit
(s 10)

Running Account Credit
(s 10)

Consumer Credit Agreements
(s 8)

Regulated Agreements
(s 189)

Exempt Agreements
(s 16)

Restricted Use CCAs
(s 11)

Unrestricted Use CCAs
(s 11)

Debtor-Creditor-Supplier
(s 12)

Debtor-Creditor CCAs
(s 13)

N.B. A number of other 'sub-species' also exist – Credit Token Agreements (s 14), Small Agreements (s 17), Non-Commercial Agreements (s 189), Multiple Agreements (s 18), Linked Transactions (s 19), Credit Agreements and Bargains (s 137), Hire-purchase and Conditional Sale Agreements (s 189).

Varieties of consumer credit transactions

Index

Index

Index

Index

Index

485

Index

Index

Index

Index

Index